1993

YALE UNIVERSITY PRESS
PELICAN HISTORY OF ART

Founding Editor: Nikolaus Pevsner

EARLY CHRISTIAN AND BYZANTINE ARCHITECTURE

Richard Krautheimer

Revised by Richard Krautheimer and Slobodan Ćurčić

Professor Krautheimer took his degree at the University of Halle-Wittenberg. He taught in Germany
at the University of Marburg and, after going to the United States, at the University of Louisville,
at Vassar College, and from 1952 at the Fine Arts Institute of New York University. He now lives
in Rome. His publications range from Early Christian, medieval, and Renaissance architecture (*Kirchen
der Bettelorden in Deutschland*, 1925; *Mittelalterliche Synagogen*, 1927; *The Carolingian Revival of Early
Christian Architecture*, 1942; *Studies in Early Christian, Medieval and Renaissance Art*, 1969) to Renaissance
sculpture (*Lorenzo Ghiberti*, 1956) and urban development (*Rome: Profile of a City, 312–1308*, 1980; *The
Rome of Alexander VII*, 1985). In the Early Christian field his main work is the *Corpus of Early Christian
Basilicas in Rome*, a monumental historical and structural survey in five volumes, completed in 1977.

Professor Ćurčić gained an M.Arch. degree prior to his Ph.D. from the Institute of Fine Arts, New
York University, where he was a student of Professor Krautheimer. He has taught at the University of
Illinois, Urbana–Champaign, and since 1982 at Princeton University. His principal publications are
Gračanica. King Milutin's Church and its Place in Late Byzantine Architecture (1979), *Art and Architecture in
the Balkans: An Annotated Bibliography* (1984), and a number of articles on the architecture and art of
Byzantium and its sphere of influence.

Richard Krautheimer

EARLY CHRISTIAN AND
BYZANTINE
ARCHITECTURE

Yale University Press
New Haven and London

First published 1965 by Penguin Books Ltd
Fourth edition 1986

20 19 18 17 16 15 14 13 12 11 10 9 8 7 6 5 4 3

Copyright © Richard Krautheimer 1965, 1975, 1979, 1981, and (with Slobodan Ćurčić) 1986

Set in Monophoto Ehrhardt, and printed in Hong Kong through World Print Ltd

Designed by Gerald Cinamon

ISBN 0–300–05296–0
Library of Congress catalog card number 72–93453

TO T.K.

CONTENTS

PREFACE

This book was difficult to write, and I can truthfully say that I have never faced a harder task. The comprehensive presentation of any subject must address itself to a broad spectrum of prospective readers, from the educated public to students and specialists, and thus must attempt to condense the largest possible amount of material into the framework of a few guiding ideas and historical lines as well as tracing, if sketchily, the political, intellectual, and religious forces which determine this development. This is never easy. In the area discussed in this volume, the difficulties increase. The scattering of the monuments over many lands and the difficulty of access make it next to impossible even for the specialist to have visited, far less to know thoroughly, more than a limited number. Reports on the monuments are often fragmentary, and not infrequently published in periodicals not easily available and requiring a linguistic knowledge surpassing that of the author as he moved into regions east of Greece. Providing illustrative material proved difficult in an area where few commercial photographers have been active. The natural unfamiliarity of the general reader with the political and religious background of the periods and territories under discussion, and of even the more important monuments, forces the author into a treatment at times more prolix than desirable. The state of preservation of the monuments – many known only in plan, others in ruins and fragmentary, hardly any preserving their original decoration and few serving their original function – requires a continuous appeal to the visual imagination and a constant effort on the part of the reader. Finally, in discussing an area as scantily known and so far from settled as Early Christian and Byzantine architecture, the summing up will always be a task even more hazardous than in other fields.

But if it has been difficult to write this book, it has also been rewarding. It was possible to spread its preparation over a number of years and to test my views in my teaching, in publications, and in discussions with colleagues and students. The numerous discoveries of Early Christian and Byzantine buildings and sites and the new interpretations of monuments and classes of monuments proffered in recent times, together with the ensuing scholarly discussion, had brought into flux the seemingly stable picture of Late Antique, Early Christian, and Byzantine architecture. Thus it was possible, I hope, to gain new insights into the involved problem and, though much remains obscure, to try out new ways of interpreting the historical sequences and of presenting the subject in its interrelations with the liturgical and political facets of the period. The reader will have to decide whether or not I have succeeded. Further studies will, I hope, again change the picture. I can but present the problems as I see them today, and I shall be content if the reader gains as much from his perusal of the book as I did from writing it.

One final word about the way in which the book relates its material to larger historical questions. The reader will find that the accent is on Early Christian and Byzantine architecture not as a prelude to medieval church building, but as essentially a last phase of Late Antique building. Contrary to many historians, I do not see Early Christian architecture as a fundamentally Western development, but rather as the final expression of the architectural concepts which were dominant in both the Western and Eastern Mediterranean centres and coastal areas of the Late Roman world. The timber-roofed, hall-like basilica, taken over from Roman civil architecture, pervades church building in the East and West up to the time of Justinian, later re-emerging in the West as part of a renascence movement. In the East, on the other hand, the building principles of the Late Empire – in this case, the vaulted, centrally-planned buildings of palace halls, funerary structures, and thermae buildings – come to the fore in the period of Justinian and continue to determine the character and development of religious building in the East for a thousand years or more. In brief, Christian architecture in the East preserves and continues principles of Late Antique building in a natural development, while in the West an Antique building type of comparatively early date dies out only to be consciously resuscitated as part of a revival movement. Consequently in the present volume I am dealing with Christian architecture in the East from the beginnings to the fall of Constantinople, while in the West I am presenting the development to the end of the sixth century, but not further. Building of pre-Carolingian and early Carolingian times represents a different trend, and must therefore be treated separately.

Like anyone, I have profited enormously from talks both with friends, too numerous to list, and with my students, and I am greatly indebted to them. The staffs of institutes and libraries have patiently supported my work, and I want to mention with particular thanks: in Rome, the libraries of the American Academy, of the Bibliotheca Hertziana, of the Pontificio Istituto Orientale, and the Vatican Library; in New York, the libraries of Union Theological Seminary, of the Metropolitan Museum of Art, of Columbia University, particularly Avery Library, and of our own Institute; in Washington D.C., the Dumbarton Oaks Byzantine Research Institute and Library of Harvard University. My more special thanks are due to Dr Djurdje Stričević and Dr Ivanka Nikolajević of the Byzantine Institute of the Serbian Academy of Sciences at Belgrade, who on inter-library loan lent me books missing from Roman libraries. Friends and colleagues from many lands, whose patience I must have all but exhausted, have nevertheless with the greatest generosity sent me photographs for publication and, in still greater numbers, for study. I list them with

gratitude: Professor and Mrs Robert J. Alexander of the University of Iowa; Mrs Selina Ballance, Eton; Dr Carlo Bertelli, Rome; Professor Luigi Crema, Soprintendenza ai Monumenti, Milan; Professor Friedrich Wilhelm Deichmann, German Archeological Institute, Rome; Professor Gerhard H. Evers, Technische Hochschule, Darmstadt; Professor George H. Forsyth, University of Michigan, Ann Arbor; Miss Alison Frantz, Athens and Princeton, whom I want to thank very particularly for the numerous special trips she made to distant monuments; Dr Hildegard Giess, Bibliotheca Hertziana, Rome; Dr Nelson Glueck, Hebrew Union College, Cincinnati; Dr Richard Goodchild, Department of Antiquities, Cyrene; Professor Josephine Harris, Wilson College, Chambersburg, Penn.; Dr Martin Harrison, Lincoln College, Oxford; Dr Vera Ivanova, National Museum, Sofia; Dr G. Kerff, Hamburg; George Kidder-Smith, New York; Professor Ernst Kitzinger, Dumbarton Oaks Byzantine Research Institute, Washington, D.C.; Professor Johannes Kollwitz, University of Freiburg; Professor Jean Lassus, Algiers; Dr H. Lenger, Liebighaus, Frankfurt am Main; Mr Lawrence Majewski, Institute of Fine Arts, New York; Professor Cyril Mango, University of California, Berkeley; Professor Mario Mirabella Roberti, Soprintendenza alle Antichità, Milan; Dr Ernest Nash, Fototeca, American Academy, Rome; Professor Neborov, Sofia; Dr Norman Neuerburg, Fototeca, Rome; Dr Ivanka Nikolajević, Byzantine Institute, Serbian Academy of Sciences, Belgrade; Professor Dimitri Pallas, Athens; Dr Walter Schumacher, Freiburg; Dr Hellmuth Sichtermann, German Archeological Institute, Rome; Dr Gerda Soergel, Landesdenkmalamt, Bonn; Professor Richard Stillwell, Princeton University; Dr Djurdje Stričević, Byzantine Institute, Serbian Academy of Sciences, Belgrade; Mr Cecil L. Striker, Vassar College, Poughkeepsie; Professor A. Tonev, Bulgarian Academy of Sciences, Sofia; Professor Paul Underwood, Dumbarton Oaks Byzantine Research Institute; finally, the librarians of the photographic collections of the German Archaeological Institute in Istanbul, of the Metropolitan Museum in New York, and of the drawings collection of the R.I.B.A. in London. Nor should the so-called 'commercial' photographers be forgotten, who, like Olga Ford, Josephine Powell, Max Hirmer, and Antonello Perissinotto – for love more than for gain – have provided splendid pictures of rarely photographed buildings.

Finally, I want to express my warm gratitude to those who helped me to beat the work into final shape. Mr Paul Lampl, a busy New York architect, generously sacrificed many hours of his time to see to the bulk of text figures, working out reconstructions, drawing and re-drawing plans and isometric perspectives, and generally adjusting the illustrations. In an end phase, Miss Sheila Gibson in London ably supplemented his work. Finally, Mrs Debra Dienstfrey, my assistant at the Institute of Fine Arts, New York, went with a critical eye over every sentence of the manuscript, supervised the typing, and took care of the appendices.

Institute of Fine Arts
New York University
1 December 1963

PREFACE TO THE SECOND EDITION

The preparation of this second edition in paperback – nine years after delivering the manuscript of the first hardback edition – has given me the opportunity to go thoroughly over the volume and to amend, revise, and correct where necessary text, notes, and illustrations. I have also looked with an eye sharpened by distance at the broader aspects of my handiwork: the overall planning and the selection, accentuation, and interpretation of the material. In this task I have been assisted by advice and suggestions proffered orally or in writing by helpful friends, often former students; and by criticism on the part of more and less benevolent reviewers.

The change in format of the new edition forced us to abandon the attempt made in the first edition to preserve common scales for the plans and elevations. The relative scales marked on each drawing will have to suffice.

Amendments and revisions of a substantive nature became necessary in the new edition through new findings made and published since the original manuscript went to the publishers in 1963. Wherever such discoveries concerned key buildings, the amendments have been incorporated into the text, footnoted, and, where possible, illustrated. Examples are: Constantine's basilica at the Holy Sepulchre in Jerusalem and the Anastasis Rotunda – the excavation of the former not yet terminated; St Peter's in Rome – the low transept and its lower wings; the Lateran basilica – the raised inner aisle; S. Tecla in Milan and the Menas Basilica at Abu Mina – both now fully excavated and redated; H. Polyeuktos in Constantinople – now in the course of final publication; the two churches at Hosios Lukas, where the relative and absolute chronology have been reversed; in Constantinople, the Fenari Isa Camii, the Myrelaion church, the Kariye Camii, and the Kalenderhane Camii – the last still under study, but all cleaned up, restored, newly investigated, and precisely dated. Such findings in a number of cases have modified for large groups of buildings either the chronology or the stylistic roots or the liturgical functions formerly envisaged and led to changes in the new edition. Such is the case at Hosios Lukas, where M. Chatzidakis has correctly assigned a tenth-century date to the smaller Theotokos church and thus by implication pushed back by almost a century the appearance in Greece of the cross-in-square plan, of *cloisonné* masonry, and of 'cufic' ornament. Similarly, R. M. Harrison's work at H. Polyeuktos has led not only to the discovery of a huge, 'domed basilica' in Constantinople, precisely dated; it also brings out convincingly the Sassanian character of large parts of the ornament and thus raises basic questions as to the origins and style of architectural decoration in sixth-century Constantinople. These questions will be answered in due time by Mr Harrison; in the present edition I could but hint at their having been posed. Fresh interpretations of material, but insufficiently known heretofore, raise comparable questions. For North Africa, P.-A. Février, N. Duval, and J. Christern have not only established a new chronology; Duval's research has also provided new insights into the liturgical factors of local church planning, while Février calls attention to the social and economic background. C. L. Striker's work on the Kalenderhane Camii has established beyond doubt the survival into the twelfth century of the cross-domed type. Again, Thomas F. Mathews, by re-evaluating the archaeological and liturgical evidence, has changed the picture, heretofore held, of the interplay of church building and liturgy in Justinian's Constantinople, in particular in the H. Sophia. So much for major amendments and the corresponding changes in the text of this edition. Supplementary evidence, such as additional buildings discovered of a known type or additional bibliography, have been relegated, in selection, to footnotes.

Suggestions and criticism have fastened on a number of mistakes which inadvertently had crept into the text. Such oversights are hard to avoid in a book encompassing a vast field; attention to detail is apt to flag under the pressure of formulating concisely one's ideas. Nonetheless they are annoying and I apologize for not having caught them at least in proof. A number I had marked myself over the past years for future correction; others were pointed out by friends and critics. I have striven conscientiously to eliminate from the present edition such blemishes and, if I have done so without footnoting the specific source of the corrections, I nonetheless remain grateful.

Basic questions, too, concerning the overall planning of the book have risen in my mind or been voiced by friends and reviewers. Some shortcomings of a general character are built into the nature of the book and its place within a series. If, for instance, the interplay of architecture and mosaic decoration in Ravenna or in Middle Byzantine Greece is insufficiently stressed, it is because – contrary to the original intention of the editor – the two fields for reasons beyond his control had to be assigned separate volumes. Still, I feel unhappy about thus divorcing two aspects of what might have been treated as an integral design. Likewise, there is some justification to my having assigned but limited space to secular building of Early Byzantine times. It continues, after all, traditions of Late Antiquity as outlined in another volume of this series. Within the limits of the space available it thus seemed preferable to focus on secular architecture in Middle and Late Byzantine times where both literary and archaeological evidence could be integrated into a somewhat consistent and, I trust, new picture. Even so, secular architecture throughout the volume remains on the sidelines and the focus is on church building. This, I admit, is a serious shortcoming. One could well envisage a future history of Early Christian and Byzantine architecture giving secular building equal place with church building, as we are used to seeing it done in the Renaissance. Russian and Bulgarian historians of art even today are inclined, indeed, to give secular building precedence. At this point, though, I doubt the possibility of achieving even as much as a fair balance in the period we are concerned with. Much opposes it: the sheer quantity of well-preserved churches as against secular structures; the poor state of conservation of the latter – except the village houses of Syria; the lack of preliminary work done on the subject, save Tchalenko's on Late Antique and Early Christian Syria, Orlandos' on monastic architecture in Middle Byzantine Greece and on Paleologue palaces and houses at Mistra, Bulgarian scholars' on Middle Byzantine palaces and housing at and near Pliska and Preslav. Lastly there is the conservative element inherent in secular building during Early Christian and Byzantine times: fortifications, palaces, urban planning, and – most outspokenly – ordinary housing resist by sheer inertia the changes which transform plan and design of church building. As it is, church building simply is a better gauge for tracing the history of architecture from Late Antiquity to the fall of Constantinople. I must leave it to future historians to redress the admittedly unfair balance.

There is perhaps an element of unfairness built into all writing of history. It means by definition to choose from a mass of material the essential and to organize the selection by placing accents – all this within the framework of a development as charted by the author in accordance with the factual historical evidence. Whoever has attempted the task knows the difficulties: charting the current; deciding what within its limits is essential; what beyond can be included without obscuring the mainstream. The difficulties naturally increase proportionately to the span of the subject – in our specific case over a thousand years of architectural history in an area comprising first all of the Mediterranean countries and eventually shrinking. Given the underlying overall concepts, numberless issues important in themselves had to be dealt with slightly or omitted outright: provinces retaining obsolete architectural concepts; regional forms, developed on the periphery of the mainstream; creations never reaching fruition. At times such shortcuts hurt badly. Armenian architecture is fascinating in its inventiveness and complexity of both design and origin, the latter far from being clear; but it still is a side branch of the mainstream. Scholars are bound to disagree on what is and what is not essential; the decision and responsibility must lie with the author who to the best of his knowledge has charted main currents and branches.

The currents, once charted, dictate also the placing of accents. As presented here, Early Christian building both in the Latin West and in the inland countries of the East must give precedence to contemporary architecture in the Aegean coastlands. There, in the core of the Eastern Empire, the new Byzantine architecture evolves, closely linked both to local antecedents, architectural and liturgical, and to Imperial demands. At the same time, in the West and the inland countries the development is cut off – by economic, social, and political collapse in the West, the Muslim conquest in the East. Hence the greater stress placed on the architecture of the coastlands seems to me historically justified and the same obtains on similar grounds regarding the stronger accent placed in Middle Byzantine times on Constantinople and her immediate dependencies as against provincial architecture.

In charting the main and side currents, in choosing and in placing accents the historian, I fear, cannot avoid giving some play to personal predilections. I will not deny that the both monumental and complex design of the H. Sophia and its sister buildings appeals to me more strongly than the delicate design of even the best Paleologue architecture – in Constantinople, Salonica, Serbia under Milutin; that, outside these court centres, it seems to me receptive rather than inventive; that even the parekklesion of the Fetiyeh Camii or the Holy Apostles in Salonica do not compare in quality with the Katholikon of Hosios Lukas; that, indeed, Late Byzantine architecture seems to me best understood as an epilogue: decorative rather than architectural; often subtle, but lacking the vigour and inventiveness of Middle Byzantine building under the Macedonians, not to speak of Justinian. Nonetheless, I think I have been unfair in the first edition in restricting unduly the space assigned to and passing all too severe judgement on Paleologue architecture. In this new edition I have tried to correct some of these shortcomings by rewriting the entire chapter. Byzantinists, if their interest is focused mainly or exclusively on the end phase of Byzantine art, will still remain dissatisfied. Within the context of a history of architecture reaching from Constantine I to Constantine XI the outlook cannot but differ from that of a historian of Late Byzantine painting.

Warm thanks go to the many who have assisted in preparing and, I trust, improving the new edition. I list them as they come to mind, disregarding titles and alphabetical order: Cecil L. Striker for much information gained over years of close connection in enjoyable talks in the monuments of Istanbul and in frequent correspondence as well as for photographs and plans of the Bodrum and Kalenderhane Camii; R. Martin Harrison for pleasant discussions on his finds at H. Polyeuktos in Istanbul and their implications; Nezih Firatli for manifold help during recent visits to Istanbul; Semavi Eyice for kindly providing

me with his numerous publications; Thomas F. Mathews for many questions regarding Byzantine liturgy and architecture in Constantinople, jointly and singly, thrashed out in long discussions and letters; Robert L. Van Nice for a new photograph and a friendly corrective note on H. Sophia; Slobodan Ćurčić for invaluable help in the field of Late Byzantine architecture both in Yugoslavia whence he procured information, photographs and plans and in Salonica where on a recent renewed visit we spent an instructive three days together; Vojislav Korać, who through Slobodan Ćurčić sent photographs and reprints on Serbian churches; Charilabis and Laskarina Bouras for numerous reprints which otherwise I might have missed, for photographs of Hosios Lukas, yet unpublished, and for help during that same visit to Salonica; Alison Frantz for acting as a permanent contact with Greece and for the generous help given time and again with camera and pen; Anastasios K. Orlandos for providing access to the first preliminary publications on the new excavations at the Holy Sepulchre in Jerusalem; Fr. Bellarmino Bagatti, OFM, for a long guided tour through the new finds at the Anastasis Rotunda; Moshe Barash and Gustav Kühnel for providing transportation to places in Palestine not accessible on previous visits; Noël Duval, Jürgen Christern, Paul-Albert Février, and Margaret Alexander and her team for numerous photographs of the North African material, for many reprints from Noël Duval and for a delightful tour through Tunisia three years ago arranged by Margaret Alexander; James Morganstern for photographs and detailed reports on Dere Ağzı and Myra; Mario Mirabella Roberti for detailed information on S. Tecla in Milan; W. Eugene Kleinbauer for extensive correspondence and for permission to peruse the first parts of the manuscript of his book, *The Aisled Tetraconch*; George C. Miles and Sir Nikolaus Pevsner for corrective notes; lastly, Friedrich Wilhelm Deichmann for a helpful – if harsh and petty – review (*B.Z.*, LXV, 1972, 102 ff., and my reply *ibid.*, 441 ff.).

To conclude I cannot thank sufficiently the indefatigable crew which has coped with the physical production of the revised manuscript and the book: in Rome, Betsy Emerick, an invaluable assistant, bright, meticulous, patient and good-humoured even when bored; in London, Susan Stow who takes care of missing photographs; Sheila Gibson and Paul White, whose drawings and redrawings of plans and sections speak for themselves; H. A. Shelley, who redrew the maps; finally, Judy Nairn who holds all the threads in her competent, firm hands.

Rome
6 July 1972

The review by Mr Hallensleben in *B.Z.*, LXVI (1973), 120 ff., dealing with Parts 6 and 7 of the first edition of the present volume, comes to my attention as I am reading proof. I have been able to revise a few mistakes kindly pointed out by the reviewer and not caught previously by myself. But I cannot enter into a controversy over the essential points he makes – the 'standing' of Late Byzantine architecture and the place held within its development by Salonica.

Rome
6 July 1973

PREFACE TO THE THIRD EDITION

The text of this the third edition has been revised in those places where new discoveries have required major changes in dating or interpretation. The footnotes have been brought up to date by eliminating obsolete and adding new bibliography.

My thanks go to all colleagues who in the course of the past years have kept me informed about research under way in the field, published and unpublished, and to those critics who have spent much of their precious time in discussing, positively and negatively, the previous editions of this book or individual monuments or problems included therein. For help in completing the new edition I am greatly indebted to Judith Calvert McClendon, Joan Barclay Lloyd, and Deborah W. Kellogg.

Rome
15 June 1978

PREFACE TO THE REVISED THIRD EDITION

This reprinting of the third edition after only two years gives me the welcome opportunity to make a few revisions in the text based on recent findings or new points of view of my own or proffered by others and to bring up to date and expand the bibliographical information provided in the footnotes.

Rome
31 January 1981

PREFACES TO THE FOURTH EDITION

The author wants to express his pleasure and his gratitude to Professor Slobodan Ćurčić for having consented to share with him work on preparing this, the fourth edition, and to take on himself the burden of revising further editions of this volume.

Richard Krautheimer
Rome, 6 July 1984

That a fourth edition of this volume was needed but four years after the revised edition was published in 1981 gives us the feeling that keeping the book up to date, eliminating errors, and possibly improving it, is worthwhile. The publication of key monuments over these last years, or their imminent publication accessible to us through the kindness of the authors – the buildings at the Holy Sepulchre in Jerusalem; S. Lorenzo in Milan; the church of Dere Ağzı; the North African churches; H. Polyeuktos and the Kalenderhane Camii in Constantinople; the Katholikon of the Great Lavra on Mount Athos; the Nea Moni on Chios, to mention but a few – have

enabled us to confirm or rectify our text, and we are most grateful to the colleagues and friends who have provided us with the information on these as well as on many other buildings under investigation. Likewise, new research on Early Christian and Byzantine liturgy and on the liturgical function of ecclesiastical buildings and their parts (twin churches, pastophories) have allowed us to modify, when needed, the corresponding passages. Moreover we have changed some of the judgements on Paleologan architecture expressed in earlier editions.

The footnotes have been brought up to date by adding the recent, and where possible, eliminating obsolete bibliography, and by including additional information and rectifications on old and new sites. Also, so as not to overload the text, we have used the notes to present arguments still *sub judice*, such as date and reconstruction of the Hagia Sophia in Ohrid, for instance. Our special warm thanks go to Mrs Ornella Francisci Osti, who, while preparing the Italian translation of this volume, has gone over the notes with a fine-tooth comb, and straightened out inaccuracies in bibliographic references.

Richard Krautheimer
Rome, October 1985

Slobodan Ćurčić
Princeton, N.J.
October 1985

FRANCE · SPAIN
ALGERIA

Germigny-des-P.

Poitiers

Grenob

Aix

Marseille

Tarragona

Cordova

Granada

Malaga

Gibraltar

Tipasa

Castiglione

Bône

Orléansville

Djemila (Cuicul)

Bénian

Sétif   Henchir

Constantine
(Cirte)   Timgad

Tebess

ALGERIA

0   300 miles

0   500 km.

ITALY · GREECE
& NEIGHBOURING COUNTRIES

ten
gne
nn
Mainz
line

ALIA
ISALPINA
Brescia Vicenza Aquileia Trieste Pécs
Verona Venice Poreč ISTRIA
Parenzo
Ravenna Pula R. Danube
Pisa (Pola)
ILLYRICUM
Zadar Salona Pliska
(Zara) DALMATIA Studenica Niš Preslav Varna
Trogir Split Gračanica Caričin Grad Nessebâr
Perugia (Spalato) Staro Nagoričino Sofia Pirdop (Mesembria)
Rome Kotor Skopje Plovdiv Adrianople Constantinople
Nerezi Peruštica (Edirne) (Istanbul)
Bari Stobi Veljusa Stanimaka Nicome
Naples APULIA Ohrid MACEDONIA THRACE (Izmit)
Salerno (Castro) Lake Salonica Philippi Ferai Nicae
Prespa (Iznik)
Kastorja Thasos Sige
Rossano Great Meteora Mount Athos
CALABRIA Trikala THESSALY Pergamon
Catanzaro Nikopolis Arta Nea-Anchialos (Bergama)
Palermo Stilo Amphissa Skripou Chios Hierapoli
Piazza Armerina Hosios Thebes Izmir (Pammuka
Patras Lukas Athens Ephesus
Syracuse Nauplion Corinth Miletus
MEDITERRANEAN PELOPONNESOS Didyma DereAğz
Mistra (Mystra) Sparta Cos
Siagu Kitta Monemvasia Paros Rhodes
la Christianou Lindos Myra
khira (Dem
Gortyna
SEA
Sabratha Tolmeita Apollonia Latrūn
(Ptolemaïs)
RIPOLITANIA CYRENAICA

TURKEY · PALESTINE
EGYPT

ska

Varna

Nessebâr
(Mesembria)

drianople
dirne)

Constantinople
(Istanbul)

Nicomedia
(Izmit)

Nicaea
(Iznik)

Sige

Ankara

Üçayak

Göreme
Valley

Kayseri (Caesarea)

Eski Andaval

Viranşehir

Gelveri

CAPPADOCIA

Trebizond
(Trabzon)

Ani

Mren

Ereruk

Eghvard

Vagharshapat

Dvin

Zvart'nots

ARME · NIA

Aght'amar

Mayafarquin

Silvan

Amida
(Diyarbekr)

TUR ABDIN

Nisibis (Nusaybin)

Edessa

MESOPOTAMIA

Pergamon
(Bergama)

Izmir

Hierapolis
(Pammukale)

Ephesus

Miletus

dyma

Cos

Rhodes

Lindos

Konya

Binbirkilise

Kanlidivane

Antalya (Adalia)

DereAǧzi

Perge

Aspendos

Korykos

Side
(Eski Antalya)

Alahan
Manastir

Myra
(Demre)

Meriamlik

CILICIA

Dar Qita

Antioch
(Antakya)

Qal'at Si'man

Kharab Shems

Turmanin

Aleppo

Qalb
Lozeh

El-Anderin

Qasr Ibn Wardan

R'safah (Sergiopolis)

Dura-Europos
(Qalat es Salihīye)

Baghdad

Ctesip

Hira

Salamis

Larnaka

Curium

Apamea

SYRIA

Damascus

Tyre
(Sur)

GALILEE

et-Tabgha

Capernaum

Beişan-Beth-Shean (Scythopolis)

Izra

Bosra

Umm-es-Surab

Gerasa (Jerash)

Sichem

Emmaus

Jerusalem

Mambre

Mt Nebo

Bethlehem

Mamshit (Kurnub)

JORDAN

Avdot

Sbeita
(Shivta)

Alexandria

Abu Mina

Hermopolis (Ashmunein)

Cairo

Deir-es-Suriani
(Natrun Valley)

Bawît

Deir Abu Hennes

R. Nile

Sohag

Denderah

Erment
(Armant)

El Khargah

Aswân

Mt. Sinai

RED SEA

Qasr Ibrîm

Faras

Adindán

Serreh (Serra)

0   300 miles

0   500 km.

EARLY CHRISTIAN AND
BYZANTINE ARCHITECTURE

PART ONE

CHRISTIAN BUILDING PRIOR TO CONSTANTINE

CHAPTER I

THE BEGINNINGS OF CHRISTIAN ARCHITECTURE

A.D. 50–150

During the first three centuries of the Christian era, two elements determine the position of Christianity: that it evolved a new faith, and that it did so primarily within the social, cultural, and religious framework of the Late Roman Empire. Christianity's organization, its needs, and even its conflicts with Rome were largely determined by conformity with or by opposition to this framework; and its architecture, as far as we know it, must be seen within the context of the Roman-Hellenistic world.[1]

Religion in Imperial Rome had split into two spheres. Public worship of the gods that guaranteed the welfare of the Empire – Jupiter, the Invincible Sun, or the Emperor's Divine Majesty – was a civic duty performed according to state ritual; worship was required only of those in the sphere or under the scrutiny of officialdom. Spiritual needs were satisfied by divinities of one's personal choice: either native tribal gods or saviour gods, frequently of oriental origin. All these cults, whether centred on Mithras, on the Great Mother, or on Isis, guaranteed salvation after death to the initiated – small, select, and segregated groups in which the brethren might forget social distinctions. No conflict need arise as long as the cult of the Emperor and the cults of personal salvation were not mutually exclusive, or as long as the mandatory worship of officialdom could be avoided. And for the masses, the latter was not difficult.

Within the sphere of Late Antique saviour religions, Christianity grew almost unnoticed for at least a generation after Christ's death. Indeed, were it not for St Paul, the first Christian congregations might well have remained insignificant heretical groups within the Jewish communities of Palestine – that obstreperous Aramaic-speaking backwater. Paul planted the seeds of a world religion in Christianity. He spread the gospel to both Jews and heathens living in the hellenized cities of Greece, along the coast of Asia Minor, and in Rome. He severed Christianity's ties to Judaism and to Jewish nationalism. And he laid down a policy of evading the social and political demands of Roman society. Converts were recruited largely from the metropolitan proletariat, with an occasional member of the middle classes – a retired non-commissioned officer, a freedman, or the like. By A.D. 100, the new faith, while largely centred in the big cities, had spread all over the East to small towns and even to villages.[2] Within the congregations a loose organization gradually developed. Business and other practical matters were taken care of by a group of volunteer administrators, the overseers (episkopoi, bishops), and stewards (diakonoi, deacons). Religious inspiration came from migrating preachers, first from the Disciples, later from 'apostles' and 'prophets'. Ritual was also loosely organized, even at the beginning of the second century. The congregation would assemble at sunrise on Sunday for prayer, and towards evening for a meal (agape) – recalling the

Jewish meal on the Eve of the Sabbath. This evening ritual opened with a blessing over the breaking of the bread and ended with a second blessing over a cup of wine. Prayers were offered either during the meal or after, hymns were sung, and at times a spiritual discourse evolved. A 'prophet', if present, would deliver a sermon or would speak ecstatically in tongues.[3]

These early believers had neither the means, the organization, nor the slightest interest in evolving an ecclesiastical architecture. They met in whatever place suited the occasion. To win proselytes, a group might assemble in a Jewish place of worship – in Jerusalem the Temple precinct, elsewhere a synagogue. But with the widening gap between old and new believers, such mission meetings became increasingly difficult.[4] Christians might assemble at a street corner, as did St Paul and his listeners in the market place at Athens. Rarely would they be able to hire a public hall, as did the congregation at Ephesus at the time of St Paul's visit.[5]

In contrast to such mission meetings – which ceased with the death of the Disciples – regular gatherings would of necessity be held in private, in the house of one or the other of the brethren, 'breaking the bread from house to house'.[6] Since the core of the service was a meal, the given place of the meeting would be the dining-room. And as the congregations were recruited by and large from the lower and middle classes, their houses would have been typical cheap houses. Such houses are known to us, if not from the first and second centuries, at least from the fourth and fifth. In the Eastern provinces, they were apparently one-family buildings up to four storeys high. The dining-room on top was the only large room, and often opened on a terrace. This is the upper floor, the *anageion* or *hyperōon* frequently mentioned in the Acts,[7] the room 'high up, open to the light', of which Tertullian still speaks after A.D. 200.[8] The furnishings would simply consist of a table and three surrounding couches, from which the dining-room takes its name in Latinized Greek – the *triclinium*. The main couch opposite the entrance was presumably reserved for

the elder, the host, and the speaker as honoured guest. The congregation might crowd the room, including the window sills, so that at Troas – from the heat of the many lamps and the length of the sermon – a young man fell from the fourth floor (the *tristegon*), only to be resurrected by the preacher, St Paul.[9] In Rome, where tenement houses with horizontal apartments were the rule, not necessarily including a dining-room, any large chamber may have served for these gatherings.[10] No other rooms would have been required by the congregations. *Postulants*, desiring to be converted, and *catechumens*, converts not yet baptized, were not admitted to 'breaking the bread', and may have left the room before that climax of the meeting. Baptism, originally administered only in flowing water, was performed in standing water, either warm or cold, as early as the beginning of the second century; it took place presumably at a fountain or well in the courtyard of the house, in a bathroom, or in a small, privately owned public bath.[11]

Until A.D. 200, then, a Christian architecture did not and could not exist. Only the state religion erected temples in the tradition of Greek and Roman architecture. The saviour religions, depending on the specific form of their ritual and the finances of their congregation, built oratories above or below ground, from the simplest to the most lavish but always on a small scale. Christian congregations prior to 200 were limited to the realm of domestic architecture, and further, to inconspicuous dwellings of the lower classes. This limitation, and particularly the evasion of the architecture of official worship, is something that becomes decisive for the early development of Christian architecture.

A.D. 150–250

The position and outlook of Christianity changed radically after the middle of the second century. By 250, Asia Minor was sixty per cent Christian. The congregation in Rome numbered thirty to fifty thousand. North Africa counted hundreds of small-town congregations.[12] Through the continuous controversies with pagans and Jews as well as among its own members, dogma became more clearly defined. The last years of the second and the first half of the third century saw the first great Church fathers: Tertullian and Cyprian in Africa, Hippolytus in Rome, Clemens and Origen in Alexandria. Men of wealth and rank rose to leadership: Calixtus, a freedman and wealthy banker, held the office of deacon in Rome, then that of bishop from 217 to 222. By 230, the congregations counted among their members high civil servants and courtiers; Christians, so says Tertullian, have penetrated town councils, the palace, the senate, the forum; and bishops, so says another Church father, had become stewards of the Emperors.[13] The congregations had become increasingly organized and expanded their activities of divine worship and care of souls to include charity, the tending of cemeteries, the administration of property, and instruction classes for proselytes. Bishops, elders (presbyters), and deacons grew into the hierarchy of a professional ordained clergy, each degree entrusted with different spiritual and administrative functions. In Rome, Bishop Dionysius (259–68) established a parochial organization and a similar set-up prevailed throughout the Empire, one bishop presiding over the Christians in each town. As early as 220, the bishops of the metropolitan centres – Rome, Carthage, Alexandria, Ephesus, and possibly Antioch – had gained actual leadership in their respective provinces.

The new strength of Christianity was bound to lead to conflicts with the State.[14] Christianity found it increasingly impossible to evade the demands and avoid the challenges of officialdom. As early as the second century, the self-segregation of the Christians and their voluntary exclusion from official worship and government service had led to suspicion and to sporadic pogroms. By and large, however, the authorities were inclined to consider the Christians harmless sectarians. Persecutions remained localized and far apart: in Rome in 64, at Smyrna in 117, at Lyons in 177. But by 250 the

situation had changed. The Christian segment of the population had grown large and influential. Their refusal to participate in sacrifice, prayer, and public rejoicing for the welfare and success of the Emperor's Divine Majesty forced the government into action. Millions of citizens were obviously subversive, refused to take an oath on the Emperor's godhead, could not be called up for military and civil service, and, indeed, began to claim future secular and political power. Closing both eyes would not do. Two bloody general persecutions, in 250 and 257–60, led to the arrest and execution of Christian leaders in Carthage, Alexandria, and Rome, and to the enforcement of sacrifice, the prohibition of assembly by Christian congregations, and the confiscation of Christian property. But the organization of the Church was too strongly built, and the trust of the faithful in ultimate salvation too strong. The Emperor Gallienus ended the persecution in 260 and restored to the Churches their property, their buildings of worship and cemeteries, and their right of assembly.[15]

The holding of property by Christian communities both before and after the persecutions, then, is assured. The legal basis for such holdings remains a moot question. Possibly the congregations were incorporated as funeral associations and held property under that title. More likely, they purchased and held property by proxy, through a member of the congregation or the bishop. All in all, except for short times of persecution, Christianity was tolerated by Roman practice, if not by law. The large Christian congregations of the Empire, by 250, certainly did not live in hiding. They held services, proselytized, baptized, buried their dead, assisted their needy – and to these ends owned property, either legally or by sufferance.[16]

The structures wanted by the congregation were to serve two purposes: the spiritual needs and social welfare of the living and the cult of the dead. Outside the cities, cemeteries had to be established and maintained where the dead could rest undefiled by neighbouring pagans, where tombs of martyrs were marked by monuments, and where the living could assemble in appropriate structures for memorial services and funeral banquets. Within the cities, congregations needed buildings suitable for assembly of the faithful, administration of the community, and distribution of charities. Small congregations might well continue to meet in private houses; leaders of large communities too would revert to this practice in times of persecution, or else assemble in the less conspicuous buildings on cemeteries. This latter apparently occurred in 250 when the Roman bishop and his deacons were arrested 'on the cemetery of Callixtus'. But as a rule, from the early third century, congregations must have held structures of their own for their manifold needs – structures within the local tradition of domestic building in the Roman-hellenistic world, yet adapted to the new needs of the Christian congregations.

These needs, both religious and social, had expanded rapidly. A rich and clear liturgy had evolved by A.D. 200. The common meal had been relegated to rare occasions: meals offered to the poor (*agapai*), or funeral and memorial banquets (*refrigeria*) held in cemeteries near sites hallowed by martyrs. The regular service consisted of two parts. The first was attended by both the faithful and catechumens and comprised scriptural readings, sermon, and common prayer (Mass of the Catechumens). The second part (Mass of the Faithful) was reserved for fully-fledged members in good standing. It consisted of three parts: the procession of the faithful bringing offerings for the Sacrifice and contributions for the maintenance of the poor and the church; the Sacrifice proper – the Eucharist; and the communion.[17] The assembly room, no longer a dining-room, had to be large, easily accessible, and divided between clergy and laymen.[18] The bishop, flanked by his presbyters, would preside over the assembly from a platform (*tribunal, solium*), seated in an armchair like a Roman magistrate. The congregation was seated outside this presbytery, supervised by the deacons and arranged in a set order. A Syrian church order of c. 250 places children in front, then men, and finally women. In Rome, men apparently occupied one side of the

room, women the other, as continued to be the custom in later times.[19] The furniture was simple, presumably wooden and movable: the bishop's chair, a table (*mensa*) for the Eucharist, and a second table for the offerings (the first table within or in front of the presbytery, the second to one side). A low wooden railing might separate the clergy from the laymen, and this railing, or another, was used to enclose the altar. An anteroom (*vestibulum*) was needed for catechumens and penitents who, dismissed after the first part of the Mass, were to hear, but not see, the Mass of the Faithful.[20] Baptism had also evolved an elaborate liturgy, preceded by anointment and followed by confirmation, requiring both a baptistery and a confirmation room (*consignatorium*).[21] All these rooms, varying in size, had to communicate with each other and allow for a smooth sequence of baptism, confirmation, and regular assembly. Moreover, auxiliary chambers had to be provided: classrooms for instruction of neophytes; a dining-room for celebration of *agapai*; a vestry in which to store altar vessels; and, at times, a library as well. The charities of the Church required the storage, distribution, and administration of food and clothing. Offices and living quarters were needed for the clergy, their families, and the clerical staff. These manifold ends could not be met either by a private house, taken over unchanged, or by an apartment temporarily at the disposal of the congregation. They could be met only by a regular meeting house, owned by the congregation in practice, if not in fact. Such a structure would be called a *domus ecclesiae*, an *oikos ekklisias*, or, in the local parlance of Rome, a *titulus*;[22] community centre or meeting house best renders the meaning of the various terms. Once purchased, the structure would as a rule have to be altered to fit the congregation's needs. Occasionally community houses may even have been built *ex novo*. But all known community houses remain bound in plan and design to the tradition of utilitarian domestic architecture, as well as subject to the regional variations of third-century building within the Roman Empire. Christianity thought of its practical needs along purely utilitarian and private lines. It shied away from the official sphere and from official and religious architecture, which was nearly all loaded with pagan connotations in third-century Rome. Temples were dedicated to the gods of the State; sanctuaries were sacred to pagan saviour gods; and public assembly halls were linked to the worship of the Emperor or the Welfare of the State. 'We have no temples, we have no altars', says Minucius Felix.[23] Inconspicuousness was both prudent and ideologically desirable for Christianity, and could be best achieved behind the façade of domestic middle-class architecture.[24]

Christian community houses of this description, formerly known only dimly from literary evidence, have come to light during the last forty years. None among those known dates from after 400, none from prior to 230. The oldest known building stood at Dura-Europos (Qalat es Sālihīye), near the eastern border of the Empire, and is representative of the position and requirements of a small-town congregation in hellenized-Mesopotamian surroundings. The community houses found in Rome, tenements remodelled in the third and fourth centuries for use by Christian congregations, are typical of the needs and position of the large Christian community in the capital of the Empire.

The meeting house at Dura-Europos is securely dated [1]. It was destroyed with the neighbouring Jewish synagogue and other houses when the town wall was reinforced in 257.[25] When built on the edge of the town, it was an ordinary town dwelling of the customary peristyle type: a courtyard, entered from an alley through a narrow passage, was surrounded on three sides by rooms of varying sizes, and on the fourth side by a portico; into the fresh plaster of one of the rooms a bored workman scratched the year: A.D. 231/2. Whether or not this house was used as such by the Christian congregation for its assemblies is uncertain. But the structure was certainly in the hands of the congregation between 240 and 250. At that time it underwent alterations designed to adapt it better to its functions as a community house. The *divan* in the south wing – the reception room, surrounded on three sides by benches – was merged

1. Dura-Europos (Qalat es Sālihīye), Christian community house, shortly after 200 and *c.* 230. Isometric view

0   40 FT

0   15 M

with the adjoining south-west room. The enlarged room – 5 by 13 m. (16½ by 43 ft) – would have seated a congregation of fifty or sixty. A dais for the bishop occupied the short east wall. Near by, a door led into a small room with wall niches which was apparently a vestry. Large doors, taken over from the older building, opened into the courtyard and into a good-sized room – 4 by 7 m. (13 by 23 ft) – in the west wing. This room, offering space for roughly thirty, would have been an ideal place for the catechumens to hear but not see the Mass of the Faithful, to receive instruction, and to prepare themselves for baptism. Its three doors open into the courtyard, the meeting hall, and into a smaller rectangular baptistery to the north. A tub surmounted by a canopy leans against the west wall of the baptistery; and the murals centre on the ideas of original sin, salvation, and resurrection – ideas closely linked in Early Christian thought to the symbolism of baptism.

Presumably community houses were similarly adapted from private residences in small towns all over the Empire.[26] The minutes of a confiscation of Christian property in a North African country town in 303 vividly reflect the plan of such a *domus ecclesiae* and the function of its several rooms. Moving through the house, the police impound chalices, lamps, and chandeliers in the meeting room; wearing-apparel for the poor in a store room; bookcases and chests in the library; chests and large jugs in a dining-room.[27] Nor were private residences only assimilated to Christian meeting houses. In Dura itself, but a few blocks from the Christian building, the remnants of a Jewish community centre prove that around 200 the Jews also housed their meeting room and needed annexes in a structure much like an ordinary Dura house: a small courtyard enclosed by smaller and larger rooms, among the larger the synagogue, among the smaller a sacristy and two divans, of which one possibly served as a dining-room and the other as a court room.[28] This building was replaced in 245 by a new community centre in which the rooms were larger, the synagogue preceded by a regular forecourt and lavishly decorated with wall paintings – the oldest surviving Old Testament cycle. But all this remained hidden behind windowless walls. Seen from the street, both the Jewish community centres of about 200 and 245 and the Christian *domus ecclesiae* were indistinguishable from any other house in the neighbourhood. This was only natural. Both congregations were small minorities, and although the environment was not necessarily hostile, there was no reason to call attention to an alien element through a conspicuously different structure. Nor is it surprising that both congregations installed their community centres in the district near the city wall, traditionally the quarter of the poor. Financial limitations, the social background of their membership, and the natural desire to be inconspicuous would have made them prefer such a location.

Community houses in the large cities of the Empire – whether Jewish or Christian – would differ from those in country towns for a number of reasons:

the greater wealth and larger size of the congregations, the metropolitan surroundings, and the tradition of large-city domestic architecture. But like their country cousins, the *domus ecclesiae* in the metropolitan centres of the Empire were rooted in domestic architecture and would preserve their unobtrusive presence among the ordinary houses of a large city. Metropolitan architecture, by the early third century, had indeed developed two distinct types, each with a number of variations. The private residences of the wealthy, the *domus*, followed the plan of the old hellenistic or Italo-hellenistic peristyle house. Far more numerous were the buildings designed for the teeming masses of the urban population: tenement houses of up to five or more storeys – either tower-like, as in Alexandria, the apartments heaped on top of each other, or forming large blocks (*insulae*), as in Rome and Ostia, with shops, small thermae, or warehouses at street level and numerous apartments on each of the upper floors.[29] Crowded along narrow, shady, smelly streets bustling with life and noise, these tenements must have looked very much like their late descendants in present-day Rome or Naples.

The Christian communities of Rome installed their *domus ecclesiae* in just such tenements. Their resemblance to ordinary tenements would have made these *tituli* as hard to identify as the meeting rooms of contemporary sects installed in the tenements of New York's Harlem or London's East End. The term *titulus* is a legal one, derived from the marble slab which bore the owner's name and established his title to a property. By the early fourth century the parish organization of Rome rested on twenty-five *tituli*, known under such names as *titulus Clementis, titulus Praxedis, titulus Byzantis*, and the like. These *tituli* exist to this day in name and law, with 'saint' prefixed to the owner's name, or with the original *titulus* name replaced by that of a saint; and each *titulus* is assigned to one of the cardinals of the Roman Church as his title church. Most of these *tituli* are now regular church buildings, laid out from the fourth to the ninth centuries, and often remodelled later. However, incorporated into their walls or preserved below their floors are, almost without exception, the remnants of large tenement houses or private thermae dating from the second or third centuries, or at least from the period before Constantine. Hence it becomes very likely that the pre-Constantinian structures were used as *domus ecclesiae* until replaced much later by regular church buildings which retained the original names of *titulus Clementis*, and so forth.[30]

It is tempting to assume that a large number of these pre-Constantinian structures incorporated into present-day title churches were Christian community centres as early as the third century. But such generalization is hazardous, since no *titulus* can yet be traced beyond the early fourth century by documentary evidence. Concomitantly, the mere presence of a pre-Constantinian tenement incorporated into a fourth-century or later title church constitutes no proof that the structure was a *domus ecclesiae* prior to Constantine. Such proof exists only where the building was remodelled for Christian use in pre-Constantinian times, either structurally or in decoration. Even where a *titulus* was installed in a pre-Constantinian structure as late as the fourth century, however, this use of a tenement or a thermae building is presumably a survival of earlier times when Christian architecture was still fully rooted in domestic architecture.

The structure incorporated into the early-fifth-century church of SS. Giovanni e Paolo offers an example of a second-century tenement house of customary type, with shops on the ground floor and apartments above, which was merged with a small neighbouring thermae, probably shortly before 250. Presumably as early as 250, the ground floor – obviously no longer used for shops – was decorated with murals including Christian subjects. The building at that time must have served as the *titulus Byzantis*, as it appears in documents. However, the evidence furnished by the distribution of windows over the third-century façade, and the strengthening of ground-floor walls and the construction of a monumental staircase (both in the third century), suggest the existence of a large hall on the upper

floor. The hypothesis that the building served as a Christian community house as early as the third century thus becomes admissible. In the last third of the fourth century, a *confessio*, sheltering relics of martyrs, was inserted on a mezzanine landing of the staircase and marked the position of the altar near the east wall in the large hall above. The structure survived until replaced after 400 by the present basilica.[31]

The situation may have been similar in other Roman *tituli*. At S. Clemente, a third-century tenement with shops and what may have been a factory hall on the ground floor gave way in the late fourth century to a basilica [132]. At the same time, a second-century thermae hall was remodelled into the basilica of S. Pudenziana.[32] Conclusive proof is lacking as to the previous use of these structures by Christian congregations, but the likelihood is undeniable. Notwithstanding uncertainty in specific cases, then, the *domus ecclesiae* of third-century Rome appear to have been installed in tenement houses and other utilitarian structures, only slightly adapted, along purely practical lines, to their new function.

Correspondingly, the funeral structures of the early-third-century Christian congregations were utilitarian in design, evolved from Roman funeral architecture of the simplest kind. Christian funeral ritual, like pagan, required both a burial place and a place for memorial services. The services included a funeral banquet at which family and friends assembled round the tomb, feasting and pouring libations into the grave through an opening, the *cataract*. The standard architectural elements were a clearly identified tomb, occasionally provided with a table top, and for the banquet either a tomb chamber with mourners' benches or couches, or a separate room.

Christian custom required slight modifications of Roman traditions, which favoured burial in family groups (including slaves and freedmen) regardless of personal religious belief. Christian usage, at least by A.D. 200, required burial of the faithful uncontaminated by pagan neighbours. Burial near the mausoleum of a pagan patron became gradually impossible. Moreover, Christianity abhorred cremation, which remained standard for the poor in Rome even after the well-to-do had returned – around 150 – to the custom of burial. Hence Christians could not use the mass graves of the Roman lower classes, the *columbaria* crowded with urns on shelves or in niches along the walls of a chamber. Finally, despite the relative wealth of Christian congregations, most members were poor in the early third century; since funeral expenses were private, arrangements for burial had to be simple. And whatever arrangements were to be made, the size of the congregations required that they be made on a large scale.

A solution was found by constructing large communal cemeteries, either open to the sky or underground. Underground cemeteries – catacombs – were advantageous in certain cases: if property values above ground were high, if a terrain of soft rock below a thin layer of soil guaranteed low labour costs, and especially if a previous excavation, quarry, or cistern offered a starting-point. The rare coincidence of such conditions limited catacombs to a few Christian sites in Sicily, North Africa, Naples, and Rome. The beginnings go back to the last quarter of the second and the early third centuries. But catacombs were enlarged throughout the fourth century and occasionally laid out anew. They went out of use during the later fifth century and early sixth century under the impact of political and economic catastrophes with resulting decreases in the labour force and the collapse of land values.[33]

Regional differences among catacombs are marked. In Syracuse, broad galleries formed a spider's web with narrow branches tightly packed with floor tombs (*formae*), and with an occasional tomb niche (*arcosolium*) in the wall of a gallery. In Naples and North Africa, a straight broad gallery forms the core of the catacomb, occasionally widened into a plaza on which rock piers support the ceiling and form a free-standing baldacchino. In Rome, narrow galleries form a tight gridiron scheme, starting frequently with an older hypogaeum group, or a tufa quarry or sandpit

(*arenarium*). Two, three, or even four storeys are superimposed and connected by narrow ramps or stairs. Into the walls are hollowed narrow shelf tombs (*loculi*), sealed with tiles or marble slabs inscribed with a name and blessing [2]. Square or polygonal chambers (*cubicula*) branch off from the corridors. Intended for affluent individuals or families, their walls were set out with *arcosolia* and niches for lamps; ceilings and walls were decorated with frescoes. This archetype is preserved in the oldest portions of the Callisto Catacomb in Rome. The first cemetery of the Roman congregation, it was apparently established before 217 by one of the great organizers of the Church, Calixtus, and enlarged in the course of the third and early fourth centuries. The same simple gridiron type prevails in the other early catacombs near Rome. Only with the increasing demand for space in the fourth century was the network of corridors converted into the maze which impresses and frightens the modern visitor.

The plain archetype derives from the pagan group hypogaeum, which is simplified, regularized, depersonalized, and enlarged for the benefit of a sizeable congregation. The congregation would pay out of its own funds for the ground and the labour of cutting galleries. The individual, poor as he might be, could at least afford a *loculus* of his own. Needless to say, no catacomb was ever intended or used for holding regular services in hiding from persecution. The idea of Roman Christians, thousands strong by 220, marching to the catacombs for Sunday services unbeknown to the police is preposterous. Moreover, the catacombs were damp, dark, intricate, and the largest *cubiculum* would take not even fifty people. Only memorial services were held in catacombs, and if attendance exceeded a bare minimum, even they and the accompanying funeral banquets had to be held above ground. In times of emergency, small groups may have occasionally tried to meet for regular services in a catacomb chamber, but even then the subsidiary buildings above the catacomb were preferred.

By and large, however, third-century Christians preferred to bury their dead in open-air cemeteries

2. Rome, Catacomb of S. Panfilo, third or fourth century. Gallery

(*areae*) rather than in catacombs. Such cemeteries are known to have existed from about A.D. 160. Later ones dating from the third to the sixth century have been found all over the Christian world, in North Africa, Asia Minor, the Balkans, Dalmatia, Rome, Spain, and the Rhineland. Simple graves, often topped by funeral banquet tables (*mensae*), alternated with free-standing sarcophagi. In between rose small mausolea (*cellae*); some have survived, transformed into crypts, in some medieval churches in France.[34] Funeral banqueting halls of varying size were at times enclosed buildings; at other times they were open to the sky; or they were porticoes bordering the area and sheltering a few *mensae* [5, 6].[35]

Such purely practical layouts gave way to slightly more monumental designs when a structure was to serve more than a private memorial function: for example, the public cult of a *martyrium* – the grave of a martyr and a witness for Christ and the Faith, or a place which bore witness through memory of a martyr's sufferings or by the Godhead's manifestation. The worship of such sites and the structures built to shelter them are closely linked to pagan antecedents and contemporary pagan custom.[36]

From time immemorial, pagan antiquity had divinized its great and occasionally its minor dead. An elaborate cult had evolved around mythical heroes, rulers – from tribal chiefs to hellenistic kings and Roman emperors – and members of well-to-do Roman families. The sites linked to their deeds and their deaths had been marked by *heroa*: structures which fused the function and design of temples and sanctuaries with those of mausolea. In their simplest form such heroa were areas open to the sky, terminated by a niche sheltered under an aedicula. In more elaborate form they were enclosed structures: either rectangular halls, longitudinal or transverse, provided with apses; or rotundas, domed like the heavens, raised on high platforms, and preceded by colonnaded deep porticoes. In the course of time, the distinction between heroa and mausolea became obliterated, and by way of heroa, the panoply of the

vocabulary of pagan religious architecture – classical orders and all – enriched the realm of Roman funerary building.

Heroa and the hero cult are the roots from which Christian martyria and the martyr cult sprang, apparently as early as the second century. The finds underneath St Peter's in Rome have unearthed what appears to be the oldest known martyrium. In the midst of a cemetery occupied by lavish monuments of well-to-do followers of oriental cults – all dating from *c.* A.D. 120–60, except for one late-third-century intruder – a small area has survived. It measures 5 by 7 m. (16½ by 23 ft) and contains a few mean graves, possibly the remnant of a poor graveyard which preceded the luxury cemetery. The area is terminated by a wall which oversails one of the poor graves. From brick stamps, the wall can be roughly dated *c.* A.D. 160. Above the grave a niche was hollowed into the wall, either when built or at least before 200. An aedicula was placed in front of the niche, formed by two columns carrying a stone plaque 1·50 m. (5 ft) from the ground [3]. The upper part of the niche continued above the aedicula, perhaps flanked by half-columns and surmounted by a gable.[37]

The archaeological evidence tallies with historical tradition. As early as *c.* 100, local Christian belief held that the apostle Peter had suffered death in Rome; by 200, his *tropaion*, the monument of his victory over death and paganism, was venerated on the Vatican Hill. This is apparently the aedicula now unearthed. Invocations scratched into an adjoining wall leave no doubt that to Christians of the mid third and presumably the late second century, this was the shrine of the apostle. By 320 the lower part of the niche was buried; but its upper part was retained, and on it Constantine's architects focused the enormous mass of their basilica. To this day, it forms the centre of veneration in the church of St Peter's below the high altar. Whether this shrine covered Peter's grave or merely a cenotaph (a fictitious tomb), or whether it simply commemorated his martyrdom, are questions the historian of architecture may well leave open.[38]

3. Rome, St Peter's,
shrine of St Peter,
late second century.
Elevation

N

0   10 FT

0   3 M

A.D. 250–313

Simple martyria abounded after the collapse of
Decius's persecution in 260, and after that, of
Diocletian's of 303–5. Two chambers inside the
Callisto Catacomb – prepared before 207 for the
common burial of Roman bishops and in use until
314 – were joined together by 250 and decorated, if
modestly, by two attached columns [4]. Inscriptions
mark the enlarged room, the 'Chapel of the Popes',
as a martyrium, and indeed in the fourth century it
was provided with an altar and chancel screens.[39]
Martyria above ground were designed as precincts,
resembling the one at the shrine of St Peter but
along quite simple lines. On the site of S. Sebastiano
on the Via Appia, a festival commemorating St Peter
and St Paul was celebrated from A.D. 258. At that
time, an open courtyard was laid out, terminated on
one side by an open loggia – a funeral-banquet hall
(*triclia*) [5]. Were its walls not covered with invoca-

tions of the Apostles (one dated 260) and with
records of feasts in their honour, the loggia might
be the *pergola* of an ordinary *osteria*. Inside the
courtyard, a niche with marble revetment formed
the cult centre.[40] A much simpler martyrium precinct was set up at roughly the same time on a
Christian cemetery found below the medieval
cathedral at far-away Bonn [6] – a rectangular bench
under the sky, surrounding two masonry blocks
rising over two tombs, one block prepared for offering libations.[41]

Numerous small martyria precincts have been
found in the cemeteries of Salona on the Dalmatian
coast.[42] They show half a dozen variants: simple
apses with a bench along their curve, the floor raised
and slightly projecting so as to cover the martyr's
tomb in front; walled-in square courtyards terminated by an apse and sheltering the graves, both of the
martyrs and others; precincts, their front wall opening in an arcade and centred on a banquet mensa,

4. Rome, Catacomb of S. Callisto, Chapel of the Popes, c. 250

0   20 FT
0   5 M

5. Rome, S. Sebastiano, triclia, c. 258. Reconstruction

6. Bonn,
memoria, c. 250

o   10 FT

o   3 M

with the martyr's tomb sheltered by a canopy. At times the precinct is surrounded by porticoes with projecting apses – their number multiplies during Constantine's reign into a maze of apsed chapels. At Salona–Marusinac an elaborate tomb precinct was laid out: a long porticoed courtyard, terminated by an apse and two mausolea projecting sideways. Superficially the plan recalls a basilica with transept, and indeed, the structure at Salona has been termed a 'basilica discoperta' and interpreted as an ancestor of all church building [143].[43] Both the precinct's late date, 426, and the rarity of basilicas with transepts make this thesis untenable. On the contrary, the plan represents a precinct plan barely

monumentalized beyond the most practical needs, and old-fashioned by fifth-century standards.

Open-air precincts apparently gave way during the fourth century to more monumental types of martyria. The Anastasius Mausoleum in Salona, dated c. 305–10, is an example [143]. Others are found in places as far distant as Pécs in Hungary and Alberca in Spain. All are small two-storeyed buildings, rectangular and provided with interior apses, barrel-vaulted and strengthened by exterior buttresses.[44] At Salona, the underground tomb vault sheltered the martyr's body under the apse, the founders' sarcophagi under the nave. The upper chamber, also barrel-vaulted, was presumably used for funeral banquets and memorial services. The type obviously derives from Roman two- and three-storeyed mausolea and heroa, but the placement of an altar over the tomb of the martyr for memorial services introduces a new element, important for the later development of Christian architecture. Simultaneously, elaborate martyria and banqueting halls were built in Rome amidst open-air graveyards above the catacombs. Some were triconchs (*cellae trichorae*), the centre bay vaulted, the façade open in a wide arch or a triple arcade or preceded by a short nave [7]. The martyr's tomb was either below the floor or in a chamber of the catacomb.[45] Other

7. Rome, Catacomb of S. Callisto, cella trichora, c. 300(?), as in c. 1850

martyria were cross-shaped, the centre square groin-vaulted, and the tomb apparently hidden underground in a circular vault enlarged by cross arms. The martyrium above the catacomb of St Praetextatus, perhaps as late as the second half of the fourth century, was a hexagon structure with low niches projecting between high buttresses, the centre room domed and lighted by narrow windows above the apses.[46] Judged by their masonry, all these buildings would seem to date from the first quarter of the fourth century; some may be pre-Constantinian. All are closely linked in plan and design to the tradition of pagan Roman mausolea and heroa of an elaborate type. In exceptional cases, Christian martyria of pre-Constantinian date seemingly absorbed an even more pretentious type of mausoleum, customary in the Eastern provinces: the *tetrapylon*, a four-arched vaulted structure, recalling a canopy such as those rising over the Emperor's throne. The connotations are significant to the placement of such a tetrapylon over the grave of St John the Evangelist at Ephesus perhaps as early as 300.[47]

Monumental forms seem to have penetrated more easily into Christian funerary architecture than into other fields of Christian building. Pagan funeral

building was by and large in the private domain and therefore lacked the religious overtones inherent in all monumental public architecture. It had absorbed from this latter the vocabulary and often the plan, but it was considered neutral and not truly religious architecture. Hence the forms of classical architecture could easily slip into Christian funerary building – whether private mausolea, banqueting halls, or martyria – when deprived of their religious and therefore unacceptable connotations.

On the other hand, the buildings where congregations met for regular services and for the administration of their affairs clung much longer to the concepts of purely utilitarian architecture. Houses, legally or practically in private hands, were used for services even in the early fourth century in North Africa. In Rome *domus ecclesiae* were purchased and remodelled far into the fourth century.[48] Occasionally, however, in the last decades of the third and the first years of the fourth century, a bishop and his congregation felt dissatisfied with the unobtrusive, utilitarian character of the community centres. Against the strong opposition of his brethren, as early as 265 the bishop of Antioch, Paul of Samosate, claimed more showy quarters and the

8. Rome, S. Crisogono,
first church,
early fourth century(?).
Reconstruction

0   30 FT
├──┼──┼──┼──┼──┤
0   10 M

appurtenances, both architectural and ceremonial, of a Roman ranking magistrate: a 'lofty throne' atop a dais, an audience chamber, and the performance of acclamations upon entering the meeting room for services.[49] Dais, throne, and chambers could have been installed, no doubt, in a community house of the old type. Complaints were raised by pagan opponents against what were felt to be pretentious Christian meeting places, such as the one in Nicomedia (Izmit), 'high up amidst large buildings'. However, this structure might still have been an old-fashioned *domus ecclesiae*.[50] On the other hand, the contemporary accusation levelled against the Christians of erecting 'huge buildings thus imitating the structures of temples' can refer only to a meeting hall of public appearance.[51] The walls of at least one pre-Constantinian Christian hall may have survived in Rome in the first church of S. Crisogono, along-side and far below the twelfth-century basilica. It was rectangular, aisleless, truss-roofed, and modest, its right flank possibly skirting a portico and a courtyard [8]. The brickwork suggests a date very early in the fourth century. At the same time, the size of the structure, 15·50 by 27 m. (51 by 89 ft), and the three-arched opening in the façade proclaim its public and to some extent monumental character.[52] The even more impressive S. Sebastiano on the Via Appia may have been laid out just prior to Constantine's occupation of Rome in 312 [20].[53] Yet while such structures have departed from the pseudo-domestic, modest utilitarianism of previous Christian building, they are still far from the concepts of Roman-hellenistic monumental architecture. Not before Constantine are Christian concepts expressed in the language of the official architecture of Late Antiquity.

PART TWO

THE FOURTH CENTURY

CHAPTER 2

CONSTANTINIAN CHURCH BUILDING

With the Edict of Milan in 313 at the beginning of his reign, Constantine recognized Christianity with open favour and granted it official standing.[1] Through word and deed during the following twenty-four years of his life he established the Church as the dominant religious power within the Roman Empire. Church and Empire became closely wedded, and the political as well as the social position of the Church changed radically, in the eyes of the world and in her own eyes. Her hierarchical organization, already strengthened in the decades of peace between 260 and 305, was tightened. It paralleled the administrative organization of the Empire. Villages and parishes had their own clergy; each town had its bishop. The bishops of provincial capitals strengthened their spiritual and administrative leadership previously held by custom. Major sees rose above them: Carthage, Trier, Aquileia, Antioch, Caesarea in Cappadocia, Milan. A few emerged as the dominant ecclesiastical centres of the Empire: Alexandria, the leading centre of Christian thought during the third century; Rome, the old capital of the world; Constantinople, from 330 the new capital and the seat of the court.

The position and organization of the Church during the decisive years from 313 to 337 pivots round the person of Constantine. Layman though he was, and baptized only on his deathbed, he considered himself the thirteenth Apostle, Christ's vicar on earth, and like his pagan predecessors – a thought abhorrent to later generations – an aspect of the Divinity incarnate, the Invincible Sun, the Seat of Justice. As he saw it, he had been divinely appointed to lead Christ's Church to victory. He presided in person at Church Councils, pressed for the settling of dogmatic controversies, and used the machinery of the government to implement decisions of the Councils. He employed the unlimited means of Imperial power to raise the standing of the Church and to draw towards it the pagan world. The Church became an official body closely linked to the Imperial administration and a political power as well. Ladies of the Imperial family, including the Empress Dowager Helena herself, had been devout Christians for some time, as were many women from aristocratic houses. Christian officials were numerous at the court, and the Imperial favour shown to Christianity led large numbers of civil servants and aristocrats to embrace the new religion. By the time of Constantine's death in 337 this interpenetration of ecclesiastical and Imperial power was complete. Christianity, under the Emperor's own auspices, had attained the highest political and social standing. In the decades preceding Diocletian's persecution Christian leaders, anticipating victory, had occasionally arrogated to themselves the insignia of officialdom. Now under Constantine bishops were granted rank, privileges, and the insignia of the highest government officials.[2]

Her new position was bound to affect the liturgy of the Church. A permanent and unchangeable liturgy was required; indeed, minor divergencies notwithstanding, the liturgy of the Mass as established in the early fourth century became nearly uniform all over the Empire. The basic lines remained those of old: the division into the Mass of the Catechumens and of the Faithful; the rite of the oblation; the separation of congregation and clergy; the presiding position of the bishop. But the ritual grew more strict and more solemn. Christ was no longer, as even in the third century, primarily the god of the humble, the miracle-worker and saviour. As Constantine viewed himself as God's vicar on earth, so God was viewed increasingly as the Emperor of Heaven.[3] Hence the liturgy became a ceremonial performed before the Lord or before his representative, the bishop, just as rigidly adhered to as the ceremonial performed before the Emperor or his magistrate. Indeed, the liturgy began to borrow an ever greater number of features from the ceremonial of Roman officialdom and the Imperial court. The bishop, clad in the garments of a high magistrate, entered the church in solemn procession, preceded by the insignia of his official rank, candles and book. Flanked by his presbyters, he was seated on a throne, the *sella curulis* of a Roman official. Every act performed in the church was permeated by this new, official flavour.

Hand in hand with the new public connotations of the ritual goes a strengthening of the hieratic element. Throughout the third century the service had increasingly eliminated the participation of laity and concomitantly insisted on the sacred solemnity of the ritual. Under Constantine, the Mass was further elaborated. At the start of the service, bishop and clergy performed their ceremonious entry into the church. The rite of the oblation at the end of the Mass of the Catechumens became a solemn procession of the congregation depositing their offerings on the altar or a near-by table. The altar, formerly a wooden table easily carried in for the Mass of the Faithful, gradually became a stable structure, often covered with gold and precious stones. Occasionally it was accompanied by a *fastigium*, an arched and pedimented lintel colonnade, like that under which the Emperor revealed himself to his subjects at court, as it survives in Diocletian's palace at Spalato (Split). The graves of the martyrs and their places of martyrdom became the object of a solemn cult and of pilgrimages. In Constantine's late years, this veneration extended to the sites where the gospels and tradition place Christ's life and sufferings.

Christian architecture of the Constantinian period developed within this framework, where practical features were inextricably interwoven with ideological elements. The new official and hieratic character of the Church required a new ground plan. The sanctuary where Mass was said and where the clergy were assembled had to be architecturally distinct from the lay part. All ecclesiastical architecture had to be differentiated from and raised above ordinary buildings. Finally, the official and hieratic overtones of the Church and the dignity of her Imperial patron demanded an architectural vocabulary corresponding to the highest class of public buildings, palaces, and temples.

The large numbers of new Christians required larger church buildings, particularly in urban centres. Concomitantly, the tighter organization of the new liturgy required a stricter differentiation between the various ecclesiastical building types and between the various sections of an individual building. Structures designed for the regular assemblies of the faithful had to be clearly set off from those primarily intended for the cult of venerated sites, and both had to be distinguished from buildings set aside for the baptismal rite or for burial. A forecourt (*atrium*) or a precinct court had to be provided, accessible even to non-believers and postulants, while other provisions had to be made for the large number of catechumens. Under instruction but not yet baptized, the catechumens could remain during the first part of the service, but during the Mass of the Faithful were required to withdraw to a segregated part of the building: entrance, aisles, atrium, or rooms attached to the flanks of the church, or to a second structure near by. The clergy also required a separate area, and this was provided, segregated by screens from the laity, containing the altar, and often raised above the nave.[4]

Church building under these new conditions could no longer remain in the realm of domestic architecture, where it had been rooted for the last two hundred and fifty years. Community centres had no future once the Church had become the Establishment of the Empire. They were too small to accommodate the thousands of new converts. Too many functions were crowded into them, religious, administrative, social, utilitarian. Situated in the slums and hidden indiscriminately behind the plain façade of an ordinary house, they were incompatible with the dignity of the Church and of its Imperial patron. For want of other facilities, the old *domus* continued to be used and occasionally even new ones were purchased. But Christianity under Constantine had to find a new architecture of a higher order, public in character, resplendent in material, and spacious in layout.

For both practical and ideological reasons it was impossible that this new Christian architecture should evolve from the religious architecture of pagan antiquity. Christianity obviously saw in paganism and all its works the very opposite of its own intentions. It shied away from pagan temples to such a degree that neither they nor even their sites were occupied by the Church before the late fourth century in the East or before the sixth century in the West.[5] Just as important, no pagan religious building was adaptable to the needs of Christian worship. The temples of the old gods, an obsolete type by 320 in any event, had been designed to shelter an image, not to accommodate a congregation of both laymen and clergy. To be sure, the sanctuaries of the Neo-Pythagoreans, of Baal, Mithras, the Great Mother, and Attys, all oriental cults, were designed to hold small congregations numbering twenty or thirty, assembled along a central passageway and subordinate to a priest officiating at an altar. The Christian communities of Constantine's time, however, comprised hundreds or thousands of members, and had to evolve their churches within a different framework.

Given her new official standing under Constantine and her new concept of Christ the King, the Christian Church in search of an architecture was bound to turn to the realm of public, official architecture.[6] Within it, she would inevitably single out a building type which combined religious connotations with the criteria of official building. Such a building type existed: the basilica. Since the second and first centuries B.C., basilicas had been built all through the Roman world. In modern architectural parlance, a basilica is a building divided into a nave and two or more aisles, the former higher and wider than the latter, and lit by the windows of a clerestory. But Roman basilicas were rarely, if ever, of this type. In their simplest form they were aisleless halls, occasionally subdivided by supports. In more elaborate form, the nave was enveloped by aisles or by aisles and galleries; or aisles and galleries were doubled; or they ran parallel to the nave instead of enveloping it. The clerestory might be high or low, the entrance could be either on the long or short side, or on both. The tribunal, the seat of the magistrate, rose on a plain dais either inside the nave or in the aisles, or in an apse of rectangular or semicircular plan. Again, this apse might project either from one of the short sides or from the long side, or the number of apses might be doubled or tripled. Open timber roofs or flat ceilings were the rule.[7]

By A.D. 300 this variety had increased even further. Much in contrast to temple architecture the basilica remained immensely alive and prone to change in plan under the impact of other building types. The Basilica of Maxentius was designed as a huge vaulted nave flanked by niches, resembling a thermae hall. Throne basilicas in Imperial palaces occasionally seem to have adopted central plans. Sometimes, though rarely, an open area surrounded by porticoes may have served as a basilica. The most common type, however, at the turn of the fourth century was apparently a longitudinal, timber-roofed hall without aisles, terminated and thus dominated by a raised apse. Huge windows in single or double rows along the flanks lit the interior. The palace basilica at Piazza Armerina, the basilica at Trier, two forum basilicas at Sétif in Algeria, and the hall, now SS. Cosma e Damiano, on the forum in Rome are examples.[8] In conformity with general contemporary practice, the exterior was dominated by plain stretches of wall, the interior was resplendent with marble revetments and gilded capitals and ceilings.

However, in Roman parlance, the term basilica applies to the function rather than to the design of the building, and despite variation the function of Roman basilicas is easily described: a basilica was but a large meeting hall.[9] The forum basilica, found in any Roman town, was but a covered extension of the adjoining market-place – a hall to transact business and to exchange town gossip and news from the Empire, a *souk* to display wares, much like the *galleria* in any modern Italian town. On a dais, the tribunal, the magistrate and his assessors would sit in court; surmounting it, a shrine sheltered the effigy of the Emperor in whose presence alone law could be dispensed and business contracts validly concluded.[10] In large cities a number of basilicas might be assigned different functions: stock and money exchanges, clothing bazaars, florists' arcades, special law courts, each designated by an explanatory epithet. Army camps had their riding and drill basilicas, opening on to a sanctuary where the eagles of the legion and the Emperor's effigy were kept. Large thermae might boast a basilica, where clients could disport themselves.[11] Beginning in the second century A.D., basilicas adapted to the demands of the specific ritual had come to be used by religious sects: the large hall in the sanctuary of Isis and Osiris at Pergamon; the basilica of the Tree Bearers in Rome; a group of synagogues in Galilee. Or again, a funerary college might gather in a tiny funerary basilica.[12] Large reception rooms in wealthy houses were likewise termed basilicas. Outstanding among these were the audience halls, within or near the Imperial palaces, where the Emperor's Divine Majesty, enthroned in the apse, would solemnly appear to his subjects.[13]

At the same time, the direction Christian architecture was to take was determined by the religious connotations which all such basilicas had carried for centuries. These sacred overtones grew stronger with the growing import of the cult of the Emperor's divinity. The palace basilica in which he sat enthroned was *ipso facto* a religious building. The drill basilica of a barracks became religious ground as the garrison paraded and swore loyalty before the Emperor's bust. In forum basilicas, his divine effigy consecrated official and private business. Even in thermae basilicas, the image of the godhead received the homage of those gathered. The borderline between the secular and religious functions of the basilica is fluid throughout Late Antiquity, and the wide variety of purposes for which the buildings served fluctuated between these two poles.

It was almost inevitable that the Church under Constantine would develop, within the framework set by the genus basilica, the buildings she specifically required for the solemn celebration of Mass amidst an assembled congregation presided over by her high dignitaries, bishop and clergy. Clearly, however, the newly-built Christian basilicas were not derived from any specific type of Roman basilica – be it the forum basilica, the Imperial audience hall, or a funerary or a religious basilica. On the contrary, the Christian basilica both in function and design was a new creation within an accustomed framework. In the eyes of contemporaries this was nothing extraordinary. The Christian assembly halls simply represented one more type of basilica created by a new demand. In Constantine's time, the Christian basilica was viewed as just another monumental public meeting hall with religious overtones. Its function had to be explained by a distinctive epithet, such as '*basilica id est dominicum*', an assembly hall that is a house of the Lord, or, 'a basilica for the Apostolic and Catholic congregation'. Or else, Constantine himself refers to the church on Golgotha as 'a basilica more beautiful than all others anywhere', and thus places it on a level with any other assembly hall built for whatever purpose.[14]

Modest basilicas may already have been built by Christian congregations in the years preceding the Peace of the Church: S. Crisogono in Rome is an example. But only under Constantine did architects meet the requirements of the Christian ritual by creating new variations on the ever variable type of the genus basilica. From this background, the Christian basilica drew three or four features which by A.D. 300 had become essential characteristics common to the majority of basilicas whatever their function: the oblong plan; the longitudinal axis; the timber roof, either open or concealed by a flat ceiling – vaulting, as in the Basilica of Maxentius, having remained exceptional in Roman basilicas; finally, the terminating tribunal, whether rectangular or in the form of an apse. Division into nave and aisles and a high clerestory with large windows became preponderant, but they remained optional; galleries remained rare. Within this framework, the Christian basilica had to be brought in line with the demands for greater dignity and monumentality newly created by the Constantinian spirit of Christianity and had to be adapted to specific liturgical requirements, to the financial means and the social standing of the patron, and to local building practice – all widely diverging. The patron might be a poor country congregation, a wealthy bishop, or the Emperor himself. Local building practices might prescribe stone, brick, or concrete construction. The liturgy, while uniform in its general lines, varied locally in implementation. As a result, the clergy might be seated in the apse or in front of it; the altar might be in the apse or in the nave; the offering tables near the altar or in adjoining rooms; the catechumens might withdraw to a forechurch, to the atrium, to the aisles, or to a separate building. Conditions varied further where a building was intended not for the regular services of a congregation, but for the sporadic meetings of local congregations and pilgrims at the tombs of their dead or at the graves of a martyr or at a holy site. Indeed, prior to 350 there was no such thing as *the* Christian basilica; there were only a large number of variants on the theme basilica, adapted to liturgical requirements, building practice, and the wishes of patrons.[15]

Churches from various provinces, built under varying patronage, illustrate the vast variety of Constantinian church planning. The cathedral at Aquileia, replacing a *domus ecclesiae*, was formed by three buildings, completed prior to 319 and perhaps as early as 313: two main halls, running parallel east and west, were connected at their western end by a transverse hall; a small, square room off the transverse hall served as baptistery [9]. The walls and the rich mosaic floors of both the north and south halls survive in large parts underneath and adjoining the eleventh-century cathedral and incorporated into its walls.[16] Each main hall, measuring roughly 20 by 37 m. (66 by 122 ft) and capable of seating several hundred, was divided into three naves of equal width. The six piers or columns of the naves supported flat ceilings; only the east bay of the south hall was surmounted by a transverse coffered barrel-vault built of cane. Set off by a marble screen and a separate floor mosaic, this rectangular bay sheltered the bishop's throne, his *cathedra* (hence cathedral, the building which houses the cathedra), and the bench for the clergy. The altar itself rose farther west, in the nave. From the exterior, the structures must have looked plain. Inside, however, mosaic floors composed of geometric panels framing donors' portraits and Christian symbols, and wall paintings with garden scenes, made for a colourful, if inexpensive decor. Singly, these halls, whether or not subdivided by supports, resemble pre-Constantinian meeting houses, such as S. Crisogono in Rome. Yet, doubled into a complex of buildings, they form a distinct local group. A large number of Constantinian and slightly later churches in the Adriatic provinces were laid out as such 'twin cathedrals'.[17]

Like Aquileia, Orléansville (El-Asnam) in North Africa was an important, although minor, episcopal see. Yet its cathedral, founded perhaps as early as 324 and thus nearly contemporary with Aquileia, shows very different features [10]. Comparatively small – it measures but 16 by 26 m. (53 by 85 ft) clear, corresponding to less than half the surface of either hall at Aquileia – it was a single, isolated building. Its rectangle was divided by four rows of square piers into four narrow aisles and a wide nave, the nave presumably higher and lit by clerestory

PRIOR TO 319, WALLS SURVIVING

PRIOR TO 319, FOUNDATIONS

C. 350 OR 400

40 FT

15 M

9. Aquileia, twin cathedral, plan,
stages of *c.* 313–19 and *c.* 350 or 400

10. Orléansville (El-Asnam) Cathedral,
founded perhaps in 324. Plan

324 (?)

BEFORE 475 (WEST APSE)
AND 6TH CENTURY? (STAIRS)

windows. Mosaics covered the floors. An apse sheltering a small crypt rose high above the floor level, pulled into the body of the building rather than projecting from it. Galleries may have surmounted the aisles; but if so, they were possibly added in the sixth century; certainly the western apse was added, perhaps about 400 and certainly before 475.[18]

The cathedral of Tyre (Sur) on the Lebanese coast, consecrated *c.* 315, represents still another approach. Eusebius's description, although rhetorical and theological in aim, outlines the plan and reflects the impression a lavish church building was designed to make.[19] A *propylaeum*, a monumental colonnade, faced east towards the street, '. . . great and raised aloft, turning the gaze even of strangers to the faith towards the first entrance. . . .' It led to a forecourt, an atrium, enclosed by four colonnaded porticoes, its centre occupied by a fountain.[20] Three portals opened from the atrium into the church. The nave, well lit by windows, towered above the two dark aisles, covered by the gilded beams of a timber roof. Colonnades, whether carrying arches or an architrave, supported the clerestory walls. At the far, western end of the nave rose the altar inside a chancel, while the clergy sat still farther west. A baptistery may have stood somewhere inside the vast precinct wall which enclosed the entire structure, including its forecourt.

Tyre, Aquileia, and Orléansville, then, represent variant types of Constantinian cathedrals. In all three, material and workmanship continued century-old local building practices: in Aquileia the walls were built of small ashlar stone, in Orléansville of small stone held in place by horizontal and vertical stone chains, in Tyre presumably of large stone blocks. The doubling of structures in the Istrian cathedrals may also be a local tradition (double temples had been frequent in that province), and the precinct wall at Tyre enclosing the church and its annexes is but the old hellenistic and ancient Near Eastern *temenos*. Of greater importance than such traditions of construction and planning were local liturgical customs, which by 300 had determined the position of altar, clergy, catechumens, and faithful within Christian meeting rooms for nearly two centuries. The clergy at Orléansville were enthroned in an apse high above the lay folk. At Aquileia they remained at the same level as the congregation, though sheltered by a vault and segregated by screens. The altar at Aquileia and Tyre was placed between clergy and congregation. At Tyre, the catechumens withdrew either into adjoining rooms or into the aisles, possibly curtained off during the

Mass of the Faithful. In the Istrian twin cathedrals, the segregation of catechumens during the Mass of the Faithful apparently determined the layout of the entire building complex. Thus at Aquileia, the transverse hall might have been assigned to the catechumens for withdrawal, while the north hall may have served both as an entrance lobby and as a classroom for instruction. The south hall was the church proper where faithful and clergy remained throughout the entire service.[21]

In other respects, however, the cathedral at Tyre stands out in comparison with its sister buildings at Orléansville and Aquileia. The propylaeum, the atrium, and the high nave filled with light are all elements which the basilica at Tyre shares with Imperial palace architecture. Eusebius's description of the building lays particular emphasis on these features. None were unknown in Late Roman architecture, but the context was different. Syrian temples were frequently preceded by propylaea and by the year 300 such colonnaded porches, their trabeation rising over the centre bay in a pedimented arch, a fastigium, had become a characteristic feature of Imperial palace architecture as well. The atrium at Tyre also has Imperial references: it is derived in all likelihood from the colonnaded courts (*xystoi*) which preceded the audience hall in Imperial palaces and villas – witness the one at Piazza Armerina. Even the high, well-lit nave may have been linked to a tradition of buildings dedicated to the Emperor's cult. To be sure, Roman basilicas with large clerestory windows had not been unknown; but the emphasis on a flood of light grows strongest where a fourth-century building shelters the Emperor, the Invincible Sun, the Sun of Justice, either in person or in effigy, as in the audience hall at Piazza Armerina, in the Basilica of Maxentius, in the Sedes Justitiae at Trier.[22] Such Imperial connotations of church design were strongly felt. After all, Christ too was identified with the Sun of Justice; He had risen at sunrise; His second coming was expected from the East; He was the light of the world. Hence, the mysticism of light would lead fourth-century Christians to think of Imperial audience halls as well

11–13. Rome, Lateran Basilica, begun *c.* 313.
Isometric reconstruction as in 320 (*below*),
foundation wall of apse (*bottom left*),
and foundation wall of nave (*bottom right*)

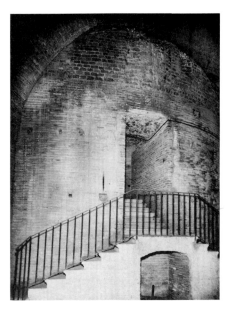

as of churches filled with light. Not that Constantinian churches were derived from palace basilicas: but Christian leaders and their architects quite naturally transferred to their church buildings large parts of the architectural panoply surrounding the Emperor's Divine Majesty. Not by chance does Eusebius view the axis of the church complex – from the propylaeum to the altar and clergy section – as a royal path: along it the congregation approaches the altar of Christ, King of Heaven.

Connotations of the Imperial cult are most patent in churches subsidized by the Imperial house. But they too were far from uniform. In Rome, possibly as

14. Rome, Lateran Basilica, begun c. 313. Reconstruction of nave erroneously arcaded; fresco by F. Gagliardi, c. 1650.
Rome, S. Martino ai Monti

early as 313, Constantine had donated an Imperial palace, the Lateran, to the Church as a residence worthy of the bishop of Rome's standing in the official hierarchy. The cathedral of Rome, the Basilica Constantiniana, now S. Giovanni in Laterano, was laid out on an adjoining site, formerly occupied by the barracks of the Horse Guard which were razed and filled in.[23] Despite fires, earthquakes, and rebuildings – the most incisive the addition of a long chancel (1876–87), the most impressive Borromini's superb remodelling (1645–9) – enough has survived of foundation and other walls and old drawings and descriptions to give an idea of the Constantinian structure [11]. A vast nave, running east and west and flanked by two aisles on either side, was supported by two rows of fifteen huge columns, surmounted by an architrave – this rather than the arcades shown in a late reconstruction [14]. The aisles were separated by low arcades, each resting on twenty-two columns of green marble placed on high pedestals. Large windows lit the outer, semicircular windows presumably the inner, higher aisles, and the practice of Constantinian architecture suggests large windows for the nave as well. A towering projecting apse terminated the nave to the west; its foundation wall is well preserved below the entrance to the nineteenth-century chancel, as are the foundation walls of the nave and aisles in their entire length [12, 13]. The tall, wide transept, however, is a medieval addition; in the Constantinian church, the inner aisles continued to the springing of the apse while the outer aisles were each cut short by a low wing. Projecting sideways, these wings may well have been repositories for the offerings; in modern parlance we would call them sacristies. The nave and aisles would be given to the congregation, the outer aisles possibly curtained off for the withdrawal of the catechumens. In the western section of the nave a chancel in front of the apse and in line with the sacristies, would shelter the altar; a long pathway, enclosed by parapets, extended from the chancel into the nave. The apse held seats for bishop and clergy. Across its opening a huge fastigium of silver may have extended, supported by a double row of columns. Standing below were silver statues: the congregation saw Christ the Teacher seated and flanked by His apostles, while the clergy were faced by a Christ Resurrected, enthroned between four angels. Like the Emperor, then, Christ revealed Himself under the upswept lintel in different but complementary aspects to the people and, as it were, to the high officials of His court.[24]

In size the Lateran basilica was not enormous. Yet with the nave and aisles 75 m. long and 55 m. wide (250 by 180 ft), it would have held a congregation of several thousand. The sanctuary, an additional 20 m. (65 ft) long, would accommodate a clergy of two hundred or more, as would indeed attend the Roman bishop on high holidays. Construction followed local building practice. Foundation walls, the bottom sections built of large fragments of stone and marble and 1·70 m. (5 ft 6 in.) thick, were sunk 10 m. (30 ft) into and below the pre-existing barracks foundations; the top was evened out by concrete masonry faced by *opus listatum* and brick. The foundation of the apse, concrete masonry faced more solidly with brick, went down even farther to reach to the bottom of a slope in the terrain. The upper walls were all concrete masonry with brick facing.

Neither the plan nor the construction of the building, however, was as decisive as its decoration. Nothing survives, but the lists of donations incorporated into the *Liber Pontificalis* speak a clear language. Contrasting with the plainest of exteriors, the interior fused colour, light, and precious materials into a resplendent design. The ceiling, whether open timber or coffered, and the half-dome of the apse shimmered with gold foil high above the yellow, red, and green-spotted marble columns of nave and aisles and the marble revetment of the arcade spandrels. Seven silver altars, six of them probably offering tables, stood in the sanctuary and presumably in the sacristies; the fastigium was of hammered silver. Five chandeliers lit the sanctuary, forty-five the nave, forty the right-hand aisle, twenty-five the left, not to mention the sixty candlesticks, all of gold or silver. The outer walls may well have been plastered, as were those of Constantine's basilica at Trier.[25]

At Trier, where Constantine's father had resided, a cathedral was laid out, some time after 326. It occupied the site of a slightly earlier Imperial palace and apparently was also an Imperial donation. Athanasius, exiled from Alexandria, tells of attending Easter Mass in the unfinished structure in 340. The original foundations of two huge halls have been traced – to the north, below the eleventh-century cathedral; to the south, below the Gothic church of Our Lady [15].[26] Apparently linked to North Italian custom, the church at Trier was

49

15. Trier, twin cathedral,
after 326. Plan

AFTER 326,
WALLS EXCAVATED

AFTER 326,
RECONSTRUCTION

11TH–13TH CENTURY
CHURCHES, OUTLINED

120 FT

40 M

N

designed as a twin cathedral. The two halls were connected by annexes, one of them a large, square baptistery. Chancels, rectangular and set off by screens as in the south hall of Aquileia, terminated the nave in both halls at Trier and were divided into a centre section and small flanking compartments. In other respects, however, the cathedral of Trier differed vastly from the modest bishop's church at Aquileia. Its two halls with a length of 73 and a width of 30 and 38 m. (240 by 100 and 125 ft) were designed to seat a total congregation not much smaller than the Lateran's. Like the Lateran and the cathedral at Tyre, both halls at Trier were also basilicas, divided by supports into a wide and presumably high nave with aisles on either side. Finally, again recalling Tyre, the Trier complex included a vast atrium in front of each hall. Colonnaded porticoes seem to have flanked rather than surrounded these courts, and the one to the north was entered through a monumental structure facing the street. Moreover, in both halls a section near the entrance was apparently screened off, possibly for the withdrawal of the catechumens. Hence,

notwithstanding the resemblance of the plan, the two halls presumably did not have the same functions as at Aquileia.[27]

The wide differences in Constantinian church building, with plans varying according to local custom, become more strongly marked where a church did not serve a regular congregation. In the Sessorian Palace in Rome, the Imperial House or possibly the Empress Dowager Helena herself established S. Croce in Gerusalemme as a palatine chapel and perhaps herself endowed it with a relic of the True Cross. A huge, rectangular hall dating from about A.D. 200 was remodelled for the purpose: an apse was added to one of its short walls and the interior was divided high up by two transverse parallel walls. These interior walls were supported by arches, presumably triple and resting on paired columns. The design fits the concept and function of a court chapel: highly monumental, its three transverse bays – narrow, wide, narrow – lent themselves to a sequence of three sections, for the servants, the court, and the altar, with the clergy presiding in the apse [16].[28]

16. Rome, S. Croce in Gerusalemme, as in c. 329.
Isometric reconstruction

0   60 FT

0   20 M

But palatine churches in Constantinian times are fascinating exceptions. They are far less significant in the overall picture than cathedrals and parish churches. And they are less significant than buildings associated with the cult of the dead, or martyria linked to the veneration of martyrs and of holy sites. These last two groups of buildings become increasingly important in church architecture during the course of Constantine's reign. To a large degree funeral architecture continued along lines laid down in the decades prior to 313, and both catacombs and open-air cemeteries were simply enlarged as the demand increased. Indeed, in Rome as well as in North Africa the great majority of cemeteries, below and above ground, date from Constantine's times and later. Inside the cemeteries, however, the new standing and wealth of the Church, the bounty of the Emperor, and the increased veneration of the martyrs led to significant changes. The tomb of a venerated martyr, such as St Lawrence in his catacomb on the Via Tiburtina, just outside the walls of Rome, was isolated from the rock of the catacomb wall; a sizeable tomb chamber was created around it to form an underground martyrium. A ring enclosing a hollow tube (*cataract*) was placed over the grave, allowing the faithful to peer down, to offer libations of oil and wine, and to lower linen strips, which would acquire the power of a relic through contact with the martyr. Imperial gifts of silver railings, lamps, and candlesticks were placed around the tomb and inside the chamber.[29] Similar changes took place near venerated graves in cemeteries under the open sky. The new spirit of Constantinian Christianity increased the desire to partake of the martyr's blessed status by burial near his tomb, and well-to-do families vied with each other in building apsed enclosures or mausolea as family tomb chapels, as close as possible to the resting place of a martyr. This was the case at the cemetery of Manastirine at Salona, where an early-fourth-century *area* was nearly doubled in size and surrounded by new exedrae, including one attached to the older apse behind the martyr's tomb [17].[30] Pre-Constantinian custom also continues where funeral

17. Salona, memoria precinct, early fourth century and later. Reconstruction

halls were built on Constantinian cemeteries for memorial services and funeral meals. Different in size, but always simply rectangular in plan and obviously timber roofed, such halls are found from Dalmatia and North Italy to the Rhineland.[31]

Different solutions had to be devised, however, by the Christian congregations in the large centres of the Empire. The space available near the shrine of a martyr either in a catacomb or on an open-air cemetery was insufficient to accommodate the huge gatherings expected for memorial services and commemorative banquets. Nor was there room for the hundreds who wanted to be buried near the martyr, coveting that vicinity as an efficacious guarantee of salvation. The funeral banquets had grown into monster kermesses. Naturally the mobs would get out of hand, and drunkenness and dancing, brawls, bawdy songs, and gobbling all became part of the revelry. The celebration of Mass in the early morning hours did little to dampen the excitement. Hence, a new type of structure was required near the tomb of the martyr, one that could accommodate burials and commemorative services as well as funeral banquets culminating in the celebration of the Mass. Large, roofed, their floors covered with graves, these buildings would shelter mensae for funeral banquets, including a mensa for the martyr which also served as an altar during commemorative services held on his feast day. Constantine's contemporaries may have considered such structures not so much churches as funeral banqueting halls and covered cemeteries. But the distinction is fluid, and in the course of the fourth and fifth centuries, these *coemeteria subteglata* absorbed more and more the functions and features of regular churches for the suburban population living near the cemeteries outside the city.[32]

These funeral halls seem to have varied in plan, again following local custom, but all were variants on the age-old genus basilica. Most extraordinary is a group of huge buildings which in recent years has come to light outside the walls of Rome. One, at S. Sebastiano on the Via Appia, is well preserved below a Baroque remodelling; others, at S. Lorenzo on the Via Tiburtina, S. Agnese on the Via Nomentana,

and SS. Marcellino e Pietro on the Via Labicana, are known from excavations. Only S. Agnese seems to date from after Constantine's death. The others are all Constantinian, mainly from the early years of his reign; S. Sebastiano, while completed possibly after 337, may even have been started prior to 313. All rose either near a site hallowed by the presence of the Apostles, as at S. Sebastiano, or near the grave of a great martyr, such as Lawrence or Agnes, situated in a neighbouring catacomb [18]. The martyrs' graves were still enclosed in underground martyria, to be replaced only later by the tomb churches, now surviving for example at S. Lorenzo and S. Agnese. The floors in all were covered with graves from wall to wall, and mausolea crowded around the building, among them at SS. Marcellino e Pietro that of Constantine's mother, Helena, at S. Agnese that of his daughter Constantina, S. Costanza. All were

18. Rome, S. Lorenzo fuori le mura, basilica and
underground memoria as in *c.* 330.
Isometric reconstruction

0   120 FT

0   40 M

huge, between 80 and 100 m. (260 and 340 ft) long [19]. All were basilicas, with nave, aisles, and, as a rule, an entrance porch (*narthex*). Piers or columns supported the clerestory walls. The decor seems to have been uniformly plain. Finally, the aisles in all these halls enveloped the apse and formed an ambulatory – a feature long known in pagan mausolea, but never on a large scale and never merged with a basilican plan [20]. Thus, these funerary halls of Constantinian Rome, intended for

19. Rome, S. Agnese, *c.* 350. Wall of ambulatory; drawing by B. Breenbergh

20. Rome, S. Sebastiano, 312/13(?). Model

mass burial, seem to have fused into a homogeneous design elements from two very different realms: the ambulatory from funerary buildings, and the basilican plan from public architecture.

The focus of veneration – the martyr's grave (*martyrium*), surmounted by an altar – in all these buildings remained in the catacomb and thus outside the structure where the faithful sought burial and assembled for funeral banquets and services commemorating the martyr. In the last fifteen years of Constantine's reign, however, the ever-growing cult of martyrs and holy sites made it imperative to merge the martyrium with the basilica. At times this merger may have been achieved by adapting an ordinary basilica to its new funeral function. On the graveyard of the Five Martyrs at Salona–Kapljuč, the martyrium dating from about 350 shows such adaptation very clearly.[33] The rear half of the structure adopted the plan of a basilica with nave, aisles, apse, and altar enclosure, providing room for the martyrs' graves and for services; the front half served as a covered graveyard for the faithful, bordered on all sides by mausolea. A bishop's tomb could also form the focus of veneration. At Tipasa, on the Algerian coast, a local bishop, Alexander, about 400 endowed the building of a covered cemetery over his tomb, making use of the precinct walls of an older, open-air graveyard. A basilica, very irregular in plan, nave and aisles filled with graves, was built, including one with a semicircular couch for funeral meals. The apse, at the west end, contained only another tomb.[34] The building may reflect early custom, for the solutions characteristic of Late Constantinian times were quite different. The old basilica of St Peter's in Rome is the outstanding example. It was replaced between 1505 and 1613 by the present church, but the excavations and old descriptions, drawings, and paintings give a clear picture of the old building and the history of its construction.[35]

It remains unknown exactly when Constantine decided to house the shrine of St Peter in a huge basilica which would hold thousands of pilgrims; nor is it known when actual construction began. But it was started certainly before 324 – possibly in 319–22.[36] At that time the tomb chambers of the large necropolis surrounding the second-century memoria of the Prince of the Apostles were filled in and their tops cut off. On the new level, a large terrace was driven from east to west and from south to north into the slope of the Vatican Hill. Only the top of the apostle's monument was left, rising near the western end of the site, the church being occidented, not oriented. On the terrace a vast basilica was laid out, enclosing the shrine and covering the entire site. In order to overcome the obstacles of the terrain, the foundation walls of nave and aisles to the south had to be built up some 8 m. (25 ft) from the slope of the hill, while those to the north and west were correspondingly sunk into the uphill slope. Construction proceeded quickly notwithstanding the size of the building and the difficulty of the task; by 329 or shortly later construction, though perhaps not decoration, was complete, and the dedicatory mosaic inscriptions on the arch of the apse and on the triumphal arch were in place. The murals of the nave, still visible in the sixteenth century, dated from the middle of the fifth century. But the original plan of the architects seems to have remained unchanged during execution: the foundation walls are of one build, apparently laid out at the very outset. In width – over seven feet – as well as in construction they recall the foundation of the Lateran, even though at St Peter's the position on the steep slope forced the masons to face the concrete from the very bottom with *opus listatum* or brick.

The expense and labour incurred in overcoming the obstacles of the site are proof in themselves, if no other existed, that the basilica was laid out to house the memoria of the apostle long since held in veneration, making it accessible to the crowds and offering space for services held over it or near by. At the same time, the building served as a covered graveyard and a funeral banqueting hall. Its floors, excavated in the sixteenth century, were found carpeted with graves, some holding fourth-century sarcophagi. Wealthy mausolea, of later fourth-century date, including the mausoleum of the Anicii adjoining the apse and an

21 and 22. Rome, St Peter's, as in *c.* 400. Isometric view (*above*) and plan (*below*)

N

0	
0	120 FT
	40 M

     C. 200

     CONSTANTINIAN

     CONSTANTINIAN (DETAILS HYPOTHETICAL)

     C. 400

Imperial tomb of about 400 built against the south end of the transept, lined the outer walls; and as late as 396 we hear of funeral banquets being held in the church.[37] This double function as both martyrium shrine and funeral hall underlies the size as well as the plan of the structure. The quick and the dead required the largest possible space: huge crowds, Romans as well as pilgrims, assembled to venerate the apostle and to attend services, hundreds desired burial near his memoria, and their relatives were wont to gather for funeral meals. Hence St Peter's had to be laid out on a grander scale than any other Constantinian church building. With a total inner length of 119 m. (391 ft), a nave length of 90 m. (300 ft), and a width of 64 m. (208 ft), it would hold a congregation one fourth larger than the Lateran basilica, the cathedral of Rome; but this had to shelter only the resident congregation of the capital [21, 22].

Likewise, the double function of St Peter's determined its exceptional plan. True, the tall, long nave and flanking aisles, two on either side, recall the Lateran's plan, despite their additional funerary functions. At St Peter's, however – in contrast to the Lateran or to any other Constantinian cathedral or parish church – the nave and aisles did not simply terminate in a chancel part. Instead they were met by a continuous transept, lower than the nave, with yet lower end bays projecting sideways beyond the aisles and undivided except for the end sections. Opposite the nave the transept terminated in a huge apse. Together, they formed an area separate in function and marked off as a distinct part of the basilica. Transept and nave were separated by a triumphal arch, transept and aisles by column screens.[38] Primarily, the transept enshrined the memoria of the apostle, the very focus of the entire construction. Rising on the chord of the apse, his monument was set off by a bronze railing. A baldacchino, resting on four spiral vine scroll columns, rose above it; two more architraved columns linked the baldacchino to the corners of the apse, the openings into the apse being closed by curtains [23].[39] The vast space of the transept would hold the crowds come to venerate the

23. Rome, St Peter's, begun c. 319–22. Shrine and baldacchino represented on an ivory casket from Pola

shrine. Only during commemorative services, it seems, was the transept given over to the clergy as a chancel. The altar, presumably movable, was separated from the shrine; it may have stood within the railing; or it rose near the triumphal arch, where it would have been easily accessible to the communicants. Behind the altar and on either side of the shrine, the assisting clergy would line up during services, bishop and high clerics emerging through the curtains of the apse. The transept was common ground for congregation and clergy, and it served as the site for all rites in which both actively participated: veneration of the shrine, communion, and oblation, the latter possibly taking place inside the low ends of the transept wings where column screens, otherwise unexplained, support dividing walls. Transept and apse, then, served as the site of martyr's shrine, altar, clergy seats, and oblation tables – all in one and poorly separated.[40] Nave and aisles, on the other hand, were a covered cemetery. Thus it recalled covered graveyards, such as S. Lorenzo and S. Sebastiano; yet St Peter's was fundamentally different: the martyrium had emerged, as it were, from the catacomb. Fused with the chancel part into the transept, it had been rendered both visible and accessible to the crowds assembled in the nave and aisles. Transept and apse on one hand, nave and aisles on the other, were different in nature, both functionally and architecturally, and the diversity in function of the two structures is apparent in the awkwardness with which they are loosely attached, rather than joined, to each other.

As in all Constantinian architecture, precious, colourful materials and furnishings focused attention on the interior and led the visitor in a crescendo towards the goal of his pilgrimage. From the river, the street, flanked by Roman tomb monuments, ascended over a slight incline to the triple entrance gate of the atrium. The pilgrim proceeded across the atrium, past the *cantharus*, the fountain. This was a second-century bronze pine cone placed under a splendidly furnished canopy: six porphyry columns, all second-, third-, and early-fourth-century spoils, carried four bronze arches curtained with grilles and surmounted by bronze peacocks [24]. At the west end of the atrium, the pilgrim would see the façade of the nave, plain like all Constantinian exteriors. Entering the nave [25], he moved between two rows of twenty-two huge columns, all spoils, ranging in

24. Rome, St Peter's, begun *c.* 319–22. Atrium; drawing by G. A. Dosio.
Formerly Florence, Uffizi

S Pietro,

25. Rome, St Peter's, begun *c.* 319–22. Interior of nave facing west; drawing by M. van Heemskerck.
Berlin, Kupferstichkabinett

material and colour from green serpentine and yellow giallo antico to red and grey granite, in diameter from 0·92 to 1·18 m. (36¼ to 46½ in). Placed at distances of only 2·50 m. (15 ft), in a proportion not very different from the Parthenon colonnade, their monumentality must have been overwhelming. Like the shafts, the capitals were spoils differing in height and type – Corinthian or composite. Likewise the entablature was composed of spoils, its cornice wide enough to serve as a catwalk for the lamp lighters, and, indeed, protected by a railing. The upper wall of the nave rose to a total height of over 32 m. (105 ft). The double tier of Old Testament frescoes, preserved as late as the sixteenth century,

and their stucco framing were evidently of fifth-century date; Constantine's architects may well have envisaged a non-figural decoration. Eleven wide windows, one to every second inter-columniation, lit the nave. As in the Lateran, the colonnades between the aisles resting on pedestals supported, above an arcade, a wall to carry the roof of the aisles. A row of openings high up in this wall lessened the weight bearing down on the columns. In contrast to the Lateran, however, the aisles seem to have been of equal height, and the inner aisles remained dark. On the other hand, the outer aisles and transept were well lit. In the transept was the shrine of St Peter, the very goal of the pilgrimage. Thus the Constantinian basilica of St Peter's was not an ordinary church, but a martyrium, bound to remain exceptional throughout Early Christian times, unless warranted by an object of veneration as sacred as St Peter's shrine. In the fourth century its plan was taken up in Rome but once – at the shrine of St Paul in 384. Outside Rome it remained equally rare. Not before the Carolingian revival did the basilica with continuous transept come into general use both in Rome and north of the Alps.[41]

St Peter's is the only large Constantinian church enclosing the shrine of a martyr. Otherwise, martyria in Constantine's day were limited to the sites where the Godhead had revealed itself. These sites were naturally all in the Holy Land. The Empress Dowager Helena had visited them on a pilgrimage as early as 326–7. Presumably at her behest, the Emperor donated church buildings on these sites during the last twelve years of his reign: at

the Grotto of the Nativity, on the site of the Resurrection and Crucifixion, at the place on the Mount of Olives and at Mambre where Christ had taught the Disciples, and near the terebinth at Mambre where the Lord had spoken to Abraham.[42] Possibly at the same time, possibly slightly later, relics of the True Cross may have been brought from Jerusalem to more distant sites – to represent, vicariously as it were, the sacred site of Golgotha.

Following the pattern set by early Constantinian funeral halls in Rome, the object of veneration in the christological martyria of the Holy Land remained outside the main hall where the faithful gathered. At the Ramet El Khalil near Mambre, the terebinth of Abraham, enclosed in a large precinct wall, had been venerated by pagans, Jews, and Christians from time immemorial. Shortly before 330, a small church was built at Constantine's behest against one wall of the old enclosure. The plan is far from clear, but a nave, an apse, aisles, and projecting side chambers recalling those of the Lateran have been traced. A long, narrow portico dividing the enclosure served as an entrance hall for the church and the two flanking courtyards. The tree where the Lord had spoken to Abraham stood in a corner of the larger plaza in the front half of the enclosure.[43]

0 |———————————| 60 FT
0   20 M

26. Bethlehem, Church of the Nativity,
as in 333. Isometric reconstruction

Planning was very different at the great sanctuaries built by Constantine to commemorate Christ's Life and Passion. At the Grotto of the Nativity at Bethlehem, as early as 333, a pilgrim from far-away Gaul saw 'a basilica built on orders of Constantine'; apparently its walls, but not its decoration, had been completed by then.[44] It was replaced in the sixth century by the present structure, but its original foundation walls built of huge limestone blocks and its mosaic floor were excavated some fifty years ago. A forecourt, a full 30 m. (100 ft) long, led towards an atrium of 45 by 28 m. (148 by 92 ft), terminated in front of the church by a colonnade raised one step as a propylaeum [26]. The nave and its four aisles covered roughly a square, 28·30 by 29 m. (93 by 95 ft), divided by four colonnades, as in the sixth-century building extant on the site. Possibly the shafts of the present columns are spoils from Constantine's church; certainly their capitals copy fourth-century models. Attached to the east side of this basilica hall rose an octagon, raised three steps and flanked on either side by shorter rooms and intermediate triangular bays. Nave and aisles communicated with this sanctuary presumably through arches. In the centre of the octagon, three steps led up to a railing which protected a wide, circular opening. Piercing the rock ceiling of the grotto, it allowed visitors to gaze into the cave where tradition places the birth of Christ. The octagon may have been lit from above by an opening in its pyramidal roof.

Much remains to be clarified regarding the history and the details of Constantine's church of the Nativity: the splendid mosaic pavements, in the octagon and the hall, were probably not laid until the end of the fourth century; the original access to the grotto may have been in front of the octagon, occupying half of the ascending steps. But the plan of the structure suggests the functions of its principal parts. The outsized forecourt would have served as a resting place for pilgrims and a place for tradespeople catering to their needs. The atrium, too, was large and possibly open to believers and non-believers alike. On the other hand, nave and aisles were barely sufficient to hold a congregation one quarter of that envisaged by the architects of the Lateran basilica. The Christian community in Palestine during the entire fourth century was, after all, small, and pilgrimages were still rare; in Constantine's day the land of Christ was missionary country. In the comparatively small space of the nave and aisles at Bethlehem, then, the congregation and pilgrims would attend services. The altar would have been set in the nave, some distance from the steps leading to the octagon. The clergy may have occupied the octagon, but it served mainly as a martyrium sheltering the site where Christ was born. The *opaion* in its roof and the opening in its floor connected the place of His birth with the sky to which He had risen. Before and after services the faithful could circulate in the octagon and look over the railing down into the grotto. As at St Peter's in Rome martyrium and basilica, then, are attached to each other, but they remain distinct both in plan and function. This distinctness of the two sections is more important than the different designs of the martyria, a continuous transept there, an octagon here.

Likewise in Constantine's basilica on Golgotha a basilica and a centrally-planned martyrium were joined to one another. The Empress Dowager Helena, when visiting in 326, was shown a rock tomb in the heart of Roman Jerusalem as the Holy Sepulchre. Constantine already knew of the find; an imperial rescript enjoined the bishop of Jerusalem to build on the site 'a basilica more beautiful than any on earth'. A reliable if late source mentions the names of the architects, Zenobius, a Syrian name, and the presbyter Eustathios from Constantinople. Begun in 325/6, the basilica – the martyrium as its contemporaries called it – was consecrated in 336 by an assembly of bishops, ordered to Jerusalem from Tyre where they had been gathered for a synod.[45]

Only scant fragments have survived of Constantine's buildings on Golgotha. The Sepulchre in all likelihood was originally one of a number of tomb chambers of traditional Jewish type in a rocky cliff, its entrance facing the rising sun. The fourth-

27(A). Jerusalem, basilica and Anastasis Rotunda on Golgotha. Hypothetical reconstruction of basilica as *c.* 335

century builders isolated it, cut it into conical shape, and decorated it with twelve columns supporting a baldacchino. The huge rotunda enclosing the sepulchre whence Christ had risen – hence Anastasis – may not have been planned from the outset, but built only in Constantine's last year or after his death. The ground extending from the sepulchre to the colonnaded Roman main street, 120 m. (400 ft) to the east, was levelled. The Rock of Calvary some 30 m. (100 ft) south-east of the tomb was shaped into a cube. Between Calvary and the Sepulchre and its rotunda extended a courtyard, enveloped by porticoes on three sides. The one to the east and, behind it, the apse of Constantine's basilica have recently been found. At the opposite, the eastern end of the entire complex, the basilica was preceded by an atrium and a colonnaded propylaeum [27]. Part of the atrium wall and two columns survive and turn out to be remains of a second-century street and adjoining structures. While, like the apse, not on axis with the Sepulchre, they yet establish the width of the complex at roughly 40 m. (130 ft). Given the distance of the atrium façade to the newly found

apse, 74 m. (243 ft), and the depth of the atrium, the basilica, restricted as it further was by the Rock of Calvary to the west, could be but short and wide. Interior and decoration are described by Eusebius but in vague terms. The nave, he says, rested on huge columns – but their hugeness is open to question – and was flanked on either side by double aisles. These in turn were separated either by piers or by a row of short columns rising on pedestals, as at the Lateran. Galleries apparently surmounted both aisles. There is no evidence for clerestory windows; but there was a coffered ceiling and it may have run all across nave and galleries. All this was crowded into a small interior one third the size of the Lateran basilica and the amassing of marble columns, gilded capitals, and ceiling coffers overwhelmed the faithful, as did the polished stone walls and gilded bronze tiles of the exterior. The apse, flanked by side chambers, backed by a straight wall and semicircular inside (or nearly so), was but 8·20 m. wide. It is hard to envision it as the 'head piece of the whole', as described by Eusebius, 'encircled as a wreath by twelve columns, like the number of the apostles',

27(B). Jerusalem, basilica
and Anastasis Rotunda on Golgotha.
Plan of fourth-century
remains

each carrying a silver vessel, the whole topped by a *hemisphairion*, a dome or half-dome. Somewhere Eusebius or – this is more likely – we got confused in trying to interpret the layout. It is not impossible, after all, that after describing the atrium he switched back to the Sepulchre and the sheltering canopy.

The plan, though, remains clear. Propylaeum, atrium, basilica, and the porticoed courtyard beyond led to the climax of the whole: the Tomb of Christ. Services were divided between the various sites and led from one to the other. Mass, except during Passion week, was said in the basilica. But sermons were delivered and hymns sung in the open courtyard as well, and processions moved from the basilica to the Rock of Calvary, to the Holy Sepulchre whence He had risen, and back into the basilica, the martyrium. The entire complex, then, including basilica, Sepulchre, and courtyard, was the martyrium of Christ's sacrifice and resurrection. There seems to be no reason to set apart the area enclosing Golgotha and the Sepulchre as a *basilica discoperta*.[46] All parts of the complex served their specific functions within the curious peripatetic service of the fourth century, more peripatetic than elsewhere at the holy sites, where the regular services of a local congregation were merged with the veneration of the testimonials of Christ's Resurrection by pilgrims come from afar, like Aetheria from Aquitaine, who has described them for us.

27(C). Bread mould, seventh-eighth century, showing buildings on Golgotha:
from left, Propylaeum(?), Basilica, Anastasis Rotunda; below, interior of Basilica(?) and paving of courtyard

St Peter's in Rome, the Church of the Nativity in Bethlehem, and the basilica on Golgotha are parallel solutions to a similar problem: merging within one building complex a meeting hall for the congregation with a monumental shelter over the martyrium. Yet the differences are equally clear. St Peter's, like the covered cemeteries of Rome, was primarily a graveyard and a funerary banqueting hall, and the shrine of St Peter enclosed in the transept represented his tomb. Hence St Peter's rose outside the town, on a graveyard. It had no permanent clergy; mass was celebrated only sporadically for pilgrims' gatherings rather than for a resident congregation. In the Palestinian sanctuaries, on the other hand, no burials ever took place. They rose inside the city limits, and they served as cathedrals where the resident congregations gathered throughout the year. And the shrines which they enclosed were not graves but, in one case, the grotto of Christ's birth, and in the other, the site of the Resurrection, the trophy of His victory.

The differences in function were rooted in different traditions, and they resulted in differences in planning. An octagonal structure, as it terminated the Constantinian church at Bethlehem, is easily traced back to the large Imperial mausolea of Late Antiquity, all of which rise on a central plan. Diocletian's mausoleum at Spalato (Split) comes first to mind: octagonal on the outside, circular on the inside, it is surmounted by the hemisphere of a dome. Eight columns stand against the walls and carry projecting entablatures. Obviously neither Diocletian's mausoleum nor any of the other Imperial mausolea of the late third and early fourth centuries were just tombs. They were heroa, tomb temples designed to commemorate the dead Emperor, raised to the Gods, and to pay him divine honours. Hence, heroa easily adopted from religious buildings such as the Pantheon the round or circular plan, the enveloping niches, the heavenly dome, and the architectural vocabulary. Christianity in Constantinian times, while omitting the actual cult of the Emperor, changed the concept of deification very little. Concomitantly, the function of Imperial heroa

was shifted only so far as to attach them preferably to the flanks or the porch of cemetery basilicas. The mausoleum of Helena, until 329 perhaps intended for Constantine himself, was thus attached to the basilica of SS. Marcellino e Pietro; the mausoleum of Constantina, about 350, was attached to the basilica of S. Agnese in Rome; and the mausoleum of the Honorian dynasty, in about 400, to the south transept of St Peter's.[47] But Constantine's contemporaries must have thought it natural to adapt the plan of Imperial mausolea to the commemoration of Christ – Man, God, and King – and to make such centrally-planned heroa the focus of churches commemorating Christ's Life and Passion. The basilican hall only houses the faithful and directs them towards the heroon-martyrium which enshrines the testimony to Christ's presence on earth. Thus it is but natural that the merger of centrally-planned martyrium and basilica at the height of Constantine's reign remained confined to those churches in the Holy Land which commemorated Christ – human born, risen as God, and reigning in Heaven. Conversely, in this light the transept of St Peter's appears as an emergency solution, newly invented because the Imperial heroon type reserved for Christ was not considered appropriate for any martyr, not even St Peter.

Constantinian church planning knows of no norm. A standard type of church building, what we might call 'the normal Early Christian basilica', evolves only during the second half of the fourth and the fifth century. The most striking feature of Christian architecture during Constantine's reign remains its variety. Christian leaders and architects experiment with the most diverse types: aisleless halls, basilicas, and centralized buildings; basilicas with and without apses; basilicas with projecting wings as at the Lateran; basilicas with ambulatories; basilicas attached to structures of central plan or to continuous transepts; twin cathedrals; structures enclosed within a precinct wall; basilicas with and without atria. Such variations were largely determined by the variety of functions as cathedrals, martyria-basilicas, and covered cemeteries. But even within one category the plans vary. Among cathedrals founded by the Emperor, buildings as different as the Lateran church and the cathedral at Trier stand side by side. Similarly provincial cathedrals and parish churches include such different structures as Orléansville and Aquileia, while martyria-basilicas include the Church of the Nativity at Bethlehem, St Peter's in Rome, and the martyrium on Golgotha.

Contemporary sources intimate some of the reasons for such variety. For the church at Mambre, upon Constantine's behest, a gathering of provincial bishops drew up specifications, obviously taking into account local liturgical custom and the function of the sanctuary as martyrium. For the structures on Golgotha, an Imperial rescript provided that simple materials and workmen were to be supplied by the local governor. Local building practices would then have determined the construction. The plan, on the other hand, may have been the work of Eustathios from Constantinople; and one is tempted to view his fellow architect Zenobius as the local supervisor.

Whether or not Eustathios brought a plan from the Imperial court, Constantine, at least by indirection, exerted his influence on the design of his churches. His letter regarding the buildings on Golgotha advises the bishop to draw on the Imperial treasury for marble columns and the gilding of coffered ceilings. No official, when offered such Imperial bounty, would have hesitated. At Mambre, Constantine enjoins the gathered bishops to plan a church 'worthy of my generosity and worthy of the catholic and apostolic church'. In one of his speeches he envisages the Christian Church as a building preceded by a façade with twelve snow-white marble columns and surmounted by a fastigium.[48] By implication, then, the Emperor recommends a religious architecture coincident with the design of public architecture of the highest class, expressive of his own power and dignity, and absorbing the panoply of the architectural vocabulary proper to Imperial palaces and to public buildings. In the same terms Eusebius had described the cathedral at Tyre: a straight path leads from the propylaeum through the atrium to the 'royal house', the nave, and culminates in the chancel, where behind the altar enclosure, bishop and clergy were enthroned. The church architecture of Constantine must be viewed within the framework of Constantinian public architecture. The massing in one complex of several structures, different in function and often in plan, is basic to Constantinian thermae and palaces no less than to twin cathedrals, martyria-basilicas, and covered cemeteries surrounded by mausolea. Similarly, in public and church complexes alike, courtyards preceded the main building as a xystos or atrium, or surrounded it as a precinct court. More often than not, the principal parts follow each other on a longitudinal axis, but at times longitudinal and transverse elements intersect as in palace buildings and in churches with projecting wings or in twin cathedrals. In church design this grouping is linked both to the variety of functions assigned to the various parts of the building and to the peripatetic character of the service: the clergy entered the church in procession; catechumens and others excluded from communion left the building; the faithful brought their offerings in procession to the sanctuary part; bishop, clergy, and congregation, in martyria churches, such as the structures on Golgotha, filed by the holy site, stopping for prayers and hymns. Today's Christmas procession from Jerusalem to Bethlehem is a last survival of such peripatetic services.

Despite this planning of elaborate complexes, the exteriors of Constantinian churches, as has been seen, were quite simple. All lavishness was concentrated on the interior: gilded ceilings, gold and silver furnishings, variegated marble columns, mosaic decoration. Columns, capitals, and architraves in the Western provinces more often than not were spoils – heterogeneous in type and material, different even in size and design. In the East, decoration apparently remained more homogeneous. But even here the concept of structural order, still prevailing throughout the third century, was gradually being replaced by a new visual approach. To be sure, colonnades supporting archi-

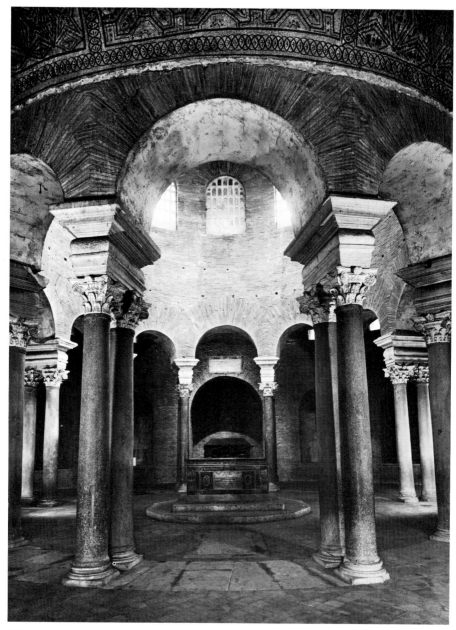

28. Rome, S. Costanza, *c.* 350. Interior

traves remained the rule, as witness St Peter's, the Lateran, and presumably the church at Bethlehem. Even superimposed or giant orders occurred, as in the basilica on Golgotha. But such residuals of the classical, static concept of orders are more frequent in the East and there, too, they are subordinated to a colouristic design which encompasses the entire wall. Constantine's churches, surviving as they do, if at all, under remodellings, have preserved this new design at best in fragments. But the design is known almost in its entirety in the mausoleum of Constantine's daughter Constantina, now S. Costanza, built about 350 against the narthex of the great covered cemetery of S. Agnese in Rome [28]. Here the round domed centre room rises from an arcade carried by twelve pairs of composite columns with splendid impost blocks. Twelve huge clerestory windows flood the centre with light. A dark, barrel-vaulted ambulatory encircles it, interrupted opposite the entrance by a high, well-lit bay, a kind of baldacchino. The 'baldacchino' rises above a porphyry plaque which, below the middle arch of the centre room, once seems to have carried the princess's sarcophagus. Of the decoration, the mosaics of the ambulatory vault have survived: in a crescendo, they lead from geometric patterns in and near the entrance bay, to panels with vine scrolls and putti, culminating in the dark area flanking the sarcophagus with panels strewn with branches and gilded vessels used for libations. These in turn led to the mosaics of the baldacchino, which represented the Heavenly Jerusalem, the Apostles as lambs, and the golden dome of Heaven. These last mosaics are known from sixteenth-century drawings, as is the decoration of the dome, where Old Testament scenes on a blue ground were framed by gilded caryatids with Bacchic panthers crouching at their feet. Between and below the windows, the walls of the centre room were sheathed with a multicoloured marble revetment. Lavish materials, light, and colour were fused into a design clear, but based on visual, not structural elements. The arches in the main axes of the centre room are imperceptibly wider and higher than the others, and again those on the longitudinal axis, above and opposite the sarcophagus, are slightly wider and higher than those on the transverse axis. The small niches in the wall of the ambulatory do not correspond to the arcades; it is only when seen from the arch opposite the sarcophagus that they become fully visible.[49]

The interiors of the great Constantinian churches must have looked similar to S. Costanza or, for that matter, to the Imperial audience hall at Trier. Visual rather than structural relationships determined the picture. The colonnades in the Lateran and at St Peter's stood against the dimly-lit foil of the aisles; the lower colonnades between the aisles in both churches also obey the laws of a visual order; the huge windows of the nave alternate with dark window piers.[50] The Constantinian decoration on the vast expanse of wall at the Lateran and at St Peter's between colonnade and clerestory is lost, if ever it existed: Constantine's architects may well have envisaged marble or imitation revetment surmounted by ornamental mosaics. Yellow and red columns in the nave of the Lateran contrasted with the green speckled columns of the inner arcade, the apse vault shimmered in gold foil. Colour and light more than anything else brought this architecture to life. Light, shining through the wide windows of the nave or during night services flickering from thousands of oil wicks and candles, shimmered on and was reflected by marble columns, revetments, mosaics, gilded ceilings, and precious metal furnishings. The lists of Imperial donations to the Roman churches abound with gold and silver chandeliers, lamps and candlesticks, chalices, patens, jugs, and jars, and with jewelled altar cloths. The rays of the sun shining through the windows of a nave, the reddish glinting of ceilings and mosaics, the shimmering marble columns are recurrent *topoi* in contemporary prose and poetry.

All these features had been increasingly characteristic of all Late Antique architecture since the second century; Constantinian Christian architecture turned out to be the last phase of the architecture of Late Antiquity.

CHAPTER 3

CHRISTIAN ARCHITECTURE IN THE CAPITALS

The political changes in the Roman Empire during the seventy years following Constantine's death were minor. Until 395, his successors ruled over an Empire united by a centralized administration and increasingly christianized. This is true notwithstanding the pagan reaction under Julian the Apostate (360–3) and the prolonged passive resistance of pagan aristocrats, notably in Rome, as well as of pagan scholars in the East. Even the division of the Empire after Theodosius I (379–95) was more in name than in fact. But, as had been the case since the third century, the defence of the frontiers and the administration of the far-flung territories forced the emperors to move their headquarters frequently. Alongside the Constantinian capitals in the East – Constantinople, Antioch, and Nicomedia – new capitals came to the fore in the West. Rome lost her political status. But Milan, Trier, and Cologne gained importance as imperial residences and, witness Milan under St Ambrose, as the sees of powerful Church leaders. At the same time, three cities became paramount in the fourth century as religious centres and pilgrimage goals: Jerusalem, with the holy sites of Christ's Resurrection and Ascension; to a lesser degree, Alexandria, the see of the Egyptian patriarch and supposedly the burial place of St Mark; finally, Rome, now insignificant as a political capital but increasingly important both as the burial place of Peter, Paul, and other martyrs, and as the see of the papacy – the latter, since the fall of the Western Empire, the only unifying political and spiritual power in the Occident.

No wonder that these secular and ecclesiastical capitals became leading architectural centres as well. The court and powerful Church leaders were eager to finance residences and churches for local use and to commemorate the sites of Christ's life and passion, and the graves of His martyrs. In the case of some of the capitals – such as Nicomedia and Alexandria – no monuments, and few sources, survive to document this building activity. Elsewhere – as in Constantinople, Jerusalem, and Antioch – the monumental material is scarce in comparison to the literary evidence available. In Rome, Milan, and Trier, on the other hand, both the monuments and the literary sources abound. Yet wherever evidence is available, it leads to the conclusion that the architects in charge of the new buildings had frequently come from abroad, presumably in the suite of the court. On the other hand, masons, as a rule, were home-bred. Hence the stylistic concepts and the vocabulary of church and palace architecture remain closely linked throughout the political and religious capitals of the Roman world. Differentiations, often conditioned by local traditions of construction technique, are ever present but they play a minor part. Certainly no marked contrast can be seen between stylistic concepts prevailing in the East and West on this highest level of Christian building in the sphere of the court. (The churches built by the congregations outside this sphere follow different lines; but we shall have to postpone their discussion.) In the stratum of the court, the architectural vocabulary likewise remained anchored firmly in the classical tradition of Late Antiquity. The strength of this tradition in the East rested with the scholars and rhetoricians, whether Christian or pagan, attached to the universities and the Imperial court. Through them Church and court were permeated by a classical spirit; and as a result, emperors, courtiers, court bishops, and court architects remained the mainstays of the classical heritage of the new Christian Empire far into the fifth century. Indeed, the classical spirit, weakened in the course of the third and the early fourth centuries, was rekindled in the ambience of the court in the course of the later fourth and the early fifth centuries. It remains obscure whether or not the Greek East led these renascences.[1] Certainly in Rome, except for a small aristocratic (and largely pagan) circle, the classical spirit remained weak for a long time. The Church in Rome remained indifferent to classical learning and culture for the better part of the fourth century; and this position changed only when, late in the century, the papacy came to the fore in the West as a powerful cultural force.[2]

Beginning with the last years of Constantine's reign and continuing through the rest of the fourth century, the increasingly complex requirements of the ecclesiastical services and the close links between Church and Empire led to the development of new church types in the political and spiritual capitals of the Empire. Martyria rise over venerated sites, no longer joined to basilican naves but independent and cross-shaped, circular, or oval in plan; in or near the precincts of Imperial palaces rise tetraconch or octaconch churches. All these types serve also for the regular assemblies of urban congregations, and they appear with only slight variations in the various new capitals of the Empire, from Constantinople to Jerusalem and Cologne, designed and promoted presumably in the migratory ambience of the court, its patrons, theologians, and architects. The majority of the new types disappeared in their original form after two or three hundred years. But their rise in the fourth century demonstrates more than anything else the creative fertility of a Christian architecture which was still firmly rooted in the stylistic concepts and the construction techniques of classical Late Antiquity.

CONSTANTINOPLE

Of Constantine's church buildings in his new capital, hardly a trace has survived. The cathedral he began next to his palace – the first H. Sophia, completed only in 360 – was it seems a large basilica with double aisles and galleries. Short, as compared to its presumably great width, it was preceded by an atrium and perhaps a propylaeum; to the north-east to this day rises a rotunda, the *skeuophylakion* (treasure house), the *diaconicon*.[3] The basilica would have resembled that at the Holy Sepulchre, except of course for its larger size. Neither is there any trace left of the fourth-century Church of the Holy Apostles, which was replaced in 536 by Justinian's church, and in 1469 by the Mosque of the Conqueror, the Fatih. However Eusebius's description of the first structure, written shortly after it had been laid out by Constantine, brings out its salient points.[4] The church rose in the centre of a wide courtyard, skirted by meeting halls, baths, and pools. It was cross-shaped, the entrance arm perhaps slightly elongated. Gilded and coffered ceilings covered all four arms, but it remains to be decided whether they were all aisleless, or divided into nave and aisles. The walls were covered with marble revetment. A drum, well lit by bronze-grilled windows, rose over the crossing and was apparently surmounted by a conical roof. Below this drum stood the sarcophagus of the Emperor, flanked by piers or cenotaphs inscribed to the Twelve Apostles. The sarcophagus and piers stood within an enclosure where Mass was read at an altar. Thus, ostensibly, the building was the mausoleum of the Emperor and a martyrium dedicated to the apostles. Its connotation, however, was that of the heroon-martyrium of the Emperor himself: where he rested in the sign of the cross – as suggested by the plan of the structure; where he was venerated as the thirteenth of the Disciples, in the company of the Twelve Apostles themselves; and where he was the centre, if not of devotion, of attention, as much as or more than the Eucharist celebrated near by. Such an unorthodox outlook apparently became intolerable when, in 356/7, real relics of apostles were brought into the church and Constantine's remains were transferred into a separate, adjoining mausoleum of traditional plan, circular, and domed. From the outset, the Apostoleion was a martyrium, much as the basilicas at the Holy Sepulchre, at Bethlehem, and at the tomb of St Peter. But in its plan Constantine's Church of the

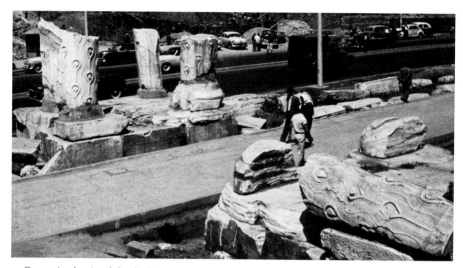

29. Constantinople, triumphal arch of Theodosius I, 393

Apostles marks a new departure. The martyrium section – rather than being appended to the nave and aisles of a basilica, as at Bethlehem, or hidden underground in a catacomb, as at S. Lorenzo in Rome – becomes the very core of the structure. To this core the four arms are appended to shelter the faithful. A new type of martyrium has sprung up, a self-sufficient structure centred on the focus of veneration.

Dozens of churches during the later fourth and the early fifth centuries copied the plan of Constantine's Apostoleion – as the term 'copy' was understood from Antiquity throughout the Middle Ages.[5] From the original Apostoleion they take over at least two paramount features: the plan with its connotation of the True Cross and the dedication to the Apostles. At times a great saint, a local apostle as it were, takes the place of the True Disciples. We shall encounter such 'copies' of late-fourth- and early-fifth-century date at Milan and Ravenna, at Ephesus and Antioch, at Gaza and Sichem; likewise, the Apostoleion of Constantine seems to have exerted at least a collateral impact on the formation of basilicas with cross transept, such as that in the city of Menas.

The types East and West differ in plan: in the East the four arms radiate from a central nucleus, while in the West two lateral arms issue from a continuous longitudinal nave.[6] However, the far-reaching impact exerted by Constantine's Church of the Apostles need not mean that already in his own day Constantine's capital was a major architectural centre. Nothing survives of the palaces, squares, colonnaded streets, and public buildings which contemporary and later writers have attributed to his building activity. In fact, what fourth-century buildings are left in Constantinople date from the very end of the period. But these mark the Constantinople of A.D. 400 as a centre of the first magnitude. There is the hippodrome, as enlarged by Theodosius I (379–95), its impressive substructure dropping twenty-odd metres (60–70 ft) into the valley. There is the base and capital of the colossal column which carried his equestrian statue; there are the remnants of a huge triumphal arch, dating from 393, supported by four clusters of columns, their shafts marked by 'tear drops' in imitation of the trunk of a cypress tree [29]. Finally, the remains of two adjoining palaces have been found north of the hippodrome, both dating probably from the first decades of the fifth century. In both, flights of steps ascend to a colonnaded curved façade, behind which lie the reception rooms. In the smaller palace the reception room is round, its wall hollowed by ten niches; a door opposite the entrance leads into a longish hall, apsed and flanked on either side by three niches: a banqueting hall of a type customary in Constantinople, as witness the (lost) Hall of the Nineteen Couches in the Imperial Palace, each couch assigned to a niche, with the apse holding the Imperial High Table. In the second palace, a hex-agonal hall occupies the centre – each of its sides over 10 m. (30 ft) wide and enlarged by a deep niche;

small roundels separate the niches, opened, it seems, towards the outside in colonnaded arcades. (The hall in the sixth century became the church of H. Euphemia.) Circular reception rooms, quite sizeable, follow the hexagon hall on either side, and were followed farther along the hemicycle of the façade by smaller octagonal rooms. The combina-tion of hemicycles, rotundas, hexagons, and octa-gons gives a faint idea of the inventiveness of Late Antique palace architecture still in fifth-century Constantinople [30]. Another circular, niched and domed palace hall of somewhat later date has come to light near the Myrelaion church: well preserved to a height of five-odd metres (about 16 ft), and pre-

30. Constantinople, palaces north of the hippodrome, early fifth century with later additions. Plan

0   120 FT

0   40 M

N

PALACE OF ANTIOCHUS, EARLY 5TH CENTURY, (HEXAGONAL HALL BECOMES H. EUPHEMIA C. 550)

PALACE OF LAUSOS, 5TH CENTURY, (BANQUETING HALL NICHES C. 530, VAULTING C. 550?)

MAUSOLEA, ADDED TO H. EUPHEMIA

ceded by a colonnaded porch, its interior diameter was 29·60 m. (100 Roman, or about 97 English feet), its walls 6.10 m. (20 ft) thick. In the tenth century it was transformed into a multi-columnar cistern, whose vaults served to carry a small palace.[7]

Better than anything else, utilitarian building in Constantinople attests to her position as an architectural centre of the first rank in the decades at the turn of and throughout the fifth century. Cisterns were built all over the city and her suburbs, the major ones open to the sky, others certainly as early as the fifth century vaulted over dense rows of columns. Most impressive among open cisterns is the Fildami cistern freed c. 1965 at Bakirköy, 127 metres long, and 75 wide (416 by 246 ft); its façade, buttressed by niches, still rises nearly to its full original height, roughly ten metres [31]. The most outstanding utilitarian structure was of course the

31. Bakirköy, Fildami cistern, fifth century

32. Constantinople, city wall, 412/13, with later repairs

land walls of Constantinople, laid out in 412/13. Four and a half miles long, the main wall rises to 30 ft; it is 16 ft thick and preceded by an advanced wall and a 60-ft-wide moat [32]. Ninety-six towers, square or polygonal in plan, project from the main wall, and six major gates gave access to the city. Barring repairs of eighth- and twelfth-century date, the whole is remarkably well preserved. It gives a splendid idea both of the working organization – the main wall was apparently completed in little more than a year – of fifth-century military engineering, and of the building techniques of Constantinople at the time. While Roman fortifications as a rule had been limited to a towered main wall and a moat, the insertion of an advanced wall creates, perhaps for the first time in military history, a *double enceinte*: a system of fortifications which in the later Middle Ages plays a large part in the military history of Western Europe. The walls are constructed in a technique which is found in the palaces of the hippodrome as well and remains customary in the capital for a long time: concrete faced with small limestone blocks and reinforced at varying distances by brick bands, each consisting of five or more courses of thin bricks – each 3 to 5 cm. (1¼ to 2 in.) high – with mortar beds of equal thickness. The towers are built in the same technique, except for the two which flank the Golden Gate and those which face the Sea of Marmara – all of huge marble blocks. Passages and stairways inside the towers are barrel-vaulted with bricks pitched on their sides; chambers are domed with concentric rings of bricks. In 439, a corresponding wall, simpler in layout, was built along the Sea of Marmara. The walls of Salonica, *c.* 450, are almost equally impressive and other fortifications around the Aegean, such as those of Nikopolis, represent the type on a smaller scale.[8]

The walls of Constantinople are one of the great sights of the Late Antique world. At the same time all these city walls are characteristic of the conservative character of building in the sphere of Constantinople during the fifth century. To be sure, the *double enceinte* fortification represented an effective innovation, as long as military tactics and siege equipment remained essentially unchanged. However, the technique of construction – mortared rubble levelled by brick bands and faced with stone – had been customary for a long time along the west coast of Asia Minor and apparently had been imported into Constantinople. It is equally important to realize that the decorative vocabulary of public architecture in Constantinople about 400 shows remarkably conservative features, and that it too appears to be rooted in a century-old tradition indigenous to Asia Minor.[9] The capitals from the arch of Theodosius are hardly distinct from classical prototypes and thus exemplify the beginnings of the classical current which – in more lively form – becomes characteristic of the art of Constantinople in the later fifth century.

JERUSALEM

Buildings surviving in Constantinople from post-Constantinian times are mostly fortifications and palaces of comparatively late date. In Jerusalem, on the other hand, and all over the Holy Land remains have survived of a number of ecclesiastical structures dating from the last years of Constantine and subsequently. The majority were erected over the sites of Christ's life and passion and are therefore martyria, in function identical to those built by Constantine at Bethlehem and on Golgotha. But in contrast to such structures of the twenties, late and post-Constantinian martyria in Palestine and all over the Christian world shun the fusion of a centralized 'head piece' with a basilican nave. Rather, the centralized martyrium becomes self-sufficient.

Two types of such central-plan martyria pre-dominate in the fourth and fifth centuries, both derived from Constantinian models. Cross-shaped martyria, with four arms of equal length or nearly so, whether aisleless or basilican are clearly variants on Constantine's own martyrium, the Apostoleion in Constantinople. In Palestine, one such structure, built – probably before 380 – over the Well of Jacob near Sichem (Shechem) where Christ met the Woman of Samaria, is known from a plan and description of a seventh-century pilgrim, Arculf, and from parts excavated. Others were built at Gaza, Antioch, Milan, and elsewhere.[10] In the Holy Land, however, unattached martyria obviously would turn to Constantine's Anastasis Rotunda as a natural prototype.[11] Built of solid ashlar blocks and sheltering the sepulchre of Christ, it faced, at the western end of a shallow three-porticoed courtyard, the apse of Constantine's martyrium-basilica. Possibly planned from the outset, but apparently not yet completed in 336, it seems to have been in use by 350. Despite frequent remodellings, its original plan has been ascertained in its main lines. A straight façade, pierced by portals, faced the courtyard where rose the Rock of Calvary. Inside, the Anastasis was laid out as a huge rotunda, 33·70 m. (110 ft) in diameter, its centre room enveloped by an ambulatory of irregular shape [27B, 33]. In the very middle of the

33. Jerusalem, Anastasis Rotunda, as in 1609. Engraving by J. Callot

structure – both its focus and its *raison d'être* – rose the cone of Christ's sepulchre below Constantine's baldacchino. The centre room was encircled by twenty supports carrying an arcade, though deprived possibly of two piers where to the east the façade cut in. Ideally, though, the circle of supports was arranged, presumably from the outset, in four

groups of three. Pairs of piers on the main axis formed a cross; the columns in the diagonals were grouped in triads, symbolizing – in the interpretation of the Fathers – the Twelve Apostles, and the four ends of the world to which they bring the four-fold gospel of the Trinity. The ambulatory, semicircular and with three niches projecting, embraced the western half of the centre nave, terminating in rectangular spaces near the façade. A gallery above the ambulatory accommodated the faithful unable to find room on the ground floor. Finally, above the clerestory zone rose a dome. It was possibly of timber construction, and – but this is not certain – open in the centre like the roof of the octagon over the Grotto at Bethlehem. The overall design was clumsy, the columns stout and placed on high pedestals, the walls extraordinarily heavy.

The Anastasis Rotunda clearly stands in a tradition of Late Antiquity with strong classical overtones. Whether or not the capitals of the columns and the profiles of their high pedestals were as classical as the old reproductions pretend, the plan is rooted in the tradition of Imperial mausolea and heroa. This is but natural in a structure designed to shelter the sepulchre and to commemorate the resurrection – dare one say the apotheosis – of Christ, the *basileus* of Heaven, the Risen Sun. The huge mausolea-heroa of Imperial Rome come to mind: that of Helena; that of Diocletian at Spalato; and finally, the mausoleum of Constantina, this latter – like the Anastasis – encircled by an inside ambulatory [28]. No doubt the same sources served the architects both of S. Costanza and the Anastasis. Indeed, one wonders whether the self-sufficient circular martyria of the Holy Land, of which the Anastasis Rotunda is first and foremost, should not be interpreted as part of a renascence movement of late- or post-Constantinian times. Against the fusion of basilican and central plan, the free-standing martyria re-establish the tradition of the Imperial mausoleum-heroon.

The Anastasis Rotunda was not the only structure of its kind among the martyria of the Holy Land. Excavations on the Mount of Olives have brought to light a few of the walls of the Imbomon, the sanctuary built in 370 by the Roman lady Pomoenia to commemorate the site from which Christ rose to Heaven.[12] A part of the circular outer wall has been found – indicating a diameter of roughly 18 m. (60 ft) for the rotunda – together with the remains of an outer colonnade. Inside, the early pilgrims saw another colonnade – that is, an ambulatory – perhaps double-storeyed. The ambulatory enveloped an enclosure, which encircled the rock with the footprints of the ascending Christ. This centre room either had no roof whatever, or its timber roof – possibly conical – terminated in a huge opaion. To the east, a chancel and apse, starting from the centre room, seem to have pierced the ambulatory. In either case, the Imbomon represented a variant on the plan of the Anastasis Rotunda. Nor was it the only variant. A sanctuary much like the Imbomon has been excavated at Beišan–Beth Shean (Scythopolis) in northern Palestine. It was no doubt a martyrium, but the event it commemorated or the relic it sheltered remains unknown.[13] Such centrally planned martyria, whether rotundas or polygons, appear in other variations on the holy sites of Palestine: possibly over the Tomb of the Virgin in the Valley of Josaphat outside Jerusalem;[14] certainly in a church which the Emperor Zeno (474–75, 476–91) dedicated to the Virgin on Mount Garizim (Gerizim) near Sichem – in plan an octagon rather than a circle and sheltering a piece from the Rock of Calvary [118].

Outside the Holy Land 'copies' of the Anastasis and of its filiations were frequent in medieval Europe,[15] but they seem to have been comparatively rare in the Christian world of the fourth and fifth centuries. One example which comes to mind is the church of H. Karpos and Polykarpos in Constantinople. Only the circular substructure survives, but it clearly suggests at ground-level a building composed of a domed centre room and an ambulatory, the latter pierced by chancel and apse. The masonry points to a date near A.D. 400, and the plan as well as a local tradition imply that the church was a comparatively early copy of the Anastasis.[16]

ANTIOCH

Excavations undertaken some years ago have provided for a fairly clear picture of the domestic architecture of Antioch (Antakya). Dozens of houses and villas, mostly of the fifth and sixth centuries, have come to light, following the age-old Greek house plan centred on a peristyle court and lavishly decorated with mosaic pavement.[17] However, few churches have been found; and only one dates from the fourth century, when Antioch was still an Imperial residence: the martyrium of the local martyr St Babylas, whose remains were exhumed during the reign of Julian the Apostate, and whose tomb became a new centre of veneration in the seventies. Built at Kaoussié, just outside the ancient city, and begun probably in 379, his new martyrium was cross-shaped.[18] The centre, square and presumably surmounted by a pyramidal timber roof, incorporated a chancel enclosure which sheltered the altar, the grave of the saint, and the graves of two of his successors on the episcopal throne of Antioch. From this centre section – a kind of towering baldacchino – extended four arms, lower, aisleless, and timber-roofed [34]. The colourful geometric designs of their mosaic floors contrasted vividly with the plain marble pavement of the centre square. The model was obviously Constantine's Church of the Apostles; in the eyes of the Antioch congregation the relics of St Babylas stood for those of the Disciples and deserved a similar resting place. Even so, some new elements penetrate the structure at Antioch. A baptistery was built against one of the cross arms, and a sacristy against another, thus adapting the martyrium for regular church services. This development, of course, had started under Constantine, the basilica on Golgotha serving both as martyrium and as cathedral of the permanent congregation of Jerusalem, and, like the martyrium of St Babylas, provided with a baptistery. The progressive absorption of the martyrium plan as a regular church type becomes obvious.

Earlier than the martyrium of St Babylas and more important among the churches of Antioch was

34. Antioch-Kaoussié, St Babylas,
begun probably 379. Plan

LATER ADDITIONS

N

0   60 FT

0   20 M

the Golden Octagon adjoining the Imperial palace on the Orontes island in the centre of the city. Begun by Constantine in 327, it was dedicated – two years after the Council of Nicaea – to Harmony, the divine power that unites Universe, Church, and Empire, and completed in 341 under his son Constantius. No trace has survived of the structure. But its outlines become fairly clear from its name, its summary representation on a floor mosaic found in a villa outside Antioch, its description given by Eusebius, and from the scattered remarks of later writers.[19] Eight-sided, it was preceded by a double-storeyed narthex and surmounted by a gilded roof. Inside, its octagonal centre room carried either a pyramidal roof or, perhaps from the outset, a dome in timber construction. This core was enveloped by colonnaded aisles – Eusebius says *oikoi* – on two levels (that is, an ambulatory and a gallery), and by niches (*exedrae*). The plan may be visualized in two alternative ways; either ambulatory and gallery directly adjoined the centre room, while the niches opened outward from the ambulatory; or the niches billowed from the centre room into the enveloping spaces of ambulatory and gallery. Both solutions are possible.

The first corresponds roughly to the plan of the church on Mount Garizim [118]; the second anticipates by two hundred years the plans of H. Sergios and Bakchos in Constantinople and of S. Vitale in Ravenna – a double-shell construction[20] in which a domed central core is enveloped by the ancillary spaces of aisles and galleries [180, 187].

The Golden Octagon has been called a martyrium.[21] But there is no evidence that it ever sheltered an important relic. From the outset it seems to have been the cathedral of Antioch jointly with the previous see of the bishop in an older church.[22] However, the location of the Octagon adjoining the palace precinct; the person of its imperial founder; and its dedication to the divine force uniting both Church and Empire, suggest that in contemporary eyes it was both the cathedral and coterminally the church linked to the palace where the Emperor, God's counterpart on earth, would attend public services jointly with his subjects. Thus the Antioch Octagon would seem to be the ancestor of a group of churches, similar in shape, function and location, as built by Justinian and in later times, from H. Sergios and Bakchos and the H. Sophia to

Charlemagne's chapel at Aix-la-Chapelle: all octagonal in plan, composed of centre room, ambulatory, and a gallery level, and all close to the ruler's palace.[23] Given the probable identity of function and resemblance in plan, a direct link between Justinian's H. Sophia and Constantine's Antioch church does not seem improbable.

However, the lines run back as well. Beginning with the first century, large centrally-planned halls become an increasingly frequent and an increasingly important component in the layout of Late Roman and Early Christian palaces and palace villas. They may be circular, like the one in the smaller palace north of the hippodrome in Constantinople, or like the huge domed rotunda in Diocletian's palace at Spalato. They may be hexagonal, like the hall – later the church of H. Euphemia – in the larger palace north of the hippodrome in Constantinople, or octagonal, as in Nero's Golden House, or even decagonal, like the structure in Rome known as the Minerva Medica. Whether round or polygonal, they may or may not be provided with niches; and these may be hollowed into the thickness of the walls or may billow outward and, indeed, open through arcades into adjoining rooms [30, 186]. Or else such centrally-planned palace rooms were triconchs: the one at Piazza Armerina may stand as an example for many others. No tetraconchs have been found so far in palaces; but it is likely that these too existed. Whatever their shape, however, these centrally-planned palace structures served closely related functions, though under a variety of names. Placed often on the centre axis and at the entrance either of the palace or of its state apartments, they may be *salutatoria*. The rotunda in Diocletian's palace at Spalato is an example: preceded by a colonnaded 'peristyle' and raised on a podium, its front is surmounted by the arcuated lintel of a *fastigium* – a glorification façade.[24] Inside the room, the Emperor would presumably receive the high court charges; later he would reveal himself below the fastigium to his subjects assembled in the open-air area in front – the *tribunalium*. Elsewhere, such centrally-planned palace rooms were apparently audience-and-throne

halls, that is, *basilicae* in contemporary terminology; a '*basilica quae trullus appellatus*' existed in the Great Palace in Constantinople. It has disappeared, but it was obviously domed and presumably of central plan. As early as the second century, the throne room of Septimius Severus with its astrological vault may well have been circular or polygonal in shape.[25] Or again, centrally-planned rooms in palaces, whether triconch, polygonal, or round, served as triclinia: not just dining rooms as the term originally implied, but State banqueting halls, where the Emperor partook of his meal as a God in the ceremony of the *coenatio Jovis*; or they were simply throne-and-audience rooms. The borderline fluctuates, but on the whole the purpose remains the same. Triconch triclinia are found from the second to the sixth century, witness the audience hall in governor's palace at Qasr Ibn Wardan of 563–4; as late as the ninth century the type is represented by the *triconchos*, known from literary sources in the Imperial Palace at Constantinople.[26] The triclinium in Nero's Golden House was an octagon.[27] Between 310 and 320, the type seems to be represented by the Minerva Medica [186]: surmounted by a dome, its decagonal core billows outward in ten niches, some of them pierced by triple arcades. A podium with heating facilities filled the rear of the centre room, opposite the entrance, and would have been suitable for a banqueting table or a throne. The building may well have been designed as a throne room and State banqueting hall for the winter. Later, two nymphaea were added on the exterior, making the structure comfortable for summer as well.[28] Needless to say, in all such triclinia, salutatoria, and basilicae, religious and secular functions interlocked, as implied in the position of the God-Emperor; in domed rooms in particular the idea of the Dome of Heaven was ever present. In the Chrysotriklinos, the Golden Triclinium, of the Great Palace in Constantinople, the type survives as late as the end of the sixth century. No trace remains of it, but the descriptions leave little doubt regarding its plan: circular, enveloped by eight vaulted niches – perhaps double-storeyed – which opened into adjoining rooms. The centre space was surmounted by sixteen windows placed into the webs of a pumpkin dome. Also, like the Late Roman audience halls, its functions were both religious and secular: it served as audience hall for the Emperor's Majesty and as palace chapel.[29]

True, this double function of the Chrysotriklinos is not documented prior to the tenth century. But the interlocking of the Imperial and the religious sphere goes far back into Late Roman times, pagan and Christian. Thus the transfer of the plan of a circular audience hall to an Imperial palace church is likely enough. If, then, the Golden Octagon at Antioch was indeed in location and function linked to the palace, its close resemblance to central plan audience halls becomes plausible, regardless of which alternative is chosen for reconstructing its plan.

If the Golden Octagon was both the cathedral and Constantine's court church at Antioch, it was the first of its kind. But such court churches in the fourth century were probably more frequent than we imagine. So far none have been definitely ascertained, but the 'suspects' are numerous. Of S. Lorenzo in Milan we shall speak soon. A tetraconch rather than an octagon, it nevertheless shares several features with the church at Antioch: the centripetal plan, the enveloping aisles and galleries, the neighbourhood of an Imperial palace. But churches linked to the palace may have differed widely. H. Georgios in Salonica is an example.[30] Its core had been built close to, and as part of, the Imperial palace layout about 300, functioning either as a mausoleum or a throne room. Covered by a huge dome 24 m. (80 ft) in diameter, it was an imposing rotunda built in the same masonry technique which a century later would serve for the walls of Constantinople. Eight barrel-vaulted niches lightened the thickness of its 12-foot walls. About 400 or 450, this rotunda was turned into a church. A chancel and apse were added, an ambulatory was built, all in brick-faced concrete, and the walls of the niches were pierced. A narthex, flanked by staircase turrets and thus probably double-storeyed, projected towards the main road, which led from the triumphal arch of Galerius and, beyond, from the palace grounds. A rich mosaic of saints standing against complex niches and fastigia covers the dome. The plan obviously recalls more closely martyria such as H. Karpos and Polykarpos at Constantinople rather than either the Golden Octagon at Antioch or S. Lorenzo in Milan. But the closeness to the palace and the central plan make it equally plausible that it was to serve as a palace or a court church.[31]

Altogether, in the fourth century, throughout the Eastern capitals of Constantinople, Antioch, and Jerusalem, we are forced to rely mostly on literary evidence and conjecture. We are on firmer ground as we turn to the architecture in the political and religious centres of the West.

MILAN

More clearly than any other centre, Milan conveys an idea of the impact exerted by the new capitals on the formation of a grandiose church architecture since the middle of the fourth century.[32] From 353 the city had frequently been the Imperial residence and, in effect, the capital of the West. In 373 it became the see of St Ambrose, and, through him, for some decades the spiritual centre of the West as well. Discoveries in recent years have shown that at one time Milan was also one of the great architectural centres of the Christian world. Its importance is demonstrated by five huge churches, three of them standing to this day at nearly their full height – S. Nazaro, S. Simpliciano, S. Giovanni in Conca, S. Tecla, and S. Lorenzo, of which only S. Lorenzo has long been known. Their widely differing plans show the inventiveness of the builders then assembled round the Imperial and episcopal courts at Milan. They have in common monumentality of design, grandeur of volumes, powerful, stark walls, and articulating pilaster strips, blind arcades, and dwarf galleries. They are covered with simple great vaults or timber roofs, and their construction is in solid masonry: high bricks, occasionally laid in herringbone patterns and interspersed with large pebbles, with low beds of white mortar.

35 and 36.
Milan, S. Lorenzo, shortly before 378.
Plan and exterior from
the south-east; to the south, S. Aquilino

37. Milan, S. Lorenzo, shortly before 378. Interior facing south-west

S. Lorenzo is a huge quatrefoil structure, of double-shell design [35]: an inner shell, formed by the centre room, is enveloped by an outer shell, that is, the ambulatories and galleries. Remodellings of twelfth- and sixteenth-century date have changed the details but not the basic design as it was laid out presumably some time shortly before 378 – a date suggested by historical circumstances and by the technique of the masonry.[33] The atrium, facing the street as today, is preceded by a colonnaded propylaeum: its trabeation, in the centre, curves up into an arch – the old symbol of Imperial power. Four towers rise at the corners of the church [36]. They are tall, but not much higher than the square drum which originally rose over the centre space instead of the present octagon of sixteenth-century date. As complex and as beautiful as this rich silhouette is the interior. A central space, 23·80 m. (78 ft – that is, 80 Roman ft) square and originally c. 27·50 m. (90 ft) high, is marked off at the corners by four L-shaped piers [37]. Covered presumably by a dome in hollow-tube or cane technique or by a groin-vault,[34] this core swings out on its sides in four wide double-storeyed exedrae – open on both floors, each in five arches. Their supports, originally either columns or square piers, in an eleventh-century remodelling were replaced by or re-cut into the present octagonal piers. In the sixteenth century, the centre square, its corners bridged by arches, was transformed into an octagon to support the present eight-sided drum and dome. The original tetraconch core – a kind of huge baldacchino – is enveloped by the ancillary zones of aisles and galleries in a double spatial belt, each lit by a row of wide windows. The double-shell construction, the ensuing complexity of the spatial design, and the overlapping views combine with the contrasts of light and shade to create an interplay of superb richness. This splendour was further emphasized by the original decoration: walls faced with marble, walls and vaults set off by friezes, window soffits by tendrils, both stucco, the vault with gold mosaic – all of it contrasting with the starkness of the exterior. Both starkness and lavish interior decoration were taken up in the adjoining much smaller structure of S. Aquilino [35, 36]. Planned at the same time as the huge quatrefoil, it seems to have been an Imperial mausoleum. It is a niched octagon with its outside walls surmounted by a dwarf gallery resting on slender piers. The interior was covered with marble revetment and mosaics, some well-preserved, and surmounted by a cloister-vault in sheer brickwork. This is a technique of

vaulting very different from that previously customary in the West, but it finds its parallels at an early time in the Aegean coastlands.[35] An Eastern architect may have been at work. Links to the East were close while the emperors resided in Milan – a Cappadocian, the Arian Auxentius, was Ambrose's predecessor. But this does not make S. Lorenzo into an Eastern building. In plan it belongs to the family of double-shell designs which had become common property of thermae and garden and palace buildings all over the Empire from the fourth century, if not before, and which, during that century already, started its migration into church architecture. Within this new church architecture, the specific function of S. Lorenzo remains still in doubt. It lay outside the city walls and thus could hardly have been the ordinary church of one of the urban congregations; nor is any important relic known ever to have been venerated in the church, and the late dedication to St Lawrence rules out the possibility of its foundation as a martyrium. On the other hand, it lies close to the Imperial palace. Thus it was possibly built as court church and cathedral for the Arian court when under St Ambrose the urban cathedral, S. Tecla, became Catholic. Indeed, its plan recalls again the possible reconstruction of the Golden Octagon and the palace churches of Justinian's time.

Among the churches of Milan, S. Lorenzo is unique. But links to the other Imperial capitals remain strong in all Milanese architecture of the fourth century. Such links become clear in the Church of the Apostles which St Ambrose laid out in 382.[36] Its walls survive to nearly their full original height, incorporated into the Romanesque S. Nazaro. A huge cross, 200 Roman feet long, is formed by four aisleless arms, each roughly 50 Roman feet wide [38]. The stem of the cross, somewhat longer than the transverse wings, continues unbroken into the head piece. The arms were lower than the nave, and communicated with it through wide arches, each subdivided by a triple arcade on columns. In the centre of the cross rose the altar, the focus of veneration, visible to the faithful who entered either at the ends of the tran-

38. Milan, Holy Apostles, begun 382.
Isometric reconstruction

sept wings or at the end of the nave. Relics of the apostles were deposited in a silver casket below the altar presumably by St Ambrose himself. In any case the dedicatory inscription, once in the church, makes it appear that for St Ambrose and his contemporaries the Church of the Apostles in Milan was a copy of Constantine's Apostoleion, intended to hold such relics, and like it – through its cross shape – intertwined with the evocation of the True Cross. Both the dedication and the implied reference of the structure made it a highly desirable burial place, as witness the tombs, one of them the tomb of an Imperial princess, placed in two niches in each of the cross arms.

The cross plan of St Ambrose's Apostoleion was taken up, with minor variations, from the end of the fourth and throughout the first half of the fifth century in more than one church in North Italy: in a church at Como dedicated to the Princes of the Apostles and buried below the eleventh-century

basilica of S. Abbondio; in the large sanctuary of S. Croce at Ravenna, built by Galla Placidia about 425, and – except for her mausoleum off the narthex – known only from excavations [144]; and in the church of S. Stefano at Verona, about 450.[37] All are cross-shaped with aisleless arms, but at Como and Verona the long head piece has been replaced by a simple apse; the original dedications show that, just as with the rotunda plan of the Anastasis, the cross plan of the Apostoleion was easily transferred from martyria to ordinary churches.

In Milan itself, still at the end of the fourth century, S. Simpliciano took up the cross plan on a huge scale.[38] Perhaps it was the *basilica virginum*, dedicated to all virgin saints by Ambrose's successor Simplicianus. The original structure survives, nearly untouched, like St Ambrose's Church of the Apostles, within a Romanesque remodelling. A cross, the nave is a full 60 m. (197 ft, and 200 Roman ft) long and 22 m. (72 ft – nearly 75 Roman ft) wide. The

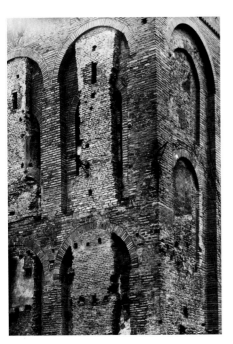

cross arms project over 50 Roman ft, and a huge apse – recently uncovered – terminated the head piece. The outer walls, built in splendid brickwork, subsist to this day to their full height of 17 m. (56 ft: nearly 60 Roman ft) [39, 40]. A narthex and low side chambers enveloped the nave on three sides. In the upper half, the walls opened in eight windows, each close to 5 m. (16 ft, and 16 Roman ft) high and framed by the upper tier of a double order of large blind arches – an articulating device widespread from the third century in the Gallic provinces, from Trier to Ravenna. With its simple, spacious interior, its powerful walls, its clear articulation by blind arches and windows, and its beautiful brickwork, S. Simpliciano remains an impressive witness to the grandeur and perfection of building not only in Milan, but in the whole Christian world of the fourth century.

39 and 40. Milan, S. Simpliciano, late fourth century.
Exterior of north transept (*left*)
and exterior from the south-west (*below*)

Alongside tetraconch and cross plans, other church types existed in fourth-century Milan. S. Giovanni in Conca, an aisleless church terminated by an apse, survives in the lower portion of its outer walls, to a length of 53 m. (174 ft).[39] The cathedral, apparently built around the middle of the fourth century and in the Middle Ages dedicated to S. Tecla, was first encountered by chance in 1943 under wartime conditions.[40] Re-explored in 1960–2, when the underground station was built on Piazza del Duomo, the outlines of the entire structure came to light: close to 82 m. long and over 45 m. wide (c. 270 by 150 ft) and not much smaller than Constantine's Lateran basilica in Rome; a nave flanked by two aisles on either side, supported by widely spread outer and inner colonnades, presumably arcaded; the nave continued as a chancel to the springing of the apse – as again at the Lateran [41]. Behind the

apse rose the eight-sided baptistery, whether contemporary with the cathedral or a couple of decades after; we shall discuss it later. An altar enclosure slightly raised above nave-level filled the area of the chancel and a narrow raised pathway projected nearly the full length of the nave. Two deep wings extended sideways, each divided into two aisles and communicating with the chancel area through a quintuple arcade. Small side chambers projected east from the outer aisles in the wings; but neither in the chancel area nor in the nave did the number of outer and inner supports coincide, again recalling the Lateran. In a remodelling after 400, a slightly narrower apse preceded by a short bay replaced the original apse. The function of the chancel wings can only be conjectured: presumably they served the rite of the offerings, just like the rooms in the Lateran basilica which projected sideways from the inner

41. Milan, S. Tecla, mid fourth century, and baptistery. Plan

aisles flanking the chancel area. The reconstruction of these chancel wings, on the other hand, remains in doubt. They may have been just low, deep wings. Or else the plan may have been analogous to that of the Lateran basilica, a high inner aisle, opening into a low outer shallow wing. Finally, they could have been tripartite transept wings with high arms, though presumably lower than the nave, shut off by arcades from the central area, their end walls strengthened by inside buttresses. Such tripartite transepts, rare in Rome, became frequent in the Aegean coastlands in the fifth and sixth centuries. On the other hand, the chancel enclosure and its long projecting pathway, known already in Constantine's Lateran basilica, disappear from Rome apparently in the sixth century; in the eastern coastlands, as *bema* and *solea*, they remain customary in the fifth and sixth centuries and far later in Byzantine architecture.[41]

All this throws a sharp light on the place of Milan in Early Christian architecture. Links to Constantine's Lateran basilica are clear. Equally clear is the transposition of such sources into long-standing local construction techniques and stylistic concepts. At the same time, Milan seems to have been the fountain-head of a transept type which was to dominate parts of the Aegean area.

TRIER AND COLOGNE

The Roman Rhineland always maintained strong ties with Milan. Analogies exist in the technique of construction – high bricks with comparatively thin mortar beds; in the use of huge windows; in the articulation of the outer walls by means of pilaster strips and blind arches; and finally, in the design of volumes and masses. The Imperial Basilica at Trier, for example, compares closely in all these respects with S. Simpliciano in Milan, despite nearly a century's interval. Teams of masons and architects seem to have travelled readily from the Imperial capital in North Italy to the capitals in the Rhineland: Trier, Constantine's residence until 312 and sporadically inhabited by his successors until the end of the century, and Cologne, the more important frontier residence used by Julian the Apostate and his successors in their defence of the Empire against the barbarian invasions. But fourth-century Christian architecture in the Rhineland seems to lack the inventiveness and forceful independence of

contemporary building in Milan. It clings more strongly to, and indeed revives, Constantinian models. Yet the location of these sources – in Jerusalem and Constantinople – shows up the close ties between the political and religious capitals all through the Empire.

About 380 the Emperor Gratian made Trier his residence, and the twin cathedral, by then nearly fifty years old [15], underwent a thorough rebuilding. The supports in the nave of the north church were strengthened by adding a pier behind each column; these doubled supports were then used to carry galleries, built above the aisles. The old chancel, either then or prior to 353–6, was done away with, and its place was taken by a centrally planned structure. It survives to this day still 25 m. (75 ft) high, incorporated into the Romanesque church: a square, tall block divided into nine bays by arches resting on four monolithic columns and on half-piers projecting from the walls [42]. A large square bay in the middle was enveloped by four rectangular bays on the axes and smaller squares in the four corners. Twenty-four large windows opened in two tiers along three sides of the block, while the fourth side communicated with the nave, aisles, and galleries through huge arches. The roofs of the four corner bays, rising above those of the axial bays and the still higher square drum of the centre bay, recall the nearly contemporary silhouette of S. Lorenzo in Milan. The singular design is obviously rooted in Late Roman architecture. The structure also certainly served as the chancel area, occupied as it was by a raised *bema* – like those at the Lateran and at S. Tecla in Milan – from which a *solea* extended into the nave and terminated near an *ambo* – a pulpit. However, the central plan of the whole structure, its fusion with the basilican nave, and the later addition of galleries to the basilica, recall as well Constantine's martyrium-basilicas on Golgotha and at Bethlehem. Indeed, the new 'chancel' at Trier may well have been a martyrium: a half-submerged circular cavity in its centre, situated below the high drum of the main bay, is encircled by twelve niches corresponding to the number of

42. Trier, north basilica,
as in c. 380. Isometric reconstruction

Apostles. Could it possibly, as a memoria, perhaps surmounted by a canopy, have sheltered a relic of Christ?[42]

The original structure of St Gereon in Cologne, incorporated into the decagon of the Romanesque church, seems to date from the very end of the fourth century. Replacing a smaller memoria, it was probably a martyrium rather than a private mausoleum, but its original dedication remains unknown.[43] A 24-m. (80-ft) oval, its sides are flanked each by four niches, horseshoe-shaped, vaulted, lit by windows,

and jutting outward. An apse to the east, a double-apsed narthex, and a large porticoed atrium complete the plan [43]. Inside, paired and tripled columns placed in front of the piers carried short pieces of entablature; piers and niches shone with marble

43. Cologne, St Gereon, c. 380. Plan of excavations

revetment. Above, the clerestory of the oval, marble-clad or painted and well lit, supported presumably a light cane dome shining with gold mosaic like that of S. Lorenzo in Milan. Imperial mausolea come to mind such as the one added to the Apostoleion in Constantinople around 360 to shelter the remains of Constantine by then displaced from their original resting place in the centre of the church. In any event, the architecture of St Gereon in Cologne recalls that of other Imperial capitals.

ROME

After Constantine's departure in 326, the old capital of the world by-passed for fifty years the problems which occupied church builders in the ambience of the Imperial court at Antioch, Constantinople, Jerusalem, Milan, and Trier. The papacy and the Roman clergy, instead of developing new types of martyria or palatine churches (these latter, in any event, unnecessary in the absence of the emperors), focused their building activity on evolving a church type serviceable for the ordinary needs of the congregations. But of this later. Likewise, they seem to have been indifferent to the classical tradition. This changes in 384, when S. Paolo fuori le mura was begun on the Ostian Way.[44] Sponsored by the three reigning emperors, it was meant to exalt the *doctor gentium*, thus countering the pagan reaction strong among Roman intellectuals, and to rival St Peter's church and grave. Over a modest mausoleum – St Paul's burial place or memorial – a small church had been built in Constantine's reign or shortly thereafter. Oriented inversely, with its entrance to the west, the new church of 384 was designed to provide a shelter for St Paul as dignified and monumental as

44. Rome, S. Paolo fuori le mura, begun 384. Interior of nave, as in 1823; engraving by L. Rossini

the basilica which enshrined St Peter – huge, lavishly built, and providing space for large crowds of pilgrims to attend services and to venerate the tomb, as well as space for burials. The backing given by the Imperial treasury makes it likely that construction was completed by 400 at the latest.

A fire razed the church in 1823, and at present we see but a sore conceit of what the nineteenth century took to be 'Classical Christian Architecture'. But size, proportions, and a few stretches of original wall survive, as do numerous old illustrations and descriptions [44]. Preceded by a colonnaded atrium, the nave – nearly 24 m. (80 ft) or 80 Roman ft wide – extended an impressive 97 m. (319 ft) in length, close to 330 Roman ft. Two aisles flanked the nave on either side, each pair equal to the width of the nave. The shrine of St Paul is located below the altar, close to the triumphal arch which separated transept and nave. (The two columns and the lower archivolt of the triumphal arch were probably added in the fifth century.) A transept, continuous but higher than that of St Peter's, shelters the shrine. Eastward, it terminated in a huge apse, like that of St Peter's. Four rows of arcaded colonnades flanked the nave and separated the aisles; in the nave they supported huge upper walls, and in the aisles low walls. As at St Peter's, the arcaded walls between the aisles were pierced by openings below the roofs. Twenty-one large windows, one above each intercolumniation, instead of the eleven at St Peter's, lit the nave. The apse remained dark, but in the transept arched windows and oculi shed a flood of light on the shrine.

The builders of S. Paolo emulated St Peter's in size and plan, including the rare form of the continuous transept. But they created a variant, not a copy. The transept was nearly as high as the nave, deeper and shorter, with its end walls barely projecting beyond the line of the outer aisles. The reasons for this adjustment are unknown, whether it was the need for more space near the shrine for clergy or pilgrims, or some other cause. The shrine, in any event, rose not on the chord of the apse as at St Peter's, but as close to the nave as possible; also, the altar rose above the shrine. The nave colonnade carried arches instead of an entablature. In contrast to the hodge-podge of architrave pieces, bases, and capitals at St Peter's, those at S. Paolo were originally homogeneous. The shafts were apparently carefully selected from among Roman spoils as were the nave capitals – those in the centre replaced after 442 by other spoils. But the aisle capitals were designed for the building. Their homogeneity and the 'correct' if dry capital types testify to a perfection of execution and predilection for classical concepts, as one would expect them in an Imperial construction of the late fourth century. We do not know whether the rest of the decoration planned in 384 would have been closer to the alive classical vocabulary prevailing elsewhere, say at Milan, in the

45. Rome, S. Maria Maggiore, c. 432–40. Nave elevation as in c. 1480; drawing. *Rome, Vatican Library*

ambience of the Imperial court. True, prior to 1823 the spandrels of the nave arcades were covered with stucco tendrils and their soffits overlaid with glass mosaic; stucco colonnettes, with shafts fluted in clockwise and counter-clockwise spirals, separated the two tiers of murals which covered the nave walls below the window zone. But this entire decoration belongs to the thorough restoration under Leo I (440–61) – the same resotration which added the mosaic of the four-and-twenty Elders and the columns to the triumphal arch and replaced part of the columns and walls in the nave.[45]

Indeed, this later decoration of S. Paolo is representative of a new departure in Roman church architecture. Its relation to the classical tradition differs wholly from that which in 384 created the conservatively dry classical capitals of the church, and, at roughly the same time, the capitals from the Arch of Theodosius in Constantinople. The new movement in Rome, on the contrary, aims at reviving the classical forms of an era long past. Nor does it limit itself to the vocabulary, but draws on the entire design of classical and late classical Roman buildings of the second, third, and early fourth centuries. This classical revival comes decisively to the fore under Sixtus III (432–40) and continues under his successors to the See of St Peter's until about 470. The basilica of S. Maria Maggiore best represents this 'Sixtine Renaissance'.[46] The wide nave [46] is flanked by only two aisles, all three designed in quiet majestic proportions. Long rows of columns with Ionic capitals carry a 'classical' entablature and lead

46. Rome, S. Maria Maggiore, c. 432–40. Interior of nave

the eye towards the triumphal arch which continued into the original apse vault. On the nave walls monumental pilasters formed an upper order, each flanked by a double tier of colonnettes with clockwise and counter-clockwise spiral fluting, and carrying a stucco frieze of the purest classical rinceaux design. Pilasters and colonnettes framed the windows as well as the mosaic panels of the nave, the latter each encased in a gabled, colonnaded aedicula [45]. Overall design and details breathe a spirit more retrospective than the live classicism of Constantinople, and reminiscent, more than anything else, of Trajanic art.

But obviously any 'classical' building of the past would equally serve Sixtus III and his architects, as witness the baptistery at the Lateran. Two remodellings of the sixteenth and seventeenth centuries are easily discounted. Laid out by Constantine as an octagon, with corner columns and lit by two rows of windows in the outer wall, and presumably covered by a timber roof, it was thoroughly remodelled under Sixtus. Two trabeated orders in the centre – each of eight columns – formed, as it were, an octagonal baldacchino over the font [47]. They were in turn surmounted by the eight large windows of a clerestory, and either a pyramidal timber roof or a light cane dome, possibly a pumpkin dome. Elegant marble panelling revetted the walls, mosaics covered the barrel-vault; also the windows in the clerestory seem to have been framed by stucco profiles. An

47. Rome, Lateran Baptistery, c. 315 and c. 432–40. Section; engraving by A. Lafréri

48 and 49. Rome, S. Stefano Rotondo, 468–83. Reconstruction and interior

octagonal and barrel-vaulted ambulatory enveloped this core. Plan and details recall S. Costanza – a century old at the time Sixtus remodelled the baptistery.[47] The same spirit of a renascence persists as late as 468–83, when S. Stefano Rotondo was built. Comparatively well preserved, it shows to this day its main components. A huge cylindrical nave rests on a trabeated colonnade with Ionic capitals [48, 49]. The high walls of the nave, originally faced with marble plaques below the twenty-two windows of a clerestory, were planned to carry a dome of light material. This core is enveloped by an ambulatory which opens into groups of five and six colonnaded arcades. These lead, alternatingly, to four deep, tall chapels – laid out crosswise – and presumably to open courtyards containing pools and terminated at the periphery by arcaded porticoes. Remnants of a classical stucco decoration have survived on the archivolts of the first ambulatory and suggest the lavishness of the decoration in general.[48]

Nothing is known of the original function of S. Stefano. Its dedication from the outset to St Stephen, the venerated protomartyr, as well as its circular form are reminiscent of a martyrium, but it never sheltered a relic of the saint. Also, the complex plan with its interpenetration of rotunda and cross shape may have been influenced by the Anastasis, and perhaps collaterally by other martyria in the Holy Land. However, Roman garden pavilions

equally appear to be among the sources of S. Stefano Rotondo, although none of the same type has come to light so far. Nor has S. Stefano had any descendants, except perhaps for the rotunda of S. Angelo at Perugia.[49]

Altogether, the Sixtine Renaissance throws light on the approach of Christian architects and patrons in Rome to the heritage of classical Antiquity. In plan and vocabulary, monumental classical architecture was traditionally linked to temples, public buildings, and palaces; it threatened Christian architecture through pagan religious connotations, including those of the Emperor cult. Christians in Rome – for the better part of the fourth century – were on the whole indifferent, if not hostile, to classical culture. Thus in contrast to their co-religionaries in the Greek East or in the northern Imperial residences of Milan and Trier, they avoided the classical heritage in their buildings as well. Only with the ultimate defeat of paganism in Rome in 395, and with the concomitant rise of a thoroughly Christian and highly educated aristocracy, could the classical past become acceptable – void of its pagan connotations. Simultaneously, the sack of Rome in 410, the weakening of the Empire in the West, and the increasing alienation from the East compelled the Papacy to absorb and, indeed, to claim both the political and the cultural legacy of Rome.

PART THREE

THE FIFTH CENTURY

CHAPTER 4

INTRODUCTION

The division of the Empire in 395 was envisaged by the Emperor Theodosius as a partnership between East and West.[1] In principle it was to be not much different from the Tetrarchy of Diocletian, but through the force of events it hardened into a schism. From the beginning of the fifth century, the West was ravaged for a hundred and fifty years by successive invasions. As early as 402, its capital had to be transferred from Milan to Ravenna, where it was protected by the fleet in near-by Classe. Rapidly shrinking in political importance, the Western Empire sank into weak dependency on the East. Rome was sacked in 410 by the Visigoths, who afterwards occupied Provence and Spain. Beginning in 429, the Vandals set up their kingdom in North Africa, threatening the Italian islands and the mainland and finally sacking Rome in 455. Central and northern France were lost to the Franks after 460. Italy fell to the Heruleans in 476 and then to the Ostrogoths, who under Theodoric (495–526) set up their strong and peaceful rule from Ravenna.

The East, on the other hand, remained comparatively strong, despite losses on the Danube and Euphrates frontiers. Internal unity was preserved through a well-run administration and protected by strong armed forces, and so the East could maintain itself as the political power of the Empire: the Emperor in Byzantium remained the *Basileus tōn Romaiōn*, the Emperor of all Romans, East and West, and his capital was the capital of the Empire. In fact, though not in law, towards the end of the fifth

century, the Western Barbarian kingdoms, now stabilized, considered themselves semi-vassals of Constantinople.

Ecclesiastically the situation was reversed. The East was torn by dogmatic strife over the definition of Christ's nature – whether only divine (monophysitism), or both human and divine (dyophysitism), or some shading of both. Related to this fundamental question was the dogma of the Virgin as God-bearer (*theotokos*), formally accepted in 431 at the Council of Ephesus. As a result of the controversy, dogmatic provinces began to oppose each other. Alexandria was monophysite, Antioch dyophysite, Constantinople held an intermediate position. After the Council of Chalcedon in 450 the division grew sharper. Egypt and Syria, led by Aramaic and Coptic monastic groups from the hinterlands, battled for monophysitism, while hellenistic Constantinople leaned towards dyophysitism. Attempts at reconciliation only resulted in further splintering. As a side effect of the dogmatic battles, the fully developed liturgies of the various provinces parted ways even further. Yet this strife strengthened the role of the Imperial power. Regardless of which faction was in power, the Church needed the protection of the Empire. A strong Emperor was given a chance to establish himself head of the Church, as finally happened under Justinian (527–65).

The West remained aloof from such theological controversies. Rome increasingly assumed spiritual and administrative authority over the Western Church, from the Balkans to France. Due to the weakening of Imperial power in the West, the Papacy was forced into a political role. Leo I (440–61), continuing the policies of his predecessor, Sixtus III, steadily increased the power of the Papal See. In fact, Rome retained its influence in the West in church matters across the newly created political frontiers and, though threatened, managed to keep a foothold even among the Arian Vandals and Visigoths. The Arian Theodoric treated the Roman Church with the greatest respect. Thus, towards the end of the century, Constantinople and Rome emerged as the two centres of the Church within the Empire. Milan, Alexandria, Antioch, and Jerusalem sank to the rank of important but provincial ecclesiastical capitals, comparable to older local sees such as Carthage or Aquileia.

The architectural history of the fifth century is no less complex. Many monuments are known, but little attempt has been made to present them in a broader perspective. A few general remarks are therefore in order.

Architects and patrons, in the last years of the fourth century, begin to concentrate on problems of church architecture quite foreign to Constantinian thought. The inventiveness and experimentation of the Constantinian age gives way to the establishment of norms, and distinct building types, which had gradually evolved for different liturgical functions, rapidly become standardized. Complementing this development, the three great regions of the Empire formulate differing plans and distinct architectural styles, all diverging in design and decoration.[2] Within each region individual provinces give preference to this or that local variant. Finally, an exchange of architectural concepts develops between provinces. These interlocking developments begin about 380 in the great architectural centres, reaching their peak in the fifth century all over the Empire. And they continue in the provinces far into the sixth century.

Throughout Constantinian and post-Constantinian times, architects, churchmen, and patrons had striven to evolve an architecture appropriate to the needs and demands of the young, powerful Church. By 380 the search for new building types and for a new style comes to an end. The complex plans of Constantinian origin were gradually eliminated. Composite martyria basilicas, huge cross churches and the like fall into disuse. 'Continuous' transepts, such as those of St Peter's and St Paul's in Rome, after 400 find hardly any following for another four centuries. Twin cathedrals, aisleless or aisled halls without apses, altars placed in the middle of the nave, and similar variants survive only in backwater provinces. Instead, clearly distinct building types come to be defined for the ordinary services of the congregation, for the cult of the martyrs, for baptism, for private devotion, for public receptions.[3]

For regular services, standard types of basilicas rise as parish churches in villages and in urban centres. Much simpler than Constantinian designs, they are composed of only a few basic elements: nave, apse, and two aisles. Local custom adds to this basic theme variations, sometimes innovations, more often Constantinian survivals: atria – that is, forecourts – as a rule enclosed by four colonnaded porticoes (*quadriporticus*); nartheces – that is, shallow vestibules – either in front of the church (*exonarthex*) or inside, preceding the nave (*esonarthex*); galleries above the aisles; a supplementary pair of aisles; occasionally, though rarely, a crypt – a subterranean chamber below or in front of the apse; and, equally rarely, a pair of towers flanking the narthex. Sometimes a cross transept or a tripartite transept intervenes between nave and apse: the former a transept with its wings enveloped by colonnades which continue the colonnades of the aisles; the latter a transept with centre bay and high arms, segregated from each other by arcades.[4] Separate areas are set aside for the auxiliary needs of the Mass and the administration of the congregation. The preparation (*prothesis*) of the Eucharist took place in the *diaconicon* (also *skeuophylakion*), where the deacons also received the offerings and kept archives, library, vestments and the church treasure.[5] Only later did the Eastern Churches set aside for that rite a separate place, the *prothesis*. Local custom determined the location of the diaconicon: whether inside the church and, in that case, in the east bays of the aisles, in the wings of a tripartite transept, or in one of two side chambers flanking the apse; or attached to narthex or atrium; or in a separate structure. Local custom, too, availability and funds decide the choice of nave supports – columns, piers, or both combined – and the shape of the windows – rectangular, round-headed, or circular. Local custom and financial means also decide the choice of a flat, coffered ceiling or an open timber roof. Conventional churches are indistinguishable from parish churches, and cathedrals of large episcopal sees differ from minor churches in size and decor but not in basic plan. They are enriched only by an added baptistery, by a *consignatorium* and further rooms for the rites supplementing baptism, and, at times, by side chapels (*parekklesia*), and a reception hall (*salutatorium*). Orientation becomes the rule. The church axis runs west and east: the apse facing east, the façade west – contrary to Constantinian church plans where the apse faced west, east, or north, subject to regional custom and local topographical conditions. The manifoldness of Late Constantinian and post-Constantinian martyria also gives way to a few formulas. In the East martyria are generally large, free-standing, and of central plan: either round and enveloped by an ambulatory, thus following the model of the Anastasis Rotunda; or octagonal, with ambulatory and chapels; or cross-shaped, the arms either aisleless or basilican. In the West, from Greece to North Africa and Italy, martyrs' graves more often than not are enclosed in basilicas of standard plan, indistinguishable from parish churches within a town. The relics of a martyr brought inside a city – in Eastern as well as Western provinces – are usually sheltered in a small cross-shaped martyrium attached to a parish church or cathedral. At times – and again this depends on local custom – the diaconicon serves simultaneously as the martyr's chapel. In North Africa the relics often occupy an apse, or a place in the nave opposite the

main apse – a counter-apse, as it were, and as a rule added later.[6]

Baptisteries likewise become standardized. In some provinces, e.g. Syria and North Africa, the Constantinian (or pre-Constantinian) square plan continues throughout the fifth century. As a rule, though, the plan is octagonal as it had been at the Lateran. However, the new baptisteries differ from Constantine's: they are often enlarged by niches or enveloped by an ambulatory, and almost always vaulted. The type apparently grew from the tradition of Roman funerary architecture, and this is understandable within the context of Early Christian symbolism: baptism is the death of the old Adam and the resurrection of the new man; eight is the symbolic number of regeneration, salvation, and resurrection, as the world started the eighth day after creation began, and Christ rose from the dead on the eighth day of the Passion. Best known from North Italy and Provence, the octagonal baptistery plan likewise occurs in Syria, in the Aegean coastlands, including Constantinople, and in Rome.[7]

At the same time, the monastic movement makes its impact felt.[8] Its beginnings in the late third and the early fourth centuries had been anachoretic and individualistic, and the eremitical life continued to play an important part in the East and the West throughout the Middle Ages, and in the Christian East up to our own time. But hermits always were exceptions. For the great majority of monks, the eremitical and hence anarchitectural life gave way by the middle of the fourth century to new rules: either a *lavra* system in which the monks, living in individual hermitages, would gather on feast days at a common centre for services and meals; or a coenobitical system (from *koinos*, meaning common, and *bios*, life) in which the monastic congregation lives together in a compound composed of living quarters (cells), a dining-room (refectory), a kitchen, a guest house, and an oratory or a church. Both systems were developed in the course of the fourth century, the *lavra* in Palestine, the *coenobium* in Egypt and Asia Minor. By the early fifth century, monasteries are found all over the Eastern part of the Empire and regular conventual buildings develop in place of the villas, country houses, or clusters of hovels which had served the first coenobitical congregations. Distinct from episcopal residences and from parish houses containing offices and living quarters for the secular clergy, these conventual buildings vary in plan according to specific monastic custom or local building tradition. Cells, kitchens, guest rooms for pilgrims, refectory, and church may form a cluster of rooms, as in Upper Egypt (Aswan, convent of St Simeon); they may be loosely arranged around an open area, as in northern and eastern Syria and sometimes in Asia Minor; or they may form a tight rectangular block, enveloping an inner courtyard, as in southern Syria; again the various chambers may be attached in a row along the flank of the church, as at Tebessa in North Africa. Different as they are, all these conventual plans become standard within the confines of larger and smaller architectural provinces.

The comparative homogeneity of the church plan in the fifth century does not preclude differences in layout determined by liturgical custom. The ritual of the service determines position and shape of the chancel, absence or presence and placement of pastophories, martyr chapels, and other side rooms. Local ritual likewise dictates the placing of altar, pulpit, clergy seats, and possibly exedrae in the nave, position of entrances on the façade or the flanks of the building, and the separation of nave and aisles, as well as the presence or absence of tripartite or cross transepts. In a leading province, such variations were no doubt determined by custom prevailing in the ecclesiastical capital, be it Constantinople, Milan, Antioch, or Rome, where new liturgical customs would originate and necessitate new planning. Backwater provinces, on the other hand, clung to Constantinian and earlier arrangements: in Africa, chancel and altar rise well forward in the nave; in Istria, a curved free-standing clergy bench is placed behind the altar; in Syria, an exedra occupies the middle of the nave, facing the altar in the apse. However, the dogmatic controversies of the fifth century and the ritual of the service are apparently

unconnected. Nor is liturgical planning necessarily linked to architectural design as it develops during the fifth century in the various parts of the Empire.

The variety and inventiveness of Constantinian and post-Constantinian church planning had been evolved within a framework of comparative uniformity in style. Whether in Rome, in Milan, in the Holy Land, in Trier, or in Constantinople, church building seems to have shared in the overall concept of an Imperial *Reichskunst*. Minor provincial centres were nourished by these same ideas, though in cruder form. The reverse is true of the fifth century. The wide variety of church plans is narrowed down. But norms in architectural and liturgical planning and notably different styles develop within each of three large regions of the Empire. These regional styles come forcefully to the front towards 380, and continue with little change until the sixth century.[9]

One region comprises the Latin-speaking West. Spiritually and to some degree politically the domain of the papacy, this area extended from Italy east to the Adriatic coastland including Dalmatia, west to southern France and Spain, south to North Africa, from western Algeria to Tripolitania. A second style prevails in the coastlands of the Aegean sea where Constantinople was the leading centre, Greek the common language, and the culture hellenistic. Thrace and Macedonia, the southern Balkans, the mainland of Greece, the coasts of Asia Minor and the Greek islands comprise the core of this region. But it also includes the shores of the Black Sea, the big trade centres, mainly on the coasts of Syria, Palestine, Egypt and Cyrenaica, and Greek towns far in mountain or desert regions of the East, where the architecture of the coastland cities penetrated because of the prevailing urban character of hellenistic culture. A third architectural style dominates the inland countries of the Near East, those provinces and borderlands of the Empire where native languages remained in widespread use: Syrian, Aramaic, Coptic, Armenian, and the dialects of Asia Minor. Predominantly rural, these areas preserved their native cultures and continued to resist the impact of hellenized city culture. They touch the sea at the Phoenician coast and extend into the uplands of Palestine, Jordan, and Syria and across the desert to the Euphrates. To the north, beyond the mountain provinces of Cilicia and Pamphylia, they cover the high plateaus of Asia Minor, Cappadocia, and Phrygia; to the south, they reach across the Negev and the Sinai peninsula into the uplands of Egypt; finally, on the borders of the Empire and beyond, they extend into Armenia and Mesopotamia.

Despite their vastness and their geographical diversity, each of these regions remains surprisingly homogeneous in its basic architectural concepts. Space and mass, light and decoration, are handled if not along the same, along similar lines from one end of the region to the other. Frequently such concepts spread from a political and spiritual centre. This seems to have been the case in the Aegean coastlands, where Constantinople with the court, the patriarch's curia, the Imperial Building Office, and the near-by Imperial stone quarries occupied that position. But a style might also form in the village and monastic centres of the hinterland in opposition to the cultural and religious capital of a region. The spiritual hegemony of Antioch or Alexandria, for example, does not guarantee them any architectural leadership in the hinterlands of the Near East.

Neither stylistic concepts nor church plans are tediously uniform throughout each region. Far from being monotonous, they are shot through with ever new variations. Rich and poor buildings stand side by side. Martyria, baptisteries, and parish churches vary in plan among each other. Indeed within one and the same functional category, the variations are numberless. Among parish churches in the Aegean coastlands, basilicas with cross transepts and tripartite transepts stand alongside ordinary basilicas with and without galleries and all become standard types.

The regional styles are determined only in part by the use of the same building materials and techniques. Even where, as is frequently the case, materials and techniques differ in various parts of a major region, the stylistic concepts remain unchanged. In design, the Menas Basilica in Lower Egypt and the church of H. Demetrios in Salonica are close, notwithstanding the use of stone in the former, of mortared rubble and brick bands in the latter structure. Similarly, the liturgical layout, while linked to the design of the building and the interrelation of its parts, is not necessarily a determining stylistic factor. No doubt, it helps to shape the stylistic development in the Aegean coastlands, where centralizing elements, under the impact of liturgical demands, become increasingly decisive in the church plan. On the other hand, in the Latin West – despite the homogeneity of stylistic concepts – the layout of the chancel, the site of the altar, and the approaches to the church vary vastly from Rome to Milan and Salona. Conversely, liturgical demands, and with them church plans, often cut across regional boundaries. To give one example: tripartite transepts become standard in Corinth and the coastal cities of Epirus, imported in all likelihood from Milan, the metropolitan see for northern and western Greece. But in absorbing the plan from the Latin West, the Greek church-planners retain all the stylistic characteristics of building in the Aegean coastlands.

Nor is there rigid separation in function among the various building types. After 450 and occasionally earlier, church types take on functions different from those originally intended and are assimilated to each other. Because of the increasing inclination to deposit relics in every church, standard basilicas in the West which were originally designed to serve as parish churches are now employed to shelter a martyr's grave and used as covered cemeteries. Conversely, in the Greek East centrally-planned structures, used both for martyria and palace churches, apparently become interchangeable among each other, and indeed interchangeable with parish churches and cathedrals.[10]

The heading of this section, 'The Fifth Century', wants to be taken *cum grano salis*. While the standard types seem to have formed all over the Empire at roughly the same time towards the end of the fourth century, their life span differs in the three great architectural regions. In the Aegean coastlands, the standard types once formed do not become common property before the middle of the fifth century. Their predominance, except in the border provinces of the Balkans, comes to an end as early as *c.* 550, with the victory of Justinian's architecture. In the Latin West, however, parish churches, cemetery basilicas, and baptisteries had become standardized as early as 420, and remained standard until the early seventh century both in North Africa, where Christian building was cut off by the Arab conquest, beginning in 640, and in Italy until the year 600. Again, in the hinterlands of the Near East, the rule of the native standard types was terminated by the Arab conquest only in Syria. In Asia Minor and Mesopotamia they lived on unchallenged into the ninth century, and in Armenia throughout the Middle Ages.

The standard church plans of the Western provinces as they were developed from the fourth to the early sixth century have been long taken to be the direct source for pre-Carolingian, Carolingian, and Romanesque church building in Western Europe from the eighth to the twelfth century. This belief has become firmly rooted, but it wants to be modified to a considerable degree. In fact, the standard plan of the Latin West, the ordinary basilica with nave, aisles, and apse, falls into disuse – even in its original habitats, Italy and North Africa – towards the end of the fifth and early in the sixth century. Nor does it during the time of its prime and shortly after spread to the christianized countries beyond the Alps. Instead, beginning with the sixth century and increasingly during the seventh and eighth centuries, the West is invaded by church types native to the East, be it the Aegean coastlands or the hinterlands. Basilicas with galleries appear in Rome at this time. Basilicas with three apses occur throughout northern Italy. In France, a small hall-church, barrel-vaulted like the churches at Binbirkilise, is found in the seventh century at Glanfeuil. Apses are flanked by pastophories, as at St Pierre at Geneva. Small cross churches, their arms either as high as the nave or slightly lower (dwarf transepts), make their appearance from Switzerland to England – possibly an Alpine or Dalmatian type, but closely resembling structures in the highlands of Asia Minor. Occasionally towers, either singly or possibly in pairs – but this wants further investigation – precede the body of the church. Only in the last decades of the eighth and during the first half of the ninth century are these Eastern types again superseded by ordinary simple basilicas or by basilicas with transepts, as had been customary in the Latin West prior to 400: a renascence closely linked to the political concepts of Charlemagne and his papal contemporaries. At the same time, however, this revival merges with the eastern current which had dominated the preceding centuries. Both Late Carolingian and Romanesque architecture continue to draw on this heritage, which fuses into one elements originating in the standard architecture of the fifth century as it developed in the three great regions of the Empire.[11]

CHAPTER 5

THE AEGEAN COASTLANDS

Stylistically, the architecture of the Aegean coastlands seems to have been closely tied to the Imperial
court and concomitantly to Constantinople.
However, the genesis of the style and its development up to 450 are hard to visualize. Archaeological
evidence of church building in Constantinople prior
to 460 has completely disappeared, and it remains
scarce up to 530. In the provinces, as well, little has
survived of buildings of before 450, owing to the
wide building activity of the later fifth and sixth
centuries and the havoc wrought on Christian architecture by Arabs, Seljuks, and Turks down to our
own days. Yet by the middle of the fifth century, the
style of the coastlands presents itself in a maturity
and with a wealth of forms in planning and detail that
testify to a long and rich tradition. The abundance
and variety of church plans along the Aegean coasts
contrast sharply with their comparative uniformity
in the Latin West, or in the uplands of the Near East.
In the Aegean the 'normal basilica' is merely one
of several types, all more complex in design:
the basilica of ordinary plan, but with galleries
surmounting the aisles; the cross-transept basilica,
the wings either enveloped by aisles on two or three
sides, or accompanied by only one aisle; the basilica
with tripartite transept; the basilica with trefoil sanctuary. Each of these plans prevails in one of the
major provinces of the Aegean region. Along with
them stand martyria and palace churches of a wide
variety of design: cross-shaped martyria, their arms
either aisleless or divided into nave and aisles; round
martyria enveloped by ambulatories, the centre
room timber-roofed, domed, or open to the sky;
finally, quatrefoil churches, either palace churches,
martyria, or cathedrals.

The architectural style of the Aegean region
becomes clear in the church of the Acheiropoietos in
Salonica, built about 450–70.[1] Basically an ordinary
basilica with galleries [50], its exterior brick walls
look simple enough. But remnants on the façade
indicate that an outer narthex (exonarthex) was
flanked by low towers, which enriched and
enlivened the silhouette. Two doors in the rear wall
of the outer narthex led to an inner narthex (esonarthex), and this in turn opens through a triple arch
(tribelon) into the nave. Corner bays help to lock the
esonarthex to the aisles, and the chain of aisles,
corner bays, and esonarthex envelops the nave on
three sides: an ancillary zone, it communicates with
the nave through colonnaded arcades; but parapets
inserted between the columns prevented direct
access. Galleries repeat the three-sided movement
in the upper zone. Their colonnades accompany
those on the ground floor in a similar rhythm, yet
differing in scale and decoration. Aisles and galleries
are lit by tripartite, sexpartite, and octopartite
windows which are subdivided by piers with two
half-columns projecting inward and outward
respectively – a pier type peculiar to fifth-century
architecture in Greece and on the coast of Asia
Minor. Whether or not a clerestory rose above the
galleries, the nave appeared depressed, delimited on
all sides by colonnaded screens, and surrounded by
the ancillary zones of esonarthex, aisles, and galleries. Yet the expansive force of the core is remarkable. It moves slowly sideways and upwards into the
outer zones across the enclosing hurdles – the high
stylobates of the ground-floor colonnades, the
parapets which blocked off aisles and galleries from
the nave, the curtains which perhaps originally hung
in the upper and in the lower arcades; everything
remains centred on the nave. The walls in the aisles
were covered with marble revetment, simple but
impressive. Mosaics covered not only the half-dome
of the apse, but also the soffits of both ground-floor
and gallery arcades. Large parts of the splendid

marble pavement are left in the nave; the aisles apparently were paved in *opus sectile*, with the nave strongly marked off against the aisles, as customary throughout the Aegean coastland. The capitals in the nave are equally splendid [51]. The ground-floor colonnades carry composite capitals of the 'Theodosian' type (a misnomer by now well rooted). Their double rows of acanthus leaves, deeply under-cut with the drill, are lacy, finely toothed, and topped by a belt of standing palmettes, the entire design based on the contrast of white marble and dark ground [52]. In the gallery zone, the blocks of the Ionic impost capitals are covered with leaves and tendrils. Within each colonnade, shafts, capitals, and bases are homogeneous. Details have parted ways with the vocabulary of classical Antiquity, but the classical concept of order pervades the building.

50–2. Salonica, Church of the Acheiropoietos, c. 450–70.
Section and plan (*opposite*),
interior of nave, south aisle (*above*),
and capital of the nave (*right*)

The nave, then, was the focus of the entire design,
and this was in keeping with the demands of a liturgy
which seems to have assigned nave and chancel to
the clergy, aisles and galleries to the congregation.
This liturgical division differs from that demanded
by the ritual of the Latin West. There (except for
North Africa), the clergy, by the time of Constantine, had withdrawn to the apse and the space
around the altar; the aisles and in large part the nave
as well – certainly since the middle of the fifth
century – were given over to the congregation. In the
Greek East, on the other hand, by the fifth century
the nave belonged mainly to the clergy, whether or
not shared intermittently with the congregation, as
may have been local custom in Constantinople. The

liturgical furniture of the Acheiropoietos, linked to the increasingly hieratic celebration of the Mass, is easily visualized from churches contemporary to it in northern Greece: a semicircular stepped clergy bench (*synthronon*) rising along the curved wall of the apse; a short chancel (*bema*) projecting into the nave to shelter the altar, curtained off and enclosed by parapets; in Greece, high stylobates and parapets between the columns to segregate the nave; and finally, far forward in the nave, the pulpit (*ambo*), linked to the chancel by a raised pathway (*solea*), the latter known from Constantine's Lateran basilica and S. Tecla in Milan.[2] Segregated as it was the nave thus became a westward elongation of the sanctuary: not as sacred as the chancel proper, where on the altar Christ revealed himself in the flesh, yet sacred enough as the place where Christ revealed himself in the word read and preached from the pulpit, and as the site of the Great and Little Entrances. The emphasis on the nave-chancel axis and on the segregation of nave and enveloping aisles is closely connected with these Entrances: processions, apparently a custom long before they were codified, in which the clergy accompanied first the bishop (later the gospel book) from the esonarthex through the nave to the chancel and in a second procession brought to the altar the elements of the Eucharist, prepared in a side room.[3] The space for the congregation was largely restricted to the aisles. In order to enlarge this area, the aisles were linked by a 'third aisle' along the short end of the nave, the esonarthex. For the same reason, galleries above the aisles (known since Constantine's day) were a welcome addition. Conversely, the nave and the entire body of the church could be kept short. The result was the basilica plan characteristic of the Eastern coastlands in the fifth century: a structure broad and short, its nave with aisles on three sides, the aisles surmounted by galleries. It was a centripetal plan, focused on the nave, where the central action of the liturgical drama took place. Concomitantly, the nave could be fully viewed only by those gathered right there, intent on celebrating the Great Mystery. From the ancillary outer zones, the nave was seen

only in fragmented views, blocked by a screen of columns, parapets, and curtains – just as the Mass, the Great Mystery, was meant to be seen but not fully understood by the layfolk.

The Acheiropoietos is representative of the style and the liturgical demands prevailing in large parts of the coastlands. The plan is variable: as a rule an atrium, terminated by an exonarthex, precedes the body of the church; rooms project sideways from the exonarthex, one often a baptistery, the other a diaconicon where the congregation deposits its offerings. Liturgical custom may require transepts of varying types; local tradition may demand the suppression of galleries; financial restrictions may call for a simpler decoration – but the stylistic principles undergo little change. In material and technique, on the other hand, the Aegean lands present a far less unified picture. To be sure, the interiors are, as a rule, covered with open timber roofs, the apses are half-domed, the walls are built of mortared rubble levelled and held in place by brick bands. But the facing of these walls differs from province to province. At times it is pure brick; in other places bands of small ashlar stone – from three to five courses high – alternate with brick bands from four to nine courses high; elsewhere the facing may consist of the rough mortared rubble itself, interspersed with brick bands.[4]

Style, plan, and building technique are easily characterized in the Aegean coastlands once they appear fully developed in structures such as the Acheiropoietos. But it is more difficult to trace the evolution of church buildings before, during, or after it reaches that climax. The great majority of buildings are known only from excavations, and these have not always been carried through with the necessary care. Documentary evidence, so plentiful in Rome, exists in the Aegean region only for a few foundations, mostly Imperial. Building inscriptions, numerous both in Italy and Syria, are rare in the Aegean region. Among the few that exist, some contain a bishop's name but remain undatable through the scarcity of bishops' lists. Thus the chronology of buildings in the Aegean region more often than not must rest on secondary evidence: the types of capitals, the design of mosaic pavements, occasionally a change of building technique. Such evidence is obviously of only limited validity, and may be contradicted almost any day by further findings. Moreover, what holds for Constantinople does not necessarily hold for the coast of Asia Minor and the near-by islands, or for the mainland of Greece, or for the coast of Egypt and Tripolitania. Thus, with all possible precautions, we shall have to present the architectural development in the Aegean coastlands in what appears to be the logical sequence, proceeding from province to province.

CONSTANTINOPLE AND VICINITY

From the fourth century onwards, the presence of the Emperor and his court was the determining factor in the architecture of Constantinople. The Imperial house, its favourites, and the great aristocratic families provided commissions and

53 and 54. Constantinople, H. Sophia, propylaeum, 404–15. Trabeation (*below*) and capital (*bottom*)

financial backing. The government-run marble quarries on the near-by Proconnesian islands in the Sea of Marmara and the brick kilns furnished materials, and the continuous building activity provided experienced teams of masons, self-perpetuating for centuries. At the same time, Imperial and aristocratic patronage promoted an architecture firmly rooted in the Constantinian tradition, and an architectural vocabulary which retained from classical Antiquity the concept of order, careful workmanship, precious materials, and elegant design.[5]

The bulk of building activity in Constantinople during the fifth century may well have been centred on palaces. But we know little about them, and the situation is not much better when it comes to church building. Between 404 and 415, the propylaeum of Constantine's Hagia Sophia was rebuilt after a devastating fire.[6] The plan – a trabeated colonnade centred on a high fastigium – remained presumably unchanged. But the architectural decoration – capitals, entablature, and the frieze on the arcuated lintel of the fastigium – shows forms quite different from the conservative ornament that still prevailed in Constantinople in the last decade of the fourth

century [53, 54]. True, the overall composition of the Corinthian capitals, of an egg-and-dart frieze, of a lesbian cyma, remains unmistakably classical. But the foliage of the acanthus leaves or of the rinceaux is cut with a new sharpness. The points of the leaves touch and the intervening ground is hollowed and begins to form an independent ornament, composed

55. Constantinople, St John Studios, founded 450s. Interior of nave

of geometric forms, triangles, rectangles, and rhomboids. The new style of the architectural decoration
was apparently rooted in a tradition firmly
established since at least the fourth century in the
Greek cities along the west coast of Asia Minor – in
Pergamon, Ephesus, Miletus. Imported into Constantinople early in the fifth century, this kind of
ornament initiates a style of decoration which was to
dominate the Imperial capital for a century.

On the other hand, the rebuilding of the propylaeum of the H. Sophia tells us nothing about
large-scale architectural concepts or church planning prevailing in fifth-century Constantinople.
Only one major church has survived from the century between 415 and 527 when Justinian ascended
to the throne. This church, St John, and its adjoining
monastery, were founded by the senator Studios
(hence St John Studios) in the 450s.[7] Though
ruined, the structure is easily visualized: the atrium,
enveloped by porticoes and accessible from the front
and the sides; the short nave with its columns raised
on stylobates not linked by parapets; the aisles with
large windows; galleries enveloping the nave on
three sides; the façades of the narthex opening
outward in a short colonnade; the apse pushing out
in a polygon; the rich decoration throughout [55].

The nave, in all likelihood, had no clerestory and
was therefore comparatively dark. Twelve-foot-
high columns of precious green marble with
'Theodosian' capitals on the ground floor are surmounted by an entablature which carried shorter,
greyish-veined columns in the galleries with elegantly designed Ionic impost capitals. Similarly
splendid 'Theodosian' capitals surmount the columns of the narthex [56]. The entablature in nave
and narthex bears a deeply undercut acanthus frieze.
The walls in the aisles were sheathed with marble
plaques, those in the galleries presumably painted,
and the apse vault carried a mosaic. Everything
speaks of the preservation and strength of a classical
tradition nurtured by Constantinian and post-
Constantinian sources. The short, almost stumpy
proportions, the centripetal design, the galleries,
the lavish materials all call to mind the basilica of
the Holy Sepulchre. The decoration recalls the
Theodosian propylaeum of the first H. Sophia.
Classical as it is in its homogeneity and in its basic
forms, however, the decoration is filled with a new
life, created largely by the contrasts of dark background and raised design, of light and shade, of
organic and inorganic forms. After all, it is only
natural that the classical and Constantinian tradition

56. Constantinople, St John Studios, founded 450s. Narthex, capitals and entablature, inside

actively continued by the court would determine the architecture of Constantinople throughout the fifth century and beyond. It is equally natural that Constantinople would develop characteristics of its own in church planning and building technique. The Studios church clearly shows these characteristics: an atrium, enveloped by porticoes, its outer wall pierced by wide openings; a semicircular apse faced to the outside by three sides of an octagon; a synthronon rising amphitheatrically along the inner curve of the apse, oversailing a barrel-vaulted corridor; a short bema projecting into the nave, presumably prolonged towards the pulpit by the raised solea; on the chord of the apse, a small, cross-shaped crypt; doors at the ends of the aisles; a slightly raised stylobate, but no parapets between the columns; wide windows, undivided and arched; finally, concrete masonry, faced by pure brick with wide mortar-beds, or by brick interspersed at regular intervals with stone bands in two or three courses – the mortar dressed with horizontal and vertical strokes of the trowel, notwithstanding the contemporary marble revetment.

Basilicas with galleries similar to the Studios church were apparently standard in Constantinople. Remnants survive of only one, the church of St Mary

in the Chalkopratiae, near the H. Sophia: a twin of the Studios church except for the presence, adjoining the flank of the atrium, of a central-plan structure, whether baptistery or martyrium. Two others are known from contemporary descriptions: H. Euphemia in Chalcedon (Kadiköy), built prior to 450; and the church of St Mary in the Blachernai, built under Justin I (518–27) and the last to represent the type in Constantinople.[8] A small martyrium completed the plan of all these churches. Designed to shelter a venerated relic, it was attached to one of the flanks of the atrium in the Chalkopratiae, of an aisle in the Blachernai church, and to the end of one aisle at Chalcedon. At Chalcedon and in the Blachernai, the martyrium was apparently round and double-storeyed, communicating with both the aisles and gallery; in the Chalkopratiae, it was either a single- or double-storeyed octagon – the niched octagonal substructure is the only remnant. Large independent martyria seem to have disappeared from Constantinople with the rotunda of H. Karpos and Polykarpos at the beginning of the fifth century.

The vast majority of church buildings in Constantinople are lost to us. However, building types and architectural decoration closely linked to what survives at Constantinople crop up during the fifth century all over the Aegean coastlands, from Meriamlik (Meryemlik) and Side (Eski Antalya) to Salonica and Ravenna. Thus it seems logical to suggest that the buildings found on these sites reflect models which existed in Constantinople and are yet to be found.

THE COASTS OF ASIA MINOR

Constantinople was always in close contact with the Greek settlements in Asia Minor, which included the cities along the western and southern coasts, such as Miletus, Ephesus, or Perge; the trade centres inland, such as Sagalassos; and the off-shore islands, from Cyprus to Lesbos. Byzantium – the small town from which grew Constantinople – had been one of these Greek Aegean settlements; and in its architecture, its Imperial successor would naturally draw on concepts and techniques long customary in its sister cities along the eastern shores of the Aegean. The building techniques employed in Constantinople in the late fourth century have their prototype as early as the second and third centuries in Ephesus, Aspendos, Nicaea (Iznik), Salonica – mortared rubble masonry levelled off by broad brick bands; mortared rubble faced with small stone blocks and brick bands; solid masonry of alternating stone and brick bands; finally, vaulting of pure brick

rather than cast concrete.[9] Certainly the architectural ornament of the Studios church and, earlier, of the propylaeum of the first H. Sophia is rooted in the building traditions of Asia Minor.

One would expect that, conversely, in the fifth century Constantinopolitan church building would dominate the ecclesiastical architecture of Asia Minor.[10] But this is not so. Only in the late fourth and the very early fifth centuries were prototypes from Constantinople taken up in the coastlands of Asia Minor. And, even at this late time, it is true only with reservations. The huge Epiphanius basilica at Salamis on Cyprus – only its plan is known – had triple aisles flanking the nave on either side, best explained as a survival of Constantinian planning.[11] The overall broad proportions are also reminiscent of Constantinian churches, such as the Nativity church at Bethlehem and presumably the first H. Sophia in Constantinople. Similarly, the cross-plan structure built after 400 over the tomb of St John at Ephesus (later replaced by Justinian's church) apparently went back, though with modifications, to a Constantinian prototype, the Apostoleion at Constantinople.[12] Four arms, radiating from the shrine of the saint in the centre, were each divided into nave and aisles [57]. While the nave arm was slightly longer than the cross arms and apparently preceded by one or two nartheces, the head piece – terminated by an apse and as long as the

57. Ephesus, St John, as in c. 450. Plan
(the sixth-century rebuilding in dotted lines)

N

0   120 FT

0   40 M

58 and 59. Ephesus, St Mary, *c.* 400 and sixth century. View facing east (*above*) and plan (*below*)

cross wings – was further enlarged in width by increasing the number of aisles from two to four. Inaccessible to the pilgrims gathered in the three other arms, it was presumably designed for a numerous clergy. But such buildings are exceptional. The rule is a standard basilica plan – as it was adopted *c.* 400, or even earlier, on a remarkable scale for the large church of St Mary at Ephesus, the cathedral where the Council met in 431 [58, 59]. It was a huge structure, 85 m. (280 ft, nearly 300 Roman ft) long; narthex and atrium added another

58 m. (193 ft). The masonry was concrete, anchored by large vertical blocks, and faced with alternating bands of brick and small stone. All walls rested on the foundations of a second-century building. The colonnades of the basilica were closely spaced. It is not clear whether they carried an entablature or an arcade, but certainly parapets between the columns closed off the aisles from the nave. The nave terminated in an apse. A baptistery adjoined the flank of the atrium, domed and with eight piers projecting from between alternatingly semicircular and shallow rec-

tangular niches; its walls were faced by brick with wide mortar joints and sheathed by a splendid marble revetment. Impressively simple large crosses mark the marble plaques of the piers, stucco shells the niches. A square outside ambulatory enveloped the baptistery. The complex has been dated in the early fourth century; the style of the mosaic floors in the narthex makes a date c. 400 appear equally possible.[13]

The plan of the cathedral of Ephesus, then, shares some features, but not all, with the standard basilica plan of Constantinople. It has no galleries. The design is simpler, the proportions lay greater stress on the longitudinal axis. If the church at Ephesus establishes what might be called the standard plan for the coast of Asia Minor, the type is in many respects closer to that of the Greek mainland than to Constantinople. In fact, dozens of churches and baptisteries along the coast and on the islands – ranging from the early fifth far into the sixth century – reflect the plan of Ephesus on a more modest scale, minor deviations notwithstanding. The churches are all basilicas with a nave and two aisles. Nartheces as a rule are tripartite and communicate with the nave and aisles only by doors, as in Constantinople.[14] Apses are at times polygonal on the exterior as in Constantinople.[15] At other times they are semi-circular as on the Greek mainland. A church ruin near Mastichari on Cos is an example [60].[16] Mosaic

60. Mastichari, basilica, fifth century. Plan

floors as customary carpet the nave, recalling the propylaeum of the H. Sophia, and (as we shall see later) occasionally bearing the inscription of the

donor or local bishop. Galleries were apparently rare in the coastal towns and on the islands of Asia Minor; but they do occur.[17] Similarly simple are the plans of baptisteries. Frequently they were square, sometimes enveloped by an ambulatory as at Miletus. At other times they were transformed internally by corner niches into octagons, as at Ephesus. Or again, as at St John on Cos, they were round and provided with corner niches, with columns either attached to or standing at a short distance from the walls.[18]

An impressive local school of architecture, somewhat different from that which flourished on the west coast, developed during the fifth and sixth centuries on the south coast of Asia Minor – in Lycia, Pamphylia, Pisidia, and Cilicia, extending north to the Greek towns in the valleys of the Taurus and Antitaurus Mountains.[19] Church plans are related to those found along the west coast, but they are not exactly alike. The simple apse of western Asia Minor gives way to elaborate chancel plans. The apse is flanked by lateral rooms, or it is preceded by a transept of tripartite or of continuous plan – possibly under the impact of liturgical customs centred in Antioch, the ecclesiastical capital for the southern regions of Asia Minor from the third century. Likewise, building practices and building materials continue local traditions which differ vastly from the techniques customary in the Aegean basin proper, from Ephesus to Constantinople and Corinth. Mortared rubble masonry with brick bands gives way to walls built of heavy stone blocks which convey an impression of stark strength and powerful massiveness. The revival of this building technique, known since Roman times, seems to be linked to neighbouring Syria, and so do some of the chancel plans. A large basilica at Side (Eski Antalya), possibly as early as c. 400, shows the apse flanked by barrel-vaulted rooms which recall the lateral side chambers of Syrian churches. In the cathedral at Korykos (Kiz Kalesi), the last two bays are segregated from the aisles by piers and cross walls, again forming side chambers – this time flanking a forechoir. A basilica of similar plan, dating

from the last third of the fifth century, survives at
Alahan Manastir. However, the elevation, with galleries, is closer than other churches in southern Asia
Minor to Aegean church types; also the splendid
sculptural decoration recalls the Acheiropoietos in
Salonica and the Studios church in Constantinople.[20] Finally, in the huge basilica of St Thecla at
Meriamlik (Meryemlik) – it measures roughly 78 by
39 m. (256 by 128 ft) and may have been financed by
the Emperor Zeno (474–5, 476–91) – an apsed
chapel was projected eastward at either side of the

semicircular main apse [61]. A straight wall linked
the two chapels at their eastern end, leaving an
enclosed space behind the apse.[21] In a number of
churches in and near Kanlidivane (Kanytilideis),
these flanking side rooms become somewhat form-
less spaces extending on either side and behind the
apse in a provincialized version very characteristic of
Cilicia.[22]

Impact from neighbouring Syria both in planning
and construction technique is only natural. It is more
surprising to find church types and decorative

61. Meriamlik (Meryemlik), St Thecla, c. 480. Plan

62. Perge, Basilica A, fifth or sixth century. Plan

forms, well known in Constantinople and Salonica, on the south coast of Asia Minor – forms singularly lacking in the cities of the west coast, such as Ephesus. At times such imports may have come directly from Constantinople. The splendid Corinthian capitals in the Thecla basilica at Meriamlik and its pavements in mosaic and *opus sectile*, all elegant, homogeneous, and of the highest quality, accord with the tradition which assigns the construction to workmen sent from Constantinople by the Emperor Zeno shortly after 476. Traces of marble revetment are still visible in one of the basilicas at Perge. Cross transepts, tripartite transepts, galleries – all elements well known in the great Aegean centres – appear in sizeable church buildings in the small towns along the south coast as well as farther inland. At Perge two churches were provided with 'reduced cross transepts' [62].[23] The plan appears to stand in a tradition which assimilates the plan of Constantine's Church of the Holy Apostles into a basilica: the main stem of the cross is turned into a nave; the head piece is replaced by an apse; finally, the transverse cross arms are enveloped by aisles, either on three sides ('full cross transept') or on two or only one side ('reduced cross transept'). So far, no such cross-transept basilicas have been traced at Constantinople. However, they frequently appear on a large scale and splendidly decorated in buildings and in localities closely linked to the Imperial court: in the last quarter of the fifth century, both in the Menas Basilica in Lower Egypt and in H. Demetrios at Salonica.[24] But it is strange to find the type also in the out-of-the-way towns along the south coast of Asia Minor. It is equally surprising to find in these same places tripartite transepts, well known on the Greek mainland, but as yet unknown on the west coast of Asia Minor. Two examples may suffice. One is found in the basilica *extra muros* at Korykos, combined with a chancel plan recalling the Thecla basilica at Meriamlik: two chapels projecting eastward and joined behind the main apse by a straight wall.[25] The other example, a basilica outside Kanlidivane, presents a tripartite transept incorporated into a basilica with galleries[26] –

decidedly a Constantinopolitan or Salonican type, quite unknown on the west coast [63]. Finally, continuous transepts, possibly derived from cross-transept plans, appear several times in the region: twice in churches at Sagalassos (Ağlasun), and twice in churches at Side.[27] But all the buildings present themselves in a solid, massive design, vastly different from the architecture of the Aegean coastlands. Constantinopolitan and other elements inextricably intermingle with local and Syrian forms in the border territory along the south coast of Asia Minor.

With few exceptions, the available publications have given an all too sketchy picture of the character and the chronology of this architecture. This is particularly regrettable since in the sixth century the south coast of Asia Minor seems to have exerted considerable impact not only along the coasts of the eastern Mediterranean, but even as far west as Italy. Apses enclosed within rectangular walls which recall the Cilician churches occur on Crete and Lesbos, in southern Palestine, and at Grado on the Adriatic shore. As at Meriamlik, projecting chapels with absidioles flank the main apse of S. Apollinare in Classe.[28]

EGYPT

In Egypt the style of the Aegean coastlands had taken a firm hold by the time the large church of St Menas was built at Abu Mîna, in the Mar'yut desert west of Alexandria.[29] A huge basilica was completed, it seems, under the Emperor Zeno by 490, not as formerly believed in 412. A first project, with a continuous transept, was abandoned: nave and aisles remained unchanged; the transept, however, was enlarged into a cross transept, subdivided by colonnades; a new apse was built and a chancel laid out in front: west of the basilica, and linked to it by a colonnaded, bi-apsidal narthex; a tetraconch later rose over the presumed burial place of St Menas; and attached to it still further west an octagonal baptistery niched, domed, and enveloped by a square ambulatory was built. Only the bottom courses survive, but the layout is clear. From the outset,

63. Kanlidivane (Kanytilideis), church, sixth century. Choir and apse

the entire complex was laid out on a huge scale, with lavish materials, designed to hold large crowds of pilgrims. The main church as completed by *c.* 490 was a cross-transept basilica, *c.* 66·50 m. (218 ft) long from the doors to the apex of the apse and 50 m. (169 ft) wide across the transept [64]. Nave and transept were thus extraordinarily long, while the aisles – compared to the width of the nave – were quite narrow. They continued into the transept, enveloping the wings on three sides with the transverse axis marked by a wider intercolumniation. Chancel, altar, and synthronon occupied the

64. Abu Mîna, St Menas, probably complete by 490. Plan

crossing, much as they must have done in Constantine's Apostle Church in Constantinople – presumably the ultimate source of all cross-shaped martyria, and indirectly of all cross-transept basilicas. One would not wonder, in fact, had the plan of the Menas basilica been sent to Egypt by the Imperial Office of Works, just as a similar plan possibly went to the shrine of St John at Ephesus at the same time, and certainly to Gaza.[30] Zeno was one of the great builders among the Eastern emperors; along with the Menas basilica he financed the construction of the Thecla basilica of Meriamlik, of Qal'at Si'man, and of the church on Mount Garizim, and it seems quite possible that the sumptuous churches built in the last quarter of the fifth century in major Greek sees were in some part due to his support and encouragement. At Abu Mîna part of the materials came from Constan-

65. Capital from the Menas basilica,
fifth century. *Frankfurt, Liebig Haus*

tinople. So did a number of the details: many of the capitals, whether of imported or local material, are of Aegean design [65]. The columns rise from pedestals, like those of the propylaeum of the early H. Sophia in Constantinople, though alternatingly square and eight-sided. As in Constantinople, the profiles of pedestals and door lintels are highly classical and finely worked. The colonnades in nave and transept, as in the Studios church, were in all likelihood surmounted by architraves and these in turn appear to have carried the colonnades of the galleries. The half-dome of the apse seems to have been covered with a mosaic on a gold ground. All these are features rooted in a tradition either specifically of Constantinople, or of the Aegean coastlands in general. Such links are not surprising in a famed sanctuary near the large port of Alexandria and favoured by the Imperial court. But it is surprising how clearly the characteristics of the Aegean style come to the fore at Abu Mîna despite a building material quite different from that employed in Constantinople or Ephesus – small ashlar, instead of mortared rubble with brick bands, and very thin walls.

From Alexandria the coastland style spread west and south. To the west, in Cyrenaica, it is manifest in the churches of Apollonia (Marsa Susa). The East Church of Apollonia – of *c.* 400 but possibly rebuilt at roughly the same date as the Menas basilica – retains the position of the chancel in the crossing, as well as the pedestals of the columns [66]. But the

66. Apollonia (Marsa Susa), East Church, *c.* 400, perhaps rebuilt *c.* 500. Exterior from the south-west

occurs here for the first time in Egypt. As it appears at Hermopolis, it perhaps represents a fusion of the cross-transept plan with the trilobe chancel – and the trilobe chancel is a form well established in Egypt by the second quarter of the fifth century. The White Monastery (Deir-el-Abiad) near Sohag far to the south shows the plan fully developed [68]. To this day the structure is extraordinarily impressive.[33] Enclosed by huge walls, slightly sloping and built of beautifully cut large stone blocks, it has the grandeur of an Egyptian temple or, for that matter, of a Roman fortress [69]. Within the tall rectangle of the

enclosure, the church is preceded by a narthex and flanked by a long hall on the south side. Both narthex and hall terminate in absidioles supported by free-standing colonnades. Inside the church, trabeated colonnades rose from high pedestals and were surmounted by a second, lower order; just as at Hermopolis, aisles and galleries enveloped the nave on three sides [70]. Profiles and capitals are crude but clearly reveal their classical ancestry, and the scanty remnants of the pavement are composed of splendid white marble and red granite plaques. The chancel is laid out along grandiose lines: a shallow

68 and 69. Deir-el-Abiad (White Monastery), c. 440(?).
Plan (*above*) and exterior from the south-east (*below*)

70. Deir-el-Abiad (White Monastery), c. 440(?). Nave, aisle, and gallery level facing north

71. Deir-el-Abiad (White Monastery), *c.* 440(?). Triconch; drawing by Freshfield

bay with a slightly raised floor terminates the nave; behind it rose the opening of a triumphal arch supported by huge columns (they are hidden within an ungainly eighteenth-century brick wall). Through the arch one enters the chancel proper: three half-domed apses extending north, south, and east from a rectangular centre bay and forming deep cavities, originally lit, one supposes, from a clerestory below the timber roof of the 'crossing' [71].

The layout, then, is clear despite the thorough remodellings the structure has undergone. The most recent alteration took place prior to the eighteenth century, when the trefoil was walled up to serve as the church by itself; what had formerly been the nave was filled with the hovels of monks and fellahin. These huts have been removed and a few columns rise in the empty area of the nave, over 7 m. (23 ft) high and some still carrying Ionic capitals [70]. Another alteration, presumably in the eleventh century, involved the placement of a brick dome over the centre bay of the triconch. In an earlier renovation, perhaps in the sixth century, the apses were possibly rebuilt or redecorated with columns, capitals, cornices, and gabled niches, mainly spoils removed from earlier structures [71].[34] The trefoil plan itself, however, may well date from about 440 when the great abbot Shenudi founded the monastery.

Free-standing trefoil memoriae had been frequent during the third and fourth centuries on pagan and Christian cemeteries. In post-Constantinian times the type was carried on by chapels, as they occur in large numbers in Tunisia, occasionally in Algeria, and as far away as Provence and the Veneto. However, thus far the first known example of a trilobe being designed from the outset to be the apse of a basilica is the new church laid out in 401/2 by Paulinus near the grave of St Felix at Nola near Naples. During the fifth century the plan was apparently widespread over the Mediterranean littoral. But it remained exceptional, save for western North Africa, Provence, and South Italy, always closely linked.[35] Thus the triconch plan may have reached Egypt from the West. It is possible that the

trilobe served the very same function in fifth-century Egypt which Paulinus had assigned to its component parts at Nola: the centre bay to hold the altar, and the conch behind it to shelter the bishop's throne; the left conch to serve for the preparation and the guarding of the Eucharist; the right conch to be used as a place for meditation and as a library – the latter being a regular function of the diaconicon.[36]

A local building technique and local workmanship, then, serve at Deir-el-Abiad to produce a design which fuses into a whole elements drawn from many foreign parts – elements distinct from those of Upper Egypt and distinct among each other. Constantinople may be one of the sources; certainly the Aegean coastlands are a general source; and presumably western North Africa or southern Italy as well. The church plan and the style which result from this fusion take a firm hold in the architecture of the Nile Valley. The plan of the church of Deir-el-Abiad was taken over by the builders of the Red Monastery, Deir-el-Ahmar. The church is slightly smaller; the conchs of the trefoil chancel are more closely tied together; the number of wall bays in the conchs is reduced from five each to four and three respectively. Capitals, cornices, and niche frames are uniform in style and suggest a possible sixth- rather than a fifth-century date.[37] Indeed, triconch chancels, aisles enveloping the nave on the entrance side, and apses articulated by niches, remain features characteristic of major churches in sixth-century Egypt.[38] But the decoration loses ever more of its classical tenor. A harder, local style of architectural decoration takes over. Alongside the classical and later, classicizing designs imported from across the Aegean, the local 'Coptic' decoration had been powerful since at least the third century, but only during the sixth does it become the dominant note of church decoration in Christian Egypt.[39]

GREECE AND THE BALKANS

Christianity had taken root in the Greek cities as early as the days of St Paul. However, among country folk as well as in educated city circles resistance remained strong even after Constantine. The closing of the temples by Imperial decree in 395 crushed only the outward signs of paganism. A faint flavour of the old faith lingered among Greek Christians for a long time. No church seems to have risen inside Athens prior to the mid fifth century, and until 529 the University of Athens made a last-ditch stand for the old gods. In the fifth century, however, Christian congregations all over the mainland increased in number, importance, and wealth. Churches of respectable size were built even by country congregations in the mountains and on the sites of the old pagan sanctuaries. Large churches were erected in the cities along the coasts, three, four, and five at a time. Their plans and their decoration mark them as a separate group, though linked to church building both in the eastern Mediterranean – from Constantinople to Egypt – and in North Italy, where Milan remained the leading centre.[40]

This double-headed impact is only natural. Greece was a seafaring country and her cities thrived on commerce. The ports along her east coast had the closest contact with the Imperial capital and with the great and small trading centres along the coast of Asia, from Ephesus to Antioch and Gaza, on the islands of the Aegean Sea, and as far south as Alexandria. Salonica soon grew to be a 'Little Byzantium', a cultural, intellectual, and architectural outpost of Constantinople. Even a minor seaport such as Nea-Anchialos (Thebes) in Thessaly apparently imported its architects and part of its architectural decoration straight from Constantinople. So did a great city such as Corinth; but here the elements from across the Aegean Sea mingled with features drawn, it seems, from Italy. No wonder this either. Like all the western ports of Greece as far north as Epirus, Corinth had close links of trade and navigation with Ravenna and Milan as well as with Constantinople and the Asian coastal centres. These commercial ties were strengthened by ecclesiastical bonds. As late as the middle of the fifth century the Balkans, including Greece, were claimed by the Roman See as its spiritual domain,

and they were in fact subject to the diocese of Milan in the last decades of the fourth century.

The twofold impact from East and West makes itself felt in church building in Greece as early as the end of the fourth and the very beginning of the fifth century. As far east as Epidauros, Eastern and Milanese features were joined in the plan of a church built on the outskirts of the sacred precinct of Aesculapius, just closed down by Imperial decree.[41] The style of the pavement mosaics in nave and narthex leaves little doubt regarding their date, about 400. Of the church complex, only the foundations and a few walls have survived, barely a foot above ground and of poor workmanship. In fact, despite its size – 60 by 45 m. (200 by 150 ft) – it can never have been very impressive; but it does show the absorption in Greece of many traits from abroad [72]. The transept is divided lengthwise by short column screens into five sections. The bema occupied the centre compartment; the adjoining sections were well adapted to hold the supernumerary clergy; and the outer sections, slightly raised above the inner ones and communicating with the aisles only by doors, lent themselves to the deposition of the offerings. Thus, the plan of the transept recalls S. Tecla in Milan, where about 350 the dwarf wings of the chancel had been raised to form a tripartite transept and repartitioned into five sections. Other traits of the plan, however, find their parallels in the architecture of the eastern Mediterranean. The plan of the nave with four aisles is obviously rooted in Constantinian and post-Constantinian custom. Yet with this tradition, the choice of supports at Epidauros – columns in the inner row, piers in the outer – points to Eastern parallels, such as the martyrium at the Holy Sepulchre. Decidedly Aegean in planning and style are, finally, the atrium enveloped by chambers – the functions are unknown; the propylaeum in front; the long, closed narthex, with its side rooms pushed outwards; the rectangular baptistery; and the mosaic carpets in atrium, narthex, nave, and outer transept.

At the same time as the quinquepartite transept at Epidauros, or not much later, a transept type of

72. Epidauros, basilica, c. 400. Plan

purely Eastern flavour makes its appearance in a church just outside the city walls of Athens: the basilica on the Ilissos Island.[42] Datable to about 400 through the pattern of its mosaic floor, and in no case later than 450, its plan is clear: a 'reduced cross transept', its wings enveloped by aisles along the western and the short sides, a dome or pyramidal roof over the centre bay. Obviously the plan, though apparently earlier, finds its closest parallel in the Menas basilica; ultimately it may go back to Constantinople.

Finally, the remnants of a third extraordinary structure dating from the early fifth century rise in the very centre of Athens, inserted into the courtyard of the Library of Hadrian [73].[43] Its quatrefoil plan calls to mind S. Lorenzo in Milan, with its square centre room, its billowing exedrae, its ambulatory and surmounting gallery. The plan is modified only slightly in Athens: the eastward lobe and ambulatory

are replaced opposite the entrance by the semicircle of an apse; the columns of the three other lobes rise from stylobates slightly raised above the level of the mosaic floor in the ambulatories; and a huge narthex enclosing a staircase leads into the building. It appears by now certain that the tetraconch was laid out as a church rather than (as previously held) a lecture hall or the audience hall of the provincial governor.

However, all three buildings – the churches at Epidauros and on the Ilissos Island and the quatrefoil in the Library of Hadrian, whatever its original function – stand out as exceptions in the architecture of late-fourth- and early-fifth-century Greece. The normal type, found in dozens of churches from the fourth far into the sixth century, was a simple basilica. Notwithstanding the usually small size and the poor decoration, this standard basilica shares some essential features with the churches along the

73. Athens, Tetraconch, Library of Hadrian, *c.* 400

74. Vravron, basilica, fifth century. From the north-west

west coast of Asia Minor. An atrium and exonarthex form the approach. The nave is flanked by two aisles. The colonnades are raised on stylobates and – a feature perhaps proper to Greece – the inter-columniations are closed by parapets. A short chancel projects into the eastern bays of the nave, a synthronon fills the hemicycle of the apse, the ambo stands in the nave, often off axis. Deviations seem to follow local Greek custom. Contrary to Constan-tinopolitan habit, the apse tends to be semicircular both inside and out. The colonnades are sur-mounted not by entablatures, but by arches resting on impost blocks. The esonarthex communicates with the nave through a triple arch, a *tribelon*. Finally, one or two rooms jut out from the end of the narthex, one apparently a diaconicon where the offerings of the congregation were received. Apparently no dis-tinction in planning was made between parish churches and cemetery basilicas. In Greece, it would seem, the two types had become fully assimi-lated to each other by the early part of the fifth century.

A rural church excavated near Vravron in Attica represents one among many such standard basili-cas.[44] The columns had fallen, but some have now been replaced on their stylobates, together with the crudely designed Ionic capitals and impost blocks [74]. Atrium, outer narthex, nave, aisles, and chancel are still clearly visible, as well as a small round baptistery adjoining the right flank. Just as typical of the Greek mainland is the masonry: mortared rubble, interspersed with brick bands and strengthened by brick corners, the surface criss-crossed by a network of wavy trowel lines. Also preserved are large remnants of a decoration remarkably rich for a small rural church: the nave is paved with marble slabs; door sills and the base of the chancel screens are of red and white marble; a colourful painted imitation of marble revetment covers the walls of aisles and narthex. Finally, on the walls of the baptistery remain traces of a genuine marble revetment, surmounted by a stucco decora-tion of twisted colonnettes, cornices, roundels, and peltae. The liturgical arrangements – altar, syn-thronon, and the footings of the bema enclosure – still exist in a good state of preservation.

Such simple plans remain standard. By the second half of the fifth century, however, they have become overshadowed by the upsurge of a new, lavish church architecture in the major centres. The size of the structures increases, the decoration becomes richer, the plans show greater complexity. Under the impact of Constantinople, basilicas with galleries come to the fore, yet with characteristic differences. The Acheiropoietos in Salonica transposes its unknown prototype – possibly the Studios church – into a looser key with a taller and longer nave, lighter arcades, more complex vistas. Basilicas with cross transepts become frequent, their enveloping aisles surmounted by galleries. Tripartite-transept plans come into common use; atria, nartheces, annexes become more elaborate; the site is integrated with the design of the building complex. The plans are not new. One recalls the quinquepartite transept plan of Epidauros, the cross transept of the Ilissos basilica, the quatrefoil in the Library of Hadrian – all dating from about 400 or slightly later.[45] But only towards the end of the fifth century are the stylistic potentials of these plans fully exploited. It is as if the earlier types had been resuscitated on a more complex level. Enriched through the double-zone elevation with galleries, the design no longer seems only a response to liturgical requirements but a sheer enjoyment of a sophisticated architecture. Few buildings of the 'new wave' are dated by inscriptions, but their capitals, friezes, and mosaic and marble pavements leave little doubt that in their great majority they were erected between 470 and 530.

The excavation during recent years of large Christian sites, each with a number of churches, testifies to the wealth of the Greek cities and the lively building activities of the congregations. It also gives visual evidence of the high standards of archi-tectural design, the inventiveness of builders and patrons, and the lasting close links of Greek to Constantinopolitan, Aegean, and Milanese church building. In Nea-Anchialos (Thebes) in Thessaly, nine churches have come to light, all sumptuously decorated with finely-worked capitals, chancel screens, floor mosaics, and marble pavements. At Corinth, three huge churches have been explored so far, and remnants of others await excavation. At Nikopolis in Epirus four churches have been found; at Philippi in Thrace likewise four are fully known so far, at Amphipolis at least three. In Salonica two huge churches of the fifth century have survived nearly in their entirety, retaining large parts of their original decoration. All these buildings have in common a complexity of design and a lavishness of decoration, but they differ in plan according to their location. Corinth and Nikopolis on the west coast retain Milanese features; Salonica turns to Constantinople and to Ephesus on the coast of Asia Minor. From Salonica, in turn, church plans spread south, east, and north: to Thessaly, Thrace, southern Yugoslavia, and Bulgaria.

Among the churches excavated at Nea-Anchialos, the largest (Basilica A) – though not the bishop's church – is close in date and plan to both the Acheiropoietos in Salonica and the Studios basilica in Constantinople. A long esonarthex, continued by rooms off either end, opened into the nave through the triple arcade of a tribelon and thus enveloped it as a short third aisle – the same plan as found in the Acheiropoietos [75]. The columns between the nave and aisles rose from stylobates elevated above the pavement level, and the intercolumniations were closed off by parapets; likewise, parapets crossing the aisles closed off the eastern bays. Arches, not architraves, sprang from the columns and a gallery surmounted each aisle – again all features found in the Acheiropoietos. However, as in the Studios church, the church at Nea-Anchialos was preceded by an atrium, far richer than that at Constantinople. Three colonnaded porticoes surrounded the open centre part, the terminating colonnade to the west curving back in a hemicycle; long apsed rooms flanked the sides – to the north a baptistery, to the south a diaconicon (or prothesis) containing offering tables. The front corners of the atrium were formed by two square rooms; they enclose staircases and have been tentatively reconstructed as low towers. The capitals, all sumptuous, were subtly chosen with

75. Nea-Anchialos, Basilica A, c. 470. Plan

different designs for different parts of the building complex. To the atrium are assigned Corinthian capitals with dry, sharply cut leaves, their points separated by the dark shapes of triangular and rectangular interstices ('leathercut' capitals) [76]. The tribelon capitals are deeply undercut with 'Theodosian' leaves in a lower zone surmounted by the half-figures of lions ('two-zone protomai capitals') [77]. The nave and galleries both have capitals with impost blocks, the former 'Theodosian', the latter, as well as those of the window piers, fused into Ionic impost block capitals [78]. Some of the capitals, of Proconnesian marble, were presumably ordered ready-made from the Imperial quarries on the islands in the Sea of Marmara. Others, of local stone, are yet so close to Constantinopolitan models as to suggest the hand of workers called in from there. No less sumptuous than the capitals were the flagstone pavement of nave and aisles, the marble revetment of the walls, and the liturgical furniture. A fountain (*phiale*) rose in the atrium, surmounted by a canopy with superbly carved foliate friezes. The chancel, projecting far into the nave, was bounded by screens carved with intricate geometric and foliage patterns. Along the sides of the chancel, two straight clergy benches supplemented the high-rising synthronon of the apse; the altar in the bema was under a canopy; the pulpit rose from its circular base outside the chancel in the nave. Following Constantinopolitan custom, doors open from the eastern ends of the aisles. The elegance and refinement of plan and decoration are in no way inferior to the Studios church in the Imperial capital.[46]

The type of the Acheiropoietos in Salonica and of Basilica A at Nea-Anchialos penetrated into southern Yugoslavia and Bulgaria. Like the Greek churches, the bishop's church at Stobi in the Vardar Valley (laid out early in the fifth century and remodelled successively until the mid sixth century) was a galleried basilica, its Ionic arched colonnades closed by parapets, an atrium, and a narthex. The narthex opened into the body of the church through doors, as in the Studios church, rather than through a

76–8. Nea-Anchialos, Basilica A, *c.* 470.
Capitals from the atrium (*top*),
the tribelon (*centre*), and from a window pier (*bottom*)

tribelon; but as in so many Greek basilicas the area of the narthex was subdivided by column screens into three bays. Mosaic pavements, wall paintings (both decorative and figural), and presumably a mosaic in the half-dome of the apse completed the picture. Similar church plans of apparently fifth- or sixth-century date, with or without galleries, have been excavated all over the Balkans. Occasionally the standard type was modified. The supports are sometimes piers rather than columns.[47] At Stobi, a crypt extended below apse and chancel, its semicircular core ringed by a colonnaded corridor. Now and then the outer narthex seems to have been flanked by twin towers, pushed sideways much as in the Acheiropoietos, or else sacristies extend sideways from the ends of the aisles, thus recalling the plan of Constantine's Lateran basilica.[48]

Sumptuous though they are in their best examples, in Salonica or Nea-Anchialos, such basilicas remain comparatively simple in plan. Alongside

79. Salonica, H. Demetrios,
late fifth century. Plan and reconstruction

them, however, basilicas with cross transepts come to the fore as a hallmark of fifth- and early-sixth-century church building in northern Greece and the Balkans. When the plan was first taken up in the Ilissos basilica early in the fifth century, its elevation may have been quite simple. In the last years of the century it appears fully matured in H. Demetrios in Salonica; from there it spread shortly after 500 into Thrace and northern Macedonia, and then on into Bulgaria as far as the coast of the Black Sea.

H. Demetrios in Salonica represents the type of the cross-transept basilica at its best, its most complex, its most lavish.[49] To this day it remains one of the most impressive churches in the Aegean coast-lands, more than 55 m. (180 ft) long [79]. The building burnt down in 1917 and was replaced by a replica, incorporating the ruined remains, but both purist and pretentious – the interior whitewashed,

the exterior faced with intermingled brick and stone blocks. To distinguish original parts, early rebuild-ings, and modern additions, is fraught with diffi-culties. However, the plan, considerable stretches of the outer walls, large numbers of columns and capitals, transept and apse, and finally the tribelon wall at the west end of the nave, splendidly decorated, substantially survive from the original fifth-century structure; until 1917 also the arcade between the two north aisles remained in place. An esonarthex, now flanked by low towers, precedes the body of the structure. Transept wings slightly lower than the nave project sideways in front of the apse [80]. Nave and wings are enveloped by the con-tinuous flow of esonarthex, aisles (doubled along the nave), galleries, and low clerestory windows. The chancel encloses the altar, and was originally linked by a solea to the pulpit far down near the beginning

80. Salonica, H. Demetrios, late fifth century. Exterior of apse and transept

81 and 82. Salonica, H. Demetrios, late fifth century.
Interior of nave as in 1960 (*above*)
and north wall of nave prior to 1917 (*opposite*)

of the nave. The grave of the saint is relegated to a crypt: extending below the south transept wing, it was the spiritual but no longer the architectural focus of the building. In the nave, a sophisticated rhythm of supports, arcades, windows, and a sumptuous decoration reinforce this complex plan

[81]: an alternation of pier and column groups gives a sequence of four, five, and four – a rhythm echoed by that of the gallery zone. In the clerestory zone, the rhythm of the windows originally planned remains in doubt. To be sure, the nave was rebuilt after a major catastrophe in the first third of the seventh century

[82]. Column shafts, bases, capitals, and the marble revetment of the arcade are spoils, hastily thrown together. Except, though, for a few fold capitals of clearly sixth-century date – twins of those at H. Sergios and Bakchos – the majority of the capitals appear to have come from the original fifth-century

83. Salonica, H. Demetrios,
late fifth century. Capital of the nave

church: Theodosian capitals, double-zone capitals
with protomes, eagle capitals, capitals with wind-
blown leaves [83]. The capitals in the gallery zone –
copies at present – were originally all Ionic impost
capitals. Indeed, the rhythm of piers and columns,
too, may have been planned from the outset and
have been retained in the rebuilding. The original
decoration of the nave is best reflected by its western
tribelon wall: *verde antico* columns on Attic bases,
Theodosian capitals, marble-sheathed piers and
voussoirs, alternatingly red and green, elegant dwarf
pilasters rising from the spandrels. Large parts of
the decoration and certainly the plan would still
seem to date from the fifth century, including a
change already during construction: arcades and
walls, projecting eastwards on either side of the apse,
suggest that at first, instead of the apse, a rectangular
chancel enveloped by an ambulatory was envisaged.

The foundation of H. Demetrios has been traditionally assigned to the years 412–13, but all
evidence points to a date in the last (or perhaps the
third) quarter of the fifth century for the original
building – the capitals, the patterns of the marble
revetment as preserved in the tribelon wall, the
brickwork of the piers with broad mortar joints. The
seventh-century rebuilding, in our opinion, did not
alter the original design in its essentials.

The impact of H. Demetrios made itself felt
throughout northern and eastern Greece and the
Balkans. In a cross basilica on Thasos, the aisles not
only envelop the transept wings, but continue along
the chancel arm much as was planned at first for H.
Demetrios. At the same time, the reduced cross-
transept plan makes its appearance at Tropaeum on
the Black Sea coast, and at Philippi, midway
between Salonica and Constantinople – one of the
greatest Christian sites in the Aegean and still under
excavation [84].[50] Of Basilica A at Philippi only the
plan and fragments of the decoration – suggesting a
date about 500 or somewhat earlier – have survived,
and they give the impression of extraordinary
splendour. The vast atrium, preceded by a forecourt, was approached from the south by stairs. Its
west wall, articulated by niches, formed a
monumental fountain. Across the entire east end of
the atrium ran a broad flight of stairs ascending to
the narthex. Components of the building complex
were all laid out on different levels, and the visitor
gradually ascended to exonarthex, esonarthex,
aisles, and galleries to view the celebration of the
Great Mystery which was performed in the central
space of nave, transept, and apse, the former two cut
off from the aisles by parapets. At the same time,
even more exceptional church types make their
appearance at Philippi. In the 1960s a large and
splendid octagonal church came to light dating
perhaps from about 500 or even somewhat later.
Columns supported the walls and the roof of the
centre room [85]. The encircling ambulatory, likewise octagonal, is supplemented by niches in the
four corners and by an apse projecting from the wall
of the enclosing square. Huge marble plaques cover
the floor of the centre room, the apse, and the
intervening bay of the ambulatory, while its other
seven sectors are paved with an elegant *opus sectile*.
Columns and window piers carried splendid
capitals. A narthex linked up on either side with a
colonnaded street was entered by a sumptuous
gabled triple portal. A richly decorated baptistery, a
fountain court, a small bath, and other rooms
adjoined the church; the bishop's palace, if that it

84. Philippi, site facing south. Basilica A, c. 500; octagonal church, c. 500; Basilica B, shortly before 540

85. Philippi, octagonal church, c. 500. From the north-west

was, extended behind. The type of the church is rooted in the tradition of centrally-planned martyria, such as the church of the Virgin on Mount Garizim (Gerizim) (484) or the martyrium of St George at Izra (Zorah) (515) in Syria. However, by 500 the plan had long migrated from the realm of martyria into that of ordinary churches and, indeed, the liturgical layout of the Philippi octagon – the bema projecting from the apse and piercing the width of the ambulatory; the ambo near the middle of the

86. Peruštica, Red Church, early sixth century

centre room – suggests in no way that it served as anything but a parish or bishop's church, despite its extraordinary plan.

Quatrefoil structures with ambulatories are likewise revived around 500 in the eastern Balkans, possibly within the framework of a renascence of building types well known a century earlier but only now fully exploited. The ruin of one such structure, called the 'Red Church', still towers high on a hill near the village of Peruštica (Peroushtitsa) in Bulgaria, not far from the town of Plovdiv [86].[51] The plan with its outsize narthex and simple apse at the opposite end at first glance recalls the quatrefoil at Athens. But it has been greatly reduced by limiting the ambulatories to the north and south lobes, by replacing the colonnades of the exedrae with heavy piers, and by renouncing the galleries above the ambulatories. The brickwork and the few remnants of capitals and chancel screen suggest a date in the early sixth century. A fully developed quatrefoil church, on the other hand, possibly of the same time or earlier, still stood with ambulatories and galleries at Adrianople only eighty years ago. But it has since been razed, and only a few photographs and a sketchy plan testify to its grandeur.[52]

Cross-transept and quatrefoil plans were revived around 500 apparently in north-eastern Greece and in the eastern Balkans. At the same time, tripartite transepts came to life anew in the architecture of the Greek west coast, from Nikopolis in the north to Corinth in the south. This is not too surprising. A tripartite transept plan had been developed by 350 in Milan and taken up in Rome by 450 – and western Greece maintained close trade links across the Adriatic Sea. Three churches in Nikopolis – dating from roughly the same time (Basilica B, the 'Alkison basilica', prior to 518, Basilica D, perhaps contemporary, Basilica A, the Dumetios basilica, from the second quarter of the sixth century) – show the layout of such tripartite-transept basilicas.[53] The transept wings, possibly lower than the nave, communicate with the centre bay through either a triple arcade or a single wide arch [87], with the aisles

narthex to the nave and aisles; the apse is raised a few steps above the chancel and buttresses both strengthen and articulate its walls; piers, counter-piers, and arches clearly set off the separate spatial volumes. Even the walls convey an impression of clarity and solidity quite different from the thinner, heavily pierced walls of churches in north-eastern Greece. The thick, solid walls at Nikopolis are built of pure brickwork, with bricks, as at Milan and Ravenna, up to 8 cm. (3 in.) high. Only the rich figured pavement mosaics link Nikopolis to the colourful architecture of the Aegean coastlands.

In the great church of H. Leonidas at Lechaion, the harbour suburb of Corinth, this tripartite-transept plan was transposed into a less rigid and

87. Nikopolis, Basilica A
(Dumetios Basilica),
sixth century (second quarter). Plan

N

0   40 FT

0   15 M

(doubled in Basilica B) through simple or double arches, the latter closed, it seems, by parapets; a diaconicon (or prothesis?), as a rule, is attached or close to the narthex. The churches of these port cities are less monumental than those of either Philippi or Salonica, but they are more precisely outlined. Doors, not column screens, lead from the

far richer key. The ruin of the basilica was excavated from 1955 to 1965 and is preserved but two feet above ground, but it is still one of the most impressive sights of Early Christian Greece.[54] Forecourt, atrium, and basilica followed one another – totalling 186 m. (610 ft) in length, 600 Byzantine feet. The basilica consisted of nave and aisles, tripartite tran-

88 and 89. Corinth-Lechaion, H. Leonidas, 450–60(?)
and 518–27. Plan (*above*) and view from the west (*below*)

sept with projecting wings, and a huge half-domed
apse [88]. Two rows of large windows originally
pierced the wall of the apse; fragments of their
arches and of the spandrels of the apse vault survive.
A row of niches along the foot of the apse sheltered
thrones for the clergy in lieu of a simple synthronon.
Four huge piers and columns in the corners of the
centre bay of the transept would have supported a
timber-roofed tower or a wooden dome on four
arches. The bema below is well preserved; altar site,
chancel screens, lateral clergy benches, and solea
remain – the solea projecting far into the nave and
terminating at the foot of the pulpit. The transept

wings, set off from the centre by arches, fall into two
sections. An inner section, communicating with the
aisle through a triple intercolumniation closed by
parapets, was possibly intended for the offertory,
while the narrow outer section, raised one step – but
screened off by columns and thus similar to the
transept arrangement in the Constantinian St
Peter's in Rome – possibly served as a sacristy.
Along the nave, high stylobates carried the colonnades and their marble shafts, 0·61 m. (2 ft) in
diameter [89]. Parapets closed the intercolumniations, pierced only by two entrances near the
façade. Galleries may have risen above the aisles, but

90–2. Corinth-Lechaion, H. Leonidas.
Pavement (*top*),
nave capital (*centre*),
and Ionic capital (*bottom*),
450–60(?)

this is not certain. The esonarthex opened towards the nave in a quintuple arcade while the exonarthex was approached across the atrium – a monumental colonnaded hemicycle which curved behind a fountain and was preceded by an outer forecourt.

Within this grandiose layout every detail was executed with superb workmanship. The walls – mortared rubble with a criss-cross mortar design at the bottom, and pure brickwork higher up – were built with mortar-beds up to 6 cm. (2⅓ in.) wide and were covered with fine plaster. The apse vault carried a mosaic; even the outer wall of the apse was painted. The pavement of nave and chancel, still preserved, is composed of huge marble plaques – grey streaked with green, framed by dark grey marble battens, while in the aisles and transept wings plaques of dark and light marble form geometric designs of diamonds and squares [90]; the capitals throughout the basilica point to a fifth-century date [91, 92]. Some are of 'Theodosian' design, others are Ionic impost block capitals with varying foliate design. A date between 450 and 460 seems likely for the start of building; construction on a building of its size may have gone on for a long time; the atrium and forecourt might well have been completed just prior to the earthquake which ravaged Corinth in 551. Indeed, every detail of the structure is so splendidly preserved as to raise doubts whether the building was used for any length of time.

The Lechaion basilica presents the plan of a basilica with a tripartite transept in an extraordinarily rich and sophisticated language. The sections of the transept, the aisles, and the centre bay are all placed on different levels, and the screens of columns which originally separated them display a variety in rhythm, spacing, and height. Light and shade play over the deep carving of the capitals. The patterns of the pavement slabs in purple and light and dark grey must be visualized against the lively colours of mosaics and wall paintings, of which only scarce remnants survive. All told, the rich and complex architectural concepts of the Lechaion basilica rival the architecture of the other great Aegean centres, whether Constantinople, Salonica, Ephesus, or Philippi. By 500, Christian architecture has reached a peak in Greece – was it due to Imperial support? – and, except for Constantinople, it far outshines the other provinces of the eastern coastlands.

CHAPTER 6

THE INLAND COUNTRIES

The architecture of the Aegean coastlands, both ecclesiastical and domestic, left its traces all over the Near East. Even on the high plateaus inland, fertile throughout antiquity, and across the desert, its impact is felt wherever the Imperial administration took a hand in backing lavish building activities. Its influence is seen even more clearly in the hellenized cities dotting the coast and the caravan routes from Antioch to R'safah on the Mesopotamian border. Yet even in the most hellenized buildings of the inland countries, the architectural designs absorbed from the coastlands were clothed in a vocabulary and built in materials and in a technique alien to the style in which they had originated: a construction in heavy stone blocks encasing a narrow core of rubble masonry; and a solid, somewhat rustic ornament. It becomes clear that in such buildings designs drawn from the Aegean coastlands were constantly vying with, and threatened by, an architecture which was rooted in local tradition.

The native architecture of the Near East drew its strength not from the cities, but from the vast rural areas of the hinterland.[1] Autochthonous in custom and population, speaking Syrian, Aramaic, Cappadocian, or other native dialects, the countryside – beyond a narrow coastal strip – remained relatively impervious to the culture of the Roman-hellenistic cities. Concomitantly, the architecture of these rural areas shows a style distinctly its own. It has been suggested that the style, the plans, and the vocabulary of these country buildings – houses as well as churches – had migrated into the countryside from the great urban centres. True, these rural areas occasionally absorbed architectural forms from Greek cities, such as Antioch or Constantinople. But such outside inspiration seems to have been subsidiary. It is just as likely that the architecture of the hinterland was locally conceived by rural masons

active in the market towns, villages, and monastic centres all over the area; numbers of these masons are known by name from building inscriptions.[2]

The strength of the village organization, at least in Syria, and of the monastic movement all over the Near East cannot be overrated. Monophysite monasticism, strongly opposed to hellenization, romanization, and the dogmatic compromises of Constantinople, was nourished from Nisibis (Nusaybin) from the late fourth century and dominated the hinterlands of the East. Even now hundreds of their monasteries are preserved in ruins. Monastic congregations and villagers were jointly responsible for the majority of church buildings, and the borderline between parish and monastic churches is, if traceable, as a rule insignificant.

The usual building material of this inland architecture is the local stone, cut into large blocks [95]; small stones or rubble masonry are used but rarely. These blocks, in Anatolia and Armenia, encase a core of rubble masonry; in Syria they comprise, as a rule in double courses, the full thickness of the wall. The supports are piers, columns, or piers with half-columns attached. Bases, column shafts, and capitals are of local execution, not imported as they often are in the Aegean area, and but rarely pilfered from older buildings as was the rule in Rome. Where wood was available, timber roofing was the rule. Elsewhere, buildings were vaulted – groin-vaulted or domed, as was the custom from the second and third centuries. Occasionally roofing is achieved by huge stone slabs. Vaulting, however, was the result not of choice but of necessity. Writing about 380, Gregory of Nyssa pointed out to the bishop of Iconium (Konya) 'since in our part of the world we have no timber, we will have to vault the octagonal chapel projected'.[3] To consider vaulting an improvement over timber roofing is a nineteenth-

136 · PART THREE: THE FIFTH CENTURY

century prejudice and must be discarded in this context.

Building materials and practices support the architectural style of the inlands, but they do not create it. Whether full ashlar or rubble faced with stone blocks, the impression remains unchanged. Interior space is played down: arcade and clerestory zones are poorly articulated, supports heavy and squat, windows small. While the interiors need not always have looked as stark as they do today, their wall paintings and floor or apse mosaics (where, and if, they existed) were quite simple. The exterior of the building, on the other hand, becomes the basis of a design of powerful composite masses, joined together in block units. The units are strongly articulated. Nave and aisles, base zones, walls, and roofs, and the successive storeys of a tower are set off against each other by cornices, eaves lines, and string courses, just as openings, windows, and doors are set off by strong frames.

The profiles of frames and cornices, capitals, and the bases of columns and piers are classical, if crude in design. Yet in contrast to the alive and ever-evolving classical approach of Constantinople, the Aegean coastland, and the hellenized cities of the hinterland, the classical vocabulary of the rural areas remains by and large stationary. Always a foreign element in the Near Eastern hinterland, Roman-hellenistic architecture and its vocabulary are used for centuries in unchanged provincialized form to denote the higher strata of architecture, temples and public buildings. Forms created in the provincial art of Roman Syria in the second and third centuries are retained often into the sixth century. The conservative populations of the uplands cling to the same vocabulary in decorating their sacred buildings, be they dedicated to a local divinity, to a Greek, a Roman, or the Christian god.

Notwithstanding the common stylistic characteristics, a multitude of church types develops in the hinterland of the Near East: timber-roofed basilicas, supported by colonnaded arcades; barrel-vaulted basilicas and barrel-vaulted hall-churches; cross-shaped churches; octagons; aisleless churches,

covered by barrel-vaults or by stone slabs placed on transverse arches. Given the vastness of the area and its fragmentation by mountain chains and deserts into isolated districts, it is natural that types and variants in building technique should become standard within their own comparatively small districts – northern and central Syria, the Haûran in southern Syria, Central Lycia, Lycaonia, Cappadocia.

As in the Aegean coastlands, the architecture of the cities in the Near East is known primarily through the fragmentary evidence of excavations. In the hinterland, on the other hand, great numbers of buildings have survived to this day, many almost fully preserved. This is due in part to the depopulation of the countryside from the seventh to the end of the nineteenth century. As a result of re-population, the number of surviving buildings – numbering many hundreds half a century ago – is rapidly diminishing through popular ignorance and governmental indifference in many, though not all, parts of the Near East. Church architecture in the uplands of Syria and Asia Minor, nevertheless, presents a more complete picture than in most other regions of the Early Christian world. Moreover, many of these buildings bear inscriptions giving the date of construction and at times the names of the founder and the architect. Thus the historical development in a province such as Syria becomes remarkably clear.

The chance preservation of large numbers of buildings in regions abandoned or sparsely settled for centuries has led to a curious situation. Rediscovered in the formative days of a modern history of architecture – Syria in the 1850s, Asia Minor between 1890 and 1910 – the frequently untouched structures of the hinterland became better known than buildings in large parts of the Latin West and the Aegean coastlands. Moreover, the customary nineteenth-century approach to the history of architecture, still surviving in the twentieth century, was grounded in a concept of technical progress. It worked with vague analogies between building types or details, established on paper without regard to context, scale, quality, concrete design, or historical situation. Hence the heavy, cramped, but as a rule small Syrian churches with their twin-tower façades could be viewed as leading up across a gulf of six hundred years to the huge Romanesque cathedrals of France with their freely organized plans and memberings. This misconception was reinforced by the impact which the first scholarly publication on Syrian building made on French and American architects of the last third of the nineteenth century, such as Labadie and Richardson. During the last eighty years such misjudgements on the architecture of the inlands of the Near East – as to quality, size, and its historical place within the context of both Early Christian and medieval church building – have continued and proliferated. The small cross churches in the highlands of Asia Minor have been interpreted as the fountain-head whence sprang all the decisive elements of medieval church building in Europe. Cappadocia, it is said, gave to Early Christian Palestine, Greece, and Italy, the cross martyrium, the cross transept, and the tripartite transept; to Byzantium, the 'domed basilica'; and to Romanesque France, England, and Germany, the crossing tower, the segregated crossing, the fully developed individual three-bay transept, and the 'square schematism' of the church plan.[4]

Individual features could easily have penetrated without a time lag from the inland countries to the West. The motif of the centre tower could have been carried from Asia Minor to Central Europe and taken root in pre-Carolingian times in the context of small cross churches. Similarly, the twin-tower façade could possibly have penetrated Carolingian Europe from Syria.[5] But by and large, the champions of the Eastern hinterlands as *the* fountain-head of Early Christian, Byzantine, and Western medieval architecture have overshot the mark. Resemblances of plan on paper, regardless of scale, are not historical reality. Gaps of half a millennium between the putative forebear and the offspring are not easily bridged, unless there are unquestionable intermediaries. Nor are links between countries far apart in place and culture – such as Muslim Syria and the Christian West –

lightly postulated in the absence of evident means of transmission. Is it, after all, really necessary to speak of dependence and influence wherever a resemblance exists between two styles distant in time and place? Is not a design in solids simply one of the possible architectural concepts which repeats itself in history? We leave the question open and turn to a discussion of the buildings.

SYRIA

Syria had been among the most flourishing provinces of the Roman Empire. Permeated by Roman-hellenistic culture, its great urban centres rose on the coast and along the caravan routes. The hinterland had been one of the rich agricultural reservoirs of the Roman world, producing grain and oil. Nor did its economic or cultural situation change from the fourth into the early seventh century. Only after the conquest of Syria by the Muslims did its rural economy collapse.[6]

The architecture of the cities is closely linked to that of the Aegean coastlands. In culture, nationality, and speech, the upper strata of the urban population were romanized Greeks, and in their buildings, as well, they naturally leaned towards the plans and the architectural concepts which prevailed all along the shores of the Aegean Sea. Indeed, houses and churches in the large cities of Syria are nearly indistinguishable in plan from those known in Constantinople, Ephesus, and the Greek islands.

From the fourth to the end of the sixth century, the wealthy city houses of Antioch on the Orontes, with peristyle courts and elaborate, colourful mosaic floors, held to a type which had been traditional for nearly half a millennium. The situation holds for church buildings as well. The standard basilicas in the cities were of established Aegean plan: their naves wide, preceded by atria and colonnaded nartheces, their floors carpeted with mosaics, their apses closed outside in three sides of a polygon.[7] At times, basilicas with galleries appear inland even in minor urban centres along the caravan routes. But the type may just as well have been brought to Syria from Constantine's basilica at the Holy Sepulchre, itself apparently a product of the court architecture of Constantinople.

Little is known about the ecclesiastical buildings in post-Constantinian Antioch. The only major churches known at least from excavations are a basilica at Antioch-Ma'chouka, the cross martyrium at Kaoussié, and a late-fifth-century quatrefoil at Seleucia-Pieria (Samandağ), another suburb.[8] Roughly 36 m. (120 ft) in diameter, the quatrefoil must have been an imposing structure, richly decorated and spacious [93]. In plan it recalls the

the structure was a martyrium is likewise open to conjecture. Clearly, the quatrefoil of Seleucia-Pieria does not represent the style of the inlands of the Near East. Plan and design are based on concepts well established in the Aegean by the end of the fifth century: a double-shell design; spaces freely expanding in contrasting volumes – cubes, half-cylinders, cylinder segments; column screens rather than walls; colourful decoration; complex interior views. Plan and design, however, may be rooted in a Constantinian tradition firmly established at Antioch: the Golden Octagon, notwithstanding its octa-

93. Seleucia-Pieria (Samandağ), martyrium(?), late fifth century. Plan

earlier and somewhat larger church of S. Lorenzo in Milan, with the only difference that a deep chancel or apse projected from its eastern wall. The four exedrae of the inner quatrefoil expanded freely, supported by columns. Marble pavements covered the centre room, mosaics paved the ambulatory. No evidence of galleries was found, and it is quite possible that the ambulatories, like those at Peruštica, were single-storeyed and, like the centre room, covered with a timber roof. Whether or not

conch plan. In the sixth century, possibly in a revival, the type took root in the hellenized urban centres: at Apamea (Qalaat el Mudiq) a quatrefoil church has been excavated in the centre of the town; another has survived in large parts incorporated in the mosque el-Halawiya at Aleppo; at Bosra (Bosra Eski Sham), the ruins of the cathedral, dated 512 through an inscription, were well preserved until some fifty years ago; finally, the walls of a quatrefoil church, possibly the cathedral, rise amidst the ruins of

R'safah in eastern Syria.[9] Only rarely are central plans transposed into the local dialect of the hinterland, as in the church of St George at Izra (Zorah) (515): an octagon on piers, with ambulatory and corner niches – the whole encased in a square, and

94. Serjilla, village, fifth century. Plan

SARCOPHAGI

PRESS

BATH   'CAFE

CHURCH

Terrace   Terrace

PRESS

◻ PYRAMIDICAL TOMB

0 — 120 FT

0 — 40 M

crudely built. The egg-shaped dome over the centre room suggests an awkward substitute for the timber dome or pyramid of a centrally-planned structure of Aegean type.[10]

However, both the ecclesiastical and the domestic architecture of the great Syrian cities remain largely unknown. On the other hand, rural Syria is studded with the ruins of churches, monasteries, villas, houses, and stables, and with the remains of entire villages and small towns, all dating from the fourth

95. Ba'udeh, house façade, fifth century

(and earlier) to the end of the sixth century. Three major regions stand out clearly: the north, beyond Antioch and Aleppo; central Syria, surrounding Apamea and Damascus, and extending east across the desert; and finally the Djebel Haûran around Bosra in the south. While the first two are closely related, the Haûran stands by itself.

Building in the Syrian countryside had little in common with the architecture of the hellenized cities. The plans of the rich houses of Antioch are on the whole as unknown in the villages and small towns of the uplands as are their mosaic decoration and their technique of construction in concrete faced by small stones. In many places, as at Serjilla, entire villages – composed of farm-houses, barns, and stables dating from the fifth century – were reasonably well preserved as late as 1910.[11] Blocky, massive, and with classical, though crude, profiles, capitals, and door frames, their buildings – including thermae and churches – gave impressive testimony of the level of architecture in the north and central Syrian countryside [94]. Houses are laid

out as rectangular cubes, two and three storeys high, and divided on each floor into two or more rooms. Walls are built of large blocks of ashlar. Tiers of porticoes, one per floor and supported either by columns or piers, provide access and light through doors which lead to the single rooms; in the hot season they presumably also served as sleeping porches [95]. Windows in the rear walls of the houses or towards the porticoes are rare, and generally of sixth-century date when they do appear. The blocks, as a rule, open on to a courtyard. They are often built in pairs, standing at right angles or facing each other. A tower occasionally surmounts the courtyard gate or rises at one end of the block.

Conventual buildings in the region differ from ordinary domestic architecture mainly in three respects: the individual buildings are internally undivided, as one would expect in monastic dormitories and refectories; the porticoes often envelop the block on three or even on four sides; and, together with the church, the conventual buildings enclose the four sides of a courtyard.[12]

In the Haûran, to the south, building is even more conservative than in the countryside of central and northern Syria. Little distinguishes church buildings from secular basilicas or even from houses and stables, and nothing sets apart structures of the second or third from those of the fifth or sixth centuries. Construction is based on the principle of a rectangular space covered with stone slabs which rest on a series of transverse diaphragm arches. When over-large, the span was crossed by two or even three parallel rows of arches, the one in the centre full-height, the flanking ones narrower and providing for a double tier of aisles and galleries. Two third-century structures at Tafḥa and El Qanawāt, both presumably secular basilicas, manifest this style. Churches, as a rule, were aisleless; when provided with apses they should probably be assigned a date not before 400.[13] In the course of the fifth century, the uniformity of Haûran design was altogether broken up by an invasion of church types from central and eastern Syria and from the Roman-hellenistic cities along the trade routes. Towards the end of the century, colonnaded basilicas are found even in Haûran villages, such as the Klaudianos church at Umm-el-Jemal. Exceptionally, a basilica is even provided with galleries, such as one at Umm-es-Surab in the Haûran of 489 [96]. At El Bāra in northern Syria just this type took local root: four churches are all provided with galleries and esonarthex and one of them with a transept, to boot. An enclave of the 'Aegean' church type seems to have formed itself far in the interior of Syria.[14]

In northern, central, and eastern Syria, on the other hand, a wealth of church buildings are known – many dated through inscriptions. Aisleless chapels occur in the north as well as in the Haûran: timber-roofed, small in size, and built at any time from the fourth to the end of the sixth century.[15] They have been interpreted as the aboriginal Syrian church type, but this is by no means certain. It is equally doubtful whether ecclesiastical architecture evolved from domestic building in Syria more directly than elsewhere in the Roman Empire.[16] Nor is there any indication that aisleless chapels antedate the earliest

96. Umm-es-Surab, church, 489, and monastery. Plan and section

0   40 FT

0   15 M

basilicas in the Syrian uplands, or for that matter, that these latter were brought in from the hellenized urban centres.[17] The basilica appears fully developed in an insignificant village church as early as 372 at Fafertin, and becomes rapidly standard: at Kseidjbe (Hsedjeh) (414), at Kharab Shems, at St Paul and Moses at Dar Qita (418) [97].[18] The plans of such basilicas do not differ fundamentally from those of simple country churches elsewhere in the Christian world. The nave is flanked by aisles; the upper walls of the nave rest on arcades; the squat columns are surmounted by crude provincialized Corinthian capitals [98]. However three features distinguish these earliest North Syrian churches: the entrances, two as a rule, are on the south flank of the building; the apse, semicircular both inside and outside, is flanked by two square chambers; finally, the middle of the nave is frequently occupied by an

97. Dar Qita, St Paul and Moses, 418. Plan

exedra – a raised rectangular enclosure, its curved end opposing the main apse [113].[19] No doubt, all these features reflect local liturgical custom. The exedra in the nave as it survives in Nestorian churches was reserved, at least in northern and western Syria, for the clergy during the Mass of the Catechumens. The altar site in the apse was approached only during the Mass of the Faithful by the procession of the clergy conducting the celebrant. Again, the doors on the flank coincide with Syrian upland custom, which precluded a western entrance by separating men and women, the former in front of the exedra, the latter behind.[20] The side chambers, as yet, remain liturgically inexplicable. The traditional term, *pastophories*, would reflect their use as sacristies, but functionally they cannot be established as such prior to the sixth century. On the other hand, tripartite sanctuaries were customary in Syrian temples still in the third century, and church buildings may have followed such models.[21]

The cramped, austere space of the interiors is as pronounced in these churches as the impressive blockiness of the exterior. Plain profiles set off the eaves lines of the aisles. Windows are simply cut through the thick walls even when their shape, generally rectangular, gives way to a round-headed type. Capitals are Corinthian, Ionic, or simply cylindrical in shape. In the Corinthian capitals the leaves are heavy and thick and, as a rule, outlined with only the ribs marked; the churches of St Paul and Moses at Dar Qita (418) and at Kseidjbe (414) provide typical examples. In Ionic capitals the volutes are turned into plain disks, set with a cross or a rosette, and placed high against the cylindrical core; the egg-and-dart of the echinus is generally omitted. Only

98. Kharab Shems, basilica, fifth century, as in 1900. From the north-west

on the door frames does an elegant ornament of Roman-hellenistic origin survive: guilloches, palmette friezes, and laurel patterns seem to be the hallmark of the master builder Markianos Kyris, who designed the churches at Kseidjbe and Dar Qita.[22]

The large number of dated structures makes it possible to trace the development of church building in Syria. After 430 ornamentation disappears from the exteriors. On the other hand, the starkness of the interiors becomes occasionally relieved by some slight decoration. The changes in plan likewise are minor. In central Syria piers instead of columns at times support the nave. The exedra in the middle of the nave now becomes the rule. Perhaps under the influence of urban and Aegean custom, and for no apparent liturgical reason, the main doors are now placed on the façade, while those on the flanks serve as subsidiary entrances. The function of the side chambers flanking the apse, formerly ambiguous, is now clarified. Frequently, though by no means

always, one room, as a rule the south one, opens in a wide arch towards the aisle. It functions as a martyr's chapel and frequently shelters a reliquary.[23] The opposite chamber, communicating with the aisles only through a door, would serve as a diaconicon, a sacristy. Frequently a door from one of these rooms leads to the apse as well. In that case, this side chamber – whether diaconicon or martyr's chapel – may have had the additional role of prothesis, the room where, following Eastern rite, the Eucharist was prepared. Occasionally, as at Deir Siman, a second and sometimes a third storey surmount, tower-like, one side chamber.

Baptisteries in the early fifth century were square, apsed rooms attached to the flank of an aisle. The great majority, however, are of sixth-century date – as a rule free-standing, square, and often provided with an apse; none are vaulted. Only one is hexagonal, and only the baptistery at Qal'at Si'man presents the plan known from the Aegean coastlands and the West: an octagon with corner niches,

99. Qal'at Si'man, baptistery, c. 480–90. Exterior, as in 1954

enclosed in a square and enveloped by a low ambulatory [99].[24]

Churches and baptisteries in Syria were rarely isolated in the middle or on the edge of a village or town. As a rule, they were accompanied by domestic structures, living quarters for the secular clergy, for monastic congregations or pilgrims. In planning them, North and East Syria on the one hand, the Haûran in the south on the other, follow different paths just as in their church buildings. In North and East Syria, throughout the fifth century, a number of buildings of the local house type face the area of the courtyard, in front or behind, but most frequently along one of the flanks of the church. In conventual buildings, the individual parts – dormitories, a refectory, kitchen, larder, and a pilgrims' hostel (each preceded or enveloped by corridors and sleeping porches in several storeys) – are as a rule linked by porticoes. Qasr el Benât shows the plan fully developed as early as c. 425; but it continues with little change into the sixth century. At Deir Siman it appears in three convents and a large hostelry at the end of the fifth century. At times the plan is tightened into a continuous rectangle of structures enveloping an inner courtyard; thus at Qal'at Si'man conventual and pilgrims' buildings occupy the south-east quadrant of the huge cross church [100, 101]. The rectangle plan may have reached Qal'at Si'man from southern Syria where it had been customary for monasteries from the fourth century, placed, as a rule, along the flank of the church. The monastery of H. Sergios and Bakchos at Umm-es-Surab (489) illustrates the plan [96]. In the Haûran, on occasion, the block of conventual buildings will occupy the site in front of the church so that the inner courtyard is also an atrium. But this plan seems to have been evolved only in the sixth century, under the impact of atrium plans as they were customary in the Aegean coastlands.[25]

In northern and eastern as well as southern Syria by the middle of the fifth century, the plans of churches, baptisteries, and monasteries were definitely established within regional limits. Indeed, planning changes little until the Islamic Conquest, *c.* 630. But from 480 on, a new classical style and a new vocabulary come to the fore in the great monastic centres. Qal'at Si'man, financed, it appears, by the church builder on the throne, Zeno (474–5, 476–91), is the most grandiose example of this new phase of Syrian church building [100–2].[26] It is a cross

100. Qal'at Si'man, martyrium, *c.* 480–90. Plan

N

0   60 FT

0   20 M

101. Qal'at Si'man, c. 480–90. Church and monastery from the north-east, as in 1900

martyrium, comparable to the one excavated at Antioch-Kaoussié, or to the fifth-century church of St John at Ephesus. But in execution Qal'at Si'man outstrips everything previously built on Syrian soil. It is of impressive size, 80 and 90 m. (260 and 295 ft) across respectively, designed to house large crowds

102. Qal'at Si'man, martyrium, c. 480–90. Isometric reconstruction

103. Qal'at Si'man, c. 480–90. Octagon, looking north-west, as in c. 1960

104. Qal'at Si'man, c. 480–90. Octagon and south wing

of pilgrims, and of elaborate design. With its conventual buildings, it covers many acres of ground
[101]. The centre part, originally timber-roofed,
rose over the pillar on top of which St Simeon
Stylites had spent the last part of his life [103, 104].
The four wings, instead of being aisleless, are fully-
fledged basilicas: those west and south were preceded by nartheces, while the east wing was terminated by three apses [105, 106]. All parts of the
structure are strongly set off against each other.
Clearly profiled string courses mark the base zone
and rise to frame door jambs and windows. Eaves
lines and the arches in the octagon and wings are
similarly outlined. The shafts of the columns in the
octagon rise from elegant bases and carry capitals
covered by windblown acanthus leaves with spiky
edges. In the wings the capitals are Corinthian. On
the exterior, the main apse was articulated by two
tiers of strong engaged columns and a corbel-table

105. Qal'at Si'man, c. 480–90.
Exterior of apses, as in c. 1960

106. Qal'at Si'man, c. 480–90. Interior of apses

107. Qal'at Si'man, c. 480–90. South façade, as in 1954

frieze – two small arches with scallop fillings to each intercolumniation. On the south façade, fluted pilasters carry the three arches of a triumphal entrance gate [107].

Neither in size nor in plan could the huge martyrium of Qal'at Si'man become the model for any number of ordinary monastic or parish churches. In the church built on Mont Admirable to enclose the column of St Simeon Stylites the Younger, the plan was taken up on a smaller scale; only the ornament [117] continues the elegant design of the old workshop into the early sixth century. However, it reflected in the area a sense of monumentality and a classical vocabulary unrivalled anywhere in fifth-century Christian architecture. For a generation or two these factors determine the design of a group of comparatively large church buildings in northern, central, and eastern Syria, such as Turmanin, Qalb Lozeh, Kerratîn, El-Anderin, and Ruwêha (Rueiha). Some of these 'cathedrals', as they have been called, are preserved in ruins, others known only from de Vogüé's drawings. At R'safah-Sergiopolis – one of the major garrisons on the Euphrates frontier and the pilgrimage town of St Sergius – two basilicas rose, one of them apparently the martyrium of the saint.[27] None of the churches in this group are dated by inscription, but the majority seem to fall between 480 and 520. Turmanin, now destroyed, can hardly

be later than 480 since its vocabulary is reflected in dated village churches, such as Basufân (491–2) and the east church at Kalôta (492). Qalb Lozeh, well preserved, may well date from c. 450 [108–10]. Of the two basilicas at R'safah-Sergiopolis, Basilica B was presumably built in the last twenty years of the fifth century; the basilica of St Sergius is later; but it still dates from before 520 [111–14].

Whatever their dates, all these churches are closely related and seem to be designed by one or two workshops active over a thirty- to forty-year period. At Qal'at Si'man, notwithstanding the initiative and support lent by the Imperial court in Constantinople, the cross plan chosen was that customary for martyria in Syria and Palestine from the fourth century. The other 'cathedrals' likewise follow older local custom. Their apses are framed by side chambers; entrances are placed both in the façade and along the two flanks [108, 109]. Supports vary: columns, following North Syrian custom, supported the nave of Turmanin, while those of Qalb Lozeh, of Ruwêha, or of the Sergius Church at R'safah are piers, following central and east Syrian tradition. The vocabulary, as well, is rooted in earlier Syrian church building, but the classical elements grow in number and strength. String courses with rich classical profiles mark the base of the walls and the eaves lines. Half-piers are fluted, piers are topped by foliage capitals. The crude Ionic and

108. Qalb Lozeh, church, c. 450. Plan

109. Qalb Lozeh, church, c. 450. Exterior from the south-west

110. Qalb Lozeh, church, c. 450. Interior of nave

111 and 112. R'safah, St Sergius (Basilica A),
before 520. Plan (*above*),
and interior of nave as in 1954 (*below*)

113. R'safah, St Sergius (Basilica A), before 520. Exedra

114. R'safah, St Sergius (Basilica A), before 520. Room above pastophory

Corinthian capitals of the earlier Syrian churches
give way to elaborate Corinthian, composite, or
wind-blown capitals. Their leaves are sharply cut,
with spiky edges separated by deep drill holes [115–
17]. Towards the middle of the sixth century, the
thorniness of the foliage grows sharper, and the
capitals of, for example, Qasr Ibn Wardan look as if
they were covered by a thistle growth standing out
from a dark ground.[28] But already at Qal'at Si'man
all details are of conservatively classical derivation,
transposed into harsh forms. Throughout the first
half of the sixth century, the silhouette of the buildings grows richer, the treatment of the walls sculptural. Gabled porches on columns projected over the
doors along the flanks of the Bizzos church at
Ruwêha and of the church at Qalb Lozeh [109].
Towers, slightly lower than the nave, rose on either
side of a deep porch at Turmanin, Qalb Lozeh,
Ruwêha, and – raised high on a flight of steps – at the
Sergius Basilica at R'safah. Jointly, towers and porch
form the characteristic Late Syrian twin-tower
façade.[29] Even the side chambers of the apse – two-
storeyed at Turmanin – were at times surmounted
by low towers, or by domed upper chambers. In the
Sergius basilica at R'safah the squinches of their
domes survive [114]. None of these towers seems to
have served any practical or liturgical function. But
they convey a feeling of clarity, articulation, and
monumentality far greater than is warranted by the
actual dimensions of the structures; indeed, in size
these Syrian 'cathedrals', from 35 to 50 m. (115 to
165 ft) in length, are much smaller than even minor
parish or cemetery churches in Constantinople,
Rome, Corinth, or Ravenna. Likewise, the interior
of these 'cathedrals' becomes articulated, and
monumentalized, beyond their actual proportions.
In fact, in a break with the previous tradition of
Syrian architecture, around the turn of the century,
the interior becomes an object of architectural
awareness. Widely spaced low piers and huge arches
convey the impression of a space vaster than reality
[110]. At Ruwêha, half-piers rose through the entire
height of the wall. In the Sergius Church at R'safah,
these half-piers carried an upper order,[30] dividing

115. R'safah, north gate of town, c. 530. Capital

116. Qal'at Si'man, church, c. 480–90. Capital

117. Mont Admirable (Jebel Seman),
church of St Simeon the Younger, sixth century.
Door jamb

the interior into distinct spatial units and unifying it in length, width, and height in a monumental design [112]. Certainly the rows of short columns placed on brackets along the clerestories of Qalb Lozeh, Ruwêha, and R'safah are designed to produce a monumental effect of interlocking space and wall unknown before in Syria. Since such elements for organizing the exterior mass and interior space are comparatively weak at Turmanin, but grow stronger at R'safah and at El-Anderin, one is led to view the group of 'cathedrals' in terms of a stylistic sequence leading from c. 480 to 520 and beyond.

The monumentality of this Late Syrian architecture, the new organization of space and mass, and the rich classical vocabulary are without precedent in the local tradition. Outside forces were apparently at work, and it has been suggested that the new style was first formed at Antioch. This is possible, but it is not borne out by the scanty facts known about church building at Antioch. Hence an alternative hypothesis offers itself. Beginning with the rule of Zeno (474–5, 476–91), the Imperial administration took a renewed, lively interest in the Eastern provinces. Church buildings financed by the emperors abound from Mount Garizim in Palestine to R'safah on the Euphrates, to Qartamin in the Tur Abdin, and to Qal'at Si'man. To stress the classical heritage was, we recall, a characteristic of Imperial architecture, whether secular or ecclesiastical. Imperial backing might well have led the Syrian builders to take a new look at the antique architecture of their own province, and thus towards a richer, more fully 'classical' vocabulary. Imperial backing would also have led them to absorb elements of a vocabulary customary in the milieu of Constantinople: capitals with wind-blown leaves, though less harsh in design than those at Qal'at Si'man, are known in the fifth century from Salonica, from Nea-Anchialos, from the Balkans, and from Ravenna – all sites within the sphere of influence of the Imperial capital.[31]

Twin-towered façades, too, have been taken to be symbols of rulership, from the Hittite kings to the Byzantine emperors; hence, the Syrian 'cathedral' façades have been linked to Constantinopolitan models.[32] However, it remains to be proven that such twin-towered façades surmounted the gates of the palaces of Constantinople. Proof of Imperial connexions has also been seen in the twin-tower structure, surprisingly Syrian in design, which on the wooden doors of S. Sabina in Rome (c. 430) surmounts, like a canopy, the figures of an angel and of a presumably Imperial personage.[33] In a broader context, though, the question arises whether the new feeling for an articulated interior space in the Syrian 'cathedrals' of the early sixth century may be linked to the movement which at the same time led to the victory of the domed church in Constantinople and the core provinces. Obviously the question cannot be answered, but it is one which to us seems well worth posing.

PALESTINE AND JORDAN

Three currents exert their impact during the fifth and the early sixth centuries on the architecture of Palestine and Jordan: the fourth-century buildings over the holy sites; the architecture of the Aegean coastlands in general, and of the court of Constantinople in particular; and finally, the monastic and village churches of neighbouring Syria.[34]

The impact of the buildings erected over the holy sites on the later local architectural tradition is surprisingly small. A church on Mount Garizim (Gerizim) is the only one to enrich the formula set by the fourth-century prototypes.[35] Built in 484 by the Emperor Zeno as his offering of thanks after quelling a Samaritan uprising, the church was dedicated to the Mother of God and further sanctified by a relic from the Rock of Calvary. The octagonal centre room, presumably covered by a wooden dome or a pyramidal timber roof, was enveloped by an ambulatory [118]. Beyond this centre, three shallow entrance porticoes and a deep chancel and apse on the main axes alternated with four chapels in the diagonals, one a baptistery. Eight corner piers and seven pairs of columns supported the centre room; they may have been surmounted by the upper order of a gallery. Imperial backing explains the elegance

118. Mount Garizim,
Church of the Theotokos,
484. Plan

of the construction, the masonry of carefully hewn ashlar blocks with drafted margins, and the finely worked bases and Corinthian capitals [119, 120]. The plan, extraordinarily rich in its combination of spatial forms and levels, has been linked to Constantine's Golden Octagon at Antioch; but it is more easily explained as a new variant on the type of the martyria erected since Constantine's day in the Holy Land. After all, the late fifth century was fertile in evolving such new variants: S. Stefano Rotondo in Rome at nearly the same time combines in a remarkably similar way a centre room with an ambulatory and an outer ring of alternating spatial units.

The court of Constantinople continued to subsidize church building in the Holy Land throughout the fifth century. Through these Imperial enter-

119. Mount Garizim, Church of the Theotokos,
484. Capital

120. Mount Garizim, Church of the Theotokos,
484. Wall of ambulatory

121. Gerasa (Jerash), Church of the Prophets, Apostles, and Martyrs, 465. Plan

prises the architectural concepts of the Aegean coastlands gained a firm hold. At times the impact can be directly traced. At Gaza on the Palestinian coast, a cross church was built in 401 from a plan sent, together with thirty-two columns of Greek green marble, by the Empress Eudokia from Constantinople.[36] The plan, in all probability derived from Constantine's Apostoleion, took root in the Aegean coastlands, as witness the fifth-century church of St John at Ephesus. Another variant of the cross plan appears in 465 in the Church of the Prophets, Apostles, and Martyrs which has been excavated at Gerasa (Jerash), across the Jordan.[37] There the four arms were subdivided into nave and aisles by thirty columns [121]. Similarly in Palestine and Jordan, a few major basilicas reveal the impact of Constantinopolitan and, in general terms, of Aegean architectural concepts. The plan of the church of St Stephen in Jerusalem, built between 437 and 460 by the exiled Empress Eudokia, recalls the contemporary Studios church. Like the church in Constantinople, it was a basilica, the aisles possibly surmounted by galleries, the apse polygonal on the exterior, the nave colonnaded and preceded by a colonnaded narthex and an atrium.[38] Aegean ele-

ments, such as polygonal apses, aisles enveloping the nave on three sides, rich mosaic floors, and occasionally even galleries, occur in other fifth-century basilicas in Palestine, Jordan, southern Syria: at Evron near Nahariya in Israel, where layers of mosaic pavements and rebuildings, all dated, follow one another from 415 to 492; at Shavei Zion, with a similar sequence of floors, the latest dated 486; at Ramat Rahel, just outside Jerusalem, with enveloping aisles; at Mamshit (Kurnub) in the Negev, where two basilicas rise, of fourth- and sixth-century date, preceded by atria and with rich mosaic pavements; at Madaba in Jordan; in Syria, at Umm-es-Surab about 489; and in Jordan at St Theodore at Gerasa about 494–6. On the site of the Miracle of the Multiplying of the Loaves and Fishes at et-Tabgha (Ein Ha-Shivah) near Lake Tiberias, a basilica was laid out about 500 with a splendid mosaic floor and with a 'reduced cross transept' [122]. The transept wings are accompanied by aisles along the west wall only, but otherwise the building was much like the many cross-transept basilicas in the Aegean coastlands.[39]

Such Aegean impact seems to have been strongest in Palestine and Jordan during the fifth century.

122. et-Tabgha (Ein Ha-Shivah), basilica, c. 500. Plan

Limited, however, to centres of pilgrimage and trade, it remained an alien element. The masonry technique of large ashlar blocks in Palestine and Jordan was as integral a part of architectural design as in the other inland countries of the Near East. Likewise, in plan and elevation the numberless minor parish and conventual churches in the Holy Land were closely linked to those of neighbouring Syria; the chapel excavated below the transept church of et-Tabgha had its roof supported on diaphragm arches in a technique customary in the Haûran. As a rule, however, country churches in Palestine, as in Syria, were small basilicas supported by arcades on low columns. The apse – flanked by side chambers (after 500 by lateral apses) – was enclosed within a massive straight-sided rear wall, solid or hollowed by hidden recesses.[40] One of three churches preserved to this day at Sbeïta (Shivta) in the Negev, probably of sixth-century date, may stand as an example for many similar buildings known only from remnants [226]. The walls are impressively strong, the windows small. Capitals, bases, and other ornaments are crude variations of the more elegant forms found in the hellenized urban centres of Palestine. The plan occurs

occasionally on a larger scale with slight modifications: at Emmaus (Amwas), where the apse projects outward to the east in three sides of a polygon; and at Ras as-Siagha on Mt Nebo, where the fifth-century basilica was preceded by an atrium and a raised narthex, and terminated by an older trefoil, the fourth-century martyrium, recording the site of Moses' death.[41]

Such modifications point to a phenomenon characteristic of Palestine and Jordan – the fusion of concepts rooted in the architecture of both the Aegean coastlands and the inland countries. The nine churches preserved in ruins at Gerasa manifest this fusion.[42] Dated as they are by inscriptions, they show at the same time how the impact of hellenized Aegean church architecture gives way after 500 to a resurgence of inland building. In the cathedral, c. 400, the chancel plan recalls that of the basilica at the Holy Sepulchre [123]. An atrium precedes the church; the colonnades in the nave are trabeated; the walls of the aisles are sheathed with finely polished stone plaques, and the apse is revetted with marble slabs. However, as late as the sixth century, the church builders of Gerasa and their patrons remained partial to a chancel arrangement of

123. Gerasa (Jerash),
cathedral, *c.* 400 (*right*), and
St Theodore, 494–6 (*left*).
Isometric reconstruction

0   120 FT
0   40 M

Aegean type and to a lavish interior decoration, with stone-revetted walls, glass mosaics in the apse vaults, and stone mosaic on the floors. But the overall plans are more and more assimilated to those of neighbouring rural Syria. A series of eight churches, dated by inscriptions from 464–5 to 611, shows the common features of the type and the gradual changes it underwent. All are built of heavy ashlar masonry. All are basilicas, except two: the centrally-planned church of the Baptist and the cross church of the Apostles, Prophets, and Martyrs. As in Syria, the supports are generally columns, occasionally piers. Geometrical and figural mosaics cover the floor. Atria disappear in favour of nartheces. In the second quarter of the sixth century sacristies, martyria chapels, or baptisteries flanking the apse give way to lateral apses with forechoirs recalling those of Qal'at Si'man. The resemblance to the Negev churches is close. Finally in the Genesius church (611), the side rooms are fused with the forechoir and turned into dwarf transept wings. The chancels, which at first project only into the last bays of the nave, later extend into the aisles as well.

The churches of Gerasa are extraordinarily impressive – through their size, through their number, and through their tendency to group several structures within one precinct. The cathedral was approached from the rear by a grand staircase. At the head of the staircase extended a huge courtyard, and in it a shrine of St Mary was placed against the rear of the apse. Between 494 and 496 the church of St Theodore was set up on a yet higher terrace, in front of the atrium of the cathedral and on an axis with the latter. In the group of churches dedicated to SS. John, Cosmas, and Damian (529–33), the structures are laid out along a transverse rather than a longitudinal axis: two small basilicas flank the centrally-planned church of the Baptist. But fundamentally the principle of grouping is the same, and may well be due to the impact of the building complexes which had grown on Golgotha since Constantine's times.

THE HIGH PLATEAU OF ASIA MINOR

Sizeable remnants of Christian buildings in the cities of Asia Minor have survived only on the sites along the rim of the high plateau. In the towns of the highlands proper, such as Kayseri, Ankara, or Konya, barely a few remnants of large timber-roofed basilicas remain standing. On the other hand, in rural areas a large number of church buildings were well preserved until a generation ago. They represent a variety of types, but they are small, often not more than 10 m. (30 ft) long or less. But whether large city churches or small country chapels, with few exceptions all employed the local stone, either in large well-cut blocks or in slabs, facing a rubble core; only in later structures are small chunks used. All were designed in blocky masses recalling the rustic buildings of the Syrian uplands. All were vaulted throughout, wood being difficult to obtain. Arches were frequently horseshoe-shaped in plan and elevation. The decorative vocabulary, as far as it exists, is crude yet unmistakably of classical derivation, transmitted either from the coastal cities or from Syria by way of Cilicia.[43]

Hierapolis (Pamukkale), in Antiquity a sizeable town just beyond the western edge of the high plateau, had claimed from the first century to shelter the grave of the Apostle Philip, and thus occupied a

124. Hierapolis (Pamukkale), martyrium of St Philip(?), early fifth century(?). Plan

ORIGINAL STRUCTURE   LATER ADDITIONS   NOT EXCAVATED BY 1965

leading position among Christian congregations in Asia. In the fifth and sixth centuries it was an important Christian centre, closely linked to the coastal cities along the Aegean shore. Three churches remain, and not too surprisingly, at least one reveals links to the architecture of the coastlands.[44] An octagonal structure outside the city walls, it is possibly of early-fifth-century date and was perhaps the martyrium of the Apostle Philip [124]. The centre room, 20·70 m. (68 ft, 70 Roman ft) wide, and probably timber-domed, was enveloped by deep niches lit by windows, and by entrance arms in alternation – all barrel-vaulted and connected by narrow passages and small chapels hidden inside the piers. All this was enclosed within a huge square of 60 by 62 m. (197 by 203 ft) of low chambers, perhaps pilgrims' shelters. Elements of coastland architecture are manifest throughout: in the brick and stone bands of the walls, with only the piers utilizing large blocks; in the vaulting technique in brick; in the marble revetment and marble pavements; in the few capitals preserved. All this contrasts with the pure 'inland' design of the other two churches of Hierapolis. One is a huge hall, originally perhaps a bath, flanked by three barrel-vaulted niches on either side. It was transformed into a church about 410 by the addition of three pendentive domes over the nave. The third church is a similarly large hall, its nave flanked by niches, but it dates from as late as 535. In Kayseri, remnants of a large church survived till 1957, possibly a basilica of Syrian type, dating from the end of the fifth century.[45]

In contrast to Hierapolis's huge city churches, the village churches on the high plateau are tiny. Here two centres of building activity are known. A goodly number of structures survived until recently in Cappadocia near Kayseri; another cluster of structures – nameless and undated – is located in the mountains of Lycaonia, south-east of Konya, called with Eastern fancy Binbirkilise – the Thousand and One Churches.[46] Not a single building is dated on either site, but a comparison of the architectural vocabulary with that of the neighbouring provinces

to the west and south suggests the late fifth or first half of the sixth century for the earliest known village churches in Asia Minor. As in Syrian churches between 480 and 550, orders of pilasters articulate the outer walls, string courses with classical profiles arch around windows. Basilicas are built with galleries; capitals are worked with friezes of vertical tongues, and façades may occasionally have had twin towers. All are features characteristic of either Syria or the Aegean coastlands in the late fifth century, and cannot be thought to have penetrated the backwater provinces of Lycaonia and Cappadocia before 550, if that early. Though still recognizable in the seventh century, such decorative elements gradually disappear. But unadorned or adorned in the most modest forms, church buildings in Asia Minor continued unchanged in type and overall design possibly as late as the tenth and eleventh centuries.

Throughout, builders in the uplands clung to a few basic types: timber-roofed basilicas and vaulted cross-churches in Cappadocia, vaulted basilicas and hall-churches in Lycaonia. On the coast a vaulted basilica on piers presumably preceded the extant church of St Nicholas at Myra. At Binbirkilise from at least the sixth century on, the type was standard [125–7]. Horseshoe-shaped apses, at times polygonal on the outside, echoed the horseshoe-shaped arches of the arcades. The low piers were widened sideways by half-columns, obviously purloined from the shape of window piers customary along the west coast of Asia Minor. At times side chambers projected sideways off the narthex, as in fifth-century Greece and along the coast of Asia Minor. Barrel-vaults extended lengthwise over aisles and nave with small windows high up in the upper walls. Occasionally open porches led off sideways from the aisles. The interior was dark, slightly enlivened by a mosaic floor and perhaps by wall paintings. Only the bare masses of the exterior spoke. The Syrian antecedents are clear, as is their transposition into the local language.

This standard plan appears some twenty times at Binbirkilise, varying only in details and size, from as much as 38 m. (125 ft) in length to less than 15 m.

(50 ft). A major departure from this occurs only in church no. 32: galleries surmount the aisles; towers, if such they were, push outward from the narthex; pastophories project from the aisles near the apse; and the window mullions display tongue ornament [128A]. All this points to fifth- and sixth-century models in the coastlands. Another variant occurs at Eski Andaval, across the Cappadocian border.[47] The nave, originally timber-roofed and lit by clerestory windows, was later barrel-vaulted, thus turning the basilica into a hall-church like Binbirkilise. The fully classical decoration of the apse windows and the exterior polygon of its plan suggest an early date, possibly not much after 500.

125 (*above, left*). Binbirkilise, Church no. 33, *c.* 600. Exterior of apse, as in *c.* 1960

126 (*left*). Binbirkilise, Church no. 32, *c.* 600. Interior of apse, as in *c.* 1960

127 (*below*). Binbirkilise, Church no. 1, *c.* 600 or later. Interior of nave, as in *c.* 1960

128. (A) Binbirkilise, Church no. 32, c. 600. Plan. (B) Tomarza, Panaghia, sixth century. Plan

On the contrary, in central and eastern Cappadocia cross churches were standard. They are small, never more than 20 and often only 10 m. (65 and 32 ft) long. The wings project strongly, and the apse – horseshoe-shaped inside, polygonal outside – balances the short nave. Nave, apse, and wings are of equal height and barrel-vaulted; four arches segregate the crossing; a tower rose above, sheltering a dome. The plan in Cappadocia became and remained standard for rural parish and monastic churches. Clad in sixth-century ornament, it was well preserved until 1921 in the Panaghia at

Tomarza, which was perhaps built as a parish church [128B, 129]. It still survives in the ruins of a monastic church at Buzluk near Persek, south of Kayseri, where half-piers rise from pedestals at the apse corners and recall Qalb Lozeh, and a doubled order of pilasters marks the façade corners [130]. A simpler, but very powerful church, possibly as late as around 600, rises near Sivrihisar: its octagonal and domed crossing-tower is placed on squinches, its nave is flanked to the north by an aisle [131]. The design of volumes and masses is of a stark, but impressive beauty.[48]

129. Tomarza, Panaghia, sixth century. Exterior before 1921

130. Buzluk near Persek, church, end of the sixth century. Exterior, as in 1954

131. Sivrihisar, Kizil Kilise, c. 600(?). Exterior, as in 1954

Cross buildings by 500 were obviously not new in Christian architecture. On the same small scale as in Cappadocia, they had been adapted from Roman mausolea as early as 400 by the builders of Christian martyria, presumably in Constantinople and certainly in upper Italy. Indeed, many cross-shaped martyr and tomb chapels are known in Asia Minor, at and near Binbirkilise, both on isolated mountains and in monastic precincts. However, none antedates the eighth century and some may be much later. The type may have become accepted as early as the sixth century in Cappadocia as well as in Lycaonia. But there is no proof that the vaulted cross plan was first created in Asia Minor.

At times an exceptional plan stands out amidst such standard types, whether basilicas or cross churches. A small domed octagon at Binbirkilise, with four arms projecting crosswise, is perhaps of sixth- or seventh-century date, yet it recalls the church described as early as 380 in the correspondence of Gregory of Nyssa with the bishop of Konya. At Soasa, near Aksaray, a larger octagon (now destroyed) rested on powerful piers enveloped by an ambulatory; the centre space was domed, the ambulatory perhaps timber-roofed.[49] A more remarkable church stood near Küçük Büyüngü (Sari Kilise, Skupi), until torn down in 1954.[50] The aisleless nave continued to the springing of the apse, which was horseshoe-shaped inside and polygonal outside. Attached to the flanks of the nave, before the apse, were two low chambers which projected sideways and had prominent portals facing west. Only they were barrel-vaulted. Whether porches or sacristies, these chambers were mere adjuncts to the nave; they formed, as it were, dwarf transept wings, and the structure, far from being a cross church, represented a type of its own. Four orders of pilasters flanked the nave, and the capitals, though crude, were foliate. The classical profiles of the cornice rose over the door lintels and curved over two superimposed rows of arched windows. The whole suggests the impact of Syrian buildings and a date not much after 500.

Taken by itself, this architecture in the uplands of Asia Minor – its basilicas, hall-churches, aisleless structures, octagons, or cross churches with or without flanking chambers – is but a backwater offshoot of the greater architecture of adjoining Syria, Cilicia, and Pamphylia. Yet it occupies an important place in the history of Early Christian architecture, not only in the inland countries of the Near East, but throughout the Mediterranean world. It has preserved in remote mountains and high plains a variety of church types of the Early Christian East, which in more accessible regions have been overlaid by later architectural forms; and between the seventh and ninth centuries it has contributed plans, techniques, and an architectural vocabulary towards the formation of an architecture in Western Europe.

CHAPTER 7

THE LATIN WEST

With the beginning of the fifth century, the Latin West increasingly becomes a sphere of its own, both in its political aspects and in its intellectual, artistic, and religious life. Contacts with the two great regions in the eastern half of the Empire continue, but the West gradually drifts away. After Alaric's Sack of Rome (410), the papacy assumes spiritual and cultural leadership with ever greater decision in the Latin-speaking world: Italy, Dalmatia and the northern Balkans, southern France, Spain, Sicily, and North Africa. And although Rome's political influence on North Africa ceases with the Vandal conquest, this loss is countered towards the end of the century by the expansion of Roman orthodoxy to pagan or Arian territories beyond the Alps in France and southern Germany.

Christian architecture in the West falls into two distinct geographical spheres: to the north, central and northern Italy with her border-countries east and west; to the south, North Africa and her dependencies across the sea – South Italy, Sicily, the Balearic Islands, and the coasts of Spain. In the northern half of the Latin countries, Rome and Milan are the leading architectural centres; Ravenna, beginning c. 425–50, holds a straddling position between the Latin West and Greek East. As early as 385, a standard basilican plan spreads presumably from Rome to Milan, slightly later to Ravenna, Istria, and Dalmatia. At the same time, the octagonal baptistery plan, with a possible origin in either Rome or Milan, becomes standard in Provence, Ravenna, and Dalmatia. In the southern half of the West, on the other hand, Africa takes the lead, but no one city can be identified as a great architectural centre. Nevertheless, standard types develop for basilicas and baptisteries very different from those customary in central and northern Italy and her borderlands. Yet whatever the divergencies in planning and workmanship, churches from Milan to North Africa differ surprisingly little in style.

Early Christian church building in the Latin West has been comparatively well explored. In Rome, Milan, and Ravenna a significant number of buildings are fully or nearly fully preserved. In addition, excavations have brought to light foundation walls and pavements which reveal the characteristic plan and design of churches and baptisteries in cities, villages, and monasteries from Spain to Dalmatia and from southern Algeria to the Alpine regions.[1]

The plan of the standard basilica in the Latin West is simple. The nave was long, generally flanked by aisles, and terminated by a semicircular apse. Whether or not an atrium or a narthex preceded the church depended on local custom, vicinity of streets, and funds available. The supports of the nave were columns, which were either made to order, or, together with capitals and bases, were spoils from Roman buildings, as was the custom in Rome. Surmounted by arcades, the columns carried the high upper walls of the nave; these walls were topped by a band of wide windows in the clerestory. As a rule, the number of clerestory windows corresponded to the intercolumniations below. The windows were variously filled: either by stone plaques perforated with numerous holes, or by costly mica, coloured glass, or alabaster panes set in stucco and wood gratings. In every case, the light filtering into the churches was abundant but opaque, not the clear white light which fills them today. Below the clerestory, mosaic panels or, more frequently, less expensive frescoes covered the walls. As a matter of course, the vault of the apse carried a mosaic or fresco. The use of windows in the aisles depended on local custom. All parts of the structure, except for the half-dome of the apse, were covered with open timber roofs, on rare occasions

with coffered ceilings, both often gilded. The floors
in Rome were paved with flagstones; in Milan they
were apparently overlaid with marble; in the eastern
parts of North Italy, and in Istria and Dalmatia and
in Africa, they are carpeted with mosaics. A chancel
enclosed by parapets extended from the apse into
the nave; wing walls projected sideways into the
aisles, forming a barrier at which the congregation
handed its offerings to the clergy. Since until the
sixth century sermons were not required in the
West, ambos are found neither in Rome nor in
North Africa.[2]

Plan and design, then, are both quite plain. Much
in contrast to contemporary architectural concepts
in the Greek East, the interior was composed of
three spatial units clearly designed and neatly
separated from each other. In the nave a controlled
channelled space moved from the entrances to the
apse. It was accompanied by the similar units of the
aisles, but the spatial units did not flow into each
other. Curtains seem to have closed off the intercolumniations and supported the impression of
three parallel but separate space channels. Indeed,
contemporaries likened the nave of the fifth-century
basilica to a river, flowing slowly along, filled with
the broken light filtered through the windows. The
walls of nave and aisles neither dissolved into
screens, as in the Greek East, nor were they viewed,
as in Syria, as massive solids. They want to be seen
as surfaces, cardboard-thin and ideally designed to
support frescoes or mosaic. The colours of these
paintings and mosaics were meant to fuse with the
opaque light of the windows, with the tints of the
pavement, the gilded timber roofing, the mosaic of
the apse vault, the precious furnishings. At night the
entire building would shimmer in the flickering light
of oil-wicks and candles. Many a contemporary
letter and poem speaks of the jewelled golden and
silver altars and altar vessels, the gilded roof beams,
ceiling coffers, and capitals, the gold mosaics, the
shining marble revetments of fifth-century churches
in the Latin West.[3]

In contrast to such interior wealth, the exterior of
these same churches was utterly plain. The walls

and the roofs of nave and aisles nowadays extend in
the stark bareness of stone, brick, and tiles, their
surfaces broken only by the greyish-white stucco
gratings of the windows; whether or not they were,
or were intended to be, covered with plaster,
remains an open question. Materials and methods of
construction vary locally: concrete faced with brick;
concrete faced with alternating courses of brick and
stone; small stone held in place by stone chains or
standing by itself; thin or thick bricks and
mortar-beds.

By the last quarter of the fourth century this
standard type of basilica was in use in all major
centres of the Latin West. Given the plan's uniformity, it may well have spread from a single centre,
possibly Rome. Indeed, in Rome, as witness the first
structure excavated below the church of S. Marco, it
may have been common among parish churches
even prior to 350.[4] Certainly this standard plan has
determined the picture of Early Christian Rome
which we have today.

ROME

Never until the seventeenth century did church
building flourish in Rome as it did in the century
from 380 to 480.[5] On one hand, there are four huge
foundations of the Imperial and Papal courts,
designed in the spirit of a classical renascence: S.
Paolo fuori le mura, S. Maria Maggiore, the Lateran
baptistery, S. Stefano Rotondo. Alongside such
monumental structures stand a dozen parish
churches in the city, the suburbs, and on the great
estates. Less pretentious and luxurious, they are still
impressive by their size, their clear and simple
design, their balanced proportions. By sheer number alone they determine the picture of fifth-century
Christian Rome as much as the far more ambitious
Imperial and papal foundations. S. Sabina is a
superb example, well preserved and well restored.
But other churches have likewise survived in large
portions, hidden below medieval and Baroque
remodellings: S. Clemente, S. Sisto Vecchio, S.
Pudenziana, S. Anastasia, SS. Giovanni e Paolo, S.

Lorenzo in Lucina, S. Vitale, S. Pietro in Vincoli, S. Agata dei Goti. Of still others, such as S. Marcello inside the city walls, S. Stefano on an estate on the Via Latina, and the basilica of Pammachius at Ostia, at least the plans are known, wholly or in part. Most, it seems, were designed to replace the obsolete community centres of 'pre-Constantinian tenor or time. All are standard basilicas, composed of nave, aisles, apse, and atrium. The columns, as a rule, are spoils, the walls built of concrete and faced with pure brickwork, the bricks likewise looted from older buildings. The width of the mortar-beds and joints progressively changes throughout the century and thus gives a clue for the chronological sequence of the buildings and their parts. More than elsewhere, in Rome such technical data are supported by a wealth of documentary evidence.

S. Clemente not only conveys a good idea of the design of a standard basilica in Rome about 380; it also impressively exemplifies the relationship of these fourth- and fifth-century churches in Rome to earlier buildings on the site, as well as to their later remodellings.[6] The present church, slightly below street level, is a twelfth-century structure, redecorated in the Baroque. The Early Christian church rose from a level more than 4 m. (13 ft) farther down, occupying the site of three earlier buildings [132]. Its apse oversails the ground floor of a second-century house which encloses a mithraeum of third- or early-fourth-century date. Its nave and aisles are inserted into the walls of a third-century structure, possibly used as a Christian community centre; and this in turn rises on the podium of a public building of first-century date. Yet within this maze the remains of the fourth-century basilica are easily discerned. The columns of the nave, eight on either side, are enclosed into the foundations of the upper church; the arcades, clerestory, and façade are absorbed into the wall of its right aisle. An atrium, in front of the fourth-century church, is buried below the present twelfth-century forecourt. From these remains the first basilica is readily envisaged: the nave was broad, comparatively short, and remarkably low – in metres 15 by 35 by 13·50, in Roman feet 50 by 120 by 45 (50 by 115 by 45 English feet); the columns were all different in size and material, their wide arcades springing from wedge-shaped impost blocks; the clerestory windows were wide, separated by narrow piers and enveloping the nave on three sides; the atrium included a colonnaded *quadriporti-*

132. Rome, S. Clemente,
c. 380. Isometric reconstruction

o   60 FT

o   20 M

cus; and finally, an open arcade led from the nave
into the portico along its façade – the esonarthex, as
it were – with the result that the nave was encircled
on three sides by the ancillary spaces of aisles and
esonarthex. The church plan which prevails during
the fifth century in the Aegean coastlands, in the late
fourth century seems to have been equally characteristic of Rome.

This standard plan at first glance seems to have
been retained unaltered by Roman church builders
throughout the fifth century. A more critical look
reveals the changes the plan underwent during those
hundred years. The proportions of the nave become
narrower, longer, and higher: as a rule *c.* 50 by 150
by 60 Roman feet.[7] The number of arcades and
windows increases, and their proportions become
steeper, while the individual window becomes wider
and higher than before. The façades, as late as the
first quarter of the fifth century, opened towards the
narthex in a series of arcades; the narthex in turn

133 (*below*). Rome, SS. Giovanni e Paolo,
c. 410–20. Façade

134 (*above*). Rome, S. Vitale, 401–17.
Reconstruction of façade, narthex, and nave

opened in a colonnaded arcade towards the atrium, and thus functioned both as an exo- and an esonarthex [133, 134]. As a result a double screen of columns intervened between atrium and nave, the first perhaps open, the second certainly hung with curtains, much like the tribelon of a fifth-century church in Greece. In the Roman churches, the faithful were led through these screens into the nave, not barred from it as apparently was Aegean custom. Only after 430, such arcaded façades and 'exo-esonartheces' disappear from Rome and with them the airiness of construction which their openness imparted to the building. Instead the narthex communicated with the nave only through doors. The space of the nave appears to be more compact and the ancillary units of aisles and narthex give way to the parallel flow of nave and aisles towards the apse. The impression of parallel currents of space is further strengthened when, as early as the second decade of the fifth century, the continuous window band breaks into a separate design in the façade, be it

a huge five-arched opening, as at S. Vitale and SS. Giovanni e Paolo [133], or a row of oculi, as at S. Pietro in Vincoli.[8]

In this development, S. Sabina on the Aventine represents a high point of Roman church building.[9] Built between 422 and 432, and incorporating remnants of earlier buildings, it typifies in plan and proportion the new Roman standard basilica of the fifth century, quite different from the older variant of the type represented by S. Clemente. At the same time, in elegance of design and lavishness of decoration, S. Sabina partakes of the very beginning of the classical renascence under Sixtus III [135-7]. The twenty-four columns of the nave, of beautiful Proconnesian(?) marble, and their Corinthian capitals and bases are spoils obviously all removed from a second-century building, but they have been selected with loving care so as to match in every detail. The marble revetment in the spandrels shows in beautiful design chalices and patens, the ensigns of Christ. The tendril friezes painted in the aisles are

135. Rome, S. Sabina, 422–32. Exterior of apse and clerestory

136 and 137. Rome, S. Sabina, 422–32. Interior of nave (*opposite*) and of right-hand aisle and nave (*below*)

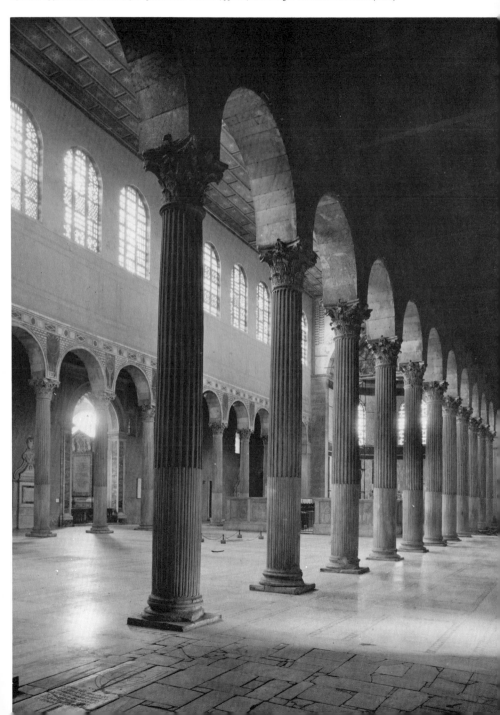

forceful and elegant, and the splendour of the original decoration in the nave is still shown in the monumental mosaic panel across the interior façade with its dedicatory inscription. The lateral walls of the nave apparently carried mosaics above the marble revetment of the spandrels.[10] But all this lavishness is applied to a simple standard plan, albeit of the new variety which comes to the fore in Rome about 420. The nave is extraordinarily high, long, and narrow, its elegant slenderness supported by the narrowness and the length of the flanking aisles, and set off by the lighting. Arcades of thirteen bays on either side of the nave lead the eye rapidly from the entrance doors to the apse. The arches, closely spaced, swing easily from one tall column to the next. Huge windows, 8 Roman feet wide, 14 feet high, and a bare 4 feet apart, form the clerestory, one above each intercolumniation. Three more windows open in the apse and five in the façade, these latter perhaps replacing an original five-arched window. Together the thirty-four windows bring a flood of light into the nave, presumably filtered through mica panes set into stucco gratings.[11] The aisles, on the other hand, remained windowless and dark, and from nave and aisles only doors communicated with the narthex and the preceding atrium.

None of the other fifth-century parish churches of Rome could apparently vie in elegance with S. Sabina, but at least until the middle of the fifth century they all adhered to the standard plan. Only round the middle of the century was the type modified anew: the windows grew narrower, the distances between them larger, and as a result, the light dimmer. The nave of S. Pietro in Vincoli, as rebuilt apparently *c.* 450, and the small basilica of S. Agata dei Goti, of 462–70, represent this later phase. At the same time outside influences modify church building in Rome: the tripartite transept, which is included in the remodelling of S. Pietro in Vincoli, recalls that of S. Tecla at Milan, while S. Agata dei Goti corresponds in both plan and elevation exactly to the Arian cathedral of Ravenna, S. Spirito, and was laid out in Byzantine instead of Roman feet.[12]

The standard basilicas of the fourth and fifth centuries in Rome are by no means as complex, nor for that matter as subtle and splendid, as those designed at the same time in Constantinople or Salonica. Nor are they as powerful as the churches of Qalb Lozeh or of R'safah in Syria. To western eyes they appear rather ordinary, and the overall picture seems uniform. However, the impression of over-simplification and monotony is hardly fair. We are led to it largely by the strong imprint exerted by the Roman standard type on nearly all medieval church building and even on much later architecture. Revived in the ninth and again in the eleventh and twelfth centuries, the type spread all over Europe and was taken up again in fifteenth-century Italy. The many derivatives have blinded us to some degree to the forceful, simple grandeur of the original design.

NORTHERN ITALY AND SOUTHERN FRANCE

In contrast to Rome, churches of standard plan in northern Italy and southern France are known only through fragmentary excavations.[13] Yet there is sufficient evidence to show that in the old provinces of Gallia Cisalpina and Narbonensis, too, the wealth of earlier church types, as we know it from Milan, was replaced from the late fourth century on by a 'normal' basilica of the type found in Rome. Obviously the new buildings were erected in the traditional techniques of the Po Valley: a concrete masonry faced with high bricks set, as on occasion in Milan, in a herringbone pattern and interspersed with huge pebbles; the vaults composed of brick or of hollow tubes. At times distinguishing features set off the plan of such northern Italian standard basilicas from those in other regions of the Latin West: a rectangular apse, or no apse at all; a martyr's chapel attached to the rear of one of the aisles; the doubling of churches to form a cathedral, a carry-over from Constantinian times.

A huge church, named from the outset after himself, was laid out by St Ambrose about 385 on a Milan cemetery. His burial place was to be located below the altar next to the relics of two local martyrs, appropriately dug up for the consecration in 386. The remnants of this original church have been traced below the present Romanesque S. Ambrogio: a nave and aisles, two colonnades of thirteen or more supports each, the bed of a marble floor, the springings of a stilted semicircular apse, the four columns of a baldacchino over the high altar; the position of the façade, and thus the original length of the nave, remain unknown. The narthex and atrium of the Romanesque structure, unusual in the High Middle Ages, suggest that they too rest on fourth-century foundations and complete the picture of a huge building complex, more than 300 Roman feet long and 100 feet wide, comparable in plan but larger than contemporary standard basilicas in Rome. The plan of S. Ambrogio becomes standard in the fifth century throughout northern Italy, from Vicenza to Verona, Brescia, Pavia, and Turin [138]. Its layout,

cathedral is a simple rectangular hall; at S. Trinità at Vercelli the basilican nave terminates in a trefoil apse, and once, at Pavia, the basilica is composed of a nave and four aisles.[14]

A main characteristic of the northern Italian standard basilica is the martyr's chapel attached near the end of one aisle: a feature either planned from the outset or pre-existing or, indeed, added slightly later. At S. Ambrogio, the tomb cella of the local martyr Victor, remodelled when the basilica was built and altered a second time about 500, is a small trapezoidal domed room, its apse pierced by two tiers of three windows. More often, however, these chapels are cross-shaped, their arms barrel-vaulted and, like the centre dome, in tube construction. One such structure, presumably a martyrium, is attached to the north arm of the cross church of S. Simpliciano at Milan and may be contemporary with the main structure. The cross martyrium of S. Prosdo-

138. Vicenza,
SS. Felice e Fortunato,
fifth century. Plan

including the atrium, is closely followed, often presented in the context of a twin cathedral. Local modifications are minor: the apse at SS. Felice e Fortunato in Vicenza is rectangular, at the cathedral in Verona it was semicircular. Pavements in Milan and farther west were marble, in the eastern parts of upper Italy they were mosaic. At Verona, the chancel was raised and prolonged into the nave by a solea, the columns were placed on pedestals. Throughout, major deviations from the standard plan are rare. Occasionally, as for example in the old cathedral at Brescia, one of the two structures of the twin

cimo at Padua, dating from between 500 and 507 and well restored, projects similarly from the transept of S. Giustina, a huge sixteenth-century building replacing an Early Christian church. A third cross chapel of fifth-century date, S. Teuteria, rose close to the apse of the Church of the Holy Apostles at Verona. Finally, a fourth was added to the right aisle of SS. Felice e Fortunato at Vicenza about 400. The walls were revetted with marble plaques and the dome was decorated with mosaics, of which fragments are preserved on the pendentives.[15]

The position of northern Italy within Christian architecture of the fifth century is not easily determined. The standard basilica plan of northern Italy is so close to those of fourth- and fifth-century Rome that it could very possibly have been imported from there, especially since around and after 400 Milan relinquished its political dominance to Constantinople, its ecclesiastical influence to Rome. On the other hand, the small cross chapels probably find their closest parallels on the coasts of Asia Minor. Documentary evidence prior to 450 locates the chapel of H. Euphemia at the end of the aisle of her basilica at Chalcedon (Kadiköy); and a cruciform martyr's chapel in the same position, though of sixth-century date, has survived at Alakilise (Alaja Jaila) in Lycia.[16] Indeed, northern Italy always had close links with Constantinople and Greece. One need only recall the tripartite transepts of fourth-century Milan and of contemporary and later Greece; or the mosaic floors of Greece, the Balkans, and north-eastern Italy, so different from the marble and flagstone pavements of the standard basilica in Rome. It is still in doubt whether such features were brought to northern Italy from the East, or whether upper Italy and the Aegean coastlands share a common heritage.

On the other hand, a standard type of baptistery may have spread from Milan to northern Italy and Provence.[17] In the fourth century, baptisteries as a rule had been either square or rectangular rooms, with or without apses, either unvaulted, such as the first baptisteries at Aquileia and Trier, or covered with a flat dome on squinches and attached to the end of the aisles, as at Naples about 400. Conversely, already under Constantine the Lateran baptistery was laid out on an octagon plan, its corners marked by columns; the outer walls of Constantine's structure have possibly survived to this day. The plan was taken up, enriched, when the baptistery of Milan was built behind and either at the same time with the cathedral, about 350, or thirty years later under St Ambrose. In any event, Ambrose provided an inscription alluding to the number symbolism of the building:[18] an octagon, its diagonal sides expanding

in semicircular niches, the others in rectangular niches; a domed centre room; and in the centre, the eight-sided font. In simplified form the plan survives well preserved at Grado, about 450; in elaborate shape, with columns in the corners of the octagon and with a clerestory articulated by arcades, appears at Fréjus and Albenga. At times the octagonal core expands in niches projecting outward, as at Novara; elsewhere, it is enveloped by ambulatory rooms: square at Aquileia (c. 450) and at Riva San Vitale (c. 500) [139, 140] on the southern tip of Lake Lugano; octagonal in the Baptistery of the Arians at Ravenna in the late fifth century.[19] However, no baptistery of the period has preserved its original form and decoration better than that of the Orthodox in Ravenna [141, 142].[20] The bottom parts, now deep in the ground – and with them the octagonal plan and the marble revetment – date from about 400, but this first building was not vaulted. Not until fifty years later, under Bishop Neon, were the dome and the upper part of the outer walls built – the former in tube construction, the latter articulated by pilaster strips. (The terminating corbel-table frieze contrary to former belief seems to date from an early medieval rebuilding.) Likewise, the interior received its decoration partly about 400, partly about 450. In the spandrels of the eight niches mosaic tendrils envelop the figures of prophets. In the second zone, tripled stucco arcades, part of the original design, frame windows and stucco aediculas sheltering sixteen minor prophets; they in turn are surmounted by wide arches filled with rich stucco rinceaux, both added about 450. Finally, in the dome, the mosaic, of the same date, represents in three rings empty thrones and altars, apostles, and Christ's Baptism.

Links between northern Italy and the Aegean coastlands are possibly also reflected in the dissemination of the octagonal baptistery plan. About 400, or earlier, it occurs alongside the church of St Mary at Ephesus, some time late in the fifth century near the Menas basilica [59, 64]. But this does not mean that the plan was brought from the Aegean shores or from Constantinople to Milan. In fact, it

139. Riva S. Vitale, baptistery, c. 500.
Section and plan

140. Riva S. Vitale, baptistery, c. 500.
Exterior

141. Ravenna, Baptistery of the Orthodox, c. 400–50.
Exterior from the west

remains rare in the East. On the other hand, the octagonal baptistery with corner niches is frequent in the sphere of influence of Milan. A more elaborate type develops in the fifth century. The Lateran baptistery, as remodelled by Sixtus III, fused the octagon plan with that of a Roman mausoleum of the type of S. Costanza, with domed centre room, barrel-vaulted colonnaded ambulatory, and narthex with two sideway apses [47]. This fusion need not have taken place first or exclusively in Rome. As early as c. 400, octagonal baptisteries with inner colonnade and ambulatory are found in Gallia Narbonensis, for instance at Marseille and Aix-en-Provence.[21] But in the Lateran baptistery it finds its most powerful expression: a monumental blend of Late Roman architectural concepts, of an Ambrosian Christian symbolism, and of the practical requirements of the baptismal ritual.

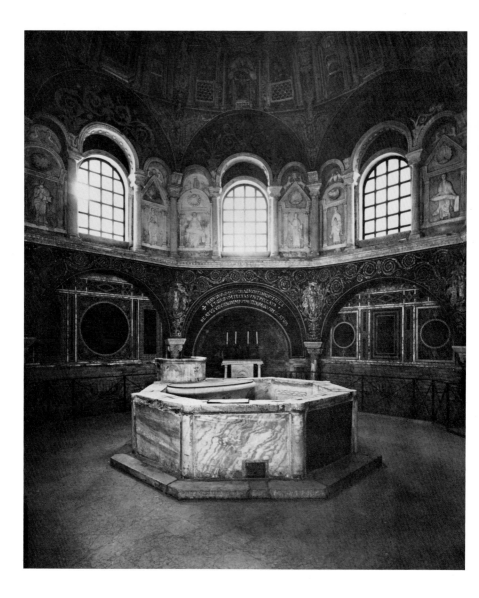

142. Ravenna, Baptistery of the Orthodox, c. 400–50. Interior

ISTRIA, EASTERN VENETO, AND CARINTHIA

The Christian congregations on the north shore of the Adriatic, in the Alpine region farther north, and as far east as Hungary and Bosnia, clung to architectural types locally established in the early fourth century or even earlier: box churches, as a rule without apse, the altar site pushed well forward into the nave, a semicircular clergy bench behind the altar. Often, even in remote places in Carinthia and Hungary, two such simple rectangular halls are coupled into a twin cathedral.[22]

In the fifth century, however, the impact of the standard basilica makes itself felt with increasing force in the larger communities along the sea shore. At Aquileia, either about 350 or 400, a new structure replaced the north hall of the old twin cathedral [9]. Following conservative local custom it lacked an apse, but was provided with a clergy bench. Yet in size the new church can be compared with the new standard basilicas of Rome and Milan; and, like these, it was divided into a wide nave and two comparatively narrow aisles and thus certainly provided with a clerestory.[23] Another feature of the standard type was purloined for the new cathedral at Pula (Pola): a triumphal arch resting on columns and cross piers, together with two minor arches, serves to separate nave and aisles from a clergy section, the latter elevated above the nave level and sheltering the customary clergy bench.[24]

A group of small churches in the Alps and in the mountains that rise from the Istrian plain, share with Istria the motif of the clergy bench. Others enrich the plan by adding an apse and laterally-projecting annexes – forming a cross plan – and by enclosing the nave within corridors or chambers. The type is found from Carinthia to Dalmatia and Bosnia-Herzegovina and from the Tyrol to Switzerland and Piedmont.[25] It may well be a provincial derivative from the Milanese cross churches spread through the arc of the Alps. From there it was possibly carried in the seventh century to the British Isles, presumably by missionaries.[26] Yet during the fifth century, church building in Istria and Carinthia had little contact with architecture elsewhere in the Christian world.

DALMATIA

The architecture of Salona on the Dalmatian coast, from the fourth to the end of the sixth century, was far from being that of a backwater town. It takes its place alongside the architecture of Rome, Milan, and Ravenna, with a character all its own. In Rome, the comparative uniformity of the standard type and its imperviousness to foreign influences are impressive. In Milan, the size of the church buildings, their inventiveness, and the close ties with both Rome and Constantinople are significant. In Salona one is struck by the manifoldness of church plans and by the willingness with which stimuli are absorbed from all over the Mediterranean area. At the same time, Salona so far remains the only sizeable Christian site to come to light along the Dalmatian coast. And even here, nothing more survives of any building than the plan, a few fragments of decorative sculpture, and some mosaic pavements. Over the last eighty years, however, excavations have been exemplarily carried out and carefully published, yielding extraordinarily rich results. They have brought to light numerous mausolea and martyrs' chapels, two baptisteries, and – between parish churches and cemetery basilicas – a dozen churches.[27]

Given the geographical position of Salona, the importance of the port, and the diversified ethnical roots of her population, it is natural that church planners would draw equally on models from the Latin West and from the Greek East, and in both territories on more than one centre.[28] For example, Constantine's basilica at the Lateran with its 'offertory rooms' projecting sideways would seem to be reflected in the basilica orientalis. Certainly the thoughts of the Salonitans were on the basilicas of St Peter's or of S. Paolo fuori le mura in Rome when, about 400, the cemetery precinct of Manastirine was remodelled as a basilica with a continuous transept to shelter the grave of the local martyr-bishop. The plan of Salona's twin cathedral, on the other hand, is obviously linked to the tradition of near-by Istria, but it consists of two regular basilicas rather than of two halls. The one to the south, the *basilica episcopalis*, has been dated as early as 350, but this remains uncertain. Whatever its date, the plan with nave, aisles, and narthex, and the proportions are close to fifth-century provincial churches all along the shores of the eastern Mediterranean. Only the short bay intervening between nave and apse in the *basilica episcopalis* is a distinctive local feature. Except for this short forechoir, the plan is retained unchanged throughout the entire fifth century in the city churches of Salona. The north church of the twin cathedral, the *basilica urbana* (begun before 405; completed by 426), with its mosaic-carpeted floors incorporates into the standard plan a free-standing clergy bench, purloined from neighbouring Istria to the north.[29]

At Salona, earlier than elsewhere, i.e. beginning with the fifth century, the cemetery basilica becomes indistinguishable from such city churches of standard Aegean type. The Anastasius basilica at Salona-Marusinac was a normal basilica like any in Greece, including the mosaic carpets in nave and aisles, the altar directly in front of the apse, the atrium enveloped by porticoes. The buttresses of the apse specifically recall the basilicas at Nikopolis in Epirus, some 500 miles south on the coast, and only the short bay in front of the apse seems derived from the local *basilica episcopalis*. Were it not for the site of the church outside the town on a cemetery, the fact that the mausoleum of the martyr is enclosed in the atrium, and the presence of private mausolea at the four ends of the aisles, nothing would reveal the cemetery function of the structure. At times the assimilation of cemetery layouts with the plan of the normal city basilica goes even further. A large open-air precinct of regularized plan, adjoining the Anastasius basilica to the north, was laid out in 426 to replace an older, small, apsed martyrium shrine [143]. A courtyard enveloped by porticoes terminated in a group of three mausolea; an apse in the centre and two oblong rooms projecting sideways, a plan which superficially evokes the transept basilica

143. Salona-Marusinac,
Anastasius Basilica, as *c.* 426 (*right*),
Anastasius Mausoleum, *c.* 300 (*foreground*),
and martyrium precinct, 426 (*left*).
Isometric reconstruction

0   60 FT

0   20 M

to such a degree that the structure has been termed a 'basilica discoperta', a roofless basilica.[30]

The impact of the Eastern coastlands remained strong in the architecture of Salona even in the sixth century. Probably about 530 the south basilica of the twin cathedral was replaced by a cross structure with four basilican arms, in plan much like the Church of the Apostles at Gerasa, and presumably that of Porphyrius at Gaza.[31] At times the apse of a basilica at Salona is flanked by rectangular rooms with one curved side: the plan known from the islands near the west coast and from the south coast of Asia Minor. Or else, as in the churches of the Negev, the aisles in one of the Salonitan churches terminate in absidioles, which in turn are followed by regular pastophories.[32] But such features intermingle with elements based on the local architectural tradition and on the increasing importance of Ravenna as the cultural centre of the Adriatic coastlands. When the baptistery of the cathedral at Salona was rebuilt towards the end of the fifth century, columns in two tiers were placed against the walls recalling the mausoleum of Diocletian at Spalato. Yet at the same time the sumptuous decoration with gold mosaics, stucco, and wall paintings (only tiny fragments were found) must have been similar to the Baptistery of the Orthodox at Ravenna.[33]

RAVENNA

In contrast to Salona, where only ruins survive, Ravenna to this day glories in a dozen or more church buildings of fifth- and sixth-century date, most of them superbly preserved, with mosaics, stucco decoration, and marble revetments. True, the gradual submersion of the city into the sea has forced successive generations, from the eighth to the end of the sixteenth century, to raise the level of the churches and their arcades and clerestories in complicated building operations which have changed their original proportions. But beneath such remodellings the original structures are easily recognizable. Ravenna presents a splendid example of a locality where Early Christian architecture

survives in all its variety in a series of buildings encompassing two centuries: apparently a closed development, were it not for the readiness with which the milieu constantly absorbed foreign concepts and a foreign vocabulary. This openness is understandable against the background of the geographical location of Ravenna at the border between the Eastern and Western parts of the Empire and of her political position: first, as capital of the Western Emperors, beginning with Honorius, who transferred the Imperial See from Milan, and continuing under his sister Galla Placidia (425–50) and her son Valentinian III (450–5); then, in ever closer contact with Constantinople and the Eastern provinces as the residence of the Ostrogothic conquerors and their highly romanized court – Theodoric (490–526) and his successors; finally, as the See of the Byzantine viceroys after the reconquest of Italy by Justinian's armies. Yet despite all political changes, a local style and a local standard plan gradually developed, and survived into the seventh and eighth centuries.[34]

Insignificant as it was prior to 402, Ravenna to our knowledge had evolved no autochthonous Christian architecture during the fourth century; its first known church buildings, erected between 402 and 425, draw on the architectural traditions of both Milan, the previous capital, and the Aegean coastlands. Under Galla Placidia, a major church was laid out on a cross plan with aisleless nave, the type common in Milan up to 400. Of the church proper, only the nave survives under the name of S. Croce, badly mauled and possibly rebuilt in the Middle Ages. But the plan is known [144], the nave enveloped by low rooms – another Milanese trait – a colonnaded portico, and a long narthex with screened ends – this latter a hallmark of church plans in Greece. To the side of the narthex rises a small structure, the so-called mausoleum of Galla Placidia, added not much after 424 [145, 146]. Dedicated to St Lawrence, it shelters three sarcophagi, once attributed to Galla Placidia, her brother, and her husband, and was hence both tomb and martyr's chapel. Indeed, like the martyrs'

144. Ravenna, S. Croce
and mausoleum of Galla Placidia,
c. 425. Isometric reconstruction

chapels in and near Milan, it is cross-shaped, with a slightly longer nave. Its arms are barrel-vaulted; its centre bay rises high and carries a pendentive dome. Strong blind arcades frame the windows, as at S. Simpliciano; classical cornices set off the pediments over the arms. Like the plan and the exterior design, the masonry with very high bricks and narrow beds of white mortar suggests Milanese workmanship. But the refined decoration of the interior is rooted in the art of the Imperial court, whether based at Milan, Constantinople, or Ravenna. Marble revetted the walls from the floor level, originally nearly 5 ft farther down. Mosaics on a blue ground cover the

upper zone: four pairs of apostles on the wall of the centre bay, St Lawrence on the rear niche, tangled tendrils on the barrel-vaults of the arms, and the starred Heaven across the dome.

The masonry technique in Ravenna remains Milanese throughout the fifth century. In design, however, from the early fifth century on, the architects of Ravenna break more and more with Milanese church planning and look instead towards

145. Ravenna, Mausoleum of Galla Placidia
and S. Croce, c. 425. Exterior

146. Ravenna, Mausoleum of Galla Placidia, *c.* 425. Interior

147. Ravenna, S. Giovanni Evangelista, 424–34. Exterior from the south-west

contemporary church building in the Aegean coast-lands.[35] The basilica of S. Giovanni Evangelista, built between 424 and 434 as an *ex-voto* by Galla Placidia, has undergone several remodellings.[36] Its nave colonnades were raised to the present level and its clerestory newly built, perhaps around 600 [147,

148]. It was thoroughly repaired again in the twelfth century and finally rebuilt in large part after a bombing in 1944. However, major portions of the fifth-century church survive: the outer walls of the aisles and their windows, the columns and capitals, and finally, the old level, now 2·25 m. (6 ft 6 in.)

below the floor. The original basilica consisted of a nave and aisles, cut shorter than those present by a narthex, the arcades widely spaced. The aisles are lit by large windows, their walls articulated on the exterior by pilaster strips. Impost blocks in the form of inverted truncated pyramids surmount the capitals, closely recalling contemporary impost blocks in Greece [148]. The narthex was apparently tripartite. Additional rooms jutted out sideways from the aisles may perhaps have been martyrs' chapels, as they resemble the jutting chambers of the Cilician coast rather than the side chambers of Syrian churches [147].

Not until the end of the fifth century, however, does a standard basilica type evolve in Ravenna: in S. Spirito (originally built as the Arian cathedral); in S. Agata, partly rebuilt in the sixth, remodelled in the eighth, twelfth, and fifteenth centuries, but first laid

148. Ravenna, S. Giovanni Evangelista, 424–34. Interior

the narthex, as in so many fifth-century churches in Greece and on the Asian coast, and were possibly surmounted by towers. The apse, too, is of Aegean type, polygonal with three windows. The arcaded opening higher up may well be contemporary. Two free-standing chambers projecting eastward from out about 470;[37] and finally in S. Apollinare Nuovo, built by Theodoric as his palace church and sixty years later dedicated to St Martin [149].

Were it only for its plan, S. Apollinare Nuovo would seem to be just one more ordinary basilica, with nave and two aisles, an apse, and arcaded

149. Ravenna, S. Apollinare Nuovo, c. 490. Interior of nave and apse

colonnades.[38] The earlier standard plans of the Latin West, of Rome, and of Salona come to mind. Also the masonry technique of S. Apollinare Nuovo follows that long established at Milan, while the hollow tube construction of the apse vault had been customary for centuries in southern Italy and North Africa. Yet into this Western plan are incorporated countless Eastern features. The exterior polygon of the apse, long at home in Ravenna, is Aegean in origin. The capitals, presumably imported from Constantinople, are exact counterparts of pieces found at Nea-Anchialos about 470 [cf. 76]. Finally, the buttress pilasters of the outer walls are crossed by a brick band arched over the windows which creates a strong pattern of vertical and horizontal elements. Reminiscent of Syrian rather than Aegean churches, this motif hints at the rapidly widening horizon of Ravenna builders in the last decade of the fifth century. Far more than such details, the proportions, the lighting, and the splendid mosaic convey an impression very different from that of a standard basilica in fifth-century Rome. The width of the nave as compared to its length is greater, the span of the arcades is proportionately wider. On the other hand, the height of the nave is conspicuously greater than its width, conveying a sense of an ample space. This impression is intensified by the lighting. While the nave windows are smaller and set farther apart than in Roman basilicas, the aisles are lit by windows as large as those of the nave. The result is an even distribution of light and shadow in both nave and aisles, as customary in the Aegean coastlands.

Nothing, however, determines the picture of S. Apollinare Nuovo more strongly than its sumptuous mosaic decoration. In Roman churches by the fifth century and replacing older non-figural patterns, the wall space between arcades and clerestory was given over to individual panels arranged in one or two tiers, each presenting a historical event from the Bible. St Peter's, S. Paolo fuori le mura, SS. Giovanni e Paolo presented examples of this Roman pattern. Instead, at S. Apollinare, long rows of figures move towards the apse: to the south, male saints advance from Theodoric's *palatium* towards Christ; to the north, female saints step forward from *Classis civitas* towards Mary. Between the upper windows, figures of apostles arrest this eastward movement, while the small topmost panels, containing gospel scenes and decorative shells, counter the height of the nave. The long rows of saints date from after the Byzantine reconquest, about 550; but they only replace original similar processions approaching from the palace and from Classe. Hence, under Theodoric the church would have looked much as today. Throughout, the mosaics balance and correct, as it were, the proportions of the interior. Their smooth expanse and their glitter of whitish-grey, green, blue, and gold, transform the walls into a bodiless tapestry.

Whether or not this concept of a mosaic decoration which envelops the entire building was originally evolved in the sphere of the Imperial courts at Constantinople and Milan during the late fourth century, it had a firm hold in Ravenna from the days of Galla Placidia. Thus S. Apollinare Nuovo represents a new standard type: a Latin Western plan executed in a building technique originating in Milan. Into it are fused elements purloined from the Aegean coastlands and as far away as Syria. The interior is clothed in a shimmer of light and colour, the whole a blend peculiar to Ravenna.

AFRICA

Large numbers of churches have been excavated in Africa: in Algeria, Tunisia, Libya, and western Cyrenaica.[39] Others are preserved across the seas in South Italy, Sicily, and the Balearic Islands. But our ignorance regarding their dates, style, or planning is appalling. It is due in part to obsolete publications and poor excavation techniques in the past, but also to a widespread propensity for aligning the architectural chronology of Mediterranean Africa with its political history: as a Roman province prior to 427; under the Vandals from 427 until the Byzantine conquest; as a Byzantine province from 534 until the Arab invasion in 647. The fact is, however, that the changing political fate of North Africa apparently exerted little impact on church planning. Nor are the religious heresies of North Africa or the concomitant contrasts of native hinterland and Roman coast reflected in her architecture. Donatist or Arian Vandal structures can be distinguished from orthodox Catholic churches only if demarcated by a distinctive religious inscription.[40] Similarly, churches look basically alike whether built in the larger centres of North Africa, or in any one of the hundreds of small towns. Barely can we start to distinguish church plans in the large administrative provinces of Late Antique North Africa: Mauretania (Western Algeria), Numidia (Eastern Algeria), Byzacene (Tunisia), Tripolitania, Cyrenaica. Carthage, long the political and spiritual centre of the territory, apparently exerted little architectural influence. On the contrary, distinctive regional features such as side chambers flanking the apse, double nave supports, or a colonnade articulating the clerestory, are concentrated in small districts and may well have spread from one or the other of those small town or village bishoprics into which the entire territory was split.

Under the circumstances, any attempt to establish a chronology for North African church architecture must be extremely tentative. Documentary sources are practically non-existent. Rarely does a date inscribed on a pavement, a lintel, or a tomb suggest the period of construction. Regional features may, but need not, be limited to one period. Only the Byzantine occupation of North Africa marks a caesura in church planning, at least in the provinces most strongly byzantinized: south-eastern Tunisia, Cyrenaica, and the Djebel Aurês.

Two currents seem to flow side by side in North African church planning. The majority of churches that have been found are ordinary basilicas of the type common in the Latin West: a high nave supported by arcaded colonnades, occasionally preceded by a narthex or an atrium, flanked by two low aisles, and terminated by a semicircular apse. Alongside this standard type, however, a distinctly Constantinian plan survives in North Africa in numerous examples. In this group the nave is flanked by four or more aisles, recalling the four-aisle Constantinian basilicas, from the Lateran to Bethlehem and, in Africa itself, Orléansville. Reasons for the expansion into six or eight aisles, as at Tipasa [150], elude us. It

and the Rhineland. At times forechurches precede the church proper, basilican in plan and roofed, but cut off by a wall and linked to the main church only by doors. The similar forechurch perhaps intended for catechumens in the Constantinian cathedral at Trier comes to mind, along with the fact that in North Africa in the fourth and fifth centuries reconciled Donatists would take the place of catechumens. Certainly the placement of altar and chancel in the nave is a liturgical fossil of pre-Constantinian and Constantinian times, as witness the cathedral at Aquileia and, in Syria, Eusebius's description of the cathedral at Tyre. Elsewhere in Africa, the opening of the apse is blocked by a triple arcade – a derivative, one suspects, of Constantinian fastigia. Baptisteries as a rule are simple rectangular

150. Tipasa, basilica, c. 450. Air view

is not limited to either cathedrals or martyrs' churches, nor does the number of aisles greatly differ in point either of locale or time. However, Constantinian elements permeate the plan of standard churches as well, and North Africa's place within the history of Christian architecture is best understood when its highly conservative character is kept firmly in mind. Likewise, twin cathedrals occur, recalling those of the early fourth century in Istria

or square rooms, attached to the rear or flank of an aisle, or occasionally free-standing. Again, this shape and position of the baptistery are features apparently widespread in the fourth century throughout the Christian world.

Likewise, Constantinian features of a specifically North African kind survive into the fifth and sixth centuries, more often than not linked to the cult of the martyrs. Indeed, at an early period, the cult of the

151. Carthage, Damous El Karita, basilica, fourth century(?), with adjacent buildings and (*foreground*) mausoleum

martyrs plays a large role in North African religious thought and hence in church planning. Nevertheless, martyria of central type are unknown, except tri- and tetraconchs and perhaps the rotunda behind Damous El Karita at Carthage [151]. On the other hand, as late as the fifth century, *areae* or open-air cemeteries were laid out, rectangular or circular and at times enclosed by porticoes, as in an *area* found outside Tipasa. And, as early as the beginning of the fourth century, martyrs' and other relics were deposited in churches, including parish churches inside towns. They would rest either in small vaults below the altar, or in a larger vault, a regular crypt, placed below the altar or below the apse, and often inaccessible. The latter arrangement, found perhaps as early as 324 at Orléansville, survives throughout the fifth century. More frequently, however, the crypt was accessible, but then it served at times as a mere anteroom, whence to view the martyr's grave in a small cella situated behind the apse. Indeed, occasionally the crypt lost all links to the martyr cult and became a baptistery. Elsewhere square or semi-circular counter-apses were laid out facing the main apse: in martyrs' churches to shelter the venerated grave, in cities as burial places for very important persons. At Orléansville such a counter-apse was added to the Constantinian (?) church about 400 and re-used in 475 for the tomb of Bishop Reparatus. But counter-apses remain rare; they are not the source for those of medieval churches in Europe.

The building material throughout Christian Africa is invariably the local stone, cut as a rule into

152. African basilica; reconstruction
of mosaic from Tabarka, c. 400

small blocks and held in place by vertical stone posts and horizontal chains; as a rule construction is poor. For fortifications and exceptionally for sizeable churches, such as Tebessa, large stone blocks are used. Timber roofing was the rule, except for the stone vaults of apses and baptisteries. The columns supporting the nave and aisles as well as their capitals are also cut mostly of the local stone. Ornament is scarce and, by and large, crudely continues a late classical tradition in carving, stucco, and decorative wall painting. Roman spoils are rarely employed. Plans, more often than not, are carelessly laid out.[41]

A standard basilica is represented in a mosaic from Tabarka, about 400.[42] Representation shifts back and forth between exterior and interior in the discursive manner characteristic of Late Antique and medieval portrayals of architecture [152, 153]. On the right, a flight of steps ascends to the church portal which is closed by a curtain leading into the nave. A triangular gable, pierced by one arched and two round windows, terminates the façade; however, these windows may well be intended to be farther down in the wall of the façade proper. Columns support the upper wall of the nave, presumably surmounted by arches; the horizontal which runs

153. Mosaic from Tabarka showing a basilica, c. 400. *Tunis, Bardo Museum*

154. Haïdra, 'Melleus' church, towards apse, *c.* 400

above the columns in the mosaic is the bottom line of the outside clerestory and not an architrave, an element rarely, if ever, used in North African churches. Rectangular windows open in the clerestory and are closed with stone slabs pierced by round holes. The roof of the nave is covered by tiles, the floor by a mosaic pavement of bird and floral motifs enclosed in squares. A few steps ascend to the apse and a triple arcade runs across its opening. On the left, the half-dome of the apse is pierced by a huge oculus visible from outside; it has probably slid down in the rendering from its actual place in the rear gable of the nave. Yet the apse does not shelter the altar. With altar cloth, antependium, and three candles, the altar rises in the nave above a funerary vault, a confessio, presumably containing the sarcophagus of a martyr.

In plan and design, then, the standard basilica of Christian North Africa differed little from other basilicas in the Latin West: the space was channelled, the light dimmed by window panes of alabaster

or mica. Volumes of aisles, apse, and nave built up in steps. Floor mosaics such as those shown in the Tabarka mosaic recall Aegean or Adriatic rather than Roman Christian architecture. However, the altar placed in the middle of the nave and the triple arcade in front of the apse are hallmarks of African church planning about 400. Examples of the standard type are plentiful from western Algeria to Tripolitania. On a large scale, preceded by a fore-court, it appears at Haïdra in Tunisia about 400, in the church of Melleus [154], presumably the cathedral; the apse is flanked by side chambers, the altar and chancel project far into the nave; a second altar and chancel (was it so from the beginning?) occupied the bays near the entrance.[43] At Djemila (Cuicul) in south-eastern Algeria, a basilica of standard type took the place of an older community centre [155].[44] Its nave, two aisles, and colonnades are easy to trace. The floor is carpeted with mosaics of geometric and floral design, framing animals in large octagons. Possibly from the start of construc-

155. Djemila (Cuicul), basilicas and 'Christian quarter', c. 400–11. Air view

tion, or later, a larger basilica was built alongside with floor mosaics of even richer design, four aisles, and paired supports rather than single columns; an inscription names as the founder one bishop Cresconius, mentioned but once, in 411 – hence the church may be earlier or later. Spacious crypts, accessible from the outside through a connecting corridor, extend below the apses of both churches. The baptistery to the west is extraordinarily impressive and exceptional in Christian North Africa through both its size and its monumentality. The core of the structure is round and domed. In its centre, four columns carry a square canopy rising above the font. This core is in turn enveloped by a barrel-vaulted ring corridor, its two walls moulded by niches, pilasters, and a strong cornice. Stucco

revetment covers the walls; the columns surmounting the font rise from high pedestals; the column shafts are fluted, the capitals elegant; and a mosaic covers the floor. The whole design breathes the spirit of a classical survival. Thermae, a small basilica, and two open courtyards, all presumably linked to the rites preceding and complementing baptism, are attached to the structure. Indeed, an entire complex of buildings envelops the twin basilicas – a large Christian quarter given over to the administrative functions, living quarters, and utilitarian needs of a large clergy.

Cresconius's buildings are not the only ones in North Africa to be permeated by the spirit of a still Constantinian classicism. The church complex at Tebessa in its present form dates from about 400

156 (*below*). Tebessa, church and monastery, *c.* 400 and sixth century. Plan

157 (*bottom*). Tebessa, basilica, *c.* 400. Propylaeum

and is strongly imbued with Constantinian concepts.[45] A broad flight of steps ascends from a forecourt (it is of later date) towards a colonnaded propylaeum [156, 157]. From there, three doors lead into the church. All this recalls, if anything,

Tyre, or the basilica at the Holy Sepulchre, or the first H. Sophia in Constantinople and its propylaeum. In the nave, the piers – the rear members of the paired supports – carried arches above which appeared the openings of a gallery and presumably of a clerestory. The front columns, all spoils, as are the capitals, were surmounted at gallery level by the projections of a cornice [158]. This cornice in turn supported a second and third order of columns ascending to the roof beams. Mosaics covered the floors in the nave and aisles. The sculptured ornament is – an exception in North Africa – remarkably fine. From the right aisle, a broad staircase descended to a trefoil martyrium, built about thirty years before the main church and replacing a yet earlier memoria. A chancel barrier in the last bays of the nave enclosed the altar, and a second 'chancel' was laid out near the entrance. The slightly raised apse is flanked by side chambers, both of which communicate through doors with the aisles as well as the apse.

158. Tebessa, basilica, c. 400. Nave from east

For the side chambers Tebessa hardly drew on Syrian models. Apparently North African architects had independently developed such side rooms in the fourth century; possibly they derived them from Constantinian models such as the row of side chambers which flanked the chancel of both halls of the twin cathedral at Trier, as well as S. Tecla at Milan [15, 41]. Other features at Tebessa likewise recall Constantinian church building. Galleries, for example, marked the basilica of the Holy Sepulchre and probably the first H. Sophia at Constantinople. Occasionally, as in Greece, the aisles are separated from the nave by parapets or high stylobates – at Tebessa as early as the late fourth, elsewhere, for instance at Tigzirt and in the fortress church at Haïdra, as late as the sixth century. An impact from Greece on North Africa is unlikely and one wonders whether the separation of nave and aisles both in Greece and Africa had an early common source. On the other hand, 'counter-chancels' and 'counter-

apses' placed opposite the main altar, at the entrance side of the nave, appear to be germane to North Africa. At times laid out from the outset, more frequently installed in the late fifth or the sixth century, the duplication was probably determined by yet unknown demands of the local liturgy.

The largest church in North Africa, at Damous El Karita, a suburb of Carthage, may also belong among such derivations from the Constantinian past [151]. But like all of Carthage it is poorly explored. What survives are but the outer walls and the pier-like substructures of the columns. Clearly, though the building is exceptional in more than one respect: its size – over 65 m. (215 ft) the length of the basilica, 150 m. (490 ft) the length of the entire complex; its semicircular atrium; its eight aisles; the 'transept' cutting across the centre, its eight piers at the intersection carrying a dome or, more likely, a pyramidal timber roof; the structures which extend behind the basilica – several large halls, one six-aisled and sheltering a font; numerous small mausolea; another hall, composed of nave and aisles; finally, a circular structure, half-subterranean, domed, niched, and colonnaded inside, a mausoleum or martyrium. Smaller mausolea clung to the flanks and the atrium of the church. No doubt, Damous El Karita was a covered cemetery, like the Constantinian ones outside the walls of Rome, and, indeed, its features suggest a date well inside the fourth century.[46]

All such Constantinian features are, as a rule, limited to small districts. Crypts are common only in Algeria. The screening of apses by triple arcades is confined to buildings along and near the coast, from Bénian to Sabratha. Likewise, the doubling of the nave supports seems to be a local phenomenon: from the fourth to the end of the sixth century, paired piers and columns – as in the larger of the basilicas at Djemila – or double columns spread through Numidia, Tunisia, and Tripolitania. The outer row of supports carried the nave arcade as well as, in many cases, a gallery, and always a clerestory. The inner row of supports (towards the nave) supported a second colonnade along that upper wall; the Great Church at Tigzirt, like Tebessa, is an example.[47] This changes only when, in vaulted churches in South Tunisia about 550, arcades and clerestory were placed on the inner supports, and the outer ones carried a vault over the aisles.

Church building in North Africa, then, until the Byzantine conquest in 530, evolves largely in a retrospective clime. Hence, it appears most unlikely that so provincial an architecture should have transmitted to Carolingian Europe such motifs as the counter-apse. A re-invention for different functions is far more plausible. Concomitantly, however, the conservatism of the African provinces may well be responsible for a feature of church planning which is more clearly marked in North Africa than in any other region of the Roman Christian Empire. As pointed out recently, nowhere in North Africa can the church building be viewed as an autonomous structure. On the contrary, it ought to be seen as part of a building complex which comprises the bishop's

palace, dwellings for the clergy, dining-rooms for community banquets, often of trefoil plan, libraries, store rooms, bakeries, oil presses, and the like. The 'Christian quarters' unearthed at Djemila and at Bône ('Annoba) – St Augustine's Hippo – are two of many examples [155].[48] They provide a picture of community life in the fifth century far more lively than it can be visualized elsewhere. At the same time, they suggest that conservative North Africa preserved tenaciously the concept of the pre-Constantinian community centre with its fusion of secular-utilitarian and sacred elements in one and the same structure.

SOUTHERN ITALY, SICILY, AND SPAIN

Church architecture in southern Italy, Sicily, the Balearic Islands, and Spain, from the fourth to the end of the sixth century, is perhaps even less known than that of the North African provinces. True, in contrast to the ruins and excavation sites of Christian Africa, a small number of churches and baptisteries have survived in southern Italy, wholly or in large parts. But the number of Christian buildings known in this transmarine zone of African influence is small, and no attempt has been made so far to sift the material and establish a chronology, even for so outstanding a centre of fourth- and fifth-century Christianity as Naples and Campania.[49] Roughly speaking, in Naples a regional architecture with pre-Constantinian features was apparently overlaid by 400 by large-scale structures with Roman and North African characteristics, as would be natural in the greatest seaport south of Rome with its close African connexions. When Paulinus retired in 394 to his estate at Cimitile-Nola outside Naples, he found, above and near the grave of the martyr Felix, a few modest structures:[50] column screens north and south of the tomb, marking off the martyrium; a small basilica with an apse attached to its eastern end; opposite, a larger western apse, opening in two arched exits towards the adjoining cemetery; finally, two chapels near by, one perhaps remodelled as early as c. 300 from a Roman mausoleum. The whole gives a good idea of the somewhat disorganized layout of a cemetery and pilgrimage centre of a pre-Constantinian kind, though of fourth-century date. The changes wrought by Paulinus by 401/2 are characteristic of the drive of the new generation towards stricter organization and greater monumentality [159]. The nave, aisleless or basilican, are rare. However, they occur, if spottily, from the Crimea to Crete, Egypt, and North Africa. From these Paulinus may have purloined the plan of his church.[51] The building technique, on the other hand, is local, an *opus listatum* in small blocks of volcanic stone, with arches of brick or stone, singly or in alternation. Assembled,

159. Cimitile-Nola, martyrium precinct of St Felix, fourth century and 401/2. Plan

column screens were transformed into a square aedicula-martyrium, enclosed and subdivided by colonnades, their arches covered with mosaics. To the north, a larger colonnaded basilica was added, its façade opening in a triple arcade towards the martyrium, its aisles each flanked by two chapels. The apse formed a trefoil, the right-hand lobe serving as prothesis for the preparation of the Eucharist, the left one as a chapel for meditation. While trilobe mausolea and martyria are frequent in Early Christian building, trilobe apses fused with a it seems, in some hurry, the masonry is not quite as good as that of the older structures.

These building techniques continue apparently unchanged in Campania and in Sicily throughout the fifth and sixth centuries. So do local features of planning, such as arched openings in the curve of an apse. At S. Gennaro extra moenia in Naples, the apse of a single-naved cemetery church of about 400 opens in two arcades towards the near-by catacomb. But the feature was apparently accepted also in a major town church such as S. Giorgio Maggiore in

Naples, where it served no evident function whatever. A huge structure wholly altered in the Seicento, it apparently had a tripartite transept; to this day, it has preserved its late-fourth- or early-fifth-century apse with a triple arcade on columns opening towards a street or courtyard [160]. In S. Giovanni Maggiore, as late as the sixth century, the apse was even further punctured by two double arcades and one quintuple one.[52]

If open apses are a local feature, other architectural elements in Early Christian Naples point far afield: the impost blocks above the columns in the apse at S. Giorgio Maggiore to the Aegean coastlands, the tripartite transept to Milan. However, North Africa exerts the strongest impact. At Salemi

160 (*left*). Naples, S. Giorgio Maggiore, *c.* 400. Apse

161 (*below*). Naples, S. Restituta,
fourth century (last third). Interior of nave

162. Nocera Inferiore, baptistery of S. Maria Maggiore, sixth century(?). Interior as in c. 1770;
engraving by F. Morghen

in Sicily a basilica has been found with wide aisles
and nave, the floors covered with tomb mosaics. The
cathedral at S. Maria di Capua Vetere is a huge
structure, its core possibly still of fifth-century date.
Very wide in proportion to its length and divided into
a nave and four aisles, it recalls North African
basilicas. In S. Restituta at Naples the same plan has
survived, dating from the last third of the fourth
century.[53] The apse with its floor raised high above
the nave and its triumphal arch supported by two
columns pushed far inward, recalls African
churches, such as the one at Sabratha. As late as the
fifteenth century, the chancel of S. Restituta rose in
the nave, as customary in Christian Africa [161].
The square baptistery placed at the end of the right-
hand aisle is also characteristic of North Africa; and
while found in Pammachius's basilica at Porto,
Rome's harbour, it may have come there straight
from North Africa.[54]

Rome, then, apparently exerted little impact on
late-fourth- and fifth-century church building in
southern Italy. However, by the end of the sixth
century, the impact of Rome came to be felt alongside that of North Africa in the Christian architecture of Campania. The two currents show perhaps
most clearly in the baptistery at Nocera Inferiore,
probably dating from the sixth century. The circular
plan, the barrel-vaulted ambulatory, the centre
dome, the fifteen pairs of enveloping columns, the
eight columns placed on the rim of the font – all
recall the baptistery at the Lateran [162]; but at the
same time a North African parallel comes to mind,
the baptistery at Siagu (Ksar Er Zit, near Bir Bou
Rekba) in Tunisia. Elsewhere, Roman Christian
models come more strongly to the fore. The baptistery at Canosa combines elements purloined from
the Lateran baptistery and others taken from S.
Stefano Rotondo: a double-apsed narthex precedes

the structure; inside, a colonnaded centre room is enveloped by an ambulatory; four arms project outward and are linked by corridors accessible from the ambulatory. A structure of similar plan, though with variations, and much smaller in scale, adjoins the cathedral of S. Severina near Catanzaro in Calabria: while serving now as a baptistery, the rotunda at S. Severina – built perhaps not before the seventh century – may originally have been a martyr's chapel.[55]

Likewise, two churches in Spain show this balance of architectural power between Rome and North Africa along the northern shores of the Western Mediterranean. A church at S. Pedro de Alcántara (Vega del Mar) between Gibraltar and Málaga on the south coast dates from after 365 and was perhaps originally a parish rather than a cemetery church. It shows the African plan with apse and counter-apse, its opening screened by a triple arcade as on the Tabarka mosaic, and a baptistery to the right of the main apse. On the other hand, at Tarragona on the Catalonian coast, a basilica of a date after 409 has come to light, apparently with continuous transept and thus following the Roman type of a combined martyrium and cemetery church.[56]

PART FOUR

EARLY BYZANTINE BUILDING

CHAPTER 8

INTRODUCTION

In 527 Justinian ascended the throne of East Rome to shape for forty years the destinies of the Empire.[1] He was a remarkable man:[2] stocky and ugly; an autocrat deeply conscious of the prerogatives and duties of his exalted position close to God; self-controlled and ascetic in his personal life; unfettered by social mores, as witness his marriage to Theodora – a show girl of extraordinary beauty, courage, and brains; a shrewd diplomat and a first-rate organizer admirably gifted in selecting the best collaborators and in tightening the administrative and legal set-up of the Empire. Profoundly religious, he was permeated by the conviction of his divine mission to re-establish orthodoxy and to guide the Church throughout his dominions and beyond. Very intelligent, but not far-sighted, he was blind to the impossibility of solving religious problems by vacillating political compromises. Unable to stem the progressive exhaustion of the economy, unwilling to form long-range plans for the future to secure the eastern and northern frontiers against Persians and Slavs, Justinian was intent on the immediate present. He occupied himself with grand propaganda schemes to promote his own glory: easy, or seemingly easy conquests; a trade in luxury goods with far-away countries – China, India, Abyssinia; a grandiose building activity largely concentrated in his capital, directed at both intellectuals and the populace, and providing employment for the masses; a well-planned publicity campaign directed at the intelligentsia throughout the Empire, entrusted to his court historian Procopius, and later to his court poet, Paul the Silentiary.

Procopius has set forth the aims of Justinian's policies: quelling all inner unrest; wresting large parts of the Empire from Barbarian usurpers and expanding the Empire 'to the farthest shores of the ocean'; securing the frontiers; re-establishing religious orthodoxy; re-organizing the law; finally, reviving prosperity. The achievements fall short of these aims, but the direction makes the picture more specific. The bloody repression of the Nika Insurrection of 532 marks the last popular resistance to autocratic rule; the Marcellinus Conspiracy in 556 is the last of the aristocratic uprisings. Related aims underlie Justinian's administrative and religious policies. An autocratic system requires a dependable administrative bureaucracy; and in theory at least, Justinian's Minister of the Interior, John of Cappadocia, succeeded in establishing a reliable and nearly bribe-proof civil service. The universities in Constantinople and Beyrouth, staffed by outstanding faculties, supplied the young men. An autocracy also requires a well-disciplined army; Belisarius and Narses created it. Autocracy requires a uniform creed. Hence the suppression of the last residues of paganism, the elimination of Arianism, linked as it was to the Ostrogothic usurpation of Italy, and the attempt to bring, under the leadership of Rome, the orthodox of the Greek East, the monophysites of the Semitic provinces, and the dyophysite West to a compromise formula regarding the nature of Christ.

The compromise was palatable to none, but its proposal was inevitable in a society in which religion and politics were so closely interwoven that religious divergence struck at the core of absolute Imperial power. Finally, an autocracy requires a uniform code of law, and this was formed by Tribonianus in the early years of Justinian's reign, 529–34: the *Corpus iuris*; it, more than any other of Justinian's achievements, has survived him.

Justinian's code aims at unifying the administration of law and tightening autocratic rule; it strives equally to revive the law of Rome. That most of it was written in Latin and translated into Greek is of limited significance. Greek had never developed a legal terminology. What is significant is that the *Corpus* resurrected a Roman tradition extending from the Twelve Tablets to Theodosius, and thus stressed both the continuity of the Roman State up to the time of Justinian and, by implication, the Western root of the Empire. The revival of Rome and the turn to the West interlock, and the same *Drang nach Westen* underlies to a large degree Justinian's policy of expansion. In the East he aimed at maintaining, even under sacrifices, the *status quo*. A truce with Persia secured an uneasy frontier along the Euphrates. Yet, this appeasement policy freed Justinian's hands for his main goal, the conquest of the West. North Africa was taken over from the Vandals in a short campaign in 533–4; Sicily, Sardinia, and Dalmatia were occupied the year after. Italy was wrested from the Goths in a long-drawn-out and costly war. Finally, in 554 a foothold was gained in the seaports of south-east Spain – not on, but at least not too far from 'the farthest shores of the ocean'. To be sure, three years after the Emperor's death, Italy was lost again, to the Longobards. Nevertheless, by Justinian's last years, the Mediterranean was a Roman lake. Roman – not Byzantine, for in Justinian's eyes these conquests were reconquests; the *Basileus tōn Romaiōn*, the Roman Emperor, reasserted his inherited right to provinces illegally occupied by barbarians and, worse, heretics. He waged a crusade against them in the name of both orthodoxy and Rome. He ruled from Byzantium; his funds and manpower were drawn from the Eastern provinces. But the Empire as he viewed it was centred round the Mediterranean. Ravenna was to be a sub-capital, subject to Constantinople yet vying with it in splendour; Rome was to be a spiritual centre, balancing the see of the patriarch in Byzantium. New Rome, Constantinople – 'the daughter more ravishing than the mother' – strove to revive the glory of old Rome. Ideally, though not in reality, Justinian's Empire was the Roman Empire, the Empire of old, with its power shifted to the East.

Building was one of the means by which Justinian's autocracy attempted to impress the peoples both inside and outside the Empire and to unify its territory. Where Constantine had promoted church building by moral and financial support, Justinian was the sole driving force behind gigantic architectural undertakings, certainly in his capital and possibly throughout his Empire. Thus, Justinian's is an Imperial architecture in a true sense. Only the Emperor could provide the immense funds needed for his building programme, and he was well aware of the programme's significance. After all, he must have been the one to insist that his court historian dedicate an entire volume to this programme, the *Buildings*. And Procopius leaves little doubt that in the Emperor's mind the architectural enterprises ranked with the restitution of religious orthodoxy, the revival of jurisprudence, the reconquest of the West, the re-establishment of prosperity, and security of the frontiers. Within these propagandistic aims, it was only natural for Justinian's architects to strive towards a style of building, standing in an old tradition, yet newer and bolder than any created earlier.

The time of Justinian marks a turning point in architectural history rivalled by few other periods. The change is noticeable not so much in palace building or in the architectural vocabulary of capitals and decorated friezes as in church planning. Until the beginning of Justinian's reign, the majority of church building, East or West, with but few exceptions, had been based on one building type: the basilica, a timber-roofed hall with or without aisles.

Age-old, its plan had been evolved, one recalls, for civic buildings in Italy presumably as early as the third or second century B.C. All changes that developed in later Roman public building, and afterwards in church architecture, were but variations on the old theme. Galleries, apses, multiplied aisles, nartheces, atria, and the like were simply designed to adapt the type to new functions. Similarly, the new vocabulary which gradually evolved – capitals, colonnaded arcades, mosaics on walls, vaults, and pavements – at closer view turn out to be mere adaptations of a basic type to the changing taste of the times and the preferences of the various regions of the Empire, whether in the Latin West, the Aegean coastlands, or the Semitic hinterlands of the Near East.

The situation changes decisively with the sixth century. The West continues to view the basilica as the only appropriate form of church building through the entire Middle Ages and beyond. The vaulting systems of the Romanesque and Gothic centuries and their changing vocabularies leave the principle unaltered. On the other hand, Justinian's architecture in the East breaks with the tradition of the basilica and thus with a tradition going back to early Roman times. Turning to vaulted centrally-planned church buildings, Justinian's architects base themselves on architectural concepts which had been evolved and had certainly matured in the architecture of the Late Empire: in palace halls, in funerary structures, in thermae and garden buildings, ever since at least the second and third centuries. From these roots Justinian's builders create a church architecture which is invariably based on a central plan and nearly invariably vaulted, culminating in a central dome. To be sure, centrally-planned churches, roofed or domed in timber or occasionally perhaps groin-vaulted, had been built since the fourth century. But until the second third of the sixth century they were rare and designed only for specific and extraordinary functions: as palace churches or as martyria. About 500 the type becomes slightly more frequent beyond these narrow confines. But only Justinian's architects make the domed brick-

vaulted central plan the rule in church building in all the major centres of his Empire, and without regard to special function. Thus they set out on a path radically different from that chosen by the West. The choice of Justinian's architects was destined to determine the character and the development of religious building in the East for a thousand years and more. First Byzantine church builders, later Balkan and Russian architects developed it in ever new variations. So did the builders of Persian, North Indian, and Turkish mosques. The schism between East and West in the realm of architecture, then, starts earlier and it is as deep as, if not deeper than, the religious schism.

Within this broader view, it is of but secondary importance whether the centrally-planned churches of Justinian's time and their immediate forerunners were evolved from martyria, from palace churches, or from both. More important than either – and possibly the truly determinant factor – is, in my opinion, the Christian liturgy as it had developed in the Aegean coastlands. The elaborate celebration of the Mass with the gradual development of the processional entrances had apportioned the nave primarily to the clergy since the early fifth century, if not before. The congregation in many parts of the eastern coastlands seems to have been relegated for large portions of the service to the ancillary spaces enveloping the nave, whether aisles, galleries, or esonarthex. Throughout the fifth century, this liturgical situation appears to be reflected through the extension of the chancel and its solea far into the nave and nearly all over the Aegean through the use of parapets to close off the nave and make it, wholly or in part, inaccessible from the ancillary spaces. Yet such adaptation of the basilica plan to local liturgical needs remained necessarily a solution chosen for want of a better one. A centrally-planned building, on the other hand, was ideally suited to the requirements of a service in which the performance of the Mass occupied the central area both liturgically and architecturally. Hence, it seems to me, Justinian's architects and churchmen – preceded perhaps by a lone maverick two or three decades before – took up with enthusiasm the central plan for their church buildings. Without physically closing off it seems by parapets the nave from the aisles, they focused the structure on the area where the action took place. How right they were from their point of view is demonstrated to this day by the service as performed in any Greek church: the clergy entirely filling the nave, the congregation crowded into whatever there is of the aisles, into the narthex, and into the porticoes running along the flanks of the tiny building.[3]

With the sixth century, then, the architectural concepts of Classical Rome, as they had survived in the Early Christian basilica, finally come to an end in the Eastern Empire. Their place is taken by a new architecture, rooted in Late, not in Classical, Antiquity and developed far beyond. Byzantine architecture starts with Justinian.

CHAPTER 9

THE HAGIA SOPHIA AND ALLIED BUILDINGS

The foremost task that Justinian set himself and his architects was the building of the Hagia Sophia.[1] The first basilica, completed in 360 and remodelled from 404 to 415, had been burnt to the ground in 532 in the Nika Riot, except the skeuophylakion outside to the north. Justinian, victorious, decided to build – perhaps as a monument of his triumph – a new church on a plan and of a size and lavishness hitherto unheard of. Columns and marbles were brought from all over the Aegean lands and from as far as the Atlantic coast of France. (That these columns were spoils from Rome, Ephesus, and Cyzicus is a later embellishment of the tradition.) The marble workshops of the Proconnesian islands were kept busy furnishing capitals, cornices, and huge pavement plaques. Thousands of labourers

163. Constantinople, H. Sophia, 532–7. From the south-west

were 'gathered from all over the world' to work on the building site, in the brickyards, and in the quarries. The task of organization and logistics, performed by Anthemios, was as phenomenal as that of the Imperial Treasurer. The equivalent of £130,000,000 or $180,000,000 (as per 1986) was spent; and after five years the structure, though without its furnishings, could be consecrated.[2] Correctly or not, tradition has transmitted Justinian's words on the day of consecration: 'Solomon, I have vanquished thee!'

An architecture out of the ordinary requires an architect out of the ordinary. Master builders had long dominated the profession and continued to design and execute the bulk of the building in Justinian's Empire. But, well trained though they were, they were apparently not considered up to the task of supervising the construction of the H. Sophia. Instead, the Emperor chose two men who stood on a different plane both in training and social status: Anthemios of Tralles and Isidorus of Miletus. They were what their contemporaries called *mechanopoioi*, grounded in the theory of statics and kinetics and well versed in mathematics. Such architect-scientists are occasionally, if rarely mentioned in Late Antiquity; but Anthemios and Isidorus appear to have been more scientists than architects. Anthemios was the author of a work on conical sections, an expert in projective geometry, and an inventor who knew the principle of steam power and of the burning mirror. Isidorus taught stereometry and physics at the universities, first of Alexandria, then of Constantinople, and wrote a commentary on an older treatise on vaulting.[3] They were skilled in a theoretical knowledge that could be applied to the practice of either engineering or building, be it a steam engine, a burning mirror, or the complex vaulting system of the H. Sophia. They could organize the work, draw up the plans – including possibly sections and perspective renderings – and train the assistants necessary for executing the building. They were, one would like to think, not architects to start with, but they turned into architects when called upon to devise the plans and statics

of a building never before considered viable on a large scale.

As it stands today, the H. Sophia is no longer quite the structure that was dedicated on 27 December 537 [163]. The first dome, quite low and possibly continuing the curve of the pendentives, collapsed in 558. It was replaced by a steeper ribbed dome, completed in 563, and the construction of this new dome carried with it a number of other changes. Its base had been deformed by the thrust of the first dome – which caused the piers and buttresses to tip backward, the east and west arches to expand, and the lateral arches north and south to bend outward. It was regularized by broadening inward the crowns of the arches to the right and left, and partially reconstructing the pendentives. Likewise, the clerestory walls below the lateral arches were rebuilt and the original window pattern – seven, wider than at present, and topped by one single large segmental opening, divided by piers – gave way to the present one; but whether this happened in 558–63 or much later, in 869, is yet undecided. Simultaneously, in any event, the gallery arcades and the wall they supported were shifted back to the perpendicular.[4] Possibly also in the ninth century, the west façade was reinforced with four flying buttresses which projected into the atrium.[5] The western portion of the second dome again fell in 989 and was repaired by an Armenian architect, Trdat; and finally the eastern portion collapsed in 1346. More incisive changes were wrought by the Turkish conquerors after 1453: minarets were planted at the four corners, beautiful in themselves but countering the broad curve of the dome; Turkish mausolea were clustered about the flanks of the structure. In the interior, the figural mosaics, all dating from after Justinian, were covered with yellow paint; and four enormous shields, inscribed with verses from the Korān, were hung from the piers flanking apse and entrance. All this has marred, but nothing has destroyed the incredible beauty of the building.

The structural system of the H. Sophia is bold but simple. A huge rectangle was laid out, measuring 71 by 77 m. (230 by 250 ft), equalling roughly 225 by

60 FT

20 M

BAPTISTERY

NARTHEX

EXONARTHEX

ATRIUM

N

5TH CENTURY

JUSTINIAN (WESTERN HALF, ATRIUM, RECONSTRUCTIONS)

LATER ADDITIONS

165 and 166. Constantinople. H. Sophia, 532–7.
Isometric view and
exterior of dome and western half-dome

167. Constantinople, H. Sophia, 532–7. Interior of nave, from the west

240 Byzantine feet. Inside it, four huge piers, run-ning north and south, rise at the corners of a square, 100 Byzantine feet on each side [164, 165]. Seventy feet from the ground, four arches swing across, those to the east and west free-standing, those north and south embedded in the side walls of the nave and hardly noticeable inside, but strongly projecting above the roof on the outside [163]. Four penden-tives, slightly irregular in shape, link the arches [167]. From the apex of the arches and the four connecting pendentives rises the main dome, a shell scalloped by forty ribs and forty curved webs. It is buttressed on the outside by forty closely-spaced

short ribs which frame small windows [166, 168]. The piers to the north and south rise above the roofs of the aisles to abut the lateral thrusts of the east and west arches and, indirectly, of the main dome. Possibly as an afterthought during construction, tower-like excrescences were placed on top of these buttresses to secure them against the thrusts of dome and arches. On the other hand, it is debatable how far the longitudinal thrusts are countered by the two huge semi-domes which open east and west and which rest on the main piers and on two pairs of subsidiary piers flanking the entrance and chancel bays. True, these semi-domes are too thin to exert

168. Constantinople, H. Sophia, 532–7. Interior of dome

much counterthrust, and indeed, their apices have collapsed time and again. Nevertheless, as witness the deformation of the dome base, their strength was sufficient to withstand the thrust of the first, lower dome. On the other hand, the smaller conchs that open on diagonal axes on the bays of the half-domes, inserted between their supporting piers, simply lean their thin shells against the semi-domes without abutting them. Nor is the structure strengthened by the barrel-vaults which project on the centre axis

from the huge semi-domes, that to the east ending in the half-dome of the apse, that to the west terminated by the wall of the narthex and its upper gallery.[6]

Hazardous in its statics, this core – composed of piers, arches, domes, half-domes, and conchs – forms the inner focus of the double-shell design. A baldacchino, it stands free in space, independent of the enveloping ancillary spatial units. Similarly, aisles, narthex, and galleries remain on the whole unconcerned with the structural workings of the inner nucleus. Their vaults – domical groin-vaults in the lower, pendentive domes in the gallery zone – rest on free-standing columns and piers and are linked to the main piers and walls merely by tiny groin- and barrel-vaults. The construction is both simple and bold, and equally simple and bold are the building methods employed. Only the eight main piers are built of large blocks of ashlar.[7] The walls, through their entire thickness, are built of thin bricks set in mortar-beds up to 7 cm. (2¾ in.) high, interspersed with limestone courses placed apparently at the springing of the vaults [172]. Bricks pitched on their sides, instead of being radially placed, and embedded in thick beds of mortar form

169. Constantinople, H. Sophia, 532–7. North-west conch

170. Constantinople, H. Sophia, 532–7. View from the south aisle facing north-west

extraordinarily thin and light vaults. They fuse with the walls into a nearly homogeneous resilient mass, though not as resilient or homogeneous as a Roman concrete construction.

Defying all laws of statics, shaken by successive earthquakes, collapsing at its weak points and being repaired, the H. Sophia stands by sheer miracle. Experienced master builders of 537 must have stood aghast at the disregard of sound building practices by those two non-professionals to whom the Emperor had entrusted his greatest building. True, Anthemios and Isidorus went to the very limits of

what we call the safety coefficients. Their first project was apparently bolder still and corrections were forced on them during construction: openings towards the nave perforating the main piers were walled up; arches to buttress the piers were thrown across aisles and galleries, resting on half-piers added to the main piers; the main buttresses surmounting these piers were raised to provide added weight; and the number of arcades in the gallery zone, planned in five as on the ground floor, was increased to seven, thus diminishing their distances and heights.[8] In building the first, flatter

171. Constantinople, H. Sophia, 532–7. View from the gallery, south-west bay, facing north-east

dome, they still went too far and it collapsed within twenty years. Yet at the risk of failure they had to employ hazardous techniques – techniques which were the necessary tools for developing the design they meant to create. Perhaps they could envisage both design and techniques only because they were not professional architects.

The design unfolds itself from the centre of the structure. Standing under the apex of the dome, the visitor begins to grasp the huge space [167]. At first glance amorphous, it gradually falls into shapes and the shapes fall into place. From the vertical centre

axis, space expands longitudinally into the huge niches to the east and west. It expands beyond, to the east into the forechoir and its apse, to the west into the entrance bay. From the niches, the space moves into the conchs that open diagonally on either side. It rises vertically into the main dome, gropes along its rim, sinks into the half-dome, widens and moves farther into the quarter spheres of the diagonal conchs. The sequence of spatial shapes develops both centrifugally around a middle axis and longitudinally from the entrance bay to the apse. The huge piers that support the arches of the main square and the subsidiary piers to the east and west are pushed aside into the aisles and galleries. In their place the eye encounters smooth, vertical planes; higher up rise the curved surfaces of arches, pendentives, domes, and half-domes; and between the piers, two orders of arched colonnades open into aisles and galleries. The involved yet simple rhythm of colonnades and window openings forms an accompaniment ᵗhe spatial design. Arcades of five bays flank the nave on either side, surmounted by arcades of seven bays in the gallery zone. These in turn were succeeded, it would seem, in the clerestory zone by seven windows, surmounted in turn by an upper one, with five intercolumniations. In the east and west conchs, three arches on the ground floor support seven in the gallery zone [169]; these are followed by five windows along the rim of the conch vault, and this rhythm is repeated by five more windows at the foot of the western and eastern half-domes. The rhythm of three is again taken up by the three openings which lead into the nave from the west gallery, and by the double row of windows, three to each row, which pierce the wall of the apse.

Clearly articulated by this rhythm of threes, fives, and sevens, and clearly disposed, the spatial units are, nevertheless, not clearly delimited. All expand beyond what seem to be their natural borders. The

172. Constantinople, H. Sophia.
Masonry, sixth century (*centre*),
tenth century (*left*), and Turkish (*right*)

eye wanders beyond the centre square into aisles and galleries whose shapes cannot be grasped. The gaze of the viewer is drawn beyond the curved arcades in the conchs and into the outer bays; yet the overlapping of these arcades with the windows in the outer walls precludes a ready understanding of the relationship between ancillary and main spaces [169]. Within the inner shell, both the spatial volumes and their sequence are all intelligible. But beyond this core, space remains enigmatic to the beholder who is restricted to the nave. The form and interplay of spatial shapes is first established, then denied. Indeed, none of these spatial shapes are contained by the enveloping solids, be they piers, straight or curved walls, or vaulted surfaces. The term solids – in this architecture at least – is a misnomer. The piers are massive enough if seen from the aisles; but they are not meant to be seen. Their bulk is denied by their marble sheatʰing. The column shafts are huge, measuring two and a half to three feet in diameter, but the colourful marble counters the feeling of massiveness.

Precious materials, subtly graded, shimmer over the interior. From the dark grey marble plaques of the pavement rise high grey marble pedestals carrying columns of green marble with large white veins – both on the ground floor and in the gallery arcades. Reddish porphyry columns stand in the conchs that flank apse and entrance. The piers and walls in the nave are covered by marble plaques in three zones: first, green marble slabs flanked by grey-yellowish plaques with purplish veins; above, porphyry slabs enclosed by dark bluish marble with yellow veins; finally, a third tier repeating the first [169]. Slabs have been sliced in two and the sections fitted together so that the veins form a symmetrical pattern along a central axis. The capitals are all overspun with foliage, their shiny marble leaves and branches standing out against the deep shadows of the ground [173, 185]. A lacework of tendrils overlays the spandrels of the arcades; elsewhere, white mother-of-pearl rinceaux are inlaid into black marble. Silver, gold, and mosaic are joined in this wealth of colours and shades. Silver sheathed both the

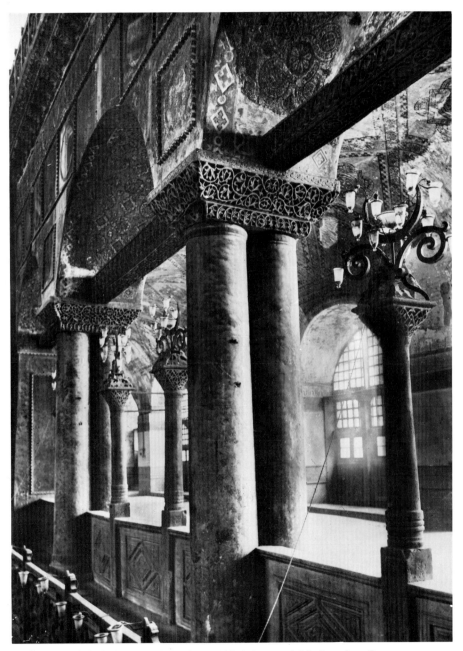

173. Constantinople, H. Sophia, 532–7. Twin columns with Ionic impost capitals in the narthex gallery

synthronon, rising in three tiers in the apse, and the column screen of the chancel, the latter projected westward from the arch of the forechoir and continued by the long solea, both protected by parapets. Golden lamps dangled in the intercolumniations; others rose from the trabeation of the chancel screen.[9] Domes and half-domes, vaults, and soffits gleamed with mosaic. A few fragments survive: golden tendrils on a bluish-green field, purple crosses on a gold or silver ground.[10] Figurative mosaic was apparently missing. The first dome, we know, was covered with plain gold mosaic, while the new dome of 563 carried a huge cross. The windows were filled with glass panes, presumably coloured, like those found at S. Vitale, at Ravenna: deep blue, greenish, dark purplish brown, off-white, yellow, light purple.[11] The light would have risen in gradations from the darkest zone in the aisles, to the lighter zone of the galleries, and finally into the window zone of the nave. But always subdued, the light remained darkish in tone. At night services, lamps were strung along the rim of the dome, chandeliers hung from its cornice, and candlesticks stood in the arcades of aisles and galleries.[12]

The principle of a design which proceeds by statement and denial acts with equal force throughout the building. It applies to the proportions of the nave, where the soaring height of piers, walls, and domes is countered by the horizontal layers of marble veneers, arcades, window zones, and cornices. It applies equally to the relationship between principal and subordinate spatial units. At first sight, aisles and galleries seem to be independent spaces. Yet this impression holds only if the aisles and galleries are viewed lengthwise – a view never intended to be seen. On the contrary, they are intended as places whence to view the nave. But seen from the aisles and galleries, the nave remained always half-hidden behind screens of columns; screens doubled in the centre, where two extra columns carry the vaults of the double bay; or equally confusing, convex in the end bays [170, 171]. Curtains hanging between the columns may have provided a further screen. Hence the nave, from the

aisles and galleries, presents itself only in fragments. Parts of the main dome, parts of the half-dome, parts of the concave conchs or straight arcades, parts of piers are seen by the beholder, who is never allowed to understand the whole design of the nave, or, indeed, of the building. In short, the beholder relegated to aisles and galleries sees the nave, but is denied its intelligibility. Only those gathered in nave and chancel are permitted to understand the spatial design. Fragmentation of views and of a space which is nevertheless whole, marks the design of the building and its component elements. The first, large windows in the clerestory of the nave were cut across by the lateral arches under the dome; the groin-vaults behind the curved exedrae are likewise cut by the arched colonnades, and demand a completion never to be attained [171].

Such an interpretation of the H. Sophia in dialectical terms is anything but arbitrary. Procopius proceeds along the same lines in describing the church. The building, so he says, forms part of the city, but at the same time it stands very much by itself. It is exceedingly long, yet extraordinarily wide. It is bulky, yet harmonious. Light seems to flood the interior from the outside, yet it seems generated inside as well. The structure is solid, yet it engenders a feeling of insecurity. The columns perform in a choral dance, the piers are sheer mountain peaks. Vaults seem to float, the dome seems suspended from heaven. Vistas change and yet the spatial shapes follow each other in a clear sequence. Statement and denial are at the basis of Procopius's description just as they are at the basis of the architects' design.

To design a shockingly bold interior was, no doubt, the primary concern of Anthemios and Isidorus. Yet the exterior is equally impressive. The volumes are stacked on top of each other and the eye is led subtly towards the forechoir, from there towards the eastern half-dome, and finally up towards the dome [163, 166, 174]. Surrounded by palace buildings to the south and east and by city buildings to the north and west, the Great Church towered above the city and the Sea of Marmara.

174. Constantinople, H. Sophia, 532–7. Exterior from the east

With this picture still vivid, the visitor entered the atrium to be enclosed by porticoes in which one pier rhythmically alternated with two columns.[13] Finally, after passing through the transverse barrier of the long but shallow esonarthex, he entered the church proper through one of five doors, the royal gate in the centre. Only then did he see the nave revealed, focused on its huge dome and half-domes, and only then did he understand as relations in space what had been but half-intelligible from the outside.

However this revelation was reserved for the principal actors on the stage of the nave: the clergy led by the patriarch, and, to a lesser degree perhaps, the Emperor accompanied by his court. The faithful, most of them gathered in aisles and galleries, saw only fragments of the building, just as the solemn celebration of the services was revealed to them only in fragments. The strict segregation of aisles and nave by parapets customary in the Aegean coastlands suggests that the liturgical custom in those provinces kept the faithful out of the nave, reserving it for the performance of the service by the clergy, starting with the Lesser Entrance when bishop, clergy, and people entered, the latter to fill the aisles, the former to bring the gospel along the solea to the altar. In Justinian's reign, a second procession – no doubt previously customary but not codified – became a main element in the Mass of Constantinople.[14] This was the Great Entrance, in which the elements of the Eucharist were fetched from the outside skeuophylakion by the deacons emerging from the chancel through the north aisle and returning through the aisle into the nave and along the solea to chancel and altar. In the H. Sophia both Entrances were, probably long before Justinian's time, solemnized and interwoven with the appearance of the Emperor and his court.[15] The nave, then, was a stage on which the procession moved along a solemn path from the royal gate towards the solea, and along the solea into the bema. Thus it would seem that in principle in Constantinople as well, aisles and galleries were assigned to the faithful, women to one side, men to the other. If at the high points of the celebration or in their aftermath, when the nave was empty, the faithful surged in – there being no parapets in Constantinople – the principle of segregation still remained inviolate. During much of the Mass, indeed, the clergy remained inside the chancel. At stated points in the celebration of the liturgy however, clergy and patriarch re-entered the nave, both with and without their secular counterparts of Emperor and court. The two powers entered the church together during the Lesser Entrance to take their appointed places, the patriarch and clergy in the sanctuary, the Emperor and court in the Imperial enclosure in the south aisle. The clergy emerged for the reading of the scriptures and moved to the ambo, the pulpit, which rose at the entrance to the solea, below the eastern rim of the great dome. On solemn occasions, the patriarch and clergy would proceed a second time to the pulpit to deliver the sermon. The Mass of the Faithful would open with the solemn procession of the Great Entrance, when the patriarch, preceded by the clergy, would proceed from the bema along the solea and into the nave, and return into the chancel to deposit the elements of the Eucharist on the altar – accompanied by the Emperor, the one

layman apparently allowed inside the sanctuary.[16] After the sacrifice had been performed, the patriarch would emerge from the sanctuary a fifth time, to meet the Emperor and exchange with him the Kiss of Peace. Returning to the sanctuary, the patriarch would continue the Mass, emerging one last time towards the end in order to carry the communion to the Emperor. To the faithful, all these appearances of the clergy and the Emperor – epiphanies would be a better term – were but fragments of a celebration which as a whole remained incomprehensible. In sixth-century Byzantium, then, the ceremonial of the Mass fell into two parts: one, removed from profane eyes, took place inside the chancel – in Greek church parlance, the Great Mystery; the other, public and meant to be seen by all, was staged in the nave where clergy and Emperor met to perform their respective roles below the eastern rim of the great dome – the Dome of Heaven.[17]

This ceremonial is closely linked to the exalted place which sixth-century thought assigned on one hand to the clergy, on the other to the Emperor. The clergy – so say the writings of the Pseudo-Areopagite about 500 – reflects the nine celestial hierarchies of the angels; indeed, the hierarch, that is the patriarch, is actually close to the angels. The visible ceremonies he performs with the assistance of the clergy are intended to evoke the image of the invisible world which centres around the divinity. Similarly, the Emperor, one wants to recall, had his assigned place in the celestial hierarchy as mirrored on Earth. Since Constantine's time he had been considered equal to the apostles, and perhaps more than equal. Certainly in the tenth century he acted the part of Christ on solemn occasions – breaking and blessing the bread and raising the cup of wine to his lips after state dinners; swathed in white bands as Christ resurrected and surrounded by twelve apostles on Easter Sunday. Emperor and patriarch were the 'two halves of God'.[18] And if the patriarch reflected the religious aspects of the Godhead, the Emperor mirrored the secular aspects, power and justice. The interaction of Emperor and priesthood was essential for establishing and maintaining a Christian Empire, and their meeting under the great dome of the H. Sophia becomes a symbol of the interaction. Both the ecclesiastical and secular hierarchies were permeated by the light of the Divinity which emanated from the centre of heaven and spread to the angels, patriarch, clergy, and Emperor. Thus in the H. Sophia the spatial shapes, the light, and the colours all emanate from the centre dome. The ordinary people in the aisles and galleries remained hidden in the shadows. Only from afar were they allowed to see the light, the colours, and the glory that streamed from the centre, the seat of the Godhead.

Such a symbolic interpretation of an architectural design, in both theological and political terms, was less fantastic to men of the sixth century than it seems today. A hymn written in Syria only fifty years after the building of the H. Sophia describes the cathedral of Edessa (Urfa) in very similar terms.[19] Small though it is, says the poet, it resembles the universe. Its vault expands like the heavens and shines with mosaics as the firmament with stars. Its soaring dome compares with the Heaven of Heavens, where God resides, and its four arches represent the four directions of the world, with their variegated colours like the rainbow. Its piers are like the mountains of the earth; its marble walls shine like the light of the image not man-made, the Godhead; three windows in the apse symbolize the Trinity, the nine steps leading to the chancel represent the nine choirs of the angels. In short, the poet concludes, the building represents heaven and earth, the apostles, the prophets, the martyrs, and, indeed, the Godhead.

The H. Sophia forms a key element within Justinian's architecture, but only a very few other structures are designed along similar lines. In recent times the foundations and hundreds of pieces of architectural sculpture, belonging to an astonishing structure, have come to light in Constantinople.[20] Identified by a long inscription, in parts preserved on the fragments found, as the church of H. Polyeuktos, it was built in 524–7 next to her palace by Anicia Juliana, the last descendant of the former Imperial House, and a great patroness of the arts. The foundations, a massive platform of solid walls, brick-vaulted corridors, and fill raised the church high above street level, outlining a 52 m. (170 ft) square, two-thirds the size of H. Sophia. Two walls, over 7 m. wide and deep, run the length of the foundation and mark off a nave and aisles, terminated by an apse and flanking side structures of undetermined shape. A small cross-shaped crypt was sunk into the foundation of the apse, continued west by corridors and walls supporting chancel screens, ambo, and solea, the latter possibly extending to the very doors of the nave, the ambo midway between apse and façade. The narthex, reached over a high flight of stairs, was preceded at ground level by an atrium, to the northward restricted by a structure, chapel, baptistery, or part of the palace. The huge lengthwise foundation walls would have carried piers and colonnades both on the ground-floor and gallery level – the latter referred to in the inscription; on the upper level would have fitted in six peacock niches, found in the excavation. Plan and elevation, however, remain conjectural. Vaulting is suggested by the bulk of the foundations, and a plan anticipating that of H. Sophia, with a dome 20 m. (65 ft) in diameter, has been suggested as one alternative. However, a lengthwise plan is more likely: a domed basilica, composed of a barrel-vaulted entrance bay and a domed main bay, and thus related to H. Irene, as built after 532, and possibly to Meriamlik – buildings to be discussed later on.[21] As interesting as the plan is the decoration of the church. The walls were sheathed and the floor paved with precious marble slabs. Capitals, cornices, and furnishings were sumptuously covered with figural, vegetal, and geometric design, splendidly executed, but widely differing in type. There are niches, each filled by a peacock and bordered by part of the dedicatory inscription, the spandrels covered with vines of a classical type [175]. There are column capitals densely spun over by spiky acanthus with free-standing corner handles; on others, shaped to truncated cones, a fleshy lotus palmette is framed by a broad

175. Constantinople, H. Polyeuktos, 524–7, peacock niche. *Istanbul, Archaeological Museum*

wicker band. There are pier capitals, the faces marked with palm trees, the corners with thin ivy tendrils, the upper border with a fleshy heart pattern, far removed from any classical tradition. Cor-

176. Constantinople, Zeyrek (Mollazeyrek) Camii, chancel plaque from H. Polyeuktos, 524–7

nices and impost blocks carry similarly unclassical palmettes, fleshy stylized acanthus, vines, and star flowers. Comparable designs occur on parapet slabs, now dispersed at the Zeyrek (Mollazeyrek) Camii [176], and convincingly this type of ornament has been linked to Sassanian rather than Late Antique or classical sources. Both types stand side by side in the fragments of two piers found on the site, the capitals carrying a sparse, quite unclassical acanthus on the four faces, the piers covered with rich highly classical vines. Their exact counterparts in size and design, but fully preserved, stand on the Piazzetta in Venice, south of S. Marco [177], obviously brought there from H. Polyeuktos, after the conquest of 1204. Finally, there are column shafts inlaid with amethyst and coloured glass in an intricate pattern. The type, common in Justinian's Constantinople – splendid examples formed the chancel screen set up when the hexagon hall [30] in one of the palaces

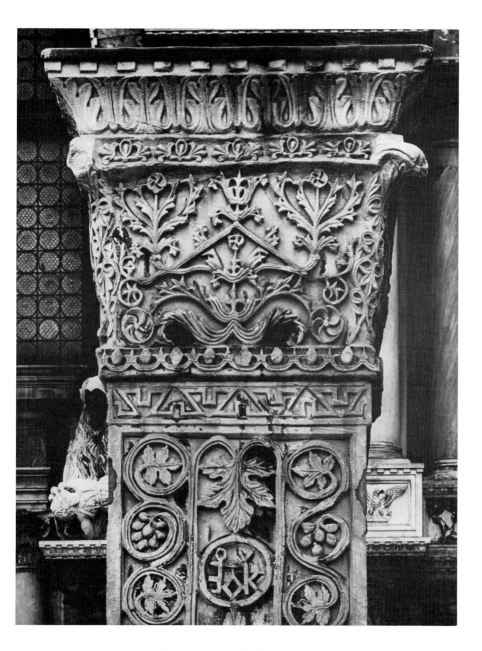

177. Venice, Piazzetta, pier and capital, from Constantinople, H. Polyeuktos, 524–7

178. Column with inlay, from Constantinople,
H. Euphemia, sixth century.
Istanbul, Archaeological Museum

179. Column with inlay, from Constantinople,
H. Polyeuktos, 524–7.
Istanbul, Archaeological Museum

north of the hippodrome became the church of H.
Euphemia – survived into or was possibly revived in
the ninth century [178, 179].

All told, the architectural ornament of H.
Polyeuktos only in part anticipates that of H. Sophia.
The Sassanian elements are an intrusion, eliminated
by the designers of Justinian's Great Church. Much
closer to this latter, in plan and details, though not in
quality, is the church of H. Sergios and Bakchos, a
simpler variant on the double-shell compositional
system [180–2]. Octagonal in plan, it seems at first
glance different from the composite plan of the H.

Sophia [180]. But the difference is only apparent,
and the H. Sophia contains all the elements of a
double-shell octagon: the domed core, the billowing
niches, the enveloping aisles and galleries. But these
components have been, as it were, broken up and
rearranged lengthwise – for the simple reason that
the size required for Justinian's Great Church made
radial expansion of an octagonal plan impracticable.
The octagon of H. Sergios and Bakchos and the plan
of the H. Sophia belong to the same family. Also,
they are nearly contemporary. H. Sergios and Bakchos, indeed, was begun by Justinian apparently

A

B

180. Constantinople, H. Sergios and Bakchos,
completed prior to 536. Plans (A) of ground floor, (B) of gallery

N

0   60 FT

0   20 M

181. Constantinople, H. Sergios and Bakchos,
completed prior to 536. Exterior

182. Constantinople, H. Sergios and Bakchos, completed prior to 536. Interior

early in his reign and completed prior to 536. The structure was squeezed in on an irregular site between the Hormisdas Palace, Justinian's residence as heir to the throne, and a church of St Peter and St Paul, a basilica with galleries which had been begun before 519. The addition of the church of H. Sergios and Bakchos made of the two churches a double church, a common narthex, atrium, and propylaeum extending in front of both buildings.

Moreover, H. Sergios and Bakchos communicated with both the basilica and the palace through open arcades on both floors and thus formed the focus of the entire complex. Incorporated into the south flank of H. Sergios and Bakchos, the north wall of an older structure survives; but whether it be the church of St Peter and Paul or part of the palace, must remain open.[22] Built in the full brick masonry with broad mortar-beds by then customary in Constantinople, and, like the H. Sophia, strengthened with chains of ashlar, the structure is supported by eight piers, which form an octagon placed inside an irregular square [182]. Alternatingly rectangular and semicircular niches link the piers and project into the enveloping ancillary spaces of an ambulatory and upper gallery, both pierced opposite the entrance by a forechoir and apse. Pairs of columns in the curve of the niches carry an architrave on the ground level and triple arcades on the gallery level. Over the centre space rises a sixteen-sided pumpkin dome in which the straight sides, flush with the wall, alternate with scooped segments. The scooped segments rest on the corners of the octagon; the straight sides spring from the centres of its sides and are pierced by windows.

The principle of the architectural design, then, compares with that of the Hagia Sophia. The centre space, at first easily understood, loses its clarity when viewed from the ambulatory and galleries. The space expands into the niches and from the niches out into the ambulatory, but it is bounded by mere screens. Indeed, the intercolumniations in the niches as well as, behind them, the arcades in the outer walls (originally perhaps leading into the neighbouring palace and into the aisles and galleries of St Peter and St Paul) drew the eye from the centre room, through the ambulatory, into rooms whose relation to the centre room remains unintelligible. Yet, while the principle of planning is subtle, the execution is strangely ambivalent. No attempt has been made to counteract the irregularity of the site, and even the seemingly regular octagon of the piers has sides of different length. The proportions are unpleasantly low, even if the columns on the ground floor were originally placed not only on hexagonal bases (one still shows), but also on pedestals now perhaps buried in the Turkish pavement. Even disregarding the eighteenth-century decoration, the arches of the niches, their triple arcades, the webs of the dome, and the windows seem clumsy. On the other hand, the original ornament of the building is superbly fine and delicate [184]. On the ground floor, the folded capitals are spun all over by tendrils

of sharp-toothed acanthus surrounding the monogram of Justinian and crosses – these latter chiselled off by the Turks. The Ionic impost capitals in the galleries are of similar elegance. The soffits of the architrave are coffered and decorated with rosettes, squares, and diamonds. Above, the fine triple architrave of the entablature is surmounted by a bead-and-reel motif, and this in turn followed by an egg-and-dart and tendril design, deeply undercut so that leaves and tendrils stand out sharply against the dark ground. The dedicatory inscription of Justinian and Theodora on the frieze is done in a bold, beautiful lettering, set in white against a greyish ground and topped by the deeply shadowing cornice [184]. The disturbing contrast between this elegant ornament and the subtle planning on the one hand, and the awkward proportions and the clumsy use of the building site on the other is hard to explain. Is it perhaps possible that an excellent plan was handed over to a master mason who was unable to adapt it skilfully to the site, and that, moreover, he was provided with beautiful capitals and entablatures ordered ready-made from the workshops of the Proconnesian quarries? Variants on the plan were indeed frequent in Justinian's Constantinople; witness St John in the Hebdomon, built shortly before 560 in place of an older church in the Hebdomon Palace, and St Michael in Anaplus. Both are known, from Procopius' description and from a few remains of the Hebdomon church demolished but recently, to have been double-shell domed octagons with seven half-cylindrical niches projecting into an enveloping ambulatory.[23]

The roots of the style which dominates the H. Sophia and H. Sergios and Bakchos have been sought far and wide: in the vaulting techniques of Mesopotamia and in the domed and groin-vaulted structures of Imperial Rome;[24] in the 'de-materialized' wall decoration of Parthian and Sassanian architecture; and in a fusion of all or any of these.[25] Their centralized plans have been traced back to Armenia,[26] or to Rome. The H. Sophia has been explained as a merger of the Basilica of Maxentius with the dome of the Pantheon.[27] Or, its plan has been linked to the tradition of Christian martyria of the fourth and fifth centuries.[28] Its handling of space has been thought to derive from Western-Roman or from Roman-hellenistic concepts of architecture or from principles first evolved in the Roman West, but which had 'long become part of the wider heritage of late classical architecture [and] had incorporated many other elements'.[29] And in opposition to all these attempts at finding origins, the architecture of the H. Sophia has been presented as a break with tradition, as the 'first medieval architectural system'.[30] It has been discussed in terms of its structural problems, its vaulting, abutting, and supports; in terms of its spatial design, its rhythm and decoration; in terms of its function – and depending on these different approaches, different hypotheses have been put forward regarding its origin.

Structure, function, and design are inseparable in the H. Sophia, as they are in any great architecture. But they need not have the same historical origin. The full brick masonry, either strengthened by horizontal stone chains – as at H. Sergios and Bakchos – or chains combined with heavy stone piers – as at the H. Sophia – had been customary since the second and third centuries in the Greek cities along the coasts of Asia Minor, from Aspendos to Miletus, Ephesus, and Pergamon. Also customary was the masonry of mortared rubble – open or faced with small stones, and interspersed with brick bands – of which, e.g., the city walls of Constantinople were built. All three methods of construction had gained a firm foothold in Constantinople and its vicinity by the end of the third and the beginning of the fourth century – a natural development, since Constantinople then became the centre of gravitation for the entire Aegean region. From the fourth to the end of the fifth century these techniques of construction were constantly employed in the buildings of the new capital, and by Justinian's time they were the approved practices known to the mason crews of Constantinople.[31]

Similarly, the vaulting techniques employed in the new churches of Justinian's early reign had been brought long before from the coastal cities of Asia

Minor to the metropolitan centres of the northern Aegean – Constantinople and Salonica. Groin- and barrel-vaults were constructed, not of concrete, but of a single layer of bricks, slightly pitched, laid across the axis of the vault, and embedded in very thick mortar [183]. The result was an extraordinarily

183. Constantinople, Yerebatan Cistern, fifth century. Vault

light vault. Whether or not the technique has Mesopotamian and Egyptian roots, it was at home in the third century in the Greek cities of Asia Minor. From there it penetrated into Salonica around 300, as witness the barrel-vaulted niches in the rotunda of Galerius, now the church of H. Georgios. By the early fifth century, it was employed in the towers of the city wall of Constantinople, and remained in use throughout the century and later. The domes and half-domes of the H. Sophia and the pumpkin dome of H. Sergios and Bakchos are in their construction but an outgrowth of this age-old practice: thin, light, and built of a single layer of bricks, pitched on their sides and embedded in thick mortar. But the transfer of this technique to domes and half-domes of wide span in Constantinople need not have occurred prior to the first years of Justinian's reign.

The architectural ornament of H. Sergios and Bakchos and the capitals and friezes of the H. Sophia certainly evolved in Constantinople, or

184. Constantinople, H. Sergios and Bakchos, completed prior to 536. Capitals and entablature

185. Constantinople, H. Sophia, 532–7. Composite capital

rather, in the marble workshops of the nearby Proconnesian islands. They are rooted in a tradition which, shortly after 400, had been imported into Constantinople from the same Aegean cities whence had come the techniques of masonry and vaulting. One recalls how closely the ornament of the propylaeum which between 404 and 415 was added to the first H. Sophia was still linked to third-century prototypes at Miletus and Ephesus.[32] But this ornament was further developed by the stonemasons of Constantinople. By 450 in the Studios church, the undercutting of leaves and tendrils had grown much deeper, the contrast of raised, white foliage and black ground much sharper, and the leaves spikier than ever [53, 54, 56]. Seventy years later the ornament has again changed. As among the capitals of H. Polyeuktos, the foliage on friezes and capitals at H. Sergios and Bakchos is worked completely à jour. More important, the classical proportions, still present in the Studios church, have been abandoned: in the relations of architrave, frieze, and cornice of the entablature, and in the ornamental motifs – rope, egg-and-dart, tendril and dentil friezes, and rows of brackets. Correspondingly, in the capitals, the traditional Corinthian, composite, or Ionic forms have given way to fold capitals, overspun by twigs with spiky leaves raised high from the black, undercut ground. Even where – as in the H. Sophia – the foliage and volutes of a composite capital remain recognizable in residual form, the leaves have been turned into a dense growth of thorny thistles. As at H. Polyeuktos, possibly under the impact of Sassanian art, the capital itself has been transformed from an organic growth into the geometric shape of a truncated cone, and its decoration continued without a break into that of the impost block, eliminating the difference between support and burden, capital and block [184, 185].[33]

The techniques of masonry and vaulting, and the architectural ornament of Constantinople, are, then, ultimately derived from the same source – the hellenistic cities of the Empire situated along the coasts of Asia Minor. But their development in Constan-

tinople differs. The masonry construction remains conservative. In vaulting, the technique of thin brick vaulting is applied, perhaps first by the architects of Justinian, to forms of vaulting previously built in hollow tubes, concrete, stone – pendentive domes, domes on pendentives, ribbed domes, pumpkin domes. The ornament, while gradually changing during the fifth century, is finally radically transformed in Justinian's early years.

It is but natural to suspect that plan and general design of Justinian's churches, as epitomized in the H. Sophia, were evolved by Anthemios, Isidorus, and their contemporaries along similar lines, i.e. by radically changing forms long accepted in Constantinopolitan church building. But church building in Constantinople prior to 525 knows no structure remotely comparable to those which now suddenly sprang up. Plan and design of H. Sergios and Bakchos and of the H. Sophia, and the concepts of space, boundaries, light, colour, and rhythm which they embody draw on a multiform tradition in which many threads are interwoven. Different though they are, they have been fused into perfection by the genius of the architects who designed the new structures of Justinian.

Stylistic concepts which by 525 had prevailed for a century or more in Constantinople no doubt play an essential part in this process of fusion. Architects in the northern Aegean coastlands, since the early fifth century, if not before, had been thinking of church buildings in terms of a space which spread sideways, subdivided rather than contained by curtain walls. They had been designing lavish interiors with marble revetted walls, deeply undercut friezes and capitals, and with column shafts of precious colourful marble. By the early sixth century, then, patrons, architects, and the educated public in Constantinople were accustomed to view architecture along lines which, in general terms, also describe a structure such as the H. Sophia. However, such background resemblance is but one constituent element, and all too vague at that. Similarly, the elements of construction, the masonry, and the vaulting practices of Constantinople were but one constituent factor in generating the new structures. The technique of building lighter vaults enabled the architects to think of bolder skeleton constructions, of fewer and thinner supports, and of wider vaulting spans. Like the general concepts of style prevailing, the methods of construction at the disposal of the architects are but part of the background. So are the demands of the liturgy which for centuries had exerted their impact on church planning in the eastern coastlands. As a result of these demands, the traditional basilica plan had been marked by new accents. The nave where Christ revealed Himself in the word and in the flesh, accompanied by the processions of the clergy, was turned into the central element of the design. The dome rose above it, chosen perhaps 'because in the ancient Near East it already had a clear and specific symbolic meaning . . . the canopy of Heaven'.[34] Aisles and esonarthex enveloped the nave on three sides and imparted to the whole design a centripetal note. This was reinforced by the superposition of two ancillary enveloping zones, aisles and galleries, both sheltering the worshippers. Strengthened and codified in the early sixth century, these liturgical demands and iconographic connotations were presumably an essential constituent element in creating the new designs of H. Polyeuktos and H. Sergios and Bakchos. Certainly they were best fulfilled by breaking with the tradition of the basilica and turning instead to a centrally-planned building composed of a freestanding baldacchino and an enveloping ambulatory, possibly two-storeyed, in short, double-shell designs.

By 525, double-shell designs had been employed in church architecture for nearly two hundred years, beginning with Constantine's Golden Octagon at Antioch. But octagonal double-shell designs, one recalls, remained rare. From the late fourth into the sixth century and sometimes beyond, the majority are tetraconchs, as they rise in all the provinces of the Christian Empire: at Milan in the late fourth century; at Peruštica (Peroushtitsa) in the Balkans in the early sixth century [86] and possibly earlier at Adrianople; in Syria, at Seleucia-Pieria (Samandağ)

[93], Apamea (Qalaat el Mudiq), Bosra (Bosra Eski Sham), and Aleppo, shortly before and after 500.[35] The list could easily be enlarged. Near Canosa in southern Italy, the remnants of a tetraconch structure of uncertain date await further exploration. Another one has been dug up near Ohrid in southern Yugoslavia; provided with atrium, narthex, baptistery and diaconicon, it would seem to have been a bishop's cathedral.[36] At R'safah, on the Euphrates frontier, stands the ruin of a quatrefoil, like its Syrian neighbours of early-sixth-century date [221]. As late as the seventh century the type survives in the church which the patriarch Narses III (641–61) built at Zvart'nots in Armenia, adjoining his palace [287].[37] The common features of plan and construction are easily listed: the inner core in tetraconch shape, supported at the corners by four L-shaped piers; the four huge lobes expanding from the core; the enveloping ambulatories and galleries. The covering of the central core remains in doubt, but timber construction seems to have been the rule, either a pyramidal roof or a wooden dome. Variants in plan are insignificant: at Bosra the walls of the ambulatory are circular inside and square outside, instead of repeating the inner tetraconch curve; at Zvart'nots the ambulatory wall, both inside and outside, is circular; at R'safah the eastern and western lobes are elongated, creating a longitudinal axis.

Given the background of stylistic concepts firmly established in the Aegean coastlands, architects and patrons in early-sixth-century Constantinople and throughout the great cities of the region would naturally be attracted by such double-shell designs. They must have been intrigued by the interlocking of spatial volumes, the fragmented views, the change of boundaries into mere screens, the expansion of the core into the lobes of the exedrae and into the envelope of aisles and galleries. Certainly it is not by chance that, in the decades prior to and during the first third of Justinian's reign, tetraconch churches became so frequent in the hellenized cities of Syria and in the Balkans, where Constantinople exerted its strongest influence. Still, compared to H. Sergios and Bakchos or to the H. Sophia, all tetraconch churches are simple in design. A closer look at their liturgical functions leads somewhat further.

It has long been taken for granted that tetraconch churches were without exception martyria.[38] Some probably were: the tetraconch at Seleucia-Pieria may have sheltered apostle relics; and the murals at Peruštica, though apparently a century later than the structure, represent martyrdom scenes. The liturgical functions of the tetraconch churches at Apamea, Adrianople, Aleppo, and Canosa, however, so far remain unknown. On the other hand, the tetraconch at Bosra was certainly the cathedral of the local bishop, as was the one near Ohrid. The one at R'safah has long been termed the martyrium of St Sergius, but recent findings suggest that it too was the cathedral of the city.[39] Likewise the tetraconch at Athens, if indeed it was built as a church (as now seems certain), was the *Megali Panaghia*, the Great Church of Our Lady, and thus the cathedral [73].[40] Still others were presumably both cathedrals and palace churches, beginning with the Antioch Octagon. Certainly the latest church of the group known to date, the one at Zvart'nots, was a reliquary shrine – a martyrium – and both cathedral and palatine chapel of the patriarch. The tetraconch cathedrals at Bosra and R'safah are both so closely linked to the adjoining episcopal palaces that they too must be considered not only cathedrals, but the bishops' palace chapels as well. This throws light also on Justinian's early church buildings. After all, the H. Sophia was both the cathedral of Constantinople and the church of the adjoining Great Palace, and its ceremonial was geared to the participation of the Emperor in the services. H. Sergios and Bakchos was built inside, and communicating with, the palace which Justinian inhabited when heir to the throne. It functioned as his palatine chapel, but at the same time it enclosed, like the H. Sophia, relics, and thus also carried the connotation of a martyrium. St John in the Hebdomon, too, rose inside an Imperial palace, this one outside the city. The interplay of functions parallels that found in many a contemporary tetraconch church.

The differences are, of course, obvious. Justinian's churches in Constantinople are not tetraconch structures. H. Sergios and Bakchos rises on an octagonal plan, and the H. Sophia is a variant on the octagon. However, it is likely that octagonal double-shell designs, as well, had their place in church architecture ever since Constantine's Golden Octagon at Antioch. Like the tetraconch, the octagon plan was used occasionally for martyria: about 350, Gregory of Nazianz (Nenezi) built in his native city a martyrium in memory of his father. An octagonal structure, it was enveloped by aisles and galleries like the church at Antioch. A similar structure, dedicated to the Baptist and possibly also a martyrium, rose at Alexandria in Egypt.[41] Neither survives, and nobody can tell whether or not niches billowed into the enveloping spaces of lower and upper ambulatory. On the other hand, there is a good likelihood that this was the case in Constantine's Octagon at Antioch, which was both the cathedral and the palace church and no doubt well known to Justinian and to his architects. Neither they nor the Emperor, in designing new churches closely linked to the palace at Constantinople, could disregard the model set by the great Constantine at Antioch.

True, the plan of the Golden Octagon – whether or not its niches billowed from the core – remains in doubt. Certainly the structure was timber-roofed, not brick-vaulted, as were Justinian's early churches. But then, one recalls, centrally-planned palace churches – since Constantine's day – were in all likelihood derived from centrally-planned audience halls. Such halls, it will also be recalled, were laid out as triconchs, rotundas, hexagons, octagons and decagons. They were frequently provided with niches, placed either in the thickness of the wall, or expanding from the core into adjoining spaces as in the Minerva Medica in Rome [186]. And they were always vaulted: with regular domes resting on the circular wall, as in the salutatorium at Spalato; with ribbed domes, as in the Minerva Medica; and presumably with pumpkin domes or with domes composed of straight and concave webs

186. Rome, Minerva Medica, c. 310, as in c. 1800. Exterior; etching by F. J. B. Kobell. *Munich, Graphische Sammlung*

in alternation, as they seem to have covered the Chrysotriklinos, the golden audience hall of the Great Palace at Constantinople. With its pumpkin dome and its niches opening into contiguous spaces, the Chrysotriklinos belongs to the same family as H. Sergios and Bakchos and, ultimately, the H. Sophia.[42]

The late date of the Chrysotriklinos, presumably forty-odd years after H. Sergios and Bakchos, does not necessarily mean that its plan was descended from that of Justinian's church. The Chrysotriklinos itself apparently was descended from H. Sergios and Bakchos, but it is one among many examples of vaulted palace halls with complex central plans of sophisticated design – and a late example at that. Nor is it by chance that the niched hexagon hall in the palace north of the Hippodrome at just that time

was transformed into the church of H. Euphemia by simply inserting the requisite liturgical fixtures: synthronos, altar, and chancel barriers, the latter provided with splendid inlaid columns [178]. Given the intertwining of Imperial and religious functions in the Sacred Palace, it seems but natural for Justinian's church builders to have drawn on this living source, palace halls, which continued to flow from the second and third to the sixth century, and even later. In doing so, they revitalized the type of the timber-roofed palace church, tetraconch or octaconch, which had come down from the fourth century practically unchanged and thus somewhat obsolescent.

None of this fully circumscribes the framework within which Justinian's early church buildings should be placed. The new stylistic concepts of expanding and interlocking spaces could be achieved to perfection only by applying techniques of construction never before used in such combination and on such a scale. Double-shell churches – whether tetraconchs or octagons – had with few exceptions been covered with timber constructions. Palace halls had been vaulted, but even in the fourth century in Rome they were vaulted in a concrete construction requiring heavy support from walls or piers, as witness the Minerva Medica [186]. We do not know at present whether fifth-century builders in Constantinople already employed the new techniques of brick vaulting for large spans, as they would be required by an audience hall or church of huge dimensions. In all likelihood this was done only by the architects of Anicia Juliana between 524 and 527 and of Justinian between 527 and 537. Through the use of thin brick shells they adapted to large-scale construction the complex shapes of vaults previously executed only in concrete and over comparatively small spans. The huge stone piers of the H. Sophia, combined with the thin brick curtains of the enclosing walls, allow for the interplay of a solid skeleton and diaphanous screens infinitely more efficient than that of Roman skeleton buildings constructed in their entirety of concrete masonry. The brick vaults are made so thin and light that they exert but a minimum of thrust. They can be shaped on the largest scale into complex forms which continue into the vaulting zone the contraction and expansion and the convex and concave space volumes enclosed by walls and colonnades of the building.

The change in the vaulting techniques throws into relief the relation of Justinian's architecture to the preceding tradition. It rarely breaks radically with the past. Only in its ornamentation does it approach such a break; but even there the principle is rather that of a thorough change in the mutual relationships of traditional forms. More frequently, Justinian's architects translate a form, long used and still much alive, into a different language. The complex vaults of traditional palace building are transposed into the technique of thin brick shells,

and are thus made more flexible and capable of covering wider spans. The design of centrally-planned audience halls is transposed from palace architecture into church building, and is thus adapted to the requirements of the sixth-century liturgy of Constantinople. Construction and design, ecclesiastical and Imperial ceremonial interlock. The traditional forms are a source to be tapped, placed into new contexts, adapted to new demands, transformed, and imbued with new life. Such revitalization of a living tradition is a basic trait of Justinian's architecture as it is of his policies.

Only one building outside Constantinople is close to Justinian's early court churches: S. Vitale in Ravenna.[43] When it was completed in 546–8, it was certainly considered as standing within the ambience of the Imperial court: the mosaics in the chancel – Justinian and Theodora offering gifts – speak for themselves. But no Imperial backing seems to have been forthcoming when construction started, still under Ostrogothic rule. Building was apparently financed by a wealthy local banker, Julianus, and commissioned by Bishop Ecclesius (521–32). However, construction started in earnest possibly only after 540, under Bishop Victor (538–45), whose monogram appears on the capitals of the ground floor. The mosaics in chancel and apse followed in 546–8, and were the only element of the building to be executed under Archbishop Maximian, who stands next to Justinian on the mosaics of the chancel walls.

S. Vitale has often been considered a sister building of H. Sergios and Bakchos. Indeed, the plan is close enough: the octagonal core, vaulted and resting on eight piers and arches; the enveloping superimposed zones of ambulatory and gallery; the seven niches, between the piers of the centre baldacchino, billowing into the enveloping ring; and on the eighth side, the square chancel, and the lower, projecting apse, which breaks through the zone of ambulatory and gallery [187, 189, 192]. Nor is there any doubt that column shafts and capitals were imported from the Proconnesian workshops. One wonders, however, whether the most up-to-date

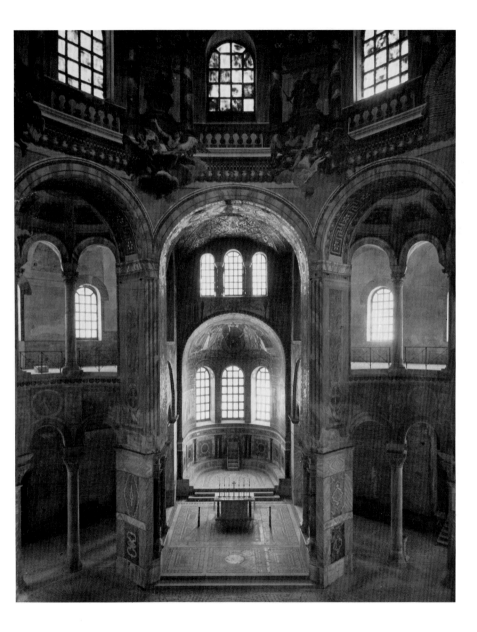

187. Ravenna, S. Vitale, completed 546–8. Interior, facing apse

models were provided for the capitals; composite capitals as used throughout the gallery, in Constantinople were long out of date; truncated cones with wicker-framed fleshy lotus palmettes hark back to H. Polyeuktos, 524–7; and only the dense spiky tendril designs on other truncated cone- or on fold capitals recall the decorative vocabulary of H. Sergios and Bakchos rather than of the H. Sophia. Also, if S. Vitale is a variant on the octagonal double-shell plan which also underlies H. Sergios and Bakchos, it is a very independent variant. It was obviously executed by local workmen and built largely with local materials. The bricks, to be sure,

188. Ravenna, S. Vitale, completed 546–8.
Masonry

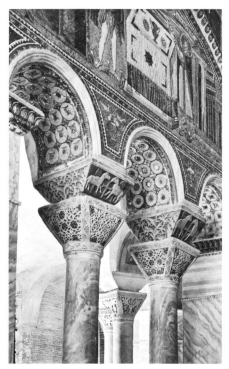

189. Ravenna, S. Vitale, completed 546–8.
Capitals in the chancel

are different from the high bricks previously used in Ravenna and in all of northern Italy. Thin and long, they imitate those of Constantinople, and were manufactured locally for all the construction financed by Julianus in Ravenna – S. Apollinare in Classe among others [188]. The vault over the centre baldacchino is built not of pitched bricks, but in the western techniques of hollow tubes inserted into each other.[44] A local western crew, then, was at work. But plan and elevation also differ from H. Sergios and Bakchos. Ambulatory and gallery zones were not vaulted – the present vaults date from the Middle Ages – and as a result greater emphasis is given to the core, the centre baldacchino, and the chancel – the parts of the building where the mosaic decoration, the richly veined marble revetment of

the piers, the most elaborate capitals, and the *opus sectile* of the pavement are concentrated [189–91]. The rhythmical alternation of rectangular and semi-circular niches which marks the plan of H. Sergios and Bakchos is abandoned. Instead, the sequence of semicircular niches produces a new unity of design. This impression of unity is furthered by the proportions of the building, which are much steeper than those of H. Sergios and Bakchos, by the placement of arcades in both the upper and lower zones of the niches, and by the slenderness of the surmounting arches. It is further stressed by the flood of light from rows of huge windows in the ambulatory, gallery, and the clerestory zone of the centre room which ties together all the parts of the building. As contrasted with the sister buildings of Constan-

190. Ravenna, S. Vitale, completed 546–8. Vault of chancel

191. Ravenna, S. Vitale, completed 546–8.
Reconstruction of original marble revetment

tinople, the design seems simplified. But this seeming simplification is counterbalanced both by greater clarity of articulation and greater complexity in the interlocking of volumes and spatial vistas. On the exterior, low circular chapels – each provided with a still lower rectangular absidiole and a higher rec-

tangular turret – flank the polygonal apse [192]. From the apse the eye ascends to the roofs of the gallery, of the chancel, and finally to the roof of the centre room: a graded arrangement of volumes not inferior even to the H. Sophia. Likewise in the interior, unification and complexity interlock. The marble revetment [191], restored on the basis of fragments surviving; the mosaic pavement, reconstructed in two triangular sections of the inner octagon; the mosaic on the walls of the forechoir, on its vault and on that of the apse – all pull the interior together. At the same time, the overlapping of vistas is superb. As the visitor passes through the wide square quadriporticus of the atrium and into the long shallow narthex, he is unaware of the anomalous position of the narthex. Standing off-axis, it touches only a corner of the outer wall of the structure. It communicates with the ambulatory through subordinate triangular spaces, the one to the left leading into the bay opposite the chancel, the other leading into the adjoining bay. Thus the vistas become immensely complex, and the visitor standing behind the convex screens of the niche arcades remains uncertain of his true position with regard to the chancel and altar – eager to clarify it by proceeding to the core of the structure.

The architect of S. Vitale was, I think, a Westerner. But he was intimately acquainted with the new architecture which was being created at that time at the court in Constantinople. He strove to translate into his own terms this new architecture of Justinian. Equal to Anthemios and Isidorus, or nearly their equal, he designed the one truly great building of the West in the sixth century.

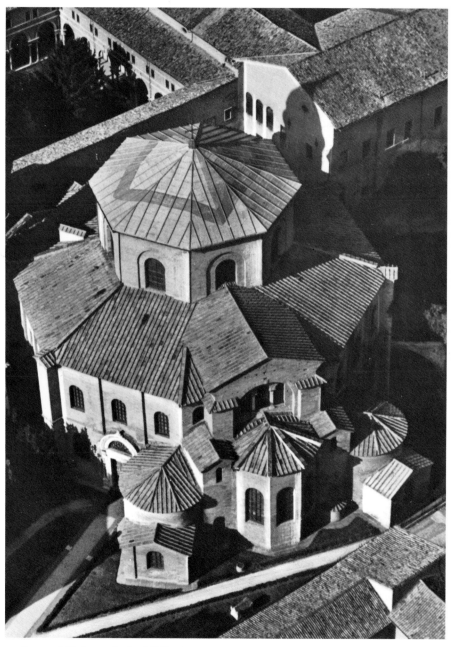

192. Ravenna, S. Vitale, completed 546–8. Exterior

CHAPTER 10

STANDARD BUILDING IN THE AGE OF JUSTINIAN

The bold construction and the sophisticated design of H. Polyeuktos, H. Sergios and Bakchos, and H. Sophia remained confined to Constantinople and to a few years – roughly 524–37. They found no real following and broke off as suddenly as they had started, as would any *tour de force*.[1] By the time the H. Sophia was completed, the style had given way to more sober, less daring, and – as its contemporaries no doubt felt – sounder concepts of construction and design. These concepts were not newly created by the master builders of the sixth century. They are rooted in a tradition which extends back into Roman times, and which had been absorbed into church building long before Justinian's architects had designed their bold and innovative structures. Indeed, one wonders whether H. Sergios and Bakchos and the H. Sophia should perhaps be viewed as a protest against an ever-broadening current of vaulted church buildings of standard design, sober and sound in plan and construction. In any event, it is not the imaginative architecture of Anthemios and Isidorus that dominates the future. On the contrary, it is the plainer, easily intelligible, and more commonplace concepts and the simpler techniques of construction which underlie the vast majority of sixth-century buildings – even in the capital and the core provinces of the Empire. Easily spread, this standard architecture decisively determines the further course of Byzantine architecture.

The master builders and architects who designed this architecture worked with a few basic elements. From the wealth of Late Roman vaulting – which had remained alive in palace, utilitarian, and funeral architecture – they selected the simple, fundamental types. They shunned such complex forms as pumpkin domes or domes with alternatingly flush and concave sides, and concentrated instead on barrel- and groin-vaults, known from time immemorial, and on pendentive domes (sail-vaults) and domes on pendentives as they had been in frequent use in the utilitarian and funeral architecture of the Aegean coastlands and the Syrian provinces. A thermae building at Gerasa (Jerash) and the 'East Mausoleum' at Side (Eski Antalya) – the former of second-, the latter of early-fourth-century date – are two examples among many.[2] Both in utilitarian buildings and in mausolea, such vaulting forms continued from the fourth into the sixth century and later. Gradually, however, in the course of the fourth and fifth centuries, the technique of construction changed from solid stonework or concrete to thin brick shells reminiscent of the vaults of the H. Sophia. Slender supports become sufficient; and long rows of columns, surmounted by capitals with or without impost blocks, can carry the endless numbers of small groin-vaults and pendentive domes in the cisterns of Constantinople. The Yerebatan Cistern [183] and the cistern near the Studios church, both fifth-century, and the sixth-century Cistern of the Thousand-and-One Columns, the Binbirdirek, are a few of the many examples of this type.[3] Likewise, pendentive domes or domes on pendentives constructed in thin shells of brick easily span large spaces, while resting at the corners on comparatively light supports. Piers hollowed out on the inside, dissolved into a cluster of supports, or, indeed, sheltering inner chambers, replace the now unnecessary solid piers.

All such elements of vaulting are geared to cover a square bay. The sides of the bay may be closed by walls, solid yet weaker than the corner supports; or they may be open, to continue the main bay in four directions by subsidiary spatial units, groin- or barrel-vaulted. The vaulted square bay is thus easily enlarged into a cross shape by four subordinate barrel-vaulted bays, all supported by corner piers.

This cross-shaped compound, as a rule surmounted by a pendentive dome or a dome on pendentives, becomes the basic unit of a standard architecture of the early Byzantine centuries: free-standing and, in that case, enclosed by walls; doubled and tripled; combined into a cruciform cluster; or fused into the plan of a basilica with galleries and transept. Whatever combination is chosen, however, the architects of the new standard buildings insist on sobriety of design, on simple plans, and on easily understandable relationships of the building parts. They shun the expansion of the core by billowing niches or by domes and half-domes flowing into one another. They abstain from double-shell designs and the ensuing interplay of spatial units. They strive towards a clear relation between the spatial units and their boundaries. Walls are solid, and where screens of columns are employed in the openings of a gallery or a huge window, they appear to be used as alien features rather than as integrated elements of an overall design. Mosaics and marble veneers are played down, and throughout the buildings shun the enticing ambiguity of statement and denial, wholeness and fragmentation, on which rests the design of the H. Sophia. When deeply undercut foliage ornament on capitals and friezes is absorbed into this standard architecture, as in Church B at Philippi [213], it stands in sharp contrast to the overall design of the building – a decoration ordered ready-made or done by workmen imported from the Imperial quarries.[4] When on the other hand it is locally made, though, more often than not the architectural ornament also takes on more sober forms.

Sound, but somewhat unimaginative, this standard architecture stands alongside the complex and imaginative buildings of Justinian's early years, and continues long after. Its beginnings, however, go farther back. On a small scale, the cross-shaped basic unit has its antecedents in Roman architecture. Cruciform mausolea, their corner piers either solid or hollowed, abound all over the Empire from the first and second to the end of the sixth century. Their centre bay is, as a rule, surmounted by a groin-vault. But in Syria and the eastern coastlands, from the fourth century on, not infrequently this groin-vault is replaced by a dome on pendentives or by a pendentive dome. The 'East Mausoleum' at Side, the mausoleum of H. Leonidas adjoining the Ilissos basilica at Athens, a mausoleum at Hass and another one at Ruwêha (Rueiha), both in Syria, are a few domed cross mausolea chosen at random.[5]

By the beginning of the fifth century, this basic element – the domed cross unit – had long penetrated, on a small scale, church architecture all over the Christian world. The mausoleum of Galla Placidia at Ravenna is but one example of many, as are the martyria attached to S. Simpliciano in Milan and to SS. Felice e Fortunato at Vicenza [138, 144, 145].[6] But regular churches of somewhat larger size – fully domed, with side chambers replacing the solid corner piers of earlier small martyrs' chapels – seem also to have existed prior to 500. The earliest surviving examples appear in the Aegean provinces: in Macedonia and on the coast of Asia Minor. Hence it is possible that these standard types originated in the provinces and were transferred to the capital only in the thirties of the sixth century, after the great churches of Justinian's early reign had been built – and failed. But it is equally possible that the early provincial examples which chance has preserved are but derivatives of prototypes in the capital, now lost.

The church of H. David at Salonica shows the cross type fully developed by the last third of the fifth century [193].[7] The centre bay was surmounted by a dome, of which the pendentives survive to the

193. Salonica, H. David, fifth century (last third). Isometric reconstruction

0   40 FT

0   15 M

present day. The cross wings are comparatively deep and, except for the east arm, accessible through doors. The entrance to the west is slightly recessed. The corner piers have been replaced by small rooms surmounted by pendentive domes, the two rooms to the east terminating in small apsidal niches. No

documents record the time of construction, but the splendid mosaics surviving in the apse and on its arch suggest a date shortly before 500. This date is likewise suggested by the few architectural details, such as the poor rubble masonry, with brick voussoirs used only over the double-arcaded window of

A

194. (A) Constantinople, Chalki gate, 532–6. Reconstruction
(B) Constantinople, Senate House, porch, after 532. Reconstruction

B

the apse, and by the one surviving capital over the column of the apse window. The type may well be older. Two churches in the Syrian uplands, one at Shaqra, the other the martyrium of St Elias at Izra (Zorah), both dating from the sixth century, present it in a provincialized version, dome and barrel-vaults replaced by timber roofs. Likewise the type appears in the Byzantine West, witness the church of the Saviour at Rometta near Messina, a structure of undetermined date.[8] But the plan is that of a domed cross enclosed in a square and resting on the walls of corner chambers. Given the poor construction and the location in the hinterland, these churches may well reflect domed cross buildings of earlier date in one of the great architectural centres. In any event, simple standard buildings of this basic type continue to be built throughout the sixth century. An example near the end of the century was apparently the cathedral of Edessa – a building known only from a poetic and somewhat vague description.[9]

The church of H. David is small. Its centre bay measures but 4·50 m. (15 ft), the entire structure

14·75 m. (49 ft) on each side. The size of the cathedral at Edessa (Urfa) is unknown. But by 530, the standard unit had become the basic element from which monumental architecture – both secular and ecclesiastical – was developed in the capital and all over the Empire. In Constantinople both the main entrance to the Imperial palace – the Chalki – and the porch of the near-by Senate House were evolved from the domed cross unit [194, A and B]. These structures have disappeared, but Procopius's descriptions are clear.[10] In the Chalki a pendentive dome rested on the arches of four barrel-vaults. To

195. Constantinople, Holy Apostles, c. 536–50, as in c. 1100–50. *Paris, Bibliothèque Nationale*

the east and west, these arches sprang from piers projecting inward; to the north and south, from the backs of lower, narrow barrel-vaults which linked the sides of the piers to the outer walls [194A]. In the porch of the Senate House, a dome on pendentives was carried right and left by deep barrel-vaults; in front and along the façade of the building proper, it seems to have rested only on arches [194B]. In contrast to the solid walls which enclosed the Chalki, barrel-vaults and arches in the porch of the Senate, which, like the Chalki, was rebuilt after 532, were supported on the exterior by huge columns.

In church building, as well, during Justinian's reign, the domed cross became the standard unit on a monumental scale. It lent itself to easy combinations of large size, and the number and variety of such combinations are surprising. Repeated five times and arranged in a Greek cross pattern, it formed the plan of Justinian's Church of the Holy Apostles. The church is known only through a skimpy description by Procopius, through the reflections it has left in the provinces – from Ephesus to Venice – and through representations in late manuscripts [195].[11] Still, both its building history and its pattern are clear. Laid out on the site of Constantine's Apostoleion, it was apparently begun about 536 and dedicated on 28 June 550, the eve of the feast day of the Princes of the Apostles. Fallen into disrepair, it was remodelled after 940, and before 1004, along lines slightly different from Justinian's. Damaged again about 1300 and hastily repaired, it survived until 1469. It then gave way to a mosque, the Fatih, erected in honour of Mehmed the Conqueror (el Fatih); and this first Fatih was in turn replaced by the present, larger mosque in the third quarter of the eighteenth century.

From its Constantinian predecessor Justinian's building took over the cruciform plan, the entrance arm possibly extending slightly farther than the other three. Five domes rested on solid piers in the corners of the cross and surmounted the arms and the centre crossing. Aisles and galleries enfolded each of the four arms on three sides, and opened towards the naves in two tiers of colonnades. A cross-shaped chancel rose below the centre dome, the only one to be lit by windows. The other domes were dark and apparently slightly lower, possibly simply pendentive domes.

In its plan, S. Marco in Venice more or less follows the pattern of Justinian's Apostoleion, but the design is reflected just as closely in his church of St John at Ephesus [196–8].[12] Prior to Theodora's death in 548 – both her monogram and Justinian's appear on the capitals – the Imperial couple had apparently decided to replace the fifth-century cross structure over the tomb of John the Evangelist by a new vaulted building. Completed by 565, its walls and piers survive to a height of 5 and 6 m. (16 and 20 ft). It was cross-shaped and, moreover, preceded by a narthex and an atrium. Its entrance arm was considerably longer than the other three. Hence, while the crossing, the transept arms, and the chancel were surmounted by one dome each, two domes of oval or slightly elliptical plan covered the bays of the nave. These domes rested on heavy piers built of beautiful blocks of ashlar. Arcades supported by columns inserted between the piers separated nave and aisles, the aisles being carried round the four arms of the building, and segregated from the nave by parapets. Galleries surmounted these lower arcades; smaller column shafts and capitals, found in the excavation, prove their existence. The wall of the nave rose above the galleries, presumably pierced by a series of grouped windows. Barrel-vaults covered aisles and galleries. Not all details of the reconstruction are necessarily correct, but the overall impression is of individual spatial units – aisles, galleries, nave, and the individual bays within the nave – clearly segregated from each other, much in contrast to the design of the H. Sophia. The plan is simple, plain, sober. The spatial units, rather than emanating from a centre in a fluid movement, stand by themselves. The bays, cut off from each other by the wide barrel-vaults and the strong projecting piers, seem to stand side by side. The domes rise vertically above the transverse spans of the arches further to stress this *staccato* movement. Nor did the nave, seen from aisles or

196 and 197. Ephesus, St John, completed by 565. Plan (*above*) and south wall of west bay during rebuilding in 1963 (*below*)

244 · PART FOUR: EARLY BYZANTINE BUILDING

galleries, force itself to be viewed as the essential element of the architectural design. The ornamentation shows a similar change. The Ionic capitals are not just provincialized and poor versions of greater prototypes; even where they are of higher quality, they have become simple and sober, with floral decoration limited to a few elements.[13] As in the design of the building itself, a somewhat unimaginative standard style prevails in every single detail.

The plan of the Holy Apostles and of St John at Ephesus was based on the concept of multiplying the standard element, using short barrel-vaults to expand the square, domed bay into a cross shape. But this solution remains rare. More decisive for the

198. Ephesus, St John, completed by 565.
Reconstructions of interior (*right*)
and exterior (*below*)

development of Byzantine architecture is the fusion of the standard element, the domed cross, with the transept or the chancel section of a basilican plan. In cross churches and cross-transept basilicas since Constantine's Apostoleion, a timber-roofed tower

had, as a rule, risen over the crossing, where normally chancel and altar were located. In the course of the fifth century, this timber-roofed tower was fused into the plan of an ordinary basilica with galleries. Placed over the bay preceding the chancel and the altar, it surmounted the area where the clergy entered into, and emerged from, the sanctuary carrying the elements of the Eucharist and spreading the Word of the Gospel.

This blend occurred as early as the late fifth century in a church at Meriamlik (Meryemlik) on the

tive reconstruction has been proposed for Meriamlik: the first bay covered by an ordinary timber roof, the second bay by a pyramidal timber construction.[16] The question still awaits a final solution. Certainly, however, basilicas with short naves and tower-like square bays preceding chancel

199. Meriamlik (Meryemlik), 'domed' basilica, 471–94. Plan

south coast of Asia Minor.[14] The date is known from contemporary reports, 471–94, and is confirmed by the style of the capitals. The building lies in ruins, but its plan is clear [199]. Preceded by a huge, semicircular forecourt and an outer narthex, the short nave was flanked by barrel-vaulted aisles and galleries. Piers, dividing the nave into two nearly square bays, interrupted the sequence of the short arcades, each of which was formed by only five arches on columns. A short forechoir surmounted by a shallow barrel-vault – hardly deeper than an arch – linked the nave to the semicircular apse. The aisles were also barrel-vaulted – traces of the vault were still visible in 1907[15] – and the general consensus used to be that the nave was likewise vaulted, the first bay being surmounted by a barrel-vault, the second bay in front of the chancel by a stone dome. Thus the church at Meriamlik would have been the first known example of a 'domed basilica'; fifty years later H. Polyeuktos in Constantinople would have been laid out on the same plan. Recently, an alterna-

and apse, all timber-roofed, are frequent in southwestern Asia Minor. The plan of the east church at Alahan Manastir (Alahan Klissi, Koja Kalessi) is the same as that of Meriamlik, and throughout the building was timber-roofed [200-2]: truss roofs over the aisles, galleries, the first bay of the nave, and the forechoir; a pyramidal roof over the tower-like final bay of the nave.[17] Rising at the eastern end of a long rock terrace, halfway up the steep cliff, the church is preceded farther west by a sculptured gate and two buildings, one the basilica, previously discussed, the other a baptistery, and all belonging to a monastery. The east church, which still stands to nearly its full height, may thus have been the main church of the monastery, a suggestion supported by its size – roughly 20 by 13·5 m. (65 by 45 ft) interior length and width – as well as its clear volumetric design, its excellent masonry, and the fine workmanship of its capitals. The date of its construction seems no longer in doubt. Inscriptions found on the terrace to the west of the main church suggest a

200–2. Alahan Manastir (Alahan Klissi, Koja Kalessi),
east church, late fifth(?) century.
Plan (*below*), interior of nave facing west (*right*),
and exterior from the south-east (*bottom*)

0
├──┼──┼──┼──┤ 40 FT
0
└──────────┘ 15 M

203. Qasr Ibn Wardan, church, c. 564. South flank

foundation in the late fifth century; none the less some of the ornament of the church would seem to anticipate a sixth-century date.[18] The ruin of a similar church rises a few miles away at Dağpazari.[19]

It is of course possible that such buildings simply transposed into timber construction a model which was entirely vaulted, with a barrel-vault over the first bay, and a dome over the second bay of the nave – in short a genuine 'domed basilica', to use the accepted term. Such a model may well have existed in Constantinople as early as the third quarter of the fifth century and thus prior to Meriamlik. In all likelihood it existed when, in 524–7, H. Polyeuktos was laid out in the capital. Indeed, it has been suggested that the plan for Meriamlik was designed in Constantinople. Certainly the style and quality of the decoration suggest the activity of a workshop imported from the capital. So far no genuine domed basilica has been found in Constantinople prior to the sixth century.

Nevertheless, it is plausible that it did exist and was carried from the capital into the farthest provinces.

The church of Qasr Ibn Wardan occupies the centre of a desert fortress in Eastern Syria together with a palace – this latter dated through an inscription of 564.[20] Rather short, the nave of the church is surmounted in the centre by a dome on squinches; aisles and galleries open on to the centre bay in triple arcades [203–6]. Short barrel-vaults, hardly more than broad arches, continue the domed bay east and west; wall arches carry it on either side. A semicircular apse – flanked by side chambers and embedded with them into the straight rear wall following Syrian custom – terminates the building. To the west, aisles and galleries are carried along and form an inner narthex and narthex gallery, both opening into the nave through a triple arcade. All this is compact in design, compressed into an area only 13 by 17 m. (43 by 56 ft).

At Qasr Ibn Wardan, then, the plan of the 'domed basilica' has been reduced and condensed – one might term it a 'compact domed basilica'. The nave, comparatively long at Meriamlik, has become a mere fragment. Recalling the H. Sophia, the domed bay has been turned into the focus of the entire design. The short arches east and west take the place of half-domes; aisles and galleries open on to the centre bay; even their continuation into a western narthex and gallery recalls the H. Sophia. Indeed, the decorative and the structural vocabulary of Qasr Ibn Wardan is permeated with elements imported from Constantinople. The slight pointing of the lateral arches supporting the dome is possibly native; certainly it becomes characteristic of later Syrian building. The undercut, thistle-like foliage of the capitals in the gallery stood blinding white against the deep shadows of the ground.[21] The design recalls the capitals of the H. Sophia and of H. Sergios and Bakchos, but the execution is that customary throughout Syria since Qal'at Si'man [205]. On the other hand, exactly as in the H. Sophia, the windows high up in the centre bay have been turned into fragments cropped across by the lateral arches below the dome. The masonry – rather than being composed of huge blocks of stone as are all other Syrian churches – consists of alternating broad bands of ashlar blocks and bricks, three and eleven per band respectively. The technique is typical of Constantinople from the fifth century, as is the brickwork, with its very high mortar-beds and long, thin bricks laid in very regular courses [207]. The bricks themselves are of the type used in Justinian's buildings in the capital. Among the very rare bricks in all Syria, they were presumably made on site but following Constantinopolitan models and in moulds imported

204. Qasr Ibn Wardan, palace, c. 564. Interior of apse

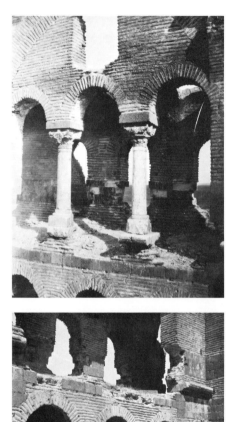

standard buildings of Justinian's age. The spatial shapes, rather than expanding, are confined. They do not interpenetrate, but stand side by side. The walls, solid, are strongly stressed as elements of design; the steep proportions support this impression. It is a standard type which appears elsewhere as well: with slightly lengthened east and west arms, for example, in the church which was inserted into the (abandoned) church of St Mary at Ephesus of *c.* 400(?) [59].[22] Indeed, a 'domed basilica' just prior to Justinian is represented in Constantinople by the recently excavated church of H. Polyeuktos. Another from the very first years of

205–7. Qasr Ibn Wardan, church, *c.* 564. North gallery, as in *c.* 1900 (*left*), ground-floor level (*below, left*), and masonry (*below*)

from the capital. It looks as if a plan sent from the Imperial metropolis had been executed, although with some variants, by a crew which mingled local builders and workmen from Byzantium.

Though it recalls in certain details the H. Sophia, the plan of Qasr Ibn Wardan falls in with the

Justinian survives in large parts in the H. Irene in Constantinople,[23] south of the H. Sophia. Begun in 532, perhaps on the site of the first cathedral of the capital (it had burned down without trace in the Nika Riot), the new church was thoroughly remodelled after an earthquake in 740; thus it survives, minor changes notwithstanding [208–10]. Of Justinian's church the ground floor remains in its essential parts, and based on it, the church is being envisaged

church complex are in pure brick construction: a double-storeyed narthex, vaulted on both levels; and an atrium, enveloped by four porticoes, those on the

208. Constantinople, H. Irene, begun 532. Exterior from the south-west

as a 'domed basilica' with galleries: the nave composed of two major bays, the first subdivided into two unequal barrel-vaulted halves, the second square and domed; a barrel-vaulted forechoir; and an apse closed on the outside in three sides of a polygon; vaulted aisles, ending in side chambers; and both surmounted in the first building as they are today by vaulted galleries. While all this is built in huge limestone blocks, the western portions of the

ground floor barrel-vaulted. Despite the difference in material, nave, narthex, and atrium are now being assigned to one building phase, that of 532. The first H. Irene then would have been a regular 'domed basilica' much like the churches at Meriamlik and Alahan Manastir, except for its being vaulted throughout. Admittedly, evidence for envisaging the upper level of the domed bay, the key element of the plan, is scarce. It may have had triple arcades

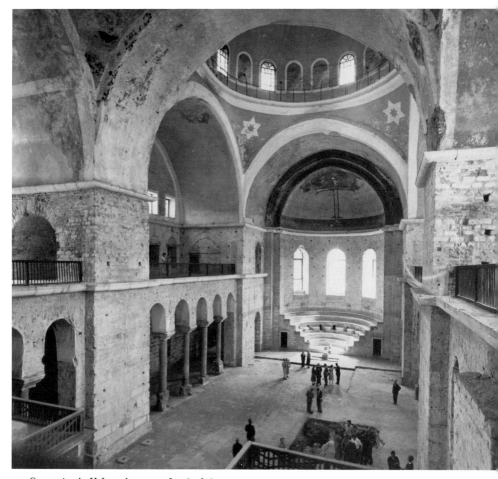

209. Constantinople, H. Irene, begun 532. Interior facing east

opening into the galleries, surmounted by a 'fragmented window' in the clerestory wall and lateral
arches to carry the dome. But the reconstruction is
by no means proven.

In the present H. Irene, as remodelled after 740,
the main dome rather than on lateral arches rests on
deep transverse barrel-vaults, extending to the outer
walls and thus oversailing the galleries. The component elements of a 'domed basilica' – domed bay,

barrel-vaulted nave and chancel, vaulted aisles and
galleries – have been re-assembled into a new
design. Churches, much like that, did indeed exist in
the sixth century in the sphere of influence of
Constantinople. During the last third of the sixth
century at Pirdop, not far from Sofia in Bulgaria, an
ordinary timber-roofed basilica of fifth-century
date, the Stag's Basilica, was thoroughly remodelled. Two strong piers were inserted into each of its

210. Constantinople, H. Irene, begun 532. Exterior from the south-east

colonnades to support the east and west arches of a dome over the east half of the nave. North and south of the dome, transverse barrel-vaults were extended to the outer walls, presumably oversailing the galleries placed over the aisles; the eastern end was rebuilt as a triple sanctuary and upper chambers were superimposed over the side chambers flanking the apse; obviously also, after the remodelling, the aisles and the western half of the nave must have been barrel-vaulted.[24] Everything suggests Justinian's Constantinople as the source of the plan.

The number and variety of such combinations in Justinian's architecture is ever surprising. I mention one more, known only from the detailed description of a contemporary, Choricius: the church of St Sergius at Gaza, built prior to 536. A short nave, barrel-vaulted and enveloped on three sides by aisles and an esonarthex, led to the domed bay;

squinches resting on four pierced corner piers carried the dome; a forechoir and apse extended to the east, short barrel-vaulted arms to the north and south. Galleries were lacking. Thus the plan might have been that of a simple Greek cross, as at H. David in Salonica; with the difference that the domed centre bay and the cross arms were separated by colonnaded arcades forming sheer screens. Surmounted by the huge barrel-vault high up, they produced an effect, one would suppose, much like the trabeated gallery colonnade in the cross arms of the second H. Irene. But it is equally possible that the core of the structure was expanded into cross shape; enveloped by aisles and esonarthex on three sides, it would have anticipated the plan of a cross-domed church.[25] Nor must the decoration of St Sergius be forgotten: the dome and the upper walls of the centre bay carried mosaics which represented in eighteen scenes the life of Christ from the Annunciation to the Resurrection – the first such monumental cycle known, though not preserved.

In the 'domed basilicas' so far discussed the component elements are fairly simple: on the one hand, the basilica with galleries but without transept, on the other, the domed cross unit. The fusion becomes more intriguing where the domed cross is blended into a basilica with deep transept wings.

The architect who shortly before 540 built Church B at Philippi in Macedonia based himself on the plan typical of local timber-roofed basilicas: atrium and esonarthex; nave and aisles surmounted by galleries; a transept enclosing a huge chancel; and finally, an apse [84, 211].[26] He superimposed on this plan a system composed of standard vaulting elements; barrel-vaults over the aisles and galleries, a ribbed pendentive dome over the crossing, transverse barrel-vaults over the transept wings, a huge groin-vault over the single bay of the nave [212]. No doubt, the plan as transformed by the vaults is based on the standard idea of a dome over the centre bay – that is, the crossing – extended by the barrel-vaults over the transept wings. But to this plan the architect applied concepts of construction and design which seem to refer much more closely to the H. Sophia and H. Sergios and Bakchos than to ordinary standard buildings. As in Constantinople, the piers are built of heavy marble blocks; the filling walls are of solid brick masonry or of mortared rubble with brick bands, and, wherever possible, these walls were dissolved into rows of colonnaded arcades or into huge colonnaded windows. The decoration, as well, was obviously intended to compete with that of the great churches of Justinian's early years. Marble sheathing covered the walls. The capitals, all over-

211. Philippi, Basilica B, shortly before 540. Plan

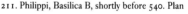

0   60 FT

0   20 M

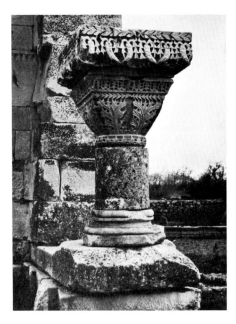

212 and 213. Philippi, Basilica B, shortly before 540.
Interior facing west (*above*),
and base, capital, and impost block (*left*)

spun by deeply undercut, thorny acanthus leaves
[213], were possibly done by the same workers who
had carved those of the H. Sophia slightly earlier.
Nowhere among surviving buildings has a standard
plan been more thoroughly transposed into the
language of Justinian's early churches – churches
which are, after all, the very opposite of a standard
architecture.

The plans of the church at Philippi and that of
Justinian's Apostle Church at Constantinople have
been blended, it seems, in two churches on the
Greek islands, one fully preserved and recently
restored, the other an imposing ruin. In the
Katapoliani (Hekatontapyliani) on Paros (Our Lady
of the Hundred Gates),[27] four barrel-vaulted arms
radiate from a domed centre bay. However, nave and

chancel are considerably longer than the transept wings; and barrel-vaulted aisles, galleries, and esonarthex enfold the nave and cross arms on three sides. The cross plan of Holy Apostles has been fused with that of a basilica. A date for Paros not much after 550 is suggested: by the colonnaded arcades of the lower tier and their Ionic impost capitals; by the finely profiled archivolts, the short piers, the impost blocks, and the trabeation of the upper tier; and by the simple, forceful decoration of the parapets as well as by the marble revetment above the arcades, and the carefully bonded marble masonry. The ruin of H. Titos at Gortyna on Crete varies the plan further.[28] Only the nave is enveloped by aisles and galleries [214]. The cross arms, barrel-vaulted like the nave, each terminate in an apse. The chancel is a triconch which communicates with flanking pastophories, each enlarged by an ante-room and apse. The complex chancel plan points to a late date, whether the very end of the sixth or, indeed, the tenth century.

the cathedral of Sofia, the basilican element decidedly predominates over the barrel-vaulted cross and its dome. Indeed, the dome has been perfectly integrated into the plan of a basilica with nave, aisles, transept, and chancel bay [215, 216]. The triple-storeyed narthex was flanked by tall towers pushed sideways. Flat groin-vaults covered nave, transept wings, and chancel; barrel-vaults covered the aisles. Only the galleries (if indeed they existed) were perhaps timber-roofed. A dome, hidden inside a higher octagonal drum, rose over the crossing, which was segregated between nave, transept wings, and chancel. The nave piers were enlarged by double responds facing nave and aisles; transept and chancel walls were articulated by blind arches. Minor changes excepted, the original structure is perfectly preserved in its major elements; but its date remains in doubt. No documentary evidence exists and the surprisingly 'Romanesque' plan and details have led to datings as late as the eleventh century. However, the building technique – brick

0   40 FT
0   15 M

214. Gortyna, H. Titos,
late sixth century. Isometric view

At Philippi, on Paros, and at Gortyna, the large-scale domed cross unit has incorporated, as it were, the basilican plan. Conversely, towards the end of the sixth century at the outer edge of the Empire, in

with broad mortar bands – points to the ambience of the architecture in the Balkan provinces of Justinian's last years, and if not to the sixth, then not after the early seventh century. The dedication to

215 and 216. Sofia Cathedral,
sixth-seventh centuries(?). Exterior and plan

Holy Wisdom, H. Sophia, establishes a link with
Constantinople. Finally, the gradual loss of the
Balkans to pagan Slavs and Bulgars from the mid
seventh century establishes a *terminus ante quem* for
the cathedral of Sofia.[29]

Such fusions of the barrel-vaulted domed cross
unit on a large scale with the plan of a transept
basilica or of a cross church are far more attractive
and intriguing than ordinary domed basilicas, such
as the churches at Qasr Ibn Wardan or the H. Irene
of 532. But within a history of Byzantine architecture they appear to be freaks, and it is the ordinary
domed basilica which exerts a decisive impact on the
future course of building in the Byzantine Empire
and its satellite countries.

A wealth of church types created by combining
standard elements in a variety of permutations is one
of the principal characteristics of Justinian's age,
taking the term broadly. So far it does not seem
possible to state what, if anything, determines the
choice of specific types for individual buildings. No
geographical pattern emerges, nor can any chronological sequence be traced. Neither does the function of the building clearly determine the choice of
the plan. On the other hand, both the variety and the
spread of the standard types clarify the position of
Anthemios's creation. The H. Sophia, to be sure, in
spatial design, in the concept of wall, in the handling
of light, and in every detail is fundamentally different from the mass of standard building. It might
well be interpreted as a protest by its 'non-pro-
fessional' architects against a tide rising under the
hands of professional builders. If this be true,
however, it is a protest which employs the very
structural elements – though not the stylistic
principles – which had been evolved by the standard
builders. Exception that the H. Sophia is, its origins
become intelligible and its design possible only
against the background of the standard buildings.
Conversely, the plan of the H. Sophia exerts its
impact occasionally on the later phases of this
standard architecture. Different as they are, the two
currents of Justinian's architecture interlock.

CHAPTER 11

THE ARCHITECTURE OF THE AGE OF JUSTINIAN

IN THE PROVINCES

The security of the Empire under Justinian and his successors entailed a vast building programme lasting until the turn of the century. Strong-points or small fortified towns were laid out or older ones modernized along the frontiers of old provinces in the East and reconquered provinces in the West, from the borders of Syria into North Africa, Dalmatia, the lower Danube valley, Liguria, and Spain. Interior fortifications were built to protect caravan routes against unruly mountain and desert tribes. Procopius presents an impressive picture of the building programme by listing hundreds of such frontier posts from the Balkans and the Caucasus to

the Euphrates and the Lybian desert. Chains of strong-points formed a new kind of *limes* along the vulnerable borders.[1]

Dozens of these frontier posts have survived. Square or rectangular as a rule, they could be as small as 40 m. (130 ft) and as large as 300 m. (1,000 ft) square, such as the citadel of Tebessa; but as a rule, they were rarely larger than 60 by 80 m. (200 by 260 ft). Their exterior walls were from 1 to 3 m. (3 to 10 ft) thick and up to 8 m. (25 ft) high. The corners and the single main gate were protected by projecting towers, square or occasionally round. (Where nature afforded protection, a wall across the neck of

217. Qasr Ibn Wardan, palace, *c.* 564. Exterior from the south

a hill or a tower on top of a steep rock might suffice.)[2] Barracks leant against the inner wall. Somewhere within the enclosure there would be a church, often dedicated to the Virgin, the 'guardian of the safety of the cities and of the true faith'.[3] The defence of Throne and Altar coincided, and against the barbarians – both pagans and heretics – the church and its relics afforded as much protection as walls and gates. The remnants of Qasr Ibn Wardan in the Syrian desert are not typical, but most impressive. On a hillock, enlarged by terraces, rose three buildings: a block of barracks, fortified and provided with store rooms; the church, discussed previously; and the governor's palace [217]. Its four wings formed a square, 50 by 50 m. (165 by 165 ft). The narrow north wing contained the entrance gate, the west wing perhaps the private apartments and offices. The south wing, higher than the rest, was apparently the State Apartment. Surviving to nearly its full height, its centre part shelters a triconch room on either floor; the one on the upper level was presum-

ably the audience hall, where the governor sat enthroned as the Emperor's representative [204]. The date 564, inscribed on the palace, no doubt applies to the entire complex.[4]

But such juxtaposition of a fortified barracks with an unprotected church and palace is anomalous. The norm is a fortified enclosure surrounding church, barracks, and other structures. On Mount Garizim (Gerizim), in the unruly territory of the Samaritans, Justinian surrounded Zeno's church of the Virgin with a wall and towers.[5] On Mt Sinai (Gebel Mûsa), he built a huge fortress – enclosing church, conventual buildings, and barracks – to protect Palestine against the desert nomads. It was apparently dedicated to the Virgin.[6] The fortified walls, extraordinarily thick, are fully preserved, including the only entrance, a small postern gate facing west [218]. The conventual buildings as they stand today are of late date. But in their majority they occupy the site of the original structures lining the inside of the walls, both living quarters and common

218. Mount Sinai (Gebel Mûsa), monastery, founded *c.* 540. Air view

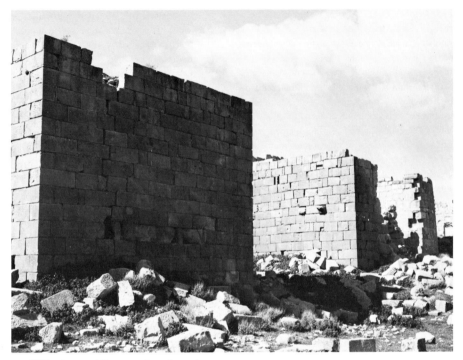

219. Haïdra, fortress, sixth century. From the north

rooms for the monastic congregation and barracks for the protecting garrison. Fortress and monastery were joined in a symbiosis strange only to us. Similarly, places such as Avdot (Ab'de) in the Negev were simultaneously monasteries, fortified garrisons, watering places, and caravanserais, whether securing a lonely strategic point or placed protectively on the outskirts of town. Fortified garrisons and small towns were the rule along the frontiers of the Empire. Haïdra [219] and Timgad in North Africa, Caričin Grad in the Balkans, R'safah and Dara on the Euphrates are impressive examples.[7]

Such fortified posts and garrisoned sanctuaries of the fifth and the sixth centuries apparently provided the model for major monasteries even where no military protection was needed. At Daphni in Greece, an area 97 m. (320 ft) square was enclosed within a huge wall strengthened on the outside by projecting towers; against the inside of the wall were built conventual buildings, cells, and larger rooms – whether dormitories, a refectory, or stables. The church would have stood in the open area much as does the present eleventh-century church. At Tebessa in North Africa, as early as the early fifth century, the church was similarly enclosed by a fortified wall with projecting towers [156].[8] True, since the beginnings of monastic building, whether in Egypt or in northern or southern Syria, it had been customary to enclose the conventual area by a wall. But only from the sixth century was this enclosure fortified and the interior layout regularized and centred on the church. A number of decrees issued by Justinian enjoined strict rules on the monastic congregations regarding their common life and insisted on the building of common dormitories and refectories.[9] In some cases such decrees may have but codified existing custom. But the monasteries built after these regulations laid down a plan which became standard throughout the Empire, and as late as the fifteenth century remained in force at Mistra and on Mount Athos.

At times fortified sanctuaries would be set up as pilgrimage centres on a lavish scale. At R'safah, outside the walls of a small second-century fort, two impressive churches had been built between 480 and 520. Basilica A probably housed relics of St Sergius and was linked to a large ecclesiastical establishment, monastery, or pilgrims' hostel.[10] Under Justinian's building programme, the entire area was enclosed by a huge fortified wall nearly 12 m. (40 ft) high, equipped with square, wedge-shaped, and round towers, and forming a trapezoid roughly 540 by 380 m. (590 by 415 yds) [220]. Two colonnaded streets crossed the interior, baths were erected, 'houses and stores and the other structures which are wont to be the adornments of a city'. A third church was laid out as an elongated tetraconch, built of huge stone blocks in the beautiful technique

customary locally [221–3]. Windows and walls were marked by sparing classical profiles. Nave and ambulatory billowed outward in conchs on three sides, those of the nave opening towards the ambulatory through colonnaded arcades. All these parts were apparently timber-roofed. The fourth side, on the other hand, was occupied by a vaulted chancel, and this is still preserved to its full height. An apse, slightly raised above nave level, encloses a synthronon and a bishop's chair. It is flanked on either side by two-storeyed side chambers. The one to the north shelters, on the ground floor, a baptismal font. Both baptistery and cathedra make it likely that this tetraconch church was the cathedral, not a martyrium, as former opinion had it, and an inscription giving a bishop's name suggests a building date prior to 553. A fourth building, outside the city wall, has turned out to be not a church at all, but the audience hall of a local chieftain, the Ghassanid Al-Mundir, who in the third quarter of the sixth century defended the frontier in the Emperor's name [301]. Piers and arches divide the square

220. R'safah, sixth century. Air view of town

221. R'safah, tetraconch,
before 553. Plan

interior into nine bays: a large centre bay, presumably supporting a timber pyramid; four rectangular
bays on the main axes, barrel-vaulted in stone
blocks; and four small corner squares, covered with
pendentive domes. An apse opposite the entrance
probably served as throne niche, and the flanking
side chambers illustrate the interplay of church
building and 'ruler's architecture' in the late sixth
century. Of the four gates of the city, the one facing
the pacified parts of the Empire to the north was
decorated with engaged columns and blind arcades,
all richly ornamented. At the same time, Caričin
Grad (Justiniana Prima) was laid out as the small
fortified capital of a frontier province in the Balkans.
A small fortress on the mountain top shelters the
cathedral, the baptistery, and apparently the
bishop's palace [224]. Spread out on the slope below
was the open town with a colonnaded main street, a
circular piazza, more churches, and 'lodgings for
magistrates, great stoas, fine market places, fountains, streets, baths, and shops' – an elegant mini-
capital far in the backwoods.[11]

Fortifications were laid out and built by the army,
perhaps with local help. Army crews, as a rule, also
built the structures inside the enclosure: barracks,
conventual buildings, and church. An exception may

be Qasr Ibn Wardan, where the plan of the church,
unique in Syria, was perhaps sent from Constantinople. In general, however, both materials and
workmen in such frontier posts were drawn from the
army, and non-military buildings in the provincial
backwaters remained bound to the local tradition.
Churches along the Balkan and Carinthian *limes*
took up the plan used locally since the early fifth
century: an aisleless nave with apse and side chambers, two of the side chambers projecting sideways
or parallel to the nave.[12] Similarly, in the Syrian
desert, the standard church plan of the area was
used unchanged by Justinian's military engineers: a
colonnaded basilica, its apse flanked by side chambers. The 'cathedral' at El-Anderin diverged little,
either in plan or design, from Qalb Lozeh, despite a
time lag of eighty years [225]; the bricks used to face
the apse vault recall those at Qasr Ibn Wardan.
Again, churches in the Negev followed the local
tradition of enclosing the three apses in a solid mass
of masonry, lightened by hidden chambers. This
type is remarkably well preserved in three churches
at Sbeïta (Shivta), two at Avdot (Ab'de), and two at
Mamshit (Kurnub) [226].[13]

The strength of the local tradition was not limited
to such outposts in frontier territory. Even in the

222 and 223. R'safah, tetraconch, before 553. View from the east (*above*)
and interior facing east (*below*)

metropolitan centres of the old provinces, throughout Justinian's reign and after, ecclesiastical and domestic building often developed along lines which had been laid down in the fifth century or earlier. City residences and country houses, in Antioch and its suburbs, laid out in the fifth and sixth centuries follow the old hellenistic and Roman tradition of the eastern provinces in plan and

224. Caričin Grad, sixth century. Air view, as in *c.* 1960

225. El-Anderin Cathedral, sixth century. Apse facing north-east, as in *c.* 1900

226. Sbeïta (Shivta), church, sixth century(?). Apses

decoration, including the use of splendid mosaic floors. Likewise, in the Syrian uplands, sixth-century houses and villas are indistinguishable from their earlier predecessors.[14]

However, not all provincial building under Justinian remains purely local. True, neither the court architecture of the capital nor the structural types spread beyond the Aegean region, except S. Vitale. To complete the Nea in Jerusalem Justinian sent an architect from Constantinople; a basilica with galleries, atrium, and propylaion, lavishly built and praised, it was pre-Justinian both in foundation and plan, the latter based either on the Golgotha basilica or on the H. Sophia as rebuilt in 404–15. The church, too, which it seems between 560 and 603–4 replaced Constantine's at Bethlehem, may or may not have drawn on a model in the capital [227].[15] Plan and proportions of atrium and nave

able. Constantine's octagon over the grotto of the Nativity, however, was replaced by a trefoil transept and chancel. Composed of the strongly marked centre bay, the three arms of transept and chancel, the three attached apses, and the fragmentary aisles in the corners, it provides an intricate spacious design of a type apparently alien in Palestine. Superficially, to be sure, the sixth-century transept at Bethlehem resembles the triconch endings of fifth-century churches in Egypt or the one at Cimitile-Nola; or else it recalls sixth-century churches in Epirus, where apses project from the ends of tripartite and continuous transepts.[16] A closer scrutiny reveals the essential differences. In Egypt, the triconch is but a trefoil apse attached to the forechoir; in Epirus the apses were small, low, and far apart – exerting little impact on the spatial design. On the other hand, at Bethlehem, transept, chancel,

227. Bethlehem, Church of the Nativity, between 560 and 603–4. Plan

0   40 FT
0   15 M

were taken over from the fourth-century church with only minor changes. The capitals, in fact, seem to have been so faithfully copied from their Constantinian predecessors as to be hardly distinguish-

and apses are fused into a unified trefoil. It is as if a cross transept of the type of the Menas basilica had been merged with the three apses of a triconch. Possibly following a similar design, the chancel part of the great church of the Virgin in the Blachernai in Constantinople was apparently remodelled into a trefoil transept under Justin II (564–76).[17] Whether or not the trefoil transept at Bethlehem drew on the remodelled Blachernai church, it is certain that the design was executed by local workmen in a technique traditional to the highlands of the Near East. The heavy blocks of hewn stone, the hook-shaped joggled voussoirs, and the simplified classical cornices are unmistakable characteristics of this tradition.

However, building in the provinces under Justinian and his successors rarely shows the full impact of the contemporary architecture of the capital, either in plan, building technique, or decoration. The wholesale export, if it ever occurred, of a metropolitan masons' crew with their building techniques and possibly their material, remains a rare phenomenon. Only the precious marble decoration and furnishings were in many cases provided wholesale from the Imperial quarries in the Proconnesos. A sunken ship has been raised off the coast of Sicily, loaded with columns, bases, capitals, ambo, and chancel screens of Proconnesian marble, apparently the entire furnishings of a church to be delivered ready-made to some place in the North African, Sicilian, or Italian possessions of Justinian's Empire.[18] Similarly at Latrūn in Cyrenaica, two churches, both built after 550, were provided with column shafts and chancel screens of Proconnesian marble and with capitals of the same marble and of Constantinopolitan, if somewhat old-fashioned, design.[19] The materials issued to provincial clients were apparently not the most modern; perhaps they were even remainders. However, as a rule, metropolitan models – if they reached the provinces at all – were executed by local workmen in materials locally available and concomitantly altered in design. The numerous capitals from the ruins at Caričin Grad were obviously drawn from metropolitan models, brought inland either from Constantinople or from Salonica, perhaps in the pattern book of a migrant journeyman.[20] As in the metropolitan prototypes, the blocks of Ionic impost block capitals are covered with foliage, while a

228 and 229. Caričin Grad Cathedral
and Baptistery, sixth century. Ionic capital (*top*)
and composite capital (*above*)

protomai capital shows two rows of acanthus leaves, an abacus, and four rams' heads [228, 229]. But the relation of the elements has been completely and almost perversely changed: the Ionic volutes rise in a sharp angle and invade the impost block; the rams' heads have attached themselves to the abacus instead of to the capital proper; the execution is miserably crude; and the models themselves are obviously types long obsolescent in the leading architectural centres by the second third of the sixth century, when Caričin Grad was built.

Similarly, provincial architects would frequently absorb building types long obsolete in the metropolitan centres of Justinian's Empire. Basilicas with galleries, for example, standard in the Aegean coastlands in the fifth century, went out of fashion in Constantinople and the near-by provinces by 530, but apparently continued in the Balkan provinces. In the ruin of the Old Metropolis at Nessebâr (Mesem-

date, such as the Studios church. In the Latin West, basilicas with galleries, rare before, spread with the westward movement of Justinian's conquering armies. In North Africa, where the type had been well established by the end of the fourth century, as witness the great church at Tebessa, it is revived in

230. Nessebâr (Mesembria), Old Metropolis, sixth and tenth centuries(?). Interior facing east

bria), on the Black Sea coast of Bulgaria, clumsy stone and brick piers carry the five low arcades between nave and aisles [230]. An upper tier of arches and piers, built of brick but otherwise similar, feigns a gallery. However, the aisles rise high, uninterrupted by a gallery floor, and the upper tier serves only to support the continuous roof of the nave and the high aisles. As it stands, though, it may well have been rebuilt in the tenth century on the old plan, though without the original galleries.[21] Certainly, the shortness of the nave and the lack of a clerestory suggest a Constantinopolitan model of fifth-century

the sixth century along new lines, small, compact, and steep; the fortress church at Haïdra is one example [231], a church at Latrūn in Cyrenaica another. A radical innovation in that province, the plan of Latrūn may well have been sent from Constantinople together with the decoration, column shafts, and furnishings of Proconnesian marble. In some cases, galleries were possibly added in the sixth century to older churches, such as Orléansville and S. Salsa at Tipasa.[22] Contemporaneously, basilicas with galleries penetrated into Rome, as witness the east church (now the

231. Haïdra, fortress church, apse, sixth century

chancel part) of S. Lorenzo fuori le mura, erected between 579 and 590, and S. Agnese, 625–38 [232, 233].[23] Both were designed to meet a special situation. In order to alleviate the crowding of the faithful around the tomb of the saint down in the dark catacomb corridors, the hill housing the catacomb was scooped out, and the basilica was sunk into the hill. The galleries were thus level with the crest of the hill, and could hold the overflow of the faithful or make it easy for the aged and lazy to attend Mass and offer prayers from the upper storey. The ground floor, enveloped on three sides by aisles, displayed

the tomb in its centre and could be reached by the clergy and the faithful – at S. Lorenzo from the side, at S. Agnese by a descending flight of stairs built into the hill.

In all likelihood these galleried basilicas reached Rome not direct from Constantinople, but from the provinces where the type was still alive. Indeed, architectural stimulus frequently came to the border provinces, the vassal states, and the newly conquered Western provinces of the Empire from provinces in the East rather than from the capital. Theodoric's mausoleum, built at Ravenna before or

232 (*opposite*). Rome, S. Lorenzo, 579–90. Interior facing east

233 (*below*). Rome, S. Agnese, 625–38. Exterior

around the time of his death in 526, shows the complexity of the situation.[24] Sombre and impressive, it is built of huge blocks of ashlar [234]. Inside, a cross-shaped vaulted chamber on the ground floor is surmounted by a circular room with a flat dome hewn from a single enormous block. Outside, the

234. Ravenna, Mausoleum of Theodoric, c. 526

lower storey is articulated by ten deep arches resting on strong half-piers. A gallery of short transverse barrel-vaults seems to have enveloped the upper storey, carried by a ring of colonnettes and alternating semicircular and trapezoidal 'arches'. The massive dome, its edge set by twelve pierced spurs, rises above a low, windowless drum. The entire structure recalls double-storeyed imperial mausolea such as the fourth-century tomb of Romulus on the Via Appia. Theodoric, intent on being both chieftain of his Ostrogoths and ruler of Rome, may well have wanted to ally himself with these traditions. But in the Latin West, the tradition of stone building had died out with Diocletian's palace at Spalato. It had remained alive, however, in the Eastern interior, and the joggling of the voussoirs – so evident on Theodoric's tomb – while customary among Roman builders, had survived in the sixth century only in the East. Hence an Eastern crew may well have been entrusted with the construction of the mausoleum because of their familiarity with building in stone. S. Michele in Africisco still in 547 transfers to Ravenna the wide-arched Syrian basilica on piers, type Qalb Lozeh, albeit in brick. Moreover, double-storeyed tombs, although surmounted by pyramids rather than circular upper storeys, were common in Syria and Asia Minor as late as the sixth century, with their lower storeys cross-shaped and vaulted much as in Theodoric's mausoleum.[25] The flat dome, on the other hand, with its pierced, projecting spurs (the holes may have served to lift the block in place), recalls, *ante litteram*, as it were, the Hagia Sophia. Only its manufacture from a single stone block may be a residue of the tradition of the stone-covered tomb mounds of Germanic chieftains.

Such fusion of elements widely different in origin is characteristic for provincial architecture in Justinian's Empire. Elements drawn in fragments from Constantinople or some other leading centre, and by that time often obsolete in their native habitat, merge with features purloined from some far-away province and with other elements rooted in a local tradition – and among these latter borrowings, a revival of Roman building types, both pagan

and Christian, is not infrequent. In Central Lycia, inland from the south coast of Asia Minor, a basilica at Alakilise (Alaja Jaila), of sixth-century date, was provided with a double-storeyed narthex, presumably galleries and an apse of Constantinopolitan type; but the spiky floral ornament recalls Syrian prototypes. At Karabel, not far away, ornament, similar, though perhaps later, covers the cornices of a triconch sanctuary, a plan locally widespread.[26] The interplay from many different sources becomes very clear in another province, southern Yugoslavia, where at Caričin Grad as many as eight church buildings have come to light (including a martyrium or baptistery), all of sixth-century date.[27] All differ in plan, but the majority seem to go back to prototypes of earlier date, drawn from Constantinople or Salonica and merged with local elements [224]. As in fifth-century Constantinople and Greece, all are preceded by atria, enclosed by porticoes, and sometimes entered through a propylaeum. The apses are of Constantinopolitan type, the exterior pushing out in three sides of a polygon. All are executed in the brick technique customary in Salonica and in the southern Balkans in the late fifth and the sixth centuries [235]. In major churches, mosaic pavements cover the floor, as in Greece. But

235. Caričin Grad, croft church, sixth century. Masonry

the wealth of building types in this provincial town is amazing. Along with models from Constantinople and Salonica, far-away buildings of early date exert their impact as well. 'Pastophories' (or transept wings) jut sideways from the aisles in the south basilica at Caričin Grad, much as in Constantine's Lateran Basilica in Rome; the *basilica orientalis* at Salona might have transmitted the type to the builders of Caričin Grad. The cathedral of Caričin Grad, inside the fortress, seems at first glance a basilica with atrium, colonnaded aisles, and galleries – the type customary in Constantinople and northern Greece [236A]. The chancel, however, is deep

and flanked by side chambers which terminate in absidioles. All this recalls the Thecla basilica at Meriamlik on the Cilician coast in the late fourth century and S. Apollinare in Classe outside Ravenna, a near contemporary of the cathedral at Caričin Grad.[28] Another small church at Caričin Grad was vaulted and cross-shaped, and thus recalls Cappadocian church building [236B]. With far greater likelihood, however, it goes back to Roman mausolea of similar plan, as they were frequent all over the Roman Empire. So does presumably a fourth church building at Caričin Grad, a barrel-vaulted triconch cemetery chapel. For other build-

A

B

0 ____ 40 FT
0 ____ 15 M

N

236. (A) Caričin Grad,
cathedral and baptistery, sixth century. Plan
(B) Caričin Grad,
cross church, sixth century. Plan

ings at Caričin Grad, parallels elsewhere are hard to find. One is a twin chapel with two apses. In the north-east church, the supports are solid walls which carried the three barrel-vaults of nave and aisles; the 'croft' church, a columnar basilica, rests along its entire length on a vaulted crypt. Finally at Konjuh near Caričin Grad a sixth-century round

church has been traced: nave and ambulatory supported by four piers framing pairs of columns, the
chancel flanked by chambers, it looks like a crude
version of an elegant central-plan structure such as
the hexagon church at Amphipolis[29] under excavation. It remains open how such plans were transmitted. But within the narrower confines of a single
province plans were apparently handed from workshop to workshop. Indeed, it has been demonstrated
that the triconch plan of the cemetery chapel outside
Caričin Grad recurs with exactly the same measurements in Byzantine feet – though of slightly varying
length – in two other funerary churches near by: at
Kuršumlija and at Klisura. Further, systems of
proportions were likewise transmitted, based on the
root of two and three, and their variants.[30]

However, fragmentary rather than wholesale borrowing was the typical way for architectural elements
to reach the provinces from the great architectural
centres of Justinian's Empire. In Rome, S. Giovanni
a Porta Latina, with forechoir, flanking side rooms,
and three-sided apse recalls the chancels of
churches in Constantinople and along the shores of
Asia Minor.[31] Provincial basilicas, from Asia Minor
to the Balkans and from Tripolitania and Tunisia to
Sicily, were frequently vaulted in the sixth century,
either wholly or in part. But while vaulting in the
deforested uplands of Asia Minor, at Binbirkilise for
instance, was a necessity forced upon poor village
masons, it was elsewhere apparently a matter of
preference. A basilica at Belovo in Bulgaria carried
barrel-vaults over both nave and aisles; and the
solid, if squat, piers, the arches of arcades and
windows, and the brick-faced concrete construction
testify to the highly developed building techniques
of Justinian's time. In a church at Tolmeita
(Ptolemaïs) in Cyrenaica, a similar plan is executed
in the local masonry technique of ashlar, nave and
aisles barrel-vaulted and a pendentive dome covering the side chamber which flanks the apse on the
left [237].[32] More frequently in a group of churches
in Tripolitania and Tunisia, vaulting was limited to
the aisles, while the nave carried a timber roof. The
inner row of a succession of paired columns sup-

237. Tolmeita (Ptolemaïs), church,
sixth century. Diagonal view from the south-west

ported the clerestory wall; the outer row, together
with a series of piers projecting from the aisle walls,
carried a barrel-vault or a series of groin-vaults over
the aisle. Such vaulting, exceptional in the West,
obviously depends on the vaulted architecture of
Justinian at Constantinople. Certainly the poor village architecture of the Cappadocian and Lycaonian
highlands was not the source for the architects of the
powerful basilica at Belovo and of the elegant
churches of Cyrenaica, Tripolitania, and Tunisia. In
the same corner of North Africa, apses were
occasionally covered by scalloped half-domes,
reminiscent of the dome of H. Sergios and Bakchos
at Constantinople. Apse walls in Algeria and Tunisia
are at times hollowed out by a series of niches, as in
the churches of the Nile Valley. The church, known
as Dar El Kous, at Le Kef carries all the characteristics of the group: paired columns, groin-vaulted
aisles, scalloped apse vault [238]. Singly, the
features occur time and again in Tunisia: a scalloped
apse vault in the citadel church with galleries at
Haïdra; groin-vaulted aisles either on piers as at

238. Le Kef,
Dar El Kous, facing apse, sixth century

Henchir Rhiria (near Beja), or, more frequently, on paired columns, for instance in the Dermesh (Douimēs) Basilica at Carthage, and the Candidus church, in its last, sixth-century phase, at Haïdra. At times, domes were inserted into older basilicas, as possibly at Damous El Karita. Once, in Tripolitania, at Lepcis Magna, a fully vaulted cross church seems to have been laid out, the arms and crossing rising high over the aisles.[33] As a rule, though, such foreign elements are grafted on to buildings which are essentially of traditional local design. Such bastardized types spread from North Africa across the Mediterranean. In Syracuse and surrounding territory, a few small basilicas with barrel-vaulted aisles have survived much like their North African cousins, though less elegant.[34] Scalloped half-domes appear as far north as Grenoble in France.[35] The use of side chambers to frame the apse is another case in point. The arrangement had long been traditional in North African churches and there is no need to derive it from Syrian prototypes. Only with the Byzantine conquest do the doors open

both towards aisles and apse – the arrangement followed in contemporary Syrian churches.

Vaulting and chancel plans, however, are but forlorn fragments of the high-class architecture of Justinian grafted on to provincial buildings. Of greater significance for Early Byzantine provincial church design is the fusion of a plain local plan and an often poor construction with a splendid decoration either directly imported from, or closely linked to, the mosaic and sculpture workshops of Constantinople. The church of the Virgin on Mount Sinai (Gebel Mûsa) presents an example. Remarkably preserved, its nave still carries the original beams, carved in relief and bearing the dedicatory inscriptions of Justinian, Theodora, and the governor. The mosaic of the Transfiguration in the apse, untouched since Justinian's day, is the superb creation of a workshop brought either from Gaza or some other major centre. But the capitals are of poor local workmanship, the columns squat and crude. The plan remains bound to local tradition except for the towers, which project beyond the narthex on either side, and the placement of the martyrium – the Burning Bush – under the open sky behind the apse.[36]

Apparently the distinction between imported and local materials in the Sinai church followed the lines laid down in Constantine's letter on the Golgotha buildings.[37] In fact, the same contrast between local construction and imported decoration marks the churches built or completed in Ravenna and Istria after the Byzantine reconquest. There, a provincial Byzantine architecture of true grandeur comes into being with a building such as S. Apollinare in Classe, the harbour town of Ravenna, where the high quality of both local and foreign workmanship achieves a superb blend.[38] S. Apollinare was founded between 532 and 536 with the backing of the financier Julianus Argentarius while Ravenna was still under Gothic rule. In 549 the church was consecrated by Maximian, the first archbishop of Ravenna following the Byzantine reconquest. The insertion of a crypt in the ninth century and the concomitant raising of the apse level high above the nave floor have slightly altered the original plan [239]. The marble revetment of the walls in the aisles, except for small traces, and the sixth-century mosaic floor have been removed. Yet, unimpaired by these losses and by extensive repairs of the clerestory in the eighth century, S. Apollinare in Classe has preserved all the beauty of its original spatial design: the spacious proportions of nave and aisles; the luminous interior

239. Classe, S. Apollinare, 532/6–49. Interior facing east

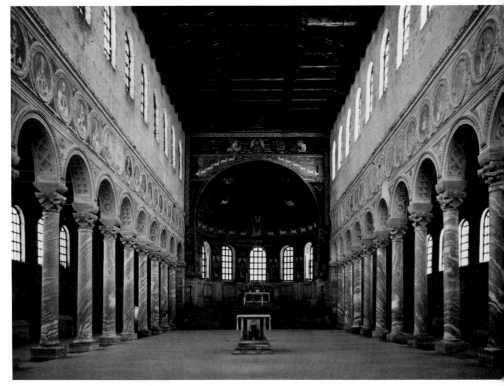

flooded with light from fifty-three wide windows in nave and aisles, not counting the five in the apse; the arcades of thirteen bays; the twenty-four column shafts, possibly of Hymettus marble, and certainly imported; the sparing, yet forceful decoration on the pedestals of the columns; the capitals with wind-blown leaves and their impost blocks; finally the decoration in the apse – marble veneer in the bottom zone and mosaics between the windows, on the piers, and in the half-dome, in part seventh-century and later. The plan continues the building traditions of Ravenna, permeated as it had long been by elements of Aegean origin. In fact, as early as 430 S. Giovanni Evangelista had shown a number of the elements which characterize S. Apollinare in Classe: the narthex and its two low towers projecting side-

ways; the seven-sided outer polygon of the apse; the projecting side chambers; and the blind arches which frame the windows of nave and aisles on the exterior – ultimately a Milanese feature [240].[39] Only the absidioles of the side chambers at S. Apollinare in Classe recall an Eastern prototype, such as the Thecla basilica at Meriamlik. On the other hand, the decoration of S. Apollinare, directly or indirectly, came from Constantinople: marble veneers, pedestals, and capitals were furnished by the Imperial workshops in the Proconnesos.

The picture of this architecture of Justinian's circle along the northern shore of the Adriatic is exemplified by a large number of churches. The cathedral of Poreč (Parenzo), built about 550 [241, 242], has preserved not only the complete layout of a

240. Classe, S. Apollinare, 532/6–49. Exterior from the west

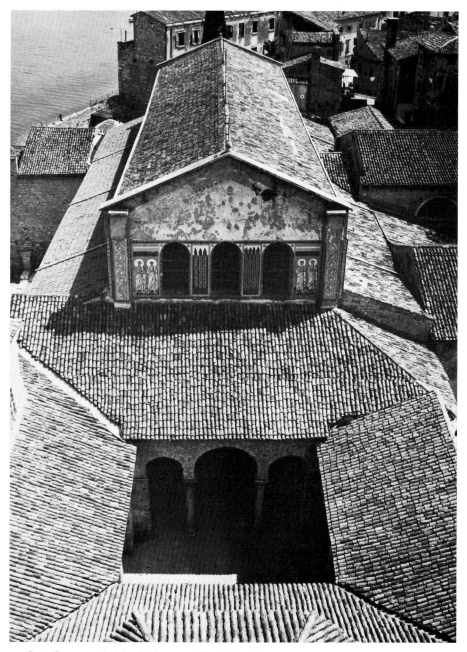

241. Poreč (Parenzo), cathedral and atrium, c. 550. Exterior from the west

242. Poreč (Parenzo), cathedral,
baptistery, and salutatorium, c. 550. Plan

major bishop's church, including a tiny atrium, a
baptistery opposite the cathedral, a triconch martyr's
chapel attached to the north aisle, and the lavish
two-storeyed episcopal audience hall north of the
atrium, the salutatorium; it has also preserved the
Proconnesian marble shafts of the columns in the
nave, the stucco decoration of the soffits in the north
arcade, the columns of the altar canopy, the chancel
plaques of Proconnesian marble, the mosaics
between the windows and in the vault of the apse,
and even an incrustation of marble and mother-of-
pearl below the windows [243]. The capitals –
composite, pyramidal or in two zones with protomai
– were probably imported from Constantinople. But
in the church itself, they were arbitrarily distributed,
apparently by local workmen. The masonry of small
stones is crude, and the proportions lack the easy
flow of the church at Classe. At the same time, a
profusion of precious materials is spattered all over
the building, even on the outside, where the gables

of the façade and above the apse is covered with a
glittering mosaic.[40]

Negligence of construction combined with elegance of decoration can be seen to an even greater
degree in the cathedral at Grado, built between 571
and 579 to replace a fifth-century structure. But as it
rises in the tiny town, the largest of three sizeable
churches, it remains an impressive example of sixth-
century 'Adrio-Byzantine' provincial building
[244].[41]

These Adriatic cathedrals show the fragmentary
use of Eastern architectural elements in Western
churches of the sixth century far more clearly than S.
Apollinare in Classe. At Poreč, the aisles terminated
in absidioles as at Qal'at Si'man, about 480, and at
Gerasa in 526/7 and 540. The triconch martyrium,
adjoining the cathedral of Poreč, recalls that of
Basilica B at R'safah (490–520). Of the cathedral of
S. Maria Formosa at Pula (Pola), built by Archbishop Maximian, a cross-shaped martyrium has

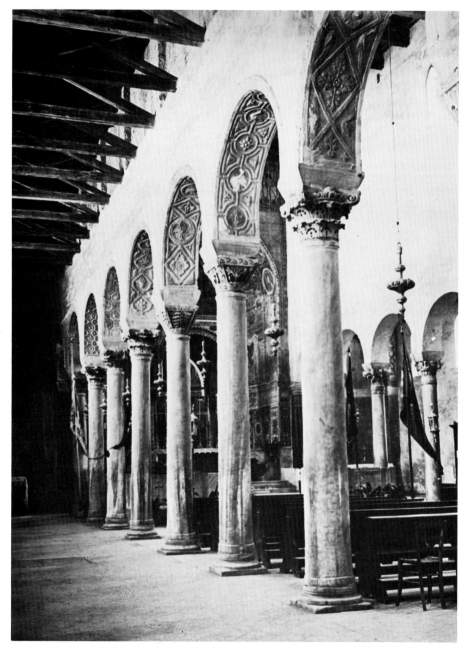

243. Poreč (Parenzo) Cathedral, c. 550. Interior of north aisle facing east

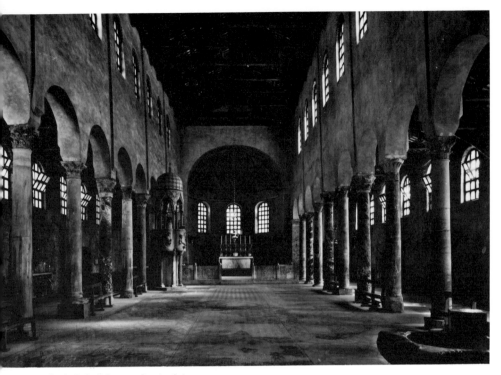

244. Grado Cathedral, 571–9. Interior facing east

survived, one of two originally flanking the main building, but these martyria recall the pair of domed pastophories with niches of *c.* 500 which project at R'safah from the ends of the aisles in both Basilica A and B.[42] At S. Maria delle Grazie at Grado the exterior of the apse is enclosed within a straight wall, as was customary from the fifth century on the Aegean islands and along the south coast of Asia Minor. On the other hand, the profiled band which, towards 490, at S. Apollinare Nuovo cuts across the buttresses and curves over the aisle windows, points to links between Ravenna and contemporary Syria; so do plan and elevation of S. Michele in Africisco and possibly the stone technique of the Mausoleum of Theodoric.

During the second half of the fifth, during the sixth, and perhaps still in the seventh century, Ravenna and Istria were two of the gates through which Eastern elements penetrated into the early medieval architecture of Western Europe.

PART FIVE

CHURCH BUILDING AFTER JUSTINIAN

CHAPTER 12

INTRODUCTION

Justinian's Empire survived barely fifty years after his death.[1] Starting in 568, Italy, except for Ravenna, Rome, and the far south, fell to the Longobards. The Holy Land, Syria, northern Mesopotamia, and large parts of Asia Minor were overrun by the Persians in 614. Reconquered by Heraclius between 622 and 630, these same lands, except for Asia Minor, were lost for good to Islam in 636–8. By 700, the Muslims also held the entire North African coast, including Egypt, which had fallen in 646. In 678, Constantinople itself was besieged by an Arab fleet and saved only by a naval victory won by Constantine IV. The Slavs made inroads in the Balkans and as early as 577–82 ravaged places as far south as Corinth. In 680 the Bulgarians crossed the Danube and established a powerful kingdom throughout the northern Balkans. The far-flung Byzantine Empire, by the second half of the seventh century, had thus been reduced to its Greek-speaking core, focused on Constantinople and the Aegean Sea, and including Asia Minor, the Southern Balkans, Greece, the city of Rome, and a few naval stations along the Adriatic coasts. By 750, even large parts of Greece, though not her coastal settlements, were occupied by Slavic tribes, to be reconquered only in the ninth century. In the East, the vassal states of Armenia formed a temporary buffer against the Islamic onslaught. But naval incursions continued: Cyprus was forced into a state of uneasy neutrality; Crete was lost; Rhodes and the coastal cities of Asia Minor remained threatened throughout the ninth century. For two hundred and fifty years, then, Byzantium was forced on to a precarious defensive.

Nor was the domestic situation in less of an upheaval, marked as it was by the decline and disappearance of the cities and concomitantly of trade and industry. Urban life had been flourishing all over the Empire from Augustan times through nearly the whole sixth century. Few cities to be sure – Constantinople, Alexandria, Antioch, Salonica in the East – were *Grossstädte*, sprawling and housing up to half a million. Most were smallish towns sheltering but a few thousand. But they were urban in administration, mentality, and economy, closely though the latter was linked to the rural surroundings in the majority of cases. The emperors in the early part of the sixth century had pursued in fact a policy of founding new towns in the border provinces – Caričin Grad, Dara – or rebuilding and strengthening those devastated by hostile incursions or natural catastrophes, for instance Antioch, twice shattered by earthquakes. By the early seventh century all this had changed. The Slavic invasions starting around 580 laid waste the towns of the Balkans and Greece: Stobi, Caričin Grad, Philippi, Nikopolis, Nea-Anchialos were and remained abandoned and forgotten until excavated in our time; Corinth, Thebes, Patras, Athens, shrank to settlements close to their defensible acropolis or port. The inhabitants fled to the country, and this ruralization coincided with the peaceful spread of the invaders during the seventh century, as witness the many Slavic toponyms of Greek villages.

However, de-urbanization and ruralization were equally predominant in the core provinces of the Empire. Excepting Constantinople and, though on a much reduced scale, Salonica, population figures, trade, banking, and industry dwindled, and so did the towns, through the seventh and well into the eighth century. The affluent withdrew to their estates; craftsmen and small traders likewise fled to become tenant farmers. Sardis and Miletus shrank to nothingness, and what inhabitants remained at Ephesus withdrew to the dockside or to the fortified hill of Aya Soluk around the church of St John; Ankara and Nicaea contracted to village size, lost within the wide ring of their ancient walls, agricultural in economy, character, and outlook. The countryside was apparently better off. To be sure, taxation was heavy, and military drafts a strain. Repeated attempts at maintaining a class of freeholder farmers failed and the majority of peasants were tenant farmers and serfs. Most of the lands were in the hands of the government, of aristocratic families, and of large monasteries. Nonetheless, the peasant class eked out a living, and the owners, frequently absentee landlords resident in Constantinople or some other town, drew an income, at times large, from their holdings.

Within this framework, strained by wars and a declining economy, theological controversies created new stresses. Ever sharpening through the seventh century, they culminated by the third decade of the eighth in the Iconoclastic Movement.[2] Except for an interlude from 786 to 813, the dispute rent the Empire asunder for more than a hundred and thirty years. Nonetheless, by the mid eighth century, the economy was apparently back on the upswing. Trade and industry revived and building activity, Iconoclasm notwithstanding, was lively. From the start of the eighth into the early ninth century, impressive churches rose again in Nicaea, Ankara, Salonica, as well as in the country serving monasteries such as Dere Ağzı. In Constantinople, where the evidence for church-building is nil, the emperor-tinker Theophilos added much-admired structures to the palace. Church design to be sure changed under the impact of Iconoclasm. Figurative murals and mosaics gave way to plain huge crosses; and church plans were altered. The growing emphasis on the Great Mystery, where in the Mass the invisible and undepictable God reveals himself, assigned the predominant role to the officiating clergy, and the space given over to their action becomes the very focus and *raison d'être* of the entire building. Hence it is only natural that from that standard element of sixth-century church-building, the domed bay with short, barrel-vaulted arms, would spring the church plan of the iconoclastic century – the cross-domed church.

CHAPTER 13

THE CROSS-DOMED CHURCH

Any attempt at clarifying Byzantine church building between 600 and 850 invariably brings to mind the architectural types and concepts of the age of Justinian. At present, however, it is next to impossible to trace a development either from one church type to another, or between types within a single group. Not more than a dozen churches in all have either survived inside the Empire from the 250 years after Justinian or are known satisfactorily from older publications. None are dated through documents or inscriptions, and only two can be given a *terminus ante quem* through such evidence. Worse luck, they are scattered all over the area of the Empire. Thus, the masonry technique, an excellent guide for dating in *one* locale, must be used with a good deal of discrimination. At the same time, the wide spread of the various types from Macedonia to the southern coast of Asia Minor and to the Euphrates presents another problem – that of determining the priority of the capital or the provinces in originating the cross-domed plan. Rather than attempting rash answers to such questions, it seems preferable for the time being simply to present the material.

Among churches of the centuries after Justinian the ruin of Dere Ağzı, tucked away in the south-west corner of Asia Minor, comes close to Justinian's own architecture.[1] But while Dere Ağzı apparently dates from the early ninth century, it is no mere provincial throwback [245–8]. Indeed, its plan recalls one of the great churches of Constantinople built in Justinian's time and remodelled after 741: the H. Irene. As at the H. Irene, the aisles are surmounted by galleries, both groin-vaulted; the nave of Dere Ağzı is divided into three, rather than two bays, the first short and barrel-vaulted, the second square and originally surmounted by a pumpkin dome, the third

repeating the first. From the domed bay, too, barrel-vaults extend sideways and oversail the gallery, its centre section protected by a trabeated colonnade. This core is preceded by an esonarthex, again as at the H. Irene, and extended eastward by a chancel. Side chambers flank the chancel on both the ground and gallery level. In contrast to the H. Irene, thus, the chancel appears remarkably long – composed as it seems of two bays preceding the apse and slightly diminishing in width. The esonarthex communicates with the nave not through arcades, as in the Constantinopolitan church, but only through a door. Thus at Dere Ağzı the domed centre bay truly forms the focus of the entire plan. In this respect the church recalls, rather than the H. Irene, 'compact domed basilicas' such as Qasr Ibn Wardan. Yet it shares, both with these churches and with Justinian's architecture in general, a feeling for elegant proportions and light, airy design. And this lightness and elegance comes to the fore even more strongly in the two octagonal buildings, possibly martyrs' chapels, which project from either flank. Throughout, the parallels for the plan of Dere Ağzı are found in late-sixth-century architecture and all point to Constantinople as an ultimate source. But none seem to date that early: a church near Vize closely related in plan to Dere Ağzı, though far distant, in Turkish Thrace, has been tentatively dated prior to 902–3.[2] Indeed, also at Dere Ağzı, details such as the pumpkin domes point to a date as late as the ninth century. Hence, a possibly early plan seems to have survived for centuries.

The continued vitality of sixth-century architectural concepts becomes manifest in the modifications imposed by builders of the centuries after Justinian on standard plans of Justinian's own age. The H. Irene itself displays such a variant. In about

245 and 246. Dere Ağzī, church,
early ninth century(?). Plan (above)
and west end from the south-west (below)

247 and 248. Dere Ağzı, church, early ninth century(?). Chancel, north side (*above, left*), and pendentive (*above, right*)

740, when the vaulting structure was thoroughly remodelled, the first bay of the nave, untouched since its building in 532 was replaced by a domed bay [208–10]. A low drum was built to hide this dome; the dome over the second bay was rebuilt and raised at the same time. The barrel-vault and the true galleries marking the original plan in this bay were remodelled so as to become nearly identical with the second bay of the nave as designed in 532: barrel-vaulted arms expanded sideways to the outer walls, oversailing a low trabeated column screen at gallery level. The masonry of the new parts utilizes bands of five ashlar courses alternating with an equal number of brick courses, with mortar-beds ranging from 6 to nearly 8 cm. (2⅜–3 ins.) in height – a technique of construction possibly characteristic of the eighth and ninth centuries.

The variation of a late-sixth-century design simply by duplication, as achieved in the H. Irene, is not very attractive. It is far less relevant within the overall picture of church building from the seventh to the end of the ninth century than other solutions. Three churches in Asia Minor present variants on Justinian's standard type exemplified by Qasr Ibn

249. Ankara, St Clement, ninth century(?). Plan at gallery level

0   40 FT

0   15 M

Wardan. They are St Clement at Ankara, wantonly
destroyed in 1921, but known from surveys,
photographs, and descriptions [249]; St Nicholas at
Myra (Demre) on the south coast, badly restored in
1862, but well preserved in its main lines [250, 251];
and perhaps – though this is open to doubt – in
atrophied form in the Church of the Archangels at
Sige, on the south shore of the Sea of Marmara.[3] All
show essentially the same plan. A square domed bay
forms the centre of the design; south and north the
dome rests on narrow lateral arches, hardly deeper
than wall arches, while east and west it is carried by
deep barrel-vaults. The east bay, the chancel, is
terminated by an apse, polygonal on the exterior.
The west bay, equally deep, communicates through
a door with an esonarthex. Two tiers of triple

250 and 251. Myra (Demre), St Nicholas,
eighth century(?).
Ambo and apse, as in 1906 (*right*), and plan (*below*)

N

0   10M

▨ Earlier building   ■ c. 1118

■ Eighth-century(?) church   ▨ Earlier infill

▨ Middle Byzantine additions   ☐ c. 1862/3

▨ Before 1118   ▨ Later rubble walls

arcades, communicating sideways with the centre bay, lead into aisles and galleries. Square rooms on two levels fill the corners of the square and open into the chancel and west bay, through simple apertures. Clearly, both churches are variants on the type of the compact domed basilica as reflected at Qasr Ibn Wardan. However, they modify the prototype in different ways. True, both enlarge the core element – the domed bay – ever so slightly sideways by replacing the wall arches in the pendentive zone by shallow true arches. However, both at Ankara and Myra, the west arm was filled by a third unit of aisle and gallery, both provided with triple arcades like those to the north and south. Thus to the west the centre dome rested on an arch nearly as shallow as those supporting it north and south. Aisles and galleries became merely ancillary spaces enfolding the dome core on three sides. Differences in size, building technique, and design between Myra and Ankara are nevertheless manifest. At Ankara the structure was small and all details were elegant: the arcades rested on slender rectangular marble piers, the pumpkin dome was subtly designed, the entire structure light and airy. The masonry of the inner domed core was brick, finely pointed, the mortar-beds sloping down and outward; the outer walls were built of alternating bands of brick and ashlar. Piers and capitals were covered with geometric and foliage ornament of metallic sharpness and delicacy; and all this elegance was concentrated in quite a small area, 14 by 20 m. (46 by 66 ft). St Nicholas at Myra is not only larger, 18 by 25 m. (59 by 82 ft), but much heavier, not to say crude. The arcades rest on clumsy brick piers. But the building preserved, still early in this century, some of the original furnishings *in situ* [250]: in the apse, the synthronon for the clergy and the bishop's cathedra; in the chancel, a trabeated canopy on four columns above the altar site; at the entrance to the chancel, the high columns of a *templon*, a trabeated colonnade; finally, in the centre of the nave directly below the dome, an ambo.

St Nicholas at Myra has been dated cautiously to the eighth century based on its plan, the techniques of masonry and vaulting, and the comparison with

churches such as H. Sophia in Salonika and H. Irene in Constantinople. For St Clement in Ankara, the masonry seems to suggest a building date near the middle of the ninth century. Bands of brick and rough stone blocks alternate on the exterior, each composed of four courses; inside piers and arcades,

252. Ankara, city walls, 859

built of thin bricks, rise from bottom courses of rough blocks. As at St Clement and in the walls of the citadel at Ankara, dating from 859, the mortar-beds are high and slope down and out [252]. The comparable method of construction at Dere Ağzı suggests a similar ninth-century date, despite the occasional substitution of mortared rubble masonry for ashlar bands. After all, the stylistic features of Dere Ağzı find their counterparts at St Clement as well: the elegant, steep proportions, the subtly gored pumpkin domes, the niched side chambers of the chancel which form true quatrefoils at Dere Ağzı. The church at Sige may date from 780, or possibly a century earlier or later.

Whatever their dates, both St Nicholas at Myra and St Clement at Ankara preserve or revive after two or three centuries the sixth-century plan of the compact domed basilica, and modify it by deepening ever so slightly the lateral arches of the domed centre bay. The true cross-domed church is fundamentally different. Four strong piers mark the

corners of the centre square. Solid or pierced on two
levels and sheltering small groin-vaulted bays, the
piers carry the barrel-vaults of four cross arms, each
clearly marked off and of equal or nearly equal
depth. A dome on pendentives rises from the apices
of the barrel-vaults and is enclosed in a low drum
pierced by only a few windows. The east arm, at
times continued by a second short bay, serves as a
chancel. Terminated by an apse, it is flanked by side
chambers with absidioles. Like the main apse, they
form on the outside three sides of a polygon. This
cross-shaped, domed nucleus is enveloped north
and south by barrel-vaulted aisles and galleries; to
the west it leads into an esonarthex, likewise surmounted by a gallery. These ancillary spaces then
form a square outer shell, comparable to the outer
shell of Justinian's H. Sophia, though very much

253 and 254. Nicaea (Iznik), Koimesis,
early eighth century(?), rebuilt after 1065.
Section and plan (right) and exterior as in 1906 (below)

255 and 256. Salonica, H. Sophia,
early eighth century(?). Isometric view
and exterior from the north-east

o   40 FT

o   15 M

257. Salonica, H. Sophia, early eighth century(?).
Interior facing east, as in 1906

simpler, or of Qasr Ibn Wardan. The north and
south aisles and the three galleries open in arcades
into the adjoining arms of the cross core. Only the
esonarthex opposite the chancel is at times closed off
by a wall, pierced by but a single door. Aisles and
esonarthex on the ground floor as well as the galleries on the upper level inter-communicate, con-
stituting, as it were, a two-storeyed ambulatory.
Indeed, the term ambulatory church is occasionally

used synonymously with the term cross-domed
church. All told, it is a compact and simple plan.

Only a handful of genuine cross-domed churches
have survived or are well known from earlier surveys.
There is the church of the Koimesis at Nicaea
(Iznik) [253, 254]; there is the H. Sophia at Salonica
[255–7]; and finally, there remain in Constantinople
two cross-domed churches: the Kalenderhane and
the Gül Camii, the first perhaps the church of St

Mary Kyriotissa [258, 259], the second perhaps St Theodosia.[4] Only the structure in Salonica still stands fully preserved, although thoroughly restored; I use a photograph of the interior taken early in this century. The Koimesis church was destroyed in 1920 in an act of vandalism. Only the bottom parts of walls and piers survive, but previous tions of earlier structures and later Byzantine and Turkish alterations. Differences within this group of buildings are minor. The cross core is fundamentally the same. Only in the Gül Camii are the lateral arms somewhat shallower than those on the longitudinal axis. The side chambers flanking the chancel bay at Salonica and in the Kalenderhane are

258. Constantinople, Kalenderhane Camii (Church of St Mary Kyriotissa?), twelfth century. Exterior from the south-west, as in 1972

surveys and earlier and later studies have clarified the aspect of the original structure and the extent of subsequent changes; the removal of the galleries above the aisles and the addition of an outer narthex some time after 1065. Of the Gül Camii the substructures of the original building have been traced; they suggest that the building retains at least the original plan. Of the Kalenderhane Camii the entire core remains, incorporating both large sec- concealed behind the corner piers. At Nicaea and in the Gül Camii they line up with the north and south aisles and communicate with the chancel bay through longish tunnels east of the corner piers. The corner piers, solid at Nicaea and in the Gül Camii, in the Kalenderhane enclose tiny groin-vaulted bays on the ground level. At Salonica, only the west piers enclose such bays; the east piers are solid, except for a tunnel leading from the aisles to the chancel bay.

N

	30 FT	
0		
0		10 M

	Bath 4th–5th centuries		Melisinos Chapel 11th–12th centuries
	Apsed building mid 5th century		Main church late 12th century
	Presentation phase 6th–7th centuries		Later Byzantine additions 13th–15th centuries
	East Bema 7th–9th centuries		Turkish 15th century and later
	Francis Chapel 10th–11th centuries	—	Structures above ground

259. Constantinople, Kalenderhane Camii (Church of St Mary Kyriotissa?), twelfth century, incorporating earlier structures. Plan

Finally, at Salonica, aisles and galleries open into the cross arms of the core through two twin arcades, while at Nicaea and perhaps in the Gül Camii, aisles and galleries rested on triple arcades; at the Kalenderhane, the existence of aisles and triple arcades has been ascertained, but galleries, while likely, remain to be proven. However, all these differences seem to be variations on a common theme rather than clues towards tracing a development.

No definite date of construction exists for any of these cross-domed churches. For one, however, a date, for another a *terminus ante quem* have been established. In the H. Sophia in Salonica the mosaics of dome and apse bear inscriptions referring to the foundation of the church, the latter framed by the monograms of Constantine VI and the dowager Irene (780–97). The huge Iconoclast cross originally in the apse mosaic and the tenor of the inscriptions, all linked to foundation rather than redecoration, date both inscriptions and construction before the iconodule second council of Nicaea in 787, hence between 780 and 787.[5] The Koimesis church at Nicaea, on the other hand, dates from no later than the first quarter of the eighth century and possibly earlier. The mosaics in apse and chancel, dated 843, bore traces of two earlier stages. In one of these, a huge cross previously occupied the place given over to the Virgin in 843. This cross decoration had itself been substituted for a still earlier figurative decoration – the footstool of an image of the Virgin shows in photographs – which therefore antedated the Iconoclast Movement. The church, then, must have been built prior to 726.[6] How much earlier is hard to tell, but the very thin bricks and high mortar-beds suggest a date perhaps in the late seventh century. On the other hand, the recessed brickwork both in the substructure and the rising walls of the Gül Camii dates the building between

the early eleventh and the late twelfth centuries when that particular technique was customary in Constantinople. (The use of amphorae vaulting in the substructure is a remarkable survival of a much older, Western technique.) Convincingly, too, the core of the Kalenderhane Camii has been assigned a twelfth-century date.[7]

The type of the cross-domed church, then, lives on long beyond the first millennium. In Constantinople, the Atik Mustafa Paša Camii, originally perhaps the church of St Peter and St Mark, modifies the canonical plan.[8] Corner piers and enclosed tiny bays are replaced by spacious barrel-vaulted corner rooms, much like those known from fifth-century buildings such as H. David in Salonica. As late as the eleventh century Russian visitors were so deeply impressed by the cross-domed plan of Constantinopolitan churches as to make it canonical all over Russia, from the Desyatinna (1039) and the H. Sophia (1037–46) in Kiev to the Preobrašenskij in Černihov (1036), and as far north as Novgorod.[9]

General opinion nowadays derives the plan of the cross-domed church more or less directly from the compact domed basilica of Justinian's late years. However, the longitudinal element inherent in such structures differs fundamentally from the perfectly centralized plan of a cross-domed church. To bridge the gap, churches such as St Clement at Ankara and St Nicholas at Myra have been interpreted as connecting links – compact domed basilicas which utilize slightly broadened lateral arches to carry the centre dome. However, this hypothesis meets with a chronological discrepancy: the cross-domed plan of the Koimesis church at Nicaea dates from before 726 and perhaps from as early as the seventh century, a hundred or a hundred and fifty years before the appearance of the type at St Clement. In fact, the plan of St Clement could well be viewed not as a forerunner, but as a derivative of the cross-domed plan, a 'shrunken cross-domed church' as it were. But neither of such one-track interpretations of history seems plausible. More likely, the plans of Qasr Ibn Wardan, of St Sergius at Gaza, of the Katapoliani (Hekatontapyliani) on

Paros, of H. Titos at Gortyna, of St Clement at Ankara, and of Dere Ağzı, are all independent and nearly contemporary variants of standard types which had been evolved in the sixth century, if not before, and persisted into the eighth century and far beyond.

The cross-domed plan, it seems to me, belongs to the same lineage. True, the Koimesis church is the first dated example of the type known to us at present. But the plan may have been created much earlier, possibly as early as the sixth century. It could well have existed alongside such variants as the compact domed basilica, with or without encroaching transverse cross arms, or the domed cross church. In fact, the domed cross plan is known from two churches of early date in far-distant provinces of the Empire. One, now gone, stood at Mayafarquin (Meyyafarikin, Silvan) in northern Mesopotamia,

and was presumably built by the Persian king Chosroës II after 591; the date has been questioned, but it seems to be confirmed by the rich late-sixth-century Syrian-looking capitals and carved brackets.[10] The other early survival, incorporated into the ruins of the Cumanin Camii at Antalya (Adalia) on the south coast of Asia Minor, can be assigned a similar date on the evidence of its capitals; the solid stone masonry, too, is comparable [260].[11] To be sure, neither of the two churches was vaulted. The centre room in both carried a pyramidal roof and the other bays were surmounted by sloping timber roofs. But the basic plan is exactly that of the cross-domed churches at Nicaea or Salonica: a centre cross with deep arms, esonarthex, and chancel; enveloping aisles and galleries opening in triple arcades towards the arms of the core; and at Mayafarquin, though not at Antalya, corner piers pierced on both levels.

SURVIVING PARTS

260. Antalya (Adalia), Cumanin Camii, late sixth century. Isometric reconstruction

0   40 FT

0   15 M

Two explanations offer themselves regarding the relation of these unvaulted cross-domed churches of late-sixth-century date to the fully vaulted domed structures of the late seventh and eighth centuries, such as Nicaea and Salonica. One explanation is that they are forerunners, created in the provinces in the sixth century and transferred to the capital in the course of the seventh century. There, in Constantinople, the plan would have been vaulted and thus assimilated to Justinian's standard types. In its vaulted form it would then have spread to near-by Nicaea and Salonica. The theory is not implausible. After all, plan and elevation of Antalya and Maya-farquin differ only superficially from the quatrefoil churches of sixth-century Syria and her border-lands. Like Mayafarquin and Antalya, the Syrian martyria were timber-roofed and focused on a centre bay. This centre bay was axially enlarged by cross arms, which were provided with rectangular exedrae at Mayafarquin and Antalya, with semi-circular exedrae in sixth-century Syrian quatrefoils. In both this core is enveloped by aisles and, sometimes, galleries. Nor is it a priori unlikely that a building type from the provinces should have been taken up in Constantinople. From the seventh to the end of the ninth century, the constant need for defending the frontiers gave greater importance to the border provinces and in particular to those provinces from which armies could be drafted. Con-dottieri from northern Syria and Phrygia ascended to the throne, such as Leo III (717–41) and Michael II (820–9), and brought along their fellow-countrymen, laymen and clergy. Builders from Isauria had been active in Constantinople (and in northern Syria) as early as the latter sixth century.[12] Thus a transfer of architectural types, or for that matter of architects, from the provinces to the capital is not a priori impossible. On the other hand, it is just as possible that buildings such as Mayafarquin and Antalya are but provincial replicas of a fully vaulted and domed prototype, lost to us, which existed prior to 600 at Constantinople. After all, it is quite poss-ible that the church of St Sergius at Gaza, which Choricius saw as early as 536, may have represented

the type, vaulted and domed, though without galleries.

Regardless of which hypothesis turns out to be correct, it is clear that the cross-domed plan goes back far beyond the late seventh or early eighth centuries, when it was taken up in the Koimesis church at Nicaea; it may well be a creation of Justinian's reign, possibly dating from his last years. However, the plan as it presents itself at Salonica is cast in a style quite different from that of the sixth century. The masses – walls and piers – are solid and heavy. Openings, whether windows or arcades, are comparatively small. The proportions are wide and easy. The exterior becomes squat, almost awkward: a plain cube, surmounted by a low, square drum which conceals the dome. Only apse and centre bay are lit, and they only dimly because of the smallness of the windows; aisles and galleries, as seen from the nave, remain shadowy, in parts dark. The marble sheathing is sombre in colour; the light greens, greys, and yellows of Justinian's churches are gone. Only the vaults shimmer with the gold ground of the mosaics [257].

Whatever its time and place of origin, however, the cross-domed church was splendidly adapted to the practical demands and the symbolism of the liturgy as they became firmly established during the centuries after Justinian. The architectural and the liturgical plan have been integrated to perfection. Aisles, esonarthex, and galleries envelop the core on three sides as an outer zone from which the faithful participate in the service, visually and spiritually, but passively. Within the core, the naos is domed and central in plan. The chancel bay preceding the apse is deep and barrel-vaulted. And the side chambers – the pastophories – which flank the chancel are domed, fused with chancel and apse into a triple unit, and communicating with aisles and chancel through doors. Plan and placement of all these elements are closely tied to the final codification of the Byzantine liturgy which must have taken place between the late sixth and the early eighth centuries. More specifically, they are tied to the ritual of the two Entrances – the Lesser Entrance, which by the eighth century accompanies the gospel book, rather than the bishop, to the altar; and the Great Entrance, which as of old transfers to the altar the elements of the Eucharist. In particular, the architectural changes are tied to the places assigned for safekeeping of the gospels and the species of the Eucharist before their actual use in the Mass.

The gradual formation of the triple sanctuary leads into the problem. In Byzantine usage, by the eighth century the gospels are kept in the south room adjoining the chancel – the *diaconicon* – while the north room serves as the *prothesis*, where the species of the Eucharist are kept and prepared before they are brought to the altar during the ceremony of the Great Entrance. However, this was not so from the beginning. In the fourth century, the diaconicon was also the place where the faithful deposited their offerings, and it was situated near the chancel, as presumably in the Lateran basilica and at Epidauros. It is unknown whether or not at that time the species of the Eucharist chosen from among these offerings were prepared in a special ceremony before being brought to the altar; if so, the preparation took place in the diaconicon, which thus would also have served as prothesis. In Syria, from the late fourth century, this room was placed on one side of the apse and thus easily accessible to the faithful, since the entrances of Syrian churches were originally on the flank, not on the façade.[13] The diaconicon, as a rule, had its counterpart in these Syrian churches in a second side chamber, adjoining the apse on the opposite side. But this room was apparently a martyr's chapel sheltering relics. Indeed, while the diaconicon communicated with the aisle and at times the apse through doors, the martyr's chapel opened in an arch.[14] Placement of the two rooms in Syria remained apparently unchanged even after the portals of the church were moved to the façade. In the Aegean coastlands, on the other hand, where the ceremonial preparation of the eucharistic species early may have become part of the liturgy, the diaconicon also served as prothesis. As early as the fifth century, a room serving both purposes was placed near the entrance of the church, accessible to

the faithful, but far from the chancel. It opened either off the narthex or off the atrium. The apsed room projecting south from the narthex in Basilica A at Nikopolis exemplifies the first solution; the apsed room south of the atrium in Basilica A at Nea-Anchialos, the second solution, both in elaborate form.[15] This placement of the diaconicon–prothesis made sense, as long as the faithful actually deposited their gifts there at the beginning of the service. But it also meant that in both the Lesser and the Great Entrance, the procession of the clergy moved back and forth the entire length of the nave. Nor did the situation change when, apparently in the second third of the sixth century in the Aegean coastlands, the prothesis was separated from the diaconicon and assigned another room adjoining the narthex. By then, however, the custom of the faithful bringing their offerings had long become obsolete, and as a result the position of the corresponding rooms on the entrance side of the church had become an atavism.

It was only natural that – beginning in Justinian's time – churchmen and architects strove to place prothesis and diaconicon closer to the sanctuary, where they could be more easily serviced by the celebrating clergy.[16] S. Vitale in Ravenna seems at first glance an early example of the change; but the side chambers at S. Vitale were primarily martyrs' chapels, whether or not they concurrently served also as pastophories. The side chambers of Syrian churches may have furnished the model. Whatever the beginnings, however, the new placing of the pastophories seems to start in the sixth century. Beginning at that time, prothesis and diaconicon in large parts of the Eastern Empire were ever more closely linked to the chancel. They were made to flank it and thus joined with apse and forechoir in the triple sanctuary which in its final, perfect form characterizes the cross-domed churches as we have come to know them, starting with the early eighth or possibly the late seventh century. In that form the triple sanctuary becomes a hallmark of Middle and Late Byzantine church planning. However, the first instances known so far appear in churches of basilican plan dating from the middle of the sixth century or shortly after: the cathedral at Caričin Grad; the 'Stag' basilica at Pirdop in its final phase; a church excavated at Sebaste (Selçikler Köyü) in Phrygia; Dağpazari in Pisidia; possibly S. Apollinare in Classe and the Euphrasius basilica in Poreč (Parenzo), but the function of the apsed side chambers in Classe, of the side apses in Poreč, remains to be clarified. The triple sanctuary, then, was widespread by 600 within the sphere of Byzantium. But Constantinople seems to have shunned it.[17] Its liturgy possibly differed from that in the provinces on this point as it did on the question of separating the nave from the aisles.[18] In any event, though, as a result of the transfer of diaconicon and prothesis, so as to flank apse and forechoir, the Entrances no longer moved along a longitudinal axis through the church, from the door to the sanctuary, as had still been the case in the H. Sophia. Now they proceeded from diaconicon and prothesis – the Lesser Entrance from the former, the Great Entrance from the latter – to the chancel, moving briefly into the naos in order to exhibit the gospel book and the eucharistic elements to the faithful. Any reminiscences of a lengthwise procession and a longitudinal building were eliminated, and the central plan of the naos was fully integrated with its liturgical function. The congregation is relegated to the aisles, the esonarthex, and the galleries. The cross-domed centre bay, on the other hand, becomes an anteroom to the sanctuary – a stage, as it were, visible to the faithful, but open primarily only to the clergy. On this stage, below the dome, Christ reveals Himself to the people in twofold form: as the species of the Eucharist, carried by the celebrant, which appear before their eyes during the Great Entrance and transformed into His body and blood during Communion; and as the Revelation, the Word, pronounced from the ambo in the very centre of the naos.[19]

Concomitantly, the chancel, the site of the altar and the eucharistic sacrifice, became fully integrated into the plan of the cross-domed church. One recalls how, throughout the fifth and often long into the

sixth century, its enclosure had projected far into the nave. In Justinian's early years, the plans of the H. Sophia, of H. Sergios and Bakchos, of S. Vitale, change this situation. A deep barrel-vaulted bay is inserted between the apse and the domed centre bay, to shelter, as a forechoir, at least the site of the altar. But the solution is not yet perfect. In the H. Sophia, the chancel still projected from the forechoir into the area of the eastern half-dome, and no prothesis and diaconicon were joined to the sanctuary. At S. Vitale in Ravenna, the integration has gone much further: the pastophories – or rooms much like them – are now integrated with the sanctuary group; and the chancel seems to have extended to the very beginning of the forechoir, but not further. Finally, in the cross-domed churches of the eighth and ninth centuries – but perhaps starting earlier – full integration has been achieved. The forechoir contains the full expanse of the chancel, and it communicates with the pastophories through doors of its own. Thus it has become a solemnly closed precinct, provided with elaborate annexes. The *templon* rises on the very borderline of forechoir and nave and hides, along the architectural boundary, the sanctuary where the ministrant clergy surround the altar. The church of St Nicholas at Myra until the beginning of this century still preserved its original furniture – templon, altar canopy, ambo – and thus illustrates better than words the function of the individual parts of the building.

The interrelations between liturgy and building were not lost on contemporary intellectuals, who interpreted church structures through an elaborate symbolism.[20] As early as 630 Maximus the Confessor presents an interpretation of the church building and of the liturgy it houses. The entire church is an image of the Universe, of the visible world, and of man; within it, the chancel represents man's soul, the altar his spirit, the naos his body. The bishop's Entrance into the church symbolizes Christ's coming into the flesh, his Entrance into the bema Christ's Ascension to Heaven. The Great Entrance stands for Revelation, the Kiss of Peace for the union of the soul with God; indeed, every part of the liturgy has a symbolical spiritual meaning. About 700, Germanos, the patriarch of Constantinople, summed up ideas presumably current for some time and which continued as late as the fourteenth century. The church building to him was the Temple of the Lord: the sacred precinct, the Heaven where God resides, the sacred cave where Christ was buried and whence He rose, the place where the mystical sacrifice is offered. The chancel, in particular, and the altar (the two are used interchangeably) was viewed as the Seat of Mercy. They were the manger of Christ, His tomb, and also the Table of the Last Supper. Equally, they were seen as the Heavenly Altar on which the hosts of Angels offer the eternal sacrifice. The apse was a symbol of the Cross; the seats of the clergy were the raised site and throne where Christ sat among His disciples. They foretell His second coming and the Last Judgement. The columns of the templon revealed the division between the assembly of the people and the Holy of Holies where the clergy gathered; the architrave over these columns symbolized the Cross. The canopy with its four columns stood for the site of the Crucifixion, and also for the four ends of the earth. Finally, the dome represented Heaven.

It is obvious that such interpretations were not applied exclusively to any one part of the church; the same meaning may be represented by several parts of the structure. It is equally obvious that the interpretations chosen were only in part freshly invented by the theologians of the late eighth century. Many are *topoi*, developed over centuries. Likewise, no doubt, only a small group of laymen was fully conscious of all this sophisticated symbolism. The general ideas, however, permeated to a wider public. In entering the church, the average believer was aware, we may be sure, that he entered Heaven; and he saw, in the procession of the clergy, the angelic host about to offer the sacrifice on the Heavenly altar.

CHAPTER 14

THE BORDERLANDS

Builders and patrons in Justinian's Empire, one recalls, created a new domed architecture – whether staid and standard or boldly experimental – and with it fresh concepts of building. New church plans were evolved; new uses of volume and mass, surface and colour, space and light were achieved. But this architecture of Justinian's circle was limited to a few great centres, and above all to Constantinople. Provincial architecture under Justinian, and for some decades following, absorbs elements of the new vocabulary, torn from context, and fuses them with traditional basilica plans. And even this piecemeal use of elements of Justinian's style is directly related to the impact of the central government: through Imperial donations or through its organs – the army, the civil administration, the Established Church. Much in contrast to such official organs and to the upper class, the popular forces beyond the pale of the Establishment consistently oppose Constantinople's demands for monolithic rule and cling to isolationist folk ways in language, religious custom, and art. This grass-roots reaction is reinforced by clerical, and above all, monastic – monophysite as well as Nestorian – resistance to the central government's religious policy. As a result, the architecture of village churches and monasteries in the borderlands of the Empire is apt to slide back into, or retain for centuries, the ways of a primitive folk architecture, in construction techniques as well as in plan and design. Alternatively, church plans rooted in the higher strata of provincial architecture are transposed into the language of primitivism and carried out in crude methods of construction. It is but natural that such reaction would be strongest where governmental rule was weakest: in remote mountain and desert regions, or along the borders of the Empire. Always slightly in flux, such border populations were never quite integrated within the

Empire; nor were the garrisons of *foederati* that protected the borders – Sassanian, Arab, Nubian, Slavic, and Germanic mercenaries, together with kith and kin.

MESOPOTAMIA AND THE TUR ABDIN

Such folk architecture, religious and secular, was widespread in the outer provinces of the Byzantine Empire as well as in territories beyond its borders. It was an architecture carried by native forces, unrelated to political frontiers. The Byzantine Empire was in a nearly continuous state of war with the Sassanian kingdom and later with the Umayyad caliphate which in 636 replaced the Sassanians as rulers of Mesopotamia and Iran. Nevertheless, Nisibis (Nusaybin) on the Byzantine side of the border remained the spiritual centre of vast numbers of both Nestorian and monophysite congregations extending far into Mesopotamia and Persia. Conversely, church plans and techniques of construction seem to have penetrated from the Mesopotamian plain north-west towards Nisibis and the hills of the Tur Abdin on the south slope of the Taurus range. Certainly Mesopotamia and the Byzantine border provinces worked with similar architectural concepts both before and after the fall of these provinces to the Persians, then to the Muslim. Space was cramped, lighting dim, the exterior plain, the interior vaulted. The church plan was determined by local liturgical custom – different in monastic and parish churches – and by local prototypes in both sacred and secular pre-Christian architecture. Building techniques likewise followed native tradition. In the Mesopotamian plain with its rich clay deposits, brick walling and vaulting were the rule. Northward in the hilly Tur Abdin, stone construction was the norm.

Christianity had early roots in Mesopotamia and in the Tur Abdin. At Edessa (Urfa) by the early third century, Christianity was declared the state religion.[1] Indeed, a church existed there as early as 201, but it remains open to question whether this was a regular church building or a community centre.[2] However, no church buildings of such early date have survived anywhere in Mesopotamia or the Tur Abdin. In general, church building in Mesopotamia is known only from a very few excavations, and none of the buildings can be safely dated. They may have been built at almost any time between the fourth and the ninth century, or later. They are, as a rule, longitudinal halls, terminated by a tripartite sanctuary – a square chancel flanked by corresponding rooms, all three accessible from the nave through narrow doors.[3] Supports, either low columns or piers, project from the side walls into the nave and form a series of niches, covered by short transverse barrel-vaults. From their backs sprang the longitudinal catenary barrel-vault of the nave. Two churches of this type have been excavated at Ctesiphon, one replacing the other [261]. Two other

Constantinian church building from the ambience of secular basilicas, both forensic and palatine.[4]

While early church buildings on the Mesopotamian plain are known only from excavations, a comparatively large group of village churches, monastic churches, and martyria still survive in the Tur Abdin and the adjoining regions, and at least a few are dated by inscriptions and other historical evidence.[5] Situated as the region is between Mesopotamia to the south, Syria to the west, and the Anatolian high plateau to the north, its architecture draws on all three neighbour provinces and adds some features of its own. Some churches share with those of Mesopotamia the longitudinal nave, either truss-roofed or barrel-vaulted, with inward-projecting wall piers. However, a stilted semicircular apse replaces the triple sanctuary. As in neighbouring Anatolia, the walls are built either of blocks or of small stones. Piers, arches, and occasionally the springings of the vault are of finely cut blocks. The apex of the vault, on the other hand, is frequently of brick construction, the bricks pitched on their sides and often laid in decorative

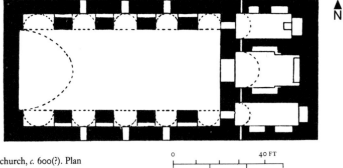

N

261. Ctesiphon, church, c. 600(?). Plan

0   40 FT
0   15 M

churches were found at Hira, one with transverse side barrel-vaults so deep as to require wall piers as well as free-standing columns. The plan has been linked to royal reception and judiciary halls in Sassanian and Umayyad palaces. If true, this derivation would constitute a neat parallel to the origin of

patterns – both hallmarks of Mesopotamian building tradition. Occasionally plans and decoration are taken over from prototypes on a less provincial level. Martyria as a rule are square or octagonal [262] and surmounted by domes or wooden roofs resting on corner squinches;[6] the plans find their parallel in

262. Qartamin, monastery of Mâr Gabriel with churches and martyrium, c. 512(?). Plan

Syria, e.g. at R'safah in the martyria attached to Basilicas A and B. Other churches, possibly monastic, have a plan of their own invention, utilizing elements drawn from both Syria and Mesopotamia. The nave is transverse and vaulted, preceded by a narthex and terminated either by an apse flanked by lateral chambers of Syrian type, or by a Mesopotamian triple sanctuary [262].[7] Very rarely, the barrel-vault gives way to two half-domes placed at the ends of the nave and supporting a dome in the centre, all three resting on squinches.[8] To such plain native plans is often applied a splendid ornament, obviously of Syrian derivation: strong profiles, vine scrolls, festooned Corinthian capitals, and colonnaded shell niches hollowed into the wall of the apse. Buildings such as the martyria of Mâr Yaqub at Nisibis and of el'Adhra at Ḥaḥ or the church of Mâr Azâzaël at Kefr Zeh serve to illustrate this impact [263]. Pilasters and capitals are excellently carved. At Mâr Gabriel at Qartamin a mosaic decorated the chancel, and the tradition is credible that the church was built about 512 with Imperial subsidies. Certainly, the church plans continue unchanged, both in the Tur Abdin itself and in bordering Commagene, into the eighth and ninth centuries.[9] Likewise, the classical vocabulary

263. Ḥaḥ, martyrium of el'Adhra, sixth century(?); upper part of drum 1907. Exterior

imported from Syria may well have survived until long after the sixth century. Only gradually does the construction diminish in elegance. The finely cut stonework of the piers and the decorative brick design of the vaults give way to a construction in small, barely hewn stones, until the designs gradually slide back into the realm of a primitive folk architecture. But without much basic change, church building in the Tur Abdin continued along the old lines as late as the twelfth century, and perhaps later.[10]

EGYPT AND NUBIA

Throughout the Empire and its borderlands, folk architecture differs locally in plan, technique, and decoration. Among the Copts in Egypt during the fifth and sixth centuries plan and construction of cemetery buildings and monasteries are tied to primitive local custom. (The term Coptic, coined for Christians resident in Muslim Egypt, is customarily applied to pre-Muslim Egypt as well.) In the ruins of Apu Jeremiah at Saqqâra, living quarters, a refectory, courtyards, and three churches – the major parts dating from the first half of the sixth century – were chaotically crowded into the area of the monastery. Rows of cells and storerooms were huddled together, as in an Egyptian village. All were barrel-vaulted, the walls built of stone at the bottom and of mud bricks higher up. Only the main church, as originally built in the sixth century, adhered to a basilican plan of Aegean type, as adopted in Egypt from at least the fifth century. An apse and three colonnaded aisles enveloped the timber-roofed nave. Column shafts and bases were imported from the Proconnesian quarries, with capitals elegantly carved by local craftsmen. The abbey of St Simeon at Aswân to this day shows the same characteristics as the monastic buildings at Saqqâra: mud brick walls, a fortified enclosure, barrel-vaulted rooms

264. Aswân, St Simeon, monastery, fourth-nineteenth centuries. Exterior

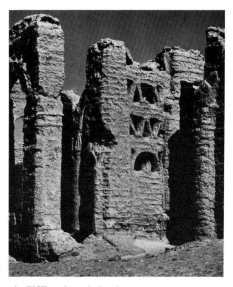

265. El Khargah, tomb chapel, fourth century(?). Exterior

and corridors [264]. At El Khargah (El Khârga) in the Libyan desert west of Sohag and at Bawît near Ashmunein, large necropolises have survived, composed of many dozens of free-standing mausolea and funeral banqueting halls [265]. All are small, built of mud brick and barrel-vaulted or domed. The architectural decoration in general points to a date between 450 and 550; but some may be earlier, given the foundation date, 386–8, of the convent at Bawît.[11] In contrast to the primitive construction and the native design of the buildings, however, their architectural ornament is highly sophisticated and drawn from the vocabulary of the Aegean coastlands [266–8]. Alongside Corinthian capitals of a late-fifth- and early-sixth-century type stand basket capitals overspun by tendrils and thus recalling the capitals of Justinian's time in Constantinople and Ravenna. A sixth-century date is, then, indicated for most of this ornamentation. But in contrast to their Aegean prototypes, the foliage of the Coptic capitals is cut either lancet-sharp or cardboard-stiff, very

266. Capital from Bawît,
sixth century. *Cairo, Coptic Museum*

268. Pilaster and demi-column from Bawît,
sixth century. *Cairo, Coptic Museum*

267. Capital from Hermopolis (Ashmunein),
sixth century. *Cairo, Coptic Museum*

different from the true pliable and naturalistic ornament of Justinian's buildings which occasionally
penetrates Egypt – probably as an import from
Constantinople.[12] Shafts and friezes are covered
with geometric and foliate designs. Chevrons,
rinceaux, overlapping tongues, stars, and rosettes
crowd each other with an abundance characteristic
of a popular taste. The late-classical tradition of the
Eastern Mediterranean has been absorbed by the
Coptic masons and provincialized; it has been
applied to the crude architecture which supported it
in much the same fragmentary manner that
prevailed in other provinces when Justinian's ornament was applied to local building.

The aversion to Constantinople, shared by the
native populations of the border provinces and their

monophysite clergy, eventually led to an exchange of architectural ideas among the border populations. The 'Syrian' church plan – an apse, semicircular or square, flanked by lateral chambers – was brought into Egypt by the monastic congregations of the Tur Abdin. Deir Abu Hennes is an early example, probably still of sixth-century date.[13] The isolationist tendencies of the outlying native Christian communities and, concomitantly, the interchange between them, increased in the seventh century with the Muslim conquest of Egypt and the Near East to the south and east of Asia Minor. Independent Christian territories, such as the Nubian kingdom in Upper Egypt and the Sudan, disappeared behind the Muslim curtain. In either case, the Christian congregations lost the last contact with Byzantium and the Aegean area and their architecture. Isolated, they clung to obsolete church designs in which local traditions intermingled with elements previously absorbed from abroad. Proportions are awkward, details clumsy, the construction poor. From Cairo to the far south, a basilican plan was predominant, with crude round or square piers as supports and with timber roofs. At St Simeon near Aswân, the chancel was formed of three arms of a Greek cross, each surmounted by a half-dome on squinches – obviously a simplified version of the trefoil plan of Deir-el-Abiad. At Deir-es-Suriani (Monastery of the Syrians) in the Natrun Valley, this trefoil chancel

plan has been modified by a square domed bay replacing the centre apse. At near-by Amba Bishoï the cross arm of the trefoil becomes a transverse forechoir. The naves were originally timber-roofed in all these churches; subsequently they were vaulted (and perhaps parts of the chancels later revaulted) with longitudinal or transverse barrel-vaults, or with domes.[14] From such beginnings there springs, it would seem, what might be termed the Coptic standard type: nave and aisles are barrel-vaulted and supported by piers; a forechoir resembling a transept terminates the nave and carries a transverse barrel-vault; the chancel (*haikal*) is composed of three square apses. Developing during the ninth and continuing to the end of the twelfth century, the plan obviously relates to North Mesopotamian types; but it is modified in that all three apses, or at least the centre apse, are domed. By the twelfth century, Deir-Baramus in the Natrun Valley shows the type fully developed.[15] It apparently continues for centuries unchanged, notwithstanding local deviations. But exceptions do occur. The churches of Old Cairo in the eleventh and twelfth centuries – witness Abu Sargeh (St Sergius) – revert to the plan of a colonnaded basilica with continuous or tripartite transept and three apses [269].[16] In upper Egypt a church plan is developed, very short, terminating in five and more apses, and divided into wide rows of domed bays.[17] The type obviously

o   30 FT

o   10 M

N

269. Cairo, Abu Sargeh,
twelfth century. Plan

draws on the customary plan of mosques – and is no concern of a study of Early Christian and Byzantine architecture.

Such late Coptic building, however, exerts no impact on the church architecture of the Egyptian south and of the Sudan. There the Christian kingdom of Nubia notwithstanding occasional invasions held out against the Muslim and for centuries continued an architecture ultimately still rooted in the Aegean tradition of the fifth century. At Qasr Ibrim in the sixth or seventh century, the nave, on columns, was flanked by double aisles, the outer ones on piers and enveloping nave and inner aisles on three sides, the whole built of fine ashlar and apparently timber-roofed. The same high-quality masonry marks the contemporary cathedral at Faras. However, the customary type in Nubia is a basilica with galleries, barrel-vaulted throughout. But the technique of construction is native: the materials are stone in the bottom courses, mud brick in the upper parts; the supports are broad piers; the arcades narrow; the gallery openings reduced to the size of small rectangular windows. Columns, if used at all, serve only to support the triumphal arch. Sacristies flank the apse on either side and a synthronon fills its curve. The last bay of the nave is occupied by the chancel and set off by slightly projecting piers. In plan, liturgical arrangement, and design, Aegean, Syrian, and local elements have been fused and thoroughly transformed. The interiors are dark; the exteriors form squat, unadorned blocks. Capitals are of a much debased composite type, unrelated to the elegant Coptic decoration. The remains of the North Church near Adindân are one example among many ruins apparently still preserved. Few are dated. Only for the second cathedral at Faras, the foundation before 707 is secured through an inscription; and in the north church outside the citadel at Faras, a graffito provides a *terminus ante quem* of 881. Others can be dated only approximately through ceramic finds; they were apparently built beginning with the latter sixth century, when Nubia was christianized, to the eleventh and twelfth centuries, when it finally fell to the Muslims. But still

prior to that conquest, Byzantine architecture exerted an ephemeral impact on Nubia: witness a centrally-planned church at Serreh (Serra) which translates the plan of domed cross churches, such as H. David in Salonica, into the native technique of construction [270].[18]

Both before and after the Muslim Conquest, then, Christian builders along the southern fringes of the Empire clung to the outmoded formulas of what might be called 'sub-Byzantine architecture'. The outlook was very different in the independent or semi-autonomous border states along the northern and eastern frontier – the Slavic kingdoms in north-eastern Yugoslavia and Dalmatia; the Bulgarian Empire in the north-eastern and central Balkans; finally, the kingdoms of Armenia extending into north-eastern Asia Minor to the foot of the Caucasus mountains. All these territories develop architectural styles of their own – national *Sonderstile*. Different among each other, these styles are yet at the same time related to, and independent from, Byzantium. In Armenia, and to a lesser degree in the Bulgarian Empire, rulers, churchmen, and architects seem to have striven quite consciously towards rivalling the best, boldest, and most impressive designs of their Byzantine contemporaries. Their buildings might be described as 'para-Byzantine architecture'.

THE BALKANS

Byzantine power in the Balkan provinces lost its grip in the course of the seventh and eighth centuries. The Church and the military and civil administration clung precariously to a few garrisoned cities along the coasts of Dalmatia and Bulgaria, and in the river valleys inland. In the 640s, Slavic Croatian tribes conquered Salona on the Adriatic coast, laid siege to Salonica, and swept as far south as Corinth. Gradually they settled down, with their biggest concentration along the west coast, and were converted to the Church of Rome. Then in 811, the Bulgars, long settled south of the Danube, began pushing south and west to eliminate the last

270. Serreh (Serra),
centrally-planned church, tenth century. Exterior

remnants of Byzantine suzerainty in the Balkans. They subjugated the Slavic squatters, except for those on the Dalmatian coast and in Croatia, and formed a new powerful state.[19] Rapidly spreading, this First Bulgarian Empire was reconquered only in 1018 by the Byzantines, led by Basil II, the Bulgar-Killer. The Bulgar czars – converted to Eastern Christianity in the last third of the ninth century – were perpetually at war with Constantinople both before and after conversion. Yet they were deeply impressed by the culture, wealth, and art of the Byzantine court – more so than the Slavic chieftains along the west coast ever were. The palaces and churches built by the Bulgars, and some of the churches built by the Slavs, are certainly linked to Byzantine concepts of court life and of aulic and ecclesiastic ceremonial. Whether Bulgarian or Slavic, however, building in the Balkans throughout the ninth and tenth centuries has a note of its own. It is quite different from contemporary Byzantine architecture both in style and construction.

Among the Croatian Slavs in Dalmatia, permanent church building seems to have started in the seventh and continued with little change until the eleventh and twelfth centuries.[20] What has survived is quite unconnected with the Early Christian tradition of Salona, and traces of Byzantine impact are equally scanty. Hall-churches such as Sv. Barbara at Trogir are frequent, but they obviously do not represent a Byzantine type. Even more common are single-naved churches covered with a barrel-vault into which a dome has been inserted: Sv. Luka at Kotor is one of many examples.[21] The dome may, but need not, be a Byzantine element. The barrel-vaulted aisleless nave, on the other hand, recalls a local tradition of Roman mausolea, such as the Anastasius martyrium at Salona. Equally frequent in ninth-century Dalmatia are centrally-planned churches: cross-shaped, trefoil, or frequently round, with six projecting niches, as at Sv. Trojce near Split, and nearly always very small structures. Again, none of these plans are Byzantine. On the

0 _____ 40 FT
0 _____ 15 M

▲ N

271 and 272. Zadar (Zara), Sv. Donat,
early ninth century(?).
Plan and exterior

impact on the architecture of the western Balkans as early as the sixth century: on the orthodox baptistery at Salona with its double order of columns curtaining the walls; on small trefoil churches of Justinian's time, at Kuršumlija, Klisura, and Caričin Grad; and on round churches with ambulatories, such as Konjuh.[22] It would seem but natural for the builders of the first Croatian centrally-planned churches to fall back either on the same Roman models, or on their sixth-century local descendants. Indeed, like their plans, the construction, the style, and the vocabulary of the Croatian churches point to a Roman tradition. The designs are compact; the masonry has a stoniness due only in part to the use of roughly-hewn chunks of rock; the exterior walls are articulated by pilaster strips or blind arcades. Possibly the long rows of niches hollowed into the outer walls also point to Rome. The back-to-Rome movement, as has been suggested, may be rooted in the opposition of the Roman Catholic Croatians to the attempted encroachment of the Church of Constantinople. A Roman renascence is certainly present in Croatian ninth-century architecture, possibly to some degree sparked by the impact of Lombard architecture across the Adriatic Sea.[23] At the same time, however, Croatian architecture maintains – at least in the function assigned to certain building types – contact with Byzantium.

The church of Sv. Donat at Zadar (Zara), probably of early-ninth-century date, illuminates the situation [271, 272].[24] Circular in plan, its centre room is enveloped by the two tiers of an ambulatory and a gallery, both ring-shaped. Six broad piers and two columns carry the arcade of the ground floor; a second order supports that of the gallery; and three horseshoe apses project from the ambulatory. The ambulatory is barrel-vaulted; the centre room was originally covered by a dome. On the exterior, blind arches articulate the apses. The gallery was originally linked to some adjoining structure, presumably a palace. The double-storeyed central plan seems to reflect the tradition of palace churches come down from Constantinian times. Sv. Donat is a cousin several times removed of H. Sergios and

contrary, they apparently revive mausolea types as they were scattered all over the Roman world, including presumably Dalmatia. Such mausolea, both Christian and pagan, had exerted a strong

Bakchos in Constantinople, of S. Vitale in Ravenna, of Charlemagne's palatine chapel at Aix-la-Chapelle, and presumably of palace chapels in Constantinople, now lost. But the impassive solidity of the Dalmatian structure recalls – far more than Byzantine models – Roman buildings or possibly Constantinian churches, such as the Anastasis Rotunda in Jerusalem.

BULGARIA

The situation differs in the eastern and central Balkans. A specifically local architectural note had come to the fore as early as the late sixth century in the Byzantine provinces in the area of present-day Bulgaria. Even then, dark vaulted hall-churches had begun to vie with the elegant but old-fashioned basilicas of Caričin Grad and with the rare domed churches of metropolitan standard type – such as the 'Stag's Basilica' at Pirdop as remodelled in the late sixth century. Squat, broad piers took the place of marble columns; the arcades became low and nar-

row. The nave, poorly lit by a few windows in the façade, carried a barrel-vault, and groin-vaults covered the aisles. Such modification of a simple basilican plan through vaulting and heavier supports, parallels similar sixth-century currents in Tunisia, Cyrenaica, and Sicily. However, in the eastern Balkans the type does not remain stationary, and perhaps as early as the late sixth century in the cathedral of Sofia, a dome and transept were fully integrated into the plan of a vaulted basilica with galleries.[25]

The further development – if indeed any building activity continued through the seventh and eighth centuries – came to an end with the Bulgar invasion. The new Bulgarian empire quickly expanded over present-day Bulgaria and southern Yugoslavia. However, little is known about the chronology or the character of architecture in this Greater Bulgaria under the rule of the First Empire. Few, if any, buildings are dated beyond question, and the development is as obscure as the links to other styles

273. Ohrid, St Sophia, late ninth and mid eleventh centuries(?). Exterior of apses

– be it architecture previously rooted in the Balkans, contemporary building in Constantinople, or the art of Mesopotamia, Persia, and Armenia. Indeed, what little seemed to be ascertained some forty years ago has recently again come into flux – so much so that a large number of the great palaces and churches excavated in Greater Bulgaria oscillate in date from as late as the ninth, tenth, and eleventh centuries to as early as the sixth. Any attempt at presenting Bulgarian architecture is therefore bound to be quite tentative.[26]

Among the church types of Greater Bulgaria, one appears to be characteristic, new, and unique: a hall-church, supported by heavy piers and low arches, and terminated by three powerful apses. Nave,

aisles, transept wings, and chancel bay are barrel-vaulted; a dome surmounts the segregated crossing. The church of St Sophia at Ohrid in southern Yugoslavia [273] seems to have followed this plan, if with variations; but both reconstruction and date, whether late ninth or mid eleventh century, remain in doubt, and rebuildings have much altered the original plan.[27] However, whether or not built as the see of a new Bulgarian patriarch under Czar Boris (852–89), in plan and style the first H. Sophia does not stand alone. It seems to have a counterpart in the church of St John the Baptist (Sv. Ivan Kristutel) at Nessebâr (Mesembria) on the Black Sea coast, which to me looks a late-tenth- or early-eleventh-century building [274].[28] It finds an even closer

274. Nessebâr (Mesembria), Church of St John the Baptist, c. 1000. Exterior from the south-west

counterpart far to the south, in Central Greece: the church of the Panaghia at Skripou[29] [275–7]. Similar in plan and far better preserved than the original St Sophia at Ohrid, the Panaghia is dated 873/4 by an inscription. It is a most impressive building – 26 m. long and 16 m. wide (85 by 53 ft), not counting the projecting transept wings – and thus nearly the exact size of St Sophia at Ohrid. The design is heavy, solid, and beautifully proportioned. Outside, nave, transept wings, and chancel are sharply set off against each other and culminate in the circular drum of the dome. The aisles, east and west of the crossing, and the three semicircular apses are subordinate elements. String courses curve above the windows, subdividing the outer

275 and 276. Skripou, Panaghia, 873/4. Plan (*top*) and view of apses, transept, and dome from the north-east (*above*)

walls at a level corresponding to the vault springings and reflecting the perfect integration of the interior space with the exterior volumes. Inside, aisles and

277. Skripou, Panaghia, 873/4. Interior facing east

nave are separated by walls four feet thick, pierced only by a low, narrow arch on either side. Nave and transept arms rise steeply to the dark barrel-vaults, encased by the massive walls. Their bleak darkness contrasts beautifully with the bright light in the sharply segregated crossing. All this is built in heavy stone blocks, largely spoils from classical Orchomenos near by.

One has to look far afield in order to establish the place of buildings such as St Sophia at Ohrid and the Panaghia at Skripou in the history of architecture after Justinian. The resemblance to the cathedral of Sofia, with its long nave, aisles, and perhaps its galleries all built of brick, is only skin-deep; and the interval of 250 years is hard to bridge. The contrast to the complex and refined brick architecture of Constantinople, as customary long before the early-tenth-century examples surviving, is apparent as well in the design of spaces and masses. And while building activity in Greece may have been considerable in the latter ninth century, as the Byzantine political position was reconsolidated, the architectural roots of Skripou do not lie in Greek art. True, in the course of the tenth century the type of Skripou was taken up in modified form by Greek and Balkan country churches. The walls between aisles and nave are supplanted by heavy piers and low arcades, much as in St Sophia at Ohrid. But in the ninth century Skripou so far seems to be unique or almost unique in Greece. In none of the comparable tenth-century churches is the nave quite that long; and only rarely are the openings towards the aisles quite that low and narrow.[30] Its design in masses and its building technique seem to me best understood in the context of Balkan architecture, as revealed by the fortresses and palaces built for the still pagan Bulgar czars for nearly a century. Such dependence of a ninth-century church in Greece on the contemporary Bulgarian tradition is not impossible. The court of the Bulgar czars and their buildings must have made a deep impression on the neighbouring Byzantine provinces. The immediate frame, then, for churches such as Skripou and St Sophia at Ohrid seems to be the architecture of the Bulgar court.

The broader frame leads farther – to the hinterlands of the Near East and to Armenia.

What survives of Bulgar court buildings is impressive to this day. At Pliska, the walls of a huge palace precinct have been uncovered – including the substructures of throne room and living quarters – presumably dating from 814–31.[31] Within the enclosure of the walls, the buildings are loosely scattered. They are of very large blocks of stone, perfectly hewn with a core of mortared rubble, and apparently designed in clear, solid masses [278, 279]. The throne room may serve as an example. Raised high on a podium, its floor rested on two parallel barrel-vaults in the substructure. The hall itself was presumably aisleless, preceded by a porch and terminated by an apse. On the outside it was probably enveloped by a terrace, either open or covered by a portico.[32] The living quarters of the palace were each laid out as a large rectangular block, divided inside into a main hall – square or rectangular – and rows of flanking rooms. Similar plans prevail in other palaces, at Madara and at Preslav, but the splendid masonry technique appears to have rapidly deteriorated.

In layout, the throne room of Pliska obviously vies with the audience halls of the Byzantine emperors at Constantinople as they are known, less from excavations than from contemporary descriptions: an aisleless, apsed hall is found in the palace complex south and downhill from the Sultan Ahmet Mosque; the high position on a podium and the enveloping terrace (heliakon) echo the triclinium of the Magnaura.[33] Indeed, the Bulgarian palaces provide a basis for envisaging, at least in plan, the lost palaces of Constantinople – throne rooms as well as possible living quarters. But the builders of the Bulgarian palaces translated the Byzantine models into a building technique of their own, and re-designed them in terms of an architecture composed of clear-cut solids.

Despite the obvious relationship of such palace designs to Byzantium, the origins of the palace architecture of Pliska have been sought far and wide. Their heavy stone work has been attributed to the

278. Pliska, palace, 814–31. East gate

skill of the Bulgarian conquerors or to craftsmen called in from Byzantium.[34] Neither is plausible: nomads, as the Bulgarians were until the beginning of the ninth century, are not builders, and stone masonry was never in the Byzantine tradition. The plans of the throne rooms and living quarters at Pliska have also been compared to Sassanian palace halls. Undeniably Bulgar buildings, of tenth-century date, often show ornament closely reminiscent of Sassanian art: griffins, winged lions, palm trees, palmetto-and-grape friezes – motifs which, in the Muslim art of Iran and Mesopotamia, survived far into the eleventh and twelfth centuries and beyond; their appearance in sixth-century Constantinople at H. Polyeuktos seems to have remained ephemeral.[35] Indeed it is perfectly possible and even likely that some such decorative motifs migrated directly from Muslim countries to Bulgaria. But it is equally possible that the migration took a detour. In fact, Sassanian motifs had penetrated the art of Christian Armenia since at least the early seventh century, and this influx continued from the Muslim Caliphate which in 638 succeeded the Sassanian Empire and

in 640 subjected part of Armenia. Sassanian ornament could thus just as likely have reached the Balkans from Armenia, and this likelihood is strengthened by the fact that the beautiful masonry of Pliska – with no link whatever to the brick architecture of Mesopotamia – nowhere finds in appearance so close a parallel as in Armenia.[36] Ties to Armenia would explain also the plan and construction of St Sophia at Ohrid and the Panaghia at Skripou. The plan, a domed hall-church, and its design in solid masses have often been linked to Armenian and Georgian building. The stonework too recalls, if loosely, Armenian stone building. Finally, the ornament of Skripou – from the bands curving over the windows to the series of decorative plaques along the apse [280] – shows, intermingled with substantially Byzantine elements, decorative devices of Sassanian origin.[37] Immigrants, either coming across the Black Sea from Armenia or northern Asia Minor, or long settled in Thrace, could easily have brought to Bulgaria such Sassanian ornamental devices, whence they would have drifted down into Central Greece.[38] Thus both St Sophia at Ohrid and the

279. Pliska, palace, 814–31. Substructure of throne room

Panaghia at Skripou seem to represent, *c.* 870, a style linked to the architecture of the Bulgar court at the time of its conversion to Christianity and permeated by elements of decoration and construction brought

from afar. During the following half-century the architecture of Greater Bulgaria takes a new turn. On the one hand it looks more decisively than ever towards contemporary Byzantium – a development

280. Skripou, Panaghia, 873/4. Ornament frieze, apse

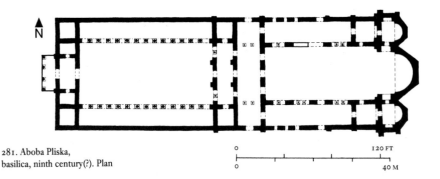

281. Aboba Pliska,
basilica, ninth century(?). Plan

0   120 FT

0   40 M

we shall discuss later. On the other hand, it models itself on the far distant local past, both the great churches of the sixth century and Roman Late Antique monuments.

From the late ninth to the end of the eleventh century large basilicas were laid out in Greater Bulgaria, some with, others without galleries, and all much like those built in the Balkan provinces of Justinian's days.[39] At times, in fact, doubts have arisen regarding either a sixth- or ninth-century date for such buildings. The episcopal church at Aboba Pliska, for example, has occasionally been assigned to the sixth century, reversing a contrary dating of 864–86, just after the conversion of the Bulgar czars. Indeed the scale – 99 m. (325 ft) in length – and the main lines of the plan resemble those of any major church of Justinian's time in the Balkan provinces, including atrium, narthex, alternating nave supports, galleries, vaulted chancel, pastophories, and, possibly, six towers [281]. Other features, however, suggest the ninth century: the rooms inserted between aisles and pastophories, presumably dressing rooms (*mitatoria*), as they are known from the Imperial ceremonial at Constantinople;[40] and the construction technique of well-hewn stone blocks, like those at Pliska, albeit alternating with brick bands. Other basilicas in Greater Bulgaria are undoubtedly of ninth-century date and later: H. Achilleos, prior to 1002, on an island in the Prespa Lake, with semicircular apse, flanking pastophories, colonnaded tribelon, and heavy piers, carrying the arcades of nave and galleries; a basilica,

dating possibly from the ninth century still, found below the fourteenth-century Bogorodica Ljeviška at Prizren in Yugoslavia; and, not far from there, another basilica, erected in 1067–71, parts of its stark outer walls of ashlar blocks incorporated into the lower portions of the fourteenth-century church at Staro Nagoričino [393].[41]

It has been suggested that these basilicas represent a renascence of sixth-century prototypes, not a survival, as formerly maintained. Indeed it is hardly plausible that the tradition of building large and lavish basilicas could have weathered nearly three hundred years of unbroken pagan occupation. On the contrary, a late-ninth- and tenth-century renascence of Justinian's style in Greater Bulgaria finds a natural explanation in the desire of the czars, by then fervently Christian, to claim legitimacy and, indeed, succession to the throne of Byzantium. Consistently (much like the Carolingian emperors a century before) they would strive to revive the Imperial architecture best known to them – Justinian's buildings in the Balkans.[42] Similar concepts of a 'renascence' could have been operating when the Round Church at Preslav was laid out [282]. The traditional date in the first third of the tenth century and the identification as the palatine chapel of Czar Simeon (893–927) have been questioned at times; however these still seem more convincing than the proposed sixth-century date.[43] Comparatively small, the church complex at Preslav opens with a forecourt, 13·50 by 16·50 m. (44 by 54 ft) [282–4]. Narrow niches billow from its walls, linked on the outside by semicylindrical buttresses. Inside, small columns, one foot in diameter, line the walls at a distance of only 50 cm. (20 in.). From this atrium one entered a two-storeyed forechurch, the upper floor, perhaps the ruler's gallery, reached by

corner stair-turrets. Recent soundings suggest that both forechurch and atrium were added, perhaps during construction, to the church. Circular, domed, and small, this latter was enveloped by eight niches, not counting apse and chancel, billowing

282 and 283. Preslav, Round Church
and fortification, early tenth century(?).
View from the east (*above*)
and reconstructed section, with plan (*below*)

284. Preslav, Round Church, early tenth century(?). Atrium from the south-west

outward between strong projecting buttresses. Its walls were lined by two tiers of colonnettes, barely ½ m. in diameter, 3 m. high, and only 60 cm. apart (1 ft 6 in. by 10 ft by 2 ft). In the upper tier the octagonal shafts were decorated with variegated inlay. The walls were revetted with glazed tiles painted with floral and geometric motifs. Much of this is rooted in older Byzantine tradition; other elements derive from the principles and the vocabulary of Middle Byzantine building, the new style which was just developing at Constantinople at the turn of the tenth century. Indeed, the Round Church at Preslav has numerous elements in common with the first churches built by the Macedonian Emperors, and with their palaces – elements known either from extant buildings or from literary sources. To begin with, there is its very function, presumably as a palace chapel – that eminently Byzantine architectural type which is referred to time and again in the court ceremonial of the tenth century. There is the *kyptikon*, the ruler's gallery, above the entrance porch; the colourful decoration of walls and colonnettes; and finally, the small scale of the structure – the rotunda measuring but 10·30 m. (34 ft) across. But these elements stand within the framework of an

overall design of a very different tenor. The egg-and-dart, palmette, and half-palmette friezes carved on the cornices of the church at Preslav are often of a design so classical as to suggest copies from Greek or Roman models rather than the drier and more formal ornament of Middle Byzantine Constantinople; others recall the fleshy patterns of Sassanian decoration [285]. Inlaid columns were customary in Constantinople from the sixth century, as witness those from H. Polyeuktos and H. Euphemia [178, 179]; it is likely that the type continued into Middle Byzantine times. More important, the circular plan

285. Preslav, Round Church, early tenth century(?). Cornice

with billowing niches is so close to Roman mausolea of the third and fourth centuries that a revival of such prototypes, Imperial or believed to be Imperial, seems most plausible to explain the Round Church at Preslav. Specifically, the double tier of columns which curtains the walls recalls the Mausoleum of Diocletian at Spalato. It may be premature to speak of a 'Bulgarian Renaissance' of the tenth century.[44] But a resurgence of elements from Rome and Justinian in tenth-century Greater Bulgaria is highly likely. Whether or not this resurgence was sparked by the parallel movement in Dalmatia during the ninth century is a question unanswerable at our present stage of limited knowledge.

ARMENIA AND GEORGIA

The kingdom of Armenia was a border state, divided in 387 into Roman-Byzantine and Sassanian spheres of influence. From 301 on, Christianity was the State religion. The eastern parts of Armenia came under Persian rule in the fifth century, under Muslim suzerainty in the seventh. But even then the country remained semi-autonomous in her policy and emphatically Christian, though opposed to the dogma and the political claims of the Church of Constantinople. However, relations with the Byzantine Empire remained close, and Armenians rose to high positions in the Imperial administration long before a family of Armenian descent came to occupy the throne of Byzantium – in 867 with Basil I. Armenia herself, split into smaller principalities in the ninth century, survived until the late eleventh century. When at that time she fell to the Seljuks, Armenian nobles emigrated to Cilicia and set up a new kingdom which lasted to the end of the fourteenth century.

To this day Armenia is studded with churches, monasteries, and fortifications – in ruins or well preserved – reaching from the fifth or sixth to the fourteenth century, long after the Seljuk Conquest. A remarkably large number of buildings are dated by dedicatory inscriptions or by contemporary chronicles. In our context we shall focus on the period prior to the eleventh century and on the relation, as I see it, of Armenian to Early Christian and Byzantine architecture.[45]

The beginnings of Armenian church building in the fifth and sixth centuries have long been linked to Syria. However, the ties to the highlands of Asia Minor south and west of the Armenian border, from Cilicia to the Tur Abdin, were close; Sassanian impact, too, made itself felt in building techniques.[46]

286. (A) Ereruk, church, c. 500. Plan
(B) Ptghavank', church, c. 600. Plan
(C) T'alinn, church, c. 662–85. Plan

A

B

C

↑ N

0   60 FT
0   20 M

In the church at Ereruk, unmistakable features point to Syria, and to a date near to or even before 500: the twin-towered façade, the chambers flanking the apse, the gabled portals along the flanks, the classical profiles framing the windows. But the towers are pushed sideways – an Anatolian rather than a Syrian feature [286A] – and aisles and nave were barrel-vaulted, as in the many small hall-churches still surviving on the high plateau of Asia Minor (and presumably in large churches which have been lost). The beautiful masonry of large stone blocks, facing a narrow core of rubble, is linked to Cappadocian and Cilician building techniques, and ultimately goes back to Roman provincial tradition. A group of hall-churches in Armenia, contemporary with or later than Ereruk, shows the Syrian element in decline and the impact from Asia Minor further increasing: at Eghvard (574–603) – as at Tekor in its first, fifth-century phase – the decorative details, including

horseshoe arches, are so close to those of Cappadocian churches as to suggest the activity in Armenia of Cappadocian mason crews.[47]

The seventh century sees a break with this earlier tradition. Hall-churches and barrel-vaulted basilicas give way to a wide variety of centralized longitudinal churches and truly centrally-planned buildings. The impact of Syrian and Cappadocian architecture, however, does not immediately cease. The double-shell quatrefoil, so frequent in Syria in the sixth century – at Bosra, Apamea, Aleppo, R'safah – was taken up in the palace martyrium built at Zvart'nots, possibly before 652, by the Armenian patriarch Narses III (641–61) [287].[48] The decoration also reveals Syrian as well as North Mesopotamian sources: basket capitals surmounted by Ionic volutes, recalling Mayafarquin; eagle capitals; vine-scroll friezes; classical profiles. The doubled colonnettes which supported the circle of

287. Zvart'nots, tetraconch church, 641–61, possibly before 652. View of remains

blind arches on the outer wall could equally derive from Mesopotamia.

The late sixth and the seventh centuries are indeed the great centuries of church building in Armenia. Immensely productive in the sheer number of structures, incredibly rich in the variety of central church plans, this architecture is yet hard to define as to its place within the network of Roman, Early Christian Syrian, Early Byzantine, and Sassanian building. At Tekor, a dome and high cross arms were raised over nave and aisles of the older hall-church. The churches of Ptghavank' (Ptghni), T'alish (Aroudz), and Mren were laid out from the outset with aisleless naves, barrel-vaulted and flanked by three niches with transverse barrel-vaults; the centre bay of the nave was surmounted by a dome on pendentives; the flanking middle niches correspondingly were raised transept-like, thus forming a cross-domed hall with niches [286B].[49] All these buildings and rebuildings have been dated to the last third of the sixth and the early seventh centuries; rightly, it seems, since the cathedral excavated at Dvin, as rebuilt in 608–15 and solidly dated, and the similar church at T'alinn [286C], only vary the plan of the cross-domed hall-church by adding three apses, one each to the ends of the nave and the cross arms.[50] Equally frequent are genuine central plans. There is a group of free-standing cross churches.[51] There are cross-in-square structures, divided into nine bays; the cross arms radiate from a domed and towered centre bay and are raised high above the corner bays. The shape of these latter – squarish as in the Gayané church at Vagharshapat (630), or slightly elongated, as in the cathedral at Mren (629–40) – determines the square or rectangular plan of the entire building [288A]. At Bagaran, dated, though insecurely, 621–8 or 624–31, the corner bays are shrunk to the size of tiny squares, while apses project from the cross arms and transform the structure into a quatrefoil [288B].[52] The church type which more than any other has been called specifically Armenian appears in the seventh century at Avan (after 611?) and at St Hrip'simé at Vagharshapat (618) [288C, 289, 290].[53]

A

B

C

288. (A) Vagharshapat, St Gayané, 630. Plan
(B) Bagaran, church, 621–8 or 624–31(?). Plan
(C) Vagharshapat, St Hrip'simé, 618. Plan

The core is formed by an octagonal centre bay. From it radiate four cross arms terminated by apses. In the diagonals four narrow cylindrical bays end in

Lake Van (915–21) [291, 292].[54] Finally, the cathedral of Zoravar near Eghvard, dated 662–81 and now in ruins, forms an inner octagon with eight

289. Avan, church, after 611(?). Interior

squinches to support the round rim of the dome. The interior, then, forms a kind of cross-octagon, and the corner niches may well have been designed to abut the diagonal thrusts of the dome. Four sacristies(?), square or round, are placed behind the niches and fill the spaces between the arms. All this – octagon, cross arms, corner niches, and sacristies – is enclosed within a massive masonry cube, allevi-ated only by steep triangular slits on the exterior between apses and sacristies. The type continues (or is it revived?) nearly unchanged into the tenth cen-tury and beyond when it is found at Aght'amar in

niches projecting, but caught in the massive enclosure of an outer octagon.[55]

Building materials throughout are large, well-cut stone blocks facing a narrow core of rubble masonry. The decoration is kept to a minimum: three or four steps at the foot of the walls; flexed arches surmoun-ting, or a band curving above the windows; a row of brackets or a profile marking the eaves lines; 'cube capitals' with semicircular faces, with or without crude foliate or geometric decoration; Ionic capitals transposed into geometric shapes. It is a rustic, though anything but simple architecture, impressive

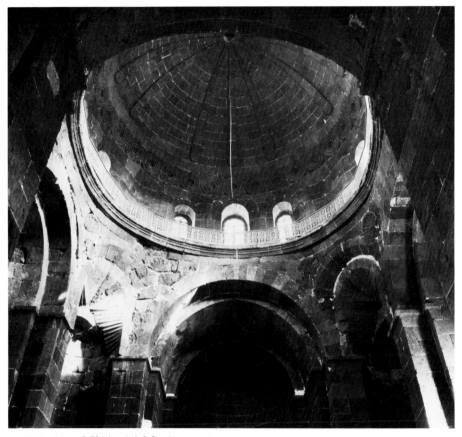

290. Vagharshapat, St Hrip'simé, 618. Interior

because of its massiveness and its sparseness of detail. But this impressiveness is counter-balanced by the comparatively small size of the structure. The cathedral of Mren, one of the largest churches in seventh-century Armenia, measures but 20 by 29 m. (65 by 95 ft). Barely larger than a minor Syrian village church such as St Paul and Moses at Dar Qita, and a good deal smaller than the Syrian 'cathedrals', St Hrip'simé covers an area 17 by 21 m. (56 by 69 ft), comparing in length and width with the cross church of Tomarza in Cappadocia, and covering just about one third the surface of the H. Sophia at Salonica. Armenian church building of the seventh century, then, in material, decoration, and size, continues traditions established in the inlands of the Near East by at least the fifth and sixth centuries, if not indeed since Roman times. Even less complex types among the churches of Armenia still recall the architecture of Cilicia and Cappadocia, in individual features or even as a whole. Apses or forechoirs may be flanked by lateral chambers, apses enclosed in the mass of a straight wall or terminated on the exterior by three or five sides of a polygon. The cross-in-square plan itself of the

Gayané church and of the cathedral at Bagaran, at first glance anyway, recalls the audience hall of Al-Mundir at R'safah, of *c.* 560. Free-standing cross chapels such as Ashtarak in Armenia were common in Cappadocia. To some extent, then, Armenian centrally-planned churches of the seventh century – like their longitudinal predecessors – are embedded in a tradition of church building basic to the inlands of the Near East for two and three hundred years.

On this everybody agrees. But opinions are widely split regarding the further implications of such a consensus: on the one hand, the remote background of the common Near Eastern heritage is in question; on the other, the argument concerns the possible impact of Armenian on Byzantine, or vice versa, of Byzantine on Armenian seventh-century architecture. Based on Strzygowski's theories, a section of scholarly opinion insists that Christian building in the interior of the Near East in general, and Armenian architecture in particular, is rooted in Sassanian and, further back, in Central Asian building traditions. In particular, the technique of dome construction in Armenia is stressed to support such hypotheses. Indeed, Armenian masons used a device unknown to Rome and rare in Byzantium but customary in Parthian and Sassanian buildings in Iran and Mesopotamia: squinches thrown astride the corners to support the dome, always used in conjunction with an octagonal bay and frequently, though not exclusively, when the dome surmounts a square bay. The steep cylindrical corner niches which support such squinches and buttress the dome in a church such as St Hrip'simé have likewise been attributed to Iranian models. Church plans in Armenia are also traced back to Parthian and Sassanian architecture. The cross-in-square plan, for instance, is supposed to be rooted – whether directly or by way of buildings such as the audience hall of Al-Mundir at R'safah – in the design of Iranian Fire Temples.

We need not concern ourselves unduly with the wider claims which have mushroomed from the soil of such hypotheses. That the Iranian domes on squinches derive from wooden houses in North India and Central Asia, or from the tents of Mongol tribesmen, is neither demonstrable nor plausible. Nor is it likely that S. Lorenzo in Milan or the H. Sophia in Constantinople were designed by Armenian architects. All such exaggerations reveal dangers constantly present in this line of thinking: ahistorical reasoning; overstress on technical devices; paper resemblances of plans; and an outlook isolating Eastern, that is Sassanian or Asian, from Western, that is Roman or Byzantine, architecture. Primitive huts are much the same, from the igloo of the Eskimo and the yurte of the Mongolian to the hovel of the Egyptian fellah and the round home of the Etruscan farmer as reflected in the tomb mounds; derivations of complex building types from primitive forms have little validity. Nor is it admissible to postulate the presence in Armenia of building types three or four centuries before their first proven appearance in dated structures. Secondly, technical devices alone are not style-generating, and the design of St Hrip'simé could not have been evolved only from squinches and corner niches. Thirdly, comparison between such buildings as the cross-in-square of Bagaran and of Sassanian Fire Temples, or, for that matter, between these and the audience hall of Al-Mundir, is tempting on paper, but they are quite different in the design of radiating cross arms in the case of the audience hall and of Bagaran, and of enclosing corridors in the instance of the Fire Temples. Lastly, it is unthinkable that Roman and Sassanian architecture should not have influenced each other; or that Armenian centrally-planned churches, when they first appear in the seventh century in highly complex forms, should not have also experienced the impact of the great Byzantine central-plan articulation of the time of Justinian and after.

To me this seems the decisive question. By the seventh century, the architects of Armenia have shifted from longitudinal to central plans, or else they fuse centralizing elements into longitudinal hall-churches and into aisleless churches with flanking chapels. No preparatory steps can be traced anywhere in Armenia; likewise attempts at tracing a development from longitudinal to central church plans have so far failed. Architectural developments beyond the Armenian borders therefore inevitably come to mind. The fusion of a domed-cross plan with the aisleless and hall-churches of Armenia might well be interpreted as a variant of Justinian's standard cross-type superimposed on the building tradition of the inlands of the Near East; the more so since not infrequently (at T'alinn for example) the dome in these Armenian buildings rests on pendentives, not on squinches. The cross-in-square plan – we will revert to it – had been absorbed, or in fact developed, by Roman architects as early as the second century, and no doubt by the seventh century was common property of the Byzantine provinces in the East. Finally, octagonal buildings with projecting niches enclosed in a massive cube of masonry, as at Zoravar, call to mind Roman mausolea. This type was common, but to date has not been found either on the high plateau of Asia Minor, in Cilicia, or in Armenia. At this point we can only wait patiently for further evidence. The cross-octagon plan with quatrefoil apses and corner sacristies, as it appears at St Hrip'simé, presents an even more complex problem. It has been compared, to be sure, with Roman mausolea plans, but the confrontations remain vague and unsatisfactory.

On the basis of our present knowledge we should much rather view these centrally-planned churches in Armenia as the creation of a local school of architects. After all, central plans in Armenia came to the fore during the last years of the sixth century in innumerable variations, and cross-octagons such as St Hrip'simé are only the most complex among a plethora of central plans. All these churches evolve almost simultaneously and without manifest ancestry on Armenian soil. Obviously they originated within the complex mesh of political, religious, and cultural relationships in which Armenia was involved. The links to neighbouring Georgia are obvious and the question of precedence still under discussion.[56] Technical devices, such as the squinch and the corner niche, very possibly Iranian in origin, certainly played their part in shaping the new

centrally-planned churches.[57] Roman mausolea types may have been influential. However, it seems more important to recall that the new central plans gain momentum in Armenia shortly after they had become the only church types truly acceptable to patrons and builders in the Byzantine provinces and in the capital. The cross-in-square plan in Armenia, although in all likelihood linked to Syrian precedents, has been transformed so as to recall – with equal or indeed greater strength – cross-domed churches and their timber-roofed ancestors – or followers, whatever they may be. The tall, powerful corner piers bear little resemblance to the stumpy cross piers of Al-Mundir's audience hall; they call to mind the corner piers of the Cumanin Camii at Antalya and, even more strongly, the powerful corner supports of the H. Sophia in Salonica and the dark, tiny spaces concealed in them. No doubt, Armenian and Byzantine centrally-planned churches differ vastly in their basic concepts. Armenian architects think in terms of cramped space and of solid mass. The interiors are hemmed in; quatrefoils or octagons are prevented from expanding. The basic idea of a structure on a central plan, engendered as it is in my opinion by the development of building of Justinian's age and that following his, conflicts in Armenia with the architectural tradition of the inlands of the Near East from which Armenian architecture had originally sprung. Armenian building thus remains torn between two conflicting concepts: that of the Early Christian Near East, conservative and ever bound to Roman provincial custom, and that of Justinian's Byzantium, immensely fresh and progressive.

This dichotomy remains inherent throughout the further history of Armenian architecture. The development through the eighth and ninth centuries remains somewhat obscure, but the tenth century experiences what appears to be a renascence of seventh-century building types and concepts. The church of the Horomos Monastery at Goshavank, built in 928–53, and the cathedral of Ani (Kemah) of 989–1001 – it was built by the architect Trdat – both take up the plan of the cathedral of T'alish with only

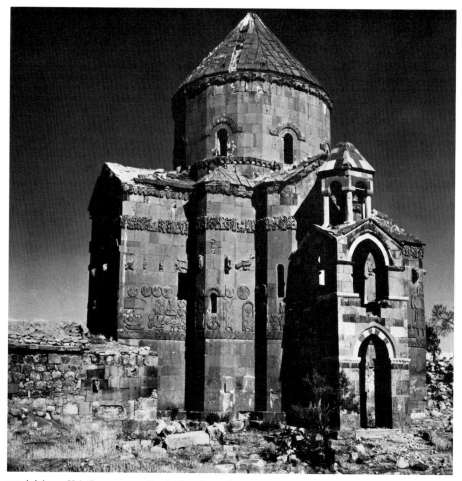

291. Aght'amar, Holy Cross, 915–21. Exterior from the south-west

minor differences. The church of the Holy Cross at Aght'amar, built in 915–21, revives after three hundred years the cross octagon plan of St Hrip'simé, with the difference that the exterior mass expresses more clearly the volumes [291, 292]. But the principal changes in all these later buildings concern the vocabulary. The piers are more complex in design; half-columns take the place of half-piers. The exterior walls are covered with decorative

sculpture, as at Aght'amar; or they are articulated, as at the cathedrals of Ani and Marmashen (986–1029), by blind arcades resting on slender colonnettes, single or in pairs.[58] Arches and capitals are covered with a web of geometric or floral ornament. Beginning with the eleventh century, church porches are frequently covered by a system of intersecting cross-arches, recalling Lombard rib-vaults. Despite such innovations in vocabulary, however,

292. Aght'amar, Holy Cross, 915–21. Interior facing north

the design of space and mass and the relation of solids and volumes remain basically unchanged. More often than not, Armenian churches of the tenth and eleventh centuries recall the Romanesque cathedrals of Western Europe. As a result, Armenian church building has been given, at least at times, the position of a life-spending source for much of later European and Byzantine architecture.

Romanesque builders supposedly received from Armenia the stone technique and the articulation of the wall by blind arcades resting on colonnettes. Gothic builders supposedly acquired the rib-vault by way of Armenia; Byzantine architects, the dome placed on squinches to cover an octagon; and Leonardo and Bramante, the central plans they employed for their churches, including St Peter's in Rome.[59]

Such sweeping claims have rarely been accepted.[60] The comparisons are as a rule ill-defined. St Peter's in Rome and St Hrip'simé at Vagharshapat resemble each other but vaguely, and only on paper. The cross-arches of Armenia are not Lombard rib-vaults. Leonardo was certainly not in Armenia, nor were the Gothic architects of France acquainted with Armenian vaulting. But it would be foolish to deny that Armenian architecture could occasionally have exerted its impact on Western, and, above all, on Byzantine building. It is perhaps of lesser importance that Trdat, the architect of the cathedral of Ani, was called to Constantinople to rebuild the dome of the H. Sophia, badly damaged in 989 by an earthquake. He might have been summoned as a technician. Yet it is undeniable that the plan of Skripou – a hall-church with inserted cross arms and dome, its design in solid masses and confined interior volumes, its sparse decoration, and its technique of heavy stone construction – is as customary in Armenia as it is exceptional in ninth-century Greece. Similarly, in the tenth and eleventh centuries the dome carried by corner squinches above a square bay may well have reached Greece – and, I would add, Constantinople – from Armenia, where it had been well established since the seventh century.[61]

Of all the border countries of the Empire, Armenia is the only one to deal with Byzantine architecture on an equal footing. But the differences between Byzantine and Armenian building – in design, construction, scale, and decoration – cannot be too strongly stressed.

PART SIX

MIDDLE BYZANTINE ARCHITECTURE
FROM THE MACEDONIAN EMPERORS
TO THE LATIN CONQUEST (864–1204)

CHAPTER 15

INTRODUCTION

The rule of the Macedonian, Comnene, and the shortlived intervening dynasties, from 867 to 1204, marks a high point on many fronts: in learning, in the arts, in religion and politics. The period has been called the 'Macedonian Renaissance'. But the term Renaissance is ambiguous, because of its primary and almost exclusive implication of a rebirth of Roman-hellenistic antiquity. On the other hand, the new flourishing of Byzantine culture certainly starts before the ascendancy of the Macedonian House, and its effect remains throughout the reigns of the Dukas (1059–81) and the Comnenes (1081–1185), up to the conquest of Constantinople by the Latins in 1204.[1] In the arts, the period has been called the Middle Byzantine Age. This term is not fortunate either. It recalls too closely the Western Middle Ages. Yet we shall use it in this book. It does, after all, isolate as a separate entity art from the ninth to the end of the twelfth century, setting it off against Early Byzantine art, from Justinian to the end of the century of iconoclasm (726–843), on the one hand, and on the other Late Byzantine, from the resurgence of the Empire, c. 1250, following the Latin occupation, to the conquest by the Turks in 1453.

The beginnings of the Middle Byzantine Age are clearly marked. Iconoclasm collapsed in 843, and the Church was pacified. The refusal of Photius, the patriarch of Constantinople (858–67 and 877–86), to recognize the supremacy of the Roman See was no definite break with the West; the definite schism between the Churches of Rome and Byzantium was to come only in the second half of the eleventh century.[2] But it established Constantinople – the only patriarchate left outside Islamic domains – as the supreme spiritual authority in the East, and from the time of Photius, the patriarch was considered the spiritual, the Emperor the temporal head of the *oikumene*, the inhabited world, as far as it was ruled from Byzantium.

In temporal affairs the power of the Emperor theoretically was unlimited. In practice, the intrigues of bureaucracy, army, navy, harem, and court led to continuous palace revolts and functioned as a check to Imperial strength. On the other hand, the efficient, continuous administration of the capital and the provinces was guaranteed by a permanent civil and military service: the officers' corps and the higher administrative and diplomatic ranks – drawn largely from the landed nobility – balanced by a hierarchy of court charges.

Reforms in the administrative and legislative areas stand alongside new activities in the applied sciences, the humanities, and the arts. Under Basil I (867–86) and Leo VI (886–912) the Code of

Justinian was reorganized, brought up to date, put into Greek, and thus adapted to contemporary use. The Emperor Theophilus (829–42), possibly stimulated by Arab technique, built a number of complex automata. Presumably at the same time, 'Greek fire' was invented, the dreaded weapon of the Byzantine navy. The university of Constantinople, closed during the iconoclastic centuries, was reopened and successively reorganized, with the primary aim of training an efficient and knowledgeable civil and diplomatic service. Its education was based on a thorough reading of the Greek classics, philosophers, dramatists, poets, historians, rhetoricians, mathematicians, geographers, and medical writers. The reading programme of Photius gives an idea of the astonishing breadth and depth of Byzantine learning, just as his sermons demonstrate the sophistication of Byzantine language and thought. The writings of that encyclopedist on the throne, Constantine VII Porphyrogenetos, not only illustrate the involved court ceremonial of the tenth century; they also show a remarkable political acumen and a thorough acquaintance with foreign countries, especially the Slavic world, acquired by way of diplomatic reports. In causing the Chronicles of Theophanes to be continued, he provides for posterity a thorough account of the Macedonian House and its deeds.[3] Michael Psellos recounts the court intrigues of the mid eleventh century in vivid, classicizing Greek.[4] A popular eleventh-century epic, *Dighenis Akritas*, glorifies the ninth- and tenth-century wars against the Caliphate, and the princess Anna Comnena composed the hundreds of pages of the *Alexiad* in praise of the deeds of her father, Alexius I (1081–1118), in war and peace.[5] All this rests on the tradition which, since the sixth century, in the cultural centres of the Byzantine Empire and particularly at Constantinople, had blended a classical vocabulary with Christian thought; a tradition which, from the ninth century on, was immensely strengthened in the figurative arts as well as in literature and learning. The illuminated manuscripts, from the Paris Psalter (Bibl. Nat., gr. 139) to the *Menologium* of Basil II (Vat. gr. 1613), speak as

clearly as the ivory plaques and caskets and the goldsmiths' and silversmiths' work of the late ninth to the end of the twelfth century.

This high level of culture was evolved and retained regardless of domestic upheavals and the political fortunes of the Empire abroad. The position of Byzantium in the Middle East, the Balkans, and eastern Europe was not primarily determined by the changing fortunes of war. It was not seriously checked by defeats, such as the rise of the Bulgarian Empire and the repeated Russian incursions against Constantinople during the ninth and tenth centuries, and finally in 1071 the catastrophic loss to the Seljuks of Asia Minor except for the Black Sea coast and a few isolated cities along the south coast. Nor was the standing of the Empire impaired by decades of military and palace revolts from 1030 to 1080 or, for that matter, enhanced on the international scene by military successes: counter-offensives in Dalmatia and South Italy under Basil I (867–86) and Nicephoros Phocas (963–9); the temporary reconquest of Syria under Nicephoros Phocas and John I Tzimiskes (969–76); and the reoccupation of the Northern Balkans under Basil II, the Bulgar-Killer (1018). In fact, regardless of the military situation, the position of the Empire both in the East and the West is as firmly established as ever, if not more firmly, during the reigns of the Porphyrogenetos (912–59), of Romanos I Lekapenos (920–44), and finally of the Comnene Emperors Alexius I (1081–1118), John II (1118–43), and Manuel I (1143–80).

For the standing of Byzantium in these centuries rests on very different circumstances: its position at the crossroads of the Western, Islamic, and Slavic worlds; its diplomatic skill coupled with the marriage policy of the Imperial houses; its trade east, north, and west; the expansion of its religious and cultural sphere of influence. Negotiations and payments to its underdeveloped neighbours and trade agreements rather than wars became the principal weapons of the Empire. Commercial relations with the Arab countries, though as a rule illegal, continue. Of greater importance are the trade routes which, from the ninth century, cross Russia to link Byzantium with the Scandinavian countries, and traverse the Balkans to connect with the valley of the Danube and with Central Europe. Simultaneously the young merchant republics of Italy, from Venice to Genoa, Amalfi, and Pisa, establish compounds in Constantinople, and their fleets export to Western Europe goods collected from all over the North and East. In the last third of the ninth century, two missionaries from Salonica, Kyrillos and Methodios, christianize the Serbs, Bulgars, Moravians, and Czechs and thus become the Apostles of the Slavs. Owing to their mission the Balkan peoples, Serbs and Bulgars, submit permanently to the spiritual domination of Constantinople. One hundred years later, the principality of Kiev, its ruler converted to Christianity in 967, is turned from an unruly foe into a close ally of the Empire, both spiritually and politically. Through Kiev, Byzantine influence is carried as far north as Novgorod and Vologda. The Princes of Kiev as well as the Bulgarian Czars – whether at war or peace with Byzantium – take Constantinople as their model both in court ceremonial and in art. In the West, Venice in the tenth century begins increasingly to model her diplomacy on that of Byzantium. By the late tenth and the early eleventh century, Byzantine building types reach Lower Saxony, presumably by way of the Balkan borderlands rather than directly from Constantinople. By the late eleventh century Byzantine mosaicists work at Monte Cassino, Byzantine metalworkers all over southern Italy. In 1063 an architect with a possibly Greek name, Busketos, lays out Pisa Cathedral, and as early as the tenth century the Caliphs of Cordova call mosaic workers from Constantinople to Spain, as the Umayyad Caliphs in the seventh century had called them to Damascus and Jerusalem.[6]

Indeed, despite the Muslim onslaught, the Macedonian emperors maintained close diplomatic relations with the infidel rulers of at least southern Spain. To the Caliphs of Cordova, the Byzantine Emperor was still a major political figure and his capital a cultural centre of the first magnitude. The esteem which the 'barbarians of the West' bestowed on Byzantium is thrown into relief by the marriage negotiations which Otto I eagerly pursued to obtain for his son the Byzantine princess Theophanou – apparently a poor cousin of the Imperial house. The reports of Otto's envoy to Byzantium, Liutprand of Cremona, are filled with ill-concealed admiration of the impressive, if slightly shoddy, glories of the Byzantine capital and court.[7] To pilgrims on their way to the Holy Land, whether Westerners or Russians,[8] Constantinople was *the* Imperial city: Micklegarth or Czarigrad, filled with countless treasures, relics, reliquaries, icons, buildings. To the Byzantines, on the other hand, Bulgars, Russians, Italians, Germans, and French alike were powerful, uncivilized barbarians. Mistrust, well justified, marked the Byzantine attitude towards the Crusaders. Seen as fellow Christians, but dangerous allies and protectors, from 1096 to 1192, they became outright enemies in 1204 when they occupied Constantinople.[9] In Byzantine eyes, one must remember, the Emperor of Byzantium always remained the only true Emperor, the *basileus tōn Rōmaiōn*; his domain, ever smaller and feebler, remained the Roman Empire; his court was the one Imperial court; his capital, the one Imperial capital on earth.[10]

Such political and cultural resurgence was based on economic prosperity revived and steadily increasing from the mid eighth century for another three hundred years. Towns half-abandoned were repopulated: Patras and Sardis returned to life; in Corinth the central agora was built over by shops and housing; in Nicaea the population had regained its previous level and around 1015 the city walls were repaired and a large church, H. Sophia, was built; in Athens the town expanded to the ancient walls, if loosely settled, and some forty churches rose from the tenth to the twelfth century; at the same time in the small town of Kastoria, a dozen or so churches were built out of thirty-two surviving. In the countryside, based on their landholdings, large monasteries flourished; Hosios Lukas, Daphni, Hosios Meletios, Sagmata; the first to rise on Mount

Athos; on Chios the Nea Moni, on Patmos the fortress-monastery of St John the Evangelist – all dating within two hundred years, starting in the mid tenth century. Also, by the ninth century, precious metalwork and weaving were produced at Patras, in the twelfth century silk stuffs at Thebes. Ivories and splendid illuminated manuscripts abounded from the ninth and tenth centuries on, and mosaics covered again the walls and vaults of churches.[11]

Constantinople was the hub of that revival – call it renascence or not. The population, sorely depleted, climbed from the mid eighth century. Whether it ever reached, as in the sixth century, the four-hundred-thousand mark, the city was the one metropolis in the Empire. Shipping was active, the streets were thronged, wares were plentiful. Building, revived since the 850s, reached a peak a generation later and remained there for two hundred years. Basil I (867–86) is said to have built a hundred churches – a rhetorical figure. But he did repair scores, starting with H. Sophia; and he built within the palace half a dozen churches, one of them the Nea, the New Church, with its colonnades, porticoes, and fountains, and clamorous state chambers – of which more anon. In town, the Atik Mustafa Paša Camii, whatever its Christian dedication, may date

from his reign. The Macedonian and Comnene Emperors from 867 to 1185, their wives, and high-ranking officials vied with one another in founding and building churches, monasteries, mansions, welfare institutions: in the first half of the tenth century alone, the Myrelaion, the nearby palace of Romanos I, another one near the Holy Apostles, the church and convent of Constantine Lips; two old people's homes, a hospital, and a handful of other churches were lost. In a new resurgence of church building from the late eleventh century on, the complex of the Pantocrator rises (Zeyrek Camii), the Eski Imaret Camii, the core of the Pammakaristos (Fetiyeh Camii), and that of the Chora church, the Kariye Camii; and, still at the end of the twelfth century, the Kalenderhane Camii – to name just a handful among those surviving. Of the roughly six hundred churches and monasteries listed from the foundation of Constantinople to its fall, roughly half were built in Middle Byzantine times. Also, from the very start this architecture spreads from the capital over the empire and beyond, to South Italy, to Venice, to Bulgaria and Russia. Macedonian and Comnene building represents the height of Byzantine influence from Calabria to the Black Sea, Kiev, and Cyprus.

CHAPTER 16

THE NEW BUILDING TYPES

AND THE 'MIDDLE BYZANTINE RENAISSANCE'

With the middle of the ninth century, the church plans of the times immediately after Justinian generally disappear from the architectural centres of the Empire. Their place is taken by new types, widely differing among each other in plan, yet closely related in stylistic concept. The nomenclature of the new types is often confusing, and some explanation is in order. Likewise their origin is far from clear. In their great majority the new Middle Byzantine church types are either freshly invented, or they transform older types so radically that they are as good as newly created.[1]

Older plans of the period after Justinian are nevertheless retained or revived, mainly along the borders of the Empire and its sphere of influence in politics and culture. Military architecture remained practically unchanged. When the city walls of Nicaea (Iznik) [293] were rebuilt after an earthquake in 1065, the eleventh-century parts differed from the original Early Byzantine sections only in their masonry technique and in very minor details. In church buildings such conservatism is less frequently found. Timber-roofed basilicas provided with galleries had been outmoded for nearly five

293. Nicaea (Iznik), city wall, south, near Yenišehir Gate, rebuilt after 1065

hundred years in Constantinople and the core provinces of the Empire. From the late ninth to the eleventh century, they stage a comeback at the courts of the 'barbarian princes' in the Balkans and in the West. In Bulgaria, this reversion has been explained as the revival of a plan firmly rooted locally throughout the entire sixth century. The reasons for this 'renascence' remain in doubt. One reason may have been the desire of the newly converted rulers and their ecclesiastical advisers to impress a still pagan population with huge, if simple, church buildings; another may have been the desire to emulate the great rulers of the past, primarily Justinian, himself a native son of the Balkans. At the Ottonian court in Lower Saxony, the church of Gernrode was completed after 971 by adding a nave with galleries above the aisles, a feature previously quite unknown north of the Alps. Attempts have been made to link its appearance to the intervention of the Byzantine-born Empress Theophanou.[2] Considering obsolescence of the type in tenth-century Constantinople, the explanation is not very satisfactory, and we wonder whether the builders of Gernrode did not rather have in mind the churches built at just that time by the flourishing court of the Bulgarian czars. However, basilicas were built or remodelled even in the very heart of the Byzantine Empire when local conditions demanded such obsolete plans. As late as c. 1065, the church of the H. Sophia at Nicaea (Iznik) was rebuilt as a basilica on the foundation walls of an older similar building, presumably of the fifth or sixth century.[3]

Other obsolete types are also resuscitated in the eleventh century in the Empire and beyond its borders. Cross-domed plans, long out of date in Constantinople and the central provinces, were carried by Constantinopolitan masons to the courts of South Russia from the first half of the eleventh century onwards; and after 1070 – beyond the western frontiers of the Empire – Justinian's five-domed church of the Holy Apostles was copied, although transformed, at S. Marco as the palatine church of the Veneto-Byzantine oligarchy.[4] As a rule, then, such revivals of early church types are based on mixed ecclesiastical and political considerations.

Very different in character from reversions to obsolete plans in the sphere of the court are survivals of old-fashioned building types on a popular provincial level, either as a persisting local type or as a borrowing from another remote province. Examples are the small basilicas of north-eastern Greece, southern Yugoslavia, and Bulgaria, barrel-vaulted or timber-roofed, as witness the church of the Anargyroi at Kastoria [294], H. Theodora at Arta, the Kato Panaghia near by.[5] With their steep naves and wide arches, these structures dating from the tenth to the end of the fourteenth century recall nothing so much as the tiny basilicas and hall-churches at Binbirkilise – far distant in time and space. But then small churches, aisleless or basilican, must have been frequent from the fourth to the tenth century, barrel-vaulted in remote deforested mountain regions all over the Christian world.

Likewise, the plans of Late Roman and Early Christian mausolea and martyria apparently survived or were revived in the small trefoil and quatrefoil churches of Middle Byzantine times. Their number is large to this day, both near the capital and in the provinces: Greece, the Balkans, Cappadocia. The Kubilidike at Kastoria, whether of about 900 or eleventh-century, is one [295], a church at Heybeliada on Chalki in the Sea of Marmara another of many examples. The wide spread of the type in Middle Byzantine times becomes clear when one realizes that the great majority of the structures were apparently either funeral chapels or chapels sheltering an important relic. They were objects of special popular veneration, just like the martyria of Early Christian times, or for that matter, the marabouts of Islamic saints. Their appearance in remote parts of the Empire in Middle Byzantine times may be explained as expressive of popular opposition to the sophisticated court architecture both within and on the outskirts of the Empire, the same popular conservatism which created the small vaulted basilicas of the ninth to twelfth centuries in the Balkans.[6]

294 (below). Kastoria, Anargyroi, first third
of the eleventh century. From the east

295 (right). Kastoria, Kubilidike, c. 900(?)
Exterior from the south-east

Nevertheless, such survivals and revivals of obsolete church plans remain confined either to special circumstances or to local predilection. The core of Middle Byzantine architecture is formed by building types either newly created or purloined from the outlying borderlands of the Empire and eagerly adopted by Middle Byzantine builders: the atrophied Greek cross plan and its variants; the octagon-domed churches; the related Greek-cross octagon; the ambulatory church; finally, the cross-in-square or quincunx plan.

The atrophied Greek-cross plan consists of but a centre bay with four shallow arms and single or triple apses, the apses at times preceded by short fore-choirs. The barrel-vaults over the arms of the cross are hardly more than wide arches, and the dome over the centre bay is pierced by large windows. Groups of windows are also placed high up in the end walls of the cross arms. The type is represented in Constantinople in the early twelfth century, for example, by the Chora church (Kariye Camii) in its central core. But the plan was in wide use long before: near Constantinople at Ereğli and Yuša Tepesi, ruins of the ninth or tenth century, and at Sige in the eighth, at Vunitsa (Vinitsa) in Bulgaria in the tenth century.[7] The type was long-lived and still favoured in Paleologan times. Possibly such atrophied Greek-cross churches were known as early as the eighth century. In any event, the plan seems to have developed from a more elaborate type, either from the Greek-cross churches of Justinian's time with deeper cross arms and corner bays, or from the cross-domed churches of the time immediately after Justinian. The atrophied Greek cross is, after all, but the isolated core of a cross-domed church: domed centre bay, shallow arms and chancel parts. But whatever their origin, the churches built on the atrophied Greek-cross plan do not determine the picture of Middle Byzantine church building. To understand more fully its character and its wealth, one wants to turn to octagon-domed churches, to combined Greek-cross and octagon plans, and to quincunx structures.

The octagon-domed church is laid out on a square plan [296]. Pilasters, cornices, and marble panelling divide the walls into two tiers, each tier

296 (*above*). Nea Moni, Chios, Katholikon, 1042–56. Plan

297 (*below*). Hosios Lukas, Katholikon, consecrated 1011 or 1022, and Church of the Theotokos, tenth century. Plan

comprising three bays: narrow, wide, and narrow. On the third tier, small stilted half-domes – hemispherical squinches – are thrown across the corners to form an octagon, while shallow arches rise in the main axis over the wider bays. Jointly, the bases of the squinches and arches form an octagon of unequal sides, inscribed in the main square. Finally, eight pendentives fill the space between arches and corner squinches, and create a circle from which rises the hemispherical dome, enclosed in a low drum. The type has survived in only a few examples, such as the Nea Moni on Chios and a handful of later churches on the same island [318, 319]. But we know that it was brought to Chios from Constantinople.[8] It was thus presumably more widespread in Middle Byzantine times, both in the capital and the provinces, than is indicated by surviving examples.

The Katholikon at Hosios Lukas and the church at Daphni are the best-known and probably the most beautiful representatives of the Greek-cross-octagon plan. The core of the plan is again formed by the octagon-domed square, but the corner squinches are carried by L-shaped piers [297 *bottom*, 298, 344, 345, 347, 351, 352]. This core is then enclosed within a larger rectangle. Four tall cross arms, set between the piers, issue from the centre towards the outer walls of the second rectangle. Each arm is barrel-vaulted, and measures half the width of the centre square; the arm to the east projects in an apse.

IOTH CENTURY

IOII OR IO22

LATER ADDITIONS

Between the four cross-arms, the corners of the outer rectangle are filled by an ancillary belt of groin-vaulted or domed bays, including prothesis and diaconicon on either side of the chancel arm. As a rule – as at Daphni – this ancillary outer belt is one-storeyed and thus subordinate to the cross arms and the domed centre [351]. But occasionally, as at

298. Hosios Lukas, Katholikon, consecrated 1011 or 1022. Interior facing north-east

Hosios Lukas, the outer bays are surmounted by a gallery, closed at the corners but wide open below the encroaching barrel-vaults of the cross arms. In either case the dominant features remain the wide, expanding octagon, the broad dome placed on corner squinches, the subordinate, tall, narrow arms of the cross and their interpenetration with the outer belt. The overall spatial effect is overwhelmingly beautiful in its complex interplay of higher and lower elements, of core and ancillary spaces, of clear, dim, and dark zones of lighting. The Greek-cross-octagon is perhaps the most impressive Middle Byzantine church plan. It is revived in the thirteenth century, both with and without galleries. But like the octagon-domed plan, it is not widely spread. The surviving examples are confined to the mainland of Greece.[9]

The Greek-cross-octagon plan is but an enlargement of the domed octagon, and the origin of both plans has long been sought in Armenia.[10] Corner squinches used to support a dome were a permanent feature of Armenian church building from at least the seventh century, and they could easily have come to the attention of Middle Byzantine patrons and builders. After all, Armenian architects were active in Constantinople around 1000. But there is no need to focus narrowly on Armenia. By the tenth and eleventh centuries, domes on corner squinches were widespread in Islamic architecture. They could have penetrated into Byzantine construction from Islamic countries as well as from Armenia. Whatever the origin of the dome on squinches, however, the importance of the question, it seems to me, has been vastly overplayed. Squinches are an element of construction which can be incorporated into almost any kind of architecture. Where the Armenian builders stressed the massive bulk of the structure and cramped the space of the interior, the Byzantine architects played on the expanding space, the pervading light, and the membrane-like enclosing walls. Complex as their plans are, the spatial design of the Middle Byzantine Greek-cross octagons differs most emphatically from the earlier Armenian domed churches. Both the octagon-domed church

and the Greek-cross octagon – a domed centre expanding into a cross and interpenetrating with an enveloping belt of subordinate spaces – are, instead, closely linked to the structural principle and the spatial design of cross-domed churches of the time after Justinian and to other designs of the late years of Justinian and the years after him. The principle of allowing the barrel-vaulted arms of a cross design to encroach upon the space of aisles and galleries is exemplified, after all, by churches such as the H. Irene after its remodelling towards the middle of the eighth century. The Greek-cross octagon, then, is rooted in a Byzantine tradition which may have absorbed a borderland element of construction.

The ambulatory church, in plan, recalls the cross-domed churches of Byzantium, known from the late seventh or early eighth centuries, as witness the Koimesis church at Nicaea (Iznik), to its latest known twelfth-century examples, such as the Kalenderhane Camii. A domed centre bay is screened off from an enveloping ambulatory by triple arcades inserted between the corner piers. In elevation, though, the differences are marked: the cross arms are reduced to mere wall arches; and the gallery zone, integral to the cross-domed church, is missing. Indeed, one of the earliest examples would have been the Koimesis at Nicaea, if indeed rebuilt shortly after 1065 by removing the galleries and replacing them by clerestory walls. At the same time or shortly later, though, the Fetiyeh Camii in Constantinople was laid out from the outset on the ambulatory plan.[11]

The quincunx or cross-in-square is the most widely spread Middle Byzantine church plan. Small, steep, and enclosed in the outline of a square, its core – the *naos* – is composed of nine elements: a tall centre bay, resting on four supports, either columns or piers; a high, well-lit drum of a dome rising as a rule from pendentives; subordinate to it, four short barrel-vaulted cross arms expanding in the main axes; lower, in the diagonal axes, four corner bays, groin-vaulted, barrel-vaulted or domed [297, *top*, 299, 303, 309, 312, 327A, 328A, 338, and *passim*]. Jointly these corner bays, sometimes surmounted on

299. Hosios Lukas, Theotokos,
tenth century. Interior

the exterior by the high drums of lesser domes, and the taller main dome, form the five spots of a quincunx. At the same time, the term 'cross-in-square' is justified by the way in which the arms of the cross issue from the centre bay and meet the outer square of the structure. Three apses project eastward from the naos. This core is at times enveloped by a narthex, by lateral open porticoes, or by closed side chapels (*parekklesia*). But regardless of such additions or variations, the quincunx or cross-in-square plan becomes the church type almost universally accepted all over the sphere of Byzantine and dependent architecture, from the ninth century to the Fall of Constantinople, and surviving in Russia and the Balkans far beyond.

The origins of the type remain in dispute, both as to its antecedents and the time and place of its first appearance. General consensus lists the Nea, consecrated in 881, as the first known quincunx church in Constantinople. This, though, is less than certain. Granted, none of the many quincunx churches so far known in Greece and the Balkans are earlier. But not far from Constantinople at Tirilye on the southern shore of the Sea of Marmara, a quincunx church has been dated tentatively 780–813. Certainly forerunners do exist outside the capital and the core provinces of the Middle Byzantine Empire. As early as the eighth and throughout the ninth century, the quincunx plan was known in the West: at Germigny-des-Prés on the Loire after 800; at S. Satiro in Milan in 868, and apparently at the same time at S. Miguel at Tarrasa in Spain; finally, as early as the late eighth century at S. Maria delle Cinque Torri at S. Germano near Cassino (778–97) in an unvaulted variant with triple arcades supporting the four walls of the centre bay.[12] Similarly, quincunx churches of the eighth and ninth centuries survive in the outlying provinces of Asia Minor and Thrace. At least one of the quincunx cave churches in the wilderness of Göreme in Cappadocia bears, covered by the frescoes of a cycle of the Passion, an iconoclast decoration of crosses. It is thus possible that its plan dates from before 843, if not from the eighth century. Another quincunx church stands among the ruins of Side on the south coast of Asia Minor. The final destruction of the city in 886 supplies the church with a *terminus ante quem* – how long before remains open. At Peristerai, in the mountains at the base of Mount Athos, a quincunx plan forms the core of a church built in 870/1 [328B].[13] All these examples – and many more could be listed – raise the question as to whether the type originated in Constantinople long before the Nea and was transmitted to the provinces, or whether at the time the Nea was built, the quincunx plan was imported from the provinces into the capital.

An origin of the quincunx plan either in the Byzantine provinces or beyond the borders of the Empire has been frequently suggested. The plan has been derived from Iranian architecture, either by way of Armenia, or directly from Sassanian Fire Temples.[14] However the resemblances to Iranian building are but superficial. The so-called 'cross arms' of the Fire Temples are part of an ambulatory covered by longitudinal barrel-vaults, and the dates of the Fire Temples are vague. Others have postulated two types of quincunx churches with different origins: one rooted in a hellenistic tradition, the other originating in the highlands of Anatolia.[15] But the sixth-century date claimed for the Anatolian quincunx churches cannot be substantiated. Two hypotheses at present contend with one another. One views the quincunx plan as a shrunk version of cross-domed churches such as H. Sophia in Salonica: the core, dome and arms, reduced; the spaces inside the piers turned into the corner bays of the quincunx, the piers into columns, the ancillary envelope into outer porticoes and esonarthex. Or else the quincunx is derived from domed transept basilicas such as Skripou: the nave shortened, the walls separating nave and aisles reduced to oblong or square piers – a quincunx as frequent in provincial Greece. Neither hypothesis satisfies.[16] Both depend on vague resemblances in plan and disregard essential differences in size and proportion. It is hard to draw any comparison between the slender columns of a quincunx and the massive piers of a cross-domed church or the dividing walls of Skripou, between the open bays of a quincunx and the enclosed spaces of cross-domed or basilican vaulted structures, the compactness of the former and the expansive design of the older types. The steep, lithe elevation of the first, the squat proportions of the second, are entirely different.

On the other hand, quincunx structures had existed from the second century on in the Roman and Byzantine Near East. As early as A.D. 180, a small building in the Roman camp of Mousmieh (Mismiye) in Syria was divided into the nine bays of a quincunx. Its centre bay, covered either by a cloister-vault or a timber roof, rested on four slender columns [300].[17] It may have been a temple or a praetorium, that is either a religious building, or a secular building imbued with religious connotations. Similar structures are known in the East in later centuries as well. A quincunx building outside the walls of R'safah, with barrel-vaulted arms,

300. Mousmieh (Mismiye), temple(?), 180. Interior. Drawing, c. 1860

groin-vaulted corner bays, and a timber-roofed centre bay, is identified by an inscription as the audience hall of a local chieftain, one Al-Mundir, dating from c. 560 [301].[18] Construction and details

301. R'safah, audience hall of Al-Mundir, c. 560. Interior facing east

leave no doubt that the training of the builders had been in provincial Byzantine conventions. Nonetheless, the links of the Middle Byzantine church type to such early 'quincunxes' are questionable and the further history of the type remains to be established. Armenian seventh-century churches, such as the Gayané at Vagharshapat and the church at Bagaran [288, A and B], bear only a paper resemblance to Al-Mundir's audience hall, and thus cannot be taken to be the missing links between the use of the type in semi-religious secular building and in ecclesiastical architecture. But it seems a plausible hypothesis, though so far unproven, to assume that at some time between the sixth and the ninth centuries the plan of the quincunx audience hall was transferred to ecclesiastical building. The cross-domed plan might well have exerted a collateral impact on the transfer, but the exact time of the transfer, and its place – whether Constantinople, the borderlands, or the provinces – for the time being must be left open.

Whether quincunx churches, basilicas, octagon-domed structures, tri- and tetraconchs, or Greek-cross octagons, all Middle Byzantine churches are remarkably small. The cross-octagon churches are somewhat larger and their expansive space makes them appear more sizeable. However, even the naos in the cross-octagon church of the Katholikon of Hosios Lukas, not including the narthex, covers an area of only 270 sq. m. (295 sq. yds), just slightly more than twice the adjoining quincunx church of the Theotokos, or the north church in the Fenari Isa Camii in Constantinople, each with an inner area of 115 sq. m. (126 sq. yds) [297, 312]. On the other hand, the area of the Katholikon at Hosios Lukas is not even one third that of the H. Sophia in Salonica, which measures nearly 900 sq. m. (985 sq. yds), not to mention Justinian's churches. Some of the complex factors underlying this predilection for small church buildings should at least be considered.

Monasticism was always supreme within the Eastern Churches. The parish and metropolitan structure remained underdeveloped and subordinate to the monastic organization. Frequently parishes and bishoprics were subject to some great monastery; to this day the high Greek clergy is as a rule drawn from the monastic ranks. Thus it is but natural that among Middle and Late Byzantine church types monastic sanctuaries took the lead,

designed as a rule for small congregations. Indeed monastic communities in Middle Byzantine times had shrunk incredibly.[19] While before 800, like those in the West they often counted many hundreds, two centuries later a congregation above eight was considered large. Groups of three and four hermits or monks, living under a *lavra* system in caves or cells some distance apart, would use tiny churches such as those at Göreme. Congregations residing in monasteries adjoining the church, too, were small in number. The convent of Constantine Lips, one of the largest in Constantinople, housed fifty nuns between ladies and servant girls; thus a small, intimate church was sufficient. Such dwindling was caused less by the iconodule emigration from roughly 720 to 850 than by fiscal pressure of the later ninth and the tenth centuries. On the other hand the number of convents in Middle and Late Byzantine times was large.

Middle and Late Byzantine parish churches followed suit both in small size and large numbers. In a minor town such as Kastoria some thirty remain, all tiny, some only 9 sq. m. (11 sq. yds) inside. Many may have been for the use of just one family or even one individual. Smallness in church design was furthered by the increasing frequency on the one hand of commemorative services, on the other of the priest's celebrating Mass without anyone attending, as 'private liturgy'. To such ends chapels, *parek-klesia*, were built: attached to the flanks of the church; installed in or above the narthex, doubled and domed; or at roof level, domed and with altar and chancel barrier, but holding only the priest; or they stand free, a tiny structure, beside the main church, itself small enough.

Concomitantly, Eastern ritual more and more favoured small architecture. The liturgical development of the service had assigned the naos wholly or in large part to the clergy. The lay folk would crowd outside the naos: in lateral porticoes; in the outer and inner narthex; or under the open sky, as is done to this day all through Greece. The naos is Heaven, inaccessible to the laymen during services, and this is brought out in its figurative decoration.[20] The main dome carries the most exalted themes of the heavenly hierarchy: either the Pantokrator in the centre of the dome with the chorus of angels arranged along the lower curve; or at times, the Descent of the Holy Spirit; or else, the Ascension. From this heavenly zone, the themes descend in an ordered hierarchy to subordinate but still exalted subjects. The pendentives and lunettes are occupied by scenes from the life of Christ and his Passion, according to the cycle of the great festivals. Finally, the walls and barrel-vaults of the aisles carry the figures of the Witnesses, Apostles, Martyrs, Prophets, and Patriarchs. Obviously this symbolism of decoration had to be legibly presented to the clergy and monks assembled in the naos and to such laymen as would enter the naos when services were not in progress. The solution was to concentrate the programme within the smallest possible space.

Lastly, smallness, intimacy, and subtlety are basic stylistic concepts of Middle and Late Byzantine architecture. A wealth of decoration designed to overwhelm the visitor would be crowded into the tiny space of these churches: marble sheathing and precious tapestries on the walls and mosaics or murals in the vaulting zone; icons and reliquaries of gold, enamel, and glass, such as have survived in the treasure of S. Marco in Venice. In centres such as Constantinople and Salonica, these structures were built by the court and the high aristocracy, for monastic congregations often drawn from the sophisticated society of these same circles. Founders, builders, and visitors alike were trained to savour the subtle interlocking of space, its expansion or restriction, the delicate curving of a niche, the membering of a wall by fine mouldings, the carving of a profile or an ornament. This highest level of quality, to be sure, would be found most frequently in the churches of Constantinople, within as well as outside the palace precinct. But it would also be found in the provinces when monasteries and convents were founded by members of the Imperial House, by aristocratic families from Constantinople, or by high civil servants – and ruled by abbots and abbesses sprung from these same social circles.

Financial restrictions and the limitations of local master masons frequently resulted in the building of churches reduced in plan and awkward in execution. But we may be sure that, ideally, founders and builders of even such provincial churches strove to compete with the most refined churches of the most aristocratic monasteries, designed and executed on the highest level of subtle sophistication.

From the late ninth to the eleventh and twelfth centuries, then, church building in the capital and throughout the Empire continues to be immensely fertile. New types are established, and a highly developed and sophisticated Middle Byzantine architectural style is evolved. Domestic architecture, on the other hand, apparently remains fettered to age-old traditions, although current evidence allows only a tentative judgement. The dwellings of the poor, presumably hovels, as well as farmhouses are unknown. Only a few Middle Byzantine houses have come to light in Constantinople.[21] Our knowledge of middle-class dwellings is limited to a handful of residences and commercial buildings excavated in a few Greek cities. In Athens, the middle-class city house formed a block, roughly square, with a courtyard in the centre as a source of light and air; rooms enveloped this peristyle on all four sides. A number of twelfth-century houses excavated on the Agora provide examples, and at the same time demonstrate the continuity of the plan in the Aegean area for over fifteen hundred years. These twelfth-century houses are indistinguishable from the fifth-century houses which preceded them on the Agora, or for that matter, from houses in Dura-Europos (Qalat es Sālhīye) of the second century, or from city houses in Delos and Priene dating from the first, second, and third centuries B.C. Likewise the old shopping terrace of Greek and hellenistic ancestry occasionally survives into the twelfth century. Simpler houses have been found at Corinth composed of two or three rectangular rooms, parallel to each other and sometimes partitioned by a pair of supports.[22] Terraces as well as the more elaborate peristyle houses were sometimes provided with upper floors. But the smallness of the rooms and – in the terrace houses – the poor organization of the plan more often than not turned the structures into rabbit warrens.

On the other hand, domestic ecclesiastical archi-tecture – if the term applies – is more monumental in appearance. Numerous examples have come down to us in the form of monasteries in Greece, many well preserved.[23] The monasteries of Hosios Meletios near Megara, of Sagmata in Boeotia, and of the Great Lavra on Mount Athos represent the type to perfection [302–4].[24] A large rectangle or trapezoid, enclosed within a fortified wall, envelops

302 and 303. Hosios Meletios, Hymettos, monastery, oldest parts eleventh century. General view and plan

N

0   40 FT

0   15 M

304 and 305. Mount Athos, Great Lavra, eleventh century. From the south-west (*above*) and refectory (*below*)

a wide courtyard. The church rises in the centre of the courtyard. The fortified walls are lined with storerooms, stables, and workshops; against this inner row of work rooms, or directly against the wall itself, lean the cells of the monks laid out in long rows and facing the courtyard. At Hosios Meletios they were one-storeyed, but frequently they are built up on two, three, or four floors. If multi-storeyed, the cells have access from long loggias; Kutlumusíu on Mount Athos supplies a well-preserved, if late, example. One side of the rectangle, frequently that opposite the church, is occupied by the refectory (*trapeza*) and the kitchen. The refectory is generally a long hall, aisleless and terminated by an apse: the refectory in the Great Lavra on Mount Athos provides a good example [305]. A long table with benches would run along the centre axis, or else a number of semicircular tables (*sigmata*) would stand along the walls, pushed back into flat rectangular niches. At times the tables are sheltered by low semicircular niches running along the flanks of the hall. Frequently a canopy rises over the well head (*phiale*) in front of the church. Sometimes a bath house and an infirmary (*nosokomion*) stand outside the abbey walls, the latter a cross-in-square building, its centre bay surmounted by a chimney and thus serving as fireplace and kitchen for the sick. Throughout the monastery, all rooms were vaulted – cells, workshops, refectory, sick bay, kitchen, and bath.

All this obviously goes back to a tradition more than half a millennium old by the eleventh and twelfth centuries. The fortified rectangle recalls the fifth-century monastery of Daphni or that of St Catherine on Mount Sinai [218]. The multi-storeyed rows of cells preceded by open loggias derive from a Late Antique house type which is reflected equally in the small town houses of fourth-, fifth-, and sixth-century Syria [95].[25] The refectories with niches projecting from their flanks are obviously linked to Late Antique banqueting halls; one such hall – the Dekanneacubita, possibly of sixth-century date – had apparently survived in the Imperial Palace in Constantinople.[26] In short, the

plan of Middle Byzantine monasteries in Greece and their details are largely survivals of Late Antiquity – pagan as well as Christian – and of Early Byzantine times.

Monasteries are the one aspect of Middle Byzantine domestic building on which we are well informed. On the other hand, next to nothing is known about the palaces of the Byzantine aristocracy, whether in Constantinople or elsewhere, during the tenth, eleventh, and twelfth centuries. Representations in illuminated manuscripts of the period, lengthy literary descriptions, and passing hints in contemporary writings are all of doubtful value.[27] The manuscripts show, to be sure, palaces with projecting wings, sometimes surmounted by towers; balconies resting on columns; façades opened by double tiers of arcades. But the question always remains whether such elements are meant to represent existing structures, or whether they are conventional symbols handed down to the Byzantine painters by their Late Antique ancestors. On the other hand, it has long been suggested that Middle Byzantine models are reflected in the Venetian palace façades of the eleventh and twelfth centuries. The type is best represented by the Fondaco dei Turchi, built as the palace of the Pesaro family: a shallow *corps de logis*, its rooms open in a double tier of arcaded porticoes flanked by low towers. The type may well derive from Roman country houses, and its appearance in Venice has been explained as a conscious return by Venetian builders to Late Antique buildings still known to them.[28] But it seems much more likely that the type remained in use throughout the centuries both in Constantinople and Venice, not only in rural but in urban architecture as well. Indeed the foundation walls of at least the reception rooms of a palace of just that plan have been recently traced in Constantinople: the palace of Romanos I Lekapenos, built about 920 atop the rotunda – remodelled into a vaulted cistern – of the fifth-century Myrelaion Palace. The case for a Middle Byzantine origin of Venetian palace architecture is strengthened by a second palace type, known in Venice only from the

Late Middle Ages onwards. Its plan consists of a long room on the centre axis at right angles to the façade, flanked by smaller rooms on either side. It thus presents a close resemblance, strange as it may seem, to the princely dwellings found in the tenth-century palaces at Pliska and Preslav in Bulgaria and, as early as the fifth to the seventh centuries, at Dvin in Armenia.[29] If they share, as is likely, a common source, that source can only be Byzantium.

One would expect the Imperial palace in Constantinople to reflect, better than anything else, the architectural style of the Macedonian Age. Certainly building activity in the Great Palace, though it had never ceased entirely, increased anew with the second quarter of the ninth century. Beginning with Theophilos (829–42), and continuing under Basil I (867–86) and Constantine VII Porphyrogenetos (912–59), new parts were added and old ones remodelled and redecorated. No identifiable remains survive. Nevertheless, a general impression can be obtained, I think, of both the layout of the Great Palace in Macedonian times and of the design and decoration of its state apartments. Contemporary descriptions such as the hints contained in Constantine Porphyrogenetos' *Book of Ceremonies* and the short *ekphraseis* scattered in the continuation of Theophanes' *Chronicle* through biographies of the Macedonian House, while tantalizingly obscure on first reading,[30] make sense when viewed against the background of palaces built by the Bulgarian czars and the caliphs of Cordova in the ninth and tenth centuries, by the Norman kings of Sicily in the twelfth, and by the Abencerrages of Granada as late as the fourteenth century. From the *Book of Ceremonies*, the Great Palace at first emerges as a vast maze of reception halls, churches, chapels, porticoes, corridors, courtyards, pools, and staircases – impossible to disentangle. Old parts – some perhaps going as far back as Constantine's first palace on the site, but rebuilt time and again – and additions dating from the fifth on to the end of the ninth century were, it seems, inextricably interwoven. From the hill of the Sarayi behind H. Sophia a loose chain of palaces and palace parts stretched south

and west down the slope of the coastline as far as H. Sergios and Bakchos. Near the end, a few remains survive: a peristyle court on a terrace, its floor carrying a splendid mosaic with animals and monsters, hunting and combat scenes, dating in all likelihood from the late sixth century; attached to the courtyard an apsed hall, possibly of the same date, possibly earlier; finally, on the seashore just east of H. Sergios and Bakchos where the Bukoleon harbour was, the so-called 'House of Justinian'. This, grown and rebuilt ever since the fifth century, and in its final phase dating perhaps from as late as the eighth century, had been enlarged by a grand covered terrace, its marble portals high up opening on a long balcony overlooking the Sea of Marmara.[31] Still, by the middle of the tenth century, when the Porphyrogenetos wrote, the part of the palace in active use had apparently contracted to two sections: the site of Constantine's palace, the Daphne, southeast and south of the H. Sophia, and east of the northern part of the hippodrome; and the closely adjoining slopes towards the seashore. The wings, overlooking the Bukoleon harbour half a mile from the H. Sophia, were probably abandoned. On careful reading, the tangle of structures and courtyards hinted at by the *Book of Ceremonies* unravels itself into several distinct groups of buildings. Directly behind the Chalki Gate (which was remodelled into a towering chapel in 970)[32] appeared an entrance court, enclosed by guard houses, reception rooms, audience halls, and chapels. The state and private apartments of the emperors – with rectangular, octagonal, square, and circular rooms, dressing-rooms, chapels, and dining-rooms – all centred on, it would seem, or adjoined the Chrysotriklinos of Justin II (565–78). The state banquet hall (the Dekanneacubita) and a reception hall (the Consistorium) were joined by a courtyard. The Magnaura formed another, separate, throne room. Finally, near Basil's new church, the Nea, were located the polo-grounds with stables and warehouses. In short, the impression is not so much of a palace block laid out along an axial system but of a number of pavilions, or building groups, each consisting of several structures and focused on a courtyard or possibly on a domed centre room. Each of these pavilions was more or less self-sufficient and fairly compact, but they all apparently varied considerably in composition, function, and decoration. Yet none were necessarily large. On the contrary, the court ceremonial conveys the impression of fairly small units, laid out at comparatively short distances. The emperors in procession moved from room to room and from pavilion to pavilion, traversing courtyards, changing dress, receiving homage, inspecting guards of honour, venerating icons and crosses – all in the short time available before the services in the H. Sophia. At the same time, the structures, courtyards, and open areas were laid out, it seems, on terraces on the crest and the slope of the hill. They were loosely linked by colonnaded porticoes, by barrel-vaulted corridors on one or two levels, and by staircases. The Magnaura, possibly of Constantinian origin, was still used as the main throne room in Macedonian times. Whether aisleless or basilican, it was terminated by an apse and rose on a terrace (*heliakon*) enclosed by parapets.[33] Elsewhere, balconies projected from upper floors and roof pavilions, either open or glazed in to offer vistas across the city and the sea. A minor reception room, the Triconch of Theophilos (829–42), was laid out on two levels: below, a quatrefoil 'whispering' grotto, where sounds whispered in one corner of the chamber were transmitted aloud to another; above, a trefoil, its main apse resting on four columns, the façade opening in a triple arcade. Both grotto and triconch opened into a hemicycle of colonnades, superimposed on a double level, the lower sheltering an elaborate fountain.[34] All through the palace, gardens enclosed by open halls and enlivened by *jeux d'eau* extended between the pavilions. The convent in the Manganes adjoining the Great Palace (by the mid eleventh century, an Imperial summer palace rather than a monastic establishment) mirrored such landscaping. The church of St George in the centre was surrounded 'on all sides by buildings, some completely, some half surrounded by porticoes . . . then came a second

circle of buildings, . . . bigger than the first and lawns full of flowers, some on the circumference, others down the centre. . . . There were fountains . . . gardens, some hanging, others sloping . . . a bath . . . streams of water'.[35] Within the palace, the rooms newly built or redecorated in the ninth and tenth centuries gleamed with colourful materials. In the Kamilas of Theophilos, six green marble columns supported a ceiling inlaid with gold. Slabs of grey Proconnesian marble paved the floor, variegated marble sheathed the lower parts of the walls, a mosaic depicting harvesters plucking fruit covered the upper wall. In other adjoining rooms the walls opened in colonnades, and the floors were covered with mosaic pavements.[36] In the Kainourgion of Basil I, the main room was apparently laid out as a basilica terminated by an apse. The nave rested on sixteen columns, eight of green marble, six of black onyx carved with vines, two of onyx with spiral flutings. On the walls above the columns and in the apse vault, mosaics represented the deeds of the Emperor. In the adjoining state bedroom, the variegated marble floor centred on a mosaic panel depicting a peacock. The walls were covered with mosaic: floral designs in the lower zone; a floral frieze in the middle zone; finally, a zone devoted to portraits of the Imperial family. A mosaic cross occupied the flat ceiling, and the entire design formed a scheme best explained as a renascence of the iconography of Justinian's time.[37] In the banqueting hall – the Dekanneacubita – Constantine Porphyrogenetos restored and remodelled the ceiling. The building itself presumably dated from the fourth or fifth century. Its name – the Nineteen Couches – reflects its plan. It was long, terminated by an apse, and flanked on either side by nine vaulted niches, each sheltering a dining couch. Constantine VII placed over the nave a coffered ceiling, richly decorated with gilded vines and foliage, '. . . so that whoever saw it was overwhelmed'. The Great Triclinium (Consistorium) of the Lateran in Rome, built by Pope Leo III (795–816) and preserved until 1588, reflected the plan on a smaller scale with only eleven niches. A banqueting hall of the same type with but seven niches has been excavated in Constantinople as part of a sumptuous private palace north of the hippodrome; and a smaller one with but five niches was built about 450 by Bishop Neon at Ravenna.[38]

The tenor of such descriptions decidedly evokes the image of Late Antique interiors sheathed in marble and mosaic and articulated by columns, pilasters, capitals, and cornices of classical derivation – not so much revivals as survivals of Roman-hellenistic Antiquity, as one would expect in the age of the 'Macedonian Renaissance'. Indeed, such a classical or neo-classical vocabulary may well have remained alive in Constantinople from Late Antiquity. Few traces are left in Constantinople; but it may have left its reflections at Preslav in Bulgaria, where Czar Simeon built his residence in 893. In plan, on the other hand, the ninth- and tenth-century descriptions of the Great Palace in Constantinople call to mind forcefully contemporary and later Arab palaces in southern Spain.[39] In the fourteenth-century parts of the Alhambra, the buildings are grouped in many units, all fairly small. In each unit, higher pavilions and lower wings enclose a courtyard with colonnaded porticoes; domed canopies project from the porticoes into the areas of the courtyard where fountains, pools, and hedges delimit the footpaths. No axial system underlies the overall plan of the palace. The units are linked only by narrow passages or by stairs; levels change; balconies project from upper floors; a belvedere rises from above the roof; loggias open on to the far prospect of the mountains. Most of the reception rooms are domed, and all details are delicate and colourful.[40] The ornament, of course, stands in the tradition of Islamic, specifically Western Islamic, art. But occasionally an element calls to mind parallels in Middle Byzantine art. The marble shafts with black inlays at the Alhambra find their exact counterpart in the Round Church at Preslav, the common source being Byzantium, where such columns were in use as early as the sixth century [178, 179]. The resemblances between Byzantine and Western Islamic art as early as the tenth century become even clearer in the palace of

Medinat-al-Zahra near Cordova. In plan the palace is not quite as loosely laid out as the Alhambra, or presumably the Byzantine palaces of the Macedonian emperors. But like these, it consists of a number of self-contained units, each unit placed on one of the successive terraces of a hill slope, each centred on a courtyard filled with a fountain or a pool. A large reception hall at Medinat-al-Zahra strongly calls to mind those described in the Great Palace at Constantinople: a basilica on columns with splendid capitals; the lower walls of the structure sheathed with marble slabs; the pavement composed of variegated marble; the upper walls presumably covered with mosaics.[41]

Much of this similarity between the plan and decoration of the Great Palace in Constantinople, as gathered from descriptions, and the palaces of southern Spain explains itself as a family resemblance between two cousins, both descended from the palace architecture of Late Antiquity. As early as the late fifth or the early sixth century a country palace on the north shore of the Sea of Marmara scattered over its area of roughly 200 by 150 m. (650 by 500 ft) groups of buildings – square and rectangular rooms, apsed halls, a chapel, and a small bath – all assembled round courtyards and on terraces and but loosely joined to each other.[42] Obviously, then, this palace at Rhegium (Küçükçekmece) establishes a link between Late Roman Imperial villas, such as those at Tivoli and Piazza Armerina, and both the Arab palaces of southern Spain and the lost palaces of Constantinople. At times, however, the links between Middle Byzantine and Western Islamic art are of a more immediate nature. The mosaic decoration and the ornament of the Macedonian palaces are, it seems, directly reflected in the mihrab of the mosque at Cordova. Inside the mihrab niche, the cornices in profile and ornament, as well as the large marble shell in lieu of a dome, are surprisingly classical in flavour. For the decoration of the façade of the mihrab, the Caliph El-Hakim (961–76) asked for and received from the Emperor Nicephoros Phocas a present of no less than 325 tons of mosaic cubes and the loan of an artist. As they survive to this day, the mosaics – executed in extraordinarily fine cubes – can reasonably be taken to reflect contemporary Byzantine court taste. Ornamentalized plants and palmettes shine in a wealth of colours in ever new combinations: gold on blue, gold on red, green on gold, red on blue, red and green on gold. For Medinat-al-Zahra as well, the emperor allegedly sent the caliph as gifts a sculpted and gilded marble basin, a fountain with figural reliefs, and one hundred and forty columns.[43] More than two centuries later, the castles and summer houses of the Norman kings in Palermo still mirror, whether by direct transmission or by way of the Arab palaces in southern Spain, the ninth- and tenth-century palaces of Constantinople. There are the state rooms of Roger II in the Royal Palace (decorated after his death in 1152) with their marble-clad walls, their lunettes and vaults covered with mosaics in which birds, griffins, and lions are enveloped by interlace work and floral designs. There is the Zisa, a summer house containing five small rooms behind a long vestibule, and opening on to a pool. There is finally the Cuba, a pavilion originally completely surrounded by water. The anteroom of the Cuba was domed; its twelve supporting arches sprang from four columns in a cross-in-square plan. Notwithstanding their stalactite niches and arabesque stucco panels, these Arab and Norman palaces, garden houses, and pools in Cordova, Granada, and Palermo recall the descriptions of the Macedonian palaces at Constantinople.

Links between Byzantium and the Arab world had been close ever since, around 650, the rulers of Islam had established their residences in Damascus and Baghdad. As early as the last quarter of the seventh century, the Dome of the Rock in Jerusalem and the Great Mosque in Damascus were decorated by mosaicists sent on loan from the Byzantine court. Conversely, Arab sciences – theoretical and applied – certainly exerted their impact on Byzantium in the ninth century, and played no mean part in the furnishings of the Great Palace and in the court ceremonial. At the receptions of ambassadors in the audience hall of the Magnaura, silver chains were hung from columns, golden and silver organs were placed in the intercolumniations. The Emperor sat on the 'Throne of Solomon', flanked by bronze lions; before him stood gilded trees in which perched gilded birds. Upon the ambassadors' entry, the bronze lions roared, showed their tongues, and beat the ground with their tails. The birds sang, each its own tune. And while the ambassador performed the *proskynesis*, the enthroned Emperor was raised 'nearly to the ceiling' and then again revealed himself, clad in a different costume.[44] The envoy of the German emperor, Liutprand of Cremona, was duly impressed, as he was meant to be. But it is doubtful that the Cordovan ambassadors were equally baffled. To them *automata* were nothing new, and those in Constantinople, constructed in large part by Theophilos I, were quite possibly built with the help of Arab mechanics.[45] Largely on this evidence, it has been occasionally suggested that the architecture of the ninth-century palaces in Byzantium was also influenced by those of the Umayyad and Abbasid rulers, and that specifically the Triconch of Theophilos in the Great Palace and its whispering grotto followed the model of the triconch throne niches in the reception halls at M'shatta and Ukhaidir.

Nothing precludes *a priori* the possibility either that Islamic architecture could have exerted its impact on palace building in Byzantium. In fact, at least one Byzantine palace, at Bryas on the Asiatic shore opposite Constantinople, clearly followed between 829 and 843 an Umayyad model, compact and axially controlled. However, it seems an alien intruder. Like Umayyad palaces of the eighth century it differs from Byzantine palace design of earlier as well as of later date. True, Umayyad and Byzantine palaces both go back to the building traditions of Late Antiquity, but they follow different lines. The designers of the Umayyad palaces take up the plans of Roman *castra* palaces such as that at Spalato. Rigidly laid out along an axial system, the main axis culminates in an audience hall; subordinate quarters line the inside of the square fortified wall.[46] Byzantine palace design, on the other hand, continues the tradition of Roman Imperial villas, such as the Villa of Hadrian at Tivoli and the Imperial villa at Piazza Armerina. Building units more or less self-contained and only loosely linked to each other are scattered over spacious grounds landscaped with gardens, pools, and artificial creeks. This 'pavilion' design, it would seem, had been transferred to urban palaces in Rome as early as the third century A.D. It certainly continued uninterrupted in Byzantium from the fourth to the ninth and tenth centuries via the palaces of the Macedonian emperors and it apparently reached the Islamic courts of Spain, and perhaps of western North Africa and Egypt, in the ninth and tenth centuries. Later, in the twelfth century, it was taken up by the Norman court of Sicily, either directly, or more likely by way of Cordova or Cairo. Clearly this impact of Byzantine palace design of the Macedonian Age does not imply that the classical vocabulary of Islamic buildings in the eighth, ninth, and tenth centuries was in its entirety purloined from Byzantium. The triconch of M'shatta, the shell dome, the egg-and-dart and bead-and-reel cornices of the mihrab of Cordova are part of the Late Antique heritage which Islam shares with Byzantium. But it seems likely, to say the least, that this heritage was strengthened through tenth-century contacts between Islam and the court at Constantinople.

The concept of a Middle Byzantine or 'Macedonian' Renaissance was first coined with an eye to literature and the figurative arts. Illuminated manuscripts such as the Paris Psalter, ivory caskets, and an occasional stone relief were found to be brimming with scenes, figures, settings, and decorations derived from classical Antiquity both in form and content. Further research has demonstrated that this heritage of hellenism did not spring suddenly into existence. It was found to have grown from a classical tradition which had continued in secular art – and thus not necessarily blended with Christian subjects – throughout the sixth and seventh centuries. Whether or not this tradition had survived, in the non-religious sphere, the iconoclastic century as well is still an open question.

Certainly it was immensely strengthened in the Macedonian Age. But the borderline between revival and survival is fluid.[47]

It is even more questionable whether the term Renaissance applies in the realm of Middle Byzantine architecture if understood literally as a conscious revival of an art of the past, in form or content, or in both. Certainly none of the many church types designed and promoted by the Macedonian and Comnene architects in Constantinople and in the core provinces of the Empire drew on models of the Roman-hellenistic past or Late Antiquity, whether pagan or Christian. Nor can they be viewed as reverting to the time of or after Justinian, i.e. pre-iconoclastic architectural forms or concepts. Whether domed octagons, Greek-cross-octagons, or atrophied Greek crosses, Middle Byzantine church plans were in their great majority freshly invented in the Macedonian age, invented, that is, within the framework of a tradition of church planning uninterrupted and consistent since the sixth century. Only rarely during pre-iconoclast or iconoclast times was a church plan, such as the quincunx, apparently transferred from the realm of secular or semi-religious buildings of Late Antiquity. Such transfers, always rare, seem to have occurred largely in the provinces or borderlands of the Empire, taken up and refined in Constantinople, and spread from there anew over the Empire. Only on the outskirts of the Empire are sixth-century building types revived: at S. Marco in Venice, and perhaps in the basilicas with galleries built in the Bulgarian Empire. Even more rarely, if at all, did Middle Byzantine church builders revert to Late Antique building types. By and large Middle Byzantine church planners thought in terms not of old, but of radically new architectural concepts and designs.

Secular architecture of the Middle Byzantine period, on the other hand, was apparently simply Antiquity fossilized. From middle-class urban dwellings to conventual buildings and Imperial palaces, building types of Late Antiquity seem to have survived with little or no change from the fourth and fifth centuries to the time after Justinian and the iconoclast centuries. As in the realm of church building, then – though for different reasons – the term Renaissance is inapplicable to the secular architecture of Middle Byzantine times.

To speak of a Renaissance in Middle Byzantine architecture is most tempting as one looks at its ornament. Granted, our knowledge in that field is woefully limited: chronologically, since ninth- and tenth-century ornament is, with few exceptions, unknown; topographically, since little ornament has survived in Constantinople or in the poorer provinces such as Asia Minor and its dependent islands. In Greece, on the other hand, where the material is plentiful and even partly *in situ*, ornament has not been sufficiently studied to work out a chronology. In addition, the better part of Middle Byzantine ornament known so far dates from the eleventh and twelfth centuries. A fleeting impression of this decoration could be interpreted as a total conscious revival of classical Early Christian ornament or the ornament of Justinian's age. Cornices are composed of tori, cavettoes, and plinths; capitals, lintels, and chancel posts are covered with acanthus leaves, palmettes, half-palmettes, and tendril friezes. But in their great majority, such elements *all'antica* are derived from, rather than reverting back to, earlier prototypes. They transpose the heavier, fleshy, and more fully developed elements of the fifth and sixth centuries into either soft and doughy, or into spindly, hard, sharply-cut, and often feathery forms and intertwine them with elevated nodules and – perhaps only from the eleventh century – with interlace work. The remnants of the sculptured decoration of the Fenari Isa Camii in Constantinople convey as clear an idea as do the capitals of the Theotokos church at Hosios Lukas and its *templa* or the friezes of the Eski Imaret Camii at Constantinople [323, 324, 339, 340]. But as long as we are ignorant of much of the ornament immediately preceding the eleventh century, and as long as

we know even less of ornament from the seventh to the end of the tenth century, we cannot say with certainty whether we are dealing with a renascence even in the most classical examples. Only exceptionally a whole group of ornamentation suggests such a conscious renascence, such as the fragments found at Preslav in Bulgaria and the imitations of fifth- and sixth-century capitals in the eleventh-century church of S. Marco in Venice [285, 368]. But such true renascences are few and locally confined.

In a literal sense the term Renaissance, then, does not apply to Middle Byzantine architecture in general. In a broader sense it might be valid: Middle Byzantine architects work with a feeling for articulation of space and mass stronger than that of their eighth- and seventh-, and even than that of their sixth-century predecessors. The spatial units within a structure are more clearly set off and more clearly balanced against each other, be they the nine bays of a quincunx structure, all of different height and shape, or the parts of a Greek-cross octagon. The outer walls of a building are clearly articulated by pilasters and responds, by blind arches, and by string courses formed of bricks and arranged in sawtooth bands. None of this vocabulary is classical. But the feeling for articulation, for contrasts of surface and membering, and for clear relationships calls to mind concepts of classical Antiquity and its architecture. So does the blend of solidity and subtlety which marks the best of the Middle Byzantine buildings: the integration of the plain surfaces of outer walls and variegated marble and mosaic sheathing on the interior, of straight, concave, and convex planes. Finally, the inventiveness, the fertility of production, and the new vigour recall, if one wants to, the Italian Renaissance of the fifteenth century. But these are only analogies, and so – once again – it seems to me that the term Renaissance can only vaguely be applied to the architecture of Middle Byzantine times.[48]

CHAPTER 17

DEVELOPMENT AND REGIONAL STYLES

OF MIDDLE BYZANTINE ARCHITECTURE

It is decidedly possible and not even difficult to characterize Middle Byzantine architecture as a stylistic entity. But the persistence of established architectural types among churches, palaces, and monastic buildings for over three hundred years makes the chronological presentation of Middle Byzantine architecture troublesome. External evidence for dating the monuments is scarce. Rarely will an inscription identify building or founder by name. Even then, remodelled or indeed rebuilt from the ground, the structure may bear an inscription bodily transferred or copied from its predecessor. Documentary evidence, if and when available, is equally confusing for the same reasons. Difficulties increase when, as in Constantinople and Salonica, churches are known only by the Turkish names they acquired at the time of their transformation into mosques; identification, then, depends at times on topographical indications, at times on information gleaned from local Greeks by sixteenth- and seventeenth-century travellers – one or two centuries after the buildings fell to the Muslims. In either case, the result is little more than guesswork.[1] Thus, the historian of Middle and Late Byzantine architecture must glean clues from the few reliably dated buildings by which to date the mass of undated structures. Such clues, to be sure, are provided by details of plan and design; the presence or absence of lateral porticoes or *parekklesia*, side chapels; the shape and construction of windows; the details of domes and drums; the hollowing of outer and inner walls by niches; the ornament of friezes, capitals, and wall surfaces. Equally revealing obviously are the features of the masonry. The alternating bands of brick and ashlar which prevail in Constantinople from at least the fourth century continue throughout

the tenth century, and the number of courses in each band often helps to establish a date.[2] The pure brickwork used more frequently by Middle Byzantine builders in Constantinople and Salonica can be dated by the number of bricks and mortar-beds per Byzantine foot, by the height of the mortar between the brick courses, or by the tooling of the mortar – grooved or slanting, either inward or outward; the tenth-century repairs on the H. Sophia in Constantinople offer a good example [172]. From the early eleventh or possibly the late tenth to the mid thirteenth century, Constantinople and her sphere of influence – including South Russia and southern Serbia – is marked by the 'recessed brick' technique: alternating brick courses, regardless of whether the masonry is faced with pure brick or with alternating bands of brick and ashlar, are recessed from the wall plane and covered over by mortar [306, 307]. As a result, the mortar-beds, appear to have a thickness two to three times that of the brick courses.[3] From about 900 on in Greece, an equally characteristic, though different technique prevailed: the *cloisonné*. Small stone blocks were framed by horizontally and vertically placed bricks [335, 336]. The horizontal bricks were laid in single or double courses, rarely more; the vertical bricks formed either single or double courses, or geometric, christological, or 'cufic' designs. Occasionally a reticulate design was imitated. The profiling of the cornices may provide further clues, as does the shaping of dog-tooth friezes, single or double, and their location in the building: along the eaves line, as window frames, or as string courses. In some cases the chronology of such tell-tale marks has been established: a superb job has been done, for instance, regarding the architecture of the eleventh and twelfth centuries on the

306. Constantinople, Zeyrek Camii,
twelfth century. Recessed brickwork

307. Antigoni (Burgas, Sea of Marmara), ruin,
eleventh or twelfth century. Recessed brickwork

mainland of Greece.[4] Elsewhere – and this includes
Constantinople – research lags far behind, and
scholarly opinion concerning the date of an
individual building or a group of buildings often
fluctuates from one to three hundred years, much as
it did a century ago with regard to Romanesque
architecture.

In any event, however, a chronology of Middle
Byzantine architecture, based on clues of masonry
technique, decoration, or even planning, is valid as

a rule only for one region or for one workshop.
Indeed, once established, such elements are easily
transformed into permanent features of a regional
school. It is therefore not too difficult to distinguish
between the various provinces of Middle Byzantine
architecture: Constantinople; Salonica and vicinity;
Central and Southern Greece; Serbia; South Russia; Central Asia Minor. It is even comparatively
easy to differentiate between subordinate regions
such as Attica, the Argolis, Epirus. But the historian
has a hard time to trace in a more than tentative
manner the development within the regional
schools. And it seems at the moment nearly impossible to present a development of the whole of Middle
Byzantine architecture during its life span of over
three hundred years.

CONSTANTINOPLE

Middle Byzantine architecture in Constantinople
apparently entered the scene in the last quarter of
the ninth century with two churches, both built by
Basil I within the Great Palace. One was the Nea,
the New Church, completed in 880, and the other
the sanctuary of St Mary at the Pharos, consecrated
probably in 864. Both are gone, but contemporary
and slightly later descriptions convey a sketchy idea
of their plans as well as a glimpse of their decoration
and furnishings.[5] The Nea rose on a terrace, and
was supported by a substructure. The five-domed
naos was built on a quincunx or possibly a cross-
domed plan. The open area of the atrium was set
with two fountains, its walls revetted with marble
plaques. Two porticoes – long, colonnaded, and
barrel-vaulted – ran along the flanks of the church
and extended beyond to enclose a long courtyard
which reached to the polo-ground of the palace.[6]
Inside, the naos was sheathed with marble and
decorated with mosaics. A templon on columns,
surmounted by arcaded colonnettes, screened the
raised chancel from the nave. Over the altar rose a
canopy; a synthronon followed the curve of the apse.
A pattern of red and white marble slabs formed the
pavement, and silk hangings enriched the decora-

tion. Finally, openings in the floor communicated with the substructure, whence aromatic smoke would rise upon the entrance of the Emperor into the naos.[7] The Pharos church resembled the Nea in its rich decoration. Of its plan, only one feature is known: the centre dome was of the pumpkin type and covered with mosaics – in the centre, the Pantokrator; in the sections, angels.

Much admired by Byzantine and foreign visitors alike, the Nea was bound to exert a steady influence on the architecture of the capital, of near-by Salonica, and on the neighbourhoods of both cities. In Constantinople, half a dozen churches seem to reflect the Nea. All are closely linked in plan, style, and details, and all date roughly from between 900 and 1200. But few can be identified beyond question with churches known from documents, and thus dated externally. But internal and external evidence assigns at least two to the first half of the tenth century. Both in ruins and recently restored, they can be identified: the north structure of the Fenari Isa as the church of the monastery of Constantine Libs; the Bodrum Camii as that of the Myrelaion.

Both are small and steep, and both are quincunx churches. The Bodrum Camii is raised on a terrace [308–11].[8] The supporting structure, also of quincunx plan, is heavy, originally perhaps just a basement shed, and built in a pattern of alternating bands: four brick courses followed by five courses of roughly hewn stones. For the upper church the builders shifted to pure brick. Over the centre bay rises a pumpkin dome; over the corner bays, groin-vaults. The cross arms are covered by barrel-vaults with interpenetrations so deep as to approximate oblong groin-vaults. The apses, all three polygonal on the outside, project strongly. Low walls rise over those on the sides and hide their half-domes. The main dome is set on a circular drum supported by eight triangular buttresses. Blind arches frame the windows of the drum, but are held down by a horizontal dog-tooth cornice slightly higher up. The main bay of the narthex and the forechoirs of the

308. Constantinople, Bodrum Camii (Myrelaion church), c. 920, as in 1938. From the south

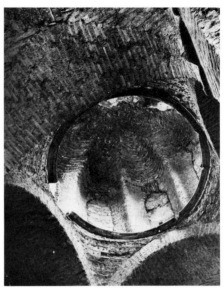

309. Constantinople, Bodrum Camii
(Myrelaion Church), c. 920.
Reconstructed perspective section
and plans of substructure and upper church

0   30 FT

0   10 M

310 and 311. Constantinople, Bodrum Camii,
c. 920. Interior of dome (*above*)
and exterior from the south-east (*below*)

N

■ ORIGINAL CONSTRUCTION PRESERVED

◢ ORIGINAL CONSTRUCTION MISSING BUT ATTESTED TO

◢ ORIGINAL CONSTRUCTION HYPOTHETICAL

lateral apses are covered by pendentive domes; the corner bays and even the cross arms are groin-vaulted. The flanks of the naos – set with strong, yet elegant half-cylindrical buttresses – were pierced all over by openings [309, 311]: huge semicircular windows, presumably subdivided by mullions high up in the cross arms; oculi or large round-headed windows further down in the corner bays; three smaller windows in the cross arms; finally at ground level, arches in the corner bays, the lateral forechoir, and in the end walls of the esonarthex, and a triple arch in the cross arms. The contrast of massive buttresses and wide open flanks, of deep shadows and lit surfaces, of rising and horizontal forces marks the exterior. Within, shallow niches billow into the side walls of lateral forechoirs and esonarthex. The concave webs of the main dome curve subtly [310]. Traces of marble revetment on the walls, of mosaic in the vaulting zone, survive all over the interior. Simple cornices, sharply profiled, mark off the lower wall and window zones on the exterior. Dog-tooth friezes mark all eaves lines.

Three parts at present compose the ruin of the Fenari Isa Camii: along the entire front and extending south, an exonarthex and a parekklesion probably of early-fourteenth-century date; in the middle and slightly earlier, the Paleologue South Church; finally, the original Middle Byzantine North Church [312–14, 325].[9] This original core is close to the Bodrum Camii in plan, style, and details; it also complements its missing parts: three bases remain of the four columns that carried the centre bay; a wealth of original ornament has survived on shafts, bases, and capitals of the window mullions and on the cornice of the centre dome, not counting the fifth-century pilaster capitals in second use; and marble sheathing can be traced not only inside, but on the outer walls as well. As in the Bodrum Camii, in the Fenari Isa too, the esonarthex terminates in shallow niches at either end; the apse and its barrel-vaulted forechoir are flanked by small lateral bays and tiny but tall absidioles, serving as pastophories, prothesis and diaconicon; the cross arms of the naos open in steep triple windows, their arches stilted,

surmounted by large semicircular windows, each tripartite. But throughout, plan and elevation in the Fenari Isa are richer than in the Bodrum Camii. Longish chapels, *parekklesia*, flanked the chancel – the one to the right now incorporated into the north aisle of the later South Church. Combined with the three steep apses of the naos, the lower apses of the parekklesia formed an impressive fivefold group of polygonal half-cylinders; terminating the original church, they opened alternatingly in rich triple and

■ NORTH CHURCH PRESERVED

▨ NORTH CHURCH EXCAVATED

⌐⌐⌐ NORTH CHURCH RECONSTRUCTED

▨ SOUTH CHURCH

▨ LATER BYZANTINE ADDITIONS

▨ TURKISH WORKS

312. Constantinople, Fenari Isa Camii. Plan

0 ⊢⟞⟞⟞⟞⟞⟞ 40 FT

0 ⊢⟞⟞⟞ 15'M

plain single windows. A stair-tower south of the narthex ascended to a narthex gallery which at vault level opens in a triple arcade into the west arm of the naos. Four tiny chapels, their walls hollowed by

313. Constantinople, Fenari Isa Camii (Church of Constantine Libs), South Church,
founded 1282/1304, and North Church, dedicated 907. From the south-east

shallow niches, rise over the four corners of the structure, domed and originally surmounted by drums high above roof level. Those to the west are placed over the end bays of the narthex gallery, those to the east above the pastophories, sheltered eastward by parapet walls and reached presumably by outside catwalks. Shallow niches billow from the forechoirs of the lateral absidioles, and their triple

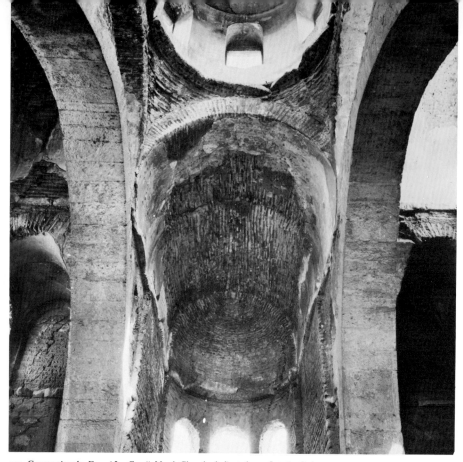

314. Constantinople, Fenari Isa Camii, North Church, dedicated 907. Interior facing east

accord is further strengthened by shaping the absidioles into tiny trefoils. As in the Bodrum Camii, the walls inside were sheathed with marble plaques, the vaulting zones covered with mosaic; ornamented glazed tiles supported the colouristic effect. Also the walling of the Fenari Isa is similar to that of the Bodrum Camii. Alternating bands of brick and roughly hewn stone, as they appear in the substructure of the Bodrum, form the walls of the Fenari Isa below the vaulting zone; the pure brickwork of the upper church of the Bodrum is duplicated by that found in the apses of the Fenari Isa [313].

The Bodrum Camii has been identified, since the sixteenth century, with the funerary church of Romanos I Lekapenos (920–44), the Myrelaion, and dated rightly prior to 923. In the Fenari Isa, an inscription on the cornice between window and attic zones of the apses gives the name of the founder – Constantine: he is Constantine Libs, killed in action in 917 as admiral of the fleet, and the Fenari Isa is the church of the monastery he dedicated in 907 to the Mother of God. Construction techniques, indeed, favour a tenth-century date for both churches. The inward–downward slant of the broad mortar-beds in the brickwork of both not only coincides with the technique used in the tenth-century portions of the H. Sophia; together with the alternating bands of brick and roughly hewn stone both in the Fenari Isa and the lower church of the Bodrum Camii, it still recalls ninth-century structures such as the ruin at Dere Ağzı. On the other hand, the 'recessed brickwork', that tell-tale eleventh- and twelfth-century device, is yet unknown.

Both the Fenari Isa and the Bodrum Camii are thus representative of an early phase of Middle Byzantine church building in Constantinople. The structures are small. The naos measures but 10·50 by 8·80 m. (34 by 29 ft) in the Bodrum Camii; in the Fenari Isa it measures 13 by 9·50 m. (43 by 31 ft), and 21 by 16 m. (69 by 53 ft) including all appendices, narthex, parekklesia, and apses. The centre and the corner bays are extraordinarily steep; the space billows into shallow niches. All parts are tiny – corner bays, lateral forechoir, and apses, whether simple or triconch – and all communicate with each other through steep arches or through doors pierced into niches. The detailing is firm and simple, but subtle and varied – cornices are strong, niches and absidioles curve subtly, windows vary from oculi to single, double, or triple apertures. Smooth exterior walls are enlivened only by broad niches in the attic zone. The centre drum and drums over the corner bays enlivened the outer silhouette. Almost all interior decoration is gone, but traces of a marble revetment have survived on the walls of the Fenari Isa, and traces of mosaic are still visible on the vaults of the Bodrum Camii.

Once established, the style continues in Constantinople, unchanged in many respects, throughout the eleventh century. As in the Fenari Isa, in the Eski Imaret Camii, the church of Christ Pantepoptes, founded after 1081 and prior to 1087 [315], the narthex gallery opens into vaulted chambers placed above the western corner bays of the naos and originally surmounted by lower outer drums like those presumably planned in the Fenari Isa.[10] As in the Bodrum Camii the drum of the main dome is strongly articulated, though by colonnettes rather than by triangular buttresses; dog-tooth friezes arched over the windows, originally, it seems, forming the eaves line in a striking rippling effect. The cross arms opened in triple arcades, their arches steeply stilted. Above, three windows were grouped, close together, yet separate, instead of the tripartite large semicircular window customary in Macedonian times. Whether or not the triple arcade was sheltered by a short flanking portico remains in

315. Constantinople, Eski Imaret Camii, founded between 1081 and 1087. Exterior from the south-east

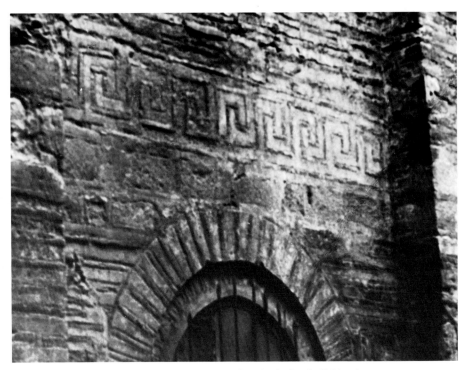

316. Constantinople, Eski Imaret Camii, founded between 1081 and 1087. Detail of brickwork

doubt. Early Macedonian elements thus are blended with new features. 'Recessed brickwork' comes into use. The detailing grows richer, but the delicate subtlety of tenth-century design decreases. The contrast between clear profiles and plain wall surfaces, between half-cylindrical buttresses and wall openings, is lost. Instead, the outer walls are set with pilasters, backed up by two or three responds, with niches and blind arches. The clear segregation of window and attic zones on the outer walls of the apses has been abandoned; instead, the facets of the apse polygon are each articulated by a wall arch; the outer arches are blind, those in the centre frame a triple window. This lower zone of arches and windows is surmounted by a tier of low, broad niches in the attic zone. The elegant pumpkin dome of the Bodrum Camii gives way to a shallow bowled dome

with heavy ribs. Niches disappear from the inner side walls of forechoirs. Wall and vaulting zones are no longer marked off by firm, simple cornices, but by running friezes: palmettes, heart shapes, or tendrils, carved precisely but without harshness. Bricks form meander patterns on the flanks of the building, weaving patterns under blind arches, zigzag ornaments in the niche heads [316]. *Cloisonné* masonry, so characteristic for Middle Byzantine building in Greece, but unknown elsewhere in Constantinople, appears in the outer walls of the exonarthex and suggests as does the rippling eaves line of the drum – if it originally existed – that by the end of the eleventh century Greek custom exerted an impact on Constantinople.

Like the Eski Imaret, the Kilise Camii, whether or not the church of St Theodore, represents the style of Comnene quincunx churches in Constantinople: 'recessed' brick masonry, with slanting mortar-beds; blind arches, triple window, and surmounting

tect, and craftsmen created one of the most beautiful structures of pure Constantinopolitan design and execution. An outer narthex, crowned by three

317. Constantinople, Kilise Camii, c. 1100. Exterior from the south; drawing by Texier, c. 1835

niches in the apse; brick ornament, including a meander; triple arcades in the cross arms, possibly an opening rather than a window, surmounted originally by semicircular tripartite windows. A date about 1100 or slightly later seems likely [317].[11]

The Nea Moni on Chios shows this same blend of earlier and later features applied to a domed-octagon plan – a plan possibly of Early Macedonian origin, though so far unknown in Constantinopolitan architecture of the tenth century [296].[12] Founded by Constantine IX Monomachos, the church was built and decorated between 1042 and 1056 under the direction of 'the Imperial surintendant des bâtiments, sent from Constantinople together with a master builder and other artists in charge of the subordinate work', presumably masons and mosaic workers. Jointly, patron, archi-

domes and terminated right and left by an absidiole, leads into the esonarthex. From there, the naos opens, only 7·80 m. (26 ft – 25 Byzantine ft) square. The tripartite articulation of its walls was effected originally by superimposed pairs of projecting octagonal colonnettes replaced in an unfortunate modern restoration by clumsy half-piers [318, 319]. This counterplay was taken up by the intervening niches: rectangular niches below, both in the centre and in the corners, followed in the second tier by deep semicircular niches in the corners, and delicate shallow, curved niches in the middle. In the third zone, elliptical dome segments in the middle alternate with high stilted half-domes in the corners to form the octagonal base for pendentives, drum, and dome. This complex and eminently refined spatial design is supported by an equally subtle decoration.

318 and 319. Nea Moni, Chios, 1042–56. Interior facing north-west (*above*) and interior facing south (*below*)

Marble slabs – also an Imperial gift – sheath the walls, framed by marble cornices à billettes. Quarter-domes, half-domes, and pendentives are covered with mosaics which rank among the best in Middle Byzantine design and workmanship; a similar decoration presumably covered the main dome as well. The floor was surfaced by interlaced opus alexandrinum. Viewed as a whole, the decoration conveys an idea of what the churches and palaces of Constantinople looked like before they fell into ruin. All this wealth and subtleness is encased in what seems a poorish shell. However, the rough masonry, enlivened by but a few blind arches, was originally clad in costly marbles. Two tiers of niches articulate the main apse: those below, steep and flanking a triple window; the upper ones squat and deep, much like those found on the apses of the Eski Imaret and the Kilise Camii.

Other church plans, whether newly invented, derived from models long obsolete, surviving or revived, come forcefully to the fore in Constantinople between 1050 and 1150. Both the Gül Camii and the Kalenderhane, the former around 1100, the latter half a century later, continue or revive the type of the cross-domed church, first known in the eighth century. Only details – the steep niches of the apses and the 'recessed' brickwork – reveal the true date of the Gül Camii; that of the Kalenderhane is given away only by finds made during excavations.[13] The ambulatory plan, too, originates in that century. It seems to derive from the cross-domed type by omitting the gallery level. The first instance, indeed, so far known might well have been the Koimesis church in Nicaea (Iznik). A remodelling in 1065 would have removed the galleries, formerly surmounting the aisles, giving over their place to clerestory walls [253], each with three windows, one full-sized and round-topped in the middle, those on either side halved and closed by a half-arch: a grouping as telling for the time of construction as the articulation of the narthex façade by three multiple-stepped blind arches.[14] At roughly the same time, as witness the Kariye Camii, churches are apt to be simplified in plan and shrunk. A single bay is topped by a dome, but provided with a full-scale chancel – forechoir, main apse, flanking apsed pastophories – wider than the nave. The interior, remarkably steep, is sheathed all over with marble plaques and mosaics: a jewel, designed to impress the visitor by sophisticated preciousness. Outside, the structure is simpler: the dome articulated by colonnettes and blind arches, the apse by a triple tier of niches, higher main tier grouped around a triple window [400]. Plan and elegance of design spread to the countryside near Constantinople: one example survives at Kurşunlu on the south coast of the Sea of Marmara. In the Toklu Dede Mescidi in Constantinople – its Byzantine name yet unknown – a nave, aisleless and barrel-vaulted, is pierced by a centre dome; the end bay, as the chancel, billows out in a trefoil plan, with shallow niches sideways and a terminating apse. The details – pilasters and responds on the flanks, outside niches on the apse – suggest an eleventh-century date. Tetraconchs, too, come to the fore in these same decades, their interior walls hollowed out by larger and smaller niches: a small sanctuary, the Panaghia Kamariotissa, at Heybeliada (Heybeli), on one of the islands in the Sea of Marmara, is the first example of the type known, near the capital and hence probably Constantinopolitan; in a complex form, moreover, in which tetraconch and Greek-cross octagon interpenetrate, and built in recessed brickwork.[15] The counterplay of subtle interior effects with a comparatively plain exterior shows even in a timber-roofed basilica such as the H. Sophia at Nicaea (Iznik), built shortly after 1065. Prior to a Turkish remodelling, two triple arcades on columns, separated and linked by an extraordinarily long pier, carried the clerestory wall with its five windows – a complex overlapping rhythm enveloped by the plainest outer wall.[16]

The end phase of Middle Byzantine architecture in Constantinople differs from the eleventh-century phase only by richer, if less subtle decorative effects. The arcades of an apse window, always tripled, or the openings of a narthex gallery grow increasingly slender, their supports thinner. The number of ribs

in a dome increases. The dome over the naos finds its counterpart in a smaller dome, rising from the upper floor of the narthex. A chapel may be crowned by two domes, placed lengthwise over its aisleless nave. Apses often push out in seven, rather than five facets. The niches surmounting the window zone on the exterior apse wall become higher and deeper than in the eleventh century. Similarly, the niches which flank the triple apse window grow tall and steep. All this is exemplified in the three structures incorporated into the Zeyrek (Mollazeyrek) Camii [320]: the large south church [321], built by the Empress Irene between 1118 and 1124 and dedicated to Christ Pantokrator; the north church, dat-

ing but shortly after 1124; finally, the chapel in the middle, completed by 1136 as the Imperial mausoleum – *heroon* is the term used in the deed of foundation. Of the splendid decoration of the south church the pavement survives little damaged: an *opus sectile* design of coloured marbles, laid out in five-spot guilloche patterns enveloping roundels, with human and animal figures inlaid. Fragments of the marble revetment remain on the chancel walls. Finally, bits of stained glass show that the windows were filled with panes showing figures of saints.[17] At times, the articulation of the apses is further heightened by a third tier of niches, added at the bottom below the steep niches of the window zone, and a cornice – composed of a dog-tooth frieze and pendant triangles – runs below the eaves line. Such detailing is found in the lateral apses of the Gül Camii [322], and, though without the terminating frieze, in the main apse of the Kariye Camii [400]. At the same time, the ornament of these Late Middle Byzantine churches appears to have changed its character. Indeed, the ornament of Comnene and

320 and 321. Constantinople, Zeyrek Camii, twelfth century. Exterior from the south-west; drawing by Texier, *c.* 1835 (*opposite*), and South Church, 1118–24, apses (*opposite, below*)

322 (*below*). Constantinople, Gül Camii, *c.* 1100(?). Exterior of apses

Late Macedonian churches in Constantinople seems quite different from earlier architectural decoration. A number of capitals and a base from the Fenari Isa Camii exemplify the earlier style of orna-ment [323–5]: leaves of foliage are scooped, and rounded at the tips; the lines of the half-wheel design on the base are wavy, the eagle on the capital is lively; the whole design is imaginative and rich. By the eleventh century, on the other hand, the orna-ment turns harder. The capitals of the Nea Moni on Chios carried on their faces an interlaced cross

323 (above). Constantinople, Fenari Isa Camii,
North Church, dedicated 907.
Capital of window in main apse

324 (right, top). Constantinople, Fenari Isa Camii,
South Church. Capital of a window
from the North Church, dedicated 907, re-used

325 (right, centre). Constantinople, Fenari Isa Camii,
North Church, dedicated 907.
Capital in the window of the north arm

326 (right). Constantinople, St John in Trullo,
twelfth century. Window capital

pattern with sharp corners. On the cornices in the north church of the Zeyrek Camii group, the palmettes have hardened, their leaves turned spiky. In the Eski Imaret Camii of *c.* 1080 the fluid forms of a Lesbian cyma have congealed into cold heart-and-arrow shapes. The clear-cut half-palmettes on a window capital in the small church of St John in Trullo end in sharply pointed leaves [326]. But so little ornament survives in Constantinople that any statement regarding the late eleventh or indeed the twelfth century is hazardous in the extreme.

NORTHERN GREECE AND THE BALKANS

Nowhere is Middle Byzantine architecture more closely linked to Constantinople than in northern Greece and the Balkan countries: in Macedonia, comprising the border provinces of Greece and Yugoslavia, and in Thrace, meaning present-day Bulgaria, European Turkey, and northern Greece east of Salonica.[18]

Before 1018

Despite continued wars, throughout the ninth century the buildings of the Bulgar czars – witness the throne hall at Pliska – had vied in plan and size, though not in style, with those of the emperors at Constantinople. With the early tenth century, the situation changed. A structure such as the Round Church at Preslav revived the plan of Roman mausolea, but fused into it features drawn from the contemporary architecture of Byzantium.[19] However, the full impact of Middle Byzantine building is felt more directly in the many dozens of parish and monastery churches founded by Czars Simeon (893–927) and Peter (927–69) around their two residences: at Preslav, where alone some thirty-odd churches and monasteries have so far been excavated – all built before the destruction of the town in 971; and at Ohrid. The ruins of churches around Preslav, in particular, seem to mirror to perfection the contemporary architecture of Constantinople. Indeed, alongside church plans known

from Constantinople appear building types and schemes of decoration no longer preserved among her churches and palaces, but presumably once extant in the Byzantine capital as well as in its outposts.

The great majority of these churches were quincunx structures, much like those built by the Macedonian House. True, they are tiny and the methods of construction differ. The building material in Bulgaria is, with few exceptions, roughly hewn blocks of rubble; the supports are piers or columns, the shafts of the columns either crude, stumpy monoliths or a rough pile of low drums. But Constantinopolitan reminiscences abound in plan and detail. Sometimes the outer walls are set with half-cylindrical buttresses, recalling the Bodrum Camii. At times the apses are polygonal on the outside and preceded by clearly marked forechoirs [327A]. Occasionally the narthex is surmounted by an upper gallery. Also as in Constantinople, the flanks of the naos often open in triple windows (or are they arcades?) towards the outside.[20] The ornament may be crudely executed, but on the capitals Ionic volutes and impost blocks are unmistakable. At times, indeed, the decoration is planned – though not carried out – along extraordinarily refined lines. Pavements are laid out in large colourful panels; hexagonal brick tiles are sometimes framed by bits of white stone and green marble; white stone octagons with four concave sides appear set between pieces of green and red stone; or again, red, white, and green materials form a zigzag pattern and are framed by a band of red-brick tiles inset with white disks.

A few churches excavated around Preslav and Ohrid, however, seem to have departed from the commonplace quincunx plan. At Vunitsa (Vinitsa), about 950, the naos was formed by a domed square.[21] Only four odd metres (13 ft) long and wide, it would seem to anticipate on a small scale the plan of the early-twelfth-century church incorporated into the Kariye Camii at Constantinople, and it may stand as an example of earlier buildings of this type no longer preserved in the capital [327B]. But at Vunitsa the type presents itself in the true language of the tenth century. Shallow niches on either side enlarge the interior square; tiny lateral absidioles project eastward, carved into the springing of the main forechoir. Outside, small niches are hollowed into the mass of the walls. Similarly, the complex tiny trefoil chapels, widespread in Macedonia and as far south as Central Greece, seem to be rooted in Constantinople. Simple trefoil chapels of Late Antique derivation were of course common from Early Christian times to the end of the sixth century, and indeed a number of small trefoil churches of Justinian's time have

been found in the Balkans.[22] But the triconch appears in far more complex form in Middle Byzantine times in a number of tiny trefoil and quatrefoil chapels of complex design of the late ninth and tenth century in Macedonia, Greece, and Constantinople, as witness the one at Heybeliada. Literary sources, too, refer to triconch structures, whether audience halls or chapels in the palace precinct.[23] At Ohrid, for instance, the church of Sv. Panteleimon (it is known only from excavations) was composed of a domed square, a forechoir and apse, and two semicircular niches, billowing out on either side and shooting forth tiny absidioles [327C].[24] Far to the

327. (A) Preslav, Bial Briag, Church 2, early tenth century. Plan
(B) Vunitsa (Vinitsa), church, c. 950. Plan
(C) Ohrid, Sv. Panteleimon, early tenth century. Plan
(D) (below) Patleina, church, 907(?). Plan

RISING WALLS ⎫
FOUNDATIONS ⎬ ORIGINAL STRUCTURE
BLOCKED ⎭

south, on Mount Varasova opposite Patras, the ruin of another trefoil church has survived: the lateral conchs are enclosed in outside polygons; domed chapels flank the short stem of the triconch; and throughout, niches are hollowed into the inner walls.[25]

Likewise, complex variants on the standard quincunx plan are frequent among tenth-century churches around Preslav, variants which in all likelihood again reflect prototypes lost at Constantinople. Such Constantinopolitan impact becomes evident in the plan of the church excavated at Patleina near Preslav and dating perhaps from 907 [327D].[26] The forechoirs of the lateral apses were separated from the naos; the walls were set with niches; the three apses terminated on the exterior as polygons. The flanks of the naos were pierced, and deep niches hollowed the walls of the narthex. Most of these features find their counterparts in tenth-century churches in Constantinople, such as the Bodrum Camii or the Fenari Isa. But the spatial design at Patleina was more subtle. Not only was the eastward pair of supports omitted from the quincunx plan, but the corners of both the apse and the corresponding western piers of the naos curve inward. Thus the dome rising from these curved corners must have interpenetrated with the barrel-vaults of the four cross-arms and transformed them into mere spatial fragments. All this was condensed into the tiny space of a naos only 5 m. (16 ft) wide and 3·40 m. (11 ft) deep. The preciousness of this jewel-box design was further enhanced by the decoration of glazed tiles which spread over floor and walls like a colourful, shiny sheet. Sassanian prototypes have been invoked for this decoration. However, glazed tiles were also known in Constantinople; and while not all the ornamental motifs painted on the Patleina tiles can be matched by what little has survived at Constantinople, the designs built from palmettes, S-shaped

leaves, and wheel-shaped blossoms placed symmetrically around a central stem find their counterparts in the mosaics designed and executed by Byzantine artists at Cordova.[27] Thus at Patleina as well, it was presumably Byzantine designs that inspired the painters of the tiles. Whether imported or locally produced, tile revetting must have appealed to the architects at Preslav as an acceptable substitute for the unobtainable marble veneer and mosaic decoration prevalent in Middle Byzantine Constantinople.

Comparable in its smallness, complexity, and crudeness of execution – though of slightly earlier date – is a remarkable church south of the Bulgarian border. Situated at Peristerai, in the mountains east of Salonica, it was built in 870/1 by a Salonican disciple of St Methodios [328A].[28] Executed in rough rubble and reduced to 15 m. (50 ft) in either direction, the core of the plan yet forms a Greek cross with five domes, recalling, on a small scale,

328 (A). Peristerai, church, 870/1.
Exterior from the east

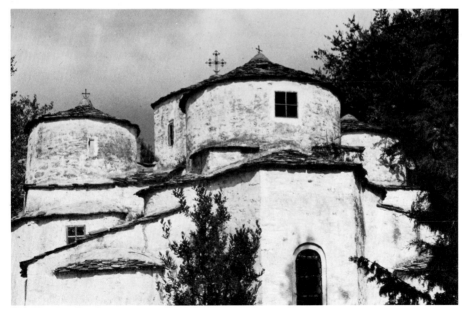

Justinian's Church of the Apostles [328B]. But this basic plan undergoes further complications: each arm has been transformed into a triconch by the addition of three steep billowing niches. Four columns placed in the corners turn the centre bay into a cross-in-square, with corner bays but 60 cm. (2 ft) wide and deep. All this calls to mind the complexity

328 (B). Peristerai, church, 870–1.
Section and plan

of Early Middle Byzantine architecture at a time when it had hardly begun at Constantinople.

Structures such as Peristerai or the churches of the Bulgarian court found at Preslav and Ohrid combine a frequently crude technique with the most elaborate spatial designs. Alongside them, however, stand churches of an extremely simple type. They are tiny hall-churches or basilicas, their three naves barrel-vaulted, carried by only one or two pairs of supports. Frequently they have been linked to similar churches in Asia Minor, but this is doubtful:

it is probably more correct to view them as the product of a folk architecture free from, and possibly opposed to, the influence of the Imperial, Royal, and Patriarchal courts at Preslav, Ohrid, and Constantinople.[29] Indeed, in the majority they date from the period after 976, when Byzantine influence in Bulgaria had much weakened. Their appearance could well be explained within the framework of a reaction directed both against the Byzantines and against the Byzantine-permeated Bulgarian court of the Preslav era. From excavations at and near Pliska, a number of such churches are known from the time of the new Czar Samuel (976–1014), when Pliska was again the capital of Bulgaria. In many cases only plans are known, making it impossible to tell how many were hall-churches, how many basilicas. Hall-churches, no doubt, did occur.[30] On the other hand, the numerous small churches with nave and aisles surviving at Kastoria in southern Macedonia are all basilicas. Starting around 900, they continue locally into the twelfth century.[31] The naves are extraordinarily high, the clerestory windows small, the supports either stumpy columns or squat piers prolonged by pilasters to carry the soffits of the arcades. Nave and aisles are barrel-vaulted, the aisles at times surmounted by galleries. A narthex, triple-naved or provided with a gallery, precedes the naos. The overall plan, then, is exactly like that of the hall-churches and basilicas to the north, in Bulgaria. Occasionally there appears amidst these small-size basilicas an equally tiny triconch chapel surmounted by the over-tall drum of its dome, witness the church of the Kubilidike [295]. But the masonry technique of the churches at Kastoria and their variegated ornament points southward, to Greece. Whether it is the church of the Anargyroi, of the Taxiarches, or that of H. Stephanos, the walls are built in the colourful cloisonné masonry shot through with cufic motifs which date the Greek churches – and hence presumably those of Kastoria as well – from the end of the ninth to the second half of the eleventh century.[32] Both this date and the fusion of Bulgarian plans and Greek masonry techniques coincide with the historical situation of Kastoria, a border town, wrested from Bulgaria in 1018 by Basil II, the Bulgar-Killer, and re-united with the Byzantine Empire. Through its geographical position, it became a well-to-do trading centre on the way from Salonica to Ohrid. To this day, the dozens of small churches – unsophisticated, colourful, and all vaulted basilicas or aisleless churches except for the trefoil of the Kubilidike – make Kastoria a site where Middle Byzantine architecture can be studied in abundance.

1018–1185

The victory of Basil II radically changed the political map of the Balkan peninsula. Of the Bulgarian Empire, only the part north of the Haemon range and east of the Struma river survived as a Byzantine vassal state, lasting until 1184, when an independent, if weak, second Bulgarian kingdom established itself. South of the mountains, Thrace returned to Byzantine rule. Likewise, Byzantium re-established herself in northern Macedonia, meaning present-day northernmost Greece and southern Yugoslavia. The Morava and Vardar valleys, from Kastoria and Ohrid to Skopje and Niš, remained indisputably Byzantine until the latter part of the twelfth century. The administrative and economic leadership of this entire vast region came to rest with Salonica, the seaport for the Central Balkans. Spiritually as well, Salonica became the true centre for the entire territory, although as early as 1020 an 'autocephalous' patriarchate was established at Ohrid as a sub-centre for the Central Balkans within and beyond the frontiers of the Empire. At about the same time, the monastic communities on Holy Mount Athos made their impact felt all through the Balkans. Architecturally the situation is less clear. The close links which always existed between Salonica and Constantinople, separated by only two days' sailing time, make it likely that prior to the mid eleventh century Salonican architecture also had strong ties to Constantinople. But this assumption cannot be proved, as no church building has survived in Salonica from the three hundred odd

years intervening between the construction of the H. Sophia and the first half of the eleventh century. Certainly the reconquest in 1018 of the vast hinterland of the Balkans gave rise to the revival of building activity in Salonica. The first witness of this new activity is the Panaghia Chalkeon, dedicated in 1028 to the Mother of God.[33] This first Middle Byzantine church surviving in Salonica remains remarkably impressive, despite its small size and notwithstanding all too thorough restorations undergone in 1934 [329]. A structure of uniform build, it is in plan a quincunx on columns, preceded by a double-storeyed esonarthex. The building material is pure brick, and the outer walls are heavily accentuated by pilasters, responds, and half-cylindrical buttresses recalling the Bodrum Camii in Constantinople. The capitals all alike show on their faces a guilloche design comparable to the nearly contemporary Nea Moni on Chios. While capitals, exterior and technique relate to practices in Constantinople, the simple handling of the interior with straight walls recalls churches in Central Greece rather than in Constantinople.[34] However, neither Greek nor Constantinopolitan custom fully determines plan and design of the Panaghia Chalkeon. On the contrary, it evolves a style characteristic, it seems, of Salonica and her territory. The walls, instead of opening in arcaded large windows as in Constantinople, are pierced by small windows, following Greek custom; but unlike Greek custom, the windows are framed by larger and smaller niches with doubly and triply recessed jambs. The façade likewise is powerfully accentuated: three huge arches spring from half-columns and pull together the upper and lower windows of the narthex gallery. Finally, the drums of three domes sprout high from above the roofs. Taken by itself, this is not a new motif: outer drums, though hidden behind parapet walls, rose over the four corners of the Fenari Isa Camii, and possibly – but this is sheer hypothesis – rose above the corner bays of the Nea. By the late eleventh century, two drums rise from the western corner bays of the Eski Imaret; four low drums rise undisguised from the corner bays of some Greek

329. Salonica, Panaghia Chalkeon, dedicated 1028.
Exterior from the west

and South Italian churches [364]; and in the Pantokrator church, the south church of the Zeyrek
Camii complex (1118–24), a single dome rises from
the narthex gallery.[35] But in the Panaghia Chalkeon
the motif takes on added significance. The drums
rise higher, they are strongly accentuated, and they
are placed not over the five bays of the naos, but over
its centre and over the two outer bays of the narthex
gallery. Throughout, the silhouette is immensely
lively. Triangular gables over the arms of the
quincunx contrast with semicircular arches rising
from the end bays of the narthex. The tall centre
dome is set with two rows of windows and is terminated by a straight eaves line; while on the two narthex

domes, slightly lower, a row of alternating windows
and niches is crowned by the rippling effect of an
arched eaves line. On the outer walls, the surfaces,
recesses, niches, windows, pilasters, responds, and
half-columns are played off against each other in a
contrast of surfaces, masses, and depth, in opposi-
tions of light and shade.

Next to nothing is known at present about church
building in Salonica for the century following the
dedication of the Panaghia Chalkeon. On Mount
Athos, perhaps as early as the last third of the tenth
century and thus prior to the Panaghia Chalkeon, a
local church type had been evolved in the main
church, the Katholikon, of the Lavra Monastery

[330].³⁶ Notwithstanding later remodellings, the core of the structure is well preserved: a cross-in-square, enlarged into a triconch by apses added to the cross arms, the dome supported by clumsy piers, the outside austere. Two chapels on a quincunx plan

heavy forms and with a comparable disdain for detail as early as the ninth century.³⁷

However, the churches and monasteries on Mount Athos always stand somewhat apart. Within the Balkans proper, Salonica and Constantinople

330. Mount Athos, Great Lavra, Katholikon, tenth century, last third(?). From the north-east

flank the narthex, all added later. All these elements, triconch plan, parekklesia, deep narthex (*liti*), become the hallmark of monastic churches all through northern Greece and the Balkans. The source on which the church of the Great Lavra drew, on the other hand, remains in doubt. The plain polygonal apses of the triple chancel call to mind tenth-century Constantinopolitan churches, such as the Bodrum Camii. The overall grimness of the design may be due both to the austerity of the founder and to his place of origin. In Trebizond (Trabzon), whence St Athanasius came to wild Mount Athos, the few early churches surviving wholly or in fragments are designed with similarly

seem to remain the two main springs – singly or combined – on which patrons and architects drew for techniques of construction, plan, and decorative vocabulary. Personal ties more than anything else may have dictated the preference for one or the other source. At Veljusa in the Struma valley, a Greek bishop, Manuel, in 1080 built his funeral chapel, following, if not a Constantinopolitan model, Constantinopolitan custom. The original structure – provided with a domed narthex and a domed side chapel – is well preserved [331]. It is a small domed quatrefoil, built of pure brick. The four foils, semi-circular inside, project on the exterior as five-sided polygons. Their three centre facets are pierced by a

331. Veljusa, church, 1080,
with later additions. Plan

■ 1080

▨ ORIGINAL;
LATER REMOVED

▨ } LATER
▨ } ADDITIONS

▲
N

row of windows, each framed by a steep blind arch; the four remaining facets are hollowed by two tiers of niches which continue the line of the windows on either side. The whole recalls contemporary churches of Constantinople, such as the Zeyrek Camii, or the Nea Moni on Chios, or the quatrefoil on Heybeliada in the Sea of Marmara; so do details, such as the herringbone patterns which decorate the half-domes of the niches in the upper tier of the main apse. Quite possibly Bishop Manuel employed a crew of Constantinopolitan workmen; for decoration and furnishings of the church also recall what little has survived in the contemporary churches of the Imperial city. A pavement in *opus vermiculatum* covers the floor in an involved, elegant guilloche pattern, and a templon with finely-carved lintel and capitals closes off the entrance to the main apse. The murals which covered all the walls complete the picture of a lavish decoration.[38]

Few such pure Constantinopolitan buildings are known in the Balkans so far. One, a variant on the quincunx, still rises at Ferai (Vira; Bera; Feredjik) near Alexandroupolis on the coast of Thrace. Dated 1152, its foundation by the Emperor's brother Isaac Comnenos explains the Constantinopolitan features: the five drums rising from the centre and

corner bays; their pumpkin webs; the 'recessed' brickwork alternating with stone bands; the high-shouldered window groups in the cross arms; the tier of niches surmounting the apse windows and their brick ornament; the colonnettes and pilaster articulation of the drums; and the elegant palmette decoration on cornices and capitals – a remarkably lavish layout for a monastic church in the provinces. More frequently, in the second half of the twelfth century in Macedonia and Thrace, Salonican and Constantinopolitan elements blend with each other; and grafted on to the blend are new features of a developing Balkan architecture. Nerezi near Skopje, in or shortly before 1164, offers yet another variant on the quincunx formula [332]. An exonarthex preceded the naos, open on the sides. The corner bays are cut off by walls from the naos: those to the east as forechoirs of the main apses, those to the west as separate chapels, accessible only from the narthex. Small drums rise from the domed corner bays in what may be the original Constantinopolitan five-spot design rather than the three-spot variant of the Panaghia Chalkeon. But at Nerezi these subordinate drums are turned into square tower-like aediculae, their gabled roofs contrasting sharply with the octagon of the centre drum – originally terminated by

332. Nerezi, near Skopje, church, c. 1164. Exterior of apses

a rippled eaves line. Much as at the Panaghia Chalkeon, this contrast of shapes is enhanced by a counterplay of wall surfaces, projecting colonnettes, responds, and windows, set into doubly recessed niches, though built in a mixture of *cloisonné* masonry and brick.[39]

The political changes in the Balkans in the last third of the twelfth century also altered its architec-

tural picture. The Serbian mountain tribes, settled west of the Morava valley and never conquered by the Empire, banded together in the kingdom of Raša, and under Stephan Nemanja (1168–97) pushed eastward into the valley towards Niš and Skopje. Their geographical position in the western mountains and their close bonds to the tribes settled along the Dalmatian littoral make it appear natural for their architecture to show close affinities to building concepts long prevalent on the Dalmatian coast and across the Adriatic Sea. A Western Romanesque vocabulary of pilasters, corbel-table friezes, and recessed portals and a masonry technique of large ashlar blocks – both drawn ultimately from Apulia and Lombardy – are applied more often than not to the church type traditional in Dalmatia: an aisleless nave, its barrel-vault pierced half-way down by a dome. It is equally natural that such Romanesque features would be blended with elements drawn from Middle Byzantine church architecture: the ribbing of a dome, the colonnettes and arches of a drum. The Church of the Virgin at Studenica, founded by Stephan Nemanja after 1183, represents this current at its best [391]. Its distinctly Byzantine dome and supporting structure notwithstanding, in general this architecture is not our concern.[40]

Conversely, it is equally natural that in the eastern parts of the Serbian kingdom recently wrested from the Byzantine Empire or close to her frontiers, Byzantine building traditions – in the form customary at Constantinople – would remain as strong as ever, though for a short time only. The ruin of St Nicholas near Kuršumlija, founded by Stephan Nemanja in 1168, is a splendid example [333]. The 'recessed' brickwork, that hallmark of Constantinople, leaves no doubt as to the origins of the builders. Possibly under the direction of a Constantinopolitan architect, this crew from the Imperial capital thoroughly re-interpreted the Dalmato-Raška plan which was presumably stipulated by the royal founder. The barrel-vaulted bays of the nave east and west of the dome were shrunk to the size of broad arches. Conversely, the centre bay, surmounted by the dome, grew in proportion. Its four supporting walls rise high, each pierced by a high-shouldered triple window of unmistakably Constantinopolitan design. Higher up rises the drum of the dome. Eight-sided and pierced by eight large windows, it has been turned into the dominant element of the entire design. A shallow esonarthex preceded a triple chancel opened from the main bay,

333. St Nicholas, near Kuršumlija, founded 1168. Exterior

recalling the atrophied Greek-cross naos of the Kariye Camii. With its alternating deep red brick courses and its broad white mortar bands, the structure presents itself as an eminently Constantinopolitan building – *in partibus infidelium*, as it were.[41]

St Nicholas at Kuršumlija and the conventual church at Nerezi reflect two contemporary versions of Middle Byzantine architecture in the Central Balkans. Behind them stand the variants of the style, as represented by the two architectural capitals of the North Aegean coast in the age of the Macedonian and Comnene emperors: Constantinople and Salonica. This is where the last phase of Byzantine architecture in the Balkans has its starting point. But Middle and Late Byzantine building in the Balkan countries after the tenth century always retains a more than slightly provincial flavour. To see Byzantine architecture of the eleventh and twelfth centuries outside Constantinople at its best, one must turn to Greece.

GREECE

Middle Byzantine church building on the Greek mainland, exclusive of Salonica and Macedonia, stands apart from the architecture of Constantinople under the Macedonian and Comnene emperors. The differences have at times been exaggerated, but they are present in the techniques of construction, in the decoration, in detailing, and, to a lesser degree, in the plan and overall design. Where the builders of Constantinople generally face their walls with pure brick, Greek builders from the early tenth century at least use a *cloisonné* facing. Quite unknown in Greece is the system of half-columns, pilasters, responds, blind arches, and niches which articulates the outer walls of churches in Constantinople and Salonica. In place of strong relief and the play of light and shade, the wall surface in Greece is determined by texture and colour. Dog-tooth friezes are used by the school of Constantinople only on drums; in Greece these same friezes serve to frame windows, to articulate the wall horizontally, or to enliven the surface – places where the masons of Constantinople would have employed projecting cornices. Straight horizontal lines set off unified walls; gables are triangular, not curved as so often in Constantinople. The drums of domes in Greece are circular or octagonal; they rarely aspire to the twelve- or fourteen-sided shapes which prevail in Constantinople from the eleventh century on. From the late tenth century, however, semicircular arches often resting on colonnettes frame the windows of the drum and form the characteristic rippling eaves line – a motif at home in Constantinople from the beginning of the century, though different from the Greek version in the use of segmental rather than semicircular blind arches. H. Sotir in Athens presents one of many examples [334].[42]

Plans also differ. The triple arcaded window openings in cross arms customary in the quincunx churches of Constantinople remain unknown in Middle Byzantine church building in Greece. Lateral forechoirs and absidioles open wide into each other and into the eastern corner bays of the

334. Athens, H. Sotir,
eleventh century. Exterior

naos, whereas in Constantinople they communicate through narrow openings, sometimes simply through doors. More often than not, the Greek Middle Byzantine designers fuse outright the lateral forechoirs with the eastern corner bays.

A firm chronology based on a few dated structures and involving a meticulous analysis of the characteristics of masonry, ornament, and window shapes has been established for a majority of Middle Byzantine churches in Greece.[43] Colouristic ornamental effects in the exterior walling start early, possibly around or before the middle of the tenth century, when chequerboard reticulate designs make their appearance in provincial churches. The patterns of the *cloisonné* walling, in particular, change in a highly characteristic way from the early tenth to the end of the twelfth century [335, 336]. Irregular to start with, the *cloisonné* was apparently fully developed by the end of the tenth century. It was composed of single or double horizontal brick courses; or of brick patterns, geometric or imitating Greek and cufic

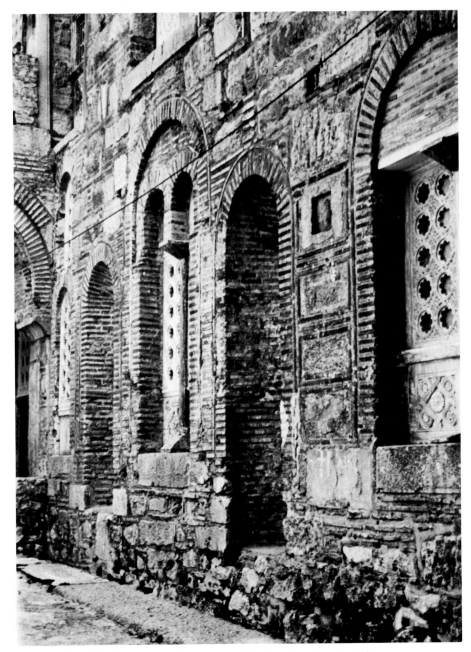

335. Hosios Lukas, Katholikon, consecrated 1011 or 1022. North flank, *cloisonné* and brickwork

336. Athens, H. Theodoroi, c. 1060–70. West façade, *cloisonné* and cufic frieze

characters, inserted vertically between the ashlar blocks. Occasionally, these cufic patterns develop into continuous friezes which, in turn, by 1070 are composed of terracotta panels inscribed with cufic characters in *champlevé* technique [336]. From the middle of the eleventh century, if not earlier, these elaborate designs are more and more replaced by simple patterns: single bricks are inserted vertically between the ashlar blocks; dentil courses, used in overabundance in the earliest buildings, are employed with increasing economy; by 1080 rows of large stone crosses take the place of the irregular stone masonry used earlier along the base of the outer walls [352]. After the middle of the century, too, meander friezes of bricks and friezes composed of cut brick come into use; local schools in the Argolis and elsewhere further develop this feature in the second third of the twelfth century [356, 357]. Other features undergo equally characteristic changes. Coupled and tripled arcaded windows gradually give way to grouped windows, with one large arch surmounting the arcades; possibly a Con-

337 (*above*). Hosios Lukas, Theotokos, tenth century,
and Katholikon, consecrated 1011 or 1022

338–40. Hosios Lukas, Theotokos, tenth century.
Vaults (*right*) and capitals (*opposite*)

stantinopolitan detail, known in Greece since the
early part of the century but rarely used, this feature
begins to prevail about 1080. Simultaneously, the
tympanum of the window arch, originally often filled
with a cufic design, presents a pattern of bricks laid
at right angles in horizontal and vertical courses.
These patterns, become curvilinear in the first half
of the twelfth century, and glazed bowls – an occasional addition since 1040 – became customary in
the design of window tympana. Concomitantly,
high-shouldered triple windows, as known from
Constantinople, become frequent in the design of
gables: a single, double, or triple window flanked by
lower semicircular arches, either blind or open.
Finally, from about 1150, arches, tympana, and
jambs of windows are dressed in stone instead of

brick. Such tell-tale features, then, establish a chronological sequence for the majority of Greek churches in the centres of building activity.

Few churches seem to have survived in Greece from the early tenth century, when Middle Byzantine architecture was first flourishing in Constantinople. What little has remained is crude: small barrel-vaulted chapels, aisleless or occasionally small basilicas on piers; or quincunx structures resting on four piers, the three apses rounded outside: a hallmark, it seems, of early church design in Greece, though possibly often as a provincial survival.[44] But in the latter part of the tenth century, the situation changes, starting from a few major centres. At Hosios Lukas, the church of the Theotokos-Panaghia – the smaller one, to the north – presents the quincunx type clad in a new, rich vocabulary.[45] Constantinopolitan impact apparently makes itself felt: the apses, outside, project in three sides of a polygon [337]; their windows are bipartite and tripartite, divided by slight mullions; and the

four inside supports are slender columns. But plan and design retain a character of their own with features destined to shape for a long time Middle Byzantine building in Greece. The inner outlines remain simple. The walls clearly delimit the interior; windows are few and narrow. Forechoirs and narthex lack the elegant shallow niches billowing into the walls, forming trefoils and quatrefoils. Cornices sharply mark the springings of the barrel-vaults in the cross arms and the centre drum; decorative ribs underscore the groins of the vaults in the corner bays [338]; templa formed by trabeated pairs of columns shut off the forechoirs from the naos. The decoration, too, on the inside, is precise and somewhat dry. Typical are a frieze of standing leaves on the sharp and hard cornices; two Corinthian capitals with long, feathery hard leaves – the *flos* replaced by globules with a cross [339, 340]; and two capitals spun all over with flat foliage, interspersed with diamond shapes and recalling – we shall revert to it – Islamic design. Hard foliage used with rosettes,

341. Hosios Lukas, Theotokos, tenth century.
Exterior of drum

diamonds, crosses, and hearts pressed into tight
patterns covers the architraves of the templa. On the
contrary, the outside is sheathed in the richest, most
colourful design. The walling is done in a lively
cloisonné, the ashlar blocks of different sizes and
shapes, framed by double and triple horizontal
courses and single vertical bricks, the mortar –
where original – rust red. Cufic inserts, including
continuous friezes, enliven the design; so do the
multiple shadow-bands of dog-tooth friezes – as
much as nine bands on the main apse. Forceful
verticals join with these horizontals in an upright
skeleton grid. A strong arch frames the cross arm.
Colonnettes project at the corners of the eight-sided
drum [341]: strongly profiled arches, slightly horseshoe-shaped, curve above, to form originally a rippling eaves line; marble panels with deeply cut
interlace design frame the windows, the ground

originally inlaid. The impact of Islamic art could not
be clearer; but it remains a matter of discussion how
this impact reached Greece – through textiles,
manuscripts, workmen – and why it reached Greece
in particular.[46]

Though more complex in plan, the church of the
Apostles on the Agora in Athens employs a vocabulary much like that of the Theotokos-Panaghia in
Hosios Lukas and is probably close in date [342,
343].[47] Here, the quincunx has been fused with an
eight-leaved rose formed by four major apses on the
main axes and four absidioles on the diagonals. Low
and high, square, rectangular and curved spaces
interlock and merge. The interior decoration is
gone. But on the outside, the combination of strong
polygonal shapes bound together by multiple dog-
tooth friezes and the red and greyish-white *cloisonné*
walling with cufic inserts conveys an impression of

342 and 343. Athens, Holy Apostles, c. 1000(?).
From the south (*above*) and plan (*below*)

Neither the Theotokos-Panaghia nor the church of the Holy Apostles achieves the sophistication and the superb quality of the Katholikon at Hosios Lukas [297, 298, 344–6]. Designed a generation later or less, and consecrated presumably in 1011 or 1022, it combines a complex spatial design, subtle lighting and colourful handling of wall surfaces. Laid out as a Greek-cross octagon, the centre bay freely expands upward under its ample dome; the steep and narrow cross arms pierce through an enfolding belt of aisles and galleries; the aisles are enclosed save for narrow entrances; the galleries open like cages. Wide and narrow, high and low, closed and open volumes thus interpenetrate on different levels [298, 344]. Double and triple windows face the west arm; double windows standing at right angles open at each of the four corners of the centre bay. At ground level, solid walls, set with

both strength and colouristic variety. At the corners of the drum, slender colonnettes are sunk into grooves; above, arches rise high and interpenetrate with the eaves line of the roof – the 'rippling dome' of Middle Byzantine Greece.

tall, flattened round-headed niches, close off the corners of the centre square. In contrast, the gap rent by the lateral cross arms is bridged on the ground floor by a slender triple arcade, on the upper level by the wide platform of an open gallery [346]. High up, the barrel-vault oversails at right angles both platform and supporting arcade. Unexpected views across the core of the naos meet the visitor who either submerges into or emerges from the caves of fragmented aisles and galleries. Alternating in clear and dim zones, light plays over the mosaics in the

dome, the corner squinches, the apse, and on the vaults of the cross arms. In darkish shades, it glides over the marble sheathing which covers wall surfaces, piers, and spandrels in a sophisticated design of light and dark grey, purple and olive slabs, framed by cornices à billettes, and set off at gallery level by a frieze of standing leaves, white against a blue-black ground and remarkably free in design [346]. If the Greek-cross octagon, indeed, harks back to the cross-domed type, the re-interpretation in terms of Middle Byzantine architectural concepts is striking: all massiveness has been eliminated; the spatial volumes, rather than being separated, interlock; the lighting, plainly defined in the H. Sophia at Salonica, has become highly sophisticated; solidity has given way to elegance and squatness to lithe slenderness.

The outer shell is simple in outline: a cube, topped by a low octagonal drum and the curve of a

344–6. Hosios Lukas, Katholikon, consecrated 1011 or 1022.
Interior facing east (*opposite*),
interior of apse and templon (*below*),
and detail of decoration (*right*)

squat dome [337, 347]. Projecting east is a single polygonal apse. Yet this shell opens like a wire screen. Single windows pierce the drum, double and triple windows are broken through the flanks. A tall, triple aperture opens at the end of the cross arms, in Greece lags nearly a century behind the first of the Middle Byzantine churches surviving in Constantinople. The precious design and costliness of the decoration make it plausible that Imperial support played a part in engendering the flowering of the

347. Hosios Lukas, Katholikon,
consecrated 1011 or 1022, and trapeza. From the south

subdivided below by colonnettes and surmounted by the group of a high-shouldered triple window. Arches resting on broad half-piers anchor the windows to the wall. The walling is an irregular pseudo-*cloisonné*: brick is used for window piers and spandrels, and it is interspersed here and there in patches between the stone blocks of the base. Only at the top of the walls is there a genuine *cloisonné*, though often framed by two courses rather than a single course of bricks. The deep-shadow bands of dog-tooth friezes in the lower spandrel zone of the main apse break up the grey and red tapestry of the walling.

Given the dates of these buildings, the latter part of the tenth and the early decades of the eleventh centuries, the new Middle Byzantine church design new style. But such support, if given, did not impose Constantinopolitan solutions on the Greek builders. The plan of the Greek-cross octagon, while not surviving in the capital, might yet have come from there. But in their vocabulary the Greek builders from the outset searched for their own solutions: lively colours, stronger accents of light and shade, rippling effects, sculptural forms.

This early style, however, seems to have lasted but a short time. The complexity of the spatial design, as seen in the Katholikon of Hosios Lukas and the Apostle church in Athens, finds no following. The colourful texture of the walling, to be sure, lives on for some decades: witness the later churches of Kastoria still long after 1100. Yet the classical phase of Middle Byzantine architecture in Greece – from

348. Athens, H. Theodoroi,
c. 1060–70. Exterior from the west

349. Athens, Kapnikarea, c. 1060–70. Exterior from the west

the last third of the eleventh to the early twelfth century – is marked by greater sobriety. As late as 1060/70 the use of multiple dog-tooth bands and the cufic *champlevé* frieze across the façade of the H. Theodoroi in Athens recall earlier custom, as do an occasional ornamental *cloisonné* and the multi-gabled roof line of narthex and parekklesion on the, presumably contemporary, Kapnikarea [348, 349].[48] The window capitals show a heart-shaped foliage ornament, still reminiscent of that on the templa of the Theotokos at Hosios Lukas [350]. By and large, however, the texture of the walling grows quieter, the exteriors simpler, the interior spaces ever more precisely marked off. At times, the design reaches a climax in an uncomplicated, beautiful, and subtle equilibrium. By the time the monastic church

350. Athens, Kapnikarea,
c. 1060–70. Capital and impost block

at Daphni was built, *c.* 1080, the masses of apses, corner bays, cross arms, dome base, and drum are as superbly balanced against each other as the wall surfaces, tile roofs, and window openings [351–3].[49] Cufic or geometrical inserts in the *cloisonné* walling are less frequent, and single bricks alone frame the stone blocks, both vertically and horizontally. The stone masonry along the base of the walls has been arranged into a series of large crosses. Indeed, in its layout as well, the cross octagon at Daphni takes on aspects very different from those of the Katholikon of Hosios Lukas. The belt of spaces enfolding the centre bay and the cross arms is but one-storeyed. There are no galleries, and the aisles are broken up into four chapels, groin-vaulted and but dimly lit. On the other hand, the centre room appears steeper: the squinches sit high up, the entrances into the aisle fragment, and the flat corner niches are extra-ordinarily tall, the proportions remarkably simple and beautiful. Where the design of the Katholikon at Hosios Lukas was based on the sophisticated counterplay of spatial units overlapping and inter-locking, of graded shades of light and dark and of variegated colours, sixty years later an impressive simplicity and balance reign at Daphni.

Similar changes affect the plan and design of quincunx churches all over the country. The com-posite plan survives well into the twelfth century. The main church of Hosios Meletios – on the Kitheron in northern Attica, built before 1100 – provides a good example, remarkable also for the rich ornament of its door lintels, templa, and capitals [302]. But the tendency from the late eleventh century onwards is towards the fusion of forechoirs and eastern corner bays of the naos into one space. This is achieved in three variants. Either corner bays and forechoirs are fused into one barrel-vaulted rectangular bay [354A]; or they are contracted into a square bay and covered by a groin- or barrel-vault [354B]. In either case, the naos with its four columns and three projecting apses remains intact. At times, however, the fusion goes still farther: the two east-ward columns of the naos are lost and the piers of the forechoirs function simultaneously as the eastern

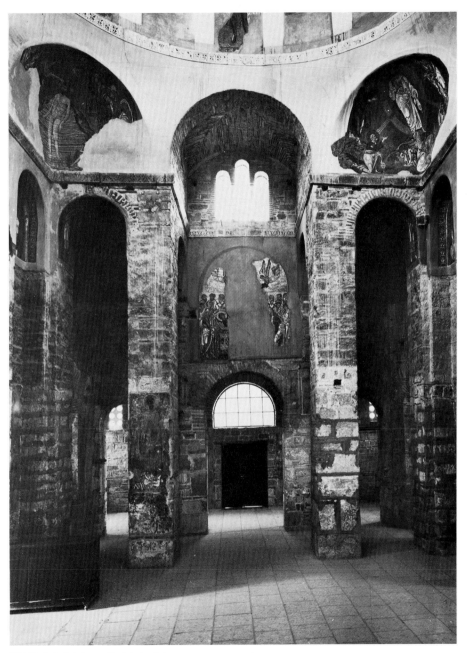

351. Daphni, church, *c.* 1080. Interior facing west

352 and 353. Daphni, church, c. 1080.
Exterior of apses (*above*) and window (*right*)

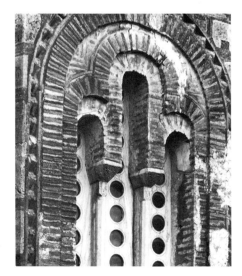

supports of the centre bay [354C]. At the same time,
in many churches the apses are shrunk to small
niches embedded in the thickness of the wall, or they
are entirely omitted. The church at Kaisariani on the
Hymettos near Athens exemplifies the first type in
the late eleventh century. The second type is
represented by the near-by church of St John the
Theologian, of c. 1120, and by St George near Kitta,
on the Mani peninsula far south in the Peloponnesus, of c. 1150. H. Sotir at Amphissa in Locris, H.
Yoannis at Ligourio in the Argolis, and H.
Theodoros at Vamvaka (Vamvakou) on the Mani
peninsula are well-preserved country churches of
the third type. The last two are dated, the first about

354. (A) Kaisariani, Hymettos, church, late eleventh century. Plan
(B) St John the Theologian, Hymettos, c. 1120. Plan   (C) Ligourio, H. Yoannis, c. 1080. Plan

1080, the second, through an inscription, 1075.[50] These few stand for hundreds of similar churches in towns, monasteries, and villages all over Greece. All are quite small. The interior surface in the Theotokos at Hosios Lukas, covering as much as 122 sq. m. (400 sq. ft), is often reduced to as little as 70 or even 45 sq. m. (230 or 150 sq. ft), with the centre bay measuring but 2·70 and even 1·70 m. (9 ft and 5 ft 6 in.) along the side. The interiors are extraordinarily steep: the vaults of the cross arms and the pendentives of the dome spring from a level twice and nearly three times as high as the centre square is wide. The dome rises to a height three and

355. Ligourio, H. Yoannis, c. 1080.
Interior of dome

four times that modulus. Special local features are frequent, as in the churches on the Mani peninsula where the nave vault of the naos projects into the narthex. Walling, as a rule, forms a simple *cloisonné* pattern, the base set with stone crosses. Vaults were cast over centering; at Ligourio the imprints and even one board of the centering are well preserved [355]. Domes with rippling eaves are still frequent, but surprisingly often they give way to a drum with a straight eaves line which holds down the blind arches framing the windows.[51]

Ornament also takes on new shapes. Cufic motifs and Islamic interlace panels, so prominent in the tenth and far into the eleventh century, by 1070 have become less conspicuous in the overall picture. Geometric forms and foliage fused and tightly compressed, as already in the templa of the Theotokos, remain in use as late as the first quarter of the twelfth century. But the geometric elements are increasingly eliminated in favour of tendril friezes with trefoil shoots. These too are tight at first, but gradually the tendrils loosen, the ground appears, and animals are inserted between the winding scrolls. By the third quarter of the twelfth century, the development is complete.[52]

At least one local school of masons, however, as early as the second third of the twelfth century renounced the sober and austere wall patterns which had come to the fore in the latter eleventh century. Four churches in the Argolis, not far from Nauplion, represent a new playful and rich design: three are quincunx churches, at Chonika, Merbaka [356], and

356. Merbaka, church, mid twelfth century(?). Exterior

H. Moni; the fourth is a charming small Greek-cross chapel at Plataniti.[53] The quincunx rests on four columns; the corner bays carry pendentive domes or groin-vaults and are small in comparison to the centre bay (in a ratio of roughly one to four). Shallow niches enlarge the chancel sideways and shelter the passages – long, dark, and barrel-vaulted – which lead to the lateral forechoirs. The esonarthex is closed off from the naos except for narrow doors. Three apses project clearly on the exterior. The upper sections of the cross arms rise only slightly over the roof of the corner bays; the drums are simple, articulated only by projecting corner colonnettes and by blind arches framing the windows. Only the H. Moni is dated, by an inscription of 1149. The church at Chonika has been assigned to the first, Merbaka to the last quarter of the twelfth or the early thirteenth century. But the measurements in all three are so nearly the same that one would like to attribute them to one workshop, active near the middle of the twelfth century. Details of walling and ornament are likewise almost identical: the simple *cloisonné* walling sparsely interspersed with dog-tooth friezes; the brick meander friezes; the triple windows in the gables of the cross arms, flanked by high-shouldered blind half-arches and filled with a brick decoration at right angles; and for the spandrels of the windows, a fan-shaped brick design. But brick ornament of this type is found beyond the borders of the Argolis as well; H. Sotir near Amphissa, not far from Delphi, shows it already early in the twelfth century [357]. Frequently ceramic bowls inserted into the walls add colour to

357. Amphissa, H. Sotir, twelfth century. Detail

the masonry. *Cloisonné* and linear elements combine to form a splendid if somewhat playful design, characteristic, it would seem, of the last phase of Middle Byzantine architecture in Greece – a design carried over into the early stages of Late Byzantine building.

ASIA MINOR

From the outset, Middle Byzantine architecture in Asia Minor stands somewhat apart. It lacks the subtlety of Constantinople and the slightly overdone elegance of Salonica and Bulgaria, and it is far less experimental and free than Greece. Caught in prov-

incial custom, its masons work with the traditional building material, ashlar blocks, and prefer the locally customary pier to the foreign column. For a long time, they cling to old-fashioned plans. But once Middle Byzantine taste caught the fancy of patrons and monastic congregations – local or immigrants from the capital – Constantinopolitan elements blended easily with native forms. The fusion presumably took place in the course of the tenth and eleventh centuries.

The loss to the Seljuks of nearly all of eastern and southern Asia Minor and temporarily as far north as Nicaea (Iznik) after 1071 seriously affected church building in the larger urban centres. In the countryside, however, Christian congregations and monasteries survived, and church building continued for some time. A number of factors, in fact, strengthened the hand of the Christian groups: the establishment of an Armenian kingdom (Lesser Armenia) in Cilicia after 1071; the passage of the Crusaders in 1097–8, 1147–8, and 1196–9; and the Byzantine re-occupation of northern and western Asia Minor by 1118 and of the southern coastline, including Lesser Armenia, from 1137 to 1176.

Vaulted chapels without aisles, cross-shaped churches, and hall-churches with nave and flanking aisles are known from the sixth and seventh centuries all through the interior of Asia Minor [128–31].[54] Unchanged, these same types apparently continued to the beginning of and into the Middle Byzantine period. Neither the masonry of well-squared large stones facing a rubble core nor the vaulting technique differ from those of the earlier buildings. Naves were covered by barrel-vaults, domes placed on squinches. Profiling and ornament likewise for centuries remained the same, and since few inscriptions have been reported, there is little evidence – external or internal – for dating the buildings. But at least three churches at Trebizond (Trabzon), on the northern coast of Asia Minor, are dated.[55] St Anne was built in 884/5 as a tiny basilica with barrel-vaulted nave and aisles; the two arches on either side of the nave rest on a single column, a spoil. The Nakip Camii, probably slightly later, was

358. Göreme, rock chapels, eighth–twelfth(?) centuries

a hall-church, barrel-vaulted and terminated by three apses. The Chrysokephalos was laid out, in the tenth or eleventh century, apparently as a large hall-church, 30 m. (100 ft) long, with galleries above the aisles. The overall plan; the barrel-vaults, longitudinal over the nave, while transverse over the aisles; and finally, the shape of the main apse, horseshoe-shaped within, polygonal without, closely link the Chrysokephalos, like the other churches, to the architectural customs that had prevailed for centuries in the interior of Asia Minor.

Needless to say, traditional plans of the ninth, tenth, and eleventh centuries were also employed in the strange cliff chapels which, from the eighth and ninth centuries, had been hollowed out by monastic congregations from the fantastic rock cones in the wild 'moonscapes' of Cappadocia [358]. Large numbers are preserved in an excellent state in the valleys of Soğanli (Soğandere), Göreme, and Menendiz Suyu (Peristrema), all south-west of Kayseri.[56] Floors, walls, piers, columns, and vaults are hewn from the living rock, as are furnishings: altar, benches, chancel screens, and, once, a fully-fledged iconostasis. In their majority, the cliff chapels are tiny, some only 2 by 4 m. (6½ by 13 ft) and rarely over 7 m. (25 ft) long or wide. All are terminated by horseshoe apses. Often they are aisleless. But double-naved churches do occur – one of the chapels is even a fully developed hall-church, its nave and aisles separated by colonnades. At times a barrel-vaulted quadriporticus, its centre open to the sky, precedes the chapel. In the Tokali Kilise, the largest of the rock churches at Göreme, a square porch leads into the nave, which in turn is laid out on

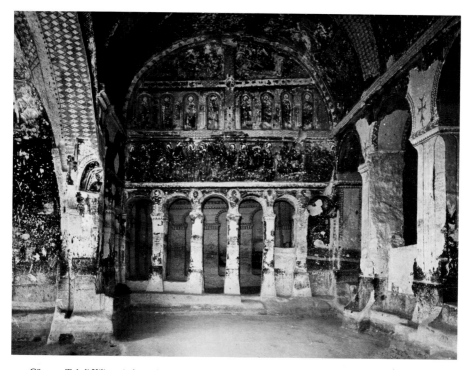

359. Göreme, Tokali Kilise, ninth–tenth centuries. Interior looking north

a transverse axis, and terminated by the five arches of an iconostasis and by three apses [359]. One is reminded of the transverse churches of the Tur Abdin.[57] The whole is most impressive, both in decoration and size – the nave alone measures 9 m. in width and nearly 6 m. in depth (30 by 20 ft).

In the great majority of the rock churches, walls and vaults are covered with extensive fresco cycles of an obviously Middle Byzantine character. A few of the cycles are dated by inscriptions ranging from the early tenth to the third quarter of the eleventh century. At times these paintings may have been executed shortly after the chapels had been hewn from the rock. Frequently, however, an older layer of frescoes appears below the Middle Byzantine murals, and this older layer often appears to be aniconic. While it is true that monastic congrega-

tions in the Cappadocian mountains could very likely have clung to the tenets of iconoclasm beyond its official end in 843, a good case can be made for a ninth- or eighth-century date for at least some of the rock churches. Indeed, a group of six, based on the style of their mural decoration, has been assigned to the iconoclastic decades 726–87. On the other hand, given the tolerant religious policies of the Muslim conquerors, the monastic congregations in the Cappadocian wilderness continued at least to paint their rock chapels until the late thirteenth century.[58]

But not all rock churches cling to obsolete plans. Middle Byzantine taste also makes itself felt in their planning, and quincunx plans are frequent [360]. Many of the churches may date from the eleventh or even the twelfth century. But one group is clearly late-tenth-century and one quincunx may be dated

360. Göreme, Elmali Kilise, tenth-twelfth centuries(?). Interior of apse and domes

into the second half of the ninth century. Such a dating would be prior to, or contemporaneous with, the building of the Nea in Constantinople. Yet the plans of the quincunx churches in Göreme differ from those in Constantinople: proportions are squat, and not only the centre and corner bays, but at least once the cross arms as well, are surmounted by domes – this latter a variation impossible in a real building, but easy in a cave. At the same time, the playful transposition suggests a date before the

quincunx type was hardened and codified in Constantinople during the eleventh century.[59]

Indeed, during the eleventh and possibly as early as the tenth century, Constantinople and her quincunx churches must have exerted a strong impact on the builders of Asia Minor. Few Middle Byzantine churches above ground have survived in the interior, but among those extant Constantinopolitan elements are paramount. In the Çanlikilise (Tchânliklisse) at the foot of the Hassan Dağ

ORIGINAL BUILDING

FIRST ADDITION

SECOND ADDITION

361 and 362. Çanlikilise, Hassan Dağ,
eleventh century. Plan (*above*)
and exterior from the south west (*below*)

south-west of Kayseri [361, 362], the walling of
alternate bands of well-cut ashlar and brick recalls
the technique well known in Constantinople from
the ninth to the eleventh century, and possibly
later.[60] The brickwork with extraordinarily broad
mortar joints either imitates or is executed in the
recessed brick technique of eleventh- and early-
twelfth-century Constantinople. Other features
equally point to the capital: the slender proportions
of interior, drum, and apses, the latter with their
polygonal exterior and semicircular interior curves.
Blind arches, twice recessed, frame the windows of
the apse, the tall drum, and the south flank, as well as
outlining the upper cross arms. Blind niches form an
upper tier high on the apse wall; the blind arches
spring from elegant colonnettes. The fan design of
bricks in the spandrels is better known from Greek
buildings, but it may well have originated in Constantinople. In short, the design of the Canlikilise –
on the wild Hassan Dağ – stems from Constantinople and was executed by a crew in which at least
some members must have been trained in the

capital. Closely related is the ruin of another church, Üçayak near Kirşehir, 90 miles north-west of Kayseri: a twin chapel, formed by two atrophied Greek-cross buildings opened towards each other and originally with a common narthex, but each provided with its own apse; the two domes, formerly on high drums, each with twelve windows; the apses polygonal outside and articulated by probably three tiers of shallow niches; the flanks opened in arcades and windows, both triple; the outer walls articulated by blind arches, three and four times stepped back; the masonry brick, throughout with broad mortar-beds, whether in genuine or imitated 'recessed' technique. Design and details closely recall either Kariye Camii or the Eski Imaret and suggest a date perhaps just prior to 1071 and Constantinopolitan building practice. Elsewhere regional building tradition perseveres. The small-stone masonry follows native custom; supports are invariably piers; the plans are limited to a naos and a triple sanctuary;

apses retain their semicircular exterior in compliance with centuries-old local custom; nartheces, lateral porticoes, and parekklesia are unknown. But the impact of Constantinople is unmistakable. The plans are cross-in-square, the chancels are set off from the east corner bays. Windows are framed by twice-recessed blind arches or by niches; upper tiers of niches encircle drums and apses. Graceful pilasters and recessed arches articulate the outer walls, and mouldings are remarkably elegant.[61]

Middle Byzantine building found its way from southern Asia Minor to the islands of the southern Aegean Sea, at times unadulterated, at other times merged with elements brought from the Greek mainland. The blend is represented on Rhodes by a number of churches,[62] but nowhere more attractively than in the ruins of H. Yoannis high up on the Acropolis of Lindos – a superb site among the Greek ruins [363]. Its cross-in-square plan clearly shows both the impact of Asia Minor and the collateral

363. Lindos, Rhodes, H. Yoannis, c. 1100. Exterior from the south-east

influence of the Greek mainland: the esonarthex has been fused with the naos as in the churches of the Mani peninsula in the Peloponnesus, and as so often in Greece, the chancel parts have been fused with the east bays of the nave. But the masonry of small ashlar, the exclusive use of barrel-vaults in the corner bays, and the recessed double frames enclosing narrow window slits link the structure to Asia Minor and suggest a date in the late eleventh or early twelfth century. On Crete, structures such as a ruin near Milopotamo and a well-preserved church at H. Myron show the same mixture of elements: stone construction, coupled with brick for the vaulting zone; a quincunx plan resting on piers, rarely on columns; domes or barrel-vaults over the corner bays; finally, blind arches, singly or doubly recessed, to articulate the outer walls. The links to church building on the mainland of Greece are weak; links to Constantinople hardly exist.[63] On Cyprus, close as it lies to the south coast, the impact of the mainland of Asia Minor is even more strongly felt.[64] Alongside the customary Middle Byzantine church types such as quincunx buildings, domed-octagon plans, and small Greek-cross structures, a cross plan with an elongated west arm makes its appearance – probably descended directly from Cappadocian and Lycaonian cross churches of the sixth to eighth centuries. Quincunx churches are almost without exception supported by heavy piers, not by columns. The masonry of remarkably well-cut stone blocks hardly ever includes any brickwork. Everything suggests the architecture of a provincial island which more and more isolates itself against Constantinople and the core of the Byzantine Empire. This is not surprising, given the political history of Cyprus: ruled by Byzantium until 648, it maintained from then until 965 an uneasy state of neutrality, bound by treaties to both Constantinople and the Arab rulers of Syria; recovered by Byzantium, it fell prey in 1192 to Western powers – Crusader kings, and later the Republic of Venice. Nor is it surprising that at least one church plan characteristic of Cyprus has its counterpart in Apulia and Sicily: a nave covered along its main axis by three domes in succession, and

flanked by barrel-vaulted aisles, which in turn are pierced by cross arms.[65] Whatever the relationship, the sea lanes of the Middle Byzantine Empire seem to have formed a link between its eastern and western Mediterranean outposts.

THE WESTERN OUTPOSTS

Middle Byzantine architecture established itself in the West in two outposts, each of a distinct character. In Venice and her vicinity, Middle Byzantine building is represented by a small number of churches and palaces. Monumental in design and lavish in execution, they are on the one hand apparently linked to the art of Constantinople and some major centres in Greece, and on the other, to the styles of Romanesque Europe. In southern Italy and Sicily a comparatively large number of Middle Byzantine churches has survived. But all are small and insignificant within the overall picture of Byzantine architecture of the tenth to twelfth centuries. Both their execution and their decoration, save for the mosaics of the Martorana in Palermo, are provincial. Finally, in plan they are related not to Constantinople, but to the more retarded provinces of the Aegean basin.

The ties of the Italian peninsula with the Byzantine world from the late sixth to the end of the eighth century, while weaker than under Justinian's rule, had never been completely broken. Byzantine officials sat in Ravenna and Naples; the policy of the papacy in Rome was oriented towards Byzantium. In other areas of religious activity, however – in hagiology, liturgy, and church architecture – it is not so much Byzantium that exerts its impact as what has been vaguely called 'the East': more precisely, a conglomeration of diverse influences, stemming from different provinces in the Eastern hinterlands and the Aegean coastlands, which penetrate the West from the sixth century on. Accumulated over the centuries, blended with each other and with Western features, these often heterogeneous elements remain active in the West as a common heritage. Eastern saints were absorbed by Western martyrologies, Eastern relics were being acquired, Eastern elements were filtering into Western liturgies. In church architecture – in Ravenna, Rome, and North Italy – galleries, alternating supports, pastophories, triple apses, polygonal apse shapes, and impost blocks are gradually fused with Western church plans. However, this Eastern heritage had spent itself by the end of the eighth century. It was replaced by a revival of Western Early Christian traditions, first under Carolingian impact, later by the awakening of the High Middle Ages and their Romanesque art. True, quincunx churches sporadically made their appearance at an early moment in the West as in other borderlands of the Empire – in Italy at Milan, near Cassino, and perhaps elsewhere.[66] But in the overall framework of the West and of Italy, the East both as a heritage and as a living force had lost its significance.

Locally, in southern Italy the picture changed again in the late tenth century. In about 970 Apulia and Calabria were reconquered by the Byzantine forces, and for the next hundred years a Byzantine governor, the *katapan*, resided at Bari. At the same time, if not earlier, small congregations of Basilian monks established themselves in the countryside. The Eastern tradition of painting they carried along with them is important enough. But the cave churches in which these murals were executed are, architecturally, of little significance. Other churches of Byzantine type do, of course, exist in the territory, at Otranto, Stilo [364], Rossano; their dates of construction, however, are unknown.[67] They may have been built either while the district was under Byzantine rule, or somewhat later. Indeed, Byzantine architectural types certainly survived beyond the Norman Conquest of the territory in 1071. But regardless of their actual dates, Byzantine structures in southern Italy are highly provincial, as one would expect in an outlying province, virtually an overseas colony, of the Empire. The materials used are invariably local stone, rarely brick; construction is crude. Plans were drawn from other provinces of the Byzantine world, distant but accessible over the seas. No doubt the buildings

364. Stilo, Cattolica, tenth or eleventh century. Exterior

have their charm. But they have attracted attention for reasons external to either quality or historical importance: by virtue of the scenery, the appealing quality of folk art, and their exceptional position as building types otherwise unknown in the West. Within the overall picture of Middle Byzantine church building the churches of Calabria and Apulia are no more significant than those of any outlying mountain province in Greece. Their significance lies only in the evidence they furnish of the links between one distant province and another along the sea lanes of the Empire. The funerary chapel of Count Bohemund at Canosa – it dates from 1101, forty years after the collapse of Byzantine rule – is a quincunx structure sliced in half to adjust it to the adjoining cathedral; given the smallness of the corner bays, it may possibly be inspired by Salonican models. Basilicas with three domes rising over the longitudinal axis of the nave, found as late as the thirteenth century in the cathedral at Molfetta, find their closest parallel in Cypriote churches.[68] Similarly, the planimetric scheme of S. Marco at Rossano and the Cattolica at Stilo, both in Calabria, has been linked to distant Crete and indeed even further east to the quincunxes in the caves of Cappadocia. Nine bays, all of equal or nearly equal size, form the cross-in-square, thus forcing the centre bay into a disproportionate narrowness and steepness. The lack of balance and proportion may well be due, both in Calabria and Cappadocia, to sheer awkwardness on the part of the local builders. Wherever the plan had originated, however, it seems to have come to Calabria by way of the Peloponnesus; there it could have absorbed a number of features which at Stilo strongly recall churches in the small harbour cities of the Greek peninsula. Sawtooth friezes articulate the wall surfaces as in the Koimesis at Tegea; as in the Pantanassa at Monemvasia, five drums rise from the roof. The use of bricks at Stilo, exceptional in South Italy, likewise suggests ties with Greece. The broad chequer bands which encircle the drums of the domes have their source in the decorative walling of churches as early as the tenth century in the Peloponnesus. This may well be when the Cattolica at Stilo, too, was built; S. Marco at Rossano, being more awkward in every respect, may be a later follower.[69] The fusion of quincunx and trefoil which characterizes the churches of Mount Athos also appears, with little change, at Castro in Apulia. In short, the small, awkward village churches of South Italy seem to have drawn, whether directly or indirectly, on quite a few provinces of Middle Byzantine architecture. There is little doubt that the builders were rustics, but one wonders whether they came from the Calabrian countryside or were migrant masons from the East. On the other hand, a large structure of decidedly Western plan, the Roccelletta of Squillace near Catanzaro, in the last third of the eleventh century or possibly after 1100, uses a vocabulary of decidedly Comnene and Constantinopolitan character, including triple-recessed niches in double tiers on the apse and similar blind arches along the flanks of its aisleless nave.[70]

Sicily occupies a very different place in the scheme of Middle Byzantine architecture.[71] Its links to the Christian East, tight in the past, had been severed by the Arab occupation in 827. The Norman Conquest of 1091, based as it was on Campania, Calabria, and Apulia, naturally established ties with these ex-Byzantine provinces, and through them with the Byzantine Empire. But these ties grew strong only in the second and the last third of the twelfth century, when the Norman court reached the highest level of contemporary aulic refinement. At that time the Norman kings and the Comnene Emperors were in constant contact. Byzantine mosaic workers were called to Palermo, perhaps from Greece and certainly from Constantinople, and their art was blended with the traditions of church planning drawn from Rome, Montecassino, and France, and the traditions of palace architecture and decoration drawn from the countries of the Islamic West. Within this wonderful and fantastic blend, Byzantine church plans are rare, unassuming, and related to provincial architecture in Greece rather than to Constantinople. What little has survived on Sicily or on the near-by islands – S. Costanzo on Capri is the northernmost outpost[72] – are quincunx structures. The supports are four columns; the apses are semicircular inside and out; the corner bays carry domical groin-vaults. The lone centre drum is extraordinarily high, and placed sometimes on Byzantine pendentives, sometimes on Islamic squinches. But the architectural design never transgresses a level of decent mediocrity.

One would expect the Martorana in Palermo to be an exception [365].[73] Dedicated in 1143 by Admiral George of Antioch to the Theotokos, and placed under the charge of the Greek clergy, it carries to this day its splendid mosaics. The dedicatory inscriptions in Greek and Arabic leave no doubt as to the love and care the founder bestowed on the structure and its decoration. The splendour of the mosaics and the pride of its inscriptions only bring out more strongly the character of its architecture; a straightforward quincunx, the inside unarticulated, a simple Greek rather than a Constantinopolitan

365. Palermo, Martorana, dedicated 1143. Interior facing east

type. True the tower – built somewhat later in front of what may have been an atrium – is extraordinarily beautiful and was much admired by contemporary travellers. Formerly believed to be a derivative of the cathedral of Laon, at this point its sources, whether western or eastern, remain uncertain.

The contrast between the rich quality of the decoration and the plainness of the architecture finds its explanation within the framework of an approach to Western and Byzantine art characteristic of the city states and courts of South Italy since the late eleventh century. Trading with the Levant, the merchant cities of Amalfi and Salerno had established close ties with Constantinople in business, politics, and art. The great lords of Norman South Italy, from the abbot of Montecassino to the king at Palermo, followed suit. From Byzantium they imported what they considered superior to Western art: bronze doors, mosaic workers, enamel work. But they insisted on building their fortresses and their churches along Western lines, probably because they rightly thought the first to be stronger, the latter more monumental, spacious, and better adapted to Roman liturgy than their Byzantine counterparts. Hence the churches at Montecassino, Salerno, Ravello, Bari, or Monreale were laid out according to, or modifying, Western custom: Roman Early Christian basilicas, Norman and Lombard Romanesque churches with galleries, basilicas with segregated crossings surmounted by a dome and drum. Only the extraordinary height of the drum recalls the tall drums of Byzantine quincunx churches. But the buildings themselves remain Western.[74] Even the cathedral at Pisa, begun in 1063 on what was long believed an Eastern plan as a huge cross-transept basilica with galleries and doubled aisles, is fundamentally Western, notwithstanding possible collateral influences from the East.

In Venice the situation differs radically from that prevailing in southern Italy and Sicily in the tenth, eleventh, and twelfth centuries. The settlements in the Venetian lagoon had long slipped from active Byzantine rule. But the growing merchant republic maintained close diplomatic and mercantile ties with the Byzantine Empire. Venetian businessmen were well established in the ports of Central Greece and the Peloponnesus, and nowhere were they more powerful than in Constantinople. Finally in 1204, by engineering the Fourth Crusade, the Republic of Venice, with the aid of her feudal allies, could take over capital and Empire. No wonder, then, that the art of Venice until the eleventh and twelfth centuries – notwithstanding an ever-growing penetration of Western Romanesque elements – remained closely linked to the Middle Byzantine art of Byzantium.

Building activity in Venice may have been extensive as early as the ninth and tenth centuries. But nothing has survived save for the foundations of the first church of S. Marco, which we shall soon discuss. The picture of Venetian architecture becomes clear only with the eleventh and twelfth centuries. At that point the penetration of Western elements into Venetian building is obvious. The building material employed is the high brick with thin mortar-beds customary in North Italy from antiquity to the twelfth century among Milanese, Ravennatic, Longobard, Carolingian, and Romanesque builders. In planning, Western liturgical demands are taken into consideration. The decoration in many of its features has been assimilated to Western custom. But it is equally obvious that Venetian building of the eleventh and twelfth centuries, in its basic plans, its spatial designs, and in a wealth of details, is tied far more closely to Middle Byzantine building in Constantinople and in the great architectural centres of Greece than to building in the West.

S. Fosca on the island of Torcello varies the Greek-cross octagon; the dome has collapsed, but two squinches superimposed in each corner and the first rings of the dome have survived.[75] In plan it gives way to Western liturgical tradition by substituting short open aisles for the closed-off forechoirs of the Byzantine rite [366]. (The eight-sided outer portico is quite possibly of later date.) Otherwise the plan might just as well have been designed in Greece; the Panaghia Lykodimou in Athens and the cathedral at Christianou, both of the eleventh cen-

366. Torcello, S. Fosca, eleventh–twelfth centuries. From the west

tury, offer parallels. For that matter, the architect of S. Fosca might have drawn on Constantinople, though no Greek-cross octagon survives at present in the Byzantine capital. In fact the decorative details of the apse are those customary in eleventh- and twelfth-century Constantinople: two tiers of niches, as in the Kilise Camii; paired colonnettes, recalling the Nea Moni on Chios; a terminating frieze of pendant triangles and saw-tooth bands, as on the lateral apses of the Gül Camii. All these elements, to be sure, are rendered less subtly than they are in Constantinople. They have been provincialized and translated, as it were, into the Venetian dialect. But this Venetian dialect of the late eleventh and twelfth centuries is essentially a variant of Middle Byzantine, not of Western Romanesque architecture.

The ties of Venice to both Byzantium and the West become most obvious at S. Marco, the main church of Venice as well as the palatine chapel of her doge.[76] But the network of relationships is more involved than usual. The plan of S. Marco draws not on a Middle Byzantine, but on a sixth-century Byzantine model – a sixth-century prototype, that is, which was apparently remodelled in the tenth century. And this remodelled prototype was transposed at St Mark's into the Middle Byzantine dialect of Venice and crossed with a number of purely Western elements.

Remnants of a first church of St Mark's, built as early as 830, apparently survive in the foundation walls of the main piers and perhaps the bottom courses of some of the outer walls of the present structure. These remnants suggest that already the first building was cross-shaped, of approximately the same size as the present church, and thus presumably laid out as a copy of Justinian's Apostoleion; this regardless of whether the Venetian church was timber-roofed or whether (as has often been rashly assumed) it, like its Constantinopolitan model, was surmounted by five domes, one over each arm and one over the crossing. The reasons for this link to Constantinople are obvious. Venice, as protectress of the patriarchate of Grado, had just abducted the relics of the Evangelist St Mark – according to the legend the apostle of the Upper Adria, and the founder of both the patriarchal sees of Aquileia and Grado, as well as of the see of Alexandria in Egypt – from their resting place in Alexandria. The abduction reveals the Venetian ambition to raise the see of Grado, now under their control, above that of Aquileia, which in turn had long been eager to supplant the see of Alexandria, to all practical purposes long-extinct.[77] Equally at issue may have been competition with the patriarchate of Constantinople, supposedly founded by St Andrew. Thus, in 830, to honour the apostle of the Adria finally returned to their shores, the Venetians built a church cross-shaped like Justinian's church of the Holy Apostles in Constantinople – the shrine which sheltered, among other relics, those of St Andrew. Indeed, Justinian's church also remained the model when the Venetians, starting perhaps in 1063, replaced this first cross church by the present structure. By the late eleventh century, however, the church of the Holy Apostles was no longer quite Justinian's original building. The five low domes of Justinian's structure – only the centre dome having been provided with windows – had been replaced by domes raised on high drums with large windows which shed light into the arms as well as the centre bay. This remodelled Apostoleion is the structure reflected in the eleventh-century church of S. Marco.[78]

Construction of this new church of St Mark proceeded speedily. Walls and piers may have been completed by 1071, and in 1073 a first consecration took place. On the other hand, the decoration dragged on, and additions were made for centuries. The

colonnades inside date from the late eleventh and early twelfth centuries, the marble revetment of piers and inside walls largely from the twelfth, and the mosaics from the twelfth and thirteenth centuries. After 1204, the narthex – originally limited to the façade – was continued along the flanks of the nave so as to envelop the western arm. The domes were given the tall and steep outer shells in timber construction and slightly bell-shaped, and surmounted – at first only the one in the centre – by open lanterns with bulbous and ribbed cupolas. Construction and design, and with them the characteristic silhouette of S. Marco, are rooted in Islamic architecture, be it the Dome of the Rock in Jerusalem or the bulbous, ribbed domes of Fatimid eleventh-century mausolea in Cairo. Also after 1204 and possibly not before the second quarter of the century, the outer walls of the narthex were sheathed in the panoply that to this day greets the visitor who approaches from the Piazza: deep portal niches, mosaics, dense rows of columns in two tiers, marble slabs, parapets, and sculptures as they appear as early as the third quarter of the thirteenth century in a mosaic above the left-hand narthex door [367].[79] Much of the decoration was looted from Constantinople, together with the four bronze horses placed above the centre portal, and the best pieces of the Treasury. The fifteenth century added the florid Gothic gables above the façade, the seventeenth the large mosaics in its upper part. These additions have carried with them elements of their own, all Western in character: Italian Baroque, International Gothic, twelfth- and thirteenth-century Lombard. But none have altered the original character of the building, its perfect integration of elements of Justinian's age and Middle Byzantine elements.

With the plan of Justinian's Apostle church, S. Marco was bound to absorb sixth-century concepts of space and mass [368, 369]. The volumes of the five bays are huge. Surmounted by the hemispheres of the domes, they are emphatically segregated by broad arches. As in the H. Sophia and at S. Vitale, the masses of piers and walls are sheathed in a marble revetment, the slabs forming a pattern and

367 and 368. Venice, S. Marco, begun 1063(?).
Mosaic on the Porta di S. Alipio
showing the church as after 1204 (*above*);
interior of nave (*opposite*)

the veins of adjoining slabs often counter-matching.
Their designs are less subtle, their materials less
precious. Yet in the handling of space and masses
and in the use of a marble covering, S. Marco
breathes much of the spirit of Justinian's art.

All the same, S. Marco is permeated by new
concepts, both Middle Byzantine and Western
Romanesque. As in the Apostoleion after its
remodelling, at S. Marco the five domes rise on low
drums. Light evenly fills the upper zones; nave,
aisles, and chancel remain dim, almost dark. As in
the Apostle church, the galleries in Venice also

originally spanned the full depth of the aisles to the
outer walls. But departing from Justinian's design, at
S. Marco the galleries were not screened by colonnades; on the contrary, the lateral barrel-vaults
supporting each of the five domed bays extended
across the aisles, much as in the mid-eighth-century
rebuilding of the H. Irene in Constantinople and at
Dere Ağzı in the ninth century. At S. Marco this
syncopation of spatial units was reinforced when, in
the twelfth century, the full galleries were replaced
by mere catwalks on top of the lower colonnades
[368]. These latter thus became screens engulfed
by the sideward expansion of the nave bays, much in
the spirit of eleventh-century church design in
Constantinople. Details also find their parallel
in Macedonian and Comnene architecture in
Constantinople and in the major churches of contemporary Greece: the palmette frieze above the
arcades; the cornices on top of the parapets in niello

369 and 370. Venice, S. Marco, begun 1063(?).
Interior of cupolas (*top*)
and decorative details of gallery (*above*)

technique – white foliage on a black ground [370];
the cubic capitals in the crypt, their sides set with a
projecting knotted nodule; the delicate marble profiles along the bases of the main piers. Where not
sheathed in marble, the walls along the façades are

articulated into delicate planes by doubled and tripled blind arches, by friezes with saw-tooth patterns,
foliage, and rows of pendant triangles. The same
decoration still covers the façades behind their later
marble sheathing. The bricks in the niche-heads are
laid out in a wicker pattern. Parallels in contemporary Byzantium come easily to mind.[80]

Perhaps one may go further. The solid masses
and clearly outlined spaces of St Mark's, forced
upon the builders by the model of Justinian's
church, coincide with the predilection for well-
defined volumes and balanced forms so evident in
Middle Byzantine structures of the late eleventh
century in Greece, as at Daphni, for example. In any
event, within the framework of Middle Byzantine
architecture, Venice is one of the centres of a
genuine renascence of the art of Justinian and
before. The evidence of the plan is confirmed by the
capitals. A large number, if not all, in the colonnades
of the interior and elsewhere are eleventh-century

copies from models of Justinian's age and slightly earlier, done so carefully that only the harsher details distinguish them from fifth- and sixth-century capitals, Corinthian or two-zone capitals with projecting figures of rams.[81] The ecclesiastical and political reasons underlying the choice of a specific Byzantine plan are fused with the sheer aesthetic enjoyment of the forms of Justinian's churches and similar early forms.

Nonetheless, S. Marco was not built by craftsmen or with materials shipped from the East. The high bricks are those used in North Italy since Roman times. Even the piers are built of bricks, facing a core of rubble masonry so poor as to create very serious problems of maintenance, and much poorer than in any genuine Byzantine construction. Contrary to Byzantine and following Western technique, the bricks of the domes are laid in concentric, not radial courses. The harsh and precise workmanship of the capitals likewise reveals Lombard, not Byzantine hands, as do the bases of the columns (the shafts are no doubt spoils), and the profiles of the revetment base along the inner walls. The plan itself seems to have been adjusted to the Western predilection for basilican patterns: the nave is pulled slightly lengthwise; a deep barrel-vault continues the nave westward; to the east, the chancel and apse are raised above nave level, supported by a huge hall crypt; along the chancel, the lateral forechoirs open towards the transept in wide arches as in any Romanesque church.

Such blending of Byzantine and Western features is only natural in Venice, the westernmost cultural stronghold of the Eastern Empire and at the same time a powerful member of both the European and Near Eastern political and economic communities from the eleventh into the thirteenth century. However, Western elements evidently penetrated much farther into the Byzantine Empire and reached, if not its provinces, at least its capital. The details of Constantinopolitan churches from the Pantepoptes church (Eski Imaret) and the Kilise Camii to the churches of the Zeyrek Camii often suggest the possibility of an impact of Romanesque architecture on the later phases of Middle Byzantine building. In particular, they recall the architecture of the so-called *premier art roman* in Lombardy. Rows of niches in the attic zone of apses, right below the eaves lines, had been a hallmark of Lombard churches since the ninth century, such as S. Pietro at Agliate and S. Ambrogio in Milan. Blind arches frame the windows and articulate the walls of apses in dozens of Lombard churches from the ninth to the end of the eleventh century. Finally, dog-tooth friezes are a common decorative element in Lombard brick construction. Such features might easily have reached eleventh-century Constantinople either directly or by way of Venice. It is too early to go beyond a mere suggestion of this possibility. But it is certainly worthwhile considering the idea that Byzantine architects were not entirely ignorant of, or disinterested in, Western development.

PART SEVEN

THE END OF BYZANTINE ARCHITECTURE

CHAPTER 18

INTRODUCTION

If historical dates are taken literally, the Byzantine Empire came to an end on 29 May 1453, with the death in action of Constantine XI Paleologos and the victorious entry into Constantinople of Sultan Mehmed. In reality the beginning of the end had started long before, and the last two hundred and fifty years of Byzantine history are but a drawn-out last phase. When the end starts is disputable. Does it begin in 1204 when the Latins – the Franks – occupied Constantinople; in 1390 when the Empire became a Turkish vassal state – limited to the capital, its immediate vicinity, and a small slice of the Peloponnesus around Mistra; or at some time in between? In political history, certainly, 1204 seems a good starting point for the Byzantine epilogue. On the other hand, the Latin Conquest lasted but fifty-odd years in the capital, and a shorter time in the few provinces where the Frankish barons had established themselves. Further, despite the fall of Constantinople, Byzantine grandees kept large strongholds in the provinces. In Asia Minor – except for the tiny north-western slice under Latin occupation and the south-eastern third (long under Seljuk occupation) – the Empire of Nicaea was established by the Laskaris and Vatatzes families. At the same time in Epirus, the dynasty of the Angeloi founded an independent despotate with Arta as its capital. From there the dynasty reconquered Macedonia and Thrace from the Franks and in 1224 usurped the Imperial title at Ohrid – only to be defeated first by the Bulgarians, then by the Vatatzes of Nicaea

and the Paleologues who became governors of Salonica. In Trebizond, finally, the family of the Comnenes founded a third state and precariously managed to hold on until 1461. But in 1204 the Empire had lost its capital, for so many centuries a symbol to the East and West. It had lost the islands, the important Greek ports, and the trade routes to the Venetians. And it had been split into a number of dwarf states, both Byzantine and Latin, all fighting one another and none able to live. The reconquest of Constantinople by Michael VIII Paleologos in 1261 and the subsequent submission into vassalage of Epirus and the entire Peloponnesus only just stemmed the tide.[1] Granted that until 1340 the Empire still held on to Thrace, Macedonia, Thessaly, Epirus, the Peloponnesus, and half of Asia Minor, yet it played only a minor part in Mediterranean and Balkan politics. To the north, powerful neighbours had grown up since the late twelfth century: Serbia since 1168, Bulgaria's Second Empire since 1184. Both grew more threatening in the late thirteenth and the fourteenth century: Bulgaria under the rule of Czar Ivan Asen II (1218–41) and a century later under Ivan Alexander (1331–71); Serbia under her kings Milutin (1282–1321) and Dušan (1331–55). To the south the Seljuks pressed ever harder. The final breakup came during the years 1340–50. Asia Minor was wrested from the Empire by the Turks; the Central Balkans, including Macedonia, Epirus, and Thessaly, were conquered by the Serbs under Dušan, and Thrace by the Bulgarians – both only to be lost to the Turks in 1388–9. What little was left of the Empire – Mistra, Constantinople, and Salonica – to all practical intents went into vassalage to the Turks. The fall of Salonica in 1430, of Constantinople in 1453, of Mistra in 1460, and of Trebizond in 1461, have symbolic more than practical significance.

As a political entity, then, Byzantium died a slow death, dragged out over nearly two hundred and fifty years. As a cultural power it survived with remarkable vigour both in the territories left to Byzantine rule – Nicaea, reconquered Constantinople, Epirus, Salonica, and Mistra – and beyond the ever-shrinking frontiers of the Empire.[2] This is but natural. In the Byzantine territories the newly established dynasties – the Angeloi, the Laskaris, and from 1260, the Paleologues – needed outward signs of their rule: court poetry, palaces, tomb chapels, churches, illuminated manuscripts, murals, mosaics, and icons were produced in a flourishing renascence of the arts in Constantinople, Arta, Mis-

tra. Yet Byzantine writing, painting, and church building remain equally strong in lands long lost politically: in the Balkan countries and in the provinces and islands under Latin and Venetian rule. Again this is natural. For many centuries Byzantine culture had been carried by the Church as much as, or more than, by the court and its nobles. The Church, one recalls, had been firmly rooted in the Slavic countries since before the twelfth century. And through the Church, Byzantine art and architecture dominated the Balkans and Russia for nearly two hundred and fifty years or more before the physical end of the Empire. Serbia and Bulgaria, and Russia to a degree, remained cultural satellites of the Byzantine world. Indeed, long after the fall of the Empire, Byzantine culture lives on with considerable strength in and through the Church, under the comparatively mild rule of the Turks. The survival of flourishing monasteries on Mount Athos is but the most striking of many examples that come easily to mind.

CHAPTER 19

LATE BYZANTINE ARCHITECTURE

The after-life of Byzantine culture in the Ottoman Empire and the architecture it produced is beyond the scope of this volume. But Byzantine art from 1200 to 1450 does concern us, and it is relevant that at this late stage the term Byzantine needs to be understood in terms far broader than the political confines of the Empire – in terms not only of the Paleologues and their predecessors, but also of the reigns of Milutin and Dušan and their families in Serbia, and of the rule of Ivan Asen II and of Ivan Alexander in Bulgaria.

Byzantine art, then, is remarkably active during the last two centuries before the fall of Constantinople. It is also remarkably far spread, from the Danube to the Peloponnesus and Constantinople, and from there to Trebizond and Crete. Nor is there any doubt that the Paleologan Age created an exciting, expressive, and monumental new style in mural painting and manuscript illumination.[1] But in architecture the situation is somewhat different. To be sure, Byzantine builders – taking the term Byzantine in a broad sense – both continue and create new variants on traditional church plans. They play with virtuosity on and enrich the stylistic concepts of Middle Byzantine architecture. New liturgical needs, come to the fore since early Middle Byzantine times and grown ever stronger, forced changes on Paleologan patrons and builders. Separate spaces were needed outside the naos for baptismal fonts, for burial of benefactors, and for the commemoration of saints and members of the monastic community: spaces in the narthex which, acquiring greater importance, was lengthened and deepened or doubled or supplemented by a second and third corridor along the flanks of the church. Or else chapels, parekklesia, were attached to the bema, the chancel part, or to the narthex.[2] The Fenari Isa in Constantinople and the Great Lavra on Mount Athos present early examples, the former of the first, the latter of the second solution. Growing ever more frequent and richer, by the thirteenth and fourteenth centuries such parekklesia might be laid out as miniature quincunx churches of traditional type, provided with double-storeyed, twin-domed nartheces; or as aisleless naves, their barrel-vaults interrupted and surmounted by high domes – a Middle Byzantine type, as witness the Imperial mausoleum in the Pantokrator, the Zeyrek Camii group, prior to 1136. Often, the spaces set aside to serve as parekklesia would be absorbed into the narthex or the narthex gallery of the main church and marked by domes – doubled or singly rising from the roof of the narthex gallery: again a Middle Byzantine feature, first known from the Panaghia Chalkeon in Salonica. Also, nartheces and parekklesia were fused into an envelope embracing the naos on three sides: as a rule opening into it by mere doors; but occasionally absorbed inside and forming a belt of aisle-like, galleried spaces. In consequence of such changes in function and plan, the church, itself often of older date, in Paleologan times rarely is viewed as a self-contained unit. Rather, it is but the core around which are grouped the appended structures, differing among each other in size and shape but, as a rule, all surmounted by domes and richly decorated. Grouping, varying, and multiplying the volumes and surfaces of the envelope of subordinate, attached elements, all on miniature scale, Paleologan architects create the vision of Late Byzantine church building. They stress the diversified, exciting silhouette of grouped domes and wavy roof lines. They accentuate the vertical axes: drums, domes, apses, and interior spaces grow narrower and steeper. They tend to fuse, regionally anyhow, basilican and central plans. They enrich the decorative patterns, both inside and outside. They strive for new colouristic and ornamental effects on the outer walls, through ever more complicated brick patterns, through combining brick, white and red stone, and glazed tiles into variegated designs, through alternating in the masonry brick and stone bands. Inside, they blend mosaic, painting, sculptural decoration, and interior space into a unit. At times – particularly in Constantinople and Salonica during the first decades of the fourteenth century – their designs are developed with remarkable subtlety and with a delicacy rarely achieved before. On this everyone agrees. But excepting Constantinople and Salonica in the early fourteenth century, the architectural production seems to us rich, varied, often interesting – but not always of high quality. This opinion contrasts strongly with that of many of the great nineteenth-century scholars who, as late as the twenties and thirties of this century, dealt with Late Byzantine architecture always lovingly, and with high praise either explicit or implied.[3] In the Balkan countries national pride may occasionally have contributed towards excessive enthusiasm. But this is less important than the 'visual habits' of late-nineteenth-century historians. Their generation was naturally fascinated by an architecture which is colourful, richly silhouetted, and complicated – qualities which underlie a good deal of late-nineteenth-century architecture as well, and which attracted other historians of their generation towards the Late Romanesque architecture of Germany. Obviously these qualities had less meaning to a generation which grew up with Le Corbusier and the Bauhaus or their followers active since the middle of this century. Quite possibly the visual habits thus engendered had caused a marked underrating of Late Byzantine architectural design. But it does seem that Late Byzantine builders depended heavily on the tradition laid down by their Middle Byzantine predecessors, looking often as far back as the early tenth century, regarding parekklesia, narthex galleries surmounted by twin domes, rippled eaves lines, brick patterns, church plans. Nor does it seem that the overall level of Byzantine building between 1200 and 1450 – certainly outside Con-

stantinople – is always of the highest. Regional differences and idiosyncrasies are more strongly marked than ever. Decoration becomes a major concern; the vocabulary rich and varied. Structural expression and spatial articulation are played down, though not entirely forgotten. Certain regional developments, as for example that of Constantinople, display a greater concern for tectonic and spatial qualities than is found elsewhere. An epilogue though it is, Late Byzantine architecture reveals surprising vitality.

EARLY PALEOLOGAN ARCHITECTURE

The characteristics of Late Byzantine building first present themselves in the last third of the thirteenth century and appear nearly simultaneously at far distant points of the various Byzantine principalities: in Epirus, Macedonia, Thessaly; in the Peloponnesus; in Asia Minor; in Constantinople. A first phase is clearly marked off; we shall call it Early Paleologan, although it starts before the reconquest of Constantinople. This first phase makes way about 1310 for a High Paleologan phase, which in turn fades out, in different places at different times but always during the century between 1340 and 1440. The first phase bears remarkably similar characteristics everywhere, both in planning and decoration. For the most part, church planning continues traditions uninterrupted since the days of the Macedonians and Comnenes: quincunx plans, triconch and tetraconch chapels, and the like – the former sometimes replacing with a high transverse barrel-vault the dome customary over the centre bay. Small tetraconchs of the type widespread in the tenth, eleventh, and twelfth centuries near Constantinople, as on Heybeliada in the Sea of Marmara, in the southern Balkans, and in Greece may have survived into Paleologan times, though major problems regarding the dating remain.[4] At other times, and apparently limited locally, central plans are blended with basilican naves; an impact that perhaps stems less from Western influence than from the small vaulted basilicas customary in Bulgaria, Epirus, Macedonia, and Thrace ever since at least the tenth century. As early as 1232 or shortly after in the Panaghia at Bryoni near Arta, a fusion has been effected between a domed quincunx sanctuary and a barrel-vaulted nave and aisles. Similarly in the Kato Panaghia just outside Arta, a quincunx is joined to a barrel-vaulted basilican nave with the difference, however, that a transverse barrel-vault, taller than the longitudinal vaults of the nave, is substituted for the domed bay of the quincunx. In the Porta Panaghia in Thessaly, both centre bay and cross arms are pulled together by one single transverse barrel-vault, high up.[5] Aisleless chapels are widespread, either as small monastery or village churches or as funerary chapels. As monastery churches and clearly of old lineage, they become frequent, it seems, in Late Byzantine Constantinople as well as in the provincial and allied centres: terminated by single or triple apses; barrel-vaulted and domed, as in the Church of the Archangels in the latter thirteenth century at Nessebâr; plain and timber-roofed or simply barrel-vaulted as in the region of Ohrid and all over Greece and the Balkans; occasionally enriched, as the small church of H. Basilios at Arta [385], by no less than four parek-klesia, two on either flank separated by a barrel-vaulted passage.[6] As funeral chapels, often double-storeyed – the lower floor serving as crypt – they appear early in Bulgaria and, possibly quite a bit later, in Constantinople. The Asen church at Stanimaka (Assenovgrad) [398A], dating from the late twelfth or the early thirteenth century, offers an example; barrel-vaulted and, on the upper floor, supporting a dome as well and terminating in apses both on the chapel and on the crypt level.[7]

As a rule, though, in the major centres and when funds were available, the demand was for larger – always relatively – and more sophisticated buildings. In the South Church of the Fenari Isa Camii in Constantinople [312], the plan of an ambulatory church, as known from Early Byzantine times on, was taken up at the turn of the thirteenth century; whether the type had survived or was revived, remains open.[8] Occasionally, however, late-

thirteenth-century builders and patrons seem to have taken up plans fallen into disuse after the eleventh century or earlier still. Thus the Greek-cross octagon last seen at Daphni was revived all over the various Byzantine principalities: in the Parigoritissa at Arta, in 1282–9 [371–4], and in H. Theodoroi at Mistra (Mystra), 1290–6 [384], to mention the two best known examples.[9] Shortly after 1300 in the Aphentiko church of the Bron-tocheion at Mistra the plan of a basilica with galleries was fused with that of a cross church with open galleries bridging the transept arms [377, 378], so as to call to mind churches of eighth- and ninth-century date. In brief, it seems not impossible that Byzantine and possibly Western contemporary concepts were fused with the concept of a revival of Early Byzantine architecture. The idea of a renascence of church plans fallen into oblivion centuries before seems a natural phenomenon in the spurt of enthusiasm accompanying the resurgence of a Byzantine Empire in the last third of the thirteenth century. It finds its close parallel in painting in the revival of Early Macedonian models in the last decades of the thirteenth century.[10]

Such 'renascence' plans, to be sure, are rarely copies after the earlier prototypes. At Arta the Greek-cross octagon is enclosed within a solid cube whose general appearance resembles a palace with its two tiers of superimposed windows. The interior at Arta, on the contrary, is far more complex, if somewhat crude, in design.[11] A triple order of colonnettes, standing at right angles, rises from projecting brackets and supports the squinches of the dome; a device which recalls the Nea Moni on Chios rather than the Katholikon at Hosios Lukas. At the same time, at Arta the cross arms are narrower and shallower than at either Hosios Lukas or Daphni. Far more important is the addition, as an afterthought during construction, of parekklesia, surmounted by galleries, and their fusion with the narthex and its gallery and the relation of this three-sided envelope to the naos. While on the ground floor parekklesia and naos remain separate units, accessible from each other and from the naos only

0   40 FT

0   15 M

through arched doorways, on the gallery level they open freely into the centre space. Correspondingly, the vaulting marks chapels and narthex on the ground floor as separate entities, each focused on a domed bay in the middle; on the contrary, on the upper level, three domes are placed over the narthex, two more over the end bays of the side galleries all surmounted by drums, the one in the middle of the façade lit by an open lantern [371–4]. Nonetheless, the Parigoritissa never crosses the threshold of provincial heaviness, and this provincial element prevails more strongly yet in the smaller churches in Epirus.

Arta, throughout the Latin occupation and until the end of the thirteenth century capital of a powerful independent state, the despotate of Epirus, was a natural centre to develop a new regional style in its buildings. It seems equally natural that new solutions, though different in planning, would be evolved regionally in at least some of the capitals of the other Byzantine states, surviving through the Latin occupation of Constantinople or set up afterwards in territory wrested from the Latins. About Salonica, occupied early by the despots of Epirus and afterwards by the emperors of Nicaea, we know little. Architecture built under the Laskarid emperors, though not in Nicaea itself, has recently come into focus. At Trebizond (Trabzon), where a semi-independent Empire survived until 1461, building activity went on; and Mistra, wrested from the Franks in 1262 and ruled, first from Constantinople, then from 1348 until 1460 as the suzerain despotate of Morea, was from the end of the thirteenth century a flourishing centre. In Trebizond, the church of H. Sophia, dating from some time between 1238 and 1263, presents a local variation on the quincunx plan, with elongated western corner bays and deep projecting porches

371–3. Arta, Parigoritissa, 1282–9.
Isometric view (*above, left*), interior facing north (*left*),
and interior facing east (*opposite*)

374. Arta, Parigoritissa, 1282–9.
From the north-west

north, south and west – all opening in triple arcades
[375, 376]. The local traditions of the highlands of
Asia Minor, reinforced possibly by Armenian or
Georgian influence, are felt in the heavy stone
construction, in the almost basilican stretching of
the nave, the profile of the windows, the sculptural
decoration outside, the spareness of detail inside.
Only the pendentives and the drum, built in brick,
betray, at least in technique, Byzantine tradition.[12]
Things were different at Mistra. Starting with the
Byzantine reconquest, a town to a large extent newly
built grew on the steep hill sloping down from the
older castle; a town complete with city walls, large
tracts added to the palace in the castle, houses along
narrow streets but widely scattered, and numbers of
churches, dating from the end of the thirteenth to
the fifteenth century. Thoroughly, though at times

perhaps too thoroughly restored, Mistra thus provides an idea of what an important if not too
populous Paleologan capital looked like.[13] At the
beginning (of houses, palaces, and of High and Late
Paleologan churches we shall speak later) stand
three churches: the Metropolis, the cathedral
founded in 1291–2; and the two churches of the
Brontocheion convent, one dedicated to the H.
Theodoroi and built in 1290–6, the other to the
Virgin Hodegetria, built between 1310 and 1322
and known as the Aphentiko. The Metropolis, in the
beginning, was apparently laid out as a simple
basilica, remodelled perhaps only in the fifteenth
century. In the H. Theodoroi, the Greek-cross
octagon was taken up in its simplest form, one-
storeyed, without the galleries and the cubical
'envelope' of the Parigoritissa at Arta, but with four

375 and 376. Trebizond (Trabzon), H. Sophia, between 1238 and 1263.
Exterior from the south and plan

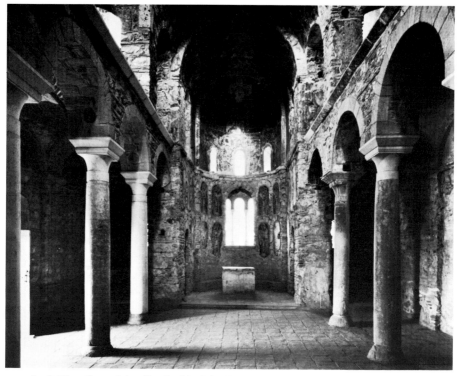

377 and 378. Mistra, Brontocheion, Church of the Aphentiko, 1310–22.
Interior of nave facing east (*above*) and exterior from the east (*below*)

corner parekklesia. As such it reveals a survival or revival of the type as first known from the Panaghia Lykodimou in Athens and from Daphni, c. 1080. In the Aphentiko [377, 378], on the other hand, and possibly as an afterthought during construction, a new building type was created. Instead of a cross-in-square, possibly first planned, the structure was thoroughly changed: preceded by a double-storeyed narthex, the ground floor was divided into nave and aisles like a basilica. The aisles were given vaults, to carry a gallery floor – laid out as a quincunx supported by piers: domed over the centre bay in the nave; barrel-vaulted the rest of the nave, west and east; the cross arms, too, barrel-vaulted and over-sailing the galleries; the four remaining corner bays in the gallery domed and surmounted outside by drums. The type locally took firm roots and has become known as the Mistra type. In its disposition it recalls the church of Hagia Sophia at Vize (Bizye) in Thrace, of questionable though certainly post-Justinianic date, with single-columned arcades below, full galleries, centre dome, and cross arms oversailing the galleries; or other churches of post-Justinianic times, such as Dere Ağzı. Though on the smallest scale – it measures inside but 11 by 8·50 m. (36 by 28 ft) – the architect of the Aphentiko seems to have reverted to a grand type of the great past of Byzantium.

The churches of Mistra, from the outset, are far more subtle in planning and design than the Parigoritissa at Arta. In their subtleness – sometimes provincial, but subtle nonetheless – they are close to Early Paleologan church building in Constantinople; but planning in Constantinople took again different lines. The South Church of the Fenari Isa Camii, founded between 1282 and 1304 by Theodora, widow of the emperor Michael VIII Paleologos, and dedicated to John the Baptist, was laid out on an ambulatory plan.[14] The traces of the steep stilted arches which screened the centre bay from the ambulatory are as clearly visible as those of the high-shouldered triple window above [312, 379]. The type, then, continues or revives earlier models, such as the Koimesis church in Nicaea

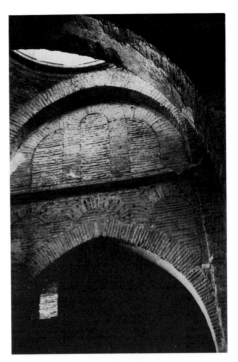

379. Constantinople, Fenari Isa Camii, South Church, founded 1282/1304. Interior of south wall of nave

(Iznik) as rebuilt after 1065 and the presumably somewhat later core of the Fetiyeh Camii, the Pammakaristos church. As already in this latter, the scale in the Paleologan church of St John in the Fenari Isa complex is small; its surface is hardly larger than the tenth-century quincunx church adjoining it to the north. Moreover the core of the structure is limited to a simple domed square bay. The church did not function in a conventional sense. Its appropriately darker ambulatory was filled with tombs and separated from the liturgical space of the naos by triple arcades. Somewhat later, as the space allotted for tombs was used up, a new burial space was added in the form of an outer envelope along the original south and west façades of the South Church. The outer walls of this 'envelope' were lined with steep niches (arcosolia) for the accommodation of tombs.

Paleologan church planning is distinguished by new 'envelope spaces' which are wrapped around the main building core: in the South Church of the Fenari Isa, to the west the exonarthex, lengthened to extend in front of the old North Church as well; to the north, the tenth-century North Church, whose southern parekklesion was incorporated into the left-hand ambulatory of the Paleologan South Church; finally to the south the funerary wing, added presumably after 1300 to the new structure; all built in a masonry of alternating brick and stone bands, characteristic for Late Byzantine Constantinople [312, 313, 380, 381]. Such belts of appended spaces, around 1300 became a hallmark of Paleologan church planning in Constantinople: witness the Pammakaristos church, the Fetiyeh Camii, where

prior to 1294 at least the corridor to the north and the small domed chapel at its east end may have been laid out; and the Kariye Camii, where the doubled narthex and both longish spaces, north and south, were built in one campaign, 1315–20.[15] Paleologan churches thus grew by a process of accretion: the whole became a 'sum of the parts', but not necessarily thought of as 'parts of the whole'. Early Paleologan 'planning' involved adding either to pre-existing buildings or to new buildings, but without any effort at formal integration. Nor was the interior decoration of the new church in the Fenari Isa complex better integrated. To be sure, only a few elements survive: the dowel holes of a marble revetment on the upper walls of the centre bay [379]; a palmette and cross frieze along the cornice of the

380. Constantinople, Fenari Isa Camii, South Church, founded 1282/1304, main apse; foreground, south apse of North Church, dedicated 907

381. Constantinople, Fenari Isa Camii, South Church, founded 1282/1304. Exterior of apse

382 and 383. Ohrid, Sv. Kliment, 1294/5. Exterior from the south-east (*above*) and detail of exterior of apse wall (*below*)

dome; in the south apse, the capitals and shafts of two window piers covered with palmette designs. But the decorative motifs are nearly indistinguishable from Middle Byzantine ornament; indeed, the frieze on the cornice of the dome so closely resembles the corresponding one in the North Church that one wonders whether it is a copy or possibly composed of Middle Byzantine spoils, and the same doubts arise regarding the window piers. Only the treatment of the wall surfaces on the Paleologan parts of the Fenari Isa Camii reveals the character of late-thirteenth-century decoration in Constantinople. The main and the south apse (the north apse was taken over from the south parekklesion of the tenth-century North Church) are covered all over with the rich panoply of late-thirteenth-century Byzantine decoration [381]. On the seven-faceted main apse three tiers are superimposed: blind niches in a sequence of low, steep, and medium high; and inserted in the centre of the tier of steep niches, a triple group of windows. Between the tiers, inside the niches and in the spandrels, the brickwork forms arch and hook patterns, meander friezes, pendant triangles, sunwheel, swastika, zigzag, and fan designs. Between these designs appear alternating bands of snow white and deep red, one course of ashlar and from

384 (*below*). Mistra, H. Theodoroi, 1290–6. Exterior of south arm and dome

385 (*opposite*). Arta, H. Basilios, thirteenth century(?). Detail of exterior of east wall

two to five courses of brick: a new colourism is announced. Around 1300 it becomes the hallmark of Late Byzantine building in Constantinople.

Indeed, all such types of Late Byzantine architecture, whether in Constantinople, Arta, or Mistra and whether traditional, newly invented, or revived and remodelled, were clad with an exterior decoration which continues, enriched and more playful, the last phases of Middle Byzantine building. At Sv. Kliment at Ohrid, in 1294/5 (originally dedicated to St Mary Peribleptos), the colonnettes of the drum project from triply recessed window frames [382, 383]. Saw-tooth friezes are doubled and tripled all along the edges, double and single brick courses alternate in the *cloisonné* walling. The brickwork forms meander friezes and chequerboard and *cloisonné* bands all along the walls. Steep, deeply recessed niches outlined by saw-tooth bands articulate the three sides of the apse, while the panels of the niches are patterned with chequerboards of dark and light diamond shapes, with hollow rhomboids between the arms of a cross.[16] Similar effects were achieved contemporaneously at Mistra and Arta: in the H. Theodoroi at Mistra by deep niches in drum and main apse, by herringbone patterns and by multiple saw-tooth bands [384]. On the outer walls of the Parigoritissa at Arta, chequerboard diamond strips were used to mark off the *cloisonné* walling, and an open tempietto, playfully contrasting with the five other drums, rises above the centre of the narthex gallery [374]. The Parigoritissa also shows more clearly than any other church the penetration of Byzantine building by a Western vocabulary: crocket capitals, pairs of intertwined columns, archivolts covered with the figures of prophets, monsters serving as brackets – strangely contrasting with the high quality of the mosaics and murals – clumsily executed and all retarded derivatives of Late Romanesque rather than Gothic design [372, 373]. The same intermingling of Western elements – long outmoded in their natural habitat – with genuine Byzantine forms dominates the architectural vocabulary in the smaller churches of Epirus, often in far richer combinations. In these smaller churches, the exterior decoration also reaches a much greater richness: chequerboard patterns in three and four shades; saw-tooth bands; fan patterns of bricks in the window spandrels; wavy lines, meanders, and broken hook friezes – all of this patterned or cut from bricks. H. Basilios and H. Theodora at Arta, H. Nikolaos at Rhodia, and the convent church of the Kato Panaghia are examples [385]. Epirotes may also have worked at Sv. Kliment and on the esonarthex of St Sophia at Ohrid.[17]

The rich brick ornament and the varied decorative vocabulary of the late thirteenth century make their appearance at almost the same time in far distant places of the Late Byzantine world – in Mistra, Arta, Ohrid, Constantinople. Their origin, on the other hand, is not clear. No doubt the beginnings go far back. Fan designs occur in Constantinople from the early tenth century, meander and wicker patterns in the course of the eleventh both in Greece and Constantinople. But such features remain isolated and comparatively simple. In all their richness, brick patterns come to the fore by the middle of the twelfth century, when local workshops in Greece decorated the outer walls of churches with the whole gamut of designs, meander and fan patterns, saw-tooth friezes, wavy lines, and others all laid out in brick [356, 357]. In all likelihood the decorative wave was widespread; by 1232 or 1238 it covers the walls of a small church, the Panaghia, at Bryoni not far from Arta in Epirus. It apparently survived until the thirteenth century in the outlying principalities on the western edge of the Byzantine world, in Epirus, in north-western Thessaly, in western Macedonia. In its fullness, it reached Constantinople and Salonica not before the last decade of the thirteenth century.[18]

HIGH PALEOLOGAN ARCHITECTURE

By that time, however, a new High Paleologan style had evolved all through the Byzantine world and that of her cultural satellites. The comparatively uniform vocabulary which Late Byzantine architecture had developed in the late thirteenth century, by 1300

gives way to numerous regional, national, provincial, and workshop variations. A western and northern group of High Paleologan buildings, in Salonica, Macedonia, and central and northern Yugoslavia, however, is easily marked off from an eastern group, centred in Constantinople and Bulgaria; and nothing is easier than to distinguish fourteenth-century hallmarks of Serbian, Bulgarian, Constantinopolitan, and Salonican building. On the other hand, though they differ on questions of planning, exterior design, and decorative vocabulary, the builders of the High Paleologan period work with common architectural concepts. The new distinctions were, in all likelihood, a result of an increased amount of construction fostering the growth of regional workshops. This is in sharp contrast with the thirteenth century, when a limited demand had resulted in a decline of building.

At Mistra, church planning remained virtually untouched by the new current. The blend of longitudinal and central plan elements, as created first in the Aphentiko, was taken up at least twice: in the Pantanassa, consecrated in 1428; and in the remodelling, at an undetermined time, but possibly in the fifteenth century, of the Metropolis. Or else the cross-in-square plan is favoured, as witness the churches of H. Sophia, of the Virgin Peribleptos, and of the Evangelistria. All date presumably from the late fourteenth century, and all show the traditional plan in a characteristic variant: the western corner bays are lengthened and inject a longitudinal element into the central plan. The vocabulary changes more visibly, presumably under the impact of ideas carried over from South Italy. Single towers recalling the *campanili* of South Italy and Sicily rise alongside the body of the church.[18a] In the Pantanassa a colonnaded open porch runs along the north flank, and five domes, with the exception of the one in the centre, are hidden below a continuous roof – contrary to Byzantine, but corresponding to Western custom [386]. Likewise construction and decoration are permeated by devices known from Salerno, Ravello, and Palermo: ribs of rectangular section in the domes; triple windows under pointed

40 FT

15 M

386. Mistra, Pantanassa, consecrated 1428.
Section, and plan of ground floor

387. Salonica, H. Katherini,
late thirteenth century(?). From the south-east

arches; blind arches carried on colonnettes and
surmounted by fan-like feathery leaves; a row of
intersecting festoons crowned by fleur-de-lis.

SALONICA AND SERBIA

Such mingling of foreign and Byzantine elements
recalls the similar blend that pervades the Parigoritissa at Arta about 1285. But it is as exceptional
in High Paleologan as it was in Early Paleologan
architecture. A purely Byzantine High Paleologan
style forms itself within the core of the Byzantine
world around 1300, and continues through the
fourteenth, and in some regions into the fifteenth
century or even beyond. An upsurge of building
activity in Salonica starts off this last phase of Late
Byzantine architecture in Macedonia, southern and
central Yugoslavia, and all over the western Balkans.
The church of H. Katherini at first glance seems
hardly remarkable [387]. Its date of construction

remains undetermined, but plan and design suggest the last years of the thirteenth century. A quincunx with tiny corner bays, its core does not essentially differ in plan from the eleventh-century Panaghia Chalkeon. Similarly its walling, a simple *cloisonné* in the chancel part, continues the construction techniques of Middle Byzantine Greece. But the dome over the centre bay, the barrel-vaults of the cross arms, and the semicircle of the apse rise more steeply than ever before in any Middle Byzantine church. This steepness is enhanced by the envelope which encloses the core on three sides and leads to two chapels at the east end. Divided into two tiers by a strong cornice, it is articulated by blind niches, windows, and double or triple open arcades of varying heights executed in brick. Four drums placed at the corners of the envelope counter the

single drum over the centre bay of the core structure. Comparatively low and set apart from the centre drum, they make for a disparate rather than a unified silhouette – very different from even the boldest Middle Byzantine design. The niches along the eastern flank, on the apse, and along the sides of the envelope display a decorative vocabulary consisting of lozenges, triangles, crosses, basket weaves, but all carefully restricted to niches alone. On the other hand, the brickwork in the colonnettes of the drums over the two chapels, and of the centre dome, is interspersed at regular intervals with white stones, reminiscent of the red and white decoration of the Paleologan Fenari Isa Camii at Constantinople, built in the last third of the thirteenth century. It seems reasonable, then, to assign the H. Katherini also to the years 1280–1300. At roughly the same

388. Salonica, Holy Apostles, 1310–14. Plan sketch

 ORIGINAL CONSTRUCTION (14TH CENTURY)

 TURKISH ADDITIONS

REMOVED BY THE TURKS

time in the church of the Chilandari monastery on Mount Athos, built by the Serbian king Milutin in 1303 as a cross-in-square triconch of the traditional Athos type, drums were placed over the corner bays of its deep monastic narthex. Links to Salonica certainly existed, but their direction so far remains unclear.[19]

The H. Katherini marks only the beginning of the new High Paleologan style in Salonica. In the church of the Holy Apostles – its narthex is dated 1310–14, and presumably the entire structure was built at that time – the three-sided envelope is narrower and higher than at H. Katherini [388–90]. Furthermore, its four corner drums are steeper and set even farther apart from the centre drum and its square base. The interior proportions of width and height of the centre bay have risen to 1:5 as against

1:3·9 at the Panaghia Chalkeon. While the flanks of the envelope to the north are marked off by simple blind arches, its front on either side of the portal, and originally its south flank as well, open in arcades [390]. In triple groups, they are arranged along the façade in an intricate rhythm: the two outer arcades are coupled under a wide blind arch, while the third inner intercolumniation is surmounted by a steep, narrow stilted arch. Along the south flank, the envelope opened in four twin arcades.

The opening of the façade in arcades, the new proportions, the new rhythm, and the new silhouette are blended with a new and richer texture of wall surface. Main dome, vaulting zones and walls inside disappear under the tapestries of splendid mosaics and frescoes presumably executed by a workshop from Constantinople, possibly the one responsible

389. Salonica, Holy Apostles, 1310–14. From the east

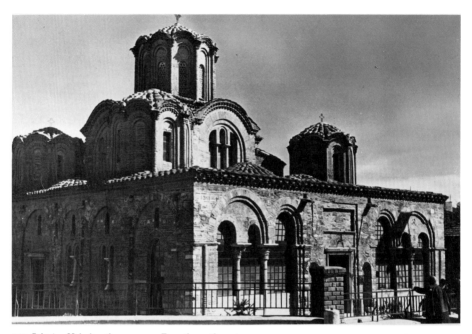

390. Salonica, Holy Apostles, 1310–14. From the north-west

for the decoration of the parekklesion of the Kariye Camii. Similarly the outer walls are covered by a decorative brick veneer. Horizontal bands of large, tightly-interwoven double zigzags, hook patterns, cross-stitch designs, and pendant triangles form a textile covering over the wall and in the niches of the apses, denying them the sense of massiveness. On the south face of the envelope, weave patterns and hexagon stars fill the spandrels of the arches. In the voussoirs, these monochrome patterns give way to a colourful alternation of white stones with groups of three and four red bricks. Neither the monochrome brick decoration nor the two-tone patterns were apparently invented at Salonica. Both were customary as early as the twelfth century in northern Macedonia and southern Thrace, on either side of the Yugoslav–Bulgarian border.[20] At Sv. Kliment at Ohrid, one recalls, the brick decoration occurs fully developed by 1295, while at the same time at Arta

the walls of small and large churches are sheathed with two-tone patterns. But Salonica seems to be the place where throughout the whole fourteenth century such decoration is fused with both the new proportions and the new silhouette into ever new designs. H. Elias, dating perhaps from 1360–85, is a triconch monastic church, like Chilandari with domed drums placed over the end bays of a deep open-arched narthex. But inside, the corner bays of the cross-in-square have been shrunk, enlarging the size of the main dome and leaving the supporting columns squeezed against the walls. Outside, domed chapels are attached to the four corners of the structure. The main dome, larger than usual, rises from among and above a wealth of arched roof lines, domed drums, apses, and high roofed barrel-vaults; all spun over with brick patterns – meanders, pendant triangles, basket weaves – and interspersed with whole stone bands. Even more strongly is the

391. Studenica, Church of the Virgin, after 1183. Exterior

vertical element stressed in the little church of H. Sotir where a single bay, enlarged by small apses into a tiny triconch, is crowned by a tall domed drum.

Certainly, Salonica is the centre from which, after 1300, the new style fans out in all directions. Southward it appears to reach as far as the Meteorite monasteries huddled on top of their rocky crags in north-western Thessaly. The buildings of the Great Meteoron – erected between 1356 and 1388, except for the sixteenth-century church – convey a good impression of the structures comprising a Late Byzantine monastery: the longish refectory (the *trapeza*) with its projecting apse; the square kitchen with its domed chimney; the infirmary, square and divided into nine bays – eight groin-vaulted, the ninth in the centre resting on four columns and opening in a domed chimney. Arches and vaults are formed throughout by alternating bands of red brick and white stone.[21] Westward, the new style creates a

secondary centre in some of the later churches in Epirus. Indeed the northward expansion from Salonica and Epirus into southern and central Yugoslavia is by far the most important.[22]

In Serbia, throughout the thirteenth century, the old West Serbian (Raška) formula of an aisleless, barrel-vaulted, and domed nave had been elaborated to include both Byzantine and Western Romanesque elements: short cross arms and Byzantine domes on pendentives; corbel-table friezes, pilaster strips, and tendril-covered window jambs of North Italian derivation; frequently, a tall tower rising from the narthex. The Church of the Virgin in the monastery at Studenica, as early as the late twelfth century, became the prototype [391].[23] By the early fourteenth century, however, this Raška architecture came into direct conflict with the new Byzantine architecture. Clearly this would happen in territory still under Byzantine occupation. To the

old church of St Sophia at Ohrid in 1313–17 an
exonarthex was added, surmounted by a gallery and
flanked by low towers, the upper floors domed and
serving perhaps as parekklesia. Seen from the outside only a few features are new: arcades in a bottom
and a top tier, separated by a row of flat blind niches;
rich textile brick ornament in the niches; drums
surmounting the corner bays, widely separated from
the older centre drum, no longer extant, of the
transept [392].[24] But it is in the central regions of
Serbia and under the rule of the Serbian kings
Milutin (1282–1321) and Dušan (1331–55), eager
to compete also as builders of churches with Byzantine emperors present and past, that the Salonican

formula bears its ripest fruit. The point of contact
may well have been Chilandari, the Serbian
monastery on Mount Athos, where in 1303
Milutin's architects seem to have encountered new
new concepts of Paleologan building of Salonica and
Constantinople. A few years later, in 1307–9, the
church of the Mother of God of Ljeviška in Prizren,
a basilica of eleventh-century date, already once
rebuilt in the thirteenth century, was entirely
remodelled under the auspices of Milutin.[25] The
outer walls and the piers and upper walls of the nave
were preserved. But the aisles were vaulted; a narthex was added, surmounted by a single tall tower;
and the wide old nave was subdivided by eight piers,

392 (*opposite*). Ohrid, St Sophia, narthex, 1313–17

393 (*below*). Staro Nagoričino, 1067–71 and 1313. From the south-west

placed so as to add two more inner aisles and to divide the remaining nave into a series of square bays. The barrel-vaulting of the nave is interrupted by two domes: one over the centre bay, the other over the chancel. A tall drum encloses the centre dome; four tiny domes surmounted by steep, slender drums rise over the western and eastern ends of the inner aisles, far distant from the main dome; and the outer walls throughout this upper zone are enlivened by white and red bands of brick and stone, *cloisonné*, embroidery patterns, meanders, scallops, and inscriptions, all laid in brick, and by the dense layering of bricks in the voussoirs of the triple-recessed window embrasures. A more restrained

decoration of walls appears in 1307 at Sv. Nikita at Čučer near Skopje.[26] Obviously plan and silhouette of the 'elongated quincunx' in the Bogorodica Ljeviška were determined by the underlying plan of the old basilica, but differ from the principles of the new High Paleologan style, as it presents itself in the Holy Apostles at Salonica. The elongated quincunx remains a basic element of fourteenth-century architecture in central and southern Yugoslavia. It reappears in a new variant at Staro Nagoričino where, in 1313, Milutin's architects solved for a second time – and in a way very similar to the Bogorodica Ljeviška – the problem of remodelling an older basilica. The outer walls of smooth stone

394. (A) Staro Nagoričino, church, 1067–71
and 1313. Plan
(B) Gračanica, church, before 1321. Plan
(C) Kruševac, church, c. 1380. Plan
(D) Ravanica, church, 1375–7. Plan

A

B

C

D

0   40 FT
├──┬──┬──┬──┤
0   15 M

blocks were preserved up to the window zone [393, 394A]. Beginning with the window level, the walling is of the fourteenth century, a *cloisonné* enriched by brick ornament in the spandrels of the windows and in the blind, flat niches on the drums. In the interior, a dome and drum, placed over the centre bay, rise high above the barrel-vaults of the short nave and the deep chancel and esonarthex. The outer envelope has been almost completely lost. The aisles are barrel- and groin-vaulted, but at both ends of each aisle a slender, tall drum shoots up from the roof zone far from the centre drum and hardly visible inside, over the esonarthex and the pastophories.[27] At Gračanica, where no old basilica had survived, a compromise solution was adopted before 1321. The plan displays an elongated core, similar to that of the Bogorodica Ljeviška, with its deep, domed bema. Its envelope, on the other hand, wraps around the core on three sides, terminating at the east end in two lateral chapels; its west part is an esonarthex, and all four corners have domes on tall drums. The link to the ambulatory-envelopes of H. Katherini and H. Apostoloi at Salonica is convincing.[28] But the proportions have been pushed far beyond anything ever adopted before [394B, 395, 396]. The dome of the centre bay rises to a height more than six times its width, the domes of the corner bays rise to nearly eight times their width. The slim drums seem to be driven higher and higher by the semicircular or pointed gables of the corner bays, drum bases, chancel, esonarthex, nave, and transverse arms which, recessed against each other, rise ever higher towards the centre of the structure. Nowhere else has Late Byzantine architecture achieved a more richly fantastic exterior design than in this, the latest of Milutin's churches.

The walling of these early-fourteenth-century Serbian churches is either a simple *cloisonné*, or brick, often pure, but at times richly patterned. With the middle of the fourteenth century, yet richer and more colourful patterns spread all over the country. But the plans turn, it seems, to greater simplicity. Ordinary quincunx plans, certainly in Macedonia, but in Central Serbia as well, take the place of the

395. Gračanica, church, before 1321. From the south-east

elongated, often enveloped quincunx. Corner domes and drums – those hallmarks of Salonican and Serbian builders in the early part of the fourteenth century – while occasionally still in use, are no longer a must. Instead a second dome is often placed over the narthex, possibly linked both to Salonican custom and to the building traditions of western Serbia, where a tower frequently rises over the narthex.[29] But whatever the plan, the decoration of Serbian churches in the second half of the fourteenth century grows ever richer and more colourful. Bulgarian churches since the thirteenth century, if not earlier, had been clad in colouristic textures; Constantinopolitan buildings of the early

396. Gračanica, church, before 1321. Apses

fourteenth century had taken up the idea and the
vocabulary of such red and white surface decoration;
and models in both Bulgaria and Constantinople
apparently exerted a powerful impact on Serbian
builders. The second narthex added between 1372
and 1389 to the early-fourteenth-century church at
Chilandari shows this over-abundant decoration at

its peak: alternating brick and stone bands neatly cut
and pointed; window tympana covered with cross-
stitch patterns, chequerboards, and fleur-de-lis
friezes; arches overlaid with interlace work; capitals
spread with eagle and floral designs.[30]

Richly decorated and often attractive, though
never great or inventive, quincunx churches and

397. Ravanica, church, 1375–7. Exterior from the north

other variants continued to be built in southern and central Yugoslavia until its conquest by the Turks. In the northern parts, independent until 1459, an autonomous architectural school had formed as early as the last third of the fourteenth century in the Morava valley. Dependent on the church type customary on Mount Athos, it adopted a triconch plan, developed round either an atrophied Greek-cross or a quincunx core. But little changes either in the spatial design, the silhouette, or the red and white texture of the walls with alternating brick and stone bands – three bands of brick to one stone – and with chequerboard patterns. Not infrequently, these traditional designs are enriched by sculptured ornament framing the windows, by twisted colonnettes, and by pointed tracery windows – these latter forms possibly drawn from Western Late Romanesque and Gothic models. Tiny, elegant, and almost riotously colourful, as at Ravanica (1375–7) [394D, 397], at Kruševac (c. 1380) [394C], at Kalenić (1407–13), and Rudenica (1402–27), these Morava churches are attractive. But within the history of Byzantine architecture properly speaking, they are of purely local interest. Their plan and decoration are reflected, it seems, only in Rumania, where, towards the end of the fourteenth century, the church at Cozia is of pure Morava type – triconch plan, blind arcades, red and white striping. Such wall texture had penetrated into Rumania at least a generation before, when the church at Curtea de Argeş was laid out as a quincunx on piers, like so many churches of much simpler design in Serbia or, for that matter, Bulgaria. To us, the territory of Rumania in the century between 1350 and 1450 seems to have been on the edge of the Byzantine world. Indeed, Byzantine seems to have been even then in competition with Gothic building. Such competition grows stronger when in the second half of the fifteenth and during the sixteenth century, Renaissance intermingle with Gothic and Neo-Romanesque forms. This mixed vocabulary is applied to buildings which have been laid out on plans still sprung from Late Byzantine antecedents in the Morava valley, albeit shot through with ele-

ments imported from Russia. The resulting cross-breed style is a side issue within the history of Byzantine building.[31]

BULGARIA AND CONSTANTINOPLE

In Bulgaria and Constantinople, High Paleologan architecture develops along lines quite different in plan and vocabulary from the style prevailing in Salonica and the western Balkans. In Bulgaria, the quincunx churches so widespread at the time of her First Empire never gained full ascendancy after her Second Empire was established in the late twelfth century.[32] The quincunx plan seems to have taken root only late and only sporadically. The churches of St Peter and Paul at Turnovo in south-western Bulgaria and those of the Pantokrator and of St John Aleiturgitos at Nessebâr (Mesembria) on the Black Sea coast are outstanding examples [398C, 399]. Both date presumably from the second quarter of the fourteenth century; but while the barrel-vaulted corner bays at Turnovo recall provincial quincunx churches in Greece, the doubling of domes in the eastern corner bays of the church of St John Aleiturgitos – the secondary domes far removed from the centre dome – possibly suggests Constantinopolitan influence. This is not surprising, given the fact that Nessebâr changed hands several times in the course of the thirteenth and fourteenth centuries.

But quincunx churches, otherwise predominant throughout Middle and Late Byzantine architecture, are not the only church type in Bulgaria. Equally frequent and perhaps more interesting is another type: an aisleless hall, its barrel-vault interrupted in the middle by a dome raised high on a drum, while a second drum, only slightly lower, surmounts the narthex. The type comes to the fore as early as 1186, in Sv. Dimitri at Turnovo.[33] In the late twelfth or early thirteenth century, it is used, fully developed, to form the upper floor of double-storeyed funerary chapels, such as the church at Stanimaka (Assenovgrad) [398A], built either by Asen I (1187–96) or by Ivan Asen II (1218–41).[34]

398. (A) Stanimaka (Assenovgrad), Asen Church,
late twelfth or early thirteenth century. Plan
(B) Nessebâr (Mesembria), Church of the Archangels,
fourteenth century (second third). Plan
(C) Nessebâr (Mesembria), St John Aleiturgitos,
fourteenth century (second quarter). Plan

Finally, and again single-storeyed, it reaches a
climax at Nessebâr, in the churches of the Archangels [398B], of the Paraskevi, of Sv. Todor – all
dating presumably from the second third of the
fourteenth century.[35] The origin of the type remains
to be clarified. The dome rising from the narthex has
its parallels in the Serbian development. The aisleless, barrel-vaulted, and domed plan of the nave
came certainly from Constantinople, where it had
been customary since at least the eleventh century.
The double-storeyed plan of the Asen church, on
the other hand, poses somewhat of a problem. The
first instance known so far in Constantinople, the
Boğdan Sarayi, is later than the Asen church: but
earlier Constantinopolitan examples may have been
lost. It has also been suggested that the double-
storeyed plan represents a revival of Roman
mausolea types; or that it reached Bulgaria from
Armenia.[36] Whatever its origin, it is characterized in
Bulgaria by a somewhat inorganic design. Nave and
narthex form a simple, longish, and low block on
which are planted the domes, unconnected with the
carrying ground floor except for the decoration. And
this decoration is antitectonic to the highest degree
as well. St John Aleiturgitos at Nessebâr is a
splendid, if late example [399]. Blind arcades
encircle the lower block, rising from pilasters and
responds, and both the arches and their supports
expand and contract as space permits. Wide on the
flanks, they become narrow on the main apse, and
narrower still on the minor apses. A corbel-table

399. Nessebâr (Mesembria), St John Aleiturgitos,
fourteenth century (second quarter). Exterior

frieze runs along the eaves line. But blind arches, corbel-table frieze, and, indeed, the entire structure are hidden under a profusion of polychrome decoration. Broad bands of white, well-carved stone blocks, one to three courses high, alternate with bands of brick in four courses. Red brick and white mortar stripes alternate in the arch voussoirs. Panels of chequerboard, interwoven brick, zigzag, and cross-stitch patterns – all in contrasts of red and white – run as a frieze along the apses. Small pieces of brick embedded into a wide mortar-bed curve as a pointillé design over the blind arches. Finally, irregularities in the bricks or the pointing of the mortar were corrected with paint by the craftsmen.

Taken by themselves, the individual motifs used in this decoration stand in the tradition represented in the early fourteenth century for instance by the narthex façade of the Holy Apostles at Salonica. But, fully developed as it appears at St John Aleiturgitos, the decoration as a whole has been translated from pure or nearly pure brick designs into a highly colourful language. Such colouristic patterns characterize – as we shall see – early-fourteenth-century buildings at Constantinople which antedate the majority of the churches at Nessebâr. No doubt the builders of Czar Ivan Alexander (1331–71) in Nessebâr drew their decorative vocabulary from the workshops in the Imperial capital. But the beginnings of this polychrome decoration do not lie in Paleologan Constantinople. They reach farther back, to Justinianic and earlier architecture both in Constantinople and in the eastern and western provinces and successor states of the Empire, and beyond that possibly to Roman provincial building techniques. Alternating bands of brick and neatly hewn stone mark, one recalls, the city walls of Constantinople and numberless buildings throughout the Byzantine Empire from the fifth to the ninth and still the twelfth century, both in the capital and in the more remote provinces: the Studios church in Constantinople; the church of Constantine Libs in the Fenari Isa complex; the Kalenderhane Camii; the Canlikilise on the Hassan Dağ [55, 314, 258, 362]. In Bulgaria, this type of masonry was equally known. Alternating red and white voussoirs appear around 1000 at the church of St John the Baptist at Nessebâr; and alternating brick and stone bands, though crudely hewn, are used in the eleventh and twelfth centuries at Bačkovo and at Sv. Dimitri at Turnovo (1186). The red and white patterns which decorate the walls of the fourteenth-century churches at Nessebâr likewise go far back. At Stanimaka, at the end of the twelfth or in the first half of the thirteenth century, 'reticulate' panels in red and white stone fill the spandrels of the blind arches along the flank of the church. Nor are such motifs confined to Bulgarian building. Chequered bands in the thirteenth century decorate the churches of Arta; but earlier still, they occur in Sicily, at the church of St Peter and St Paul at Forza d'Agro, built for Basilian monks in the twelfth century; at Stilo in Calabria, possibly in the tenth century; and certainly that early in a number of churches on the Peloponnesus. Similarly, a chequered band encircles the campanile of S. Apollinare in Classe near Ravenna – at that time still on the fringe of the sphere of Byzantine influence. But chequered and similar patterns and alternating voussoirs in red and white stone were widespread in the Carolingian and Ottonian Empires as well, from the Lorsch gatehouse to the church of St Généroux and to Bernward's church of St Michael at Hildesheim. Indeed, the tradition in the West has been traced back to Late Roman structures in Gaul and in the Rhineland. Hence it has been suggested that this polychrome wall decoration infiltrated Byzantine architecture from the West and penetrated first Epirus, later Bulgaria; a suggestion countered by the thesis that, on the contrary, vocabulary and technique were carried from the Byzantine sphere to the West. To us it seems equally possible that a Late Roman polychrome masonry technique, surviving in the West as well as in the Byzantine provinces, was reawakened in the East in Paleologan times.[37]

Whatever the origin of this and similar patterning motifs, the use of polychrome walling seems to have been transplanted to Constantinople in the early

fourteenth century from provincial Bulgarian architecture. Refined and remodelled in Constantinople
– with elegantly cut stone bands and finely pointed
white mortar-beds – this polychrome treatment
possibly found its way back to Bulgaria, and in the
second third of the century spread over the churches
of Nessebâr.

Such links between Constantinopolitan and provincial architecture throw into strong relief the
changed position of Constantinople and her court in
the fourteenth century. In Middle Byzantine as in
Justinian's times, the Imperial court in Constantinople was still a dominant centre. The provinces
led a life of their own, but time and again the court
sent builders and plans where an extraordinary
building was to be laid out and decorated. On the
other hand, the provinces only rarely, if ever, exerted
their impact on the architecture of the capital. This
changed in High Paleologan times. The impact of
Constantinople on other centres by no means
ceased. In Salonica, even in Ohrid, and certainly in
Nessebâr, Constantinopolitan elements are evident.
But just as frequently, provincial elements seem to
have been absorbed into the architecture of the
capital. Examples are easily listed: the twin-domed
narthex gallery penetrates from Salonica into Constantinople, witness the parekklesion of the Fetiyeh
Camii; also, there is, from the last years of the
thirteenth century onward, the widespread use in
Constantinople of polychrome walling. Still, Constantinople stands out with an approach to architecture much its own. Where Bulgarian builders think
anti-structurally, in terms of colourful surfaces, the
architects of Constantinople in many instances subordinate the polychrome decoration to structural
concepts. Where Salonican and Serbian churches
rise to exaggerated heights, Constantinopolitan
structures keep to reasonable proportions. Where
the provincial schools cling to one building type,
Constantinopolitan builders and patrons work easily
with a variety of plans. And whatever is done in
Constantinople is done with subtlety, gradation,
refinement, and, as a rule, with superb workmanship. Four structures in Constantinople represent

this last flowering of a Byzantine architecture in the
capital: the exonarthex and parekklesion of the
Kariye Camii; the parekklesion of the Fetiyeh
Camii; the narthex of the Kilise Camii; and finally,
the Tekfur Sarayi.

At the Kariye Camii, the twelfth-century structure was remodelled and redecorated in the very first
years of the fourteenth century by the Grand
Logothete Theodore Metochites.[38] A mosaic in the
parekklesion bears the date 1303, and work was
terminated prior to 1321. A new dome – its drum
survives – was placed over the centre bay of the main
church; both exonarthex and esonarthex were newly
laid out; and – continuing the exonarthex along the
south flank of the church – a parekklesion was added
[400, 401]. Turning the corner from the western
main wing of the exonarthex are two square bays,
covered by two low pendentive domes and forming
an anteroom. Entered through the triple arcade of a
small-scale tribelon, the nave is composed of three
units: first a deep barrel-vaulted arch; then the main
bay, surmounted by a well-lit ribbed dome on a
drum; after that a second bay, which carries a
pendentive dome similar to those in the anteroom,
but slightly higher; finally the apse. This interior
serves as a frame for the mosaics and paintings that
cover wall and vaulting zones in such profusion and
beauty as to overshadow the architectural design.
But the subtle interplay of high and low spatial
volumes, the gracefully falling and rising vaults, the
elegant relationship of anteroom to chapel, and the
gradual concentration of light towards the centre
bay, are masterpieces of refinement and architectural jewellery work. On the outer walls, the red and
white striping is subordinated to structural accents:
on the apse, responds, half-columns, and two tiers of
niches – low and high; along the flank, pilaster strips,
and recessed blind arches surmounting high-
shouldered triple windows; at the corner, a flat niche
closed by a depressed ogee arch.

The parekklesion of the Fetiyeh Camii, the
Church of St Mary Pammakaristos, develops the
new style along different lines.[39] Built either shortly
before or shortly after 1315, it is a small quincunx

400 (*above*). Constantinople, Kariye Camii, eleventh, twelfth, and early fourteenth centuries. From the south-east

401 (*opposite*). Constantinople, Kariye Camii, parekklesion, *c.* 1303–*c.* 1320. Interior looking east

with tiny corner bays and a tall drum – its height being four and a half times its width, steeper than in Middle Byzantine Constantinople but less immoderate than in contemporary Serbia [402]. A narthex precedes this small naos, double-storeyed and with a pair of domes rising from its upper gallery – the motif known from Salonica and the Balkan countries. Everything is designed with elegance on

with red and white voussoirs. On the main block, the eaves line curves up over the transverse and longitudinal barrel-vaults, and marks off on the exterior the inside volumes. Rising above these curves, the three drums are tied into the design by their own rippled eaves lines; against the background of the older dome of the main church, they form a picturesque group.

402. Constantinople, Fetiyeh Camii, parekklesion, c. 1315. From the south-west

the smallest possible scale. On the south flank, three tiers of blind arches and windows grouped in triads prevail over the alternating textile bands of red and white – one to five courses of bricks and one to four of neat ashlar blocks. A succession of low niches, steep niches, and a frieze of pendant triangles, marked off by horizontal string courses, articulate the three absidioles. On the façade of the narthex gallery, panels of polychrome chequerboard and grille patterns are anchored in place by blind arches

No other contemporary church building in Constantinople reaches the level of the parekklesia adjoining the Kariye and the Fetiyeh Camii: neither the parekklesion along the south flank of the Fenari Isa Camii, with its simple blind arches and niched pilasters; nor the Boğdan Sarayi; nor, for that matter, the envelope of structures added, probably at that time, to the Kilise Camii [403]: the exonarthex to the west; to the south, a colonnaded and arcaded portico, linking up with a possibly older parekklesion

403. Constantinople, Kilise Camii, narthex, c. 1320

next to the original bema; to the north a corridor, perhaps likewise a parekklesion.[40] In all of them, the blocks of the ashlar bands are less neatly cut, the brick bands less precisely coursed, and the mortarbeds less finely pointed. In the narthex of the Kilise Camii, the three domes rise inorganically from above the roof. Yet the structure does reveal some characteristics of High Paleologan architecture in Constantinople more clearly than the superior design of the parekklesion along the Fetiyeh Camii.

The façade opens in arcades much like the exonartheces of H. Katherini and the Church of the Apostles at Salonica and of St Sophia at Ohrid; but the rhythm is more complex. On the bottom level are steep niches at the corners, followed by open triple arcades; the portal in the centre is coupled with steep niches in a triad. On the upper floor, incongruous with the rhythm of the ground floor, are five semicircular blind arches framing windows. Inside, the succession of high pumpkin domes at the corners, low pendentive domes in the next bays, and a higher ribbed dome in the centre aims at a sharper focusing of the spatial volumes towards the middle. Reminiscences of Justinian's architecture are scattered all over the structure, whether or not in a conscious spirit of renascence: the open, colonnaded south portico – it is known from nineteenth-century drawings – with door frames inserted between the columns, like the narthex of the Studios church or the sea façade of the Bukoleon Palace; another such frame between column shafts, linking the narthex to the north corridor; and fifth- and sixth-century capitals and chancel slabs used as decorative elements. The date of the structures is undetermined, but one would like to place them after, rather than before, the parekklesia of the Kariye and the Fetiyeh Camii.

Equally undated is the Tekfur Sarayi, the only surviving Imperial palace building in Constan-

tinople [404–6]. Based on top of the city walls and projecting beyond towards the open country, it was long attributed to the reign of Constantine VII Porphyrogenetos (912–59).[41] Indeed, the short side of its ground floor is supposedly earlier than the adjoining fortification – a twelfth-century repair of the city walls. Whether or not this is correct, it affects neither the plan of the building nor its decoration and its supports. The dating of all these elements to the first third of the fourteenth century is given, in my opinion, by the textile walling and its incorporation into a pseudo-structural skeleton: the red and white bands with finely cut ashlar blocks; the alternating voussoirs of blind arches and windows; the diamond, hexagon-cross, and chequerboard patterns in polychrome treatment – all fitted into spandrels, frieze bands, and archivolt stripes. No doubt the designer of this façade was close to the architect of the parekklesion of the Fetiyeh Camii and left in

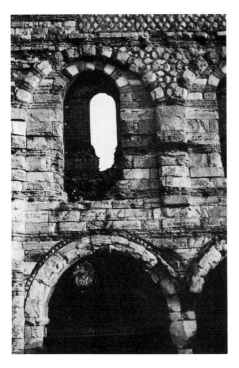

404–6. Constantinople, Tekfur Sarayi,
early fourteenth century. North-west façade (*opposite*),
detail of north-west façade (*left*),
and detail of interior, lower part towards north (*below*)

the Tekfur Sarayi a splendid example of the last stage in Late Byzantine architectural design.

But the plan of the Tekfur Sarayi is essentially not Byzantine. A solid block, it rises in three storeys. The ground floor, with groin-vaults, rests on two rows of columns. The two upper floors are undivided and were covered by flat ceilings [406]. On the main façade, two double openings on the ground floor are followed by a row of windows on each of the upper floors. Two low wings project forward from the main façade and carried terraces at the second-floor level. All this recalls the *palas* of a Romanesque or Gothic castle in France or Germany more closely than the Late Antique tradition of Early and Middle Byzantine palace building. Indeed, Western palace architecture had penetrated the Byzantine world since the thirteenth-century inroads made by the Western conquerors. At Mistra (Mystra), the oldest palace wing on the castle height

was just such a rectangular multi-storeyed block, vaulted on the ground floor. Given its narrowness, no dividing supports were needed. Whether begun prior to 1260 by the Frankish Villehardouin or after the Byzantine reconquest in 1262, it is Western in every respect. So are the two later wings, one built in the late fourteenth, the other in the first half of the fifteenth century. The fourteenth-century wing is two-storeyed, the fifteenth-century wing three-storeyed; the top floor was a long hall, lit by windows and, higher up, oculi, presumably the throne room. Likewise, smaller palaces scattered through Mistra and ordinary, if substantial houses follow a type well known in the West: the ground floor vaulted and, as a rule, dark; the upper floor occupied by a long, well-lit room, occasionally preceded by a terrace. The palaces of Frangopoulos and of Laskaris and a number of bourgeois houses offer examples.[42] The Western palace type, then, was willingly absorbed by the Paleologan courts. As early as the mid thirteenth century, an Imperial palace at Nymphaion (Nymphaeum; Kemalpaşa) near Izmir was laid out as a solid rectangular block, supported by two groin-vaulted naves and a row of supports on the ground floor.[43] In the Tekfur Sarayi, this Western palace type has been clad in the decoration of Late Byzantine architecture.

The situation is symptomatic for the end phase of Byzantine architecture. The building itself is of relatively minor interest to the architect. It may be, as in palace building, a Western type virtually unchanged. In ecclesiastical architecture any of a number of traditional church types – quincunx, cross-octagon, domed and barrel-vaulted chapels – persist with but minor variations. The proportions change; enveloping spaces, nartheces, and parekklesia are added, though not rigorously integrated with the building core. Continuous wall textures dominate the exterior, frescoes and mosaics the interior. Late Byzantine like Late Gothic patrons and builders are less concerned with space and structure than their predecessors. The focus is on colour and decoration.[44]

LIST OF PRINCIPAL ABBREVIATIONS

A.J.A.	*American Journal of Archaeology*
A.M.	*Athenische Mitteilungen (Mitteilungen des Deutschen Archäologischen Instituts, Athenische Abteilung)*
Antioch	G. W. Elderkin (ed.), *Antioch on-the-Orontes*. 4 vols. Princeton, 1934–52
Archeion	*Archeion tōn Byzantinōn Mnimeiōn tis Hellados* (all papers written by A. K. Orlandos)
Architettura Armena	G. de Francovich (ed.), *Architettura medievale armena*. Rome, 1968
B.A.C.	*Bullettino di Archeologia Cristiana*
B.C.H.	*Bulletin de Correspondance Hellénique*
B.d.A.	*Bollettino d'Arte*
Bildlexikon	W. Müller-Wiener, *Bildlexikon zur Topographie Istanbuls*. Tübingen, 1977
Bonn Corpus	*Corpus Scriptorum Historiae Byzantinae*. Bonn, 1828–97
B.S.A.	*British School at Athens, Annual*
B.S.A.F.	*Bulletin Société Antiquaires de France*
B.S.C.	*Byzantine Studies Conference Abstracts*
Bull. Arch.	*Bulletin Archéologique du Comité des Travaux Historiques*
Bull. Byz. Inst.	*Bulletin of the Byzantine Institute* (vols 1 and 2 only)
Butler, *Architecture*	H. C. Butler, *Architecture and Other Arts*. New York, 1923
Butler, *Churches*	H. C. Butler, ed. E. Baldwin Smith, *Early Churches in Syria*. Princeton, 1929
B.Z.	*Byzantinische Zeitschrift*
C.A.	*Cahiers Archéologiques*
C.A.C.	*Congresso Internazionale di Archeologia Cristiana* (Atti, Actes; preceded in Roman numerals by the number of the Congress, and followed by the place and year)
C.C.R.	*Corsi di cultura sull'arte ravennate e bizantina*
C.E.B.	*Congrès International des Études Byzantines* (preceded in Roman numerals by the number of the Congress, and followed by the place and year)
Corpus	R. Krautheimer and others, *Corpus Basilicarum Christianarum Romae*. Vatican City, 1939 ff.
C.R.A.I.	*Comptes-rendus de l'Académie des Inscriptions et Belles-Lettres*
C.S.E.L.	*Corpus Scriptorum Ecclesiasticorum Latinorum*. Vienna, 1866 ff.
D.C.A.H.	*Deltion Christianikis Archaiologikis Hetairias*
Deichmann, *Ravenna*	F. W. Deichmann, *Ravenna*. 4 vols. Wiesbaden, 1958–76
Deichmann, *Rom, Ravenna*	F. W. Deichmann, *Rom, Ravenna und Naher Osten*. Wiesbaden, 1983
Deichmann, *Studien*	F. W. Deichmann, *Studien zur Architektur Konstantinopels (Deutsche Beiträge zur Altertumswissenschaft)*. Baden-Baden, 1956
Deltion	*Archaiologikon Deltion*
Diehl, *Manuel*	C. Diehl, *Manuel d'art byzantin*. 2 vols, 2nd ed. Paris, 1925
D.O.P.	*Dumbarton Oaks Papers*
Dyggve, *Salonitan Christianity*	E. Dyggve, *History of Salonitan Christianity*. Oslo and Cambridge, Mass., 1951
Ebersolt, *Monuments*	J. Ebersolt, *Monuments d'architecture byzantine*. Paris, 1934
Ebersolt and Thiers, *Églises*	J. Ebersolt and A. Thiers, *Les Églises de Constantinople*. Paris, 1913
Ephemeris	*Ephemeris Archaiologiki*
Forschungen in Salona	W. Gerber, R. Egger, and E. Dyggve, *Forschungen in Salona*. 3 vols. Vienna, 1917–39
Gauckler, *Basiliques*	P. Gauckler, *Basiliques chrétiennes de Tunisie*. Paris, 1913
G.N.M.S.	*Godišnik. Naroden Muzei, Sofia (Annuaire du Musée Nationale de Sofia)*
Grabar, *Martyrium*	A. Grabar, *Martyrium*. 2 vols. Paris, 1943–6
Gsell, *Monuments*	S. Gsell, *Les monuments antiques de l'Algérie*. Paris, 1901
Hoddinot, *Churches*	R. F. Hoddinot, *Early Byzantine Churches in Macedonia and Southern Serbia*. London, 1963

I.B.A.I.	*Izvestija na B'lgarskija Arheologičeski Institut*
I.R.A.I.K.	*Izvestija Russkago arkheologičeskago instituta v Konstantinopole*
Ist. M.	*Istanbuler Mitteilungen* (Deutsches Archäologisches Institut, Abteilung Istanbul)
J.A.C	*Jahrbuch für Antike und Christentum*
Janin, *Églises*	R. Janin, *La géographie ecclésiastique de l'empire byzantin, première partie, Le siège de Constantinople et le patriarcat oecuménique, tome III, Les églises et les monastères.* Paris, 1953
J.D.A.I.	*Jahrbuch des deutschen archäologischen Instituts*
J.D.A.I., A.A.	*Jahrbuch des deutschen archäologischen Instituts, Archäologischer Anzeiger*
J.Ö.A.I.	*Jahreshefte des österreichischen archäologischen Instituts*
J.Ö.B.	*Jahrbuch der Österreichischen Byzantinistik*
J.Ö.B.G.	*Jahrbuch der Österreichischen Byzantinischen Gesellschaft*
J.S.A.H.	*Journal of the Society of Architectural Historians*
Kautzsch, *Kapitellstudien*	R. Kautzsch, *Kapitellstudien (Studien zur spätantiken Kunstgeschichte).* Berlin and Leipzig, 1936
Kitzinger, *Making*	Ernst Kitzinger, *Byzantine Art in the Making.* London, 1977
Krautheimer, *Studies*	R. Krautheimer, *Studies in Early Christian Medieval and Renaissance Art.* New York–London, 1969
Lassus, *Sanctuaires*	J. Lassus, *Sanctuaires chrétiens de Syrie.* Paris, 1947
L.C.L.	*Loeb Classical Library*
L.P.	L. Duchesne, *Le Liber Pontificalis.* Paris, 1881–92
Mango, *Architettura bizantina*	Cyril Mango, *Architettura bizantina.* Milan, 1974 (also, *Byzantine Architecture,* New York, 1976)
Mango, *Byzantium*	Cyril Mango, *Byzantium, the Empire of New Rome.* New York, 1980
Mango, *Documents*	Cyril Mango, *The Art of the Byzantine Empire 312–1453, Sources and Documents.* Englewood Cliffs, 1972
Mathews, *Churches*	Th. F. Mathews, *The Early Churches of Constantinople.* University Park and London, 1971
Mathews, *Survey*	Th. F. Mathews, *The Byzantine Churches of Istanbul. A Photographic Survey.* University Park and London, 1975
Mavrodinov (1959)	N. Mavrodinov, *Staroblgarskoto Isskustvo.* Sofia, 1959
M.E.F.R.A.	*Mélanges d'archéologie et d'histoire de l'École Française de Rome. Antiquité*
M.K.	*Mitteilungen des Deutschen Archäologischen Instituts, Abteilung Kairo*
N.B.A.C.	*Nuovo Bulletino di Archeologia Cristiana*
Orlandos, *Basiliki*	A. Orlandos, *Hi Basiliki xylostegos tis mesogeiakis lekanis.* Athens, 1950–9
P.B.S.R.	*Papers of the British School at Rome*
P.E.	*Publications of the Princeton University Archaeological Expeditions to Syria*
P.E.F.Q. St.	*Palestine Exploration Fund, Quarterly Statement*
P.G.	J. P. Migne, *Patrologia Graeca.* Paris, 1857 ff.
P.L.	J. P. Migne, *Patrologia Latina.* Paris, 1842 ff.
Q.D.A.P.	*Quarterly of the Department of Antiquities in Palestine*
R.A.C.	*Rivista di Archeologia Cristiana*
Ramsay and Bell, *Churches*	Sir W. M. Ramsay and G. L. Bell, *The Thousand and One Churches.* London, 1909
Recherches à Salone	E. Dyggve (ed.), *Recherches à Salone,* 1 (trans. E. Philipot). Copenhagen, 1928 ff.
Rend. Pont. Acc.	*Rendiconti della Pontificia Accademia Romana di Archeologia*
Rev. Arch.	*Revue Archéologique*
Richter, *Schriftquellen*	J. P. Richter, *Quellen der byzantinischen Kunstgeschichte (Quellenschriften für Kunstgeschichte und Kunsttechnik des Mittelalters und der Renaissance,* n.s. VIII). Vienna, 1897
R.i.P.	*Razkopki i Proučevanija*
R.K.W.	*Repertorium für Kunstwissenschaft*
R.L.A.C.	Th. Klauser (ed.), *Reallexikon für Antike und Christentum.* Stuttgart, 1950–62
R.L.B.K.	*Reallexikon zur Byzantinischen Kunst*
R.M.	*Römische Mitteilungen (Mitteilungen des deutschen archäologischen Instituts, Römische Abteilung)*

Röm. Jbch *Römisches Jahrbuch für Kunstgeschichte*
Rott, *Denkmäler* H. Rott, *Kleinasiatische Denkmäler . . . (Studien über christliche Denkmäler*, N.F. V, VI*).* Leipzig,
  1908
R.Qu.Schr. *Römische Quartalschrift*
S.A.A. *Simposio sull'Arte Armena*
Schneider, *Byzanz* A. M. Schneider, *Byzanz, Vorarbeiten zur Topographie und Archäologie der Stadt (Istanbuler Forschungen*, VIII*).* Berlin, 1936
Sotiriou, *Basilikai* G. Sotiriou, *Hai Christianikai Thibai kai hai palaiochristianikai Basilikai tis Hellados.* Athens,
  1931 *(Ephemeris*, 1929–30)
Tchalenko, *Villages* G. Tchalenko, *Villages antiques de la Syrie du Nord (Institut Français d'Archéologie de Beyrouth, Bibliothèque Archéologique et Historique*, 1). Paris, 1953–8
Van Millingen, *Churches* A. van Millingen and others, *Byzantine Churches in Constantinople, Their History and Architecture.* London, 1912
Verzone (1942) P. Verzone, *L'architettura religiosa dell'alto medio evo nell'Italia settentrionale.* Milan, 1942
Zb.R. *Zbornik Radova, Institut d'Études Byzantines*, Belgrade
Z.D.P.V. *Zeitschrift des deutschen Palästina-Vereins*

NOTES

Bold figures indicate page reference.

23. 1. Previous attempts dating back to the beginning of the twentieth century to trace the development of Early Christian and Byzantine architecture are by now obsolete due to the vast accumulation of new material, the expansion of the field, and the prevalence of new points of view. Nonetheless, some are worth consulting: O. Wulff, *Frühchristliche und Byzantinische Kunst* (Potsdam, 1918), for the superior organization of material practically unknown before; and A. Kingsley Porter, *Medieval Architecture* (New Haven, 1911), the first chapters, for the superb descriptions of buildings.

Among recent work, the few pages given to Early Christian architecture by B. Brenk in *Spätantike und frühes Christentum (Propyläen Kunstgeschichte, Supplement Bände,* 1) (Berlin, 1977) provide a concise up-to-date summary. Finally, F. W. Deichmann, *Einführung in die christliche Archäologie* (Wiesbaden, 1983), while widely different in approach, handling, and point of view from my own and frequently in disagreement with the arguments proposed by this writer, gives, if not a history of Early Christian art, a masterly survey of the field.

2. Pliny the Younger, *Letters,* x, 96 (*L.C.L.,* 11, 400 ff.); A. von Harnack, *The Expansion of Christianity* (New York and London, 1904) (*Die Mission und Ausbreitung des Christentums,* Leipzig, 1924).

The early establishment of Christian congregations in Mesopotamia, Iran, and elsewhere beyond the pale of the Empire, while important for the development of Eastern Christianity, had no impact on the rise and spread of a Christian architecture.

24. 3. Clement of Rome, 1 Corinthians 13:8; 19:4. The service in an Eastern congregation around A.D. 100 is reflected in the Didache, chapters 9 ff. (*Ante-Nicene Fathers,* ed. P. Schaff, New York, 1889, 1); a concise survey of the situation is given by J. A. Jungmann, *Missarum Solemnia,* 1 (Freiburg, 1952) (English transl., *The Mass of the Roman Rite,* New York, 1951), 7 f., and G. Dix, *The Shape of the Liturgy* (London, 1945), 78 ff.

4. Acts of the Apostles, 13:15; 17:2 ff.; 18:4, 26; 19:8.

5. Acts of the Apostles, 16:13; 19:9.

6. Acts of the Apostles, 2:46.

7. Acts of the Apostles, 1:13; 20:8; and *passim.*

8. Tertullian, *Adversus Valentinianos,* cap. 3 (*P.L.,* 11, 580): '. . . columbae . . . domus simplex in editis semper et ad lucem'. For other testimony, see also J.-R. Laurin in *Analecta Gregoriana 70, ser. facultatis Historiae ecclesiasticae, sectio A* (n. 3) (Rome, 1954), 39 ff.

9. Acts of the Apostles, 20:5–10.

10. *P.E.,* section A, *Southern Syria*; section B, *Northern Syria (Publications of the Princeton . . . Expeditions . . .)* (Leyden, 1919–), *passim*; Tchalenko, *Villages, passim*; A. Boëthius in *Die Antike,* XI (1941), 110 ff.; L. Crema, *L'architettura romana, Enciclopedia classica,* sezione 111, vol. 12, tomo 1 (Turin, 1959), *passim*; A. Boëthius, *Etruscan and Early Roman Architecture (Pelican History of Art)* (Harmondsworth, 1978), 140 ff.

11. Th. Klauser, in *Pisciculi . . . Franz Joseph Doelger . . . dargeboten* (Münster, 1939), 157 ff.

25. 12. Harnack, *op. cit., passim.*

13. Cyprian, *De Lapsis,* cap. 6, in J. Martin (ed.), *Florilegium Patristicum,* XXI (Bonn, 1930), 14: 'Episcopi plurimi divina procuratione contempta procuratores regum saecularium facti sunt.' The passage is not beyond doubt, since some manuscripts read *rerum* for *regum* (*P.L.,* IV, 484). But Tertullian's statement (*Apologeticum,* cap. 37; *P.L.,* 1, 525) is in essence the same.

14. H. Grégoire, *Les persécutions dans l'empire romain (Académie Royale de Belgique, Classe des Lettres . . .,* XLVI, 1) (Brussels, 1951); J. Moreau, *Die Christenverfolgung im römischen Reich* (Berlin, 1961). H. Mattingly, *Christianity in the Roman Empire* (University of Otago, 1955), gives a concise picture of the situation.

15. Eusebius, *Ecclesiastical History,* VII, xiii, 1 (*L.C.L.,* II, 168 f.), gives the text of the Imperial rescript.

16. G. Krüger, *Die Rechtsstellung der vorkonstantinischen Kirchen* (Stuttgart, 1935); G. Bovini, *La proprietà ecclesiastica . . . in età preconstantiniana* (Milan, 1949). The Edict of Milan as quoted by Lactantius, *De mortibus persecutorum,* cap. 48 (*P.L.,* VII, 267) returns to the Christians both the 'houses where they are used to meet and others belonging to their corporation' (*ad jus corporis eorum*), that is, to their Churches, not to individuals. Eusebius, *Ecclesiastical History,* X, v, ii, has mistranslated the passage.

26. 17. Jungmann, *op. cit., passim*; also B. Steuart, *The Development of Christian Worship* (London, 1953).

18. The arrangement and furniture of the assembly rooms

in the early centuries can be gathered from scattered references in the early Fathers and from Church orders such as the Syrian *Didascalia*, chapter 12 (ed. H. Conolly, Oxford, 1929, 120).

19. For the seating of the congregation, see H. Selhorst, *Die Platzanordnung im Gläubigenraum der altchristlichen Kirche* (Münster, 1931).

20. Tertullian, *De Poenitentibus*, cap. 7 (*P.L.*, I, 1352).

21. L. Duchesne (transl. M. L. McClure), *Christian Worship* (London, 1949), 334, quoting Tertullian, *De Baptismo* (*P.L.*, I, 1308 ff.), and Hippolytus, *In Danielem*, V, 17 (*P.G.*, X, 654); A. Stenzel, *Die Taufe* (Innsbruck, 1958); E. C. Whitaker, *Documents of the Baptismal Liturgy* (London, 1960). See also above, Note 11.

22. J. P. Kirsch, *Die römischen Titelkirchen im Altertum* (Paderborn, 1918), *passim*; L. Voelkl, *R.A.C.*, XXIX (1953), 49 ff., and XXX (1954), 99 ff.; more cautiously, Th. Klauser, *J.A.C.*, XI/XII (1968/9), 221 f., though I cannot accept his thesis that community centres in the old sense no longer existed in the fourth century; also C. Piétri, *Roma christiana* (Rome, 1976), *passim*.

27. 23. Minucius Felix, *Octavius*, chap. XXXII (*P.L.*, III, 353): 'delubra non habemus, aras non habemus'.

24. Older theories had it that the early Christians congregated in the atrium, the partly-covered central room of the Italic house; in the peristyle, the garden court of the hellenistic or hellenized Italic house; in the *basilicae privatae*, large reception rooms in the palaces of the wealthy; or in the *oikoi*, the lavish dining-rooms of such palaces. None of these suggestions holds. The atrium house had become obsolete by the middle of the first century, perhaps surviving in small country towns such as Pompeii, but not in the large cities where Christian congregations were forming; even when in fashion, it was limited to Italy, where Christianity was weakest. Furthermore the open roof of the atrium house and the pool in the centre would make it unsuitable for any gathering. The alleged resemblance of its plan, with the *alae* on either side, to that of an Early Christian transept basilica fails with the realization that the transept was always exceptional in Christian basilicas. *Oikoi*, peristyle courts, and audience halls – while hellenistic features and thus common from the first century onwards around the Mediterranean – were limited to the houses of the very rich. Hence, they were not available to the early congregations. Moreover, both garden courts and audience halls would have been utterly unsuitable for the ritual meals of the believers.

25. The definitive publication, C. H. Kraeling, *The Christian Building* (*The Excavations at Dura Europos . . . Final Report*, VIII, 2) (New Haven, 1967), with older bibliography, suggests the dates here accepted, the former thesis being that the house was remodelled for Christian use in 231/2–a minimal difference anyhow.

28. 26. M. Mirabella Roberti, in *Studi aquileiesi offerti a Giovanni Brusin* (Padua, 1953), 209 ff., discusses the poss-

ible existence of a similar community house at Aquileia, preceding the double cathedral of the early fourth century.

27. See the anti-Donatist documents, collected in Migne, *P.L.*, VIII, 673 ff., as *Monumenta Vetera ad Donatistarum historiam pertinentia*, esp. col. 231; better, K. Ziwsa (ed.), *C.S.E.L.*, XXVI (Vienna, 1893), esp. 186.

28. C. H. Kraeling, *The Synagogue* (*The Excavations at Dura Europos . . . Final Report*, VIII, 1) (New Haven, 1956).

29. See above, Note 10.

29. 30. Kirsch, *op. cit.*, *passim*; R. Vielliard, *Recherches sur les origines de la Rome chrétienne* (Mâcon, 1942). K. Gamber, *Domus Ecclesiae* (Regensburg, 1968), should be used with caution; see the review by Th. Klauser, *J.A.C.*, XI/XII (1968/9), 215 ff.

31. *Corpus*, I, 267 ff.; A. Prandi, *Il complesso monumentale della basilica . . . dei SS. Giovanni e Paolo* (Vatican City, 1953), dates the church building prior to 400.

32. E. Junyent, *Il titolo di San Clemente* (Rome, 1932); *Corpus*, I, 117 ff.; A Petrignani, *La basilica di S. Pudenziana* (Vatican City, 1934); *Corpus*, III, 277 ff.; M. Cechelli Trinci, *R.A.C.*, LVI (1974), 93 ff.; F. Guidobaldi, in *San Clemente Miscellany*, II, ed. L. Boyle and others (Rome, 1978), 215 ff.

30. 33. On the cult of the dead among third-century Christians, see the masterly presentation by P.-A. Février, *IX C.A.C. . . . 1975*, I, 211 ff.

The bibliography on catacombs is vast. For Rome, the basic work, G. B. de Rossi, *Roma sotterranea* (Rome, 1857), is to be supplemented by O. Marucchi, *Le catacombe romane* (Rome, 1933), and in particular by A. Nestori, *Repertorio topografico delle pitture delle catacombe romane* (Rome, 1975). Nearly every issue of *B.A.C.*, *N.B.A.C.*, and *R.A.C.* for the past hundred and twenty years has provided information on new findings. For the catacombs of Naples U. Fasola, *Le catacombe di S. Gennaro a Napoli* (Rome, 1974), takes the place of H. Achelis, *Die Katakomben von Neapel* (Leipzig, 1936). J. Führer, *Forschungen zur Sicilia sotterranea* (Munich, 1897), while obsolete, has not yet been replaced despite the studies of G. and S. Agnello, published in *R.A.C.*, *passim*. The North African catacombs remain to be explored.

32. 34. *Areae* are best known from North Africa; see, e.g., P.-A. Février, *C.C.R.* (1970), 191 ff., N. Duval, *ibid.*, 119 ff., and Y. Duval, *Loca Sanctorum* (Rome, 1982), *passim*. An *area* near the catacomb of Praetextatus in Rome has been studied by H. Winfeld-Hansen, *Institutum Romanum Norvegiae*, *Acta*, IV (1969), 61 ff.

Mausolea incorporated into medieval churches have survived, for instance, at Poitiers, Saint-Maximin, and elsewhere; see J. Hubert, *L'art pré-roman* (Paris, 1938), 53 ff.

35. At Cirta (modern Constantine) in North Africa, a bishop was elected 'in casa maiore in area martyrum' (*P.L.*, VIII, col. 739; see also Gsell, *Monuments*, II, 192, 397). At Tipasa, a portico with mensae has been found, adjoining the tomb basilica of one bishop Alexander of *c.* 400 (L. Leschi, *Bull. Arch.*, XL, 1938, 422 ff.; Y. Duval, *op. cit.*, 365 ff.).

Another funerary building of fourth-century date has been uncovered in a Christian cemetery situated below the church of St Severin at Cologne. But neither the reconstruction nor the date of this first building, nor of the structures succeeding it – supposedly in the late fourth and the fifth century, as proposed by F. Fremersdorff in *Neue Ausgrabungen in Deutschland* (Berlin, 1958), 329 ff. – are beyond question.

36. A. Grabar, *Martyrium* (Paris, 1948), is basic for the problems involved. See also the summary given by Grabar in *Archaeology*, II (1949), 95 ff.

37. The remnants found below St Peter's, including the large pagan necropolis, the aedicula of the apostle, the foundation walls of Constantine's basilica, and small portions of its rising walls and its colonnades have been published *in extenso* in *Esplorazioni sotto la confessione di San Pietro in Vaticano . . . 1940–1949; relazione a cura di B.M. Apollonj-Ghetti, A. Ferrua, S.J., E. Josi, E. Kirschbaum, S.J. . . .* (Vatican City, 1951). J. M. C. Toynbee and J. B. Ward Perkins, *The Shrine of Saint Peter* (London and New York, 1956), and E. Kirschbaum, *The Tombs of St Peter and Paul* (New York, 1959), present excellent summaries and clarify the situation further. The reconstruction of the aedicula as suggested by Toynbee and Ward Perkins seems preferable to that proposed in *Esplorazioni*.

38. Kirschbaum, *op. cit.*, 119 ff., and Th. Klauser, *Die römische Petrustradition* (Cologne-Opladen, 1956), *passim*, represent different points of view.

33. 39. De Rossi, *op. cit.*, I, 72 f.; II, 253 ff.; Marucchi, *op. cit.*, 185 ff.

40. Kirschbaum, *op. cit.*, and Klauser, *op. cit.* See also: P. Styger, *Römische Märtyrergrüfte* (Berlin, 1935); A. Prandi, *La memoria apostolorum in catacumbas* (Vatican City, 1936); F. Tolotti, *La memoria degli apostoli* (Vatican City, 1953); *Corpus*, IV, 114 ff.

41. Th. Kempf, *V C.A.C. . . . Aix-en-Provence . . . 1954*, 61 ff., with bibliography.

42. The exploration of Salona since 1920 has been directed primarily by E. Dyggve and R. Egger, and published in *Forschungen in Salona*, I-III (Vienna, 1914–39), and *Recherches à Salone*, I, II (Copenhagen, 1920–). A great deal of the findings, however, was published only in summary form by E. Dyggve, *History of Salonitan Christianity* (Oslo, 1951). Regarding early *memoriae*, see *ibid.*, 71 ff., and recently, N. Duval, in *Disputationes Salonitanae . . ., 1974* (Split, 1975), 83 ff., comparing those with multiple apses in similar (?) arrangements in North Africa.

35. 43. Dyggve and Egger, *Forschungen in Salona*, III (Vienna, 1939), especially 95 ff., 116 ff.

44. *Ibid.*, 80 ff., 107 ff.; for Pécs, see E. Dyggve, in *IV C.A.C. . . . Rome . . . 1938*, I, 395 f., and F. Gerke, in *Neue Beiträge zur Kunst des 1. Jahrtausends*, I (*Forschungen zur Kunstgeschichte und Archäologie*, I) (Baden-Baden, 1952), 115 ff.; for Alberca, H. Schlunk, *Cronica del III Congresso*

Arqueologico del Sudeste Español (1947), 335 ff., and *J.D.A.I.*, *A.A.*, LXIX (1954), 451 ff. The dependence of this type on Sassanian architecture, as suggested by Dyggve, is hardly tenable.

45. Best known are the cellae trichorae of S. Sotere and S. Sisto above the Callisto catacomb; see De Rossi, *op. cit.*, II, 4 f.; III, 29 f. The dates of construction and the original dedications of the various buildings await further clarification.

36. 46. A cross-shaped mausoleum, known as the chapel of SS. Tiburtius, Valerianus, and Maximus, rises over the catacomb of SS. Marcellino e Pietro, but the martyr's grave here seems to have been in the catacomb (*Corpus*, II, 191 ff.). Regarding the niched rotunda and other mausolea at the Praetextatus catacomb, see Winfeld-Hansen, *op. cit.* (Note 34 above).

47. J. Keil and H. Hörmann (ed.), *Forschungen in Ephesos*, V, 3 (Vienna, 1951), 224 ff.; also J. B. Ward-Perkins, *P.B.S.R.*, XVII (1949), 32, 40.

48. No generalization is valid regarding Christian meeting rooms or community houses in pre-Constantinian times. They apparently differed not only locally, but within the same locality. For Rome, Kirsch, *op. cit.*, in the light of these considerations should be used with caution. See now C. Piétri, *Roma christiana* (Rome, 1976), 92 and *passim*.

37. 49. Eusebius, *Ecclesiastical History*, VII, XXX, 9 (*L.C.L.*, II, 219).

50. Lactantius, *De mortibus persecutorum*, cap. 12 (*P.L.*, VII, 213 f.). Likewise, the church building at Edessa, damaged and rebuilt in 201, was presumably a *domus ecclesiae*, not, as frequently maintained, an independent church building. The same probably holds true for the 'churches of spacious dimensions' which were erected after 260, as reported by Eusebius, *Ecclesiastical History*, VIII, I, 5 (*L.C.L.*, II, 253).

51. Porphyry, *Adversus Christianos*, fragment 76, ed. A. von Harnack, *Abhandlungen Berliner Akademie der Wissenschaften, Phil. Hist. Klasse* (1916), no. 1, 98. As early as the late second or early third century the rich Jewish congregation at Sardis had installed their synagogue splendidly in a hall adjoining the public bath in the centre of town.

52. *Corpus*, I, 144 ff. B. M. Apollonj-Ghetti, *S. Crisogono* (*Chiese illustrate*, XCII) (1966), believes that the first remains belong to third-century buildings of unknown design and function which were prolonged and provided with apse and side chambers *c.* 450. While the latter observation is no doubt correct, the front part of the structure and its three-arched façade still suggest to me a former meeting hall. Proof of a pre-Constantinian date is elusive. Likewise a small church at Qirqbize (Syria) cannot be proven to date before Constantine as proposed by H. Brandenburg, *Roms frühchristliche Basiliken* (Munich, 1979), 14 f.

53. See below, Chapter 2, Note 32; *Corpus*, IV, 99 ff.

CHAPTER 2

39. 1. Writings on Constantine are numberless. His position regarding Christianity and the Church is best traced through A. Piganiol, *L'empereur Constantin* (Paris, 1928); N. H. Baynes, *Constantine the Great and the Christian Church* (London, 1929); A. Alföldi, *The Conversion of Constantine* (Oxford, 1948); H. Dörries, *Konstantin der Grosse* (Stuttgart, 1958); R. McMullen, *Constantine* (London, 1969); and T. D. Barnes, *Constantine and Eusebius* (Cambridge, Mass., and London, 1981). Primary sources are Constantine's letters and decrees (paraphrased, interpreted, and at times over-interpreted by H. Dörries, *Das Selbstzeugnis Kaiser Konstantins*, Göttingen, 1954) and Eusebius's *Life of Constantine* (*P.G.*, XX, 905 ff.; transl., ed. P. Schaff and H. Wace, *A Select Library of Nicene and post-Nicene Fathers*, second series, I, New York–Oxford–London, 1890, 473 ff.; and Eusebius, *Werke*, I, 1, ed. F. Winkelmann, Berlin-East, 1975).

2. Insignia and ceremonial of high officialdom need not all have become episcopal prerogatives at the same time. Th. Klauser, *Der Ursprung der bischöflichen Insignien und Ehrenrechte* (Krefeld, 1948), leaves in doubt whether candles, book, and fan preceded the bishop from the fourth or only from the seventh century. According to J. A. Jungmann, *Missarum Solemnia*, I (Freiburg, 1952), 51, note 21, on the other hand, both candles and the proskynesis were episcopal prerogatives from the fourth century.

40. 3. While Christ was visually represented as *basileus* first during the last third of the fourth century (J. Kollwitz, *Oströmische Plastik*, Berlin, 1941, 145 ff.), in literature and presumably in popular opinion His equation with the Emperor goes back to the time of Constantine, if not before. See K. M. Setton, *Christian Attitude Towards the Emperor* (New York, 1941), 18 ff.; K. Wessel, *J.D.A.I.*, *A.A.*, LXIX (1953), 118 ff.; P. Beskow, *Rex Gloriae* (Stockholm, 1962), *passim*; and, for Constantine's viewing himself as Christ's counterpart on earth, R. Krautheimer, *Three Christian Capitals* (Berkeley, 1982).

4. Much remains to be clarified regarding the precise forms of the liturgy in the fourth century in the various parts of the Empire. The present state of the question is summarized by Jungmann, *op. cit.*

41. 5. F. W. Deichmann, *J.D.A.I.*, LIV (1939), 105 ff.; also *idem*, *Rom, Ravenna*, 56 ff., 95 ff.

6. Numberless theories, beginning in the fifteenth century, have been propounded regarding the origin of the Christian basilica. The building type has been variously derived from the secular forum basilica; the palace basilica; religious pagan basilicas; synagogues; funerary pagan basilicas; the Italic atrium house; the peristyle of the hellenistic house; the plan of Imperial palaces; hellenistic heroa; the layout of Roman Imperial fora; or from the colonnaded streets of Roman cities. Or else it has been evolved entirely from the

requirements of the Christian liturgy, or from a combination of some or of all these factors. Summaries of the principal hypotheses have been presented in recent times in *R.L.A.C.*, I, 1249 ff.; by C. Delvoye, in *Annuaire de l'Institut de Philologie et d'Histoire Orientales et Slaves*, XIV (1957), 180 ff., and *idem*, in *C.C.R.* (1959), I, 49 ff.; by a discussion group, *Kunstchronik*, IV (1951), 97 ff.; N. Duval, in *L'Information de l'Histoire de l'Art*, VII (1962), 1 ff.; *idem*, IX *C.A.C.* . . . *1975*, 513 ff.; B. M. Apollonj Ghetti, *ibid.*, 491 ff. Leaving aside the more questionable theories, it would seem that the problem can be placed in the right perspective only by focusing not on one feature, such as the transept (an exceptional element in any event), but on plan and function in their entirety, and by thinking in terms of the creation of a new variant within the framework of a traditional genus (Krautheimer, *D.O.P.*, XXI, 1967, 115 ff.) rather than in terms of the derivation of the Christian basilica from any Roman prototype, be it religious or secular, private or public (Deichmann, *B.Z.*, LIX, 1966, 334 ff., esp. 359).

7. R. Schultze, *Basilika* (Berlin, 1928); more recently, E. Langlotz, *R.L.A.C.*, I, 1225 ff.; L. Crema, *L'architettura romana*, *Enciclopedia classica*, sezione III, vol. 12, tomo I (Turin, 1959), *passim*; and Boëthius, *op. cit.* (Chapter 1, Note 10), *passim*. Regarding the covering of the nave see F. W. Deichmann, *Felix Ravenna*, LXXV (1957), 63 ff.; *idem*, *J.Ö.B.*, XXI (1972), reprinted *idem*, *Rom, Ravenna*, 212 ff., 228 ff.

42. 8. B. Pace, *I mosaici di Piazza Armerina* (Rome, 1955); W. Reusch, *Trierer Zeitschrift*, XVIII (1949), 198 ff.; P.-A. Février, *C.A.*, XIV (1964), 1 ff., esp. 12 ff.; R. Günter, *Wand, Fenster und Licht in der Trierer Palastaula und in spätantiken Bauten* (Herford, 1968).

9. The *Thesaurus Linguae Latinae* (Leipzig, 1900 ff.), II, 1761 ff., under 'basilica', gives examples of the usage of the term with and without explanatory epithets.

10. Vitruvius, *De Architectura*, V, 1; see also R. Krautheimer, *D.O.P.* (*op. cit.*).

11. S. Pudenziana in Rome encloses the core of such a thermae basilica of second-century date; see A. Petrignani, *La basilica di S. Pudenziana* . . . (Vatican City, 1934), and *Corpus*, III, 227 ff.

12. Pagan religious basilicas known from excavations in Rome, apart from that of the 'Tree Bearers of the Great Mother and Attys' (Basilica Hilariana; see E. Nash, *Pictorial Dictionary of Ancient Rome*, London, 1961–2, I, 169 ff., with older bibliography), are the neo-Pythagorean subterranean basilica at Porta Maggiore (*ibid.*, 183) and the Basilica Crepereia known from an inscription. Synagogues of basilican plan have been discussed by H. Kohl and C. Watzinger, *Antike Synagogen in Galiläa* (Leipzig, 1916); by E. L. Sukenik, *Ancient Synagogues in Palestine and Greece* (London, 1934); and by S. J. Saller, *A Revised Catalogue of the Ancient Synagogues of the Holy Land* (Jerusalem, 1969). Their dates, whether third-, fourth-, or fifth-century, are under discus-

sion. Synagogues of the late fifth and sixth centuries adopt from church building the plan of a nave flanked by aisles and terminated by an apse (for one among many, Beth Alpha, see Sukenik, as above).
For funerary basilicas, see Ch. G. Picard, *Civitas Mactaritana* (Paris, 1957), 96 ff.; W. Seston and Ch. Perrat, *Annales de Bordeaux (Revue des Études Anciennes)*, XLIX (1947), 139 ff.; and S. Bettini, in *Studi aquileiesi offerti a Giovanni Brusin* (Padua, 1953), 307 ff.

13. J. B. Ward-Perkins, *P.B.S.R.*, IX (1954), 69 ff.

14. *Itinerarium Burdigalense*, in P. Geyer, *Itinera Hierosolymitana (C.S.E.L.*, XXXVIII) (Vienna, 1889), 1 ff., and especially 23; Eusebius, *Life of Constantine (op. cit.)*, II, 51, and III, 26. The terms used in Constantinian times for Christian cult buildings have been examined by L. Voelkl, *R.A.C.*, XXIX (1953), 49 ff., 187 ff., and XXX (1954), 99 ff., and, with special regard to North African usage, by F. J. Dölger, *J.A.C.*, VI (1950), 174 ff.

43. 15. For the main lines of Constantine's building policy, see L. Voelkl, *Die Kirchenstiftungen des Kaisers Konstantin* (Cologne-Opladen, 1964); Krautheimer, *VII C.A.C. ... 1965*, 237 ff.; G. T. Armstrong, *Church History*, XXXVI (1967), 1 ff.; and Krautheimer, *op. cit.* ((Note 3), *passim*. Regarding Constantine's part in establishing the type of the Christian basilica (a doubtful generalization) see Krautheimer, *D.O.P.*, XXI (1967), 115 ff., N. Duval, as above, Note 6, and, though controversial, U. Süssenbach, *Christuskult und kaiserliche Baupolitik bei Konstantin* (Bonn, 1977). I more and more doubt that there is such a thing as a Constantinian principle of style in church building aside from size and lavishness.

16. K. Lanckoroński and G. Niemann, *Der Dom von Aquileia* (Vienna, 1906); C. Cecchelli, *La Basilica di Aquileia* (Bologna, 1933); G. Brusin, *Aquileia e Grado* (Aquileia, 1956). More recently the buildings have been re-studied by M. Mirabella Roberti, in *Studi in onore di ... Calderini e ... Paribeni* (Milan, 1957), III, 863 ff., and in *Studi aquileiesi offerti a Giovanni Brusin* (*op. cit.*), 209 ff.; by H. Kaehler, *Die spätantiken Bauten unter dem Dom von Aquileia* (Saarbrücken, 1957); and by S. Corbett in *R.A.C.*, XXXII (1956), 99 ff. Regarding the placing of altar and cathedra, see M. Mirabella Roberti, *R.A.C.*, XXVI (1950), 180 ff.; regarding the ceilings (with painted coffers), Deichmann, *loc. cit.* (1957) (Note 7 above). Work continues and is regularly reported in *Aquileia Nostra* and *Studi Aquileiesi*.

17. Examples are found along the Istrian coast at Pula (Pola), Poreč (Parenzo), Nesactium, Trieste, and Brioni, and in Carinthia at Hemmaberg and Hoischhügel. See R. Egger, *Frühchristliche Kirchenbauten im südlichen Norikum* (*J.Ö.A.I.*, *Sonderhefte*, IX) (Vienna, 1916), with bibliography; B. Molajoli, *La basilica eufrasiana di Parenzo* (Padua, 1943); and G. C. Menis, *La basilica paleocristiana nelle diocesi settentrionali della metropoli d'Aquileia* (Vatican City, 1958). For the problem of twin cathedrals in general, see

Krautheimer, *Studies*, 161 ff., esp. 176 ff., with bibliography; and, now, J.-P. Sodini and K. Kolokotsas, *Aliki II: La basilique double (École Française d'Athènes, Études Thasiennes*, X) (Athens and Paris, 1984), 253 ff., covering the phenomenon from the early fourth to the sixth century and regionally from Trier and Aquileia into Dalmatia and Greece and across the seas to Syria, Palestine, and Algeria and Tunisia and discussing the changing functions of the twin buildings.

44. 18. Gsell, *Monuments*, II, 236 ff. The remnants are no longer visible, except for the mosaics, transferred to the modern church; G. Vidal, *Un témoin d'une date célèbre* (Algiers, n.d., *c.* 1940). The floor mosaic, according to Février and Duval (*VIII C.A.C. ... Barcelona ... 1969*, 24), dates from the late fourth century, and the inscription giving the date 324 would thus be the copy of an earlier one. It must remain undecided whether this latter refers to the church excavated in 1840 or to a lost predecessor. Until proven to the contrary, I consider the former likely. J. Christern, *VII C.A.C. ... Trier ... 1956*, 407 ff., is in doubt whether the church had galleries; if so, he considers them original rather than added (see also Deichmann, *B.Z.*, LXV, 1972, 104). Since the *corpus delicti* is gone, the decision remains suspended; in any event, the evidence for galleries at Orléansville is scanty.

45. 19. Eusebius, *Ecclesiastical History*, X, iv, 44 ff. (*L.C.L.*, II, 424 ff.); M. H. Shepherd, Jr, *Yearbook of Liturgical Studies* (1965), 73 ff. J. Wilkinson, *XVI C.E.B. ... Vienna 1983*, *Akten* IV/4 (*J.Ö.B.*, XXXII/4), 553 ff., suggests that Eusebius in his account of the church based himself on the description of the Jewish Temple in Ezekiel, chapters 40 ff., and of Flavius Josephus, *The Jewish War*, V, 184–227, both in sequence and phrasing. For the date of consecration about 315, T. D. Barnes, *op. cit.* (Note 1), 162 f. and note 108.

20. The term for the Christian atrium derives from Greek *aithrion* (an area under the open sky) rather than from the Latin *atrium*, the smoke-blackened main room of the Italic house.

21. S. Corbett, *R.A.C.*, XXXII (1956), 99 ff., and Kaehler, *op. cit.* The function of the three halls is still under debate, although general consensus seems to incline towards viewing the south hall as the church proper. But it is still doubtful whether or not the transverse hall and the north hall, or one of the two, served for the withdrawal of the catechumens and others excluded from the Mass of the Faithful.

22. H. Sedlmayr, 'Spätantike Wandsysteme', *Bayerische Akademie der Wissenschaften, Philosophisch-Historische Klasse, Sitzungsberichte* (1958), Heft 7.

47. 23. For Constantinian church building in Rome, *Corpus*, I–V, *passim*; C. Piétri, *Roma christiana* (Rome, 1976), 3 ff. and *passim*; and, in summary form, F. W. Deichmann, *Frühchristliche Kirchen in Rom* (Basel, 1948), *passim*, and Brandenburg, *op. cit.*, Chapter 1, Note 52.
On the Lateran in particular P. Lauer, *Le palais de Latran*

(Paris, 1911), obsolete. A reconstruction based on the evidence available so far is now to be found in *Corpus*, V, 1 ff., with pertinent bibliography; also, briefly, Brandenburg, *op. cit.*, 22 ff. The suggestion of half-circular windows lighting the inner aisle, though well-founded, remains conjectural, as does the reconstruction of the original façade (V. Hoffmann, *Röm. Jbch*, XVII, 1978, 1 ff.). For the choice of location, Krautheimer, *op. cit.* (Note 3), 26 ff., with older bibliography.

Regarding the chancel arrangement in Rome and the pathway leading to it (*solea*) see, in general, T. Mathews, *R.A.C.*, XXXVIII (1962, but published 1965), 73 ff. 48. 24. *L.P.*, I, 172; M. Teasdale Smith, *R.A.C.*, XLVI (1970), 149 ff., reconstructing the fastigium as a colonnaded screen, while U. Nilgen, *R. Qu. Schr.*, LXXII (1977), 1 ff., proposes a canopy resembling that of St Peter's supported by the four colossal bronze columns still at the Lateran with the statues placed in the attic.

25. *L.P.*, I, *ibid.* 'ex auro trimita', gold foil or cloth? (M. Guarducci, *Studi E. Paratore*, Bologna, 1981, 799 ff.)

26. The findings at Trier have been published by the excavator, Th. Kempf, from 1947 onward, most recently in *Neue Ausgrabungen in Deutschland* (Berlin, 1958), 368 ff.; *Germania*, XLII (1964), 126 ff.; *Frühchristliche Zeugnisse im Einzugsgebiet von Rhein und Mosel*, ed. Th. Kempf and W. Reusch (Trier, 1965), 209 ff.; *Das Münster*, XXI (1968), 1 ff. The preliminary character of the successive reports has led to occasional inconsistencies in the interpretation of the finds and the accompanying plans. For the mid- and late-fourth-century changes in Constantine's twin cathedral, see below, p. 85.

50. 27. Next to nothing is known of the cathedral in Constantine's new capital, Constantinople. It may have functioned as a twin cathedral, a common precinct enclosing both an old community centre, remodelled and dedicated to Holy Peace, Hagia Irene, and the new church founded by Constantine and dedicated to Holy Wisdom, Hagia Sophia. Doubts (G. Dagron, *Naissance d'une capitale*, Paris, 1974, 397 ff.) as to the latter's having been started 'about thirty-four years' before its consecration in 360 (*Chronicon Paschale*, *P.G.*, XCII, col. 736 ff.) seem to me unfounded given the overall reliability of that source. Construction was apparently so slow or indeed suspended that Socrates (*H.E.*, II, 16; *P.G.*, LXVII, 217) writing a century later viewed its resumption in 343 as the actual foundation by Constantius II, who completed it in 360. This first H. Sophia was burnt down in 404. But, as I see it, the walls and perhaps part of the colonnades remained and it was rebuilt on the old plan, albeit provided with a splendid new propylaeum (below, pp. 103 ff.; A. M. Schneider, *Die Grabung im Westhof der Sophienkirche ...*, *Istanbuler Forschungen*, XII, Berlin, 1941) and rededicated in 415. Finally, in 532–7 it was replaced by Justinian's great church. Scanty remains (Schneider, *B.Z.*, XXXVI, 1936, 85, though with-

drawn, *Grabung*, 6 f. and note; J. B. Ward Perkins, in D. Talbot Rice, ed., *The Great Palace of the Byzantine Emperors, Second Report*, Edinburgh, 1958, 64) and foundation walls excavated below Justinian's church suggest that Constantine's cathedral in its fifth-century rebuilding was a basilica with twin aisles on either side of the nave and galleries preceded by a wide atrium and propylaeum, in plan like his basilica on Golgotha, albeit much larger in size (below, pp. 60 ff. and Note 45; also Krautheimer, *op. cit.*, Note 3, 52 ff.).

28. *Corpus*, I, 165 ff. I no longer distinguish two phases of rebuilding, dating from 350 and 400 respectively; instead, I see only one remodelling dating from between Helena's visit to the Holy Land in 325/6 and her death probably late in 329. The proposed reconstruction with longitudinal arcades linking the transverse arches into a square (F. W. Deichmann, *Frühchristliche Kirchen in Rom*, Basel, 1948, 31) founders on the lack of longitudinal counterthrust in the direction of the apse.

51. 29. *L.P.*, I, 181, and *Corpus*, II, 6, 115 f.

30. *Forschungen in Salona*, II (Vienna, 1926), 12 ff.; E. Dyggve, *History of Salonitan Christianity* (Oslo, 1951), 76 f. and figure IV, 12.

31. At Salona two such halls adjoining an open area have been excavated under the Anastasius basilica (*Forschungen in Salona*, III, Vienna, 1939, 6 ff.). Others have been found, e.g., in Vicenza, on the site of the later cemetery church of SS. Felice and Fortunato (Verzone, 1942, 39; also M. Mirabella Roberti, as quoted below, Chapter 7, Note 14); at St Alban in Mainz (E. Neeb, *Mainzer Zeitschrift*, IV (1909), 34 ff.); and below the medieval cathedral of Xanten.

52. 32. The problem of the *coemeteria subteglata* has been taken up only in comparatively recent years. The one *ad catacumbas*, now the church of S. Sebastiano on the Via Appia, has been known in its original state since 1915 (P. Styger, *R. Qu. Schr.*, XXIX, 1915, 73 ff.; more recently *Corpus*, IV, 99 ff., proposing a new reconstruction for the building as first laid out), but was looked upon as an isolated and unexplained phenomenon until further research was found (see F. Tolotti, *La memoria degli apostoli*, Vatican City, 1953, *passim*): the covered cemetery at S. Agnese, first identified in 1946 by F. W. Deichmann, *R.A.C.*, XXII (1946), 1 ff. and further investigated by N. Perotti, *Palladio*, N.S. VI (1956), 80 ff.; the coemeterium of SS. Marcellino e Pietro at Tor Pignattara excavated in 1955 by F. W. Deichmann and A. v. Tschira (*J.D.A.I.*, LXXII, 1957, 44 ff., to be supplemented by J. Guyon and others, *M.E.F.R.A.*, XCIII, 1981–2, 999 ff., and J. Guyon, *Rend. Pont. Acc.*, LIII–LIV, 1980–2, published 1984, 27 ff., reporting on the find of a porticoed courtyard south and another enclosed area north of and both antedating the basilica and sheltering mausolea attached to its flanks and to the porticoes); the one at S. Lorenzo on the Via Tiburtina traced by R. Krautheimer and W. Frankl in 1957 (*Corpus*, II, 93 ff.). Another building of the type, yet unidentified, has come to

light in the grounds of the Villa dei Gordiani on the Via Prenestina (G. Gatti, *Capitolium*, XXXV, June 1960, 3 ff.). The monuments known by 1958 were discussed in the light of fourth-century funerary custom and martyr cult by R. Krautheimer, *C.A.*, XI (1960), 15 ff.; also *idem*, *Studies*, 35 ff.

F. W. Deichmann, *R.M.*, LXXVII (1970), 144 ff., questions my interpretation of the type as primarily covered cemeteries and funerary halls rather than regular churches. I am not denying their having served also for the celebration of the Eucharist; but I cannot overlook the paving with graves, the lack of regular clergy and services, and the location of the venerated tomb, as a rule, outside. For the entire group, also Brandenburg, as above, Note 23, 61 ff. The plan occurs outside Rome, at Andernos in southwestern France; see M. Veillard-Troiekouroff, *C.A.*, XXVII (1979), 7 ff. H. Geertman, in *Feestboendel A. N. Zadoks – Josephus Jitta* (Groningen, 1975), 277 ff., unconvincingly assigns the structure excavated at S. Lorenzo fuori le mura to the pontificate of Sixtus III (432–40).

54. 33. *Recherches à Salone*, I (Copenhagen, 1920), 176 ff., and E. Dyggve, *Salonitan Christianity* (*op. cit.*), 77 ff. and figure IV, 26.

34. Gsell, *Monuments*, II, 333, and L. Leschi, *Bull. Arch.* (1932), 422 ff.; N. Duval, *C.C.R.* (1970), 119 ff., esp. 127 ff.; P.-A. Février, *ibid.*, 191 ff.

35. The foundations and the bottom courses of apse, transept, and some of the westernmost portions of nave and aisles of St Peter's, as well as some fragments of columns, were uncovered in many years of excavations, forty years ago. Published in *Esplorazioni* (see above, Chapter 1, Note 37), these remnants form the basis of any reconstruction, supplemented by old descriptions and by the numerous drawings and prints recording the building prior to its demolition between 1505 and 1612. Outstanding among these are the plan Uffizi *dis. arch.* 20, probably by Bramante, a sketch plan by Baldassare Peruzzi, Uffizi, *dis. arch.* 11 r., a nave section by Antonio da Sangallo the Younger, Uffizi, *dis. arch.* 121, and detailed surveys of the column shafts by Baldassare Peruzzi and others listed and most reproduced *Corpus*, V, 165 ff.; the *vedute* of the church, particularly those by Marten van Heemskerck (H. Egger, *Römische Veduten*, I, 1911 (1931), plates 17 ff., and H. Egger and C. Hülsen, *Die römischen Skizzenbücher des Marten van Heemskerck*, Berlin, 1916, *passim*); finally, the minute description by Alfarano and his less reliable plan (M. Cerrati, ed., *Tiberii Alpharani De Basilicae Vaticanae . . . structura*, Studi e Testi, XXVI, Rome, 1914). Studies of these materials in recent years have clarified numerous points and led to new reconstruction proposals, most important among them that of a transept lower than the nave as convincingly suggested by J. Christern, *R. Qu. Schr.*, LXII (1967), and *idem* and K. Thiersch, *ibid.*, 133 ff., and LXIV (1969), 1 ff.; Brandenburg (above, Note 23), 126

ff. *Corpus*, V, 165 ff., gathers the material available for envisaging the structure, sums up the bibliography, and presents what we hope to be a convincing reconstruction.

36. The years 319–22 are suggested as a *terminus post* by the fact that a pagan sanctuary nearby was reopened in 350 'after twenty-eight years' and the find of a coin dated 318 in a mausoleum below the church (Josi, *Rend. Pont. Acc.*, XXV/XXVI, 1949–51, 4 ff., and Guarducci, *ibid.*, XXXIX, 1967, 142 ff.); 324 is suggested as a *terminus ad quem* by the presence among Constantine's donations to the church of large numbers of estates in the eastern provinces, estates which became available to him only after his conquest of the East in 324 (Piganiol, *op. cit.*, 112 ff.). On the other hand, a donation made still by Helena, thus prior to 329, suggests previous completion of construction. Concomitantly an Imperial decree referring to the violation of graves prior to 333 may be linked to the destruction of the old necropolis. But contrary to W. Seston, *C.A.*, II (1947), 153 ff., who first linked the decree to St Peter's, and Kirschbaum, *op. cit.*, 151 ff., it constitutes, in my opinion, a *terminus ante*, not *post*, for the construction of the church and, possibly, for completion of the atrium.

The completion of the atrium prior to 396 and possibly by 333 is confirmed by a letter of Paulinus of Nola (*P.L.*, LXI, col. 213 ff.). The date of the nave murals in the pontificate of Leo I, 440–61, is suggested by the resemblance of the surviving copies to those reflecting the murals (likewise lost) from S. Paolo fuori le mura: the latter were plausibly assigned to Leo's pontificate by J. Garber, *Wirkungen der frühchristlichen Gemäldezyklen der alten Peters- und Pauls-Basiliken in Rom* (Berlin–Vienna, 1918), 27 f.

The numerous later remodellings affected decoration and furnishings rather than plan or structure of Constantine's church. The structural changes appear to have been limited to the raising of the north exedra to the height of the transept; the addition of a *cavetto* terminating the façade under Gregory IX (1227–41), who provided a new façade mosaic; the alteration of five round-headed into pointed windows in the apse, possibly under Innocent III (1198–1216), who donated the apse mosaic; and the insertion of Gothic tracery in the windows of nave and façade, perhaps also in the thirteenth, but more likely in the fifteenth century, when Nicholas V began extensive repairs on the old structure. The fourth-century façade and its mosaic are shown in an eleventh-century Farfa Codex, now at Eton College.

56. 37. See Paulinus of Nola as quoted above, Note 36.

38. R. Krautheimer, *Art Bulletin*, XXXI (1949), 211 ff. K. J. Conant, in reconstructing Constantine's St Peter's, proposed to keep the outer ends lower than the main part of the transept (*A Brief Commentary on Early Medieval Church Architecture*, Baltimore, 1942, plate III), a suggestion now convincingly proven by Christern (see above, Note 35). Also Christern's further proposal to keep also the centre section

of the transept lower than the nave has been confirmed, see *Corpus*, V. Christern has also corrected the measurements of St Peter's as given in the first edition of the present volume, p. 35, lines 2 and 3, and I apologize for my mistake.

S. Alexander, *R.A.C.*, XLVII (1971), 281 ff., and *ibid.*, XLIX (1973), 33 ff., has rightly questioned whether Constantine's atrium of St Peter's, like that at Tyre, was already enveloped by a quadriporticus; indeed, the lateral porticoes were built shortly before 500.

39. J. M. C. Toynbee and J. B. Ward Perkins, *The Shrine of St Peter* (London, 1956), 200 ff. and figure 20.

40. Regarding the main functions of the transept at St Peter's, see *ibid.*, 207 ff., and G. Forsyth, in *Late Classical and Medieval Studies in honor of Albert Mathias Friend, Jr* (Princeton, 1955), 56 ff.; regarding the differing types of transepts in Early Christian times, see Krautheimer, *Studies*, 59 ff., esp. 67 ff. The complexity of the problem has not always been fully understood; see F. W. Deichmann, *Ravenna*, I (Berlin, 1969), 58.

59. 41. R. Krautheimer, *Art Bulletin*, XXIV (1942), 1 ff. Exceptions to the rule are S. Paolo fuori le mura in Rome (see below, p. 87); perhaps S. Eusebio at Vercelli (P. Verzone, *L'architettura romanica nel . . . Vercellese*, Vercelli, 1939, 84 ff.; T. K. Kirova, *III C.A.C. . . ., Antichità Altoadriatiche*, VI, Trieste, 1974, 323 ff., questions the Early Christian date of the remains surviving till the eighteenth century); and the basilica of Manastirine at Salona, as remodelled and dedicated to St Peter about 400 (R. Egger, *Forschungen in Salona*, II, Vienna, 1926, 18 ff. and E. Dyggve, *Salonitan Christianity*, *op. cit.*, 79 and figure IV, 30).

42. J. W. Crowfoot, *Early Churches in Palestine* (London, 1941), *passim*, with bibliography; for the buildings in Jerusalem see also L. H. Vincent and F. M. Abel, *Jérusalem nouvelle*, II, 1 and 2 (Paris, 1925). A. Ovadiah, *Corpus of the Byzantine Churches in the Holy Land* (Bonn, 1970), sums up – not always impeccably – findings and older bibliography (henceforth quoted as Ovadiah, *Corpus*).

43. E. Mader, *Mambre* (Freiburg, 1957), interprets with a good deal of fancy the solid foundation walls found.

60. 44. Regarding the Pilgrim of Bordeaux, see P. Geyer, *Itinera Hierosolymitana* (*C.S.E.L.*, XXXVIII) (Vienna, 1898). R. W. Hamilton, *Q.D.A.P.*, III (1934), 1 ff., E. T. Richmond, *ibid.*, V (1936), 75 ff., and W. Harvey, *Archaeologia*, LXXXVII (1937), 7 ff., report on the excavation of Constantine's church. B. Bagatti, *Gli antichi edifici sacri di Betlemme* (Jerusalem, 1952), has raised doubts regarding *inter alia* the existence of an opening into the grotto from the octagon; closed, it would have supported, in his view, the altar. The archaeological evidence, including traces of a canopy over the opening – appropriate in Constantinian eyes for a memoria rather than an altar – militates in favour of the traditional reconstruction. K. J. Conant's reconstruction proposal is found in his *Brief Commentary* (*op. cit.*, see above, Note 38), R. W. Hamilton's in his *The Church of the Nativity*,

Bethlehem (Jerusalem, 1947), figure 3 (both with opaion in the roof of the octagon). For the date of the mosaic pavements, see L. H. Vincent, *Revue Biblique*, XLV (1936), 544 ff., and XLVI (1937), 93 ff. (late fourth century), and E. Kitzinger, in *Kyriakon, Festschrift Quasten* (Münster, 1970), II, 639 ff. (first half of the fifth century). The bi-partition of the steps at the end of the nave, half ascending to the octagon, half descending to the grotto, proposed by Bagatti, *op. cit.*, 47 ff., has been confirmed by Kitzinger, *op. cit.*, with reference also to the flanking pavement panels, one inscribed ICHTHYS.

45. The standard work, Vincent and Abel, *Jérusalem nouvelle* (*op. cit.*), II.1, gives a survey of the remains known by 1920 of the complex of structures planned by Constantine and altered over the centuries and of the pertinent literary sources, from Eusebius through Early Christian and medieval pilgrims' reports. Their survey, necessarily incomplete, can now be replaced by that of V. Corbo, *Il Santo Sepolcro a Gerusalemme*, 3 vols. (Jerusalem, 1981–2), based as it is on a careful exploration and interpretation of the extant remains and on recent excavations undertaken by Fr Corbo and others. It presents the sequence of the structures as built by Constantine (so Corbo; in my opinion the Anastasis Rotunda dates from after 336, and perhaps after his death in 337): from west to east, first the Anastasis Rotunda, its courtyard enveloped on three sides by colonnaded porticoes: apse and side chambers of the basilica (the *martyrion* of the sources); large stretches of the foundation walls of nave and aisle colonnades; the south-east corner of the façade (did the foundation wall across the nave 5 m. (16 ft) west of the façade carry the transverse colonnade of a *tribelon*?); the atrium, uncolonnaded; and farthest east a propylaeum, using part of a second-century street colonnade.

Eusebius, who attended the consecration of the church in 336, has transmitted Constantine's rescript of 325/6 (the first edition of this volume, p. 39, erroneously gave 328) and the description of the buildings, presumably as in 336 he saw them, in his *Life of Constantine*, III, 26 ff. (*P.G.*, XX, 1316, 1410). The evidence provided by these passages as well as contemporary and later pilgrims' reports has been sifted and interpreted with great care by E. K. Wistrand, *Konstantins Kirche am Heiligen Grab . . .* (*Göteborgs Högskolas Årsskrift*, LVIII, 1952, 1). Eusebius's account of the basilica is confirmed as to its plan by the archaeological findings: the nave flanked by twin aisles on either side; the façade; the atrium with three gates; the propylaeum; and behind the basilica the courtyard with colonnades on three sides. Moreover Eusebius supplies the information available, if open to interpretation, for envisaging the elevation both inside and outside. The most obscure is his statement regarding the siting 'opposite the façade . . . at the end (or on top of) the basilica' of a *hemisphairion*, be it a dome or – improperly, but the usage occurs – a half-dome, 'encircled like a wreath by twelve columns like the number of the

Disciples, carrying silver bowls'. In the apse (being 8·20 m. or 27 ft wide, its curve measures 4.10π, 12·87 m., or 42 ft 3 in.) such columns must have been small and less than a metre from each other: an unlikely, if possible arrangement. However, it is hard to see why these columns recalling the Apostles would be placed in the apse of the basilica rather than around the sepulchre whence Christ had risen; or why that apse rather than the sepulchre should be called the 'headpiece of the whole', the *kephaleion* – the more so that at the very start of his description Eusebius twice uses that very term, '*kephaleion* of the whole', to designate the 'Holy Cave . . ., the Saviour's trophy over death . . . which the emperor adorned with exquisite columns and with divers embellishment'. To me it seems (*pace* Wistrand, 13) much more likely that Eusebius mistakenly placed 'at the end of the basilica' the twelve columns and dome he had seen around the sepulchre; or that, indeed, a scribe wrote 'ep' akron (at the end)' for 'antikrys (opposite)'.

Be that as it may, Eusebius did not see in 336 the Anastasis Rotunda encircling and sheltering the sepulchre. It is only that latter, the Holy Cave, he speaks of; and, as pointed out by Wistrand, that cave, the Holy Sepulchre, adorned by Constantine and sheltered under a baldacchino would have stood in the open, beyond the west portico of the three-porticoed western court.

Attempts at graphic reconstruction of Constantine's buildings on Golgotha, while legion, starting with Vincent and Abel, *op. cit.*, are bound to remain tentative in the face of insufficient archaeological evidence.

Certainly, as witness Constantine's letter, the Anastasis Rotunda was not envisaged at the start, nor had it been built by Easter 336 at the time of Eusebius's visit. It may have been started in Constantine's last years between September 335 and Whitsuntide 337 when the Emperor died. In any event, though, it had been built by 348 or 350 when Bishop Cyril of Jerusalem – and here I part ways with Wistrand, 20 ff. – preached his sermons to catechumens right there (see also Heisenberg, *Grabeskirche und Apostelkirche*, Leipzig, 1908, I, 50).

The names of the architects of Constantine's basilica, Eustathios from Constantinople, a presbyter, and Zenobius, apparently a Syrian, are given by Prosper of Aquitaine (*P.L.*, LI, 576) and Theophanes (*Chronographia*, ed. De Boca, Leipzig, 1883, 33). Eustathios may have been the bearer of a plan; a hypothesis based on the continued Constantinopolitan tradition of colonnaded basilicas with galleries – as witness in my view already the first H. Sophia (above, Note 27) and certainly its fifth-century rebuilding as against the rarity, not to say absence, of the type from the Holy Land (Krautheimer, *op. cit.* (Note 3), 50 ff.). Also, the late-fourth-

century Epiphanius basilica at Salamis on Cyprus has been reasonably linked to the basilica on Golgotha (below, p. 106; Delvoye, *Praktika tou protou Diethnous Kyprologikou Synedriou . . . 1969*, II, 17 ff.); or was it the first H. Sophia?

The Cleveland bread mould, first identified by W. Wixom as representing the structures on Golgotha, has been discussed by G. Galavaris, *Bread and the Liturgy* (Madison, 1970), 153 ff. As common in late antique and medieval architectural representations, the component elements are out of proportion and reshuffled, both inside and out. Hence, the interpretation of some of the elements remains in doubt. If the clerestory in the nave was really that high, a reconstruction with aisles and galleries as tall as the nave (see the earlier editions of this volume) must be eliminated; but the Cleveland mould presumably shows the basilica as rebuilt following serious damage suffered when in 613 Jerusalem fell to the Persians.

63. 46. Dyggve, *op. cit.*, in Note 45.

64. 47. Regarding the mausoleum of S. Costanza, consult H. Stern, *D.O.P.*, XII (1958), 157 ff., with older bibliography; regarding that of St Helena, F. W. Deichmann, *J.D.A.I.*, LXXII (1959), 44 ff. The two mausolea adjoining St Peter's, both rotundas with eight niches and nearly equal in size, were destroyed in the sixteenth and eighteenth centuries respectively. The one attached to the south transept and later dedicated to St Petronilla was used about 400 for burials of the Honorian dynasty. The other mausoleum, known as S. Maria della Febbre, or S. Andrea, was apparently of early-third-century date (F. Castagnoli, *Rend. Pont. Acc.*, XXXII, 1959–60, 97 ff.).

Recent excavations in Carthage have brought to light large remains of a rotunda with inner and outer ambulatory, vaulted throughout, a provincialized S. Costanza, as it were, presumably a mausoleum attached to the apse of a triconch church (*Carthage IV, Cahiers des Études Anciennes*, XII, ed. P. Senay, Trois-Rivières, Québec, 1980).

65. 48. The letter addressed to the bishops assembled at Mambre is quoted by Eusebius, *Life of Constantine*, II, 51 ff. (*P.G.*, XX, 1112 ff.); for the passage from Constantine's address to the Council of Nicaea, see Gelasius Cyzicenus, *Ecclesiastical History*, II, 7, 13 (*P.G.*, LXXXV, 1232).

67. 49. H. Stern, as quoted above, Note 47.

50. Sedlmayr, 'Spätantike Wandsysteme', as quoted above, Note 22, attempted a stylistic interpretation of Constantinian church building along similar lines, though within the framework of an all too rigid *Systematik*; see now also F. W. Deichmann, *B.Z.*, LIX (1966), 334 ff.

CHAPTER 3

69. 1. The classical spirit prevailing at the court in the fourth century has been set forth by A. Alföldi, *A Conflict of Ideas in the Late Fourth Century* (Oxford, 1952), and by J. Bidez, *Julien l'Apostat* (Paris, 1930).

2. R. Krautheimer, in *De Artibus Opuscula XL, Essays in Honor of Erwin Panofsky* (New York, 1961), 191 ff.; recently in a superb analysis by Kitzinger, *Making*, 26 ff.

3. For the first church of the H. Sophia, see above, Chapter 2, Note 27.

4. Eusebius, *Life of Constantine*, IV, 58 ff. (*P.G.*, XX, 1209 f.). The attribution of the building to Constantius rather than to Constantine, as proposed by G. Downey, *D.O.P.*, VI (1951), 53 ff., is to me unconvincing; see Krautheimer, *Mullus* (*J.A.C., Erg. Bd.*, I, 1964), 224 ff. Equally unconvincing seems to me the reconstruction of Constantine's church either as an ordinary basilica (A. Heisenberg, *Grabeskirche und Apostelkirche*, Leipzig, 1908, II, 97 ff.; still F. W. Deichmann, *B.Z.*, LV, 1972, 105) or as a basilica with colonnaded cross transept (H. Christ, *R.A.C.*, XII, 1935, 306 ff.). The texts of Eusebius and of Gregory of Nazianz (*P.G.*, XXXVII, 1258) as well as the filiations of the Apostoleion down to Justinian's structure strongly suggest the plausibility of a Greek-cross plan with arms of equal or nearly equal length for Constantine's church. For the (later) mausoleum, see R. Egger, *J.ÖA.I.*, XVI (1913), 212 ff., and suggestively C. Nordenfalk, *Gazette des Beaux-Arts*, LXII (1963), 17 ff.

70. 5. R. Krautheimer, *Journal of the Warburg and Courtauld Institutes*, V (1942), 1 ff.

6. See below, *passim*. It has been questioned whether the Apostoleion in Constantinople was really the fountain-head of all churches on a cross plan or with cross transept (Deichmann, *loc. cit.*; Ph. Verdier, *A.J.A.*, LXXIII, 1969, 255 ff., esp. 256). As to the latter category, I have modified the all-too-general statement in the first edition of the present volume; as to the former, I stick to my guns.

72. 7. Planning and growth of Constantinople from Constantine to Justinian and the squares, streets, and buildings known in their majority only from literary sources are brilliantly and concisely discussed by H.-G. Beck, *Studien zur Frühgeschichte Konstantinopels*, ed. H.-G. Beck (*Studia Byzantina Monacensia*, XIV) (Munich, 1973), 1 ff.; see also *Bildlexikon*, 19 ff.

For the palaces north of the hippodrome, see now R. Naumann and H. Belting, *Die Euphemia Kirche ... in Istanbul ...* (Berlin, 1966); *Bildlexikon*, 124 ff.; R. Naumann, *Ist. M.*, XV (1965), 135 ff.; R. Krautheimer, in *Tortulae* (*R. Qu. Schr., Suppl.* 30) (Rome–Freiburg, 1966), 195 ff., the latter two regarding the banqueting hall and related ones in Constantinople and Rome. For the Myrelaion palace, see R. Naumann, *Ist. M.*, XVI (1966), 199 ff., and *Bildlexikon*, 240 ff.; for the triumphal arch of Theodosius, R. Duyuran, *Istanbul Arkeoloji Müzeleri Yilliği*, VIII (1958), 25 ff., revising the former identification as tetrapylon, and R. Naumann, *Ist. M.*, XXVI (1976), 117 ff., with a convincing reconstruction; also *Bildlexikon*, 258 ff., on forum, arch and column of Theodosius. The botanical

prototype of the 'tear drop' columns has been established by L. Koswig, *Ist. M.*, XVIII (1968), 259 ff.

73. 8. For the cisterns of Constantinople, see P. Forchheimer and J. Strzygowski, *Byzantinische Wasserbehälter in Konstantinopel* (Vienna, 1893), supplemented by A. M. Schneider, *Byzanz* (Berlin, 1938), *passim*, R. Janin, *Constantinople Byzantin* (Paris, 1964), 201 ff., and the yearly reports of N. Firatli, *Istanbul Arkeoloji Müzeleri Yilliği* (the Fildami cistern, *ibid.*, XV/XVI, 1969, 192; also E. Tülay, in *Archaeology*, XXVII, 1974, 42 ff.). For the city walls see F. Krischen, *Die Landmauer von Konstantinopel*, I (*Denkmäler antiker Architektur, Archaeologisches Instituts des Deutschen Reiches*) (Berlin, 1938); B. Meyer-Plath and A. M. Schneider, *ibid.*, II (*Denkmäler...*, VIII) (Berlin, 1943); also R. Janin, *op. cit.*, 265 ff. For the walls of Salonica, O. Tafrali, *Topographie de Thessalonique* (Paris, 1913), 30 ff., and for a revised dating, 448–50, H. Koethe, *J.D.A.I.*, XLVIII (1933), 197 ff., M. Vickers, *Istanbul Arkeoloji Müzeleri Yilliği*, XV/XVI (1969), 313 ff., and G. Gounaris, *Makedonika*, XI (1971), 312 ff.; for those at Plovdiv, L. Botoucharova, *Latomus*, XLIV (1960), 183 ff.

9. Deichmann, *Studien*, 56 ff.

74. 10. Soundings have brought to light structures of wall and mosaic pavement, small but sufficient to establish the cross plan with a total span of approximately 30 m. (100 ft) and a width of 9 m. (30 ft) for each arm. For Arculf's report and sketch-plan see Adamnanus, *De locis sanctis libri tres*, in P. Geyer, *Itinera Hierosolymitana* (*C.S.E.L.*, XXXVIII) (Vienna, 1898), 219 ff., esp. 270 ff.; H.-M. Schenke's proposal, *Z.D.P.V.*, LXXXI (1968), 159 ff., to view the arms as basilical seems unfounded.

11. The rebuilding of the Anastasis Rotunda at present under way, while unsatisfactory aesthetically, nonetheless is based in its main lines on such data as reliably provided by the finds and supplemented by descriptions and depictions supplied by visitors from the seventh to the eighteenth centuries, such as B. Amico, *Piante et imagini di Terra Santa* (Rome, 1609), reprinted with an English translation of the original text as *Plans of the Holy Land* (Jerusalem, 1953), and E. Horn, *Ichnographiae Terrae Sanctae* (1725–44), ed. H. Golubovich (Rome, 1902), and with English translation, ed. E. Hoade (Jerusalem, 1962). Thus the clumsy proportions of the column shafts, their material – pink stone – and their high dadoes with profiles and large crosses are ascertained for the original structure. The form of the fourth-century capitals is less certain, notwithstanding Horn's drawing (*op. cit.*, 69). Also, piers and columns from the outset must have carried arches, rather than an architrave; otherwise they would not reach the fourth-century level of the gallery.

The original design of the upper parts of the rotunda, on the other hand, is less certain. Eleventh-century masonry survives in the outer walls of the gallery and in the upper parts of the façade – the latter, incidentally, in recessed brickwork (see below, p. 354, and glossary). Thus the arcades of the gallery and their alternating supports may well date from that rebuilding. For the covering of the centre room we depend entirely on early pilgrims' reports and depictions such as those on the sixth- and seventh-century Monza ampullae and the seventh-century casket from the Sancta Sanctorum, now in the Vatican Museum (A. Grabar, *Les ampoules de Terre Sainte*, Paris, 1959; C. R. Morey, in *Festschrift Paul Clemen*, Bonn, 1926, 150 ff.); always keeping in mind early medieval habits of viewing a building (R. Krautheimer, *Warburg Journal*, as above, Note 5) and the possibility of later remodellings. Thus, the conical roof shown on all except the earliest views probably dates from 1048. Prior to that, the centre room was apparently surmounted by a dome, as shown on the Monza ampullae and on the Sancta Sanctorum casket. The dome may well have been wooden. The clerestory also existed in the seventh century, as witness these same depictions.

75. 12. Recent excavations (V. Corbo, *Ricerche archeologiche al Monte degli Ulivi*, Jerusalem, 1965, 93 ff.) have made obsolete the reconstruction proposed by L.-H. Vincent and F.-M. Abel, *Jérusalem nouvelle* (Paris, 1925), II, 1. Their compilation of the sources remains, of course, valid; see also Geyer, *op. cit.*, 246 ff. Reconstruction and dating of the finds still leave room for questions.

13. G. M. Fitzgerald, *Beth Shan Excavations (Publications, Palestine Section, Museum, University of Pennsylvania*, III) (Philadelphia, 1931), 18 ff. The ruins have meanwhile disappeared. An octagon church, composed of a (roofed?) centre room, ambulatory, and porches rose in the fifth century at Capernaum (Kefar-Nahum; Tell Hum) over what is believed to be the house of St Peter; see V. Corbo, *The House of St Peter at Capharnaum* (Jerusalem, 1969), and idem, *Cafarnao*, I, *Gli edifici della città (Pubblicazioni dello Studio Biblico Francescano*, XIX, 1) (Jerusalem, 1975). Another octagon church with ambulatory, albeit of late-fifth- or early-sixth-century date, has been traced at Gadara, Jordan: niches in the corners of the aisle, the nave carried by eight columns, a mosaic floor in the aisle, the whole enclosed in a square and preceded by a colonnade (U. Wagner-Lux and K. J. H. Vriezen, *Z.D.P.F.*, XC, 1980, 48 ff.; idem, *Annual Department of Antiquities Jordan*, XXIV, 1980, 157 ff.). Is it a martyrium to commemorate the miracle of the swine?

14. Vincent and Abel, *op. cit.*, II, 2, 805 ff., and R. Krautheimer, in *Arte del . . . primo millenio* (Turin, 1954), 26; but both reconstructions are hypothetical.

15. Krautheimer, *Warburg Journal (loc. cit.*, in Note 5), 1 ff.

16. Schneider, *Byzanz*, 1 ff., has both published the remnants of the church and tentatively suggested the link to the Anastasis Rotunda; see also *Bildlexikon*, 186 f., as H. Menas.

17. *Antioch on the Orontes*, I–IV, *passim* (quoted as *Antioch*, I,

II, etc.); see also G. Downey, *A History of Antioch* (Princeton, 1961).

18. *Antioch*, II, 5 ff.; Downey, *op. cit.*, 358.

76. 19. The principal sources for our knowledge of the octagon are: Eusebius, *Life of Constantine*, III, 50, and *Triakontaetirikos*, IX, 15; Malalas, *Chronographia (Bonn Corpus*, 318, 325, 429 f.); Evagrius, *Ecclesiastical History*, VI, 8 (*P.G.*, LXXXVI, 2, 2853 ff.); finally, the floor mosaic at Yakto (*Antioch*, I, 114 f.). See also W. Eltester, *Zeitschrift für neutestamentliche Wissenschaft*, XXXVI (1937), 251 ff., and Downey, *op. cit.*, 342 ff.

20. The first solution has been proposed by A. Birnbaum, *R.K.W.*, XXXVI (1913), 181 ff., the second by Wayne Dynes, *Marsyas*, XI (1964), 1 ff.; W. E. Kleinbauer, *The Aisled Tetraconch*, Ph.D. thesis (Princeton, 1967), 253 ff., proposes, unconvincingly to me, to view the structure as a tetraconch, recalling S. Lorenzo in Milan (see below, p. 80 and Note 33). The term double-shell construction was formulated by W. MacDonald, *Early Christian and Byzantine Architecture* (New York, 1962).

21. A. Grabar, *Martyrium* (Paris, 1948), I, 214 ff.

22. F. W. Deichmann, *B.Z.*, LXV (1972), 40 ff., has come forth with a sharp critique of my views regarding the links of the Golden Octagon and of other octaconch and tetraconch churches to the nearby palaces.

Mr Deichmann is justified regarding the function of the Golden Octagon as cathedral from the outset, and I have correspondingly changed my text as against previous editions of this volume. However, this does not preclude the Octagon's having stood in a special relation to the emperor and the nearby palace. The features that set off both Antioch and the H. Sophia in Constantinople against ordinary cathedrals require, after all, an explanation: the physical closeness of palace and church; the function of the latter as both bishop's cathedral and the emperor's church, where he attends public service; and the double shell central plan, rare as it is generally in Early Christian church building except in just these churches which are closely linked to palace and emperor or to the bishop's palace. To call them palace churches leads, I admit, to confusion with churches or chapels located inside the palace and reserved for the devotions of ruler and court under exclusion of the public. I shall call these palatine churches or chapels, in contrast to what I'd still like to term a 'palace church'.

77. 23. Function, names, and symbolism of reception rooms – both centrally planned and others – in Imperial Roman palaces and their link to the cult of the Emperor have been frequently discussed during the last decades, in the first place by K. Lehmann-Hartleben, *Art Bulletin*, XXVII (1945), 1 ff.; by A. Boëthius, *B.S.A.*, XLVI (1951), 25 ff.; by H. P. L'Orange, *Symbolae Osloensés*, XXVII (1952), 114 ff., and in *Studi . . . Calderini e . . . Parimbeni*, III (Milan, 1956), 593 ff.; and by E. Baldwin Smith, *The Dome* (Princeton,

1950), and *Architectural Symbolism* (Princeton, 1956). The problem of centrally-planned palace churches and of both centrally-planned and triconch reception rooms in Roman palaces has been discussed with brilliance by I. Lavin, *Art Bulletin*, XLIV (1962), 1 ff.

24. E. Dyggve, *Ravennatum Palatium Sacrum (Kgl. Danske Videnskabernes Selskab Archaeologisk Kunsthistoriske Meddedelser*, III, 2) (Copenhagen, 1941). While Dyggve was apt to over-interpret the symbolism of architectural elements or to misinterpret their function (the 'peristyle', e.g., as a 'basilica discoperta'; see below, Chapter 7, Note 30), I feel he was right in viewing the fastigium at Spalato as a glorification façade and assigning to both peristyle and rotunda ceremonial functions.

The discovery at Spalato of a flight of stairs descending from below the centre of podium and fastigium to the basement level has kindled doubts as to the function of peristyle, podium, and fastigium and their link, if any, to Imperial ceremonial. Both the rotunda and the huge hall behind have been explained as simple thoroughfares leading to the Imperial apartments, including an audience hall in one of the wings. Indeed, it is suggested that Diocletian, in retirement at Spalato, was no longer surrounded by Imperial ceremonial (N. Duval, *B.S.A.F.*, 1961, 76 ff., and *idem, Urbs*, 1961/2, 67 ff.; G. Francovich, *Il Palazzo di Teodorico*, Rome, 1971, only restates Duval's theses, though translated from the latter's scholarly and cautious argumentation into his very own bilious language). All told, though, I am not persuaded by Duval's conclusions, the more so since he himself admits the representative character of the focal grouping at Spalato. Nor can the glorifying meaning of the fastigium be denied as easily as is done by Francovich, *op. cit.*

The interpretation of architecture, Late Antique, Early Christian, or Medieval, in terms of symbolism and iconographic meaning has often overshot the mark, as witness Dyggve, *op. cit.*, E. Baldwin Smith, *Architectural Symbolism* (Princeton, 1956), and *idem, The Dome* (Princeton, 1950). However, the negative stance taken *a limine* by the critics (J. Christern, *Ist. M.*, XIII, XIV, 1963–4, 108 ff.; Francovich, *op. cit., passim*) against any attempt at interpretation seems to me barren. Buildings in antiquity, as today, did use after all a vocabulary expressive of their function and their place in a social or religious hierarchy. To deny this means closing one's eyes to an element integral to any architecture.

25. Dio Cassius, *Roman History*, LXXVI (*L.C.L.*, IX), 60. Lehmann-Hartleben, in quoting the passage (*Art Bulletin*, as quoted above, Note 23), interpreted it as referring to a full dome rather than to the half-dome of an apse, obviously an equally valid explanation.

26. Lavin, *loc. cit.*

27. See, aside from the bibliography quoted in Note 23, A. Boëthius, *Nero's Golden House* (Ann Arbor, 1960).

28. Professors Deichmann and Stettler have promised for

many years a full-scale publication of the Minerva Medica. At this point, see M. Stettler, *Jahrbuch des Römisch-Germanischen Zentralmuseums Mainz*, IV (1957), 123 ff., and J. B. Ward-Perkins, *Roman Imperial Architecture (Pelican History of Art)* (Harmondsworth, 1981), 433 ff. For previous bibliography, see E. Nash, *Pictorial Dictionary of Ancient Rome*, II (London, 1962), 127 ff.

78. 29. The main sources for the Chrysotriklinos are Constantinus Porphyrogenetos, *De caeremoniis*, II, 15 (*Bonn Corpus*, II, 560, 586) and other passages as excerpted in Richter, *Schriftquellen*, 315 ff. See also J. Ebersolt, *Le grand palais de Constantinople* (Paris, 1910), 77 ff., and H. Fichtenau, *Mitteilungen des Instituts für Österreichische Geschichtsforschung*, LIX (1951), 1 ff.

30. The definitive study prepared by the late E. Dyggve, together with H. P. L'Orange and H. Torp, awaits publication. At present, see E. Dyggve in *Studia orientalia Johanni Pedersen* (Copenhagen, 1953), 59 ff.; *idem, in Acta Congressus Madvigiani Hafniae*, MDMLIV (sic) (Copenhagen, 1958), 353 ff.; and Ward-Perkins, *op. cit.* (Note 28), 449 ff.

31. See Dyggve, *op. cit.* (1958), as quoted above. The date of the rebuilding and the mosaic decoration, *c.* 450 rather than *c.* 400, is suggested by M. Vickers, *Istanbul Arkeoloji Müzeleri Yilliği*, XV/XVI (1969), 313 ff., and *P.B.S.R.*, XXXVIII (1970), 183 ff., and accepted by W. E. Kleinbauer, *C.A.*, XXII (1972), 55 ff., and *idem, Viator*, III (1972), 27 ff. Kitzinger, *Making*, 59, inclines towards a date 'in the decades shortly before 450', while G. Gounaris, *Makedonika*, XI (1971), 311 ff., sustains the older dating. Judgement must be suspended till the publication of the Dyggve–L'Orange–Torp volume.

32. New surveys of extant and discoveries of previously unknown buildings during the decades 1950–70 permit us to gauge for the first time the importance of Milan as a prime centre of fourth- and fifth-century architecture. See the summary presentations by Verzone (1942) and A. de Capitani d'Arzago, *Architettura dei secoli quarto e quinto in Alta Italia* (Milan, *c.* 1948); G. Traversi, *Architettura paleocristiana milanese* (Milan, 1964); S. Ruffolo, *Riv. Ist. Naz. d'Archeologia e Storia dell'Arte*, XVII (1970), 5 ff.; and M. Mirabella Roberti, *XXV C.C.R.* (1978), 211 ff. See also R. Krautheimer, *Three Christian Capitals* (Berkeley, 1982), 69 ff.

81. 33. A. Calderini, G. Chierici, and C. Cecchelli, *La basilica di S. Lorenzo Maggiore in Milano* (Milan, 1951), maintain a late-fourth-century date. The dates previously suggested, such as A. de Capitani d'Arzago in *VI C.E.B. . . . Paris . . . 1948*, II, 80: 390–408, Verzone (1942) and M. Mirabella Roberti, *VIII C.A.C. . . . Barcelona . . . 1969*, 127 ff.: fifth century, or yet later ones, can safely be dismissed; see also W. E. Kleinbauer, *Arte Lombarda*, XIII (1968), 1 ff., and D. Kinney, *J.S.A.H.*, XXXIV (1972), 92 ff., suggesting the date 355–73; S. Ruffolo, *Rivista dell'Ist. Naz. Arch. e Storia dell'arte*, N. S. XVII (1970), 30 ff., and S. Lewis,

J.S.A.H., XXXII (1973), 197 ff., counter with dates around 390 and 388–95, respectively. For the proposal 'shortly before 378', see the arguments in Krautheimer, *op. cit.* (Note 32), 181 ff. The remnants of an atrium were discovered by M. Mirabella Roberti (*Studi ... Carlo Castiglioni*, Milan, 1957, 473 ff.), and discussed at length by J.-Ch. Picard, *M.E.F.R.A.*, LXXXV (1973), 691 ff. J. B. Ward Perkins (*The Italian Element in Late Roman and Medieval Architecture, Annual Italian Lecture of the British Academy*, 1947) presents a clear and brilliant analysis of the style and construction of S. Lorenzo. The volume by Calderini, Chierici, and Cecchelli, while basic as a survey, requires cautious reading and makes evident the need of further study. See now *La Basilica di San Lorenzo in Milano*, ed. G. A. Dell'Acqua (Milan, 1985).

34. Verzone (1942), 82 f., was in doubt whether to visualize the vault of the centre room as a brick dome or as a groin-vault. Ward Perkins, Calderini–Chierici–Cecchelli, and recently Kleinbauer, *Gesta*, XV (1976), 1 ff., have decided in favour of the latter. I prefer to leave the question open, but have been toying with the idea of a dome of light material – cane or hollow tubes.

35. Deichmann, *Studien*, 36. Regarding the function of S. Aquilino as a mausoleum rather than a baptistery, and its date, contemporary with S. Lorenzo, see D. Kinney, *Marsyas*, XV (1970–1), 13 ff.

36. The documentary evidence for the Ambrosian church, including the lost inscriptions, is best found in A. K. Porter, *Lombard Architecture* (New Haven, 1915 ff.), II, 632 ff., to whom the fourth-century nucleus still contained within the Romanesque building was, of course, unknown. The original structure has been uncovered under the direction of Don E. Villa, who has published his findings in a number of papers, e.g. *Arte del primo millenio* (Turin, 1954), 77 ff. Plan, function, and symbolism of the church have been discussed by S. Lewis, *Art Bulletin*, LI (1969), 205 ff., and *idem*, *J.S.A.H.*, XXVIII (1969), 83 ff. It remains in doubt whether the head piece of the church was originally provided with an apse or terminated in a straight wall. The archaeological evidence allows for the latter solution (Traversi, *op. cit.*, Note 32, 100 ff.). Lewis, *J.S.A.H.* (*op. cit.*), 89, and recently F. Tolotti, *M.E.F.R.A.*, LXXXV (1973), 713 ff., view the apse as part of the original plan. I now consider this possible. Likewise, Tolotti's interpretation of the straight wall as support for a triple arcade spanning the apse opening analogous to the arcades in the openings of the cross arms seems plausible, although it requires further proof. Also, the plan of the western portion of the nave and particularly the form of entrance and forecourt (?) are still in doubt.

82. 37. For the North Italian cross-plan churches, see F. Tolotti in *Miscellanea Giulio Belvederi* (Vatican City, 1954–5), 369 ff.; for Como, specifically, Verzone, *Arte del primo millenio*, as in previous note, 28 ff.; for S. Croce in Ravenna,

now Deichmann, *Ravenna, Kommentar*, I, 49 ff.; for S. Stefano in Verona, Verzone (1942), 20 ff. See also below, Chapter 7, Note 25.

38. The discovery of the fourth-century nucleus enclosed within the twelfth-century structure of S. Simpliciano is due to Edoardo Arslan, who has published his successive findings in *R.A.C.*, XXIII–XXIV (1947–8), 397 ff.; *Archivio Storico Lombardo*, N.S. X (1947), 5 ff.; *VII C.E.B. ... Paris ... 1952*, 15 ff.; *B.d.A.* (1958), 199 ff.; *Arte Lombarda* (1961), 149 ff. See also P. Verzone, *Arte del primo millenio*, 28 ff., and Traversi, *op. cit.* (as in Note 32), 111 ff. The thinnish walls found in front of the façade and along either flank at a distance of 7 m. from the body of the nave (Arslan, *Arte Lombarda, loc. cit.*) suggest either enveloping side chambers or corridors. Comparable rooms seem to have existed at S. Croce in Ravenna and at SS. Peter and Paul at Como. See also M. Mirabella Roberti, *VIII C.A.C. ... Barcelona ... 1969*, 127 ff.

84. 39. L. Crema, in *Frühmittelalterliche Kunst in den Alpenländern* (Olten and Lausanne, 1954), 77 ff.; Traversi, *op. cit.*, 139 ff.

40. The discovery and subsequent first excavation of S. Tecla was due to the devoted energy of the late De Capitani d'Arzago. The results were published posthumously: A. de Capitani d'Arzago, *La chiesa maggiore di Milano* (Milan, 1952). The results of the re-excavation, directed by M. Mirabella Roberti, and the reconstruction of the plan, were published by him first in *Arte Lombarda*, VIII (1963), 77 ff., and more recently, with some revisions of his original proposals, in *Atti del Congresso sul Duomo di Milano*, I (Milan, 1969), 31 ff. The eastern parts of the church and baptistery are accessible below the steps of the fourteenth-century cathedral.

85. 41. In the light of the 1960–2 excavations, the section on S. Tecla (first edition of the present volume, 58 ff.) has been thoroughly revised: the first structure *c.* 350 instead of third quarter of the century; the remodelling, *c.* 400 instead of 450; the wings divided from the outset into two colonnaded aisles; their possible reconstruction from the first as tripartite transept wings. M. Mirabella Roberti, *VIII C.A.C. ... Barcelona ... 1969*, 134, suggests a date 'if not right after 313, so at least in the second quarter of the fourth century', a bit early in my opinion, the more so in view of the discovery of a rectangular hall, presumably Christian, below the first basilica of S. Tecla. Likewise, the existence at the Lateran of a pathway leading to the chancel and the survival of this chancel type in Rome until at least the sixth century (for the former, *Corpus*, V, 43 f., for the latter, T. Mathews, *R.A.C.*, XXXVIII, 1962 [1964], 73 ff.) required revising my former view of S. Tecla's being closely linked to the Eastern coastlands. Clearly, too, the tripartite transept of S. Pietro in Vincoli in Rome (*Corpus*, III, 178 ff., esp. 224 f.) is later than that of S. Tecla. Only the latter could thus be, if at all, the fountain-head of the Greek representatives of the type; for

this problem, see also Krautheimer, *Studies*, 59 ff., esp. the postscript, p. 67.

86. 42. Kempf, as quoted above, Chapter 2, Note 26. From later reports (*Germania*, XLII, 1964, 126 ff.; *Das Münster*, XXI, 1968, 1 ff.) it would seem that Gratian's rebuilding was preceded by two earlier remodellings of the earliest chancel of 326: a long basilical chancel which already enclosed the circular memoria and a structure much like Gratian's including the huge monolithic columns. For both a date prior to 353–6 is suggested by Th. Kempf. It seems best, though, to await the final publication.

43. For the findings at St Gereon in Cologne and the reconstruction of the fourth-century building (it is mentioned as a church first at the end of the sixth century) see now J. G. Deckers, *J.A.C.*, XXV (1982), 102 ff. The archaeological evidence presented, including excavations, has established among other things the existence of a preceding memoria and of an atrium in front of the building, and supersedes all previous publications as quoted in earlier editions of this volume.

87. 44. The archaeological and documentary evidence for the late-fourth-century basilica of S. Paolo and its mid-fifth-century repair is found in N. M. Nicolai, *La basilica di S. Paolo* (Rome, 1815); P. Belloni, *La basilica ostiense* (Rome, 1854); and particularly S. Pesarini, *Studi Romani*, I (1913), 386 ff., and *Dissertazioni Pontificia Accademia di Archeologia*, XIII (1918), 195 ff.; and now *Corpus*, V, 93 ff. More than previously suspected survives of its walls. The apse and large parts of the south transept have been identified (*Corpus*, V, 122 ff.). F. W. Deichmann and A. von Tschira, *R.M.*, LIV (1939), 103 ff., have studied the capitals and bases surviving from the fourth-century church. Based on these elements and the abundant graphic and literary evidence, *Corpus*, V, 149 ff., presents a reconstruction of that basilica as first laid out and as remodelled after 441. In particular the question of the capitals, erroneously handled in previous editions of this volume, has been clarified. On the atrium, see Ch.-G. Picard, *M.E.F.R.A.*, VIII (1975), 377 ff. For the foundation by the three emperors and its context, see R. Krautheimer, *Rend. Pont. Acc.*, LIII–LIV (1981–2), 207 ff.

Of the Constantinian church only a small piece of the foundation wall of the apse was found in 1854. Otherwise the plan as suggested by Belloni and often reprinted is sheer fantasy. Nevertheless, G. Belvederi, *R.A.C.*, XXII (1946), 103 ff., has attempted, not too successfully, to reconstruct the aspect of the Constantinian building. The evidence for the mausoleum venerated as St Paul's above the high altar has been sifted by E. Kirschbaum, *The Tombs of Saint Peter and Paul* (New York, 1960), 170 ff., *Corpus*, V, 112 ff., and most recently, presenting a new hypothesis as to its original placing in the Constantinian church, F. Tolotti, *R.A.C.*, LIX (1983), 87 ff. But only an excavation – an unlikely project – could clarify the situation.

89. 45. Pesarini, *op. cit.* (1918); also L. M. Martínez-Fazio, *La Segunda Basilica de San Pablo Extramuros* (Rome, 1972); *Corpus*, V, 122 ff.

The murals in the nave were repainted about 1300 by Cavallini; see J. Garber, *Wirkungen der frühchristlichen Gemäldezyklen der alten Peters- und Pauls-Basiliken in Rom* (Berlin–Vienna, 1918), 27 f., and J. Gardner, *Zeitschrift für Kunstgeschichte* (1971), 240 ff.

46. R. Krautheimer, in *Opuscula XL, op. cit.*, and, with postscript, in Krautheimer, *Studies*, 181 ff.; for the building of S. Maria Maggiore and its date, see *Corpus*, III, 1 ff., with bibliography; for the finds underneath, F. Magi, *Il Calendario dipinto sotto S. Maria Maggiore* (*Memorie Pont. Acc.*, XI) (Vatican City, 1972). H. Geertman, 'The Builders of the Basilica Maior in Rome', *Festoen opgedragen aan A.N. Zadoks-Josephus Jitta* (Groningen, 1976), 277 ff., proposes (unconvincingly to me) reconstructing the fifth-century basilica with an ambulatory enveloping the apse.

I remain unconvinced by F. W. Deichmann's thesis, countering my own of a classical revival in Roman late-fourth- and early-fifth-century architecture, and claiming it as a mere use of spoils (F. W. Deichmann, *Die Spolien in der Spätantiken Architektur* (*Bayerische Akademie der Wissenschaften, Phil.-Hist. Kl.*, 1975, 6).

The building can be dated neither in the second century (J. P. Richter and A. C. Taylor, *The Golden Age of Classical Christian Art*, London, 1904), nor in the fourth, as proposed by P. Künzle, *R.Qu.Schr.*, LVI (1961), 1 ff., 129 ff. Technique of construction, style, and documentation preclude any date much before 432–40, the pontificate of Sixtus III, whose inscriptions mark the mosaic decoration as well, granted even that the foundation walls may have been laid as early as 420. Later changes in the structure are easily determined: the transept and the present apse were added in 1290; the aisle vaults and the coffered ceiling of the nave were inserted in 1460 and 1500 respectively. The number of windows was halved and the mosaics deprived of their original framing aediculas and flanking stucco colonnettes; the present capitals and bases date from 1734, but the original capitals were also Ionic; finally, the chapels, façade, and apse decoration which encase the original structure date from the fifteenth to the eighteenth century.

92. 47. Superseding G. B. Giovenale, *Il Battistero Lateranense* (Rome, 1930), G. Pelliccioni, *Le nuove scoperte sulle origini del Battistero Lateranense* (*Atti Pontificia Accademia Memorie*, XII) (Vatican City, 1973), has traced below the present baptistery antecedent structures: a late-second-century house; superseding it, a third-century thermae; inserted into this, prior to 312, a circular room; and replacing it, a second circular structure, allegedly Constantine's baptistery and housing the present font; while the outer octagon wall of the present structure is assigned to a mid-fourth-century rebuilding. Notwithstanding Pelliccioni's arguments, p. 84, note 2, I view the second circular wall (are

there two, anyhow?) as the foundation of the octagon wall and both as Constantinian, with the eight spurs projecting from that foundation at the corners of the octagon designed to carry columns assembled but not used, as known from *L.P.*, I, 234, by Constantine. Sixtus III (432–40), using the columns, erected the colonnaded inner octagon surmounted by the upper order and clerestory.

48. *Corpus*, IV, 199 ff., with reference to bibliography, reconstruction proposals, and tentative explanations of the unusual plan. Its origins, to me more and more, appear to be linked to the tradition of late antique secular building, primarily villa and palace design. See my recent paper, 'Success and Failure in Late Antique Church Planning', in *Age of Spirituality. Late Antiquity and Early Christianity. A Symposium. The Metropolitan Museum of Art*, ed. K. Weitzmann (New York, 1980), 121 ff. For links to the Anastasis Rotunda, which I would now consider collateral rather than primary, see my early paper, *R.A.C.*, XII (1935), 51 ff., revised with postscript in Krautheimer, *Studies*, 69 ff. Of the two suggestions for envisaging the original structure, either with inner corridors and outer narrow courtyards linking the chapels, or with inner open-air areas and outer porticoes, the latter, accepted by C. Ceschi, *S. Stefano Rotondo* (*Memorie Pontificia Accademia Romana di Archeologia*, XV, 1982), esp. 79 ff., is anew under debate. The proposal of a domed covering in light material over the centre room is due to F. W. Deichmann, *Miscellanea Giulio Belvederi* (Rome, 1955), 437 ff.

49. For S. Angelo see D. Viviani, *B.d.A.*, V (1911), 28 ff., P. Verzone, in *Arte del primo millenio* (*op. cit.*), 28 ff., and G. De Angelis d'Ossat in *C.C.R.* (1966), 105 ff.

93. 1. For the political and ecclesiastical history of the East, see G. Ostrogorsky, *History of the Byzantine State* (Oxford, 1956), *passim*. For the West, and in particular for the position of the papacy, I rely largely on E. Caspar, *Geschichte des Papsttums* (Tübingen, 1930 ff.).

94. 2. F. W. Deichmann, *Versuch einer Darstellung der Grundrisstypen des Kirchenbaues . . .*, diss. Halle-Wittenberg (Würzburg, 1937). For the architecture of the Greek East, we have the standard works of Sotiriou, *Basilikai*, and Orlandos, *Basiliki*. No comparable summary treatment exists for the other regions of the Empire, except for individual provinces, such as Syria; see below, Chapter 6, Note 1.

3. For problems and types of martyria, see always the standard work, A. Grabar, *Martyrium* (Paris, 1948); for baptisteries, see the collection of plans (with short bibliographies) presented by A. Katchatrian, *Les baptistères paléochrétiens* (Paris, 1962). No satisfactory summary deals in general terms with the impact of the liturgy on the planning of ordinary churches in the fifth century – an extraordinarily

difficult subject, as evident from its superficial treatment in C. Liesenberg, *Der Einfluss der Liturgie auf die frühchristliche Basilika* (Neustadt a.d. Haardt, 1928). Recent attempts to link liturgy and church building have been more successful by limiting the problem to clearly defined territories and periods: to the placing of the altar, see O. Nussbaum, *Der Standort des Liturgen am christlichen Altar . . .* (Bonn, 1965); to the 'exedrae' of Syrian churches, see below, Chapter 6, Note 19; to Syrian church planning in general, see A. M. Schneider, *Göttinger Nachrichten* (1949), no. 3; to the fourth to the early eighth centuries, see T. Mathews, *R.A.C.*, XXXVIII (1962, but published in 1964), 73 ff.; to Aquileia, G. Cuscito, *Aquileia Nostra*, XXXVIII (1967), 87 ff.; to Constantinople in the fifth and early sixth centuries, Mathews, *Churches*; to Greece, D. Pallas, *X C.A.C. . . . Thessaloniki . . . 1980, Reports*, 497 ff.

4. For an attempt at differentiating the three principal transept types – 'continuous' transept, tripartite transept, and cross transept – and at determining their function, see Krautheimer, *Studies*, 59 ff., esp. 67 f.

For the rarity of 'continuous' transepts in the Latin West, see also above, Chapter 2, Note 41.

5. For the siting of the diaconicon off the atrium, as in Greece, see A. K. Orlandos, *D.C.A.H.*, X (1964), 265 ff., esp. 279 ff., and Pallas, as above, Note 3; outside church, as at the H. Sophia in Constantinople, Mathews, *Churches*, 13 ff. and *passim*; in one of the side chambers flanking the apse, as in Syria, Lassus, *Sanctuaires*, 194 ff., and more recently G. Descoeudres, *Die Pastophorien im syro-byzantinischen Osten* (Wiesbaden, 1983), clarifying their locally interchangeable functions, as diaconicon, memoria or baptistery. The adaptation of these 'pastophories' (the use of the term being of late date) as *prothesis* and *diaconicon* all over the Byzantine sphere of influence dates from after Justinian (*idem, ibid., passim*).

95. 6. The orientation of Early Christian churches has been much discussed, but no common ground has been found so far. See, however, E. Weigand, *Festschrift Sebastian Merkle* (Düsseldorf, 1922), 370 ff., and E. Peterson, *Ephemerides liturgicae*, LIX (1945), 52 ff. Regarding the North African 'counter-apses' and 'counter-chancels', their dates and functions (these latter still doubtful), see N. Duval, *C.C.R.* (1970), 119 ff.; *idem, C.R.A.I.* (1969), 409 ff., esp. 419 ff.; *idem, Sbeitla et les églises africaines à deux absides*, I, *Les églises de Sbeitla* (Paris, 1971); and Y. Duval, *Loca Sanctorum Africae* (Rome, 1982).

7. Katchatrian, *op. cit.*, for the various types of baptisteries; E. Dyggve, *V C.A.C. . . . Ravenna*, 189 ff., for the function of the rooms attached to baptisteries; Krautheimer, *Studies*, 115 ff., for the links between baptisteries and mausolea; R. Staats, *Vigiliae Christianae*, XXVI (1972), 29 ff.

8. No satisfactory publication sums up the problems and the various types of monastery building in Early Christian times. A. K. Orlandos, *Monastiriaki Architektoniki* (Athens,

1926; 2nd ed., 1958), an excellent survey, is focused on Middle Byzantine monastic architecture in Greece.
96. 9. Deichmann, *op. cit.*, as above, Note 2; Mathews, *Churches, passim.*
97. 10. Grabar, *op. cit., passim.*
98. 11. Krautheimer, *Studies,* 203 ff., with bibliography and postscript.

CHAPTER 5

99. 1. The standard works on the architecture of the Greek East are quoted above, Chapter 4, Note 2. C. Delvoye, *Revue Archéologique* (1976), 143 ff., sketches presumed regional differences between Asia Minor, Constantinople, and Greece. For northern Greece and southern Yugoslavia, the catalogue part of Hoddinot, *Churches,* provides a useful summary of the finds often published in Greek or Serbo-Croat. For the church of the Acheiropoietos (formerly known as H. Paraskevi, prior to 1911 as Eski Djuma), see in addition: J. Ebersolt, H. Saladin, and M. Le Tourneau, *Les églises de Salonique* (Paris, 1916); S. Pelikanides, *Palaiochristianika Mnimeia tis Thessalonikis* (Salonica, 1949); and A. Xyngopoulos, *Makedonika,* II (1941–52), 472 ff.; Ch. Bakirtsis, *IX C.A.C. . . . Rome . . . 1975,* II, 37 ff., proposes a date 450–60 for the mosaic decoration; and M. Vickers, *Istanbul Arkeoloji Müzeleri Yilliği,* XV/XVI (1969), 313 ff., suggests on the basis of brick-stamps a convincing date *c.* 450 (R. S. Cormack, *B.S.A.,* LXIV, 1969, 51; *c.* 450–70). Orlandos, *Basiliki,* 121, figure 159, reconstructs the nave with a clerestory. W. E. Kleinbauer has begun a Corpus of early churches in Salonica. For churches and baptisteries in Greece, D. Pallas, *Les monuments paléochrétiens de Grèce découverts de 1959 à 1973* (*Sussidi allo Studio delle Antichità cristiane,* V) (Vatican City, 1977), and J. Christern, in *Propyläen Kunstgeschichte, Spätantike und frühes Christentum* (1977), 172 ff.; for northern Greece in particular, *X C.A.C. . . . Salonica . . . 1980,* passim; for Rumania, Ion Barnea, *ibid.,* VI (Vatican City, 1977).

102. 2. Chancel arrangement, altar, canopy, solea, and pulpit as employed in the Greek East in Early Christian times are discussed by Sotiriou, *Basilikai,* and Orlandos, *Basiliki, passim,* and for Constantinople, Mathews, *Churches, passim.*

-3. Despite the excellent surveys of Gregory Dix (*The Shape of the Liturgy,* London, 1945) and J. M. Hanssens (*De missa rituum orientalium, Institutiones liturgicae de ritibus orientalibus,* II, III, appendix, Rome, 1930 ff.), the development of the liturgical ritual in the eastern coastlands is far from clear. The situation in Constantinople has been clarified regarding the Lesser Entrance by J. Mateos, S.J., *La célébration de la parole dans la liturgie byzantine* (*Orientalia Christiana Analecta,* CXCI) (Rome, 1971), and regarding the procession of the species by R. G. Taft, S.J., *The Great*

Entrance (*Orientalia Christiana Analecta,* CC) (Rome, 1978); see also *idem, D.O.P.,* XXXIV/XXXV (1980–1), 45 ff., and Mathews, *Churches, passim.* It seems certain that the Lesser Entrance was originally the ceremonial entrance of the bishop into the church, and common to the entire Christian world. Not until the eighth century was it apparently assimilated into the procession of the gospel (Hanssens, *op. cit.,* II, 10 ff.). Likewise, it seems certain that as early as 400 the Eucharistic elements were ceremonially (though silently) placed on the altar by the clergy (Taft, *op. cit.* (1978), *passim*). While no procession is specifically mentioned, it is nevertheless clear that this transfer of the species to the altar anticipates the Great Entrance. Since the species were kept in the diaconicon (*skeuophylakion*) and since in the Aegean coastlands – and in Rome as well, but not in Constantinople or in Syria – this room was customarily located off the atrium or off the narthex, during the transfer the clergy must have passed through the entire length of the nave.

4. Orlandos, *Basiliki,* 235 ff., gives a summary of building materials used in the Greek East. See also below, Note 9.

103. 5. Standard works for the churches of Constantinople are, among older publications, Ebersolt and Thiers, *Églises;* Van Millingen, *Churches;* Schneider, *Byzanz;* Janin, *Églises.* More recently, see Mathews, *Churches; idem, Survey;* the excellent summaries given in *Bildlexikon;* and Chs. Delvoye, *C.C.R.,* XXIII (1976), 147 ff., presenting a useful survey on fourth- and fifth-century building in Constantinople.

6. Schneider, and Ward Perkins, as quoted above, Chapter 2, Note 27.

104. 7. Van Millingen, *Churches,* 35 ff.; Ebersolt and Thiers, *Églises,* 3 ff.; Janin, *Églises,* 444 ff.; Schneider, *Byzanz,* 76 f.; Mathews, *Churches,* 19 ff.; *idem, Survey,* 143 ff.; and *Bildlexikon,* 147 ff. The extant remnants indicate the main lines of the original building. They are supplemented by a number of Texier's drawings in the Library of the R.I.B.A. in London (Sir Banister Fletcher Collection, Texier volumes, *Constantinople,* I) and by the limited results of an excavation undertaken a century ago (*Izvestija Russko Arkeol. Inst. K.,* XIV (1909), 36; XV (1911), 250; XVI (1912), 1 f.). Mathews, *Churches,* 19 ff., presents reconstructions of atrium and bema and suggests that the galleries were entered over outside stairs flanking the narthex. A new study of the church supported by soundings is being undertaken by U. Peschlow. C. Mango, *Byzantine and Modern Greek Studies,* IV (1978), 115 ff. has suggested a date of construction prior to 454 or 453; Peschlow, based on brick-stamps, puts it back to 449/50 (*XVI C.E.B. . . . Vienna, 1982 (J.Ö.B.* XXXII/4)), 429 ff.

105. 8. Janin, *Églises,* 246 ff., sums up the historical data for the church of St Mary in the Chalkopratiae. The remnants, described briefly by Ebersolt and Thiers (*Églises,* 256) and Schneider (*Byzanz,* 56), have been explored by W. Kleiss

(*Ist. M.*, XV, 1965, 149 ff.; *ibid.*, XVI, 1966, 217 ff.; *VII C.A.C.* ... *Trier* ... *1965*, 587 ff.) and discussed by Mathews, *Churches*, 28 ff. Recalling the Studios church in nearly all respects except the octagonal niched structure on the north side (the interpretation as a baptistery seems to me still unlikely), it probably dates from the same time. Of the homonymous church in the Blachernai, only descriptions have survived, from Procopius (*Buildings*, I, iii, 21) to the fifteenth century (Ruiz González de Clavijo, *Historia del Gran Tamerlan*, 1402, ed. F. López Estrada, *Embajada a Tamorlán*, Madrid, 1943; G. Mercati, *Memorie Pont. Accad. Rom.*, I, 1923, 23 ff.; Richter, *Schrifiquellen*, 164 ff.); see also J. Ebersolt (ed. A. Grabar), *Constantinople* (Paris, 1951); Schneider, *Byzanz*, 54 ff.; Janin, *Églises*, 169 ff. Our knowledge of H. Euphemia at Chalcedon is based only on Evagrius, *Ecclesiastical History*, II, 3 (*P.G.*, LXXXVIII, 2, 2492 ff.). A small basilica of fifth-century date in the area of the Ottoman Imperial palace, Topkapi Sarayi, is known but from meagre excavation reports (Mathews, *Churches*, 33 ff.); remains of another, possibly early basilica (with tripartite transept?) have been reported from Ereğli on the south coast of the Black Sea (S. Eyice, *C.C.R.*, 1971, 318 f.).

106. 9. The masonry techniques of fifth-century Constantinople and their antecedents have been studied with similar results by Deichmann, *Studien*, 19 ff., and J. B. Ward Perkins, *Great Palace* (as quoted above, Chapter 2, Note 27), 52 ff.

10. Orlandos, *Basiliki*, *passim*, and numerous papers in *Praktika*, *Ergon*, *Archeion*, and *V C.A.C.* ... *Aix-en-Provence* ... *1954*, *passim*.

11. Church building on Cyprus is conveniently surveyed and its place within Early Christian and Byzantine architecture discussed by A. H. S. Megaw, *D.O.P.*, XXVIIII(1974), 57 ff.; a handy summary by Chs. Delvoye is found in *XV C.E.B.* ... *Athens* ... *1976*. On the Epiphanius basilica at Salamis in particular, see Megaw, *op. cit.*, 61 ff.; on another at Kourion, provided with baptistery and other extensive annexes, *idem*, *D.O.P.*, XXX (1976), 345 ff., both excavated by Mr Megaw and dated convincingly in the last decades of the fourth century. Impact from neighbouring Syria and Cilicia on pre-Justinianic Cyprus, as pointed out by Mr Megaw, is obvious. But I question that it precludes contemporaneous links to Constantinople: the existence at Salamis of galleries, attested by staircases, points certainly to Constantinian models, but it remains open whether at Jerusalem or in Constantinople.

12. J. Keil and H. Hörmann (*Forschungen in Ephesos*, IV, 3, ed. Österreichisches Archäologisches Institut, Vienna, 1951, 200 ff.) have attempted, successfully in the main, to present a reconstruction of the fifth-century church of St John. See also P. Verzone, *Rend. Pont. Acc.*, LI–LII (1978–80), 213 ff. The baptistery, much like that of St Mary, an octagon with corner niches and enveloped by an ambulatory, the whole enclosed into a square, was

incorporated into Justinian's building complex (M. Castelfranchi, *XV C.E.B.* ... *Athens* ... *1976*, II, 1981, 129).

108. 13. *Forschungen in Ephesos*, IV, 1 (Vienna, 1932), 5, 27 ff.; F. Fasolo, *Palladio*, n.s. VI (1956), 1 ff. Keil, *Forschungen*, IV, 1, without giving his reasons, suggests a date as early as 350 for the remodelling of the second-century structure into a church. F. W. Deichmann, in *Mélanges* ... *Mansel* (Ankara, 1974), 549 ff., conjecturally proposed the 'first decades of the fourth century'. Until further proof is forthcoming it might be best to withhold judgement.

14. Examples are Mastichari (Cos) (*Ergon*, 1955, 98); Didyma (T. Wiegand, ed. H. Knackfuss, *Didyma*, I, Berlin, 1941, 29 ff.); Kourion on Cyprus (A. H. S. Megaw, as quoted above, Note 11). New soundings (W. Müller-Wiener, *Ist. M.*, XXIII/XXIV, 1973/4, 131 ff.; O. Feld, *ibid.*, 135 ff.) have brought to light at Miletus the 'Great Church', *c.* 500, the aisles surmounted by galleries, and its annexes: atrium, baptistery, the end of the south aisle, a niched mausoleum. The ambulatory enveloping the apse (Th. Wiegand, *Sitzungsberichte Berliner Akademie*, 1908, 28 f.), referred to time and again (Liesenberg, as quoted above, Chapter 4, Note 3; F. W. Deichmann and A. von Tschira, *J.D.A.I.*, LXXII, 1957, 81 ff.), has turned out to be added later: when remains open so far. St Michael's basilica, close in plan but dated by an inscription 595–605 and thus a century after the 'Great Church', would seem to have been by that time the cathedral, adjoined by a sumptuous palace (Müller-Wiener, *Ist. M.*, XXVII–XXX, 1977–80, *passim*). The large domed rotunda with inner circle of columns (Wiegand, *op. cit.*, 1904, I, 87 f., and 1911, I, 229 f.), if indeed Christian, was not a baptistery, as accepted by myself in early editions of this volume; see Müller-Wiener, *Ist. M.*, XXXI (1981), 95 ff., whose plan shows no inner colonnade. For further finds O. Feld, *Ist. M.*, XXV (1975), 197 ff.

15. For example, at Eressos on Lesbos, *c.* 431 (A. K. Orlandos, *Deltion*, XIII, 1929, 29 ff.); at the Heraeon basilica on Samos (A. M. Schneider, *J.D.A.I.*, *AA.*, 1927, 399 ff.); at Arnithi on Rhodes (A. K. Orlandos, *V C.A.C.* ... *Aix-en-Provence* ... *1954*, 115). For additional finds in the Dodecanese, see *Ephemeris* (1982), *Chronika*, 1 ff.

16. Examples, apart from Mastichari, are found, e.g., at Gülbahçe near Izmir (known through G. Weber, *B.Z.*, X, 1901, 568 ff.) and at Chalinados on Lesbos (A. K. Orlandos, *Archeion*, III, 1937, 115 ff.).

17. Wiegand (*op. cit.*, 1941, as above, Note 14, 29 ff.) has suggested a reconstruction with galleries for the church which at Didyma was inserted in the Temple of Apollo after 392. But the piers with double half-columns on which this reconstruction is based were probably window piers; see above, p. 99, and U. Peschlow, *Ist. M.*, XXV (1975), 211 ff. On the other hand, such piers served, indeed, as supports in the 'Great Church' at Miletus, as above, Note 14.

18. A. K. Orlandos, *V C.A.C.* ... *Aix-en-Provence* ... *1954*, 199 ff., reports on the baptisteries found in the

Dodecanese: the one at Mastichari, and six others on Cos, five on Rhodes, e.g. at Arnithi (see also above, Note 15), and numerous others. For those along the coast of Asia Minor, see, for Miletus, Müller-Wiener, as above, Note 14, for Gülbahçe, Weber, as Note 16. Cf. also Volanaki, as below, Note 40.

19. The church ruins of Cilicia and Isauria were explored first by G. M. L. Bell and published in a series of papers in *Rev. Arch.* (1906), I and II. She was followed by S. Guyer (*B.Z.*, XXXIII, 1933, 78 ff., 313 ff.; also *Grundlagen mittelalterlicher europäischer Baukunst*, Einsiedeln, 1950, *passim*), who with E. Herzfeld published *Meriamlik und Korykos* (*Monumenta Asiae Minoris Antiqua*, II) (Manchester, 1930), and by Keil (J. Keil and A. Wilhelm, *Denkmäler aus dem Rauhen Kilikien*, *Monumenta* . . . , III, Manchester, 1931). More recent reports are due to G. Forsyth (*D.O.P.*, XI, 1957, 223 ff., and *De Artibus Opuscula XL in honor of Erwin Panofsky*, New York, 1961, 117 ff.); to M. Gough, *Anatolian Studies*, II (1952), 85 ff.; IV (1954), 49 ff.; VII (1957), 153 ff.; XXII (1972), 199 ff.; to E. Rosenbaum, G. Huber, S. Onurkan, *A Survey of Coastal Cities in Western Cilicia* (Ankara, 1967); and to O. Feld, *Ist. M.*, XIII/XVI (1963/4), 82 ff.; *R. Qu. Schr.*, LX (1965), 131 ff.; and *idem*, in J. Borchhardt and others, *Myra* (Berlin, 1971), 401 ff.; sketching standard basilicas near Myra on the coast of Lycia, with externally semicircular or three-sided apses; to S. Eyice, in *Hommages à Charles Delvoye* . . . (Brussels, 1982), 355 ff. (two basilicas at Oküzlü, near Silifke) and as below, Note 26 – to mention but a selection.

109. 20. The few hints published so far on the ruins of Side (S. Eyice, *X C.E.B.* . . . *Constantinople* . . . *1955*, 130 ff.; more recently, with plan of transept basilica, presumably cathedral, and bishop's palace, A. M. Mansel, *J.D.A.I.*, *A.A.*, 1975, 49 ff.) only whet the appetite. On the cathedral of Korykos see, aside from Bell, *Rev. Arch.* (1906), II, 7 ff., Herzfeld and Guyer, *op. cit.*, 94 ff., and with revisions, G. Forsyth, *D.O.P.*, XI (1957), 223 ff. The date given in the pavement mosaic has been read as 429–30 (Herzfeld and Guyer, *op. cit.*, 108), 533 (A. M. Schneider, as quoted by Kautzsch, *Kapitellstudien*, 93), and 629–30 (G. Downey, as quoted by Forsyth, *op. cit.*, 137, note 32). Some basilicas in Crete represent the same type: two near Chersonesos, see *Ergon* (1955), 109 f.; *ibid.* (1956), 118 f.; *ibid.* (1959), 148 ff., and one at Kera, *ibid.* (1956), 119; a third at Panormos is provided with a tripartite transept, *Praktika* (1945–8), 112 ff., a type possibly imported from Epirus (see below, p. 131.) For the buildings at Alahan Manastir, see now *Alahan* . . ., ed. Mary Gough and others, based on the work of M. Gough (Leiden, 1985), replacing the preliminary reports quoted in former editions of this volume; but see still the summary provided by M. Gough in *Bulletin of the Metropolitan Museum of Art* (1968), 455 ff. The basilica is dated convincingly to the third quarter of the fifth century. P. Verzone, *Alahan Monastir* (Turin, 1954), published prior

to cleaning, is outdated. Gough's date for the basilica, mid fifth century, seems somewhat early.

21. On Meriamlik, see Herzfeld and Guyer, *op. cit.*, 4 ff.; Kautzsch, *Kapitellstudien*, 88, on the basis of the capitals, favours a date around 480.

22. G. M. L. Bell, *Rev. Arch.* (1906), I, 407 ff.; and with revised surveys S. Eyice, *Anadolu Arastirmalari*, IV/V (1976/7), 411 ff.

110. 23. Rott, *Denkmäler*, 46 ff., still offers the only plans and illustration published so far.

24. For another basilica with galleries at Cambazli, S. Eyice, in *Zograf*, X (1979), 22 ff.

25. Herzfeld and Guyer, *op. cit.*, 110 f.; Kautzsch, *Kapitellstudien*, 89; G. Forsyth, *D.O.P.*, XI (1957), 223 ff.

26. Forsyth, as quoted above, Note 19. For the numerous other ruins extant at Kanlidivane, see G. M. L. Bell, *Rev. Arch.* (1906), I, 404 ff.

27. The church ruins of Sagalassos are still known only through the publication in Rott, *Denkmäler*, 14 ff., those at Side through Eyice, *op. cit.*.

28. See below, p. 278.

29. C. M. Kaufmann, *Die Menasstadt* (Leipzig, 1910), has to be revised. An excavation campaign directed successively by H. Schläger (*M.K.*, XIX, 1963, 114 ff.; *ibid.*, XX, 1965, 122 ff.), M. Müller-Wiener (*ibid.*, XX, 1965, 126 ff.; *ibid.*, XXI, 1966, 171 ff.; *ibid.*, XXII, 1967, 206 ff.) and P. Grossmann (*ibid.*, XXVI, 1970, 55 ff.; *ibid.*, XXXIII, 1977, 35 ff.; see also the summary provided by P. Grossmann, *C.C.R.*, 1980, 125 ff.) has clarified the succession of structures on the site: a third-century hypogaeum, presumably the saint's burial place: surmounting it a fourth-century (?) structure; this in turn replaced by a mid-fifth-century basilica; the Great Basilica further east, first with continuous transept, then remodelled as a cross transept, this presumably from the reign of Zeno – the first phase shortly before – this rather than 412, as assumed formerly, including earlier editions of this volume. Possibly under Justinian the colonnaded tetraconch and the bi-apsidal narthex were added, the former replacing the basilica over the hypogaeum; at the same time probably the huge pilgrims' court north of the Great Basilica and the hostels beyond. On other churches at Abu Mîna, including a second, if smaller, basilica ('North Basilica'), its aisles and esonarthex surmounted by galleries, and the tetraconch East Church, of mid-sixth-century(?) date, see Grossmann, as above (1977). H. Schläger, in *Christentum am Nil*, ed. K. Wessel (Recklinghausen, 1964), 158 ff., provides a summary.

112. 30. See below, p. 158.

113. 31. J. B. Ward Perkins, *Bull. Soc. d'Archéol. Copte*, XI (1943), 123 ff.; R. Goodchild, *Kyrene und Apollonia* (Zürich, 1971), 183, 187 f.

32. A. Wace, A. H. S. Megaw, T. C. Skeat, S. Shenouda, *Hermopolis Magna, Ashmunein* (Alexandria, 1959).

114. 33. V. de Bock, *Matériaux pour servir à l'archéologie* *chrétienne de l'Egypte* (St Petersburg, 1901); Somers Clarke, *Christian Antiquities in the Nile Valley* (Oxford, 1912); U. Monneret de Villard, *Les couvents de Sohag* (Milan, 1925); E. Kitzinger, *Archaeologia*, LXXVII (1938), 181 ff.; H. G. Evers and R. Romero, in *Christentum am Nil* (as Note 29), 175 ff., with new surveys of the White and Red Convents. The proposal to reconstruct the naves as unroofed *basilicae discopertae* seems to me as untenable as the one to derive the plan from that of Egyptian temples.

117. 34. Kitzinger, *op. cit.*, 191, note 4.

35. For the church complex at the grave of St Felix at Cimitile (Nola), see below, pp. 195–6, and Paulinus's descriptions in his letters (*Paulinus' Churches at Nola*, ed. R. C. Goldschmidt, Amsterdam, 1941).

36. Paulinus as quoted in previous Note.

37. See above, Notes 33 and 34.

38. A glance at Somers Clarke, *op. cit.*, or Monneret de Villard, *op. cit.*, will provide numerous examples, such as the churches at Denderah, Erment (Armant), Deir Abu Hennes, or Deir Bagarah. However, both the chronology of Christian architecture in Egypt and the successive construction phases of individual buildings require further study; see also P. Grossmann, *M.K.*, XXIV/XXV (1969), 144 ff., and XXVII (1971), 157 ff.; also his summaries, *R.L.B.K.*, I, 61 ff., *C.C.R.* (1980), 149 ff., and *Enchoria*, VIII (*Sonderband* II) (1978), 89 (135) ff.

39. Kitzinger, *op. cit.*; see also below, pp. 305–6.

118. 40. Sotiriou, *Basilikai*, Orlandos, *Basiliki*, and D. Pallas, as above, Note 1, present good surveys of the monuments of Early Christian Greece known by 1930, 1959, and 1977 respectively, supplemented by numerous papers in *Ephemeris*, *Deltion*, *D.C.A.H.*, *Epitiris*, and *Archeion*. The annual reports in *Praktika*, *Ergon*, and *B.C.H.* provide information about new finds. A general history of Early Christian architecture in Greece is still wanting, despite the brilliant beginning made by E. Kitzinger, *D.O.P.*, III (1946), 134 ff., to establish a chronology of the churches based on the development of their floor mosaics. On types and chronology of capitals, aside from Kautzsch, *Kapitellstudien*, J.-P. Sodini, *X C.A.C. ... Thessaloniki ... 1980, Reports*, 31 ff., complementing the study by O. Farioli, *C.C.R.* (1964), 133 ff. on those at Salonica. On baptisteries in Greece, as to both function and types, J. I. Volanaki, *Ta palaiochristianika baptistiria tis Ellados* (Athens, 1976).

Regarding the ecclesiastical links to Rome and Milan, see E. Caspar, *Geschichte des Papsttums* (Tübingen, 1930), I, 309 f.

41. Sotiriou, *Basilikai*, 198 ff., Orlandos, *Basiliki, passim*, both with bibliography. On the function of the numerous annexes attached to the flanks of Greek churches and their atria recently also Sodini and Kolokotsas (as above, Chapter 2, Note 17), 142 ff. The question wants further study, notwithstanding Sodini's convincing suggestions.

119. 42. The original aspect of the Ilissos basilica is as

unclear as its date. G. Sotiriou, *Ephemeris* (1919), 1 ff., assumed a date about 400 and envisaged a dome over the crossing. M. Chatzidakis, *C.A.*, V (1951), 61 ff., and following him, Orlandos, *Basiliki*, 186, incline towards reconstructing a pyramidal roof over the crossing, and a date *c.* 500. Our own dating, *c.* 400 and not after 450, has been kindly confirmed by Mr Kitzinger, based on the style of the mosaics.

43. M. Sisson, *P.B.S.R.*, XI (1929), 50 ff., has published an architectural survey of the tetraconch, but history and function long have been in doubt. J. Travlos, *Praktika* (1950), 41 ff., saw it as a lecture hall; but, notwithstanding his stress on the absence of churches inside the city before 450, he identified it as a church in *Poleodomiki Exelixis tōn Athinōn* (Athens, 1960), 139. The inscription placed in 401–2 on the entrance by the sophist Plutarch in honour of the Governor Herculios, while suggesting a pagan context for the library (E. Weigand, *B.Z.*, XXXIII (1933), 151 f., and, with new good reasons, A. Frantz, *VII C.A.C. ... Trier ... 1965*, 527 ff.) apparently does not refer to the later tetraconch where excavations, yet unpublished, have unearthed clearly ecclesiastical features.

121. 44. E. Stikas, *Praktika* (1951), 53 ff.; (1952), 73 ff.; (1954), 14 f.

45. A tripartite-transept plan occurs at the same time at Daphnousion; Sotiriou, *Basilikai*, 207 ff., with bibliography.

123. 46. Sotiriou, *Basilikai*, 19 ff. on basilica A, 111 ff. on basilica B at Nea Anchialos; see also Kautzsch, *Kapitellstudien, passim*. Excavations on the site continue and have been reported on annually by P. E. Lazaridis in *Praktika* and *Ergon*. So far they have brought to light nine basilicas, the largest and most lavish one being Gamma: replacing a fourth-century church, it was laid out along the present lines in the fifth century preceded by a colonnaded atrium and adjoined by a splendid episcopal palace, hence presumably as cathedral; remodelled before 550, it received its final shape and decoration under a bishop Peter after the mid sixth century (*Praktika*, 1978, 54 ff.). Another major Christian site under excavation is Amphipolis in northern Greece, located between Philippi and Salonica (E. Stikas, *Praktika*, 1969–82; a summary of the early findings, *idem*, *C.C.R.*, 1972, 297 ff.). The four basilicas found so far and dated by Stikas 450–60, all with galleries, elaborate atria – one, in basilica Delta, two-storeyed – and mosaic pavements are of a type known from Nea-Anchialos and Philippi (of which more anon) and developed possibly at Salonica. On the sixth-century central-plan church excavated at Amphipolis, see below, Chapter 11, Note 29. A further site in northern Greece is being excavated at Demetrias (P. Marzolff, in *Demetrias*, I, ed. V. Milojčić and D. Theucharis, Bonn, 1976, 13 ff.). Among churches come to light in southern Greece, one at Tegea in the Peloponnesus (*Archeion*, XII, 1972, 3 ff.), and another at Corinth, the Kraneion basilica (see below, Chapter 16, Note 3), stand out. On

Thasos, at Aliki, twin basilicas have been unearthed, one of early-fifth-century date, the other about 500, replacing a small chapel, possibly a memoria; both basilicas are of normal Greek type with intercolumnar parapets between nave and aisles, and galleries; see Sodini and Kolokotsas, as above Chapter 2, Note 17.

The gradual shift in the Greek churches of the diaconicon from the entrance side to the flank and finally near the apse has been discussed by A. K. Orlandos, *D.C.A.H.*, ser. IV, 4 (1964), 353 ff.

124. 47. For the cathedral at Stobi, see R. Egger, *J.Ö.A.I.*, XXIV (1929), 42 ff.; E. Kitzinger, *D.O.P.*, III (1946), 81 ff.; Hoddinot, *Churches*, 161 ff.; and, suggesting a mid-fifth-century date based on the capitals, I. Nikolajević-Stoiković, *La décoration sculptée ... en Macédoine, en Serbie, et au Monténégro* (Belgrade, 1957; in Serbian, French résumé). Reports on extensive excavations in progress (J. Wiseman and D. Mano-Zissi, *A.J.A.*, LXXV–LXXVII, 1971–3, and *idem, Journal of Field Archaeology*, I, 1974, and III–V, 1976–9; also *idem, Studies in the Antiquity of Stobi*, II, Belgrade, 1975, 15 ff.) summed up by B. Aleksandrova, *J.Ö.B.*, XXXII/4 (*XV C.E.B. ... Vienna ... 1982*), 481 ff., and P. Hemans, *VIII B.S.C. ... 1982*, 14 f., have confirmed the existence of three churches inside and a cemetery church outside town, all basilicas, of the type found in Greece. The cathedral, of mid-fifth-century date, adjoined by a quatrefoil baptistery and a bishop's palace, replaced a fourth-century basilica likewise richly appointed with pavement mosaics and wall paintings, and parapets closing the intercolumniations – the earliest known so far. The 'Central Basilica', while contrary to former belief a church rather than a synagogue (see already Kitzinger, *op. cit.*, 129 ff.), supplants a structure marked by Jewish graffiti and murals (Wiseman and Mano-Zissi, *Journal of Field Archeology*, III, 1976, 293 ff.), presumably a synagogue. For other Early Christian church buildings in Yugoslavia, such as Suvodol, Radolište, Prokuplje, and Heraclea Lyncestia, all supported by piers rather than columns, see Hoddinot, *Churches, passim*.

48. Churches of this type are numerous, too, in Bulgaria and Rumania. For the former, such as Hisar Bania (Hisarja-Hisar; Momina Banja) and others, see V. Ivanova, *I.B.A.I.*, X (1935–6), 2, 211 ff., and Académie bulgare, Institut d'Archéologie, *Serdica* (Sofia, 1964); for the latter, such as Tropaeum, Histria, Tomis, Sucidava, I. Barnea, as above, Note 1, *passim*, with bibliography.

Towers were possibly found at Bukhovo, see V. Ivanova, *V C.E.B. ... Sofia ... 1936 = I.B.A.I.*, X (1936), 253 ff.; lateral sacristies at Deli Dyška, *idem, R.i.P.* (1949), 65 ff.

125. 49. The basic monograph, G. and M. Sotiriou, *Hi basiliki tou Hagiou Dimitriou tis Thessalonikis* (Athens, 1952), presents the findings and surveys made during the rebuilding in the 1930s and 40s. The authors correctly distinguish the original parts of the structure from those rebuilt in the

seventh century. In my opinion, though, they somewhat overestimate the extent of that rebuilding. In particular, I cannot agree either with their attribution of the alternation of supports in the nave arcade to the seventh century or with their contention that the original nave arcade was composed only of columns. Indeed, unless the columns were all shifted in the seventh-century reconstruction, the rhythm of piers and columns must go back to the fifth-century plan.

As the date of construction, the Sotiriou propose, p. 246 f., the decade 460–70 instead of 412–13, as previously accepted. (In the first edition of the present volume, p. 328, note 49, I had misread their dating.) This coincides with the dating of the surviving capitals by Kautzsch, *Kapitellstudien*, 72 ff., and E. Kitzinger, *D.O.P.*, III (1946), 63. R. S. Cormack, *B.S.A.*, LXIV (1969), 17 ff., arrives at a date near the end of the fifth century, while W. E. Kleinbauer, *Byzantion*, XL (1970), 36 ff., proposes the third quarter or even the mid fifth century, the latter being the date suggested by M. Vickers, as quoted above, in this Chapter, Note 1. None of this precludes, though, that the extant church, whether dating nearer the middle or the end of the fifth century, was preceded by an earlier one, possibly the one founded by the governor Leontios in 412–13. Might not the apse excavated below the end of the present nave be a remnant of that church, rather than of a Roman structure, as suggested by the Sotiriou?

The rebuilding as it stands differs from the reconstruction proposed by the Sotiriou and on which our isometric view, illustration 79, is based.

128. 50. P. Lemerle, *Philippes et la Macédoine orientale* (Paris, 1945), with its careful surveys of Basilicas A and B (see below, pp. 253–4; also Hoddinot, *Churches*, 169 ff., 188 ff.) is supplemented by S. Pelikanides, *Ephemeris* (1955), 114 ff. (cemetery basilica, late fourth century; also Hoddinot, *Churches*, 99 ff.) and by successive reports on the octagon church published from 1958 to 1982; work is directed after Pelikanides's death by Bakirtzis. Below the sixth-century octagon an earlier octagon church has come to light, simpler in outline, but preceded by an atrium which in the sixth-century structure remained in use. Coin finds below the splendid mosaic floor of the early octagon suggest a *terminus post* shortly after 408 for that pavement (*Ergon*, 1963; *Praktika*, 1979, 97, proposes the end of the fourth century as the date of construction). Whether or not the south-east corner niche of the sixth-century church oversails a memoria of St Paul awaits further proof. The excavations also (*Praktika*, 1969 ff.) have uncovered, adjoining the octagon, the remains of a large palace, presumably the bishop's residence, thus establishing the octagon's and its predecessor's function as cathedral. For Thasos see A. K. Orlandos, *Archeion*, VII (1951), 1 ff., who assigns to the same group of cross churches the original timber-roofed church of the Katapoliani (Hekatontapyliani) on Paros (*VI C.A.C. ... Ravenna ... 1962*, 159 ff.; *Epitiris Hetairias*

Kykladikōn Meletōn, V, 1965, 19 ff.), preceding the present sixth-century structure on the same plan; for Tropaeum, Barnea (Note 1).

130. 51. A. Frolow, *Bull. Byz. Inst.*, 1 (1946), 14 ff.; J. D. Panaiatova, *Chervenata crkva pri Peruštica* (Sofia, 1956); St. Bojadžiev, *XIV C.E.B. ... Bucharest ... 1971* (Bucharest, 1976), III, 289 ff., suggesting flat roofs over the light-weight vaults of the ambulatory.

52. A. Choisy, *L'art de bâtir chez les Byzantins* (Paris, 1883), 131 f.; N. Mavrodinov, *VI C.E.B. ... Paris ... 1948*, II, 286 ff. On another tetraconch presumably of late-fifth- or early-sixth-century date, come to light near Ohrid, see V. Bitrakova Grozdanova, *Monuments paléochrétiens de la région d'Ohrid* (Ohrid, 1975), 22 ff., with reference to earlier publications; also N. Cambi, *IX C.A.C. ... Rome ... 1975*, 141 ff., esp. 155.

R. F. Hoddinot, *Bulgaria in Antiquity* (London, 1975), provides a sketch survey of building from Thracian and Roman times to the ninth century; for Peruštica, *ibid.*, 293 ff.

131. 53. Sotiriou, *Basilikai*, sums up the findings in Basilicas A and B with reference to the original excavation reports, while E. Kitzinger, *D.O.P.*, VI (1951), 83 ff., arrives at the dating we accept for Basilicas B and A, based on the chronology of the mosaics. Two more basilicas have been found meanwhile; see *Ergon* (1956), (1959), (1961), (1962); and D. Pallas, in *R.A.C.*, XXXV (1959), 197 ff.

54. Preliminary reports have been published successively by the excavator, D. Pallas, in *Ergon* from 1956 to 1961, in *Praktika* from 1956 to 1965; *Ergon* (1961), 141 ff., gives a final plan of the complex of buildings including the baptistery and a tetraconch martyrium (?), and the date 450–60 for the church, 518–27 for the atrium – correctly I think, instead of the sixth-century date previously assigned to the entire complex.

CHAPTER 6

135. 1. The inland architecture of the Near East is comparatively well known. Syria in particular has been extensively treated in numerous publications: C. J. M. de Vogüé, *La Syrie centrale* (Paris, 1865 f.); H. C. Butler, *Architecture and other arts, Part II of the Publications of an American Archeological Expedition to Syria, 1899–1900* (New York, 1903); *idem, Publications of the Princeton Archeological Expeditions to Syria in 1904–05 and 1909, Part II, Architecture, sections A and B* (Leyden, 1910 ff.); *idem* (ed. E. Baldwin Smith), *Early Churches in Syria* (Princeton, 1929); J. Lassus, *Sanctuaires chrétiens de Syrie* (Paris, 1947); and, briefly outlining regional differences within Syria, F. W. Deichmann, *C.C.R.*, XXI (1974), 151 ff. The admirably broad picture of secular and ecclesiastical building in the economic and cultural context of northern Syria provided

by Tchalenko, *Villages*, is now supplemented by the two volumes published by the Institut Français d'Archéologie du Prochain Orient, *Documents d'Archéologie, La Syrie du Nord...*, I, *Églises de village de la Syrie du Nord, Album*, ed. E. Bacache (Paris, 1980), and *idem, Planches*, the former containing photographs, the latter architectural drawings done over the years by Tchalenko. For the side chambers flanking the apse of Syrian churches and their locally and chronologically changing functions, see Descoeudres, as above, Chapter 4, Note 5.

The monuments of Asia Minor have been published by J. Strzygowski, *Kleinasien* (Leipzig, 1904); H. Rott, *Kleinasiatische Denkmäler* (Leipzig, 1908); W. M. Ramsay and G. L. Bell, *The Thousand and One Churches* (London, 1909); and S. Guyer, *Grundlagen mittelalterlicher abendländischer Baukunst* (Einsiedeln–Zürich–Cologne, [1950]). All are out of date, and both Strzygowski's and Guyer's are loaded in favour of pet theories; but even they, not to mention the splendid factual reports of Rott and Bell, provide material since lost. For more up-to-date information, see M. Restlé, *Studien zur frühbyzantinischen Architektur Kappadokiens* (Vienna, 1979) and numerous papers in *Anatolian Studies, B.Z., Ist. M.*, and elsewhere to be quoted.

For Palestine, see Crowfoot, *Early Churches in Palestine* (London, 1941), numerous papers in *Q.D.A.P., P.E.F.Q.St., Z.D.P.V., Oriens Christianus, Israel Exploration Journal*, and the summaries in Ovadiah, *Corpus (op. cit.*, Chapter 2, Note 42), and Supplements in *Levant*, XIII (1981), 200 ff.; and XIV (1982), 122 ff.

For a view opposite to my own regarding the place of the inlands of the Near East within the overall framework of Early Christian architecture, see F. W. Deichmann, *B.Z.*, LXV (1972), 102 ff., but also my reply, *ibid.*, 441 ff., his answer, *ibid.* 448 ff. and a further attack, *idem, Rom, Ravenna*, 699 ff. I refuse to spend my last years arguing.

2. Lassus, *Sanctuaires*, 262 ff.; and Tchalenko, *Villages, passim*, for the village organization in general, and for a list of village masons.

3. The letter is published, for instance, in *P.G.*, XLVI, 1093 ff. (in English, Mango, *Documents*, 26 f.); for its interpretation see Strzygowski, *op. cit.*, 71 ff., and A. Birnbaum, *R.K.W.*, XXXVI (1913), 181 ff. Restlé's analysis (*Studien*, as Note 1, 75 ff.) seems to me misunderstood.

137. 4. Strzygowski, *op. cit., passim*; Guyer, *op. cit.* (Note 1).

5. Guyer, *op. cit., passim*, and *idem, Zeitschrift für Schweizerische Archäologie und Kunstgeschichte*, VII (1945), 73 ff., with regard to cross churches. H. Schaefer, *Art Bulletin*, XXVII (1945), 85 ff. has discussed the possibilities of origins of the Romanesque twin-tower façade. The entire question has been brilliantly posed by E. Weigand, *B.Z.*, XXVII (1927), 149 ff. in a critique of its superficial treatment by H. W. Beyer, *Der syrische Kirchenbau* (Berlin, 1925).

6. Tchalenko, *Villages*, I, 55 ff.

7. For the houses, villas, and their mosaic floors, see *Antioch*, I, II, and III, *passim*.

138. 8. *Antioch*, III, 35 ff. For Antioch–Ma'chouka see Lassus, *Sanctuaires*, 229 f. and plate XLI, 2. Other basilicas are found at Ba'albek (Th. Wiegand, *Baalbek*, II, Berlin–Leipzig, 1923, 130 ff.) and Palmyra (Lassus, *op. cit.*, 168).

139. 9. An octagon, less provincialized than St George at Izra, has come to light at Gadara (Umm Qes) in Jordan (U. Wagner-Lux and K. J. H. Vriezed, *Z.D.P.V.*, XCVI, 1980, 48 ff.). For the Syrian tetraconchs and their function as cathedrals, Kleinbauer, *D.O.P.*, XXVII (1973), 89 ff.; his tentative suggestion of the Golden Octagon at Antioch's having been a tetraconch rather than an octaconch leaves me unconvinced. For the individual tetraconchs listed, see his abundant bibliographical notes, to be supplemented by publications of more recent date: J.-Ch. Balty, in *Apamée de Syrie, Actes du Colloque . . . 1972* (Brussels, 1972), 187 ff., presenting a complete plan of tetraconch, atrium (leading to the right-hand conch), and appended buildings (bishop's palace?) and quoting an inscription of 533, possibly referring to a rebuilding (also, *idem*, in *Mélanges . . . Paul Collart*, Lausanne, 1976, 31 ff.); for Bosra, reporting on a survey under way, S. Cerulli, *Felix Ravenna* (1975), 163 ff. (masonry dome suggested rather than pyramidal truss roof), and G. Gualandi, *C.C.R.*, XXIII (1976), 257 ff. (houses, still in fifth-century use below cathedral; study of Roman city and of location of churches comparing Gerasa and Apamea). A tetraconch church with a baptistery attached has come to light east of the basilica at Abu Mîna, Egypt, possibly (like the church and the tetraconch in front) late-fifth-century (Grossmann, *M.K.*, XXVI, 1979, 35 ff., and *ibid.*, XXXVI, 1980, 220 ff.).

Whether or not the huge church of the Virgin at Amida (Diyarbekr; G. L. Bell in M. van Berchem and J. Strzygowski, *Amida*, Heidelberg, 1910, 192 ff.; Kleinbauer, *op. cit.*, 104 ff.) was a tetraconch, with circular ambulatory, so far remains as uncertain as its date.

10. Butler, *Churches*, 124 ff., and Lassus, *Sanctuaires*, 142. The church may well be a provincialized variant on a building type such as the octagon at Gadara, above, Chapter 3, Note 13.

140. 11. Tchalenko, *Villages*, 21 ff., 383 ff.; Butler, *Architecture, passim*, and *P.E., passim*; also A. M. Schneider, *Göttinger Nachrichten* (1949), no. 3, 57 f. Entire villages with similar characteristics survive in ruins, e.g. at Qirqbīze and Behyo; see Tchalenko, *Villages*, 339 ff., and plates C ff.

12. Butler, *Churches*, 49 f. (Kseidjbe-Ksedjbeh, Dar Qita); 85 ff. (Umm-il-Kutten, Umm-es-Surab, Id-Deir, Qasr el Benât); 93 ff. (Deir Termānin, Qal'at Si'man, Deir Siman); Lassus, *Sanctuaires*, 264 ff.; and Tchalenko, *Villages, passim*.

141. 13. S. Corbett, *P.B.S.R.*, XXV (1957), 39 ff.

14. Butler, *Churches*, 47, on Umm-es-Surab; Tchalenko, *Villages*, 32, note 1 and plate XII, the only source for El Bāra; Lassus, *Sanctuaires*, 67 f., goes perhaps too far in assuming

that in a great number of churches galleries were projected but not executed.

15. For example, in the double church at Umm-el-Jemal, at Brād, Banaqfur, Kfêr (Djebel el A'la), and frequently elsewhere (Butler, *Churches*, 74 ff.).

16. Lassus, *Sanctuaires*, 25 ff.; Tchalenko, *Villages*, 17 f.

17. Lassus, *Sanctuaires*, 95 f. and *passim*.

18. Butler, *Churches*, 33 f. (Fafertin); 49 f. (Kseidjbe-Ksedjbeh); 32 f. (Kharab Shems); 50 ff. (Dar Qita). See also Lassus, *Sanctuaires, passim*.

142. 19. The exedrae of the Syrian churches were first discussed by A. M. Schneider, *Göttinger Nachrichten* (1949), no. 31, 59 ff., and at greater length by J. Lassus and G. Tchalenko, *C.A.*, V (1951), 75 ff.; see also Lassus, *Sanctuaires*, 207 ff.; Tchalenko, *Villages, passim*; and, cautioning as to possible differences in the liturgical function of the bema in northern, eastern, and western Syria, R. F. Taft, *Orientalia Christiana Periodica*, XXXIV (1968), 326 ff., with older bibliography.

20. Schneider, *op. cit.*; Lassus, *Sanctuaires*, 186 ff.; Taft, *op. cit.* R. Bernheimer, *A.J.A.*, XLIII (1939), 647 ff., and H. Glück, *Der Breit- und Langhausbau in Syrien* (*Zeitschrift für Geschichte der Architekur, Beiheft*, XIV) (Heidelberg, 1916), link the lateral entrances of Syrian churches to transverse temple plans customary a thousand years before in the Ancient Near East – a far-fetched hypothesis.

21. The complex question of the changing function and place of the pastophories – that is, prothesis and diaconicon – in Syria has been explored by Lassus, *Sanctuaires*, 162 ff., 194 ff., by G. Bandmann, in *Kunstgeschichtliche Studien für Hans Kauffmann* (Berlin, 1956), 19 ff., and most recently and convincingly by Descoeudres, as above, Chapter 4, Note 5. The link with the tripartite sanctuaries of Syrian temples was first pointed out by H. C. Butler, in *Studien zur Kunst des Ostens* [for] *Joseph Strzygowski* (Vienna and Hellerau, 1923), 9 ff.

143. 22. Butler, *Churches*, 49 ff.; Lassus, *Sanctuaires, passim*, in particular, 290 ff.; Schneider, as quoted above, Note 11; Tchalenko, *Villages, passim*. A complex of two churches and a baptistery, dated 483–7 by inscriptions in the mosaic pavements, has come to light over the past few years at Huarte near Apamea in Central Syria (P. and M.-T. Canivet, *R.A.C.*, LVI, 1980, 147 ff.); parapets in the intercolumniations reflect influences from the coastlands – rare in Syria. Likewise significant are the finds of decorative mural paintings and of fragments of an apse mosaic (P. Canivet, *Rayonnement grec. Hommages à Charles Delvoye*, Brussels, 1982, 313 ff.) in the South Church.

23. Lassus, *Sanctuaires*, 162 ff., assigns this role to the south room, but points out the frequency of exceptions, in my count, nearly half. See also Descoeudres, *op. cit.*

144. 24. Butler, *Churches*, 151 ff., 207 ff.; Lassus, *Sanctuaires*, 217 ff., and *passim*; A. Katchatrian, *Les baptistères paléochrétiens* (Paris, 1962), *passim*; J. Emminghaus, in

Tortulae (R. Qu. Schr., Suppl. 30) (Rome–Freiburg, 1966), 82 ff.

25. Tchalenko, *Villages*, 159 ff., 208 ff., 235 f. For Qasr el Benât, also Butler, *Churches*, 93 ff., and P. Verzone, *C.C.R.*, XXI (1974), 249 ff.

145. 26. De Vogüé, *Syrie centrale*, 141 ff. and plates 139 ff.; Butler, *Churches*, 97 ff.; Lassus, *Sanctuaires*, 129 ff.; and Tchalenko, *Villages*, 223 ff., with detailed description, convincing dating, roughly 476 to 491, and the evidence pointing to Zeno's having initiated and supported construction. While De Vogüé, Butler, and still S. Guyer, *J.D.A.I.*, XLIX (1934), 90 ff., assumed the central octagon to have been an open-air area, D. Krencker (*J.D.A.I.*, XLIX, 1934, 62 ff., and *Forschungen und Fortschritte*, XV, 1939, 32) envisaged it with a wooden dome; Lassus, *Sanctuaires*, 135, assumes that a dome was planned, but not executed. Tchalenko, *op. cit.*, 268 ff., proposes a double-shell plan, the centre room higher and resting on an interior ring of supports; but so far no traces of such inner supports have been found. K. J. Conant, *A Brief Commentary on Early Medieval Church Architecture* (Baltimore, 1942), plate II, reconstructs a pyramidal roof spanning the width of the octagon – to my mind still a plausible solution. Whatever the covering, it collapsed in 528, turning the octagon into an open courtyard: an arrangement copied on smaller scale in the sanctuary of Simeon Stylites the Younger on Mont Admirable around 551; see W. Djoubadze, *Ist. M.*, XV (1965), 218 ff. Major repairs, including the construction of a fortress at Qal'at Si'man, were undertaken in 965 and 979, the latter by Basil II after the reconquest of the region from the Moslems (Tchalenko, *Villages*, 242 and note 4). The plan of the church as given by De Vogüé is incorrect in that it disregards the deviation of the east arm from the perpendicular (see Lassus, *Sanctuaires*, figure 46, and Deichmann, *B.Z.*, LXV, 1972, 112). Nonetheless, we reproduce it as our illustration 100, since it is the only plan to show the church not isolated but within the overall complex.

J.-L. Biscop and J.-P. Sodini, *C.R.A.I.* (1983), 335 ff., based on a new survey of the Qal'at Si'man octagon, propose, convincingly to me, a reconstruction with a drum lower than the one envisaged by Krencker and Conant (our illustration 102) and with windows, each 8 m. (26 ft) in diameter, only in its diagonal sides.

151. 27. For Mont Admirable, see Lassus, *Sanctuaires*, 133 ff.; for the 'cathedral' group, see Butler, *Churches*, 130 (Turmanin, entirely destroyed as early as 1900); 71 ff. (Qalb Lozeh; also P. Cuneo, *C.C.R.*, XXI, 1974, 115 ff.); 158 (Kerratin); 158 ff. (El-Anderin, now completely destroyed); 147 ff. (Ruwêha). See also Lassus, *Sanctuaires*, and Tchalenko, *Villages*, *passim*. For the ornamentation of Qalb Lozeh and Qal'at Si'man, see following note. Church A at R'safah, first published by H. Spanner and S. Guyer, *Rusafah* (Berlin, 1926), and then erroneously identified as the cathedral, has been newly studied in the course of a

large-scale exploration of the city started by the late J. Kollwitz. See his preliminary reports of over a quarter of a century ago, in *Neue Deutsche Ausgrabungen im Mittelmeergebiet und im Vorderen Orient* (Berlin, 1959), 45 ff.; *J.D.A.I.*, *A.A.* (1957), 88 ff.; and *ibid.* (1963), 328 ff., which deal with basilicas A and B, with the tetraconch church, apparently the cathedral, and the north gate in the city wall. On that wall, see now W. Karnapp, *Die Stadtmauer von Resafa* (Berlin, 1976); its attribution to Justinian's reign (Procopius, *Buildings, L.C.L.*, VI, as quoted below, Chapter 9, Note 1, II.ix, 3 ff.) is questioned by R. M. Harrison, *The Classical Review*, XXXIV (1984), 105 f., who considers a date in the reign of Anastasius I (491–518) possible. Tchalenko, *Villages*, 349, note 5, dates Qalb Lozeh prior to Qal'at Si'man, and perhaps as early as 450 (see also F. W. Deichmann, as quoted in the following note) as against Cuneo's dating (as quoted) of 475–90. The earlier date is correct and I have correspondingly revised my text.

A fort is being excavated at Dibi Faraj in northern Syria overlooking the Euphrates, dated by inscriptions, one church perhaps as early as 345/6, the other 429, both with mosaic floors; R. P. Harper, *D.O.P.*, XXVII (1975), 319 ff.

155. 28. F. W. Deichmann, *Qalb Lôze und Qalat Sim'an ...* (Bayrische Akademie der Wissenschaften, Phil.-hist. Kl., Sitzungsberichte, 1982, 6), brings out the increasingly rich character and the development of architectural ornamentation in Syrian church building. Stressing the liturgically prominent parts, this movement confined to northern Syria is presented as reaching its first full statement at Qalb Lozeh c. 450, its peak at Qal'at Si'man. The lost architecture of the cities, such as Antioch, may have been the fountainhead. See also C. Strube, *J.A.C.*, XX (1977), 181 ff. For Qasr Ibn Wardan, see below, p. 248.

29. Tchalenko, *Villages*, 31 ff., points out that twin-tower façades occur only in what appear to be pilgrimage churches, suggesting that the essential feature is not the towers, but the loggia in between where relics may have been exhibited. For towers flanking the apse, *ibid.*, 31, note 5. See also above, Note 5.

30. The double arches below the nave arcades are apparently a later insertion; their date remains undetermined, but is probably not much later than the completion of the original building. The reconstruction of diaphragm arches across the nave, as proposed by Butler, *Churches*, 162 and accepted by myself in the first edition of the present volume, p. 115, is erroneous.

156. 31. S. Pelikanides (*Makedonika*, II, 1951–2, 167 ff.), following Kautzsch, *Kapitellstudien*, 140 ff., has made an attempt at listing the capitals with wind-blown foliage and at tracing their origin to the second and third century. But their place of origin – whether the coastal cities of Asia Minor, Syria, or, as Kautzsch suggests, Constantinople and Salonica – remains in doubt.

32. E. Baldwin Smith, *Architectural Symbolism* (Princeton, 1956).

33. E. Kantorowicz, *Art Bulletin*, XXVI (1944), 221 ff. G. Jeremias, *Die Holztür der Basilika S. Sabina* (Tübingen, 1980), 96, views the personage as the donor. In that case, the thesis of Imperial symbolism collapses.

34. For Palestine, see L.-H. Vincent and F.-M. Abel, *Jérusalem nouvelle*, II, 1–4 (Paris, 1925 ff.), 19 ff.; A. M. Schneider, *Antiquity*, XII (1938), 172 ff.; R. W. Hamilton, *P.E.F.Q.St.*, LXXIV (1952), 83 ff.

35. A. M. Schneider, *Z.D.P.V.*, LXVIII (1944–51), 211 ff.; Ovadiah, *Corpus*, 140 ff.

158. 36. The church is described by Mark the Deacon, *Life of Porphyry of Gaza*, chapter 75, transl. G. F. Hill (Oxford, 1913), 85 ff.

37. J. W. Crowfoot, in C. H. Kraeling (ed.), *Gerasa* (New Haven, 1938), 256 ff.; Ovadiah, *Corpus*, 77 f.

38. Vincent and Abel, *op. cit.*, II, 745 ff.

39. Evron, see M. Avi-Yonah, *Israel Exploration Journal*, II (1952), 143, and Ovadiah, *Corpus*, 67 ff.; Shavei Zion, M. W. Prausnitz, *Excavations at Shavei Zion* (Rome, 1967); Ramat Rahel, P. Testini in Y. Aharoni, *Excavations at Ramat Rahel . . . 1959 and 1960* (Rome, 1962), 73 ff., and, with final plan, *idem, Excavations . . . 1961 and 1962* (Rome, 1964), 101 ff.; Mamshit (Kurnub), newly cleared and systematically excavated since 1966, A. Negev, *Raggi*, VII (1967), 67 ff., and *idem, Revue Biblique*, LXXXVIII (1974), 400 ff.; the East Church, a comparatively large basilica, apse and side chambers (with reliquaries in one, hence *memoria*) enclosed in flat rear wall, is dated by coin finds in the second half of the fourth century. The final publication is eagerly awaited. For Madaba, see U. Luz, *Z.D.P.V.*, LXXIII (1967), 165 ff.; Umm-es-Surab, Butler, *Churches*, 47; St Theodore, *Gerasa, op. cit.*, 219 ff.; et-Tabgha, A. M. Schneider, *Die Brotvermehrungskirche . . .* (Paderborn, 1934). The date suggested by Schneider, in the middle or second half of the fourth century, must be discarded. Schneider himself (*Oriens Christianus*, XXXIV, 1937, 59 ff.) found below the transept basilica an earlier chapel. The find of a coin of 395–408, in its foundation, provides for this chapel a *terminus ad* or *post quem* and this, together with the transept plan and the style of the mosaics, assigns the basilica a date in the late fifth or, better, the early sixth century (V. Corbo, *Liber Annuus*, XX, 1970, 370 ff.).

159. 40. E. Mader, *Altchristliche Basiliken . . . in Südjudäa* (Paderborn, 1918); A. M. Schneider, *Z.D.P.V.*, LXI (1938), 96 ff.; Ovadiah, *Corpus, passim*; and A. Negev, *Revue Biblique*, as above, Note 39. For churches in northern Jordan, closely linked to the Hauran and Central Syria, see M. Piccirillo, *Chiese e mosaici della Giordania settentrionale* (*Studium Biblicum Franciscanum, Collectio minor*, XXX) (Jerusalem, 1981).

41. For Sbeïta, now R. Rosenthal-Heginbottom, *Die Kirchen von Sobota* (Wiesbaden, 1982); for the urban layout, A Segal, *J.S.A.H.*, XLIV (1985), 317 ff.; for other churches in the Negev, H. D. Colt, *Excavations at Nessana* (London, 1962), and, based on coin finds and the chancel type, setting off a fourth- and fifth-century against a sixth-century group, A. Negev, *Revue Biblique*, as above, Note 39; for Emmaus, L. H. Vincent and F. M. Abel, *Emmaus* (Paris, 1932) (with the erroneous dating 'third century'); for Ras as-Siagha, S. Saller, *The Memorial of Moses on Mount Nebo* (Jerusalem, 1941).

42. *Gerasa (op. cit.)*, 171 ff. St Peter and Paul at Gerasa and the North Church at Sbeïta (Shivta) are nearly identical in plan and size.

161. 43. For bibliography, see above, Note 1.

162. 44. P. Verzone, *C.C.R.* (1965), 613 ff., with reference to the preliminary reports on his survey and clearing of the site. Of the four churches found, the cathedral was a basilica of the coastland type, colonnaded, with exonarthex and atrium, the apse outside polygonal – an exception on the high plateau of Phrygia (D. de Bernardis Ferrero, *C.C.R.*, 1983, 87 ff.).

45. F. W. Deichmann, *J.D.A.I., A.A.*, LIII (1938), col. 205 ff.

46. Rott, *Denkmäler, passim*; Guyer, *Grundlagen* (as quoted above, Note 1); Ramsay and Bell, *Churches, passim*; R. Lienhardt, *J.S.A.H.*, XXIV (1965), 300 ff. Of the forty-odd structures still seen by Ramsay and Bell but a few survive; see S. Eyice, *Karadağ ve Karaman* (Istanbul, 1971). J. Kollwitz, in *Tardo antico e alto medioevo . . . 1967 (Accad. Lincei, Problemi*, CV) (Rome, 1968), 315 ff., questions the existence of twin-tower façades at Binbirkilise. M. Restlé, *R.L.B.K.*, I, 690 ff., views the churches in the lower city (Madenşehir), such as nos. 1 and 15, as built from the fifth to the early eighth and restored from the ninth to eleventh centuries, those in the upper city (Değile), such as no. 32, as built in the eighth and ninth centuries. A thorough study is badly called for.

The vaulted basilica incorporated into St Nicholas at Myra has been identified by U. Peschlow, in J. Borchhardt and others, *Myra* (Berlin, 1975), 303 ff., esp. 323 f., and dated (*ibid.*, 341 f.) tentatively 'after 529'. See also below, Chapter 13, Note 3.

163. 47. Rott, *Denkmäler*, 102 ff.; N. and M. Thierry, *Nouvelles églises rupestres de Cappadoce* (Paris, 1963), 29 f.; recently, M. Restlé, *R.L.B.K.*, III (1978), 968 ff., esp. 982 ff.; *idem, Studien* (Note 1), surveying and summarizing the monuments, if incompletely, with revisions of some of my former views. These I have gratefully incorporated, while remaining critical of some of his theses; see my review, *J.A.C.*, XXIV (1981), 159 ff.

164. 48. Tomarza: Rott, *Denkmäler*, 180 ff.; S. Hill, *D.O.P.*, XXIX (1975), 149 ff.; Restlé, *Studien*, 67 ff. and *passim*. Buzluk near Persek: Rott, *op. cit.* 188 ff.; Restlé, *op. cit.*, 127

ff. and *passim*; *J.A.C.*, as above. Sivrihisar: Rott, *op. cit.*, 276 ff.; Ramsay and Bell, *Churches*, 441 ff.; Thierry, as above, 25 ff.; Restlé, *op. cit.*, 57 ff. and *passim*.
166. 49. For the octagon at Binbirkilise, see Ramsay and Bell, *Churches*, 99 ff., and J. Friedenthal, *Das kreuzförmige Oktogon* (Berlin, 1907); for Soasa, Rott, *op. cit.*, 249 ff.; Restlé, *Studien*, 80 ff. (Sivasa).
50. Rott, *Denkmäler*, 192 ff. (identifying the locality as Skupi; J. Lafontaine-Dosogne, *Byzantion*, XXXIII, 1963, 139, calls it Sari Kilise); *Enciclopedia Italiana* (vol. VIII, plate 209), photograph of flank of church, taken by Père G. de Jerphanion; S. Hill, in *Yaila, Report of the Northern Society for Anatolian Archeology*, I (1977), 16 ff. (a photograph of the interior, taken by Rott), points out similarities in ornamentation between Tomarza and other Cappadocian churches on one hand and Syria and Cilicia on the other; Restlé, *Studien*, 63 ff.

CHAPTER 7

167. 1. Discussion of Christian building in the Latin West has suffered in the past from an over-emphasis on Rome. The discovery of new sites, in Istria, Dalmatia, Milan, and Upper Italy in particular, has helped to correct this perspective.
168. 2. Thomas F. Matthews, *R.A.C.*, XXXVIII (1962 [1964]), 73 ff.
3. The lists of Imperial, papal, and other gifts presented to churches, particularly those inserted into the *Liber Pontificalis*, refer time and again to lighting fixtures, and beginning with the fifth century, to sets of curtains, evidently intended for the intercolumniations of the nave. See *L.P.*, CXLVII and *passim*; Prudentius, *Peristephanon*, XII, v, 31 ff.; Sidonius Apollinaris, II, ep. 10 (*P.L.*, LVIII, 486 ff.); Jerome, *Letters*, ep. 52 (*L.C.L.*, 214); Venantius Fortunatus, *Poems* (*P.L.*, LXXXVIII, *passim*); and numerous inscriptions (E. Diehl, *Inscriptiones Christianae Veteres Latinae*, Berlin, 1925 ff., 1756 ff.), provide some of the evidence.
4. Of the church of S. Marco in Rome, built in 336 as a parish church, only a few foundation walls and a splendid marble pavement have been found. They are sufficient to suggest the plan of a colonnaded basilica, its altar rising in the nave in front of a low platform, possibly intended for the clergy. It is uncertain whether the nave was terminated by an apse or a straight wall. See *Corpus*, II, 216 f.
5. For the Roman churches, see *Corpus, passim*; W. Buchowiecki, *Handbuch der Kirchen Roms* (Vienna, 1967 ff.), *passim*; F. W. Deichmann, *Frühchristliche Kirchen in Rom* (Basel, 1948); also, numerous monographs in the series *Le chiese di Roma illustrate*.
169. 6. *Corpus*, I, 118 ff.; E. Junyent, *Il titolo di San Clemente* (Rome, 1932); C. Cecchelli, *San Clemente* (*Chiese illustrate*, XXIV–XXV, 1930); M. Cecchelli Trinci, *R.A.C.*, L (1974),

93 ff.; and F. Guidobaldi, in *San Clemente Miscellany*, II (ed. Luke Dempsey, O.P.) (Rome, 1978), 215 ff., and separately, *idem, Il complesso archeologico di San Clemente* (Rome, 1978), the latter two revising on a number of points *Corpus*, I, 118 ff. In the sixth century, a chancel composed of marble screens with a long solea and an altar canopy was set up in the fourth-century church; the former are re-used in the upper twelfth-century church, while the columns and capitals of the altar canopy were re-used in the tomb of Cardinal Venerio in the left aisle (casts on the staircase leading into the lower church). Deichmann, *R.M.*, LVIII (1943), 153, suggests a seventh-century remodelling; I see no evidence. Nor can I agree with Mrs Cecchelli Trinci's (*op. cit.*, 110 ff.) suggestion of a sixth-century date for the atrium.
170. 7. The figures obviously fluctuate, but there seems to be a constant progression, as is evident from the following list (*Corpus, passim*):

	length	width	height
S. Clemente	35·00*	15·00	13·50
S. Vitale	45·00	14·43	13·45
SS. Giovanni e Paolo	*c.* 41·00	13·40	19·00
S. Sabina	48·00	13·50	19·00
S. Lorenzo in Lucina	43·84	13·25	+ 14·50
S. Agata dei Goti	22·60	9·80	13·00

*All figures are in metres.
171. 8. Open-arcaded façades are known as early as *c.* 313 at S. Sebastiano (*Corpus*, IV, 99 ff., esp. 124) and were common shortly before and after 400: at S. Clemente; S. Pudenziana (*Corpus*, III, 277 ff.); S. Vitale (*Corpus*, IV, 313 ff.); SS. Giovanni e Paolo (A. Prandi, *Il complesso monumentale della basilica celimontana dei SS. Giovanni e Paolo*, Vatican City, 1953); S. Pietro in Vincoli, first church (*Corpus*, III, 178 ff., esp. 216 ff.). The open façade of S. Maria Maggiore (Prandi, in *Atti I° Congres. Naz. Archeol. Crist.*) remains in doubt (*Corpus*, III, 46). Façades with doors are ascertained for S. Sabina, S. Lorenzo in Lucina, S. Stefano in Via Latina, the second church of S. Pietro in Vincoli, S. Agata dei Goti, all dating after the first third of the fifth century.
9. F. Darsy, *Santa Sabina* (Rome, 1961); *Corpus*, IV, 72 ff.
174. 10. *Corpus*, IV, 96.
11. Muñoz, *Il restauro della basilica di Santa Sabina* (Rome, 1938), 31 ff., believed the original stucco gratings of the windows to be of ninth-century date.
12. S. Pietro in Vincoli: transept of second church, *c.* 450 (*Corpus*, III, 209 ff., 325 f., 228 ff.); the first church, *c.* 400, may have had chambers projecting sideways, recalling those at the Lateran (*ibid.*, 224 f.). S. Agata dei Goti (A. Muñoz, C. Cecchelli, and C. C. F. Hülsen, *S. Agata dei Goti*, Rome, 1924; *Corpus*, I, 2 ff.; G. de Angelis d'Ossat, *Studi Ravennati*, Ravenna, 1962, 22 ff.). See also Deichmann, *Ravenna* (cf. Note 34, below), II, 1, 245 ff.

13. The surveys of the material then known in northern Italy as first collected by Verzone (1942) and A. de Capitani d'Arzago, *Architettura dei secoli quarto e quinto in Alta Italia* (Milan, c. 1948), are supplemented by the more recent publications of G. Traversi, *Architettura paleocristiana milanese* (Milan, 1964), and those of Mirabella Roberti, Villa, Crema, and Tamaro Forlati referred to in the following Notes. The monuments in southern France have been briefly summarized, with the older bibliography, by Jean Hubert, *L'art pré-Roman* (Paris, 1938).

A huge basilica with nave, aisles, and perhaps a semi-circular stilted apse (the fragment tentatively identified is too small to provide certainty), the floor carpeted throughout with mosaics, and with chancel and solea, has been excavated below the cathedral of Florence. Published so far only in preliminary form (G. Morozzi, F. Toker, J. Herrmann, *Santa Reparata. L'antica cattedrale fiorentina*, Florence, 1974; F. Toker, *Gesta*, XIV, 1975, 2, 17 ff.), this the first cathedral of Florence has been dated variously into the late fourth, the first half of the fifth, and the early sixth century; the mosaics, rather than being linked to North Africa (R. Farioli, in *III C.A.C. . . . 1972*, Udine, 1975, 373 ff.), appear to me closer to those known from the Veneto and Istria.

175. 14. For S. Ambrogio and the other buildings mentioned, see Verzone (1942) and De Capitani d'Arzago, *op. cit.*; and particularly regarding the nineteenth-century excavations at S. Ambrogio, Landriani, *La basilica ambrosiana* (Milan, 1889), and F. M. Rossi, *Cronaca dei restauri e delle scoperte . . . fatte (a) S. Ambrogio dal . . . 1857 al 1876* (Milan, 1889). P. Verzone, *III C.A.C. . . . 1972* (Trieste, 1974), 297 ff., proposes to reconstruct the church with arcades and, unconvincingly, with galleries surmounting the aisles. For Vicenza and Verona, see *La basilica dei Santi Felice e Fortunato a Vicenza*, ed. M. Mirabella Roberti, B. Tamaro Forlati, and others (Vicenza, 1982), and B. Tamaro Forlati, 'La Basilica paleocristiana di Verona', *Rend. Pont. Acc.*, XXX/XXXI (1959), 117 ff.; *idem* and others, *Il duomo di Vicenza* (Vicenza, 1956). For bibliography on the numerous twin cathedrals in upper Italy see Krautheimer, *Studies*, 161 ff. and postscript, the latter replying to the critique of A. de Capitani d'Arzago, in *Munera . . . Antonio Guissani* (1943), 188; J. Hubert, *Primo Congresso Internazionale di Studi Longobardi* (Spoleto, 1952), 167 ff.; G. Panazza, *Atti 4° Congresso Internazionale . . . sull' Alto Medioevo . . . 1967* (Spoleto, 1969), 479 ff.; D. Bullough, *P.B.S.R.*, XXXIV (1966), 82 ff.; Sodini and Kolokotsas, *op. cit.* (Chapter 2, Note 17), 260 ff. For the location of cathedrals outside the city walls, frequent in North Italy, see C. Violante and C. D. Fonseca, in *Atti del I° Congresso Internazionale di Studi medievali di Storia ed Arte . . . 1964* (Pistoia, 1965), 303 ff.

15. Martyrs' chapels in upper Italy have never been discussed as a type. For individual buildings see Verzone

(1942), *passim*, and Arslan, as quoted above, Chapter 3, Note 38. For S. Prosdocimo, see P. L. Zovatto, *R.A.C.*, XXXIV (1958), 137 ff. E. A. Arslan, *III C.A.C. . . . 1972* (Trieste, 1974), 307 ff., esp. 321 f., tentatively suggests for the chapel at S. Simpliciano an early medieval rather than a fifth-century date.

176. 16. For H. Euphemia at Chalcedon, see above, Chapter 5, Note 8; for Alaja Jaila, Rott, *Denkmäler*, 318 ff., and R. M. Harrison, *Anatolian Studies*, XII (1963), 126 ff., and XXII (1972), 187 ff.

17. F. Reggiori, *Dieci battisteri lombardi* (Rome, 1935), 435; Verzone (1942), and De Capitani d'Arzago, *op. cit.* (Note 13), *passim*; for the spread of the type, G. de Angelis d'Ossat, *Arte Lombarda*, XIV (1969), 1 ff.; for baptisteries in Provence, see Hubert, *op. cit.*, *passim*; for the Lateran baptistery, see above, Chapter 3, Note 47.

18. Mirabella Roberti, as quoted above, Chapter 3, Note 40. Because St Ambrose composed the verses inscribed in the baptistery, the structure, too, has been generally considered his. I think it more likely that it was built together with the cathedral, about 350, and only decorated by him. On number symbolism in baptisteries, above, p. 95.

19. Grado and Aquileia: G. Brusin and P. L. Zovatto, *Monumenti di Aquileia e Grado* (Padua, 1957), 174 ff., 399 ff.; Fréjus: J. Formigé in *Villes épiscopales de Provence* (Paris, 1954), 29 ff.; Aix: P.-A. Février, *ibid.*, 13 ff.; Albenga: C. Casalone, *Arte Lombarda*, VIII (1963), 103 ff.; Novara: U. Chierici, *Il battistero del duomo di Novara* (Novara, 1967); Riva S. Vitale: G. Steinmann-Brodtbeck, *Zeitschrift für Schweizerische Archäologie und Kunstgeschichte*, III (1941) 193 ff.; Arian baptistery, Ravenna: now, Deichmann, *Ravenna*, II, I, 251 ff., summing up critically and superseding the earlier bibliography, as listed in previous editions of this book.

20. S. Kostof, *The Orthodox Baptistery in Ravenna* (New Haven and London, 1965); Deichmann, *op. cit.*, I, 130 ff.; II, I, 15 ff.

177. 21. A. Khatchatrian, *Les baptistères paléochrétiens* (Paris, 1962), 63, 105. As far away as the Rhineland, the characteristic form of the Lateran font was taken over in the second half of the fifth century at Boppard: H. Eiden, in *Ausgrabungen in Deutschland* (ed. Römisch-Germanisches Zentralmuseum), I, 2 (Mainz, 1975), 80 ff.

179. 22. R. Egger, as quoted above, Chapter 2, Note 17; for Kekkut, N. Lajos, in *III C.A.C. . . . Ravenna . . . 1932*, 294 f.

23. Brusin, as quoted above, Chapter 2, Note 16; A. Gnirs, *J.Ö.A.I.*, XIX–XX (1919), 165 ff.; B. Molajoli, *La basilica eufrasiana di Parenzo* (Padua, 1943). For the 'post-Theodorian' north basilica at Aquileia and its date, see M. Mirabella Roberti, in *Studi in onore di A. Calderini e R. Paribeni*, III (Milan, 1956), 863 ff., and *idem*, in *Aquileia e l'alto Adriatico (Atti della prima settimana di Studi Aquileiesi . . . 1970)* (Udine, 1972), 153 ff.; also S. Tavano, *VIII C.A.C. . . . Barcelona . . . 1969*, 517 ff. The date of the

enlargement (whether about 350 or 400) is still under discussion. For the enlargement of the south basilica, after 452, see L. Bertacchi, *Aquileia Nostra*, XLII (1971), 15 ff.

24. The finds at Pula have been published by D. Frey, *Jahrbuch der K.K. Zentralkommission*, VIII (1914), 11 ff.; also, M. Mirabella Roberti, *R.A.C.*, XXIII (1947), 209 ff.

25. Examples are found in Carinthia at Teurnia (St Peter am Holz); at Duel near Feistritz; on the Hoischhügel, and elsewhere (Menis, *op. cit.*, *passim*); in the Tyrol at Lavant, R. Egger, in *Frühmittelalterliche Kunst in den Alpenländern* (Olten and Lausanne, 1954), 17 ff.; in upper Italy in the church of St Peter and Paul, excavated below the eleventh-century church of S. Abbondio at Como (C. Boïto, *Architettura del Medio Evo in Italia*, Milan, 1880, 14 ff.); in Dalmatia, on the island of Krk off the coast (A. Sonje, *IX C.A.C. . . . 1975*, II, 507 ff.), in Bosnia-Herzegovina at Mokro Polje, Majdan, Breza (near Sarajevo) (I. Nikolajević, *Zb. R.*, X, 1967, 87 ff., 97 ff.); in Slovenia at Vranje (P. Petru and Th. Ulbert, *Vranje pri Sevnici – Vranje bei Sevnica*, Ljubljana, 1975, 17 ff.); in Switzerland at Zurzach (H. R. Sennhauser, *St Verena und das Zurzacher Münster*, Zurzach, 1982); in Piedmont at S. Lorenzo, Aosta (C. Bonnet, *V C.A.C. . . . 1982*, 271 ff.); in the lake region north of Milan in the first church of S. Abbondio at Como, excavated a century ago (Boïto, *op. cit.*, 17 ff.) – to mention just a few. See now also S. Piussi, in *Aquileia e Ravenna*, ed. M. Mirabella Roberti (*Antichità alte-adriatiche*, XIII, Udine, 1978, 437 ff.).

26. Examples are found, e.g., at Reculver, at St Pancras and St Augustine at Canterbury, and elsewhere (H. M. and J. Taylor, *Anglo-Saxon Architecture*, Cambridge, 1965–78, *passim*).

A group of early medieval churches north of Lake Como, provided with two parallel apses, may be a late derivative of such small double churches; W. Sulzer, *Zeitschrift für Schweizerische Archäologie und Kunstgeschichte*, XXI (1961), 152 ff.

27. At this point, four of the church complexes have been fully published: the cathedral (*Forschungen in Salona*, I, Vienna, 1914); Manastirine (*idem*, II); Marusinac (*idem*, III); Kapljuč (*Recherches à Salone*, I, Copenhagen, 1920).

28. E. Dyggve, *History of Salonitan Christianity* (Oslo, 1951), *passim*, and E. Condurachi, *V C.E.B. . . . Rome . . . 1936*, II, 78 ff., have both stressed and overstressed the impact of Eastern church types on Salona. Syrians were apparently numerous in the congregation of Salona prior to and around 300; but indications of Syrian or Eastern impact on its architecture are few, unless the buttresses of the Anastasius mausoleum are counted as such (Dyggve, *Salonitan Christianity*, 8, 81 f.).

180. 29. Of the *basilica orientalis*, so far only a small-scale plan has been published by Dyggve (*op. cit.*, figure III, 12), who dates the structure to the fourth century; his proposed reconstruction of a cross transept does not seem to me to be borne out by the foundation walls, the only element

ascertained. The twin cathedral has been published in *Forschungen in Salona*, I. The reconstruction of its north building, the *basilica urbana*, as a basilica with nave, four aisles, and galleries as proposed by Gerber, *ibid.*, has been rightly refuted by his co-author Egger, *op. cit.*

181. 30. *Forschungen in Salona*, III (Vienna, 1939), 95, and Dyggve, *op. cit.*, 78 and figure IV, 23–5. The term 'basilica discoperta' is misleading. The late date of the structure at Marusinac militates against the hypothesis that it influenced the origins of Christian church building as suggested by Dyggve. The resemblance to Constantinian transept basilicas is based on a superficial similarity in plan; if anything, the Marusinac precinct derives from such transept basilicas. See also R. M. Milesović, *J.Ö.A.I.*, XLI (1954), Beiblatt, 128 ff.

31. *Forschungen in Salona*, I, 91 ff.; Dyggve, *op. cit.*, figure II, 13.

32. The first type is represented by the basilica in the south cemetery, Dyggve, *op. cit.*, IV, 28, the second by the *basilica orientalis*, *ibid.*, III, 13.

33. For the baptistery of the cathedral, see Dyggve, *V C.A.C. . . . Aix-en-Provence . . . 1954*, 189 ff.

34. C. Ricci, *Guida di Ravenna* (1876), frequently reprinted with revisions; *idem*, *Tavole storiche dei mosaici di Ravenna* (Rome, 1930); the periodical *Felix Ravenna* (1910–) are the older standard works. Much of their content has been summed up, critically sifted, and superseded by the new standard work, Deichmann, *Ravenna*, in publication since 1958. So far three volumes of text, one volume of plates, and a portfolio of plans have appeared. Volume I of the text presents all-too-short surveys of problems and a few selected monuments. Volume II, 1 and 2 (*Kommentar*), contains a superb catalogue of all the buildings surviving and their decoration. Volume II, 3, not yet published, promises a corresponding commentary to the chapters of volume I. G. de Angelis d'Ossat, *Studi Ravennati* (Ravenna, 1962), makes an (unconvincing) attempt at tracing the development of the basilicas at Ravenna based on their changing proportions. The older bibliographical references are conveniently collected by G. Bovini, *Saggio di bibliografia su Ravenna antica* (Bologna, 1968).

184. 35. Excavations are under way at S. Croce to clarify further plan and history of the church. See G. Cortesi, *C.C.R.* (1978), 47 ff., marking a portico south and burial chambers north of the nave; and Deichmann, *Ravenna*, II, 1, 49 ff., stressing the differences rather than the similarities with Ambrosius's church of the Apostles (S. Nazaro) in Milan. For the 'mausoleum of Galla Placidia', *idem*, *ibid.*, II, 1, 61 ff., doubting with good reasons the Imperial character of the sarcophagus and the mausoleum. Extensive descriptions of the mosaics, *ibid.*, 70 ff.; penetrating analysis of the decoration, Kitzinger, *Making*, 53 ff. The cathedral of Ravenna, built prior to 425 and remodelled in the ninth and twelfth centuries, was demolished in 1748. Old engravings

and descriptions (G. L. Amadesi, *La metropolitana di Ravenna*, Bologna, 1748) furnish the basis for a summary reconstruction (G. M. Zafagnani, *Felix Ravenna*, XCI, 1965, 5 ff., and XCII, 1965, 69 ff.; and now Deichmann, *Ravenna*, I, 128 f., and II, 1, 1 ff.). The nave was flanked by four aisles, the apse was enclosed in an exterior polygon. The colonnades, each with fourteen columns, carried arcades, presumably already in the first building; those extant until 1733, like the walls of the nave, decorated with stucco figures, dated from the ninth century, when the entire structure was raised to a level 1.50 m. higher. In that rebuilding the altar, enclosed by a chancel, occupied the centre of the nave, possibly repeating the arrangement in the first church. Many of these features – the four aisles, the position of the altar – appear to be residuals of Constantinian church planning, and the dedication of the cathedral to the Resurrection (Anastasis) carries an additional Constantinian overtone. On the other hand, the capitals with animal half-figures now in the Museo Arcivescovile – if indeed they come from the cathedral – would suggest a rebuilding of the nave *c.* 500.

36. Ricci, *Tavole*, fasc. VIII, 43 ff.; L. Scevola, *Felix Ravenna*, LXXXVII (1964), 5 ff.; P. Grossmann, *R.M.*, LXXI (1964), 166 ff.; Deichmann, *Ravenna*, I, 152 ff. and II, 1, 91 ff., with older bibliography. De Angelis d'Ossat, *op. cit.*, 14 ff., considered both the present plan, without narthex, and the clerestory to be of fifth-century date, while Deichmann, *op. cit.*, II, 1, 100, places the rebuilding about 600. He also stresses the decorated impost blocks in the nave, rare and mostly undated elsewhere in the first half of the fifth century.

185. 37. For S. Spirito and S. Agata, see M. Mazzotti, *Felix Ravenna*, XXIV (1957), 25 ff.; *idem*, *C.C.R.* (1967), 233 ff.; Deichmann, *Ravenna*, I, 207 f., II, 1, 245 ff., II, 2, 283 ff.

186. 38. Deichmann, *Ravenna*, I, 171 ff., and particularly II, 1, 125 ff., gives a full-scale description and analysis of sources, building, and decoration: the function as Theodoric's palace church, Arian of course; the provenance from the Proconnessos quarries of column shafts and capitals and the original mosaic decoration; the reconsecration around 561 to the Catholic rite and the concomitant insertion in the nave mosaics of the martyrs' processions; and the ninth-century construction of the annular crypt. The apse, demolished in a sixteenth-century remodelling, was rebuilt in 1950 on the old foundation (G. Bovini, *Felix Ravenna*, LIV, 1950, 14 ff.). The arcades in the sixteenth century were raised from their original level, 1·20 m. below the present floor, without damage to the mosaic decoration of the upper walls (*ibid.*, LVII, 1951, 5 ff.). Of Theodoric's mosaic decoration large parts survive: the groups of Christ and the Virgin near the apse; the palace and cityscape near the façade, save the king and his suite within the palace arcades and before the walls of Classe; the prophets between the windows; and the christological scenes above. Only the rows

of saints date from after the Byzantine conquest, when also the figures of Theodoric and his court were obliterated. However, these processions merely replace earlier similar representations. The hollow tube construction of the original apse vault and the history of the technique have been discussed by G. Bovini, *Felix Ravenna*, XXX (1960), 78 ff., and by De Angelis d'Ossat, as quoted, Note 34.

187. 39. For Algeria and Tunisia, Gsell, *Monuments*, II, and Gauckler, *Basiliques*, while antiquated, remain standard, supplemented by numerous papers in *M.E.F.R.A.*, *Bull. Arch.*, *C.R.A.I.*, and *B.S.A.F.* For the hinterland of Algeria in particular, see A. Berthier, *Les vestiges du Christianisme antique dans la Numidie Centrale* (Algiers, n.d., perhaps 1942). Reports on new discoveries have appeared in the successive volumes of *C.A.C.*, as have tentative summaries of the character and history of African church building; outstanding among them are J. Lassus, *VI C.A.C. ... Ravenna ... 1962*, 581 ff., and P.-A. Février and N. Duval, *VIII C.A.C. ... Barcelona ... 1969*, 5 ff.; P.-A. Février, *ibid.*, 299 ff.; N. Duval, *C.C.R.*, XIX (1972), 95 ff., 105 ff., and *idem*, *M.E.F.R.A.*, LXXXIV (1972, 2), 1071 ff., summing up in survey form the present status of our knowledge; and J. Lassus, *VIII C.A.C. ... Barcelona ... 1969*, 104 ff., a brilliant presentation of the known facts and the open questions. Re-exploration of some major sites is under way, see, in particular, N. Duval, *C.R.A.I.* (1968), 221 ff., (1969), 409 ff., (1971), 136 ff. (all on Haïdra; also, F. Baratte and N. Duval, *Les ruines d'Ammaedaera-Haïdra*, Tunis, 1974, with abundant bibliography); *idem*, *Les ruines de Sufetula-Sbeitla* (Tunis, 1973); N. Duval, *B.S.A.F.* (1969), 207 ff. (Bulla Regia, now Hammam Deradji); M. Fendri, *Basiliques de la Skhira* (Paris, 1961); P.-A. Février, *Fouilles de Sétif* (Paris, 1965).

In *Sbeitla et les églises africaines à deux absides* (Paris, I, 1971; II, 1973) Professor Duval presents in final form studies on the ruins of Sbeitla and on origin and function of counter-apses, counter-choirs, and counter-altars in North Africa, suggesting a date not before the fifth century (see, however, basilica and counter-apse at Cimitile-Nola, south and north of the grave of St Felix, both antedating 396; below, p. 195), and explains them as either sheltering privileged graves or martyrs' relics or serving, though not before the sixth century, a duplication of the ritual, favoured in North Africa, yet insufficiently known; vol. II contains a catalogue of all examples known in North Africa. Mme Y. Duval, *Loca Sanctorum Africae*, 2 vols. (Paris, 1982), has collected and analysed the martyrs' graves and clarified the cult of martyrs in North Africa.

As part of the Unesco excavation campaign under way in Carthage, the Bulgarian team has investigated the rotunda east of the basilica at Damous El Karita (S. Boyadjiev, *IX C.A.C. ... Rome ... 1975*, II, Vatican City, 1978, 117 ff.), attempting a graphic reconstruction and identifying the building as a baptistery; neither proposal seems to me quite convincing. Likewise at Carthage, the Canadian team has cleared the site of another 'rotunda', rather a dodecagon, the nave resting on piers; a memoria(?) of late-fourth-century date with later changes (*Cahiers des études anciennes*, XII, *Carthage IV*, ed. P. Sénay, Université du Quebec à Trois Rivières, 1980; *ibid.*, XIII, *Carthage V*, ed. P. Sénay, 1981; and *ibid.*, XV, 1983, 187 ff.). On urban planning in North Africa, see the pioneering paper by P.-A. Février, *C.A.*, XIV (1964), 1 ff. (Djémila, Sétif), and by N. Duval, in *Aufstieg und Niedergang der antiken Welt*, X.2, ed. H. Temporiki and W. Haas (Berlin and New York, 1982), 596 ff. and 633 ff. (Sbeïtla, Haïdra). The social, economic, and religious picture of Christian North Africa has been beautifully presented by W. C. Frend, *The Donatist Church* (Oxford, 1952), and with different emphasis by P. Brown, *Augustine of Hippo* (Berkeley, 1967), and by Février, *op. cit.*, *C.A.*, XIV (1964). For the Christian antiquities of Tripolitania and Cyrenaica, the two ancient provinces quoted in present-day Libya, see J. B. Ward Perkins, *Archaeologia*, XCV (1953), 1 ff.; *idem*, *VIII C.A.C.* ... *Barcelona* ... *1969*, 219 ff., with a list of churches known by that time; also, R. Goodchild, *C.C.R.* (1966), 205 ff.

40. The architectural remains, both Donatist and Catholic, of the interior are published by A. Berthier, *Les vestiges du christianisme* ... *dans la Numidie centrale* (Algiers, 1942).

190. 41. For the general characteristics, see Lassus, as quoted, Note 39; for the ornamentation, see L. Leschi, *IV C.A.C.* ... *Rome* ... *1938*, I, 145 ff.

42. The Tabarka mosaic (now at the Bardo Museum at Tunis) and its depiction of a basilica have been previously interpreted by R. Krautheimer (*Warburg Journal*, V, 1942, 1 ff.), J. B. Ward Perkins (as quoted, Note 39), and P. Lampl (*Marsyas*, IX, 1960–1, 6 ff.). Our illustration 152 is a revised version of Ward Perkins's drawing, figure 29.

191. 43. For the Melleus church (Basilica I) at Haïdra, see Duval, *Sbeitla*, 191 ff. Other examples of the standard type are selected at random: in western Algeria, Bénian (Ala Miliaria), prior to 439 (Gsell, *Monuments*, II, 175 ff.); Castiglione (*ibid.*, 187 ff.); in eastern Algeria, Announa, sixth-century (*ibid.*, 165 ff.); Henchir-el-Ateuch, c. 380–450 (*ibid.*, 170 ff.); Kherbet Guidra, prior to 444 (*ibid.*, 205 ff.); Sétif, c. 375 (P.-A. Février, as above); in Tunisia, Es Skhira, fourth-century (M. Fendri, as above) – the latter two sites with two basilicas each; in Tripolitania, two churches (1 and 3) at Sabratha; in central Numidia, a church (1) at Kherbet bou Addoufen (Kherbet bou Hadef) with its apse raised above nave level and a long chancel enclosing the altar in the nave.

44. Y. Allais, *Djémila* (Algiers, n.d.); E. F. Albertini, *III C.A.C.* ... *Ravenna* ... *1932*, 411 ff.; L. Leschi, *IV C.A.C.* ... *Rome* ... *1938*, I, 1940, 161 ff. Lassus, *VI C.A.C.* ... *Ravenna* ... *1962*, 591 ff., in agreement with P.-A. Février,

suggests that the two basilicas at Djemila are contemporary, not following each other as previous opinion had it – a thesis so far not generally accepted; see N. Duval and P.-A. Février, *VIII C.A.C.* ... *Barcelona* ... *1969*, 24 f.

193. 45. Superseding A. Ballu, *Le monastère byzantin de Tébessa* (Paris, 1897), and Gsell, *Monuments*, II, 265 ff., J. Christern, *Das frühchristliche Pilgerheiligtum von Tebessa* (Wiesbaden, 1976), convincingly establishes the contemporaneous construction of basilica, atrium, and triconch shortly before or around 400, and lists as related, with paired nave supports and galleries, *inter alia*, the South Church at Djemila, and two basilicas at Thelepte (S. Gsell, *Edifices chrétiens de Thélepte et Ammaedara*, Tunis, 1933). See also P.-A. Février, *C.C.R.*, XVII (1970), 164.

Side chambers, occasionally projected sideways into longish rectangles, are common in North Africa, but their functions remain unknown. Galleries, likewise, were common, the first perhaps being those at Orléansville (above, Chapter 2, Note 18), though perhaps not as frequent in the fourth and early fifth centuries (Djemila, South Church; Tipasa, Great Basilica), as proposed by Christern, *op. cit.*, 153 ff. and *passim*, and *idem*, *VII C.A.C.* ... *Trier* ... *1965*, 407 ff.

195. 46. The churches at Carthage, including the huge complex of buildings at Damous El Karita, while excavated nearly a century ago, still await scholarly publication. A sketchy survey by J. Vaultrin, *Revue Africaine*, LXXIII (1932), 188 ff., and LXXIV (1933), 118 ff., has been superseded by N. Duval's scholarly if preliminary study of a few selected problems, *M.E.F.R.A.*, LXXXV (1972), 1071 ff.

47. Gsell, *Monuments*, II, 247 ff.

48. The 'Christian quarter' and the church of Bône ('Annoba; Hippo) have come to light through the efforts of Admiral E. Marec (*Monuments chrétiens d'Hippone*, Paris, 1958); its identification with Augustine's cathedral has been questioned by P.-A. Février, *C.C.R.* (1972), 145 ff. See J. Lassus, *VI C.A.C.* ... *Ravenna* ... *1962*, 581 ff., and P.-A. Février, *op. cit.*, *C.A.* (1964), both of which brilliantly demonstrate the need for viewing North African churches as part and parcel of such 'Christian quarters'. For comparable groupings of cathedral and episcopal residence in Syria, see N. Duval, P.-A. Février, and J. Lassus, in *Apamée de Syrie*, *Actes du Colloque* ... *1972*, 215 ff.

49. A. Venditti, *Architettura bizantina nell'Italia meridionale*, I (Naples, 1967), has collected the material and the pertinent bibliography.

50. The letters and poems of Paulinus describing the buildings at Nola-Cimitile are found in *P.L.*, LXI, *passim*, and with English translation and commentary, in R. C. Goldschmidt, *Paulinus' Churches at Nola* (Amsterdam, 1940). G. Chierici has reported on his excavations in more or less final form in *Ambrosiana* (Milan, 1942), 315 ff., and *Atti III° Congresso di Studi sull' Alto Medioevo* ... *1956*

(Spoleto, 1959), 125 ff.; see also Venditti, *op. cit.*, 530 ff., and P. Testini, in E. Bertaux, *L'art dans l'Italie méridionale, Aggiornamento*, IV (Paris, 1978), 163 ff.

196. 51. E. H. Freshfield, *Cellae Trichorae* (London, 1913), is an uncritical compilation and outdated. By now triconch and tetraconch mausolea, martyria, and baptisteries (for these latter, see Katchatrian, *Les Baptistères paléochrétiens*, Paris, 1962, *passim*) are known in large numbers all over the *orbis Christianus*, from the Upper Adriatic coast to the Greek islands, as witness the memorial chapel at Concordia (near Aquileia) and the church of St Gabriel on Cos off the coast of Asia Minor. Still there seems to be a dense concentration of the type in Greece and North Africa and her dependencies, Spain and Sicily. For North Africa, see, along with Gsell, *Monuments*, and Gauckler, *Basiliques*, both obsolete, N. Duval and J. Cintas, *M.E.F.R.A.*, LXXXVIII (1976, 2), 853 ff., especially 897 ff., with particular emphasis on a tetraconch newly excavated at Cincari in Algeria, on the triconch adjoining the basilica at Tebessa (our illustration 156), and on another, free-standing, at Tebessa Khalia.

Regarding triconchs attached as apses to a nave, a summary of those in western North Africa is found in Duval and Cintas, *op. cit.*, 917 ff., including the one at Kherbet bou Addoufen (Kherbet bou Hadef) in Numidia (Gsell, *op. cit.*, 185; Berthier, as above, Note 39, 139) and another unknown heretofore, at Tebessa Khalia. Both have an aisleless nave, as does San Pere at Tarrasa on the Catalonian coast.

Outstanding among basilican naves terminated by trefoil apses and on a large scale are still the churches of the White and Red Monasteries in Upper Egypt (above, pp. 114 ff., illustrations 68–71). A large-scale cemetery basilica of the type has been recently excavated near Knossos on Crete and assigned to the fifth century (A. H. S. Megaw, *X C.A.C. Thessalonike, Communications*, 61 f., abstract). Yet another small-scale building of the type has been found at Concordia on the Upper Adria adjoining the fifth-century cathedral (G. Fogolari, *III N.A.C. . . . 1969*, 267 ff.). Finally, there is the church on Mount Nebo, Jordan (Ras-as-Siagha), where a fifth-century basilican nave was joined to the older triconch memoria, see above, p. 159 and Chapter 6, Note 41.

None appears to be as early as Paulinus's church; but the North African context of Early Christian South Italy, and the comparative frequency of the type in Tunisia-Algeria, suggest tentatively a North African root for the plan of Nola-Cimitile.

197. 52. See Venditti, *op. cit.*, 476 ff., and more specifically for S. Gennaro, E. Lavagnino, *B.d.A.*, ser. 2, VIII (1928/9), 145 ff., and IX (1929/30), 337 ff.; for S. Giorgio Maggiore, G. B. de Rossi, *B.A.C.*, ser. 3, V (1880), 144 ff.; B. Capasso, *Commissione municipale per la conservazione dei monumenti*

(1881); for S. Giovanni Maggiore, G. B. de Rossi, *B.A.C.*, *ibid.*, 161 ff., and *B.A.C.*, ser. 3, I (1876), 157.

198. 53. Most of the early churches of Naples still want a satisfactory examination; see also A. Venditti, in *Napoli Nobilissima*, XII (1973), 177 ff., and R. Farioli, in Bertaux, as above, Note 50, 153 ff. In S. Restituta (the basic archaeological evidence is still contained in A. Sorrentino, *B.d.A.*, III, 1909, 217 ff.) soundings have brought to light the original column bases and fragments of a mosaic pavement, 0·40 m. below present level, suggesting steeper proportions for the original nave; auxiliary structures, one possibly a *consignatorium*, have been found beyond the right flank; and the baptistery has been newly explored. See R. D. Stefano, *La cattedrale di Napoli* (Naples, 1975), esp. 141 ff.; see likewise *idem* and Strazzulo, *Napoli Nobilissima*, X (1976), 1 ff., and R. Farioli *IX C.A.C. . . . Rome . . . 1975*, II (Vatican City, 1978), 275, all with inconclusive results. Below S. Lorenzo Maggiore at Naples, too, a basilica, presumably of sixth-century date, has come to light (Rusconi, *VI C.A.C. . . . Ravenna . . . 1962*, 709 ff.; also Farioli, as above, in Bertaux, *loc. cit.*). For S. Maria in Capua Vetere see W. Johannowsky, *ibid.*, 149 ff. For Salemi, see B. Pace, *Memorie della R. Accademia dei Lincei*, ser. 5, XV (1917), fasc. 6, 469 ff.

54. The basilica of Pammachius at Porto has been published in *B.A.C.*, IV (1866), 37 ff., based on a report of Lanciani's. But only the apse and the adjoining baptistery were then excavated. The reconstruction of the building with nave, aisles, atrium, and side rooms, as given there, and repeated frequently, has no basis in fact.

199. 55. Nocera: M. Stettler, *R.A.C.*, XVII (1940), 83 ff., and Venditti, *op. cit.*, 550 ff.; Siagu (Ksar Er Zit, near Bir Bou Rekba): Gauckler, *Basiliques*, 17; Canosa: R. Moreno Cassano, *Vetera Christianorum*, V (1968), 163 ff., and D. de Bernardis Ferrari, *ibid.*, *Sezione Res Aquiliae*, III (1979), 163 ff.; Santa Severina, possibly as late as *c.* 700, P. Lojacono, *B.d.A.*, XXVIII (1934–5), 174 ff.

56. For early Christian architecture in Spain, see P. de Palol, *Arqueología cristiana de la España romana* (Madrid, 1967), 51 ff., 71 ff., with abundant older bibliography; H. Schlunk and Th. Hauschild, *Hispania Antiqua, Die Denkmäler der frühchristlichen und westgotischen Zeit* (Mainz, 1978), *passim*; and, for a separate group of churches, Th. Ulbert, *Frühchristliche Basiliken mit Doppelapsiden . . .* (Berlin, 1978), confirming the links to North Africa (S. Pedro de Alcántara, Casa Herrera, Torre de Palma, all now dated around 500); also S. Maloney, *Art History*, III (1980), 129 ff., questioning N. Duval's thesis as to the placing of an altar in the second apse; at Marialba, a large aisleless martyr's church, Th. Hauschild, *VIII C.A.C. . . . Barcelona . . . 1969*, 327 ff.; at Bobalá, R. Pita and P. de Palol, *ibid.*, 383 ff.

CHAPTER 8

201. 1. From among the many excellent books dealing with Byzantine history and civilization I would list: G. Ostrogorsky, *History of the Byzantine State* (Oxford, 1956); N. H. Baynes and H. Moss, *Byzantium* (Oxford, 1948; I quote from the paperback edition, Oxford and New York, 1961); L. Bréhier, *La civilisation byzantine* (Paris, 1950), with extraordinarily rich bibliography; R. Guerdan, *Vie, grandeur et misères de Byzance* (Paris, 1954), transl. Hartley, *Byzantium*, paperback ed. (New York, 1962); and C. Mango, *Byzantium* (London, 1980), a stimulating and informative introduction to Byzantine life and thought.

2. The best source on Justinian is still Procopius in his various works (*L.C.L.*, I–VI, ed. H. B. Dewing, and VII, ed. G. Downey). For a summary of his personality, see C. Diehl, *Justinien et la civilisation byzantine* (Paris, 1901); and more recently, Ostrogorsky, *op. cit.*, 57 ff., and J. W. Parker, *Justinian and the Later Roman Empire* (Madison, Wis., 1966).

204. 3. Mathews, *Churches*, has investigated with a critical eye the relation of architecture and liturgy, as reflected in the churches of Constantinople prior to and in the reign of Justinian. His findings and cautionings have led me to modify, at least in part, the views on Justinian's period expressed in the first edition of this book. The closing off by parapets of the nave, for instance, would seem not to have been customary in fifth- and early-sixth-century Constantinople, notwithstanding its use in centres as close to Constantinople and as important as Salonica, Philippi, and Ephesus.

CHAPTER 9

205. 1. As much as half a century ago the (incomplete) bibliography on the H. Sophia filled seven pages in E. H. Swift, *Hagia Sophia* (New York, 1940), despite its shortcomings (A. Keck, *Art Bulletin*, XXIII, 1941, 231 ff.) still the standard work in English. Outstanding among earlier publications are G. Fossati, *Aya Sofia* (London, 1852); W. Salzenberg, *Altchristliche Baudenkmäler von Constantinopel* (Berlin, 1877); W. R. Lethaby and H. Swainson, *The Church of Sancta Sophia* (London, 1894); E. M. Antoniades, *Ekphrasis tis Hagias Sōphias* (Athens, 1907 ff.); G. A. Andreades, *Kunstwissenschaftliche Forschungen*, I (1931), 33 ff.; H. Sedlmayr, *ibid.*, II (1933), 25 ff., and *B.Z.*, XXXV (1935), 38 ff., and the critique by E. Weigand, *I.B.A.I.*, x (1935), 145 ff. Good summaries with excellent illustrations are: A. M. Schneider, *Die Sophienkirche in Konstantinopel* (Berlin, 1939); H. Kähler, *Hagia Sophia* (New York and Washington, 1967); Mango, *Architettura bizantina*, 107 ff.; *Bildlexikon*, 84 ff.; and Mathews, *Survey*, 262 ff. Of Robert Van Nice's *magnum opus*, *Saint Sophia in Istanbul. An*

Architectural Survey (Washington, D.C., 1965), instalment one has appeared. The structural problems have been and still are under discussion: see W. Emerson and R. Van Nice, *A.J.A.*, XLVII (1943), 403 ff., *A.J.A.*, LIV (1950), 28 ff., and *Archaeology*, LV (1951), 94 ff., 162 ff.; R. Van Nice, *J.S.A.H.*, VII (1948), 5 ff.; K. J. Conant, *A.J.A.*, XLIII (1939), 589 ff., and *Bull. Byz. Inst.*, I (1946), 71 ff.; W. MacDonald, *Perspecta*, LV (1957), 20 ff.; Van Nice, *Architectural Forum* (1963), 131 ff.; R. J. Mainstone, *Transactions Newcomen Society*, XXVIII (1965/6), 23 ff.; *idem, Architectural History*, XII (1969), 39 ff.; and *D.O.P.*, XXIII/XXIV (1969/70), 353 ff.

The principal sources regarding both construction and rebuilding under Justinian are Procopius, *The Buildings*, I, i, 22 ff. (*L.C.L.*, VIII; partial translation also Mango, *Documents*, 72 ff.), and Paulus Silentarius (*Bonn Corpus*, XXXII, and *P.G.*, LXXXVI, 2119 ff.; excerpts translated in Lethaby and Swainson, *op. cit.*, 38 ff., and Mango, *Documents*, 80 ff.). Supplementary source material, in English translation, Mango, *op. cit.*, *passim*; in German translation, Richter, *Schriftquellen*, 12 ff., and *passim*.

The liturgical function and the ceremonial, both ecclesiastical and Imperial, as connected with the H. Sophia and described for the tenth century by Constantine Porphyrogenetos, *Book of Ceremonies* (*P.G.*, LXII; *Bonn Corpus*, IX–X; better (but Book I only) *Le livre des cérémonies*, ed. A. Vogt, Paris, 1935), have been discussed by Mathews, *Churches*, *passim*, and, with regard to the emperor's entry, by Chr. Strube, *Die westliche Eingangsseite der Kirchen von Konstantinopel in justinianischer Zeit* (Wiesbaden, 1973). Robert Taft, S. J., *D.O.P.*, XXXIV (1980–1), 45 ff., provides a clear picture of the performance of the liturgy in the 'Great Church' as of the eighth century and its earlier roots.

206. 2. G. Downey, *Art Bulletin*, XXXII (1950), 262 ff.

3. G. Downey, *Byzantion*, XVIII (1946–8), 99 ff.: G. L. Huxley, *Anthemius of Tralles* (Cambridge, Mass., 1959).

4. The best sources for the rebuilding of 558–63 are Agathias, *History*, V, 9 (*Bonn Corpus*, I, 1828, 295) and John Malalas, *Chronographia* (*ibid.*, XV, 489 and 495). For their interpretation in the light of the structural evidence, see Conant (1939 and 1946) and Mainstone (1965–6 and 1969/70) (both as quoted above, Note 1). While P. A. Underwood and E. J. W. Hawkins, *D.O.P.*, XV (1961), 187 and, in particular, 212 ff., assigned the present clerestory walls to the rebuilding of 558–63, Mainstone with good reasons pleads for the ninth century.

5. In listing these repairs, Swift, *op. cit.*, erroneously attributes the buttresses to the thirteenth, Antoniades (*op. cit.*, I, 141) to the fourteenth century. A. M. Schneider (as quoted above, Note 1) makes a ninth-century date seem plausible.

210. 6. In addition to Conant, MacDonald, Van Nice, and Mainstone as quoted above, Note 1, see J. B. Ward Perkins,

The Listener (1956), 746 ff. The forces and counter-forces active in the structure still need further clarification, despite the careful study given them so far by Conant and by Emerson and Van Nice, as quoted above, Note 1.
211. 7. The brick construction techniques used in the H. Sophia and their previous history have been analysed by J. B. Ward Perkins, in D. Talbot Rice (ed.), *The Great Palace of the Byzantine Emperors, Second Report* (Edinburgh, 1958), 71 ff., W. MacDonald (see also *idem, J.S.A.H.*, XVII, 1958, 2 ff.), and W. Emerson and R. Van Nice, *A.J.A.*, XLVII (1943), 403 ff. Van Nice, *Archaeology*, IV (1951), 101, has also pointed out that – contrary to Procopius (*Buildings*, I, i, 53) – the blocks of the main piers rest on hairline-thin beds of mortar instead of being fastened to each other, as Procopius thought, by metal sheets; a lead sheet is inserted only at the springing of some of the minor vaults (correction of my interpretation in the first edition of the present volume, p. 337, Note 8 end, kindly communicated by Mr Robert Van Nice).
212. 8. In reconstructing the first project W. Kleiss, *Ist. M.*, XV (1965), 168 ff., goes much too far. But some of his observations are correct; see also Mainstone (1969), 47 (as quoted above, Note 1).
216. 9. For chancel, solea, and ambo see Paulus Silentiarius, as above, Note 1 (excerpts transl. Lethaby and Swainson, *op. cit.*, 46 ff., and Mango, *Documents*, 87 ff., 91 ff.), G. Xydis,*Art Bulletin*,XXIX (1947), 1 ff., and Mathews, *Churches*, 96 ff.; green and red bands in the marble pavements may have outlined the placing of chancel screens and solea, see G. P. Majeska, *D.O.P.*, XXXII (1979), 299 ff. As to the revetment of the piers, my notes differ slightly from those of Antoniades (as quoted above, Note 1), II, 20. I retain the latter since Antoniades probably saw the marbles cleaned.
   10. Underwood, *loc. cit.*, esp. 210 ff., and *idem,D.O.P.*, XIV (1959), 209.
   11. For Ravenna, see C. Cecchelli, *Felix Ravenna*, N.S. XXXV (1930), 1 ff.
   12. See above, Note 9.
217. 13. Schneider, *op. cit.*, 22 ff., plates 8 f.
218. 14. See above, p. 102, and Chapter 5, Notes 2 and 3. Mathews, *Churches*, 117 ff., esp. 121 ff., counters my former assumption of the congregation's being entirely excluded from the nave and I have correspondingly modified my text. Indeed, the passages supporting his thesis clearly speak of the faithful at times entering the nave. Procopius, on the other hand (*Buildings*, I, i, 55 ff., as translated by Mathews, 131), with equal clarity assigns them to the aisles and galleries of the H. Sophia; Maximus Confessor, while specifically excluding them from the chancel, remains unspecific about the nave; and the occasions when the faithful are expressly mentioned as being in the nave are always moments of unusual excitement: the Lesser Entrance at the dedication of the H. Sophia in 563; sermons

by John Chrysostomus in the old H. Sophia; political trouble at the Reading of Commemorations. The sources being inconclusive, opinions differ regarding the route of the Great Entrance, and in particular its point of entering the church – centre door of the north flank, east door of the north wall, or door at the east end of the north aisle; see Mathews, *Churches*, 162, Taft (as above Chapter 5, Note 3), 194 ff., Strube, review of Mathews, *Churches*, in *B.Z.*, LXVII (1974), 408 f., and N. K. Moran, *J.Ö.B.*, XXVIII (1979), 167 ff.
   15. The main source for the Imperial ceremonial is of course Constantine Porphyrogenetos, *Book of Ceremonies* (*P.G.*, CXII; *Bonn Corpus*, IX–X; better (Book I only), *Le livre des cérémonies*, ed. A. Vogt, Paris, 1935, *passim*), which is the basis for J. Ebersolt, *Ste Sophie de Constantinople d'après les cérémonies* (Paris, 1910), as well as for my own description – *faute de mieux* and despite my misgivings regarding the use of a tenth-century source for a sixth-century situation; but, then, both religious and court ceremonial are conservative in the extreme.
   16. Mathews, *Churches*, 162 ff., points out that, contrary to former belief, the celebration of the Eucharist was not hidden from profane eyes by curtains either in the chancel screen or around the altar. Regarding the Imperial pew: *ibid.*, 96, 133 ff. The entrance of the Emperor into the sanctuary and his role there have given rise to much discussion. O. von Simson, *Sacred Fortress* (Chicago, 1948), 30, and Dj. Stričević, *Felix Ravenna*, LXXX (1959), 5 ff., maintain that the Emperor actually participated in the offertory procession of the Great Entrance. On the contrary, A. Grabar, *ibid.*, LXXXI (1959), 63 ff., is of the opinion that the Emperor entered the sanctuary only later, during Mass, to deposit a special gift on the altar. Certainly this holds true for the tenth century, when Constantine Porphyrogenetos compiled his *Book of Ceremonies*; but the lack of earlier documentation makes it difficult to judge the custom prevailing in the sixth century.
   17. K. Lehmann, *Art Bulletin*, XXVII (1945), 1 ff.; J. B. Ward Perkins, *Proceedings British Academy*, LI (1965), 175 ff. For a critique of Lehmann's argument, see T. F. Mathews, *Source*, I, 3 (1982), 12 ff. Ćurčić, *III B.S.C. ... 1977*, 49, stresses the conflict, basic in his view to Byzantine church planning, between architectural and iconographic demands regarding the placing of the dome.
   Main sources for a mystical interpretation of the liturgy are the writings of Dionysius the Areopagite, *The Ecclesiastical Hierarchy* (*P.G.*, III, 119 ff.), and *The Celestial Hierarchy* (*ibid.*, 369 ff.), *passim* (both in English translation, John Parker, London, 1894).
   18. The intermeshing of Imperial and ecclesiastical ceremonial in the H. Sophia has been frequently observed, e.g. Andreades, *op. cit.*, 58 ff. Regarding the role of the Emperor imitating Christ, see R. Guerdan (as quoted in Chapter 8, Note 1), 17 ff.

219. 19. A. Dupont-Sommer, *C.A.*, II (1947), 29 ff., and A. Grabar, *ibid.*, 41 ff.; Mango, *Documents*, 57 ff. For a new translation and an interpretation countering Grabar's, see K. E. McVey, *D.O.P.*, XXXVII (1983), 91 ff.

20. C. Mango and I. Sevčenko, *D.O.P.*, XV (1961), 243 ff.; R. M. Harrison and N. Firatli, *ibid.*, XIX (1965), 230 ff.; *idem, ibid.*, XX (1966), 223 ff.; also XXI (1967), 273 ff., and XXII (1968), 195 ff., all reporting on the excavation. Mr Harrison's later tentative reconstruction proposal in *XVI C.E.B. ... Vienna ... 1981 (J.Ö.B.*, XXXII/4), 435 ff., envisages H. Polyeuktos as 'a domed basilica ... with curvilinear open exedras ... a deliberate response to' Justinian's H. Sophia, but like this all covered with marble revetment, inlaid in agate, mother-of-pearl, and coloured glass, the vaults clothed in mosaic. *Ibid.*, as already *VIII C.A.C. ... Barcelona ... 1969*, 325, on the Sassanian elements in much of the sculptural decoration. Whether or not architect and patroness had Solomon's Temple in mind when designing H. Polyeuktos (*idem, Harvard Ukrainian Studies*, VII, 1983, 276 ff.) remains open. Publication of the final report, R. M. Harrison and others, *Excavations at Saraçhane in Istanbul*, I, *The Excavation ...* (Princeton University Press and Dumbarton Oaks), is expected in 1986. See also Mathews, *Churches*, 52 ff. F. W. Deichmann, *Rend. Pont. Acc.*, L (1977–8, 1980), 75 ff. (also *idem, Rom, Ravenna*, 643 ff.), points out that the piers in Venice came from Constantinople rather than from Acre, as tradition had it, and proposes that at H. Polyeuktos they and their counterparts carried the nave arcade rather than the altar canopy.

21. See below, pp. 249 ff.

224. 22. Van Millingen, *Churches*, 62 ff.; Ebersolt and Thiers, *Églises*, 21 ff.; Janin, *Églises*, 466 ff.; P.A. Underwood, *C.A.*, III (1948), 64 ff.; Mathews, *Churches*, 42 ff.; and *Bildlexikon*, 177 ff. P. Sanpaolesi, *Rivista dell'Istituto Nazionale d'Archeologia e Storia dell'Arte*, N.S. X (1961), 116 ff., presents a survey and structural analysis of the church correcting the older ones; he suggests that the upper portions of the dome (the lower parts are of brick, pitched on their sides) consist perhaps of some light material, cane or a mixture of straw, lime, and mortar on a wooden frame. This is possible, but so far unprovable. See also the critical remarks of O. Feld, *Ist. M.*, XVIII (1968), 264 ff. The attribution of the design to Anthemios of Tralles (H. Sedlmayr, *Kunstwissenschaftliche Forschungen*, II, 1933, 46 ff.; Sanpaolesi, *op. cit.*, note 29) rests on no historical evidence. For SS. Peter and Paul, see Procopius, *Buildings*, I, iv, 1 ff. *L.C.L.*, VII, 42 ff.), and a request by Justinian, supported by the papal legates to Constantinople, dated 519, asking for *brandea* of St Peter, St Paul, and St Lawrence for the church (*Epistolae imperatorum pontificum ...*, ed. O. Günther, *C.S.E.L.*, XXXV, Vienna, 1895, 644 f., 679 f.). Mathews, *loc. cit.*, convincingly argues for the location of the old church south of H. Sergios and Bakchos;

see also, for the location of the Hormisdas Palace at some distance from the seashore, R. Guilland, *Études sur la topographie de Constantinople byzantine*, I (Berlin and Amsterdam, 1969), 294 ff.

C. Mango, *J.Ö.B.*, XXI (1972), 189 ff., *Festschrift Otto Demus*, and again *B.Z.*, LXVIII (1975), 385 ff., views H. Sergios and Bakchos, based on a monophysite account, as built shortly before 536, primarily by Theodora, for the use of monophysite refugee monks camping in the Hormisdas Palace. I still consider it a palace church because of: Procopius' statement to that effect (*Buildings*, I, iv, 7 f.); the church's lavish construction, unlikely in a refugee context; its link by double-storeyed arcades, to St Peter and Paul on one, to other tall structures, presumably of the palace, on the opposite flank; the refugees' account's reference to services held in one of the palace halls rather than in a church; and the refugees' arrival in large numbers probably not before the start of serious persecution in 537; see also my note, *J.Ö.B.*, XXIII (1974), 251 ff. The question of central plan palace churches cannot be dismissed as lightly as Mr Mango attempts.

225. 23. R. Demangel, *Contributions à la topographie de l'Hebdomon* (Paris, 1945); Mathews, *Churches*, 55 ff. (Hebdomon); Procopius, *Buildings*, I, viii, 6 (St Michael in Anaplus).

24. Both J. B. Ward Perkins (*The Listener*, 1956, 701 ff., 746 ff., and *Great Palace, op. cit.*, especially 90 ff.) and F. W. Deichmann (*Studien zur Architektur Konstantinopels*, Baden-Baden, 1956, 38 ff.) stress the origin in Asia Minor of the vaulting techniques of Constantinople under Justinian. Following the thesis set forth by G. T. Rivoira (*L'architettura romana*, Milan, 1921) and G. Giovannoni (e.g. *V C.E.B. ... Rome ... 1938*, II, 133 ff.), G. de Angelis d'Ossat (*Romanità delle cupole romane*, Rome, 1946), S. Bettini (*L'architettura di San Marco*, Padua, 1946), and still L. Crema (*L'architettura romana*, *Enciclopedia classica*, sezione III, vol. 12, tomo I, Turin, 1956, 575) have seen the vaulting system of the H. Sophia as part and parcel of Western Roman vaulting techniques. In contrast, J. B. Ward Perkins, *Great Palace (op. cit.)*, 91 ff., and *Proceedings British Academy*, LI (1965), 175 ff., stresses the impact of Mesopotamian techniques on Late Roman building in the Aegean area and through it on Byzantine Constantinople.

25. Andreades, *op. cit., passim* and especially 85, views the design of the H. Sophia as fusing into one and further developing what he chooses to call the 'humanistic vaulted space of Rome, the Hellenistic peristyle space, the oriental cave space and the Persian principle of dematerialization'.

26. J. Strzygowski, *Origins of Christian Church Art*, transl. O. M. Dalton (Oxford, 1923), 46 ff. ('In conception the church is purely Armenian') and *passim*. The best, since balanced, interpretation of the role of the East in the formation of Byzantine domed architecture is given by J. B. Ward Perkins, as quoted above, Note 17.

27. W. R. Zaloziecky, *Die Sophienkirche in Konstantinopel* ... (Rome, 1936); Swift, *op. cit.*, 47 ff. Zaloziecky, *passim*, interprets the plan of the H. Sophia as fundamentally a composite of elements all traceable back to Roman bath and palace architecture. Rivoira's interpretation (*op. cit.*) of the H. Sophia as deriving from a fusion of the Basilica of Maxentius with the dome of the Pantheon has left its traces still in Andreades, *op. cit.*

226. 28. A. Grabar, *Martyrium* (Paris, 1948), *passim*.

29. Like the Italian scholars, quoted above, Note 24, Zaloziecky was foremost in claiming a purely Western-Roman design for the H. Sophia. Swift inclined towards a Roman-hellenistic derivation; while J. B. Ward Perkins, *The Italian Element in Late Roman and Early Medieval Architecture, Annual Italian Lecture of the British Academy 1947* (*Proceedings British Academy*, XXXIII (1947), *passim*), very correctly, in my opinion, saw its sources in the tradition of the Roman West, but long fused – with other, still unknown, elements – into the art of Late Antiquity spread all over the Empire. (The quotation incorporated in my text is from p. 21 of Ward Perkins's lecture.)

30. Sedlmayr, *op. cit.* (Note 1); and the critique of Weigand, listed *ibid.*

31. Ward Perkins, *Great Palace*, and Deichmann, *Studien*, as above, Note 24; also Sanpaolesi, as above, Note 22.

228. 32. See above, Chapter 3, pp. 103–4, and Deichmann, *op. cit.*, *passim*.

33. Deichmann, *op. cit.*, 72 ff.; Harrison (as above, Note 20), *VIII C.A.C. ... Barcelona ... 1969*. For the development of capitals in Constantinople from the mid fifth to the end of the sixth century see now C. Strube, *J.A.C.*, XXVI (1983), 59 ff.

229. 34. J. B. Ward Perkins, *Proceedings British Academy*, LI (1965), 198 ff.

35. See above, Chapter 3, Notes 20 ff., Chapter 5, Notes 51 f., and Chapter 6, Notes 9 f.

36. N.T., *Palladio*, II (1938), 149 f., on Canosa. On Ohrid, see G. Babić, *Zb. R.*, XIII (1971), 263 ff.

37. See below, pp. 230, 322–3.

230. 38. Grabar, *op. cit.*, *passim*.

39. J. Kollwitz, in *Neue Deutsche Ausgrabungen im Mittelmeergebiet* ... (Berlin, 1959), 46 ff., in particular, 69.

40. See above, Chapter 5, Note 43.

41. *Funebris Oratio in Patrem*, cap. 39 (*P.G.*, XXXV, 1037; see also, *Funeral Orations*, in L. Schopp (ed.), transl. L. P. McCauley, *The Fathers of the Church*, New York, 1953, 153 f.). A. Birnbaum, *R.K.W.*, XXXVI (1913), 181 ff., has analysed both Gregory's text and the *scholia* which refer to octagonal churches of St John at Alexandria and the Virgin at Tyre.

231. 42. See above, Chapter 3, pp. 76–7 and Note 23.

232. 43. Outstanding among older publications on S. Vitale are G. Gerola, *Felix Ravenna*, X (1913), 427 ff.; *idem*, XI (1913), 459 ff.; *idem*, XXI (1916), 879 ff.; R. Bartoccini,

ibid., XXXVIII (1931), 77 ff., and XLI (1932), 133 ff.; all superseded by F. W. Deichmann, *Ravenna*, I, 226 ff., and II, 2, 45 ff. It remains a point of contention whether or not S. Vitale was intended as a palace church – in view of its plan and decoration, a tempting hypothesis defended by G. de Angelis d'Ossat, *Studi Ravennati* (Ravenna, 1962), 59 ff., and combated by Deichmann, *op. cit.*, II, 2, 21 ff. The question is obviously linked to that of Julianus's position – whether he was just a wealthy banker or also the head of a fifth column in still-Gothic Ravenna – as well as to the significance of the Imperial portraits in the chancel – whether they merely indicate Imperial financial contributions or have a deeper significance.

234. 44. See Deichmann, *Ravenna*, I, 54, and II, 2, 60 ff., on the techniques of construction. On the hollow tube vault, see also De Angelis d'Ossat, *op. cit.*, 135 ff., and G. Bovini, *Felix Ravenna*, LXXXI (1960), 78 ff.

CHAPTER 10

238. 1. J. B. Ward Perkins, *The Listener* (1956), 748.

2. See for Gerasa, J. B. Ward-Perkins, *Roman Imperial Architecture (Pelican History of Art)* (Harmondsworth, 1981), 335 ff.; for Side, Arid Müfid Mansel, *J.D.A.I.,A.A.*, LXXIV (1959), 364 ff., and figure 3.

3. Forchheimer and Strzygowski, as quoted above, Chapter 3, Note 8; Schneider, *Byzanz* (Berlin, 1938), *passim*.

239. 4. See below, pp. 253–4.

5. The mausoleum of Leonidas, probably of fourth-century date, is well preserved, incorporated into the Ilissos basilica at Athens, in the corner between the aisle and north transept; see above, Chapter 5, p. 119 and Note 42. For the East Mausoleum at Side, see above, Note 2. The sixth-century mausoleum at Ḥass and a similar one at Ruwêha are illustrated in Butler, *Architecture*, 246 f. S. Guyer, *Grundlagen mittelalterlicher europäischer Baukunst* (Einsiedeln, 1950), 30 ff., adds other examples of tombs and martyria of this type.

6. See above, pp. 181–2, 82, 175.

7. A. Xyngopoulos, *Deltion*, XII (1929), 142 ff.; E. Kitzinger, *XI C.E.B. ... Munich ... 1959*, Berichte, 24. Both authors suggest a date shortly before 500, for the building as well as for the mosaics. But dates as early as 450 and as late as 535–40 have likewise been suggested.

240. 8. Lassus, *Sanctuaires*, 147 f.; St Elias at Izra (Ezra') is dated 542 through an inscription. For Rometta, see G. Agnello, *L'architettura bizantina in Sicilia* (Florence, 1952), 305, and P. Lojacono, *I monumenti bizantini della Sicilia* (Florence, 1951), 61 f., and figure 83 ff.; the building is of unknown date, but very possibly of the sixth century.

9. See above, Chapter 9, p. 219 and Note 19.

241. 10. Procopius, *Buildings*, I, X, 8 ff.; for the Chalki see also C. Mango, *The Brazen House (Kgl. Danske Vidensk.*

Selskab, Arkaeologisk-kunsthistoriske Meddelelser, 4, 4)
(Copenhagen, 1959), 30 ff.
242. 11. The principal sources for visualizing Justinian's
Holy Apostles are Procopius, *Buildings*, I, iv, 9 ff. (also his
comparison with St John at Ephesus, *ibid.*, v, i, 4 ff.), and the
poem of Constantine the Rhodian (E. Legrand, *Revue des
Études Grecques*, IX, 1896, 32 ff., and S. Reinach, *ibid.*, 66 ff.)
c. 940; see also Janin, *Églises*, 46 ff. Reconstructions have
been frequently attempted, for instance by A. Heisenberg,
Grabeskirche und Apostelkirche (Leipzig, 1908), II, *passim*,
and S. Bettini, *L'architettura di San Marco* (Padua, 1946), 53
ff. However both the description by Nicholas Mesarites
(trans. G. Downey, *Transactions American Philosophical
Society*, N.S. XLVII, 1957, 855 ff.) and the depictions of the
church in the *Menologium* of Basil II (the date accepted is
now 1004, rather than 979–89 as formerly; see also earlier
editions of this volume) and in two twelfth-century manuscripts refer to the church after a remodelling undertaken
between 940, when Constantine the Rhodian described it,
and 1004, when it was depicted in the *Menologium*, with five
domes on high well-lit drums (R. Krautheimer, *Mélanges
Tisserant*, II (*Studi e Testi*, CCXXXII), Vatican City, 1964,
265 ff.; *idem, Studies*, 197 ff.; the counter-arguments proffered by A. W. Epstein, *Greek, Roman and Byzantine Studies*,
XXIII, 1982, 79 ff., are not strong enough to convince).

12. Procopius, *Buildings*, v, i, 4 ff. *Forschungen in Ephesos*,
IV, 3, 19 ff. presents a careful survey of the remnants and,
157 ff., a tentative, if somewhat fanciful, reconstruction; see
also P. Verzone, *Rend. Pont. Acc.*, LI–LII (1978–80), 213 ff.
Recent excavations (M. Büyükkolanci, *Ist. M.*, XXXII
(1982), 236 ff.) have brought to light, alongside the fifth-
century baptistery, the remains of a small skeuophylakion, a
domed octagon on piers, inserted into a square and provided with a bi-apsed narthex. One side of the westernmost
bay of the church was rebuilt in 1964 – not a fortunate idea.
Regarding S. Marco in Venice and the Church of the Holy
Apostles, see below, pp. 406–11 and Chapter 17, Note 78.
H. Buchwald, *J.Ö.B.*, XXX (1981), 301 ff. has published an
aisleless, twin-bayed and twin-domed church ruin at Alaşe-
hir (ancient Philadelphia, Phrygia), clearly a variant on the
Apostoleion plan rather than on that of Justinian's H. Irene
or Philippi B with barrel-vaulted naves preceding the single
domed bay.
244. 13. Kautzsch, *Kapitellstudien*, 177 f., and figures 566 a-
f *versus* 567 a-e.
245. 14. E. Herzfeld and S. Guyer, *Meriamlik and Korykos*
(Manchester, 1932), 46 ff.; G. Forsyth, *D.O.P.*, XI (1957),
227 ff. See also, for this and the following notes, *R.L.B.K.*,
IV (1984), 182 ff.
15. Herzfeld and Guyer, *op. cit.*, figure 64.
16. Herzfeld and Guyer, *op. cit.*, 70 ff., envisage the
building as vaulted throughout as first proposed by them,
J.D.A.I., A.A., XXIV (1909), 433 ff. I no longer favour the
proposal. The reconstruction with pyramidal timber roof,

first suggested by Forsyth, *op. cit.*, has been accepted by
Gough, *Anatolian Studies*, XXII (1972), 202 f. J. Kramer,
B.Z., LVII (1963), has traced the remains of an attached
baptistery.
17. A. C. Headlam, *Ecclesiastical Sites in Isauria*, The
Society for the Promotion of Hellenic Studies, Supplementary Papers, I (London, 1893), 9 ff.; and M. Gough, as above
Chapter 5, Note 20. See also G. Forsyth, *D.O.P.*, XI (1957),
223 ff., esp. 228 ff.
247. 18. R. M. Harrison, in Gough's posthumous publication (Chapter 5, Note 20), convincingly dates the building to
the reign of the Emperor Zeno (474–5; 476–91); I am
grateful to Mr Harrison for letting me see the proofs of his
contribution. The date proposed by Forsyth, *loc. cit.*, and
Kautzsch, *Kapitellstudien*, 96 and 221, about 550 or 560 is
certainly too late. An early-sixth-century date, as accepted
in the first edition of the present volume, p. 179, seems to
me less and less likely.
19. Headlam, *op. cit.*, 20 f., who knew Dağpazari by the
name of Kestel, interpreted the remnants as those of a
basilica on piers. Forsyth, *op. cit.*, and Gough, *Anatolian
Studies*, XXII (1972), 199 ff., re-interpret the plan along the
lines of Alahan Manastir. For a thumbnail report on the
town and its buildings, including a large basilica within and
a small cemetery (?) church without the walls, see Stephen
Hill, *Yaila*, II (1979), 8 ff. (for the cemetery church already
M. Gough, *Studies in Memory of David Talbot Rice*,
Edinburgh, 1975, 147 ff.). Hill, *op. cit.*, considers octagonal
wooden domes rather than pyramidal roofs possible (M.
Gough) covering the centre bays of the East Church at Alahan
Manastir and the one at Dağpazari.
20. Butler, *Early Churches*, 191; Lassus, *Sanctuaires*, 146 f.;
see also below, Chapter 11, Note 4.
248. 21. The galleries have collapsed since the time of
Butler's visit and the capitals seem to have disappeared. My
former views regarding the import of bricks and workmen
from Constantinople have been corrected by F. W. Deichmann, *R.M.*, LXXXVI (1979), 473 ff., esp. 488 ff. For the
capitals of Qasr ibn Wardan and a number of related
buildings, their derivation and their style as opposed to that
of Constantinople, see now C. Strube, *J.A.C.*, XXVI (1983),
59 ff.
249. 22. *Forschungen in Ephesos*, IV, I, 51 ff., where the
structure is described in detail, proposes no date. C. Foss,
Ephesus after Antiquity (Cambridge, 1979), figure 19, marks
it as 'probably eighth century'. I would have thought of a
sixth- or early-seventh-century date.
23. U. Peschlow, *Die Irenenkirche in Konstantinopel (Ist. M.*,
Beiheft 18) (Tübingen, 1977), supersedes and in large part
revises the older publications, such as W. S. George, *The
Church of St Eirene* (London, 1913); Van Millingen,
Churches, 84 ff.; Ebersolt and Thiers, *Églises*, 57 ff.; Janin,
Églises, 108 ff.; Mathews, *Churches*, 77 ff.; *idem, Survey*, 102
ff.; P. Grossmann, *Ist. M.*, XV (1965), 186 ff.; H. Buchwald.

The Church of the Archangels at Sige (Vienna, 1968), note 251; and my own proposals as made in the previous editions of this volume. In particular, Mr Peschlow eliminates the attribution to a building campaign following a fire in 563 of narthex and atrium, as first proposed by W. S. George and followed by all others, except P. Grossmann, and of changes in the domed bay, as suggested by myself. Some questions still remain in my mind: the use of different building materials in narthex and nave, and their separation by deep fissures make me still wonder about their contemporaneity. But – *experti cedo*.

252. 24. P. Mutafjiev, *I.B.A.I.*, v (1915), 50 ff.; V. Ivanova, *G.N.M.S.*, IV (1922–5), 429 ff., with French résumé; Dj. Stričević, *XII C.E.B. ... Ohrid ... 1961*, and Note 18; K. Mijatev, *Die Mittelalterliche Baukunst in Bulgarien* (Sofia, 1974), 18 ff., only the sixth-century date. Professor Stričević kindly discussed with me his arguments in favour of a sixth-century remodelling of the Stag Basilica. For a critique of Mutafjiev's analysis of the structure, see D. Yasileva, *Byzantino–Bulgarica*, IV (1973), 253 ff.; her proposal to view the church as a barrel-vaulted basilica of fifth-century date does not convince.

253. 25. R. W. Hamilton, *P.E.F.Q.St.* (1930), 178 ff., and more recently C. Mango, *Documents*, 60 ff., have both translated the description of the church as given by Choricius, after 536, when building and decoration were complete; see also Pauly-Wissowa, *R.E.*, III, 2424 ff. The first reconstruction proposed is Hamilton's; the second was suggested by some of my students in a seminar discussion. Regarding a reconstruction of St Stephen at Gaza, likewise described by Choricius (Mango, *op. cit.*, 68 ff.), in particular the wooden(?) pumpkin half-dome over the apse (*ibid.*, 71 f.), see H. Maguire, *D.O.P.*, XXXII (1978), 319 ff.

26. P. Lemerle, *Philippes et la Macédoine orientale* (Paris, 1945), 415 ff.

254. 27. H. H. Jewell and F. W. Hasluck, *Our Lady of the Hundred Gates in Paros* (London, 1920); A. K Orlandos, *C.A.C. ... Ravenna ... 1959*, 159 ff. The capitals are discussed by Kautzsch, *Kapitellstudien*, 188.

255. 28. T. Fyfe, *Architectural Review*, XXII (1907), 60 ff.; A. K. Orlandos, *Epitiris Hetairias tōn Byzantinōn Spoudōn* (1926), 301 ff.; G. Gerola, *Monumenti veneti nell'isola di Creta* (1908), 11, 29; and P. L. Vokotopoulos, *Praktika Protou Diethniou Synodou Peloponnesion Spoudon* (Athens, 1976), 273 ff., all suggesting a sixth-century date against the proposal made by J. Christern in *Pepragmena toū III Diethnoūs Kretologikou Synedriou ... 1971* (Athens, 1974), 37 ff., of a tenth-century reconstruction re-using sixth-century capitals.

257. 29. Mavrodinov (1959), 30 f., St. Boyadjiev, in *Studia in honorem Acad. D. Dečev, Acad. Bulgare des Sciences* (1958), 611 ff., Dj. Stričević, *XII C.E.B. ... Ohrid, 1961, Rapports*, 176, and Mijatev, *op. cit.* (Note 24), 18 ff., all correctly maintain a sixth-century date for the church, contrary to the

medieval dates proposed by A. Protič, *Sofijskata crkva sv. Sofija* (Sofia, 1912). See also R. F. Hoddinot, *Bulgaria in Antiquity* (London, 1975), 269 ff., reporting on three churches found below the present one; *ibid., passim*, on Pirdop, Peruštica, Nessebâr.

CHAPTER 11

258. 1. Procopius, *Buildings, passim*.

259. 2. Examples are too numerous to list, but smaller and larger fortresses and forts abound from North Africa (Gsell, *Monuments*, 11, 366 ff.; P.-A. Février, *C.C.R.*, 1970, 147 ff.; see also J. Lassus, *XIV C.E.B. ... Bucarest 1971*, 11, Bucarest, 1975, 463 ff.) to Syria (Butler, *P.E., Southern Syria*, 70 f., 80 ff., 145 ff., 242 ff.; *Northern Syria*, 102; also the study of W. Karnapp, *Die Stadtmauer von Resafa in Syrien, Denkmäler antiker Architektur*, ed. German Archaeological Institute, 11, Berlin, 1976), Jordan (R. E. Brünnow and A. von Domaszewski, *Die Provincia Arabia*, Strassburg, 1904, 11, 433 ff.), the Yugoslav Danube (*Srpska Akademija Nauka, Anciennes Cultures du Djerdap*, ed. L. Trifunović, Belgrade, 1969, 88 ff.), and Carinthia (R. Egger, *J.Ö.A.I.*, XXV, 1929, 189 ff.; P. Petrie, *Arheol. Vestnik*, XXIII, 1972, 343 ff.). On a broader basis, see the numerous papers assembled in the *Actes du IXe Congrès international d'études sur les frontières romaines ... Bucharest ... 1972* (Bucharest and Cologne, 1974). In many cases, Justinian's engineers seem to have remodelled fortified posts originally built by Trajan and Diocletian as *limes* defences, e.g. Kosêr-al-Hallabât in Syria (Butler, *P.E., Southern Syria*, 70 f.) and Veliki Gradac on the Danube (Trifunović, ed., *op. cit.*, 125). Likewise, among fortified places in North Africa, some turn out to antedate the Byzantine re-conquest by a century and more, such as Henchir Faraoun (P.-A. Février, *C.C.R.*, 1970, 166 ff.).

3. Procopius, *Buildings*, e.g. 11, i, 3 ff.; III, iv, 12; V, vii, 7; V, viii, 5, etc. Regarding the Virgin as defender of the cities, also *ibid.*, I, iii, 9; VI, ii, 20.

4. See above, p. 247, and Butler, *P.E., Northern Syria*, 34 ff., 40 ff.

5. See above, pp. 156–7 (also Chapter 6, Note 35), and Procopius, *op. cit.*, V, vii, 16 f.

6. Procopius, *Buildings*, V, viii, 4 ff. Church and convent on Mt Sinai are still under study by a joint expedition, led by Professors Weitzmann and Forsyth; so far only the plate volume has appeared: G. H. Forsyth and K. Weitzmann, *The Monastery of Saint Catherine at Mount Sinai. The Church and Fortress of Justinian* (Ann Arbor, 1973). I am greatly indebted to my friend Forsyth for the information and the photographs he kindly supplied. Two main questions remain: whether the church was dedicated to the Virgin, as suggested by Procopius, or to the Transfiguration, as intimated by the mosaic; and whether the fortress mentioned by Procopius (*loc. cit.*) should be identified with the

monastery or with a fortification located further down the mountain (P. Mayerson, *Bull. Amer. Schools Oriental Research*, XXIII, April 1978, 33 ff., based on Eutychius, *Annales,P.G.*, CXI, col. 1071). For the monastery buildings, aside from Forsyth's summary in his and Weitzmann's volume, see recently I. Demakopoulos,*D.C.A.H.*, IX (1977–8), 261 ff.

260. 7. Avdot: see C. L. Woolley and T. E. Lawrence, *The Wilderness of Zin* (London, 1936), 86 ff.; Ovadiah, *Corpus*, 23 ff. Haïdra: the old publications (Gauckler, *Basiliques*, plate XIV, and S. Gsell,*II C.A.C. . . . Rome. . . 1900*, 225 ff.) are being replaced by N. Duval, *C.R.A.I.* (1968), 221 ff., *idem, ibid.* (1971), 136 ff., and *idem*, in *Aufstieg und Niedergang der antiken Welt*, ed. H. Temporini and W. Haase, II, 2, 633 ff. For Caričin Grad, see below, Note 11; for R'safah, Chapter 6, Note 27, and below, Note 10; for Dara, B. Croke and J. G. Crow, *Journal of Roman Studies*, LXXIII (1983), 143 ff., and *idem, Yaila IV* (1981), 11 ff., correcting Procopius, *Buildings*, II, i, 3 ff. (*L.C.L.*, VII, 98 ff.); for another frontier fortress in the East, F. W. Deichmann and U. Peschlow, *Zwei spätantike Ruinenstätten in Nordmesopotamien (Bayerische Akademie der Wissenschaften, Phil.-hist. Kl.*, 1977, 2).

8. G. Millet,*Le monastère de Daphni* (Paris, 1899), 4 ff. (the dating, *ibid.*, 16, is of the vaguest). The fortified wall of the church at Tebessa, formerly assigned to the fifth (Gsell, *Monuments*, 287 f.) or sixth century (Ch. Diehl, *Nouvelles Archives des Missions scientifiques*, IV, 1893, 331), is now thought to be contemporary with the church (J. Christern, *op. cit.*, Chapter 7, Note 45, 98 ff., 215 ff.).

9. A. K. Orlandos, *Monastiriaki Architektoniki* (Athens, 1958; 1st ed. 1927), 28, quoting Justinian, *Novellae*, 5, 3; 123, 36; 133, introduction.

261. 10. Procopius, *Buildings*, II, ix, 3 ff. The Sergius Basilica – that is, Basilica A – has been surveyed by Spanner and Guyer and, with corrections, by Kollwitz, as quoted above Chapter 6, Note 27; Basilica B and the tetraconch are discussed by Kollwitz, *op. cit.*, and W. Wirth, in *Tortulae (R. Qu. Schr.*, Suppl. 30), 326 ff. The building outside the walls (Butler, *Churches*, 170, as 'Central Church') was the audience hall of Al-Mundir (J. Sauvaget, *Byzantion*, XIV, 1939, 115 ff.). For the data regarding Al-Mundir's reign and fall (in 581) and his subsequent exile to Sicily, see F. Goubert, *VI C.E.B. . . . Paris,. . . 1948*, I, 103 ff. On the city walls, W. Karnapp, as quoted above, Note 2.

262. 11. Procopius, *Buildings*, IV, i, 19 ff. See also V. R. Petković, *C.A.*, III (1948), 40 ff.; A. Grabar, *ibid.*, 49 ff.; moreover the successive excavation reports in *Starinar*. The Arheološki Institut, *Caričin Grad 1912–1962* (Belgrade, 1962), has published the bibliography up to then, to be complemented by D. Mano-Zisi, *Starinar*, XV–XVI (1964–5), 50 ff.; *ibid.*, XVII (1966), 163 ff., and *ibid.*, XIX (1968), 111 ff. *Caričingrad*, ed. V. Kondić and V. Popović (Serbian Academy of Sciences, Belgrade, 1977), provides a cata-

logue of the finds brought up to date, to be complemented by N. Duval, in *Villes et peuplement dans l'Illyrium protobyzantin (Collection de l'École française à Rome*, LXXVII) (Rome, 1984), 399 ff. On the urban layout also D. Bošković, *Starinar*, XV–XVI (1964–5), 47 ff., and N. Petrović, *ibid.*, 61 ff.

12. Majdan, Mokro Polje, and Lovrečina (I. Nikolajević, *Zb. R.*, X, 1967, 87 ff.; also D. Basler, *Arhitektura kasnkoutičkog doba Bosni i Hercegovini*, Sarajevo, 1972, with German summary) in the Dalmatian mountains, Breza in Bosnia (*idem, ibid.*, 95 ff.), Duel near Feistritz and St Peter im Holz (Teurnia) in Carinthia (G. C. Menis, *La basilica paleocristiana nelle diocesi settentrionali della metropoli d'Aquileia*, Vatican City, 1958, 105 ff., 136 ff.).

13. Butler, *Churches*, and Lassus, *Sanctuaires, passim*; regarding El-Anderin, Butler, 158 ff.; for Avdot, above, Note 7; for Sbeïta (Shivta, Sobota), Ovadiah, *Corpus*, 166 ff., R. Rosenthal-Heginbottom, as quoted above, Chapter 6, Note 41, and A. Segal, as quoted *ibid.*; for Mamshit (Kurnub), see above, Chapter 6, Note 39; D. Chen, *Liber Annuus*, XXXI (1981), 235 ff., sees Byzantine builders active at Mamshit and Sobota because of the use of Byzantine feet in the planning.

266. 14.*Antioch*, I, *passim*; II, 59 ff.; III, 1 ff.; see also Butler, *Architecture*, 251 ff.; Tchalenko, *Villages, passim*.

15. The Nea in Jerusalem, dedicated to the Virgin, has been known until now only through Procopius (*Buildings*, V, vi, 1–26), who stresses the difficulties of construction, the size of the layout with atrium and propylaeum, and with two hospices on the approach, and the splendour of the columns employed, attributing the whole enterprise to Justinian; and through Cyril of Scythopolis' Life of St Sabas, who reports on the start of construction apparently prior to 513, on its completion by Justinian after 530 in the course of twelve years through the Constantinopolitan architect Theodore, locally assisted by the archbishop Peter and the bishop Barachos. Recent excavations in the south part of the old city have brought to light a few elements of the building complex (not necessarily the church), primarily a huge substructure, identified by an inscription as part of Justinian's undertaking and dated either 534/5 or 549/50; see Avigad, *Israel Exploration Journal*, XXVII (1977), 145 ff., kindly brought to my attention by Professor A. Negev, Jerusalem.

W. Harvey and others, *The Church of the Nativity at Bethlehem* (Oxford, 1910); B. Bagatti, *Gli edifici antichi di Betlemme* (Jerusalem, 1952). The date of construction is in doubt; while Procopius's silence suggests a *terminus post c.* 560 (unless one assigns the trefoil church a date before Justinian's reign), a poem datable 603–4 (Bagatti, *op. cit.*, 12; Harvey, *op. cit.*, 57, gives the date 635) provides a *terminus ante*. M. Restlé, *R.L.B.K.*, I, 599 ff. suggests a fifth-century date – unconvincingly to me, given the fifth-century date of the mosaics in the first, Constantinian church and the resemblance of the ornament on the wooden architraves in the present structure to Ummayad work.

16. E.g. at Dodona and at Paramythia; Sotiriou, *Basilikai*, 203 ff.

267. 17. Janin, *Églises*, 169 ff., in particular 175 f., quotes two epigrams 'in the apses [arches?] of the Blachernae' from the *Anthologia Palatina*; see also Richter, *Schriftquellen*, 164 ff., and Mango, *Documents*, 125.

18. G. Kapitän, *XXVII C.C.R.* (1980), 71 ff.

19. On Latrün, W. Widrig, *P.B.S.R.*, XLVI (1978), 94 ff., suggesting a date 479–518, too early in my opinion. For Proconnesian pieces found in the West Church at Apollonia, see W. Widrig and R. Goodchild, *P.B.S.R.*, XXXVIII (1960), 70 ff., especially 73. For summaries, also R. Goodchild, *C.C.R.* (1966), 205 ff., 225 ff.

20. I. Nikolajević-Stojković, *La décoration architecturale sculptée . . . en Macédoine, en Serbie et au Monténégro* (Belgrade, 1957) (in Serbian, with French summary).

268. 21. Recent finds (*B.C.H.*, LXXXIV, 1960–1, 254 ff.; St. Bojadžiev, *Byzantino-Bulgarica*, I (1962), 361 ff.) suggest for the Old Metropolis, instead of the formerly adopted tenth-century date (A. Rašenov, *Églises de Mesembria*, Sofia, 1932, 2 ff.), a sixth-century origin, and a later rebuilding on the old plan, but with changed elevation.

22. J. Christern, *VII C.A.C. . . . Trier . . . 1965*, 407 ff.; N. Duval, *C.R.A.I.* (1971), 136 ff. (Haïdra); and J. Christern, *Bulletin d'archéologie algérienne*, III (1968), 193 ff. (Tipasa, S. Salsa). See also above, Chapter 2, Note 18.

269. 23. *Corpus*, I, 14 ff. (S. Agnese); II, 1 ff. (east church of S. Lorenzo).

272. 24. R. Heidenreich and H. Johannes, *Das Grabmal Theoderichs zu Ravenna* (Wiesbaden, 1971), bring a detailed survey together with a new proposal for a graphic reconstruction. In my opinion, however, the reconstruction with upper gallery, as suggested by G. de Angelis d'Ossat, *Studi Ravennati* (Ravenna, 1962), 91 ff., still remains slightly more convincing. Earlier interpretations, often based on racial theories (A. Haupt, *Das Grabmal Theoderichs des Grossen . . .*, Leipzig, 1913), or on unchecked architectural fantasy (C. Cecchelli, *Felix Ravenna*, LXXII, 1956, 5 ff.), have been dealt with by E. Dyggve (*Studi in onore di . . . Calderini e . . . Paribeni*, III, 765 ff., and *Kung Theoderik og den nordiske runddysse*, Copenhagen, 1957), and by K. Wessel, in *Das Altertum*, IV (1958), 229 ff. A collateral relationship of the monolithic dome to megalithic tomb covers seems to me nonetheless possible. On the technical problem of setting the dome in place, also G. Tabarroni, *Felix Ravenna*, CV–CVI (1973), 119 ff.

Deichmann, *Ravenna*, II, 1, 209 ff., esp. 229 ff., views the masonry technique as related not so much to Syria in particular but in general to what I call the inland countries, and strongly modified by impact from Constantinople, the fusion possibly transmitted by Isaurian workmen (C. Mango, in *Polychronion Franz Dölger*, 1966, 358 ff.).

273. 25. E. Dyggve, *op. cit.*; for further examples of two-storeyed mausolea, S. Guyer, *Grundlagen mittelalterlicher europäischer Baukunst* (Einsiedeln, 1950), plate 1. P. Grossmann, *S. Michele in Africisco* (*Deutsches Archäologisches Institut Rom, Sonderschriften*, 1) (Mainz, 1973), analyses the remains of the church, presents a dependable reconstruction, and convincingly argues the case for a Syrian model albeit half a century older; see also Deichmann, *Ravenna*, II, 2, 35 ff. For possible Syrian impact in Ravenna as early as 490, cf. the bands arching over the windows at S. Apollinare Nuovo, above, p. 186.

26. R. M. Harrison, *Anatolian Studies*, XIII (1963), 117 ff.; also Rott, *Denkmäler*, 318 ff. Alongside Alakilise, apparently rebuilt in 812, basilicas abound in the region, their apses either semicircular or polygonal outside (Harrison, *op. cit.*). No explanation so far be given for the frequent occurrence of trefoil sanctuaries (*ibid.*).

27. See above, Note 11, especially N. Duval, *op. cit.*, and P. Spremo-Petrović, *Starinar*, IX–X (1958–9), 169 ff.; Dj. Stričević, *XII C.E.B. . . . Ohrid, Rapports*, VII, *passim*; Hoddinot, *Churches*, 204 ff.; and, providing a survey of the churches and their relative chronology and comparisons, not always convincing, with buildings within and beyond the Balkans, V. Popović, *XXVI C.C.R. 1979*, 249 ff.

It has long been noted that basilicas in the Balkans often are proportioned to a length corresponding to the diagonal of a square or a rectangle erected over its short side, i.e. an irrational number; see L. G. Dinolov, *Prinos kum metričnoto izsledvane . . .* (Sofia, 1963), with French résumé, *Contributions sur* (sic!) *l'étude de mesurage sur* (sic!) *l'architecture Médiévale Bulgare*, 186 ff. (The same seems to obtain in Cappadocian rural churches, see Restlé, *Studien*, as above Chapter 6, Note 48.) N. Spremo-Petrović, *Proporznicki . . . Basilikama Ilirski Prefekture* (Belgrade, 1971; with French résumé), suggests the use by the builders of a system approximating the values of irrational numbers rather than of these numbers themselves, e.g. 5:7 rather than the square root of 2. H. Junecke, *Proportionen frühchristlicher Basiliken des Balkans . . .* (Tübingen, 1983), proposes instead their having used 'Pythagorean triangles', e.g. 3:4 to obtain the diagonal 5. My own feeling is that the simpler method of obtaining the proportion geometrically by swinging the measuring string from the diagonal to the lengthwise direction is the most likely to have been used by the builders of these mostly rural churches: but the use of the simplified arithmetical method as proposed by Mrs Spremo-Petrović is of course equally possible. See also my review of Restlé, *Studien*, as quoted above, Chapter 6, Note 47.

274. 28. D. Mano-Zisi, *Starinar*, III–IV (1952–3), 156 ff.; Dj. Stričević, *XII C.E.B. . . . Ohrid, 1961, Actes*, 224 ff.; N. Duval, *op. cit.*, 407 ff. The reconstruction of a dome over the nave of the cathedral (V. R. Petković, *C.A.*, III, 1948, 40 ff.) is erroneous.

275. 29. S. Radojčeč, *Zb.R.*, I (1952), 148 ff., and Hoddinot,

Churches, 220 ff. on Konjuh; the comparison with the shrine of the Archangels at Fa'lul in Syria (Butler, *Churches*, 264 ff.) proposed in former editions of this volume is too vague to be sustained. The central-plan, double-shell church dug up at Amphipolis (E. Stikas, *Praktika*, 1980, plan on p. 15) seems to represent a closer prototype for the cruder variant at Konjuh. Double-shelled, the outer wall circular, the nave is hexagonal and supported by six angled piers, framing triple colonnaded arcades. A deep chancel flanked by side rooms and terminated by an apse polygonally broken outside suggests a sixth-century date. So does the atrium flanked by large rooms. The whole seems to be a one-storeyed and simplified, but still elegant version of S. Vitale at Ravenna and its relatives.

30. Dj. Stričević, *Zb.R.*, III (1953), 179 ff. (with French summary); *idem*, *X C.E.B. . . . Istanbul . . . 1955*, 171 ff.; N. Petrović, *Starinar*, VII–VIII (1956–7), 165 ff.

31. *Corpus*, I, 304 ff., and, with slightly later date, W. and R. Schumacher, *Kölner Domblatt* (1957), 22 ff.

32. Belovo: A. Frolov, *Bulletin Byz. Inst.*, I (1946), 43 ff.; Tolmeita: C. H. Kraeling, *Ptolemais, City of the Libyan Pentapolis* (Chicago, 1962), 97 ff.

276. 33. N. Duval, *C.R.A.I.* (1971), 160 ff.; *idem, ibid.*, 136 ff.; *idem, ibid.* (1969), 419 ff.; *idem, Sbeitla et les églises africaines à deux absides*, I (Paris, 1971), 63 ff.; Gauckler, *Basiliques*, plates I, XV, XXXII, XXXVIII; J. B. Ward Perkins and R. G. Goodchild, *Archaeologia*, XCV (1953), 24 ff., 70. Likewise in Cyrenaica another basilica supported by arcaded piers, but unvaulted, has come to light, datable prior to 550 (J. A. Lloyd, R. Reece, and others, *Excavations at Sidi Krebish, Benghazi*, I, Tripoli, 1982); the sanctuary, its apse flanked by side chambers and enclosed with them in a massive rear wall, suggests links to the Negev, while the narthex plan recalls Egyptian church design.

34. For example, S. Pietro at Syracuse, S. Foca near Priola Gargallo, a ruin near Palagonia, and, with triconch sanctuary, S. Pietro ad Bajas, Syracuse (G. Agnello, *L'architettura bizantina in Sicilia*, Florence, 1952, 81 ff., 93, 295; G. Libertini, *I.C.A.C. . . . 1952*, 201 ff., erroneously maintained that the arcades of the nave marked the outer limits of these churches).

35. St Laurent at Grenoble; the late-eighth- or ninth-century date suggested by J. Hubert, *Arte del primo millenio* (Turin, 1953), 327 ff., and M. Viellard-Troiekouroff, in *Karl der Grosse*, III, ed. W. Braunfels (Düsseldorf, 1965), 359 f., has not been generally accepted.

277. 36. See above, Note 6. High quality though it is, the apse mosaic is no longer attributed to a Constantinopolitan workshop. For the towers, one might compare, e.g., the Acheiropoietos in Salonica (above, p. 99). The site of the martyrium, the Burning Bush, originally under the open sky behind the apse, was apparently replaced only later by the present chapel. Comparable to the insertion of a precious apse mosaic into the crude basilica on Mt Sinai, a church at

Sabratha (Church 2) is provided with a splendid floor mosaic, obviously laid by a workshop brought into Tripolitania from overseas, although the church itself is traditional in plan and crude in execution (Ward Perkins and Goodchild, as above, Note 33, 12 ff.).

37. See above, Chapter 2, Note 45.

38. M. Mazzotti, *La basilica di Sant' Apollinare in Classe* (Vatican City, 1954); Deichmann, *Ravenna*, I, 257 ff., and II, 2, 234 ff., the latter suggesting a date after 547 for the start of actual construction and, in his analysis of both the eastern, specifically Aegean origins of 'pastophories' and narthex towers and their local continuance in Ravenna (S. Giovanni Evangelista).

278. 39. See also above, pp. 184–5.

280. 40. B. Molajoli, *La basilica eufrasiana di Parenzo* (Padua, 1943), with bibliography; M. Prelog, *Poreč* (Belgrade, 1957), 93 ff.; and now A. R. Terry, Ph.D. thesis, University of Illinois, Urbana–Champaign, 1984. See also A. Šonje, *Felix Ravenna*, XLIV (1967), 51 ff. (on the stuccoes), and A. R. Terry, *IX B.S.C. . . . 1983*, 7 f. (on the *opus sectile* panels). On the successive earlier structures, a *domus ecclesiae*(?), twin halls, and a basilica with clergy bench, flanked by consignatorium and baptistery, comparable to other fifth-century twin cathedrals in Istria (above, p. 179), see Molajoli, *op. cit.*, 17 ff.; on three successive baptismal fonts, A. Šonje, *Arheološki Vestnik*, XXIII (1972), 289 ff.

41. G. Brusin, *Aquileia e Grado* (Padua, 1956); M. Mirabella Roberti, *Grado* (Grado, 1956).

282. 42. Verzone (1942), 56 ff., and previous note.

283. 1. G. Ostrogorsky, *History of the Byzantine State* (Oxford, 1956), 72 ff., and Mango, *Byzantium*, to whose Chapter II I am greatly indebted. For the decline of the cities (and their revival, if modest as compared to their prosperity through the reign of Justinian), see also D. Claude, *Die byzantinische Stadt im 6. Jahrhundert (Byzantinisches Archiv*, XIII) (Munich, 1969); A. H. M. Jones, *The Later Roman Empire*, (Oxford, 1976), esp. II, 762 f.; and the papers by G. Ostrogorsky, R. Lopez, P. Charanis, and J. Teall, in *D.O.P.*, XIII (1959), *passim*. For the situation in seventh- and eighth-century Greece in particular, see P. Charanis, *D.O.P.*, V (1950), 141 ff., and for Athens, J. Travlos, *Poleodomiki Exelixis tōn Athinōn* (Athens, 1960). F. Gregorovius, *Geschichte der Stadt Athen im Mittelalter* (Munich, 1887) (reprint paperback *D.T.V.*, CXCVII), while obviously out of date, still makes for at times informative and always pleasurable reading.

284. 2. *Ibid.*, 119 ff., and, for the relation of iconoclasm and art, A. Grabar, *L'iconoclasme byzantin* (Paris, 1957), and E. Kitzinger, *D.O.P.*, VIII (1954), 83 ff., reprinted *idem, The Art of Byzantium and the Medieval West* (Bloomington, 1976), 90 ff.

CHAPTER 13

285. 1. Rott, *Denkmäler*, 299 ff., is now superseded by J. Morganstern, *The Byzantine Church of Dereağzi and its Decoration*, Ist. M. (1984), *Beiheft*.
2. C. Mango, *Zb. R.*, XI (1968), 9 ff.; F. Dirimtekin, *Aya Sofia Müzeleri Yilliği*, III (1961), 47 ff.; and S. Eyice, *C.C.R.* (1971), 293 ff., who suggests a fourteenth-century date, as does Morganstern, *Op. cit.*, 89 ff., in listing other examples of the type of eleventh- and fourteenth-century date (Chernihov, Leontarion, Mistra).
288. 3. H. Buchwald, *The Church of the Archangels at Sige* (Vienna, 1968), 36 ff., has taken up anew the question of type, origin, and development of the cross-domed church. He rightly points to the limitations of our present knowledge regarding the individual buildings of the group, but nonetheless suggests (p. 61) a development, perhaps overly rigid, as witness the dates, contrary to his, now secured for the Gül and Kalenderhane Camii. I still prefer my own concept of often contemporary variants. Nor can I agree on applying his term 'cross-domed basilica' (*op. cit.*, 47 and note 213) to both St Clement at Ankara and the Koimesis at Nicaea; I consider it essential to distinguish between a 'true cross-domed church' with cross arms of equal depth, as at the Koimesis, and a 'compact domed basilica' with barely developed lateral arches, as at St Clement. Indeed, both the terms 'cross-domed basilica' (Koimesis) and 'cross-domed basilica with inscribed aisles' (Dere Ağzï; *op. cit.*, 52) seem to me inappropriate and a bit clumsy.

St Clement at Ankara was surveyed before its destruction by G. de Jerphanion, *Mélanges de l'Université Saint-Joseph à Beyrouth*, XIII (1928), 113 ff. St Nicholas at Myra, badly rebuilt, in particular in its upper portions, in 1862, was published by Rott, *Denkmäler*, 324. Since then large parts of the furnishings have gone and new repairs, inside and out, have obscured the picture. A new study by U. Peschlow, in J. Borchhardt and others, *Myra* (Berlin, 1971), 303 ff., has identified the remains of an earlier vaulted basilica recalling those at Binbirkilise and clarified plan and elevation of the cross-domed church, of which O. Feld, *ibid.*, 360 ff., discusses ornament, murals, and pavement. An eighth-century date is tentatively proposed for the construction of the present church (*ibid.*, 345), a date about the middle of the eleventh century for the alterations and the redecoration.

C. F. M. Texier's surveys of St Clement at Ankara and St Nicholas at Myra (*Description de l'Asie mineure*, Paris, 1839–49, I, plate 71; III, plate 222) are unreliable. The sixth-century date proposed for St Clement by Jerphanion is untenable.

As to Sige, the reconstruction as a cross-domed church, proposed by Buchwald, *op. cit.*, seems to me far from secured, given the lack of information regarding shape and,

indeed, existence of enveloping spaces; most certainly, the church had no galleries, an element integral, it seems to me, to the basic type.
293. 4. For the Koimesis church see: O. Wulff, *Die Koimesiskirche in Nicaea* (Strassburg, 1903); T. Schmit, *Die Koimesiskirche von Nikaia* (Berlin and Leipzig, 1927), based on a survey made in 1912; P. A. Underwood, *D.O.P.*, XIII (1959), 235 ff., regarding the pre-iconoclast first state of the apse mosaic; E. Kitzinger, *XI C.E.B. . . . Munich . . . 1958*, Berichte, 1 ff. regarding the import of this observation for dating the architecture; and C. Mango, *D.O.P.*, XIII (1959), 245 ff., pointing out (250 f.) the elimination, after 1065, of the galleries and the rebuilding of the lateral tympana and the narthex. (U. Peschlow, *Ist. M.*, XXII, 1972, 145 ff., doubts the original existence of galleries and correctly denies the use of recessed brick.) For H. Sophia at Salonica, see below, Note 5.

Previous surveys of the Kalenderhane Camii and suggestions regarding its date and original dedication (Van Millingen, *Churches*, 183 ff., as Mary Diaconissa; N. Brunov, *B.Z.*, XXXII, 1932, 54 ff.; J. Kollwitz, *R. Qu. Schr.*, XLII, 1934, 233 ff., as Akataleptos and ninth-century, followed by Schneider, *Byzanz*, 51, and Janin, *Églises*, 518 ff.) can be discarded in the light of the study of the present structure and preceding buildings undertaken by C. L. Striker and Y. D. Kuban (final publication in preparation); at present see the preliminary reports, *D.O.P.*, XXI (1967), 267 ff.; *ibid.*, XXII (1968), 185 ff.; *ibid.*, XXV (1971), 251 ff.; and *ibid.*, XXIX (1975), 306 ff. My warm thanks go to Professor Striker for keeping me abreast of the latest results.

For the Gül Camii (Ebersolt and Thiers, *Églises*, 113 ff.; Van Millingen, *Churches*, 164; Janin, *Églises*, 150 ff.; N. Brunov, *B.Z.*, XXX (1929/30), 554 ff.) see now H. Schäfer, *Die Gül Camii in Istanbul*, Ist. M., *Beiheft* VII (Tübingen, 1973), establishing a date about 1100; but see the critique by T. F. Mathews, *Architectura*, V (1975), 190 ff.

A number of other structures in Constantinople were formerly listed as cross-domed churches of the period extending from the late sixth to the early ninth centuries: the core of the Chora Church (Kariye Camii), that of the Pammakaristos (Fetiyeh Camii), and the Koča Mustafa Paša Camii (perhaps S. Andrew in Krisei); see Van Millingen, *Churches*, 288 ff., 138 ff., 106 ff.; Janin, *Églises*, 545 ff., 217 ff., 32 ff. However, the eleventh- or early-twelfth-century core of the Kariye Camii was a simple atrophied domed cross church (see below, p. 337 and Chapter 16, Note 7). The Fetiyeh (below, Chapter 17, Note 14) and the Koča Mustafa Paša Camii on the other hand are of the ambulatory type like the North Church of the Fenari Isa Camii (below, Chapter 17, Note 9). Like this latter, the Koča Mustafa Paša (S. Eyice, *IX C.E.B. . . . Thessaloniki . . . 1953*, 184 ff.; *idem*, *Son Devir Bizans Mimârisi*, Istanbul, 1963, with German summary, 5 ff.) dates from the thirteenth century, while the Fetiyeh has been assigned convincingly to the second quarter or the middle of the twelfth century; see below, Chapter 17, Note 14.

295. 5. For an architectural survey of the H. Sophia in Salonica see still H. Saladin and M. Le Tourneau, *Les monuments chrétiens de Salonique* (Paris, 1918); for a first serious study M. Kalligas, *Die Hagia Sophia von Thessalonikè* (Würzburg, 1935), and *idem, Praktika* (1936–44), *passim.* S. Pelikanides, *IX C.E.B. . . . Thessalonike 1953*, 398 ff., proposed a single-storey domed narthex and low towers; further proof will be required. A thesis by K. Theocharides, based on extensive excavations and soundings inside and outside the building, is in course of publication (information kindly supplied by Professor Ch. Bouras). The date has been long in doubt. The capitals which to former students had suggested a sixth-century date for the building are spoils (Kautzsch, *Kapitellstudien*, 141 ff.), two of them close to H. Polyeuktos in Constantinople (M. Kambouri, *Epistimoniki Epetiris . . . Polytechnikis Scholis . . .*, 1974, 67 ff.). The inscriptions in the mosaics of dome and apse give, the former the founder's name, bishop Paulus, and a mutilated date, the latter the imperial monograms. Based on an arbitrary reconstruction of the date in the dome, construction has been assigned to 688–90 (Ch. Bakirtsis, *Byzantina*, XI, 1982, 165 ff.), while the apse monograms were taken to refer to a redecoration. However, as pointed out by Buchwald, *op. cit.* (as above, Note 3) and by R. Cormack (*D.C.A.H.*, ser. IV, 10, 1980–1, 111 ff.), the mosaics in dome and apse are contemporaneous. Since the former speaks of the foundation of the church; since moreover (Cormack, *op. cit.*) both inscriptions quote psalms used in foundation ceremonies; since the Imperial monograms give the time span 780–97; and since finally the original iconoclast apse decoration provides as *terminus ante* the Nicaenum II, 787, H. Sophia was built in 780–7 (Buchwald) or 783–7 (Cormack).

I gladly withdraw the objections to Buchwald's dating raised in the 1981 edition of this volume.

6. Underwood and Kitzinger, as above, Note 4.

7. See above, Note 4, for both the Gül and the Kalenderhane Camii. Regarding the recessed brick technique at the Gül Camii, see Schäfer, as quoted there, and below, p. 354 and Chapter 17, Note 3.

8. Van Millingen, *Churches*, 191 ff.; Schneider, *Byzanz*, 53; Janin, *Églises*, 416; Mathews, *Survey*, 16 ff.; *Bildlexikon*, 82 f.; Ćurčić, *J.S.A.H.*, XXXVI (1977), 280 f.; and the definitive study, T. F. Mathews and F. J. W. Hawkins, *D.O.P.*, XXXIX (1985), 125 ff., tentatively identifying the church as H. Elijah in Petrion, built by Basil I, 867–86.

9. G. H. Hamilton, *Art and Architecture of Russia (Pelican History of Art)*, 3rd ed. (London, 1983), *passim.*

296. 10. G. M. L. Bell, *Churches and Monasteries of the Tur Abdin* (London, 1913); also *Zeitschrift für Geschichte der Architektur, Beiheft*, IX (Heidelberg, 1913), 88 ff. A reprint, with commentary and notes, prepared by M. Mundell

Mango (London, 1982) (henceforth quoted as Bell–Mundell), based on the editor's own study of the buildings and on subsequent publications, updates Miss Bell's work. On Mayafarquin, see also Kautzsch, *Kapitellstudien*, 222. The structure no longer stands, see *ibid.* Miss Bell's assumption, accepted by Leroy, *op. cit.*, 480, that the church was vaulted seems to me erroneous, as witness her photographs of aisles and galleries. Only the apse and its flanking chambers carried vaults: nave and ancillary spaces were in all likelihood timber-roofed (or, the former, timber-domed). The date 591 is questioned by C. Foss in Buchwald, *op. cit.*, note 219; but the ornamentation can hardly be later.

11. M. Ballance, *P.B.S.R.* (1955), 99 ff., revising Rott, *Denkmäler*, 32 ff., and suggesting with Kautzsch, *Kapitellstudien*, 183, a date 'not much later than the time of Justinian' for the capitals.

297. 12. C. Mango, in *Polychronion, Festschrift Franz Dölger* (Heidelberg, 1966), 358 ff.

298. 13. The history of Byzantine liturgy requires further elucidation. At this point, see G. Dix, *The Shape of the Liturgy* (London, 1947), 443 ff.; J. M. Hanssens, *Institutiones liturgicae rituum orientalium* (Rome, 1930 ff.), II, III, *passim*; Mathews, *Churches, passim*; Descoeudres, *op. cit.* (Chapter 4, Note 5); and Taft, *op. cit.* (Chapter 5, Note 3).

14. See above, Chapter 6, Note 23; and regarding the placing of the entrances in Syria, Chapter 6, Note 20.

15. For other examples see Orlandos, *Basiliki*, 130 ff.

16. The older view linked the triple sanctuary to the alleged introduction of the *trisagion* in 567 (E. H. Freshfield, *Archaeologia*, XLIV, 1873, 57 ff.); but neither the date nor the link can be sustained. Present opinion on the question of prothesis and diaconicon is best summarized by Lassus, *Sanctuaires*, 162 ff.; G. Bandmann, *Kunstgeschichtliche Studien für Hans Kaufmann* (Berlin, 1956), 19 ff.; Dj. Stričević, *Starinar*, IX–X (1958–9), 59 ff.; A. K. Orlandos, *D.C.A.H.*, ser. 4, IV (1964), 353 ff.; Mathews, *Churches, passim*; Descoeudres, *op. cit.*; and Taft, *op. cit.*

299. 17. For the examples quoted, see above, *passim*; also Stričević, *op. cit.*, and (for Sebaste) N. Firatli, *C.A.*, XIX (1969), 151 ff. Within the context, H. David at Salonica (above, pp. 239–41 and Chapter 10, Note 7) presents a problem: side chambers (with niches) flank the chancel bay, but they open only into the cross arms, not into the chancel as well; hence their function remains unclear, as does that of the chambers at S. Apollinare in Classe.

Mathews, *Churches*, stresses the absence of triple sanctuaries from Constantinopolitan church planning prior to Middle Byzantine times, and points out (*op. cit.*, 84, 94) that the bays flanking the chancel in both H. Irene and H. Sophia were simply entrance bays. The corresponding areas at H. Polyeuktos (*ibid.*, 55) could have sheltered staircases; but the problem wants further study.

18. See above, pp. 217–18 and Chapter 9, Note 14.

19. For the following, see, despite their vagueness, O. Wulff, *B.Z.*, XXX (1929–30), 531 ff., and P. A. Michaelis, *An Aesthetic Approach to Byzantine Art* (London, 1955).
20. The symbolism of the church building is summed up with admirable clarity by O. Demus, *Middle Byzantine Churches and their Decoration* (London, 1948), 14 ff. The main sources are: Maximus Confessor, *Mystagogia*, *P.G.*, XCI, 660 ff. (also Urs Balthasar, *Kosmische Liturgie*, Freiburg, 1946, esp. 246 f.); Germanos, *Ecclesiastical History*, *P.G.*, XCVIII, 383 ff.; Simeon of Salonica, *Peri tou Agiou Naou*, *P.G.*, CLV, 305 ff., esp. 387 ff.

CHAPTER 14

302. 1. A. von Harnack, *Mission*, English ed. (1908), II, 142 ff.
2. The Syriac text of the chronicle, as translated by L. Hallier, *Über die edessenische Chronik* (*Texte und Untersuchungen*, IX, 1892, 1), 86, 'the sanctuary of the Christian congregation' is ambiguous. See also A. von Harnack, *op. cit.*, II, 86; J.-R. Laurin, in *Analecta Gregoriana*, LXX (Rome, 1954); E. Kirsten, *J.A.C.*, VI (1962), 144 ff., esp. 161 f.
3. D. Talbot Rice, *Antiquity*, VI (1932), 276 ff.; U. Monneret de Villard, *Le chiese della Mesopotamia* (*Orientalia Christiana Analecta*, CXXVIII) (Rome, 1940); O. Reuther, *Ausgrabungen der Deutschen Ktesiphon-Gesellschaft, 1928–1929* (Berlin, n.d.).
4. Monneret de Villard, *op. cit.*, 51 ff.; Rice, *op. cit.*, *passim*.
5. The pioneering studies for the architectural monuments of Mesopotamia and the Tur Abdin are F. Sarre and E. Herzfeld, *Archäologische Reise im Euphrat und Tigris Gebiet* (Berlin, 1911 ff.), and G. L. Bell, *Churches and Monasteries of the Tur Abdin* (Bell–Mundell; see above, Chapter 13, Note 10). Since her pioneering visit in 1911, numerous churches unknown to her have been published; see for instance J. Leroy, *C.R.A.I.* (1967), 324 ff., *ibid.* (1968), 478 ff.; F. W. Deichmann and U. Peschlow, *Zwei spätantike Ruinenstätten in Nordmesopotamien* (*Bayerische Akademie der Wissenschaften, Phil.-Hist. Kl., Sitzungsberichte*, 1977, 2), with references also to fortifications; and M. Mundell Mango, *C.A.*, XXX (1982), 47 ff. Of a new survey of churches in the region, G. Wiessner, *Christliche Kultbauten im Tur Abdin* (*Göttinger Orientforschungen*, II. Reihe, Band 4) so far parts I and II (Wiesbaden, 1982 and 1983) have appeared.
Dated buildings within our context range from Nisibis, Mâr Yaqub, 'martyrium' (359; see following note) to Qartamin (512), El 'Adhra at Ḥah (after 571), Nisibis Mâr Yaqub, main church (713–56); see Bell–Mundell, 143.
In *East of Byzantium*, ed. N. G. Garsoïan, T. F. Mathews, R. W. Thomson (Washingon, D.C., 1982), 115 ff., Mrs Mundell Mango brings out the classical Syro-Roman trend in North Mesopotamian architecture and decoration and its interlacing with Parthian–Sassanian features from the second century to the sixth. She also stresses the prevailing

Syrian character of urban church planning (Edessa, Nisibis, Amida) as against the local note of its rural counterpart – this notwithstanding the continued predominance also in the countryside of 'classical' ornamentation.
6. The type is well represented by Mâr Yaqub at Nisibis (Bell–Mundell, 96ff.). The date 359 secured for the domed structure adjoining the main church (which is later) by a Greek inscription designating it also as a baptistery (Sarre and Herzfeld, as above, Note 5, II, 336 ff.) has been challenged by Kautzsch, *Kapitellstudien*, 222 ff., who proposes a sixth-century date for the decoration. The presence of a crypt below the structure raises questions regarding the use of the building as a baptistery; unless, that is, the crypt was added later, transforming the structure into a martyrium. The niched octagon at Qartamin has been published by J. Leroy, *C.A.*, XXV (1975), 1 ff., with revised plan – deep stilted semicircular corner niches; but the plan is entirely conjectural – and interpreted tentatively as a baptistery. On longitudinal barrel-vaulted churches, see now G. Koch, ed., in *Studien zur spätantiken und frühchristlichen Kunst und Kultur des Orients* (Wiesbaden, 1982), 117 ff.
303. 7. Mâr Ibrahim at Midyat; Mâr Yaqub at Ṣalaḥ (Bell, *op. cit.*, 68 ff.).
8. El'Adhra, Ḥah (Bell, *op. cit.*, 82 ff.). The drum of the church (our illustration 263) was raised in 1907 adding a second arcade; see Bell, *op. cit.*, 82, and Leroy, *op. cit.*, 484.
9. Guyer, *R.K.W.*, XXXV (1912), 181 ff., published the ruin of a church at Surg Hagop in Commagene, but closely related to Tur Abdin architecture and dated through an inscription between 818 and 845, where the transverse nave was enveloped by projecting arched niches carrying a gallery. Based on the classical vocabulary of this late church, he suggested dates ranging from the seventh to the ninth century for the majority of the Tur Abdin churches as well, including Mâr Yaqub at Ṣalaḥ, and even Mâr Gabriel at Qartamin. Late dates for many of the Tur Abdin churches seem indeed quite plausible (Monneret de Villard, *op. cit.*, *passim*). Still, given the ornament of Qartamin, Deir Za'faran, and Ḥah, the mosaics in the chancel of Qartamin (E. Hawkins and M. C. Mundell, *D.O.P.*, XXVII, 1973, 279 ff.), and the good tradition for the church having been built in 512 by the emperor Anastasios (J. Leroy, *C.A.*, VIII, 1958, 75 ff.), a date, for these churches at least, after the sixth century is hard to accept.
304. 10. For such late examples, see in particular Leroy, *op. cit.*, and Wiesner, *op. cit.*, both as quoted above, Note 5.
305. 11. J. E. Quibell, *Excavations at Saqqarah* (Cairo, 1909), IV, 1 ff., also P. Grossmann, *M.K.*, XXVIII (1972), 145 ff.; U. Monneret de Villard, *Il monastero di San Simeone presso Aswân* (Milan, 1927); A. Fakhry, *The Necropolis of El-Bagawat* (Cairo, 1951); finally, on Bawit, *Mémoires de l'Institut Français d'Archéologie du Caire*, XII (1904), XIII (1905),

XXXIX (1916), LIX (1931); H. Torp, *Byzantion*, XXV-XXVII (1955–7), 513 ff.; *idem, Mélanges École Française*, LXXVI (1964), 137 ff., and LXXVII (1965), 153 ff.; G. Severin, *M.K.*, XXXIII (1977), 113 ff. Mr Severin dates the half column shafts (our illustration 268) to the fourth century. He has kindly pointed out the correct location of Bawît.

306. 12. E. Kitzinger, *Archaeologia*, LXXXVII (1937), 181 ff.

307. 13. For this and other examples, see Somers Clarke, *Christian Antiquities in the Nile Valley* (Oxford, 1912), *passim*; U. Monneret de Villard, *Les couvents près de Sohag* (Milan, 1926), *passim*.

14. Clarke, *op. cit.*, 95 ff.; Monneret de Villard, as above, Note 11; H. G. Evelyn-White, *The Monasteries of the Wadi'n Natrun*, III (*Egyptian Expedition Publications*, VIII) (New York, 1928); more recently, in summary form, W. Müller-Wiener, in *Koptische Kunst*, exhibition catalogue (Essen, 1963), 131 ff. In few of the structures has research as yet succeeded in definitely distinguishing original and added parts or in dating either securely; but it is possible that the original structure at Aswân dates from the late tenth or eleventh centuries. The church at Deir-es-Suriani has been convincingly assigned to the ninth century, its vaulting to about 1200. The original plan of Amba Bishoï dates from 830–49, the vaulting from 1330. See also, P. Grossmann, *Enchoria*, VIII (*Sonderband*, II, 1978), 89 (135), regarding development of types and dating.

15. Evelyn-White, *op. cit.*, 131 ff. (Amba Bishoï); 227 ff. (Deir Baramus).

16. St Sergius (Abu Sargeh), St Barbara (Barbarah), Al Muallakah; see U. Monneret de Villard, *IV C.A.C. . . . Rome . . . 1938*, 291 ff., and *idem, La chiesa di Santa Barbara al Vecchio Cairo* (Florence, 1922), superseded by Grossmann, *Enchoria*, as above, Note 14.

17. Clarke, *op. cit.*, *passim*. For churches of this and other types in Upper Egypt, S. Adli, *M.K.*, XXXVI (1980), 1 ff.

308. 18. G. S. Mileham, *Churches in Lower Nubia* (Philadelphia, 1910), 37 ff. (Adindân-Addendan with illustration); 27 ff. (Faras, churches outside citadel); 41 f. (Serreh). More recently, W. Y. Adams, *Journal Amer. Research Center in Egypt*, IV (1965), 87 ff. (attempt to trace development, 500–1400); W. H. C. Frend, *VII C.A.C. . . . Trier . . . 1965*, 530 ff. (Qasr Ibrim); K. Michalowski, *Faras* (Leiden, 1966: Faras Cathedral, 707, replacing an older church); *idem*, in *Kunst und Geschichte Nubiens*, ed. E. Dinckler (Recklinghausen, 1970), 11 ff. (Faras, south church in citadel, 'not later than 600'); T. Säve-Söderbergh, *ibid.*, 219 ff. (Serreh, south church, 600–850; Sahâba, prior to 850); M. Martens, in *Études et travaux*, XIV (1973), 263 ff. (Dongola, four churches).

309. 19. S. Runciman, *The First Bulgarian Empire* (Oxford, 1934).

20. For early church building in Dalmatia, see now V. Grozdanović, *Pre-Romanesque and Early Romanesque Archi-*

tecture in Croatia, Ph.D. thesis, Cornell University, 1972, whence also the dates now accepted in our text.

21. An eleventh-century example is Sv. Petar at Omiš; see Grozdanović, *op. cit.*, 229 ff., supplementing F. Bulič, in *Studien zur Kunst des Ostens* [for] *Joseph Strzygowski* (Vienna and Hellerau, 1923), 136 ff.

310. 22. See above, pp. 274–5, and Chapter 11, Notes 29, 30.

23. U. Monneret de Villard, *L'architettura romanica in Dalmazia* (Milan, 1910).

24. R. von Eitelberger, *Jahrbuch der K.K. Central-Kommission*, V (1861), 160 ff. The original dedication to the Trinity and a *terminus ante quem* for the construction are established by a reference in Constantine Porphyrogenetos, *De administrando Imperio*, chapter 29 (ed. G. Moravcsik and R. J. H. Jenkins, Budapest, 1949, 138 f.), but the date of construction, while presumably early-ninth-century, remains open (Grozdanović, *op. cit.*, 187 ff.).

311. 25. See above, Chapter 10, pp. 255–7, and Note 29.

312. 26. For the ninth- and tenth-century architecture in Bulgaria see Mavrodinov (1959), 89 f. (Pliska), 135 ff. (Preslav, palace and church), 184 ff. (churches around Preslav); more recently, Kr. Mijatev, *Architekturata v Srednovekovna Blgarija* (Sofia, 1965), *passim*, esp. 86 f. (small churches near Pliska), 110 ff. (churches around Preslav). A clear summary of the *status quaestionis* as of 1960 is given by Stričević, *XII C.E.B. . . . Ohrid . . . 1961*, I, 165 ff.

27. Building history and date of St Sophia at Ohrid are still under discussion; see Schmidt-Annaberg, *Deutsche Bauzeitung*, LV (1921), 193 ff., 205 ff.; D. Bošković, *God. Serb. Akad.*, XLII (1933), 164; D. Kocó, *Archaeologia Iugoslavica*, II (1956), 139 ff.; F. Forlati, C. Brandi, and Y. Froidevaux (ed. Unisco), *St Sophia of Ochrida* (1953); D. Bošković and K. Tomovski, in *Musée National d'Ohrid, Recueil de Travaux* (Ohrid, 1961), 173 ff.

Dj. Stričević, *XII C.E.B. . . . Ochride 1961, Rapports*, VII, 187 ff. sums up the discussion and provides his analysis: of an early, possibly sixth-century church of indeterminate plan, only foundation walls survive; of the 'Bulgarian' church, built by Czar Boris (852–89), the essential parts survive in the present structure – barrel-vaulted nave arcaded on piers, transept, vaulted aisles east and west of the crossing, the pendentives of the dome, chancel, lower part of apse, esonarthex on both floors; the western crossing piers are late, but the site of the original piers, slightly further west, has been established; tentatively Stričević ascribes to this building phase also the galleries above the aisles east and west linked across the transept; a rebuilding prior to 1037–56, when the frescoes in the chancel were painted (A. Grabar, *Zb.R.*, VIII, 1964, 163 ff.; also A. W. Epstein, *J.Ö.B.*, XXIX, 1980, 315 ff.) adds the upper parts of the apse and the absidioles. In the fourteenth century the two-storeyed exonarthex was built, while transept, crossing, and dome were demolished when the church was turned into a mosque.

These theses are being challenged by B. M. Schellewald, *Untersuchungen zur Baugeschichte der Sophienkirche in Ohrid*, Ph.D. thesis (Bonn, 1982) (unpublished, but made accessible to us through the kindness of Professor Hallensleben). The author argues that the original parts of the building, in cloisonné masonry, rise straight from the foundation of a fourth-to-sixth-century predecessor. The cloisonné outlines aisles, transept, nave, and three-apsed bema, the latter and the transept barrel-vaulted, the crossing domed, nave and aisles timber-roofed. The galleries ('upper chapels') both west and east of the transept, while in brickwork and originally unvaulted, belong to the first building phase. This phase, based on the character of the cloisonné in the context of a presumed continuous and all-over development of that technique, is dated by the author in the second third of the eleventh century when at Ohrid, incorporated in the Byzantine empire, a new cathedral was founded under Archbishop Leo (1037–51; see however for the use of cloisonné as early as c. 900 H. Stephanos at Kastoria (A. W. Epstein, *Art Bulletin*, LXII (1980), 190 ff.; *idem*, *J.Ö.B.* (1980), 315 ff., esp. 325 ff.). Links to Skripou or Nessebâr are being refuted (see already Hallensleben, *B.Z.*, LXVI, 1973, 125), those to Constantinople (the 'upper chapels', e.g. Fenari Isa) stressed.

A decision will have to await the results of the survey of St Sophia under way by Professor V. Korac.

28. For the church of the Baptist at Nessebâr see Mavrodinov (1959), 111 ff., with a late-ninth-century date. A. K. Orlandos, *Archeion*, IX (1961), 3 ff., suggests the second quarter of the tenth century, and lists a number of churches of similar plan to which he assigns dates ranging from the first quarter of the tenth to the second quarter of the eleventh century. Likewise, for related churches such as H. Germanos in the Prespa Lake (S. Pelikanides, *Mnimeia byzantina . . . tis Prespas*, Salonica, 1960; also Mavrodinov, 1959, 268 f.) and a ruin near Vodoča in the Struma Valley (for this latter now P. Miljković-Pepek, *Le complexe des églises de Vodoča*, Skopje, 1975, presenting the building history: east church, domed and barrel-vaulted nave, narrow aisles, seventh to ninth century, rebuilt tenth; west of it quincunx on piers, 1018–37; rebuilding c. 1100, turning west church into narthex of enlarged, domed and barrel-vaulted east church) ninth- and tenth-century dates have been proposed. Hallensleben, *B.Z.*, LXVI (1973), 124 f., favours for the entire group an eleventh-century or later date.

313. 29. J. Strzygowski, *B.Z.*, III (1894), 1 ff., was the first to call attention to the church at Skripou, followed by M. G. Sotiriou's monograph, *Ephemeris* (1931), 119 ff. A. K. Orlandos, *Archeion*, IX (1961), 3 ff., linked the plan to that of a church at Episkopi in the mountainous south-west corner of central Greece, undated, small, and rustic in design and construction. To this church in turn he linked a group of

neighbouring small quincunx churches (see Note 28) in which the supports, rather than being columns, are square or rectangular piers. Neither Episkopi nor any of the quincunxes are dated. P. L. Vokotopoulos, *Hi ekklesiastiki architektoniki eis tin dytikin Hellada kai Epeirou* (Thessaloniki, 1975), takes the same view; but based on the masonry technique and what little ornament survives, he dates Episkopi and some other churches rather than in the tenth and eleventh (Orlandos, *op. cit.*) in the second half of the eighth or the first half of the ninth century and thus prior to Skripou; see also Ch. Barla, *Charistirion eis A.K. Orlandon*, IV (Athens, 1967), 303 ff., dating a church at Suvala to the early seventh century. Along the same line of thought D. Pallas, *Epitiris Hetairias Stereoelladikōn Meletōn* (1976/7), views Skripou as intermediary between Early Christian and Byzantine church building in Greece. I remain unconvinced. Rustic construction and poor design do not necessarily denote greater age, and I cannot view the monumental church at Skripou as rooted in the architecture of these backwoods villages. The shoe, it seems to me, if any link exists, is on the other foot. As to the hypothesis of the Bulgarian–Armenian–Skripou connection suggested by me and doubted not only by the colleagues quoted above but also by A. H. S. Megaw (see following note) and S. Dufresne, *Byzantinobulgarica*, VII (1981), 359 ff., I see its flaws; but I cannot think of a proposal which better convinces me.

315. 30. A. H. S. Megaw, *B.S.A.*, LXI (1966), 1 ff., in countering my proposal, has brought out the Greek and Constantinopolitan elements in the ornament both in the templon screen and in the plaques on the exterior of the Skripou apses, and has linked the erection of the church to the Byzantine reconquest of Greece from the Slav invaders and the ensuing revival of building activity in the context of Imperial policy. Convincing though his arguments are, I still see Bulgarian and Sassanian elements, too, both in construction and in the ornamentation of cornices and wall plaques – perhaps lingering on.

31. K. Mijatev, *I.B.A.I.*, X (1936), 136 ff., and XIV (1940–2), 73 ff.; Mavrodinov (1959), 37 ff.; and Mijatev, *Baukunst*, 30 ff., 47 ff. The identification of the site with Pliska, the residence of Czar Krum, and hence the date of the buildings found has however been questioned; D. Kranažalov, in *Sbornik Vysoké školy pedagogické v Olomouci, Historie*, III (1956), 43 ff., and V (1958), 35 ff., as quoted by Dj. Stričević, *XII C.E.B. . . . Ohrid . . . 1961*, I, 180 ff. See also S. S. Vaclinov, *C.C.R.*, XV (1968), 241 ff.

32. See however the reconstruction with aisles proposed by B. D. Filov, *Die altbulgarische Kunst* (Zürich and Leipzig, 1919), and *B.Z.*, XXX (1929–30), 523 ff., and by Mijatev, *Baukunst* (*op. cit.*, Chapter 10, Note 24), 50.

33. Apsed halls were common in Byzantine palaces from the fifth and sixth centuries; see D. Talbot Rice (ed.), *The Great Palace of the Byzantine Emperors, Second Report*

(Edinburgh, 1958), 24 ff., and A. M. Mansel, *VI C.E.B*. . . .
Paris . . . *1948*, II, 255 ff. The triclinium of the Magnaura,
known only from descriptions (Richter, *Schriftquellen*, 294
ff.), and the throne room at Pliska have been linked by
Mijatev, as above, Note 31, contrary to Filov's thesis, above,
Note 32.

3 16. 34. Filov represents the former, Mijatev the latter view;
see, however, St. Stančev, *XII C.E.B*. . . . *Ohrid* . . . *1961*, I,
345 ff.

35. Mijatev, *Baukunst*, 54 f., and A. Grabar, *Les influences
orientales dans l'art balkanique* (Paris, 1928), 1 ff. The
penetration of Sassanian decorative motifs, pure and unas-
similated, as at H. Polyeuktos (see above, pp. 219 ff.), was an
isolated case as far as we can tell today.

36. Differences between the full stone masonry of
Bulgarian palaces, the stone plaques facing mortared rubble
in Armenia, and the re-used stone blocks of Skripou are
clear. Nonetheless, the same appearance is aimed at.

37. G. Millet, *L'école grecque* (Paris, 1916), 84 f., regarding
the resemblance in plan of Skripou to Armenian churches;
as to the decoration, both Megaw (as above, Note 30) and A.
Grabar, *Sculptures byzantines de Constantinople* (Paris, 1963),
90 ff., incline to view it as Byzantine and, indeed, Constantinopolitan pure and simple; however, the mingling with
Sassanian elements (e.g. heart-shaped leaves, griffins)
seems to me undeniable.

38. Runciman, *op. cit.* (above, Note 19), *passim*, has noted
the forced resettlements of Armenians in Thrace – beginning in 755 and continuing perhaps in 784 and certainly in
872 – as well as their impact on Bulgaria, both in commerce
and religion, whether orthodox or sectarian. (I am indebted
to Professors Garsoian, Columbia University, and Caspary,
University of California, Berkeley, for calling my attention
to these points.) Runciman, *op. cit.*, 231 f., and with greater
precision in N. H. Baynes and H. Moss, *Byzantium* (Oxford,
1948; paperback ed. Oxford and New York, 1961), 343 has
also alluded to links between Armenian and Bulgarian
architecture.

3 18. 39. Dj. Stričević, *XII C.E.B*. . . . *Ohrid* . . . *1961*, I, 165
ff.; *idem, Zb. R.*, VIII (1964), 399 ff.

40. N. Mavrodinov, *I.B.A.I.*, XIII (1939), 246 ff.
(*mitatoria*). The ninth-century date favoured by V. Ivanova,
I.B.A.I., XII (1938–9), 365 ff., and Mavrodinov (1959), 92
ff., is accepted by Mijatev, *Baukunst*, 77 ff., while Stričević,
op. cit., 180 ff., after weighing the pros and cons arrives at a
sixth-century date.

41. Regarding basilicas in Yugoslavia and northern Greece
in general, V. Korać, *XII C.E.B*. . . . *Ohrid* . . . *1961*, I, 173 ff.
For H. Achilleos, Pelikanides (as above, Note 28), 64 ff.,
proposing a date 1020–30; A. Grabar, *Zb. R.* (1964), 163 ff.,
prior to 1002; N. K. Moutsoupolos, in his monograph
Anaskaphai tis Basilikis tou Agiou Achilleiou (Thessaloniki,
1969), arriving at a date still under Czar Samuel, prior to
1014. In contrast, Stričević, *op. cit.*, suggests a ninth-century

date with the exception of the supposedly eleventh-century
upper chambers of the pastophories. For Staro Nagoričino,
V. Korać, as above; for the Bogorodica Ljeviška at Prizren,
Stričević, *op. cit.*, 201 ff., and S. Nenadović, *Bogorodica
Ljeviška* (Belgrade, 1963), proposing a ninth-century date;
see also below, pp. 434 ff.

42. Stričević, *op. cit.*, 207 ff.

43. K. Mijatev, *B.Z.*, XXX (1929–30), 561 ff.; *idem,
I.B.A.I.*, VI (1930–1), 187 ff.; A. Rašenov, *ibid*, X (1936),
216 ff.; G. Millet, *C.R.A.I.* (1933), 169 ff.; Mavrodinov, *op.
cit.*, 150 ff.; and Mijatev, *Baukunst*, 89 ff., all favour a date
under Czar Simeon, around 900. Dj. Stričević and I.
Nikolajevič-Stojković (*XII C.E.B*. . . . *Ohrid* . . . *1961*, I, 212
ff. and 241 ff.) attempt to prove the correctness of a sixth-
century date previously proposed by D. Bošković (*Starinar*,
VIII–IX, 1933–4, 331 ff.) and S. Radojčeč (*Zb. R.*, I, 1952,
156 f.). They reason that the classical elements of the
building, both in plan and decoration, survived into the sixth
century, when in their opinion the church at Preslav was
built. However, it remains to be proved that structures so
completely corresponding to third- and fourth-century
architectural concepts were ever designed in Justinian's
time; this quite aside from the improbability of a structure so
complex and lavish being laid out in the sixth century in
what was then the farthest corner of a frontier province.
Equally implausible is the hypothesis (Millet, *op. cit.*) that
round structures of the type of Preslav were common among
the churches of Constantinople under Justinian and later.
Hallensleben, *B.Z.*, LXVI (1973), 125 f., on the other hand,
suggests an eleventh-century date. Still other roots are
suggested by E. Schwartz, *VII B.S.C. 1981*, 42 f. To me the
elegance and smallness of the many-niched plan suggest an
early-tenth-century date, coincident with Preslav's becom-
ing the capital of the Bulgar czars.

Soundings undertaken by St. Boyadjiev (*I'S.A.A.*, 15 ff.)
show that the foundations of atrium, forechurch, and
rotunda were not built in the same phases of construction;
rather the former two were added to the rotunda in two
successive campaigns. Likewise the wall of the inner colonnade of the rotunda fails to bond with that of its niched wall.
However such divergences often only indicate the customary builders' reluctance to bond walls of different height and
carrying function. The author's view of these additions
having transformed an early 'Armenian' rotunda into the
present building does not convince. See also *idem*, in St.
Boyadjiev, N. Tchaneva Detchevska, and L. Zaharieva,
Recherches sur l'architecture du Moyen Âge bulgare (Sofia,
1982), 5 ff.

321. 44. Mavrodinov (1959), *passim*.

45. J. Strzygowski, *Die Baukunst der Armenier und Europa*
(Vienna, 1918), while outdated, remains indispensable as
the first gathering of the material. S. Der Nersessian,
Armenia and the Byzantine Empire (Cambridge, Mass.,
1945), V. M. Harutiunian and S. A. Safarian, *Pamiatniki*

Armianykogo Zodchvestva (Moscow, 1951; in Russian), and *Architettura medievale armena*, ed. G. de Francovich (Rome, 1968) present good surveys, the latter in catalogue form (we shall quote it henceforth as *Architettura Armena*). *C.C.R.*, XX (1973), *passim*, contains selected papers on the topic by members of the Italian team. Likewise the *I° S.A.A.* . . . *1975* contains a number of corresponding contributions. A. Khatchatrian, *L'Architecture arménienne du IVᵉ au VIIᵉ siècles* (Paris, 1971), examined the early 'basilican' phase with an eye also to revising previous misdatings of centrally planned structures; while the work of Michel, Nicolle, and Jean-Michel Thierry over the past fifteen or twenty years has greatly contributed to our knowledge, focused as it is largely on central-plan churches and their sculptured and painted decoration and on new discoveries: Mren (M. Thierry, *C.A.*, XXI, 1971, 43 ff.); Arcuaber (J.-M. Thierry, *ibid.*, XXV, 1976, 39 ff.); Kars (*idem*, *La cathédrale des Saints-Apôtres à Kars*, Louvain–Paris, 1978; the classification of architectural types and the elaboration of stemmata to me carries little conviction). R. W. Thompson, *The Journal of Theological Studies*, N.S. XXX, part I (1979), has dealt with the references in Armenian early writing to architectural symbolism, closely as it seems related to Syrian parallels.

G. J. Tchubinashvili, *Razbiskayia po Armenskoja Architekture* (Tiflis, 1967: in Russian with German summary), claims chronological precedence for Georgian over Armenian building; also R. Mepisachwili and W. Zinzadse, *Architektura Grusini-schidla Kartli* (Tiflis, 1975), and *Art and Architecture in Medieval Georgia*, ed. A. Alpago-Novello and others (Louvain, 1980). See further *R.L.B.K.*, I, 306 ff., on Armenia (Khatchatrian) and II, 668 ff. on Georgia (W. Ponomarew).

In recent years there has been a spate of picture books with informative text in western languages on the architecture of Georgia and its links to that of neighbouring Armenia, such as G. M. Gabridašnli, *Ancient Monuments of Georgia* (Leningrad, 1975), and E. Neubauer, *Altgeorgische Baukunst* (Vienna, 1976).

46. Der Nersessian, *op. cit.*, 58 f. stresses the links to Asia Minor and Mesopotamia, Khatchatrian, *op. cit.*, 93 ff. those to Syria. Clearly, both regions would exert their impact. *Architettura Armena*, esp. 17, 21, insists on the autochthonous character of Armenian building in both plan and technique, while F. De Maffei, *C.C.R.*, XX (1973), 287 ff., M. and N. Thierry, *C.A.*, XXI (1971), 43 ff., and in a broad survey of the architectural links between the East Roman provinces and Byzantium on one hand and the successive Sassanian, Umayyad, and Seljuk empires on the other, W. Müller-Wiener, *J.Ö.B.*, XXXI/2 (*XV C.E.B. . . . Vienna . . . 1981*) (1981), 575 ff., all bring out the transmigration from Sassanian to Armenian and from there possibly into Greek building of technical features, possibly the trump (squinch), to effect a transition from square to octagon.

322. 47. Ereruk: *Architettura Armena*, 78, with fourth- or

fifth-century date, Khatchatrian, *op. cit.*, 43 ff., fifth-century. Both datings on stylistic grounds only seem early, as compared with Syrian building; see, however, in neighbouring Georgia, the Sion's church at Bolnisi, dated 479–93 (N. Aladshvili, *Monumentalvija Skulptura Grusii*, Moscow, 1977, 10), a groin-vaulted hall church. Tekor: *Architettura Armena*, 84; Khatchatrian, *op. cit.*, 48 ff., convincingly proposes a basilican plan for the first building phase, datable 486, though perhaps timber-roofed; see also A. Alpago-Novello, *Ererouk* (1977). Eghvard: *Architettura Armena*, 77; Khatchatrian, *op. cit.*, 43 ff. Dvin cathedral, in its first state: below, Note 50. Also, more recently, F. Gandolfo, *Le Basiliche armene* (Rome, 1982); reporting *inter alia*, 13 ff., on the first 'patriarchal' basilica, perhaps fourth-century.

48. *Architettura Armena*, 102; Strzygowski, *op. cit.*, 108 ff. and *passim*. Zvart'nots – before 652(?) – W. E. Kleinbauer, *Art Bulletin*, LIV (1972), 245 ff. For a related tetraconch, *c.* 900, at Penǝk, R. G. Edwards, *D.O.P.*, XXXIX (1985), 15 ff.

323. 49. Tekor, rebuilding: Khatchatrian, *op. cit.*, 48 ff. Ptghavank' (Ptghni): *Architettura Armena*, 82; Der Nersessian, *op. cit., passim*; Tchubinashwili, *op. cit.*, 191, with tenth-century date. T'alish (Aroudz): *Architettura Armena*, 83; Tchubinashwili, *op. cit.*, 194, proposing a mid-tenth-century date as against the otherwise accepted date 670. Mren: *Architettura Armena*, 86, and M. and N. Thierry, *C.A.*, XXI (1971), 43 ff., first third of the seventh century, possibly 629–40. Also Bagaran and Odzun, *Architettura Armena*, 85.

50. Dvin: Khatchatrian, *op. cit.*, 53 ff., distinguishing fifth-century first basilica and the seventh-century rebuilding; M. D'Onofrio, *Le chiese di Dvin* (Rome, 1973). T'alinn: *Architettura Armena*, 88.

51. *Architettura Armena*, 89 ff., including chapels at Ashtarak and T'alinn (St Mary), the latter dated prior to 783.

52. Gayané church: *Architettura Armena*, 87; Tchubinashwili, *op. cit.*, 181 (the church was rebuilt in 1651 on the old plan). Bagaran: *Architettura Armena*, 97; Der Nersessian, *op. cit.*, 66; Tchubinashwili, *op. cit.*, 182, refers to the similar church of Zromi in Georgia with a good date 626–34, see *idem, Zromi* (Moscow, 1969; in Russian).

53. Avan: *Architettura Armena*, 99; Tchubinashwili, *op. cit.*, 179 f., views the plan as derived from the Djuari church at Mzchet in Georgia which may date from 585/6–604/5. Hrip'simé church: *Architettura Armena*, 100; Tchubinashwili, *op. cit.*, 186 ff., with ninth-century dating. Arcuaber: M. Thierry, *C.A.*, XXV (1976), 43 ff., with a list of related churches, classified into sub-groups and ranging from the early seventh into the early eleventh century. Soradir: T. Breccia Frattadocchi, *La chiesa di S. Ejmiacin a Soradir* (Rome, 1971); also *Architettura Armena*, 98.

324. 54. S. Der Nersessian, *Aght'amar* . . . (Cambridge, Mass., 1965); *Architettura Armena*, 103. See also Varagvank', Church of the Virgin, eleventh-century, *ibid.*, 142.

55. *Architettura Armena*, 97.

327. 56. Tchubinashwili, as quoted above, Notes 45 and 52, and *idem* in *Vseobščaya Istorija Arhitektury*, III, *Arhitektura vestočnoj Evropy, Srednie veka*, ed. J. S. Jaralov and others (Moscow, 1966), 300 ff.

57. Strzygowski's thesis, though modified, is taken up emphatically in *Architettura Armena*, 19 ff.

328. 58. Goshavank: *Architettura Armena*, 148 (related churches, *ibid.*, 144, 146, 155). Ani, cathedral: *ibid.*, 108; Der Nersessian, *op. cit.*, 73 ff. Aght'amar: see above, Note 54. Marmashen: *Architettura Armena*, 106.

330. 59. Strzygowski, *op. cit., passim*.

60. Der Nersessian, *op. cit., passim*.

61. Millet, *op. cit.* (Note 37), *passim*.

CHAPTER 15

331. 1. G. Ostrogorsky, *History of the Byzantine State* (Oxford, 1956), *passim*, in particular, 175 ff.

2. S. Runciman, *The Eastern Schism* (Oxford, 1955).

332. 3. The *Myriobiblion* of Photius *(P.G.*, CIII, 42 ff.; CIV, 9 ff.) has been translated by J. H. Freese, *The Library of Photius* (London, 1920). For Constantine Porphyrogenetos' writings, aside from the *Book of Ceremonies* (above, Chapter 9, Note 15), see *De administrando Imperio*, as quoted in Chapter 14, Note 24. The continuation of Theophanes' history (*Theophanes Continuatus*), written on Constantine's behest (*P.G.*, CIX, 15 ff.; *Bonn Corpus*, XLVIII), presents the history of the Macedonian House and its immediate predecessors.

4. Michael Psellos (trans. E. R. A. Sewter), *Chronographia* (New Haven, 1953).

5. Anna Comnena (trans. E. Dawes), *The Alexiad* (London, 1928).

333. 6. See below, Chapter 16, pp. 350–1.

7. Liutprand of Cremona, *Legatio ad Nicephorum*, and (ed. J. Becker) *Antapodosis* (*M.G.H. in usum scholarum*) (Hanover, 1915), *passim*; see also *The Works of Liutprand of Cremona* (trans. F. A. Wright) (New York, 1930).

8. S. Khitrovo, *Itinéraires russes en Orient* (Geneva, 1889); for later visitors, G. P. Majeska, as below, Chapter 17, Note 5.

9. S. Runciman, *A History of the Crusades* (Oxford, 1951–5; paperback, New York, 1964–7).

10. In a few stimulating pages C. Mango, in *Travaux et Mémoires Centre de Recherche d'histoire et civilisation byzantine*, VI (1976), 351 ff., sketches some of the social and economic factors impinging on Middle Byzantine church building. I can only agree with the emphasis he gives to the greater number of constructions in the ninth and eleventh as against the tenth century and to the prevalence of monastic as against parish churches founded after 1000. The economic reasons suggested for this deserve further study.

334. 11. Mango, *Byzantium*, 81; F. Gregorovius, *Geschichte der Stadt Athen im Mittelalter* (Munich, 1980), 109 ff.

CHAPTER 16

335. 1. Regarding Middle Byzantine architecture, see, aside from the old but still useful handbooks (O. Wulff, *Altchristliche und byzantinische Kunst, Handbuch der Kunstwissenschaft*, Wildpark-Potsdam, 1918, *passim*; Diehl, *Manuel*, *passim*), the summaries by Ch. Delvoye, *XIII C.E.B. ... Oxford ... 1966*, 225 ff., and by A. Grabar, *C.A.*, XVII (1967), 257 ff., esp. 261, and the presentation of problems and monuments by Mango, *Architettura bizantina, passim*. The dendrochronological survey being undertaken by Cecil L. Striker and P. J. Kuniholm and covering the coastlands of the Aegean is likely to produce fundamental contributions to the chronology of architecture from Justinian to the Late Byzantine period. See the preliminary report by the two authors, *Journal of Field Archaeology*, X (1983), 413 ff.

336. 2. K. J. Conant, *Carolingian and Romanesque Architecture (Pelican History of Art)*, 3rd ed. (Harmondsworth, 1974), 68. While the galleries date from a second phase of construction, after 965, the intervention of Theophanou is not documented; see *Vorromanische Kirchenbauten*, ed. F. Oswald and others, I (Munich, 1966), 98 ff.

3. Regarding the H. Sophia at Nicaea, see below, Chapter 17, Note 16. A number of large, old-fashioned basilicas, supported by arcades on piers and dating from the sixth to the thirteenth and fourteenth centuries, are scattered over Greece, the islands, and the Balkans. They include a large sixth- or early-seventh-century cemetery church at Kraneion just outside Corinth, carried by rectangular piers and lavishly appointed, preceded by a porticoed atrium, likewise on piers, and with a square baptistery and a triconch martyrium(?) attached (*Praktika*, 1972, 205 ff.; completed plan, *ibid.*, 1976); two medium-sized churches excavated on Crete, one at Vizarion with a date around 800 assigned to it (*Ergon*, 1956, 123 ff.) and another of tenth- or eleventh-century date at Vera (*ibid.*, 1959, 153 ff.); one dug up near Sparta, formerly dated 1033 (Sotiriou, *Praktika*, 1934, 132, and *ibid.*, 1939, 107 ff.), now assigned to the seventh century (Vokotopoulos, *Praktika Protou Diethnou Synedriou Peloponnesiōn Spoudōn*, II, 273, Athens, 1976); and another at Tigani on the Mani peninsula, small and crooked in plan, of twelfth-century date (*ibid.*, 1978, 1980, 183 ff.); finally in the fourteenth century, the basilica at Trikkala in Thessaly (*Archeion*, III, 1937, 156 ff.). For a summary, V. Korać, *XII C.E.B. ... Ohrid ... 1961*, III, 173 ff. The list of basilicas given in *Archeion*, IX (1961), 21 ff., suffers from the intermingling of the 'old-fashioned' with the small-scale 'Kastoria' type.

4. See G. H. Hamilton, *Art and Architecture of Russia (Pelican History of Art)*, 2nd ed. (Harmondsworth, 1975), 8 ff., and, for S. Marco in Venice, below, pp. 406–11 and Chapter 17, Notes 76 ff.

5. Kastoria: *Archeion*, IV (1939), *passim*, and now A. W. Epstein, *Art Bulletin*, LXII (1980), 190 ff., with revised

dating: H. Stephanos, Kubilidiki, Taxiarches, *c*. 900, a date challenged again by Schellewald, as above, Chapter 14, Note 27; Anargyroi, eleventh century; H. Nikolaos, twelfth century – all barrel-vaulted. Arta: *Archeion*, 11 (1936), *passim* (Kato Panaghia, 1250–70, barrel-vaulted, 70 ff.; H. Theodora, eleventh- or twelfth-century(?), timber-roofed, narthex late-thirteenth-century, 88 ff.). See also below, pp. 372 ff., and S. Mihailov, *R.i.P.*, IV (1949), 171 ff., especially regarding a sociological interpretation of this revival.

6. A first list of Middle Byzantine triconchs and tetraconchs as given by A. K. Orlandos, *Archeion*, I (1935), 105 ff., is supplemented by S. Bettini, *V C.E.B. ... Rome ... 1936*, II, 31 ff., and by Dj. Stričević, *XII C.E.B. ... Ohrid ... 1961*, *Rapports*, VII, 224 ff., with rich bibliography. Regarding the Heybeliada church, see S. Eyice, *Son devir bizans mimârisi* (Istanbul, 1967; with German summary), 44 ff.; T. F. Mathews, *D.O.P.*, XXVII (1973), 115 ff.; and A. Pasadaios, *Ephemeris*, CX (1971), 1 ff. The towering drum of the Kubilidiki is entirely rebuilt; see S. Pelikanides, *Balkan Studies*, III (1962), 463 f.

337. 7. For the Kariye Camii, see the structural analysis in P. A. Underwood, *The Kariye Djami* (London, 1967): a late-eleventh-century structure, preserved only in foundations; the core of the present church, probably *c*. 1120; and the nartheces and parekklesia, 1315–20/1; for further details on the excavation of 1957/8, D. Oates, *D.O.P.*, XIV (1960), 223 ff. R. G. Ousterhout, *The Architecture of the Kariye Camii in Istanbul*, Ph.D. thesis, University of Illinois, 1982 (unpublished, accessible to us through the author's kindness), after further scrutinizing the evidence, tentatively proposes (*op. cit.*, 102 ff.) a quincunx plan for the eleventh-century structure; see also H. Belting, *Pantheon*, XXX (1972), 263 ff. We suggest leaving the question open. The succeeding early-twelfth-century church was built on an 'atrophied domed Greek cross' plan (*ibid.*, 106). For the fragments of architectural sculpture found during excavations, see Ø. Hjort, *D.O.P.*, XXXIII (1979), 199 ff. For Vunitsa, see S. Stančev, *I.B.A.I.*, XVIII (1952), 305 ff., Mavrodinov (1958), 58, and S. Boyadžiev, *Byzantino-Bulgarica*, II (1966), 241 ff.

The ruin of the church near Ereğli (Marmara-ereğlisi) on the European shore of the Sea of Marmara, now apparently destroyed, has been dated 'near 1000 ... or at the time of Basil I ... or perhaps as early as Heraclius' (J. Strzygowski, *J.ÖAI.*, I, 1898, Beiblatt, 1 ff.), or 'not after the ninth century' (Wulff, *Handbuch*, 453 f.); the similar ruin at Yuša Tepesi on the Asian side of the Bosphorus has been equally vaguely dated 'sixth or ninth century' (S. Eyice, *IX C.E.B. ... Salonica ... 1953*, 184 ff.). For Sige, see above, p. 288, and Chapter 13, Note 3. For a church of the type near Drama, and a list of similar churches in northern Greece, southern Yugoslavia, and Bulgaria, assigned to the thirteenth century, G. Velenis, in *Epistomoniki Epitiris tis polytechnikis Scholis ... Thessalonikis*, VI (1973), 83 ff.

338. 8. On Chios, below, pp. 363–5 and Chapter 17, Note 12; on later variants of the type, Ch. Bouras, *D.C.A.H.*, ser. IV, IX (1977–9), 23 ff.

340. 9. G. Millet, *L'école grecque* (Paris, 1916), 105 ff., terms the type 'église à trompes d'angle'. He lists, apart from Hosios Lukas and Daphni, the Panaghia Lykodimou in Athens (ruined in a nineteenth-century restoration; see A. Couchaud, *Choix d'églises byzantines*, Paris, 1842, plates 11 ff., for the original building); the cathedral of Christianou (E. Stikas, *L'église byzantine de Christianou*, Paris, 1951); and four examples which he dated into the late thirteenth century: H. Sophia at Monemvasia (R. Traquair, *B.S.A.*, XII, 1905–6, 273 f.; however, H. Kalligas, *D.C.A.H.*, IX, 1977–9, 217 ff. on good grounds proposes a mid-twelfth-century date), H. Theodoroi at Mistra (G. Millet, *Monuments byzantins de Mistra*, Paris, 1910, plates 20 f.), the Parigoritissa at Arta (see below, p. 417 f., and Chapter 19, Note 9), St Nicholas-in-the-Fields, near the former Lake Kopais (*Ergon*, 1960, 240 ff.).

C. Mango, *D.O.P.*, XXVII (1973), 128 ff., tentatively suggests the existence in Constantinople of a Greek-cross-octagon plan with a dome in two lost churches, St George in the Manganes (1042–55) and St Mary Peribleptos (1028–34), the former the principal foundation of Constantine IX Monomachos, the builder of the Nea Moni on Chios.

10. Millet, *loc. cit.*; Stikas, *op. cit.*, 34 ff.

11. See Chapter 13, Note 4; Chapter 17, Note 14.

341. 12. The term quincunx was coined by K. J. Conant (as quoted Chapter 2, Note 38), *passim*. For the Nea, see below, pp. 355–6, and Chapter 17, Note 5; for Tirilye (Trilye), F. W. Hasluck, *B.S.A.*, XIII (1906/7), 215 ff., and C. Mango and I. Ševčenko, *D.O.P.*, XXVII (1973), 235 ff., reporting also on further church and monastic buildings on the Asiatic shore of the Sea of Marmara; for Germigny-des-Prés, P. Clemen, *Romanische Monumentalmalerei in den Rheinlanden* (Düsseldorf, 1916), 54 ff., and J. Hubert, *L'art pré-roman* (Paris, 1938), *passim*; for S. Satiro, G. Chierici, *La chiesa di S. Satiro a Milano* (Milan, 1942); for Tarrasa, J. Puig y Cadafalch, *VI C.E.B. ... Paris ... 1948*, II, 343 ff.; for S. Maria delle Cinque Torri (now destroyed), H. W. J. Schulz, *Denkmäler der Kunst des Mittelalters in Unteritalien* (Dresden, 1860), II, 106 ff., and E. Scaccia Scarafoni, *R.A.C.*, XXIX (1946), 139 ff. For another early example, at Armasi in the mountains of Soviet Georgia, dated by inscription 864, Mepisachwili and Zinzadse, *op. cit.* (above, Chapter 14, Note 45), 17 ff.

13. Göreme, see below, pp. 396–7 and Chapter 17, Note 56; Side, see S. Eyice, *X C.E.B. ... Istanbul ... 1955*, 130 ff., and *Anatolia*, III (1958), 35 ff.; Peristerai, below, Chapter 17, Note 28.

14. J. Strzygowski, *Die Baukunst der Armenier und Europa* (Vienna, 1918), 849 ff. The status of the question as of 1925 has been summarized by Diehl, *Manuel*, II, 460 f. More recently, see K. Erdmann, in *Spätantike und Byzanz (Neue*

Beiträge zur Kunstgeschichte des ersten Jahrtausends) (Baden-Baden, 1952), 53 ff., with bibliography.

342. 15. Millet, *op. cit.*, 62, 72; Ramsay and Bell, *Churches*, *passim*, in particular, 397 ff.; and critically, Diehl, *Manuel*, II, 437, note 2.

16. For the former (obsolete) thesis see Wulff, as quoted above, Chapter 13, Note 4; Diehl, *Manuel*, II, 460 f.; N. Brunov, *B.Z.*, XXVII (1927), 63 ff., and *Vizantiskij Vremmenik*, XXVII (1949), 150 ff.; W. R. Zaloziecky, *B.Z.*, XXVIII (1928), 372 ff., and *ibid.*, XXIX (1929), 248 ff. For the latter thesis we refer to Orlandos, *Archeion*, IX, 1 (1961), 3 ff., and Vokotopoulos, as above, Chapter 14, Note 29.

17. The structure, demolished in 1890, is known only from illustrations (C. J. M. De Vogüé, *La Syrie centrale*, Paris, 1865 f., plate 7; J. W. Crowfoot, *Early Churches in Palestine*, London, 1941, plate VIIIa; and on old photographs recently discovered, S. Hill, *D.O.P.*, XXIX, 1975, 347 ff.). E. Weigand (*Würzburger Studien zur Altertumswissenschaft*, XIII, 1938, 71 ff.) maintained that the building was erected as a temple (not a praetorium), and that the columns and covering dated only from the fifth century, when it was supposedly – but there is no evidence – transformed into a church. The second part of his thesis carries, for me, little conviction; so also S. Hill, *op. cit.*, 348 f., who however considers possible a change of the roof structure in the fifth or sixth century.

18. See above, pp. 261–2, and Chapter 11, Note 10. A structure of related form (quincunx) and possibly function is reported at Old Dongola (Sudan). The nine-bay plan of the main hall features four (three are preserved) free-standing columns. The building was converted into a mosque in 1317. It is tentatively dated to the end of the ninth or early tenth century. See W. Godlewski, *XVI C.E.B. ... Vienna, 1981, Akten*, II, 4 (*J.Ö.B.*, XXXII/4, 1982), 69 ff.

343. 19. G. Ostrogorsky, *History of the Byzantine State* (Oxford, 1956), 231 f., 245 f., regarding the reasons for the dwindling of monastic congregations; Janin, *Églises*, for the convent of Constantine Lips; for Kastoria, Epstein, as above Note 5, stressing the role of family foundations as one cause for the smallness of churches. Chapels both flanking the church and at roof level are found for instance at the church of Constantine Lips (Fenari Isa) in Constantinople, on the narthex gallery at the Panaghia Chalkēon in Salonica, free-standing beside the Nea Moni on Chios. Regarding the function of chapels, G. Babić, *Les chapelles annexes* (Belgrade, 1969); S. Ćurčić, *Zb. R.* (1971), 333 ff. (commemorative services); T. F. Mathews, *C.A.*, XXX (1982), 125 ff. (private liturgies).

20. O. Demus, *Middle Byzantine Mosaic Decoration* (London, 1948), 14 ff.

344. 21. L. M. E. de Beylié, *L'habitation byzantine* (Paris, 1902), though outdated has not been replaced. T. Kirilova Kirova, *Felix Ravenna*, CII (1971), 263 ff., links Middle Byzantine to Syrian fifth- and sixth-century houses and, like de Beylié (and Diehl, *Manuel*, 423 ff.), focuses on palaces rather than ordinary domestic building. Ch. Bouras, *XVI C.E.B. ... Vienna ... 1981 (J.Ö.B.*, XXXI, 1981), 611 ff., is a major 'state of research' article on questions of urban architecture in the Byzantine world. See also *idem*, *D.C.A.H.*, series IV, IX (1983), 1 ff. Bulgarian excavations near Preslav have brought to light foundation walls of many modest dwellings of ninth- to eleventh-century date.

22. J. Travlos, *Poleodomiki Exelixis tōn Athinōn* (Athens, 1959), 154 ff.; R. Scranton (ed.), *Corinth, Medieval Architecture in the Central Area*, XVI (Cambridge, Mass., 1957), 128 ff.; similar houses (with shops) at Hierapolis, undated, see T. Kirilova Kirova, *Felix Ravenna* (1972), 275 ff., esp. 295 ff. The finds at the Point of the Saray (E. Unger, *J.D.A.I.*, *A.A.*, 1916, 1 ff.; also T. Kirilova Kirova, *Felix Ravenna*, 1971, 263 ff.) are obviously the remains of the ground floor of an elegant house with colonnaded openings both on the façade and separating the rooms and an attached bath. See also L. Zaharieva, in *Recherches* (*op. cit.*, Chapter 14, Note 43), 204 ff.

345. 23. A. K. Orlandos, *Monastiriaki Architektoniki* (Athens, 1926, reprinted 1958).

24. *Archeion*, V (1939–40), 34 ff., and *ibid.*, VII (1951), 72 ff. See also *Archeion*, VII (1951), 72 ff. (Sagmata), and E. Stikas in *Charistirion eis A.K. Orlandon*, II (Athens, 1966), 309 ff. (Moni Agrounton), both twelfth-century; and for thirteenth-century examples, A. K. Orlandos, *Hi Parigoritissa tis Artis²* (Athens, 1963), and *Archeion*, II (1936), 70 ff. (Kato Panaghia).

347. 25. See above, pp. 140, 259, and Chapter 11, Notes 6 and 8.

26. See below, p. 349 and Note 38.

27. De Beylié, as above, Note 21, *passim*; P. Kukules, *Byzantinos bios kai politismos*, IV (Athens, 1951), 258 ff.

28. K. M. Swoboda, *Römische und romanische Paläste* (Vienna, 1925); G. Lorenzetti, in *Miscellanea ... in onore di I.B. Supino* (Florence, 1933), 23 ff.; J. S. Ackerman, *Acts XX Internat. Congress History of Art ... New York ... 1960*, II (1963), 6 ff.

348. 29. Mavrodinov (1959), 38 ff., 144 ff. For the palace of Romanos Lekapenos, see R. Naumann, *Ist. M.*, XVI (1966), 199 ff.; for Dvin, Khatchatrian (as above, Chapter 14, Note 45), plates 18 f., and *Vseobščaya Istorija Architektury*, III (as *ibid.*, Note 56), 203 ff.; for Pliska, also St. Stančev, in *Antike und Mittelalter in Bulgarien*, ed. V. Beševliev and J. Irmscher (Berlin-East, 1960), 226 ff., and a related structure at Old Dongola (Sudan); see above, Note 18.

30. The sources, excerpted in English translation, are found in Mango, *Documents*, *passim*; in German translation and impeccably arranged, in Richter, *Schriftquellen*, 253 ff. Their interpretation, over the last decades, has been undertaken by A. Vogt (as above, Chapter 9, Note 15), by R. Janin, *Constantinople byzantine* (Paris, 1950), and by R. Guilland in numerous articles, collected in R. Guilland, *Études sur la*

topographie de Constantinople byzantine (Berlin and Amsterdam, 1969), I, 1 ff., unfortunately without taking into account sufficiently the archaeological finds.

31. *The Great Palace of the Byzantine Emperors (The Walker Trust)*, I, ed. G. Brett (Edinburgh, 1947), and II, ed. D. T. Rice (Edinburgh, 1958). The mosaic pavement, of the peristyle court, once dated after 410 and before 430 (*Great Palace*, I, 91), has since been assigned dates reaching from the late fifth century (*ibid.*, II, 160) to about 530 (D. T. Rice, *Charistirion eis A. K. Orlandon*, I, Athens, 1965, 1 ff.), to the end of the sixth century (I. Lavin and C. Mango, *Art Bulletin*, XLII, 1960, 67 ff.) and as late as A.D. 700 (P. Nordhagen, *B.Z.*, LVI, 1963, 58 ff.). New excavations are under way. For the apsed hall, see *Great Palace*, II, *passim*, and for its (uncertain) date, 161 ff.; for the 'House of Justinian', *ibid.*, 168 ff., esp. 192 f.

32. Mango, as quoted above, Chapter 10, Note 10; Guilland, *op. cit.*, I, 7 ff. and *passim*.

349. 33. Richter, *op. cit.*, 294 ff.; Guilland, *op. cit.*, I, 141 ff.

34. Mango, *Documents*, 161 ff.; Richter, *op. cit.*, 342 ff.; Guilland, *op. cit.*, I, 95 ff. and *passim*.

35. Michael Psellos, book 6, chapter 185 (as above, Chapter 15, Note 4, 188 f.; also Mango, *Documents*, 281 ff.).

36. Mango, *Documents*, 163 ff.; Richter, *op. cit.*, 349 ff.

37. Mango, *Documents*, 196 ff.; Richter, *op. cit.*, 363 ff.; A. Grabar, *L'empereur dans l'art byzantin* (Paris, 1936), *passim*.

350. 38. Mango, *Documents*, 208, 210; Richter, *op. cit.*, 288 ff.; Guilland, *op. cit.*, I, 82 ff. For the great Lateran triclinium, R. Krautheimer, in *Tortulae* (*R. Qu. Schr.*, Suppl. 30) (1966), 195 ff.; for the banqueting hall north of the Hippodrome, R. Naumann, *Ist. M.*, XV (1965), 135 ff.; for the *quinque dagubitas* at Ravenna, A. Weis, *Tortulae, op. cit.*, 300 ff.; for another one with seven niches in the Hormisdas Palace at Constantinople, N. Alemanni, *De Lateranensibus parietinis* (Rome, 1625), 18, where – as I see belatedly – the Lateran Triclinium already was linked to the Dekanneacubita.

39. On the relations between Byzantium and the Islamic world, see *D.O.P.*, XVIII (1964): M. Canard, 33 ff. (political and commercial contacts); O. Grabar, 67 ff. (Umayyad and Byzantine art); G. C. Miles, 1 ff. (Aegean area, in particular 'cufic' ornament on Greek churches); F. Gabrieli, 57 ff. (Sicily and South Italy); and, more recently, Müller-Wiener, *XV C.E.B.*, as above, Chapter 14, Note 46.

40. L. Torres Balbas, *La Alhambra y el Generalife* (Madrid, 1949).

41. L. Torres Balbas, *La mezquita de Cordoba y las ruinas de Medinat-al-Zahra* (Madrid, 1960).

42. A. M. Mansel, *VI C.E.B. . . . Paris . . . 1948*, II, 255 ff.

351. 43. Torres Balbas, *op. cit.* (Note 41), 76 f., and E. Lambert, *VI C.E.B. . . . Paris . . . 1948*, II, 225 ff.; Canard, *D.O.P.*, XVIII (as above), 36, note 5 (but also O. Grabar, *ibid.*, 70, note 3, where the statement regarding Medinat-al-Zahra is questioned).

44. Constantine Porphyrogenetos, *The Book of Ceremonies* (as above, Chapter 9, Note 15) and Liutprand of Cremona, *Antapodosis*, VI, 5 (trans. Wright as above, Chapter 15, Note 7, 207 f.); also Mango, *Documents*, 209 ff., and Richter, *op. cit.*, 301 ff.

45. See, however, for the reverse dependence of Arab on Byzantine scientific manuscript illumination, K. Weitzmann, in *Archaeologica Orientalia in memoriam Ernst Herzfeld* (Locust Valley, 1952).

46. O. Grabar, *D.O.P.*, as above, Note 39. For the palace at Bryas, see Mango, *Architettura bizantina*, 194, based on S. Eyice, *Belléten*, XXIII (1959), 79 ff. (which had escaped my attention in preparing the earlier editions of this volume). A related 'fortified' royal palace may be seen at Geguti, Georgia. Presumably dated to the tenth century, the palace displays a squarish fortified enclosure with a large, centrally located octagon-domed hall; R. Mepisaschwili and V. Zindzadse, *Die Kunst der alten Georgien* (also in English) (Leipzig, 1977), 58.

352. 47. The interweaving of survival and revivals in the 'Middle Byzantine Renaissance' is discussed clearly and imaginatively by E. Kitzinger, *VI C.E.B. . . . Paris . . . 1948*, II, 209 ff., and *idem*, *XI C.E.B. . . . Munich . . . 1958* Berichte, IV, 1, *passim*; see also *ibid.*, *Diskussionsbeiträge*, 55 ff. More recently the question of a 'Macedonian Renaissance' and of later Byzantine 'renascences' has been broached, with some scepticism in particular as to its applicability to architecture and mural painting, by Mango, *Byzantium*, 272 ff.

353. 48. Ch. Bouras, *D.C.A.H.*, ser. IV, 5 (1964), 247 ff., on the existence and extent of a 'renascence' in Middle Byzantine architecture, with similar results, though with slightly greater stress on an actual revival of Late Antique spatial proportions (Nea Moni, Chios) and of the technique of stone construction (Greece, eleventh and twelfth centuries).

CHAPTER 17

354. 1. A perusal of Janin, *Églises*, Schneider, *Byzanz*, O. Tafrali, *Topographie de Salonique* (Paris, 1912), and C. Diehl, H. Saladin, and M. Le Tourneau, *Les monuments chrétiens de Thessalonique* (Paris, 1913), reveals the difficulties of correlating the monuments and the documentary evidence even in centres such as Constantinople or Salonica.

2. Schneider, *Byzanz*, 13 f., is but a first, tentative attempt.

3. C. Mango, *D.O.P.*, XIII (1959), 245 ff., in particular 249 ff., also with reference to A. M. Schneider and W. Karnapp, *Die Stadtmauer von Iznik (Nicaea) (Istanbuler Forschungen*, IX) (Berlin, 1938). The earliest examples quoted by Mango are buildings in Kiev, the Golden Gate, the second Desyatinna church, and the church of St Sophia, all dating from 1037–9. Meanwhile, excavations have made it

likely that already the first Desyatinna church, under construction since 989, was built in 'recessed' brickwork by
masons called from Constantinople (H. Schäfer, *Ist. M.*,
XXIII–XXIV, 1973–4, 197 ff., quoting M. K. Karger,
Drevnij Kiev, Moscow and Leningrad, 1958–61). For other
examples see the parts of the Anastasis Rotunda in
Jerusalem as built by Byzantine masons under Constantine
IX Monomachos, about 1045 – for that rebuilding and
replanning of the rotunda, see R. Ousterhout, *IXB.S.C....
1983*, 61 ff. The question of 'recessed brickwork' has been
taken up anew by P. L. Vokotopoulos, *J.Ö.B.*, XXVIII
(1979), 248 ff., with reference also to examples of
thirteenth-century date.

355. 4. A. H. S. Megaw, *B.S.A.*, XXXII (1931–2), 90 ff., and
ibid., XXXIII (1932–3), 137 ff.; *idem, Charistirion eis A. K.
Orlandon*, III (1966), 16 ff.

5. The church described in Photius's Homily X has been
correctly identified as that of St Mary of the Pharos instead
of the Nea by R. Jenkins and C. Mango, *The Homilies of
Photius*, Cambridge, Mass., 1958, 177 ff. (likewise Mango,
Documents, 185 f.), who have established also the dates of
consecration, 864 for the Pharos church, 1 May 880 for the
Nea. For a description of the Nea, see *Theophanes Continuatus*, v, 83 (Mango, *Documents*, 194; Richter, *Schriftquellen*,
354) and Anthony of Novgorod (S. Khitrovo, *Itinéraires
russes en Orient*, Geneva, 1889, 98 f.). For an English
translation of Russian texts dealing with Constantinople
with commentaries, G. P. Majeska, *Russian Travelers to
Constantinople in the Fourteenth and Fifteenth Centuries* (Dumbarton Oaks Studies, XIX) (Washington, 1984), 247 (text)
and 247 f. (commentaries). S. Ćurčić, *VI B.S.C. ... 1980*,
11 f., points out that the description could refer as well to
a cross-domed as to a quincunx plan; I hesitate. K.
Wulzinger, *Byzantinische Baudenkmäler zu Konstantinopel*
(Hanover, 1925), 48 ff., identifies (unconvincingly to me) a
cistern in the Saray ground with the quincunx substructure
of the Nea. Other churches in the palace grounds and
without are known, either in general terms or with specific
reference to their decoration, through consecration
sermons delivered by Leo VI the Wise (886–912) (A.
Frolow, *Études byzantines*, III, 1946, 43 ff.).

6. Their barrel-vaults were covered with mosaics, showing
martyrs thrown to wild beasts (Mango, *Documents*, 195) – an
ecclesiastical adaptation of the old motif of circus games
performed before the Emperor. (See also A. Grabar,
L'empereur dans l'art byzantin, Paris, 1936, 61 ff.)

356. 7. Anthony of Novgorod, as above, Note 5.

8. Van Millingen, *Churches*, 196 ff.; Schneider, *Byzanz*, 65;
Bildlexikon, 103 ff.; Janin, *Églises*, 364 ff. The definitive
monograph, C. L. Striker, *The Myrelaion (Bodrum Camii) in
Istanbul* (Princeton, 1981), provides all necessary information regarding the structure and its history. The basement in
Paleologan times became a burial chapel. Our illustration
309 is due to Professor Striker's kindness. The restoration

of the structure was in the hands of the Aya Sofia Müzesi.
358. 9. Van Millingen, *Churches*, 122 ff.; Schneider, *Byzanz*,
61 f.; Janin, *Églises*, 318 ff.; *Bildlexikon*, 126 ff. The conclusive study on which I depend, Th. Macridi, A. H. S.
Megaw, C. Mango, and E. J. Hawkins, *D.O.P.*, XVIII
(1964), 249 ff., results in a graphic reconstruction of the
building, based on the observations and soundings undertaken during its restoration and consolidation directed by
the late Paul A. Underwood on behalf of the Byzantine
Institute Inc. and Dumbarton Oaks, 1960–3. For the ornament, see also A. Grabar, *Sculptures byzantines de Constantinople* (Paris, 1963), 100 ff. Against Megaw's reconstruction proposal, N. Brunov, *J.Ö.B.*, XVI (1967), 245 ff.

361. 10. *Bildlexikon*, 120 ff. Outer porticoes along the flanks
have been proposed for the Eski Imaret Camii (Brunov,
Byzantinisch-Neugriechische Jahrbücher, IX, 1930–2, 129 ff.;
see, however, Schneider, *loc. cit.*) as well as for the Bodrum
and the Fenari Isa Camii, a suggestion accepted by me in the
first edition of the present volume, *passim*. Meanwhile it has
been proven that such porticoes did not exist in either the
Bodrum or the Fenari Isa Camii. I still consider it possible,
though not certain, that in the Eski Imaret at least the cross
arm was flanked by a sheltering portico, as witness the
projecting cornice above; no such traces are visible further
east or west.

363. 11. The Kilise Camii wants further study. At this point,
see Van Millingen, *Churches*, 243; Ebersolt and Thiers,
Églises, 149 f.; Schneider, *Byzanz*, 77 f.; Janin, *Églises*, 149 f.;
Hallensleben, *Ist. M.*, XV (1965), 208 ff.; *Bildlexikon*, 169 ff.
A set of drawings of c. 1835 (London, R.I.B.A., Sir Banister
Fletcher Library, Texier volumes I, Église de St Théodore;
see now C. Mango, *J.D.A.I.*, LXXX, 1965, 305 ff., esp. 323
ff.) shows the church as of that time. The colonnaded
portico along the south flank, shown in these drawings,
contrary to the belief formerly held, is probably a
fourteenth-century addition (Hallensleben, *op. cit.*, 211 ff.;
Mango, *op. cit.*, 330) to the Paleologue exonarthex.
Schneider, *Byzanz*, 77 f., dates the building into the tenth or
eleventh century; however, the recessed brick technique
and the ornamentation suggest a late date in the period
1050–1150. The exonarthex and presumably the drum of
the main dome are of Paleologue date; see below, pp.
446–8.

12. J. Strzygowski, *B.Z.*, V (1896), 140 ff., where also the
text of the sources, A. K. Orlandos, *Monuments byzantins de
Chios* (Athens, 1930; plates only), and more recently Ch.
Bouras, *Nea Moni on Chios* (Athens, 1982). A restoration
some fifty years ago rebuilt the dome and repaired the
marble revetments of the naos; but it has also replaced the
paired colonnettes of the ground-floor zone with clumsy
half-piers. While Vokotopoulos, *J.Ö.B.*, XXVIII (1979),
249, note 16, is right in stating that the exonarthex of
the Nea Moni is built in *cloisonné* masonry (Bouras,
op. cit., figures 26, 45 f.), Strzygowski's photograph shows

what may have been recessed brickwork in the pendentive zone.

365. 13. See above, Chapter 13, Note 4, regarding both Kalenderhane and Gül Camii. The identification of the Gül Camii as the church of H. Theodosia is questionable.

14. For the Koimesis, see above, pp. 292–5 and Chapter 13, Note 4, and particularly for its rebuilding, C. Mango, *D.O.P.*, XIII (1959), 245 ff., supplemented by the plan and elevation, Schmit, *op. cit.*, plates IV and IX, and by Peschlow, as quoted Chapter 13, Note 4.

The Fetiyeh Camii, St Mary Pammakaristos, has been discussed recently in two different studies: R. Hallensleben, *Ist. M.*, XIII/XIV (1963/4), 128 ff.; and C. Mango and E. J. W. Hawkins, *D.O.P.*, XVIII (1964), 319 ff. Both reconstruct the original core as an ambulatory church supported by a cistern and distinct from the enveloping elements. But they disagree on the date: Hallensleben inclining towards 1067 for the foundation; Mango and Hawkins, on stylistic grounds and convincing to me, suggesting an early-twelfth-century date for the construction. See also S. Eyice, *Son devir bizans mimârisi*, 2nd ed. (Istanbul, 1980; with German summary), 22 ff., 106, though with a thirteenth-century date. The monograph by C. Mango, H. Belting, and D. Mouriki, *The Mosaics and Frescoes of St Mary Pammakaristos . . . at Istanbul* (Washington, D.C., 1978), includes an extensive chapter on the history of the building.

15. For the Kariye Camii, see above Chapter 16, Note 7; for Kurşunlu, C. Mango, *D.O.P.*, XXII (1968), 169 ff. A ruin at Yuša Tepesi above the Bosphorus (S. Eyice, *C.E.B. . . . Salonica . . . 1952*, 184 ff.), while of similar plan, need not be of Middle Byzantine times. For the church at Heybeliada, see above, Chapter 16, Note 6; the thirteenth-century date suggested by Eyice has been revised by Mathews, *D.O.P.*, XXVII (1973), 115 ff., based on the 'recessed' brickwork, found incidentally also at Kurşunlu; for the Toklu Dede Mescidi, see A. Pasadaios, *Ephimeris* (1969), 80 ff.; *Bildlexikon*, 206 ff. C. Mango, *D.O.P.*, XXVII (1973), 128 ff., tentatively suggests a tetraconch plan surmounted by a dome on squinches for the Church of Christ above the Chalki Gate, built about 972.

16. A. M. Schneider, *Die römischen und byzantinischen Denkmäler von Iznik-Nicaea* (*Istanbuler Forschungen*, XVI) (Berlin, 1943), has established the sequence of building periods. A fifth- or sixth-century structure, built of ashlar at the bottom and of brick in the window zone, has survived in the present aisle walls. This was followed, *c.* 1065, by: the present nave, with its piers and, originally, four groups of triple arcades on columns; the apse; and, possibly, the domed chambers flanking the apse. (N. Brunov, *R.K.W.*, XLIX, 1928, 51 ff., esp. 60 f., has dated these domed chambers to the fourteenth century, perhaps correctly.).

367. 17. A. H. S. Megaw, *D.O.P.*, XVII (1963), 335 ff., has

established the structural history of the three churches incorporated in the Zeyrek Camii and brought to light pavement, wall decoration, and fragments of the stained-glass windows formerly in the south church. The older bibliography (Van Millingen, *Churches*, 219 ff.; Schneider, *Byzanz*, 68 f.; Janin, *Églises*, 529 ff.) has become obsolete as well as my own previous statements in the first edition of this work, p. 265. See also Mathews, *Survey*, 71 ff., *Bildlexikon*, 209 ff., and for the function of the three churches and the (lost) monastery, A. Taylor, *III B.S.C. . . . 1977*, 47 f.

369. 18. S. Ćurčić, *Art and Architecture in the Balkans . . .* (Boston, 1984), provides an up-to-date annotated bibliography of Middle and Late Byzantine material in Albania, Bulgaria, and Yugoslavia. Comprehensive treatments of architecture in the same period and area are, for Bulgaria, N. Mavrodinov (1959), *passim*; idem, *Ednokorabnata i krstovidnata crkva (L'église à nef unique et l'église cruciforme en pays bulgare jusqu'à la fin du XIVe siècle)* (Sofia, 1931); Kr. Mijatev, as quoted above, Chapter 14, Note 26, all with (now out-of-date) references to monographs and to papers in *I.B.A.I.* and *R.i.P.*; for Yugoslavia, G. Millet, *L'ancien art serbe* (Paris, 1919), on many points obsolete, but still basic; A. Deroko, *Monumentalna i dekorativna arhitektura . . . Srbiji* (Belgrade, 1953), with all-too-short French and English summaries and a wealth of plans, detail drawings, and photographs; V. Petković, *Pregled crkvenih spomenika kroz povesnicu srpskog naroda* (Belgrade, 1950), *passim* (in Serbian), with concise building histories; and, summarily, S. Radojčić, *Geschichte der serbischen Kunst* (Berlin, 1969); *idem*, as quoted above, *op. cit.*, 257 ff., and Dj. Bošković, *C.C.R.*, X (1963), 13 ff., and *ibid.*, XVII (1970), 23 ff.; see also the running reports and papers in *Starinar* (1910 ff.), *Zb. R.* (1952 ff.), and *Godišen Zbornik. Filosofski fakultet, Univerzitet Skopje* (1947 ff.).

19. See above, pp. 318–21, and Chapter 14, Note 43.

20. Half-cylindrical buttresses were found in a church (no. 1), excavated at Bial Briag near Preslav, of early-tenth-century date; V. Ivanova, *R.i.P.*, III (1949), 148 ff. Another church excavated near by and attributed to the second third of the tenth century (Avradaka, no. 1) seems to have opened into lateral porticoes and to have been provided with polygonal apses and apparently a narthex gallery; *idem*, *ibid.*, 13 ff. and *XII C.E.B. . . . Ohrid . . . 1961*, III, 141 ff.; also Mavrodinov (1959), 186 ff.; see also St. Bojadžiev, *Premier Congrès d'Études balkaniques*, II (1969), 599 f., questioning the open flanks of Avradaka, no. 1. A quincunx on piers, the 'Church of the Boyars', has been found in the citadel at Pliska, *I.B.A.I.*, XXVI (1963), 5 ff.

21. S. Stančev, *I.B.A.I.*, XVIII (1952), 305 ff., and Mavrodinov (1959), 185 ff.; St. Bojadžiev, *Byzantino-Bulgarica*, II (1966), 241 ff., proposes instead a reconstruction on the quincunx plan.

370. 22. Dj. Stričević, in *XII C.E.B. . . . Ohrid . . . 1961*,

Rapports, VII, 224 ff.; N. C. Dečevska, *Arkheologija*, XII, 4 (1970), 8 ff.
23. See above, Note 15, and Chapter 16, Note 34.
24. D. Bošković and K. Tomovski, *Musée National d'Ohrid, Recueil des Travaux* (Ohrid, 1961), 85 f.; D. Koco, *Godišen Zbornik . . . Filozofski fakultet*, I (1948), 129 ff. (French summary).
25. *Archeion*, I (1935), 105 ff.
26. Mavrodinov (1959), 167 ff., with bibliography.
371. 27. A. Grabar, *Les influences orientales dans l'art balkanique* (Strasbourg, 1928), stresses the resemblance of Bulgarian and Sassanian ornament on glazed tiles. However, tenth-century tiles of very similar type, both with ornament and figures of saints, have come to light at Constantinople (D. Talbot Rice, *Byzantine Glazed Pottery*, Oxford, 1930, *passim*; K. Mijatev, *V C.E.B. . . . Rome . . . 1936*, 266 ff.; and E. S. Ettinghausen, *C.A.*, VII, 1954, 79 ff.); see also the group of tiles acquired in 1959 by the Walters Art Gallery, Baltimore, Maryland, and those found in the Fenari Isa Camii (see above, Note 9). Regarding the mosaics in the mosque of Cordova, see above, Chapter 16, Note 41.
28. *Archeion*, VII (1951), 146 ff. Also Ch. Tsiumi and A. Kountoura, *Klironomias*, XIII, 2 (1981), 487 ff., who argue that an Early Christian structure was incorporated into the ninth-century construction, a suggestion that awaits further proof. Professor James Morganstern has kindly provided photographs.
372. 29. S. Mihailov, *R.i.P.*, III (1948), 171 ff., who has excavated a number of these structures, discusses their implications for the political and social history of tenth-century Bulgaria.
30. The ruin of such a hall-church survives at Vračanica near Ljutibrod in the Struma region; Mavrodinov (1959), 272.
31. *Archeion*, IV (1939), 1 ff.; A. K. Orlandos, in *Archeion*, IX (1961), 21 ff., lists vaulted and unvaulted Middle Byzantine hall-churches and basilicas found in Greece and Macedonia, dating from the tenth to the thirteenth century. See more recently Vokotopoulos, Chapter 14, Note 29.
32. See below, pp. 379–81, and A. H. S. Megaw, *B.S.A.*, XXXII (1931–2). While A. K. Orlandos, *Archeion*, IV (1939), dated the Kubilidike to the end of the tenth century, A. W. Epstein, as above, Chapter 16, Note 5, proposes a late-ninth-century dating. For the Anargyroi she arrives at an early-eleventh-century date as against Orlandos, *op. cit.*, who favoured an attribution to the second or third quarter of that century.
373. 33. C. Diehl, H. Saladin, and M. Le Tourneau, *Les monuments chrétiens de Salonique* (Paris, 1918), 153 ff., and D. Evangelidis, *Hi Panaghia tōn Chalkion* (Salonica, 1954), with new survey. The date 1044 for the dedicatory inscription, suggested by Evangelidis, is incorrect. The date is

1028, as read by earlier students; see *Praktika* (1933–4), 88 ff. *Monuments of Thessalonike*, ed. S. Molho (Salonica, 1957; reprint 1972) is a handy little guidebook.
34. See below, pp. 388 ff.
374. 35. *Archeion*, I (1935), 139 ff. For the forerunners of Middle Byzantine twin-domed narthex galleries, as in the Panaghia Chalkeon, and their Late Byzantine descendants, many-domed, single-storied nartheces, S. Ćurčić, *Zb. R.*, XIII (1971), 333 ff.
375. 36. Picture books about Mount Athos are frequent, such as R. Coate, *Mount Athos* (Grenoble-Paris, 1948), with unpleasant romantic, and F. Doelger, *Mönchsland Athos* (Munich, 1943), with equally unpleasant political, over-tones. A scholarly discussion of the buildings and their history is still wanting, despite the architectural surveys included in A. K. Orlandos, *Monastiriaki Architektoniki* (Athens, 1958), and notwithstanding the pioneer work done by H. Brockhaus, *Die Kunst in den Athosklöstern* (Leipzig, 1898; reprinted 1924), and F. W. Hasluck, *Mount Athos* (London, 1924). Professor Paul M. Mylonas is preparing a full scale architectural survey of the lavras on Mount Athos. See his preliminary report, *XV C.E.B. . . . Athens 1976*, II, 2 (Athens, 1981), 529 ff., and focusing on two monasteries of Middle Byzantine date, *ibid.*, 545 ff.
37. On the Katholikon of the Great Lavra see now P. M. Mylonas, *C.A.*, XXXII (1984), convincingly analysing its long building history, starting in 962/3. See also Ch. Bouras, *J.Ö.B.*, XXIV (1975), 229 ff., assigning the bronze door of the church to the first five years of the eleventh century. On the Protaton at Karyes, supposedly the oldest Athos church, *c.* 900, P. M. Mylonas, *C.A.*, XXVIII (1978), 143 ff. On the church at Trebizond, S. Ballance, *Anatolian Studies*, X (1960), 141 ff.; especially regarding St Anne, dated 884–5, and the possibly contemporary Nakip Camii.
376. 38. P. Miljković-Pepek, *Veljusa* (Skopje, 1981), replaces the earlier publications and, as already Hallensleben, *B.Z.*, LXVI (1973), 125, views naos, narthex, and side chapel as being of one build.
377. 39. For Ferai (Feredjik, Bera, Vira), A. K. Orlandos, *Thrakika*, IV (1933), 3 ff.; and now S. Siros, *Die . . . Kosmosoteira in Bera (Vera)* (Munich, 1985); for Nerezi, V. Ivanova, *G.N.M.S.* (1925–6), 430 ff.; Mavrodinov, *op. cit.* in Note 18 (1931), 66; and P. Miljković-Pepek, *Zbornik za likovne umetnosti*, X (1974), 313 ff., though the postulated sixteenth-century reconstruction of the dome is highly questionable. Equally problematic is the recent heavy-handed restoration of the building superstructure. An inscription on the murals gives the year 1164 as a *terminus ante* or *ad quem*, confirmed by the name of the founder, Alexis Comnenos, not the Emperor of this name, but presumably a relative.
378. 40. For Studenica and the related buildings of the Raška School (Djurdjevi Stupovi, 1170; Žiča, 1207–19)

508 · NOTES TO CHAPTER 17

see Millet, *op. cit.*, *passim*, Deroko, as quoted above, Note
18, *passim*, and M. Kašanin, V. Korać, D. Tasić, and M.
Šakota, *Studenica* (Belgrade, 1968). See also the
photogrammetric survey published by G. Vojnovic, *Zb. R.*, x
(1967), 149 ff. For the origins of the so-called 'Raška
School' see S. Ćurčić, *II B.S.C. . . . 1976*, 21 f. W. Saš-
Zaloziecky, *Die byzantinische Baukunst in den Balkanländern*
(Munich, 1955), 25 ff. has stressed the increasingly Romanesque and Western character of the Raška group.
    41. Millet, *op. cit.*, 50 ff.; B. Vulović, *Zbornik Arhitekonskog
Fakulteta Beograd*, III (1957), 3 ff., setting off the twelfth-
century core against later additions, such as the twin-
towered forechurch, once extant; Dj. Stričević, *XII C.E.B.
. . . Ohrid . . . 1961*, VII, 226 and note 13, refuting the
possibility, considered also by Vulović, *op. cit.*, of St
Nicholas' being rebuilt on Early Byzantine foundations.
    379. 42. G. Millet, *L'école grecque* (Paris, 1916), was the first
to point out (and sometimes to overstress) the characteristics of Greek as against Constantinopolitan church building. While some of his theses are outdated, such as the
antithesis of hellenistic and oriental roots in or the impact of
Armenia on Middle Byzantine church building in Greece,
his book remains basic. For the needed revisions, see, for
example, *Archeion*, I–XII (1935–73), *passim*, or Ch. Bouras,
C.A., XXI (1971), 137 ff.
    Information on church building in Greece, too, has grown
enormously over the past fifty years. In addition to Megaw,
op. cit., as quoted above Note 4, *Archeion*, as above, where
A. K. Orlandos has presented single-handed his remarkable
knowledge of the material accumulated over a busy lifetime.
For a handy survey, see *Alte Kirchen und Klöster Griechenlands*, ed. E. Melas (Cologne, 1972).
    H. Hallensleben, *B.Z.*, LXVI (1973), 126, has corrected
the mistake made in the earlier editions of this volume
regarding the appearance in Constantinople 'not before the
end of the [tenth] century' of the rippling eaves line of
domes.
    P. L. Vokotopoulos, *XVI C.E.B. . . . Vienna . . . 1980*
(*J.Ö.B.*, XXXI, 1981), 551 ff., has discussed convincingly
the impact of Constantinopolitan building methods and
ornamental details on the provinces, focusing primarily on
Greece (and Yugoslavia) during Middle and Late Byzantine
times.
    43. Megaw, as quoted above, Note 4. I cannot do better
than to summarize his results; the relative chronology
proposed by him remains valid, notwithstanding the shift in
absolute chronology caused by the late-tenth- rather than
eleventh-century dates recently established for the buildings grouped around the Theotokos-Panaghia at Hosios
Lukas.
    Regional differences and developments still want investi-
gating. For Athens a chronology based on the type of dome
is proposed by L. Philippides (Bouras), in *Epistimonika
Epitiris Polytechnikis Scholis . . . Thessalonikis*, V (1970), 79 ff.;

for western Central Greece, P. L. Vokotopoulos, as above,
Chapter 14, Note 29; for Thessaly, N. Nikonanos, *Byzan-
tinoi naoi tis Thessalias* (Athens, 1979).
    383. 44. In general, Megaw, *op. cit.*, and R. Traquair,
B.S.A., XV (1908–9), 177 ff. Among churches in Athens, the
Kapnikarea is being dated 1060–70 (Megaw, *op. cit.*, 107);
H. Sotir (Metamorphosis tou Sotirou), early, between 1050
and 1125 (L. Philippides, as above, Note 43); while the
Gorgoëpikoos (Mikra Metropolis), contrary to A. Struck,
A.M., XXXI (1906), 281 ff., dates from no earlier than the
late twelfth century (Megaw, *B.S.A.*, XXXII, 1931/2, 100
ff.; M. Chatzidakis, *Byzantine Monuments in Attica and
Boeotia*, Athens, 1956, 23, with the date 1180–1204).
    Tenth-century churches on the cross-in-square plan
probably survive in larger numbers in Greece than formerly
assumed; see, for instance, A. H. S. Megaw, *Charistirion eis
A. K. Orlandon*, III (1966), 10 ff. (Nikli near Tegea);
Vokotopoulos, as above, Chapter 14, Note 29, and *idem*,
D.C.A.H., ser. 4, V (1966–9), 149 ff. (H. Jason, Corfu); M.
Sotiriou, *ibid.*, ser. 1, II (1960/1), 101 ff. (Petraki church,
Athens); Ch. Bouras, *ibid.*, 57 ff. (Episkopi, Skyros).
    Regarding the survival (or revival?) of basilical types in
Middle Byzantine Greece, see *Archeion*, IX (1961), 38 ff.,
and Vokotopoulos, as Chapter 14, Note 29; also, starting
from a small tenth-century example in the Peloponnesus,
Ch. Bouras, *C.A.*, XXI (1971), 137 ff. See also Chapter 16,
Note 3.
    45. R. W. Schultz and S. H. Barnsley, *The Monastery of
Saint Luke of Stiris* (London, 1901), superseded by E.
Stikas, *To oikodomikon chronikon tis monis Osiou Louka
Phokidos* (Athens, 1970), *idem*, *C.C.R.* (1972), 311 ff., and
M. Chatzidakis, *C.A.*, XIX (1960), 127 ff., the latter setting
straight the relative chronology of the Theotokos and the
Katholikon and suggesting an absolute date, 1011 or 1022
for the Katholikon. As to the Theotokos Panaghia, Mrs L.
Bouras in her study of the architectural sculpture of the
church, *Ho glyptos diakosmos tou naous tis Panagias sto
Monastiri tou Osiou Louka* (Athens, 1980), proposes on
stylistic grounds a date around 960, and close links to
Constantinople transmitted possibly by Constantinopolitan
workmen sent under the patronage of the emperor
Romanos II. The doubts expressed in former editions of
this volume regarding so early a date are herewith gladly
withdrawn.
    See also Mrs Bouras's earlier studies on the lost exonar-
thex of the Katholikon, *D.C.A.H.*, ser. 4, VI (1972), 13 ff.,
and on twelfth- and thirteenth-century architectural sculpture in Greece, *ibid.*, ser. 4, IX (1977–9), 63 ff.
    For the possible (and to me probable) Constantinopolitan
origin of the Greek-cross octagon plan, see C. Mango,
D.O.P., XXVII (1973), 128 ff., although the examples
proposed date considerably later than the Katholikon at
Hosios Lukas.
    384. 46. G. C. Miles, *XII C.E.B. . . . Ohrid . . . 1961*, III,

281, and *D.O.P.*, XVIII (1964), 17 ff., with long lists of Islamic elements in Middle Byzantine Greek architecture, sculpture, and painting, stresses the impact of textiles, manuscripts, and ceramics as well as Moslem craftsmen resident in the western Aegean area; A. Grabar, *C.R.A.I.* (1971), 15 ff., focuses on architectural Islamic models, transmitted through Byzantium; L. Bouras, as above, Note 45, suggests transmission through Greek workmen active in Moslem countries. On the use of 'Kufesque' in Greece and the West, see R. Ettinghausen in *A Colloquium in Memory of George C. Miles* (New York, 1976), 28 f.

47. A. Frantz, *The Church of the Holy Apostles (The Athenian Agora*, XX) (Princeton, N.J., 1971).

390. 48. A. H. S. Megaw, *B.S.A.*, XXXII (1931–2), *passim*, and for the H. Theodoroi, *B.S.A.*, XXXIII (1932–3), 163 ff. An inscription of 1065 provides a *terminus ad quem*; the cufic frieze on the façade is perhaps not contemporary with the building (information kindly supplied by the late George C. Miles). The Kapnikarea is undated, its narthex and parekklesion slightly later than the naos. See also J. Travlos, *Poleodomiki Exelixis tōn Athinōn* (Athens, 1960), 149 ff., and L. Philippides, *Epistemoniki Epitiris Polytechnikis Scholis Thessalonikis*, V (1970), 81 ff., on H. Sotir with a date 1050–1125 (H. Hallensleben, *B.Z.*, LXVI, 1973, 126, mistakenly fourteenth century). The simplification of the cross-domed octagon becomes evident prior to 1044 in the Panaghia Lykodimou in Athens; see above, Chapter 16, Note 9.

49. G. Millet, *Daphni* (Paris, 1899); A. H. S. Megaw, *B.S.A.*, XXXII (1931–2), 93 f. The cathedral of Christianou, at roughly the same time, shows the plan of Daphni with slight variations; see Stikas, as above, Chapter 16, Note 9.

393. 50. Regarding the variants on the quincunx plan in Greece, see *Archeion*, V (1939–40), 3 ff.; for Hosios Meletios, *ibid.*, 34 ff.; for H. Sotir, Amphissa, *ibid.*, I (1935), 181 ff.; for Kaisariani, *Ephemeris* (1902), 54 ff.; for St John the Theologian, G. Sotiriou, *Evretirion tōn Mnimeiōn tis Ellados*, I (Athens, 1927 ff.), 168 f., with the erroneous date, thirteenth or fourteenth century; for the churches at Kitta and Vamvaka, R. Traquair, *B.S.A.*, XV (1908/9), 177 ff., and A. H. S. Megaw, *B.S.A.*, XXXIII (1932–3), 137 ff.; for Ligourio, *idem*, *B.S.A.*, XXXII (1931–2), 114, and Ch. Bouras, *D.C.A.H.*, ser. 4, VII (1974), 1 ff. For further material, *Archeion*, VIII (1955–6), 3 ff., on Andros; *ibid.*, IX (1961), 3 ff., on the provinces of Aetolia, Evretania, and Akarnania; *ibid.*, XI (1969), 3 ff., on the region around the Gulf of Ambrakia, all in central western Greece; and more recently Vokotopoulos, as above, Chapter 14, Note 29.

51. At times, e.g. at Ligourio, the rippling eaves line was transformed into the straight type in a late rebuilding.

52. D. Pallas, *Anaglyphos Stili tou Byzantinou Mouseiou* (Athens, 1961), has been the first to place the Byzantine ornament of Greece in a chronological context. We list a few examples in which foliage and geometric forms are fused: the capitals in the windows of the Kapnikarea; the ornament

on doors and templa at Hosios Meletios, c. 1100 (*Archeion*, V, 1939–40, 71, 97 ff.); the decoration of H. Sotir at Amphissa (*Archeion*, I, 1935, 194, figure 11), first quarter of the twelfth century. Tendril friezes of the early, freer type, still recalling the templa of the Katholikon at Hosios Lukas, are found in the third quarter of the eleventh century at Christianou (Pallas, *op. cit.*, figure 8, and Stikas, *op. cit.* in Chapter 16, Note 9, figures 36 ff.) and, perhaps later, at Kriezoti (*Archeion*, V, 1939–40, figures 8–13).

394. 53. A. Struck, *A.M.*, XXXIV (1909), 189 ff., and A. H. S. Megaw, *B.S.A.*, XXXII (1931–2), *passim*. The church at Chonika (*Ergon*, 1960, 246 f.), to judge by its simpler masonry, may well date from the end of the eleventh century, that is, earlier than the other Argolis churches. Merbaka, because of the use of 'Gothic' jamb colonnettes in the window of the main apse, has been assigned a date after 1205, under its first Frankish bishop (A. Bon, *Charistirion eis A. K. Orlandon*, III, 1966, 86 ff.). For H. Sotir near Amphissa (the detail [357] was mistakenly identified in the first edition of the present volume, plate 163B, as belonging to the H. Moni near Nauplion), see *Archeion*, I (1935), 181 ff., and G. C. Miles, *D.O.P.*, XVIII (1964), figure 29.

395. 54. The material between Kayseri and Konya and in Lycaonia was first gathered by Rott, *Denkmäler*, and Ramsay and Bell, *Churches*; for Binbirkilise in particular, see above, Chapter 6, Note 46. Our knowledge has not advanced much farther, while the monuments are disappearing. Aisleless chapels are reported, e.g. at Viranşehir and Sarigül (*ibid.*, 325 ff., 332 ff.); cross-plan churches at Helvadere (Rott, *op. cit.*, 265 ff.), Kurşuncu (known through Ramsay and Bell, *op. cit.*, 353 ff.), and Viranşehir (*ibid.*, 363 ff.). Hall-churches with barrel-vaults, mostly of small size, were built at Binbirkilise still after 850 (no. 3, *ibid.*, 53 ff.). Perhaps at the same time a sixth(?)-century church at Tilköinsar (Kemerhisar) (reported on by Rott, *op. cit.*, 287 f. and G. de Jerphanion, *Les églises rupestres de Cappadoce*, Paris, 1928 ff., I, plate 22) was remodelled as a barrel-vaulted hall-church resting on heavy piers.

55. S. Ballance, *Anatolian Studies*, X (1960), 141 ff. The church of the Chrysokephalos at Trebizond, originally a basilica with galleries of tenth- or eleventh-century date(?), was transformed in the thirteenth century by inserting into its centre a barrel-vaulted cross, surmounted by a dome (*ibid.*, 146 ff.).

396. 56. Standard works are Jerphanion, as above, Note 54, and M. Restlé, *Byzantine Wall Painting in Asia Minor* (Greenwich, Conn., 1967), the latter to be supplemented by the review of S. Kostof, *Art Bulletin*, LII (1970), 88 ff. The number of rock churches known to Jerphanion, *op. cit.*, and Rott, *op. cit.*, 204 ff., has now been vastly enlarged; see N. and M. Thierry, *Nouvelles églises rupestres de Cappadoce* (Paris, 1963), and also *C.A.*, XV (1965), 97 ff., and *ibid.*, XVIII (1968), 33 ff.; J. Lafontaine, *ibid.*, XII (1962), 263 ff.

The late dating of the churches and their murals once proposed (E. Wiegand, *B.Z.*, XXXVI, 1936, 33) can be disregarded, but arguments regarding their chronology continue, see N. Thierry, *C.A.*, XVII (1967), 161 ff., and *C.R.A.I.* (1971), 144 ff.; M. Restlé, as above, *passim*, and *R.L.B.K.*, III (1978), col. 968 ff.; A. W. Epstein, *C.A.*, XXIV (1975), 115 ff.; and G. P. Schiemenz, *Ist. M.*, XXX (1980), 291 ff., contesting Epstein's dating and rightly pointing out that the painted decoration provides only a *terminus ante*, possibly far removed for the building. Most handily, S. Kostof, *Caves of God* (Cambridge, Mass., and London, 1972), presents a clear survey of the chapels and their murals, provided with good plans and a catalogue, chronologically arranged according to the *status quaestionis* at the time of writing.

For the links of the Cappadocian rock churches, in particular those of quincunx plan, and their paintings (for which latter see already Jerphanion, *op. cit.*, *passim*) see now A. W. Epstein, *J.W.C.I.*, XLII (1975), 28 ff.

397. 57. Rott, *op. cit.*, 224 ff.; Jerphanion, *op. cit.*, I, 262 ff. For a reassessment of the Tokali Kilise (three building phases, the main hall mid-tenth-century, relation to the 'Macedonian Renaissance'), A. W. Epstein, as above, Note 56, *J.W.C.I.*, XLII (1975), esp. 36, note 34, and *VIII B.S.C.* ... *1982*, 29 f.

58. A number of aisleless chapels, sometimes doubled and as a rule with horseshoe apses, are provided with *termini ante* through inscriptions ranging from the early tenth century to 1060–1 (Thierry, as above, Note 56, *C.A.*, XV; Jerphanion, *op. cit.*, II, 2, 412 ff.; Epstein, as above, Note 56, *C.A.*, XXIV; and, with a caution regarding possibly long intervals between building and decoration and of repeated re-paintings, Schiemenz, as above, Note 56, *Ist. M.*, LXXX). A group of churches indeed has been assigned to the eighth and possibly the seventh century; see N. Thierry, *C.R.A.I.* (1971), and *idem*, *C.A.*, XVIII, 33 ff., both as above, Note 56; also, Kostof, as above, Note 56, Catalogue.

398. 59. Among the quincunx rock churches known so far, only the cycle in the Direkli Kilise (in the Melendiz Suyu Valley, near Belisirama) is dated, within the reign of Basil II (976–1025), the Thierrys inclining towards the last quarter of the tenth century, Restlé, *loc. cit.* (Note 56), towards the years 1020–5. Outstanding among quincunx churches are the Elmali Kilise, the Çarikli Kilise, and the Karanlik Kilise (Qaranleg, Analipsis), all three at Göreme (Rott, *op. cit.*, 219 ff.; 218 ff., 212 ff.; Kostof, *op. cit.*, Catalogue, nos. 57–9; Epstein, *op. cit.*, 121 ff.; and Schiemenz, *op. cit.*, *passim*). In contrast to late datings, previously proposed, present opinion inclines towards dating the murals (not the architecture, Schiemenz, *op. cit.*) all three either between 965 and 1050 (Epstein, *loc. cit.*, giving the Karanlik precedence) or between 1020 and 1130 (Kostof, *loc. cit.*). My notes taken in 1954, on the spot, mention an earlier aniconic layer with

simple crosses in the Elmali Kilise (see also Schiemenz, *op. cit.*, *passim*, pointing to the original linear decoration of many of the chapels). Does this suggest a date possibly as early as the eighth or ninth century?

399. 60. J. Strzygowski, *Kleinasien* (Leipzig, 1904), 156; Rott, *Denkmäler*, 258 ff.; Ramsay and Bell, *Churches*, 404 ff.; N. and M. Thierry, *Nouvelles églises rupestres* ... (as quoted above, Note 56), 21 f., suggesting a tenth- or eleventh-century date for the original building, a date in the second half of the eleventh century for the narthex. The 'recessed brick' technique (or imitation?) leads us to think of an eleventh- or twelfth-century date for the original core as well. See also N. Thierry, *D.O.P.*, XXIX (1975), 80 f., with a date in the second quarter of the eleventh century.

400. 61. For Üçayak, see S. Eyice, *C.A.*, XVIII (1968), 137 ff. Quincunx churches in a simple local style are known from Konya and vicinity: H. Amphilochios on the citadel at Konya (Ramsay and Bell, *Churches*, 403 ff.); the Ala Kilise on the Ali Summasi Dağ, and the Ilanli Kilise (Karadjedik Kilise) in the Ihlara Dere in the Melendiz Suyu Valley near Belisirama (known through *ibid.*, 399 ff., 418 ff.; Rott, *Denkmäler*, 274 ff.); a church near Fisandün (Strzygowski, *op. cit.*, 154; and N. Thierry, *D.O.P.*, XXIX, 1975, 80 ['possibly tenth century']); then the mosque, formerly the church of H. Gregorios Thaumaturgos, at Gelveri (Ramsay and Bell, *op. cit.*, 421 f.). Except for this latter, which I visited in 1954, I do not know whether these churches survive. Another quincunx, replacing a small sixth-century basilica, with rich sculptural decoration and of tenth-century date has been excavated at Selçikler Köyü (Sebaste) near Uşak in western Asia Minor (N. Firatli, *C.A.*, XIX, 1969, 151 ff.; *idem*, *Türk Arkeoloji Dergisi*, XIX–XX, 1970, 109 ff.). A list of quincunx churches in Asia Minor, though both incomplete and uncritical, has been compiled by G. Dimitrokallis, *Mikroasiatika Chronika*, XIII (1967), 81 ff.

62. See Orlandos, *Archeion*, VI (1948), 55 ff., on the numerous Middle Byzantine churches on Rhodes: aisleless chapels, with barrel-vaults, sometimes tripled; atrophied Greek crosses with slightly projecting arms; a few quatre-foils; and four quincunx churches – one on Mt Phileremos, H. Yoannis in Lindos, the Panaghia in the castle (almost totally destroyed in 1943), and the Demirli Camii in the town of Rhodes. None are dated by external evidence, and stylistic evidence hardly justifies the dating proposed by Orlandos: *c.* 1000 for the Phileremos church, the thirteenth and fourteenth centuries for the other three.

401. 63. G. Gerola, *Monumenti veneti nell'isola di Creta*, II (Venice, 1908), 79 ff.

64. G. Sotiriou, *Ta byzantina mnimeia tis Kyprou* (Athens, 1935); A. I. Dikigoropoulos, in *Report of the Department of Antiquities, Cyprus, 1940–1948* (Nicosia, 1958); A. Papageorgiou, *XVI C.E.B.* ... *Vienna 1981, Akten II*, 4 (*J.Ö.B.*, XXXII/4, 1982), 468 ff., on the impact of Constantinople;

and *idem*, in *Le rayonnement grec, Hommages à Charles Delvoye* (Brussels, 1982), 437 ff.

65. G. Sotiriou, *V C.E.B.* . . . . *Rome* . . . *1936*, II, 401 ff., proposing an impossibly early fifth-century date for the three-domed churches of Cyprus, such as H. Lazaros at Larnaka and H. Barnabas at Salamis, is superseded by A. H. S. Megaw, *D.O.P.*, XXVIII (1974), 57 ff., esp. 78 ff., suggesting rebuildings possibly of tenth-century date and financed by the Imperial court. Possible links to Egypt (P. Grossmann, *Mittelalterliche Langhauskuppelkirchen* . . . in *Oberägypten*, Glückstadt, 1982) warrant further exploration. **402.** 66. See above, p. 341, and Chapter 16, Note 12. For the Byzantine cultural input in Italy see now G. Cavallo *et al.*, *I Bizantini in Italia* (Milan, 1982).

67. E. Bertaux, *L'art dans l'Italie méridionale* (Paris, 1904), and *idem*, *Aggiornamento*, IV (Paris, 1978), *passim*; P. Orsì, *Le chiese basiliane della Calabria* (Florence, 1929), is like Bertaux' original text by now obsolete. Reliable surveys and discussions of the churches at Rossano and Stilo are found in H. Teodorou, *Ephemeris Daco-Romana*, IV (1930), 149 ff.; P. Lojacono, *V C.E.B.* . . . *Rome* . . . *1936*, II, 183 ff., and more recently Venditti (as above, Chapter 7, Note 49), *passim*, and M. Rotoli, *Arte bizantina in Calabria e in Basilicata* (Cava dei Tirreni, 1980), *passim*. Resemblances to the cave churches of Cappadocia, suggested by G. de Jerphanion, *V C.E.B.* . . . *Rome* . . . *1936*, II (1940), 572 ff., are certainly of an accidental nature.

The dates of construction for the Cattolica at Stilo as well as for S. Marco at Rossano are uncertain. C. Bozzoni, *La cattedrale di Stilo* (Chiaravalle Centrale, 1977), countering a thirteenth-century dating proposed by G. Dimitrikallis, *Archivio storico per la Calabria*, XXXV (1967), fasc. 2, 31 ff. (also *idem*, *Contribution à l'étude des monuments byzantins et médiévaux en Italie*, Athens, 1971, 27 ff.), suggests a date in the eleventh or early twelfth century. A. H. S. Megaw, *Charistirion eis A. K. Orlandon*, III (1966), 17 ff., based on resemblances of the ornamentation to churches along the Greek west coast, proposes for Stilo a tenth-century date which I consider very possible. M. Rotili, as quoted above, 113 ff., suggests a tenth- or eleventh-century date and points out that the remains of the quincunx church of S. Lucia del Aspromonte may date from as early as the mid tenth century. A list of South Italian quincunx churches has been compiled by G. Dimitrokallis, *Epitiris Hetairias Byzantinōn Spoudōn*, XXXVI (1968), 247 ff.

403. 68. G. Ionescu, *Ephemeris Daco-Romana*, V (1935), 50 ff.; for the Bohemund Chapel at Canosa, now A. W. Epstein, *D.O.P.*, XXXVII (1983), 79 ff.

69. *Archeion*, I (1935), 139 ff., for Monemvasia. For the 'reticulate' chequer bands and their early beginnings (e.g. the Palaia Episkopi at Nikli near Tegea), A. H. S. Megaw, as quoted above, Note 67. Examples dating, however, from as

late as about 1150 are found at H. Georgios near Kitta and at H. Varvara near Eremos on the Mani peninsula; see *idem*, *B.S.A.*, XXXIII (1932–3), 137 ff., and plates 17a, b, and 19d. The links to the churches of Arta suggested by Teodorou, as quoted above, Note 67, are less likely, given the late date of the Arta churches.

70. Links between South Italy and the Mani peninsula are also suggested by the plan of S. Pietro at Otranto, of late-eleventh-century date (for illustration, see P. Lojacono, *B.d.A.*, XXVII, 1933–4, 381). For Castro, see R. Bordenache, *ibid.*, 169 ff. For Squillace, see Bertaux, *op. cit.*, 126 ff.; Venditti, *op. cit.*, 899 ff.; H. M. Schwarz, *Röm. Jbch. der Bibliotheca Hertziana*, VI (1942–4), 1 ff., with the correct reference to Comnene building style in Constantinople. For the eleventh- and twelfth-century architecture see also C. Bozzoni, *Calabria normanna* (Rome, 1974).

71. G. Agnello, *L'architettura bizantina in Sicilia* (Florence, 1952); G. di Stefano, *Monumenti della Sicilia normanna*, 2nd ed., ed. W. Krönig (Palermo, 1979); O. Demus, *The Mosaics of Norman Sicily* (London, 1949).

72. L. Serra, *B.d.A.*, XXX (1936–7), 253 ff.; Venditti, *op. cit.*, 666 ff.; *idem*, in *Bizantina Sicilia II, Miscellanea G. Rossi Taibbi* (Palermo, 1975), 513 ff., dating it convincingly in the late tenth or early eleventh century. A monograph by E. Kitzinger and S. Ćurčić is in preparation.

73. Demus, *op. cit.*, 73 ff.; Di Stefano, *Sicilia normanna* (*op. cit.*), 41 ff. with extensive bibliography.

405. 74. For Monreale Cathedral, E. Kitzinger, *I mosaici di Monreale* (Palermo, 1960), *passim*. Mrs Christine Smith convinces me that contrary to former belief, including my own (first edition of this book, p. 286), the cathedral of Pisa depends in plan and elevation, rather than on Byzantine, largely on French late-eleventh-century models, meaning the churches along the pilgrimage roads. See also *idem*, *J.S.A.H.*, XLIII (1984), 195 ff., on the roots in Lombardy of the dome of Pisa Cathedral.

75. R. W. Schultz, *Die Kirchenbauten auf der Insel Torcello* (Berlin, 1927), 37 ff.

406. 76. O. Demus, *The Church of San Marco* (Washington, 1960), supersedes the numerous older treatments of the building and its history, which he lists. We mention only C. Boïto, *La ducale basilica di San Marco* (Venice, 1886); L. Marangoni, *L'architettura ignoto di San Marco* (Venice, 1933); and S. Bettini, *L'architettura di San Marco* (Padua, 1946).

407. 77. I am giving a simplified – and probably oversimplified – version of the complex relationships, involving Venice, Aquileia, and Grado, as presented in full by Demus, *op. cit.*, 3 ff.

78. For the first church, as known through Forlati's excavations of 1949 ff., see Demus, *op. cit.*, 64 ff., based on Forlati's reports, and B. and F. Forlati in *Alto Medioevo*, II (c. 1970), 17 ff. For the dependence of the present, 1063, S. Marco on the Apostle Church in Constantinople, as remod-

elled some time between 940 and 1004, see above, Chapter
10, Note 11, complementing Demus, *op. cit.*, 88 ff., esp. 91,
note 129. A. W. Epstein, *D.O.P.*, xxxvii (1983), 79 ff.,
proposes to date the cathedral of Canosa (Apulia), in plan
close to S. Marco, prior to the latter and hence to derive it
directly from the Constantinopolitan Apostoleion.

79. For the marble sheathing of the façades, see Demus,
op. cit., 100 ff., for the use of spoils, *ibid.*, 120 ff. The date of
the outer shells of the domes and their dependence on
Islamic models have been discussed by G. Fiocco, *Bollettino
Centro Internazionale . . . Andrea Palladio*, viii (1968), 222
ff., with reference also to U. Monneret de Villard, *Architettura e Arti decorative*, 1 (1921), 315 ff. See also *idem,
Introduzione allo studio dell'archeologia islamica* (Venice,
1966), 201 ff. (Dome of the Rock); K. A. C. Creswell, *A
Short Account of Early Islamic Architecture* (Penguin Books,
Harmondsworth, 1958), 37 ff.; and *idem, The Muslim Architecture of Egypt* (Oxford, 1952), i, plate 80 and (for wooden
domes), ii, 237 and note 7.

For the capitals employed on the façade, Roman, Early
Byzantine, and later, see *Corpus der Kapitelle der Kirche von
San Marco zu Venedig*, ed. F. W. Deichmann (Wiesbaden,
1981).

410. 80. Demus, *op. cit.*, 83 f. (galleries reduced to catwalks),
76 ff. (brick façades); H. Buchwald, *J.Ö.B.G.*, xi, xii
(1962–3), 169 ff., and xiii (1964), 137 ff. (niello inlay,
plaques, capitals).

411. 81. Demus, *op. cit.*, focuses his attention only on the
capitals in the narthex. But many of those in the interior
likewise date from the late eleventh or the early twelfth
century; see T. Krautheimer-Hess, *Art Bulletin*, xxvi
(1944), 152 ff., esp. 172. Buchwald, *op. cit.*, xiii (1964), 137
ff., differentiates between two groups of capitals, one late-
eleventh- and early-twelfth-, the other thirteenth-century.

CHAPTER 18

413. 1. See however G. Ostrogorsky, *History of the Byzantine
State* (Oxford, 1956).

414. 2. The cultural atmosphere of the Paleologan era is
brought out concisely and brilliantly by A. Grabar, in P. A.
Underwood, *The Kariye Djami*, iv (London, 1975), 3 ff., and
by I. Ševčenko, *ibid.*, 17 ff.

CHAPTER 19

415. 1. O. Demus, *XI C.E.B. . . . Munich . . . 1959, Beiträge*,
iv, 2, *passim.*

2. G. Babić, *Les chapelles annexes des églises byzantines* (Paris,
1969; review by S. Ćurčić, *Art Bulletin*, lv, 1973, 448 f.) on
iconography and function of parekklesia; T. Gouma-Peter-
son, *Art Bulletin*, lviii (1976), 168 ff., on the parekklesion
attached to H. Demetrios in Salonica in 1303 and reflecting
pro-monastic Paleologan policies; S. Ćurčić, *J.S.A.H.*,

xxxvi (1977), 94 ff., on origin, development, siting, and
design of parekklesia (starting ninth century, flanking narthex and/or aisles or placed atop the narthex with domes
rising from roof); *idem, Zb. R.*, xiii (1971), 333 ff., on
parekklesia and twin-domed nartheces.

416. 3. Diehl, *Manuel*, 735 ff., 754 ff.; G. Millet, *L'ancien art
serbe* (Paris, 1919); *idem, Monuments byzantins de Mistra*
(Paris, 1910 ff.), and *L'école grecque* (Paris, 1916), *passim.*
Hallensleben, *B.Z.*, lxvi (1973), 129 f. objects to the
distinction proposed in our text of Early and High Paleologan architecture.

4. S. Bettini, *V C.E.B. . . . Rome . . . 1936*, ii, 31 ff.; S.
Eyice, *Son devir bizans mimârisi*, 2nd ed. (Istanbul, 1980), 54
ff. The thirteenth-century date for the Mugliotissa in
Constantinople (Janin, *Églises*, 222 f.) is questioned by
Mathews, *Survey*, 366–7, who proposes a tenth- or
eleventh-century date. The church of the Kamariotissa on
Heybeliada (Chalki) has turned out to be of eleventh- or
twelfth-century date: see above, p. 365 and Chapter 17,
Note 15.

417. 5. *Archeion*, i (1935), 5 ff., 41 ff.; *ibid.*, ii (1936), 51 ff.,
70 ff. The impact of South Italian transept basilicas, suggested by Hallensleben, *B.Z.*, lxvi (1973), 129, seems to
me unlikely given the differences in elevation, vaulting, and
particularly size. For a brief survey and characterization of
the architecture of the period in Epirus, Trebizond, Russia,
and Serbia, see V. Korać, in *L'art byzantin du XIIIᵉ siècle*
(Belgrade, 1967), 11 ff.

6. Simple aisleless chapels are too numerous to list; for the
group in and around Ohrid, see D. Bošković and K.
Tomovski, in *Musée National d'Ohrid, Recueil de Travaux*
(Ohrid, 1961), 71 ff., esp. 89 ff.; for H. Basilios at Arta,
Archeion, ii (1936), 115 ff.; for examples in Constantinople,
S. Eyice (as above, Note 4), 34 ff. (Manastir Mescidi,
perhaps late-thirteenth-century; Isa kapisi Mescidi (Esa
Kapi Camii), early-fourteenth-century), and *Bildlexikon*,
passim.

7. A. Grabar, *I.B.A.I.*, i (1921), 103 ff. (Asen church at
Stanimaka); *idem, L'église de Boïane* (Sofia, 1924) (Boïana:
small cruciform church, eleventh-century, enlarged in 1259
by attached double-storeyed mausoleum church). The
Boğdan Sarayi chapel in Constantinople, too, possibly of
fourteenth-century date, may have been a funeral chapel
with crypt and domed and barrel-vaulted upper floor (Eyice,
op. cit., 32 ff.; Brunov, *B.Z.*, xxvi, 1926, 358, note 4),
whether or not attached to a monastery. The church of the
Taxiarches in Salonica (A. Xyngopoulos, *Tessares mikroi
naoi tis Thessalonikis*, Salonica, 1952, 5 ff.), certainly
monastic, likewise rises over a crypt – a timber-roofed nave,
enveloped by a portico, open except on the north, the bema
flanked by projecting pastophories.

For chapels of the barrel-vaulted and domed type in
Bulgaria, serving neither monastic nor funeral functions,
see below, p. 440 and Note 32 (Nessebâr), and (Červen) –

both of fourteenth-century date – Kr. Mijatev, *Arkhitekturata v srednovekovna Blgarija* (Sofia, 1965), 176.

8. See below, p. 423 and Note 14, for the Fenari Isa Camii. A church of similar plan at Labovo in Epirus (now Labove in Albania) is discussed by P. Vokotopoulos, *Hi ekkliastiki architektoniki eis tin dutikin . . . Hellada . . .* (Thessaloniki, 1975), 86–92, who dates it to the tenth century; and also A. Meksi, *Monumentet*, IX (1975), 77–105, who provides new drawings and proposes (erroneously) a thirteenth-century date on the basis of the plan and the building technique.

9. A. K. Orlandos, *Hi Parigoritissa tis Artis*[2] (Athens, 1963); for the other buildings mentioned, see above, Chapter 16, Note 9, for bibliography.

10. Demus, as above, Note 1; see also H. Buchthal, *D.O.P.*, XX (1966), 103 ff., for the parallel development in Sicily.

11. See above, Note 9; for the addition of the parekklesia as an afterthought during construction, see Orlandos' supplement in the second edition, as quoted, p. 165 f. Recent excavations at Philippias, near Arta, have brought to light the remains of the Katholikon of the Pantanassa monastery. The building closely resembles the Parigoritissa at Arta in scale, planning principles, and architectural and decorative details. For preliminary excavation reports see P. Vokotopoulos, *Archaiologika analekta ex Athinōn*, V, no. 1 (1972), 87 f.; *ibid.*, VI, no. 3 (1973), 402 f.; and *ibid.*, X (1977), 149 f.

420. 12. For an introduction to Laskarid architecture see H. Buchwald, *J.Ö.B.*, XXVIII (1979), 261–96. For H. Sophia, *The Church of H. Sophia at Trebizond*, ed. D. Talbot Rice (Edinburgh, 1968), especially *idem* and S. Ballance, 'Historical Introduction', 1 ff.; and S. Ballance, 'The Architecture', 8 ff. For other, earlier and later, churches in Trebizond, S. Ballance, *Anatolian Studies*, X (1960), 141 ff.

13. G. Millet, *Monuments byzantins de Mistra* (Paris, 1910; plates only); M. Chatzidakis, *Mystras* (Athens, 1956); H. Hallensleben, *Marburger Jahrbuch für Kunstwissenschaft*, XVIII (1969), 105 ff., on the genesis of the Mistra type (his suggestions regarding the general framework seem to me all too theoretical); S. Dufrenne, *Les programmes iconographiques des églises byzantines de Mistra* (Paris, 1970), 1 ff., with summaries regarding the dates of construction or remodelling of the major churches. It still remains unclear when the Metropolis was transformed into the 'Mistra type' (the fifteenth-century date assigned to the Metropolitan Matthew who financed the rebuilding rests on no sound foundation); see also D. A. Zakythinos, *Le despotat grec de Morée*, II (Paris, 1953), 284 ff., giving the list of metropolitans with wide gaps in the fourteenth century as well.

423. 14. For the North Church of the Fenari Isa Camii complex, see above, pp. 358–60, and Chapter 17, Note 9; the investigations of A. H. S. Megaw did not extend to the South Church. For this latter and its parekklesion, see Van Millingen, *Churches*, 122 ff., Janin, *Églises*, 318 ff., Th.

Macridy, *D.O.P.*, XVIII (1964), 265 ff., and *Bildlexikon*, 126 ff. For the structures appended to the Kariye Camii, I refer to Underwood (as quoted above, Chapter 16, Note 7), 17 ff., and now also R. G. Ousterhout (as quoted above, Chapter 16, Note 7).

424. 15. The structures attached to the Pammakaristos, the Fetiyeh Camii, are discussed by both Hallensleben and Mango and Hawkins (as above, Chapter 17, Note 14): esonarthex; end corridor, and end chapel; south parekklesion, that is the funerary chapel of Michael Glabas; exonarthex and south corridor. But sequence and dating of these additions remain under discussion. Hallensleben assigns an older esonarthex, now lost, and the north corridor with its end chapel to shortly before 1294; the funerary chapel to the south, to 1315; exonarthex and south corridor to the years 1326–41. Mango and Hawkins, on the other hand, date the Glabas mausoleum about 1310, and consider all the rest, north corridor, end chapel, exonarthex, and south corridor, as added around the middle of the fourteenth century.

A church, composed of a domed one-bay core with chancel and apse, enveloped by narthex and flanking parekklesia, has come to light at Nicaea (Iznik) (S. Eyice, *C.C.R.*, 1971, 309 ff., esp. 314 f. and figure 2).

426. 16. Bošković and Tomovski, *op. cit.*, 87 ff. More recently, H. Hallensleben, *Zbornik. Arheološki muzej na Makedonija*, VI–VII (1975), 297–316, who compares St Clement with a partially ruined church of Panaghia Bellas at Boulgareli in Epirus.

428. 17. On Epirus, see *Archeion*, II (1936), 70 ff., 88 ff., 115 ff., 131 ff.; D. M. Nicol, *The Despotate of Epiros* (Oxford, 1957), 196 ff. On Arta see P. L. Vokotopoulos, in *Alte Kirchen und Klöster Griechenlands*, ed. E. Melas (Cologne, 1972), 135–61. On the link to Ohrid, H. Hallensleben, *B.Z.*, LXVI (1973), 130 ff.; also *idem*, Note 16, above.

18. Early examples in Constantinople are the Fenari Isa North Church, 907; the Eski Imaret Camii, *c.* 1080; the apse of the Kilise Camii. A useful corpus of decorative patterns in Byzantine (mostly Paleologan) architecture of Constantinople is A. Pasadaios, *Ho keramoplastikos diakosmos tōn byzantinōn ktiriōn tis Konstantinoupoleōs* (Athens, 1963). For Greece, we refer to Megaw, *op. cit.*, *B.S.A.*, XXXII (1931/32), 90 ff., esp. 102 ff. For the Argolis churches, see above, pp. 393–4, and Chapter 17, Note 53; for Bryoni, *Archeion*, II (1936), 51.

18a. Belfries appear in Byzantine architecture in the aftermath of the Fourth Crusade. During the thirteenth and fourteenth centuries they were fairly widespread, though many of the examples were subsequently destroyed. The only attempt at dealing with this material comprehensively is Ch. N. Barla, *Morphi kai exelixis tōn byzantinōn kōdōnostasiōn* (Athens, 1959), but this study is outdated in many respects.

431. 19. For H. Katherini, see C. Diehl, H. Saladin, and M. Le Tourneau, *Les églises de Salonique* (Paris, 1916), 179 ff. and plate 58; for the Holy Apostles, *ibid.*, 187 ff., V. V.

Laurent, *Revue Études Byzantines*, VII (1949), 149, and A. Xyngopoulos, *Thessalonique et la peinture macédonienne* (Athens, 1955). Unfortunately M. Rautman, 'The Church of the Holy Apostles in Thessaloniki ...', Ph.D. Diss., Indiana University (1984), was not yet available for our inspection. The building has recently been surveyed by the Striker–Kuniholm team (see above, Chapter 16, Note 1), who have determined that the building core and the envelope are, in this case, homogeneous. This interpretation supersedes that expressed in the previous editions of this book. G. Velenis, *XVI C.E.B. ... Vienna, 1981, Akten*, II, 4 (*J.Ö.B.*, XXXII/4, 1982), 569 ff., also suggests that the core and the envelope are of one build. Furthermore, he proposes that the church originally had an axial belfry. (See also above, Note 18a.) Hallensleben, *B.Z.*, LXVI (1973), 130 f., on stylistic grounds views the H. Apostles as the earlier, H. Katherini as the later building. So far I fail to see his point. For the smaller fourteenth-century churches of Salonica, see A. Xyngopoulos, as above (Note 7); S. Pelikanides, *Balkan Studies*, III (1962), 463 ff.; V. V. Laurent, *Revue Études Byzantines*, XIII (1955), 109 ff.; and G. I. Theocharides, *Makedonika*, IV (1955–60), 315 ff., the latter two regarding the church of H. Elias and its date of construction c. 1360–80. The corner chapels at H. Elias were rebuilt after World War II on the extant foundations and their upper parts do not necessarily represent the original solution. The Katholikon of Chilandari (Hilandar) has been published by S. Nenadović, *Hilandarski Zbornik*, III (1974), 85–152 (French summary, 197–202), with a series of good drawings. Two additional surveys of the building are now independently in progress by architectural teams from Belgrade and Salonica. For the two-domed narthex see S. Ćurčić, *Zb. R.*, XIII (1971), 333 ff. In other respects the church is conservative and reveals strong ties with the architecture of Constantinople; see *idem, IV B.S.C.* ... *1978*, 14 f.

432. 20. Examples are found, for instance, at Sv. Dimitri, Turnovo, 1186 (N. Mavrodinov, *L'église à nef unique et l'église cruciforme en pays bulgare*, Sofia, 1931, 38 ff.), and in the Asen church at Stanimaka (see above, Note 7). See also N. Mavrodinov, in *I.B.A.I.*, VIII (1934), 262 ff., and below, Note 32.

433. 21. A. K. Orlandos, *Monastiriaki architektoniki* (Athens, 1958), *passim*; D. M. Nicol, *Meteora* (London, 1963).

22. For general bibliography, see above, Chapter 17, Note 18. Regarding the replacement of Epirote by Salonican models in Serbia, see Hallensleben, *B.Z.*, LXVI (1973), 131 f.

23. M. Kašanin, V. Korać, D. Tasić, M. Šakota, *Studenica* (Belgrade, 1968); other examples are the churches at Mileševa of 1234–5; at Sopoćani of c. 1255; at Dečani of 1327–35. See Millet, *op. cit., passim; idem*, in *L'art byzantin chez les Slaves, Recueil Théodore Uspenski*, I (Paris, 1930), 147 ff.; and Deroko, *op. cit., passim*.

434. 24. Bošković and Tomovski, *op. cit.*, in Note 6. The resemblance of the façade of St Sophia at Ohrid to Venetian and Late Antique palace façades has been often remarked on; but one wonders whether any direct link exists.

25. S. Nenadović, *Bogorodica Ljeviška* (Belgrade, 1963). D. Panić and G. Babić's book with the same title (Belgrade, 1975), reiterates Nenadović's analysis of the architecture; see S. Ćurčić's critique, *Art Bulletin*, LIX (1977), 632 ff., suggesting two building phases for the fourteenth-century remodelling and stressing the conservative character of the five-dome arrangement at Bogorodica Ljeviška as against the progressive Paleologan pattern prevailing contemporaneously at Salonica.

435. 26. Millet, *L'ancien art serbe*, 110 ff., and Mavrodinov, *op. cit.* (Note 20), 85.

436. 27. For Staro Nagoričino, see Millet, *op. cit.*, 98 ff.; Mavrodinov, *op. cit.*, 88; Bošković (*Art chez les slaves*, as above, Note 23), 195 ff.; and Deroko, *op. cit.*, 185.

28. For Gračanica, see Millet, *op. cit.*, 105 ff.; V. Korać, *Zbornik Svetozara Radojčića* (Belgrade, 1969), 143 ff., and now the comprehensive monograph by S. Ćurčić, *Gračanica. King Milutin's Church ... Late Byzantine Architecture* (University Park and London, 1979).

437. 29. Deroko, *op. cit.* (Chapter 17, Note 18), *passim*. For certain developments in Serbian architecture during the first half of the fourteenth century see S. Ćurčić, in *L'Art byzantin au début du XIVe siècle*, ed. S. Petković (Belgrade, 1978), 17 ff.

439. 30. Millet, *L'ancien art serbe*, 95 ff. For the architecture of the Chilandari (Hilandar) exonarthex and its impact on the subsequent development of Serbian architecture see V. Korać, *Hilandarski zbornik*, IV (1978), 75 ff., and Dj. Bošković, *Starinar*, XXVIII–XXIX (1977–8), 69 ff. Also Nenadović, *op. cit.* (as above, Note 19).

440. 31. Millet, *L'ancien art serbe*, 152 ff., Deroko, *op. cit.*, 314 ff. Dj. Stričević, *Starinar*, N.S. V–VI (1954–5), 115 ff., has re-established the chronology of the Morava churches. See also W. Saš-Zaloziecky, *Die byzantinische Baukunst in den Balkanländern* (Munich, 1955), 59 ff.

For Rumanian architecture, I refer to the chapter written by G. Ionescu in *Vseobščaya Istorija Arhitektury*, III (as quoted above, Chapter 14, Note 56), 453 ff.; to V. Vatasianu, in W. F. Volbach and J. Lafontaine-Dosogne, *Byzanz und der christliche Osten (Propyläen-Kunstgeschichte*, III) (Berlin, 1968), 275 ff.; and to the summary by I. D. Stefanescu, *XIV C.E.B. ... Bucharest ... 1971, Rapports*, IV, 93 ff.

32. For Late Byzantine architecture in Bulgaria, see the bibliographical references given above, Chapter 14, Note 26, and Chapter 17, Note 18; for the churches at Nessebâr, see A. Rašenov, *Églises de Mesembria* (Sofia, 1932), and *V C.E.B. ... Rome ... 1936*, II, 352 ff., Saš-Zaloziecky, *op. cit., passim*, I. Galabov, in Beŝeljiev and Irmscher, *Antike und Mittelalter in Bulgarien* (Berlin, 1960), 306 ff. St John

Aleiturgitos, the Pantokrator church, and the Church of the Archangels at Nessebâr were destroyed in an earthquake in 1913 and have been under restoration ever since. St. Boyadžiev, *Byzantino-Bulgarica*, VII (1981), 351 ff., proposes a hypothetical reconstruction of St John Aleiturgitos with four domes elevated on tall drums atop cubical bases. The archaeological evidence presented by him, however, leaves some doubts about this reconstruction.

33. Mavrodinov, *op. cit.*, 38 ff.

34. A. Grabar, *I.B.A.I.*, I (1921), 103 ff.; Kr. Mijatev, *Architekturata v Srednovekovna Blgarija* (Sofia, 1965), 171 ff.

441. 35. The best general overview of the problem is still that of Mavrodinov, *op. cit.*, 3–57, but see also Rašenov, *Églises*, 26 ff., 79 ff., 99 ff.; Mijatev, *op. cit., passim*.

36. For the links between churches with domed and towered nartheces in Bulgaria and Serbia see G. Bošković, *I.B.A.I.*, X (1938), 57 ff. Early examples of barrel-vaulted and domed aisleless churches in Constantinople are the middle church in the Zeyrek Camii complex and the Toklu Dede Mescidi; see above, pp. 367 ff., 365, and Chapter 17, Notes 15 and 17. For the Boğdan Sarayi, see Van Millingen, *Churches*, 180 ff., S. Eyice, *Son devir bizans mimârisi*, 2nd ed. (Istanbul, 1980), 43 ff., and *Bildlexikon*, 108. The Armenian hypothesis is proffered by Grabar, as above, Note 34.

442. 37. The importance of polychrome reticulated and chequerboard masonry in Roman Gaul and the Rhineland and its survival in the eighth and ninth centuries was first brought out by H. R. Hitchcock, *Art Studies*, VI (1928), 175 ff. N. Mavrodinov, *I.B.A.I.*, VIII (1934), 262 ff., S. N. Bobčev, *ibid.*, XXIV (1961), 153 ff.; and M. Čanak Medić, *XV C.E.B. . . . Athens 1976*, II (1981), 107 ff., suggest that it was known as well in the Roman Balkan provinces and thus survived in Bulgaria, but this remains to be proven. S. Bettini, *V C.E.B. . . . Rome . . . 1936*, II, 22 ff., assumes that from the West it penetrated the Balkans via Epirus in the thirteenth century; the opposite view is taken by Megaw, as quoted above, Chapter 17, Note 69. For Forza d'Agro, see F. Basile, *Chiese siciliane del periodo normanno (I monumenti d'Italia*, XV) (Rome, 1938).

443. 38. On the fourteenth-century remodelling of the Kariye Camii (narthex, north extension, lateral apses, parekklesion), see, apart from P. A. Underwood, *The Kariye Djami*, I (London, 1967), 17 ff., more recently Ousterhout (as above, Chapter 16, Note 7), 123 ff. On the paintings in the parekklesion, O. Demus, in Underwood, *op. cit.*, IV (London, 1975); also Mango and Hawkins, and Hallensleben, as quoted above, Chapter 17, Note 14.

39. Van Millingen, *Churches*, 138 ff.; Janin, *Églises*, 217 ff.;

P. A. Underwood, *D.O.P.*, XIV (1960), 215 ff.; Mathews, *Survey*, 346 ff., esp. 358 ff.; *Bildlexikon*, 132 ff. Regarding the date of the funeral chapel of Michael Glabas, 1310 as suggested by Mango and Hawkins, *op. cit.*, or after 1315 as generally accepted, see Hallensleben, *op. cit.*

The two capitals surviving in the parekklesion (Van Millingen, *Churches*, plate 40) are covered, one with stiff thorny acanthus leaves, the other with tendrils issuing from a pair of crossed cornucopias – both obviously attempts at reviving the vocabulary of the sixth century. But it is doubtful whether they were carved for their present position. They may be eleventh-century spoils, comparable to capitals of that time in and near Venice.

447. 40. See above, Chapter 17, Note 11.

448. 41. For instance, by K. Wulzinger, *Byzantinische Baudenkmäler* (Hanover, 1925), 86 ff. F. Dirimtekin, *Istanbul Arkeoloji Müzeleri Yilliği*, V (1952), 45, assigns the ground floor of the palace to the time of Constantine Porphyrogenetos, the upper floors to a restoration of undetermined date. But as far as I can see, the structure of the palace is of one build. Schneider (B. Meyer-Plath and A. M. Schneider, *Die Landmauer von Konstantinopel*, II, Berlin, 1943, 95 ff.) believed the precinct wall of the palace to be later than the fifth- and earlier than the adjoining twelfth-century parts of the city walls. This is possible; their further intimation (*ibid.*, 99 and note 3) of an eighth- or ninth-century(?) date for the palace proper remains tentative and unproven. To us a Paleologan date seems unquestionable. C. Mango, *J.D.A.I.*, LXXX (1965), 305 ff., esp. 330 ff., arrives at the same conclusion; so does O. Feld, *Ist. M.*, XIX–XX (1969–70), 359 ff., in a study on the capitals of the Tekfur Sarayi.

449. 42. *Archeion*, III (1937), 1 ff.; also A. K. Orlandos, in *Art et société à Byzance sous les Paléologues (Actes du Colloque . . . Études Byzantines . . . Venice . . . 1968)* (Venice, 1971). But see also the so-called bishop's palace at Nikosi, Georgia, allegedly built in the ninth or tenth century; R. Mepisaschwili and V. Zindzadse, *op. cit.* (Chapter 16, Note 46), 56–7.

450. 43. S. Eyice, *XI C.E.B. . . . Munich . . . 1958*, Akten, 150 ff.; H. Buchwald *J.Ö.B.*, XXVIII (1979), 261 ff.; and in greater detail, T. Kirilova Kirova, *Felix Ravenna* (1972), 275 ff., where a date of 1206–22 is tentatively suggested and both masonry technique and vaulting (on ground floor and first upper floor) are described.

44. O. Demus, *XI C.E.B. . . . Munich . . . 1958*, Berichte, IV, I (Munich, 1958), and *idem, J.Ö.B.G.*, XIV (1965), 139 ff.

GLOSSARY

Acanthus. Architectural ornament resembling the leaves of the acanthus plant.

Aedicula. A frame, as of a niche, formed by a pair of columns, piers, or pilasters supporting a gable, a lintel, or a plaque.

Agape. In the Early Christian church, a meal of semi-ritual character shared by the Christian congregation as a whole, or, later, offered to the poor of the congregation.

Ambo. Pulpit.

Ambulatory church. A church plan in which a domed centre bay is enveloped on three sides by aisles (see also *Cross-domed church*).

Aniconic. Without idols or images.

Architrave. A lintel in stone or timber carried from the top of one column or pier to another; the lowest member of the entablature.

Ashlar. Cut stone masonry.

Atrium. In Early Christian, Byzantine, and medieval architecture, the forecourt of a church; as a rule, enveloped by four colonnaded porticoes (quadriporticus).

Baldacchino. A free-standing canopy rising above a throne, an altar, or a tomb.

Barrel-vault. A half-cylindrical vault, as in a continuous arch; also, a tunnel-vault.

Basilica. An assembly room; in Christian parlance, a church; as a rule, longitudinal and composed of nave and aisles, the former lit by a clerestory.

Basilica discoperta. A basilica type supposed to consist of covered aisles and an unroofed nave.

Basket capital. A capital of hemispherical or nearly hemispherical shape, decorated with a wicker design imitating a basket.

Bema. The chancel part of a Greek church.

Camii. In Turkish, mosque.

Catechumen. In the early church, a convert to Christianity, under instruction but not yet baptized.

Cathedra. The throne of the bishop.

Ciborium. See *Baldacchino.*

Cloisonné masonry. A decorative use of masonry in which small stone blocks are framed by bricks placed vertically and horizontally in single or double courses.

Cloister-vault. A vault composed of four, eight, or twelve curved surfaces, as would result from the interpenetration of two, four, or six barrel-vaults of equal height and diameter (Brit. *domical vault*); also, a four-sided, eight-sided, etc., dome.

Coenobite (cenobite). In monasticism, the designation for communal life (see *Coenobium*).

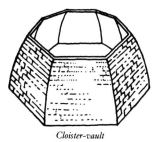

Cloister-vault

Coenobium (cenobium). A monastery arranged for the communal life of a monastic congregation.

Conch. A semicircular niche surmounted by a half-dome.

Confessio. In a church, a subterranean chamber or recess located below or near the altar and sheltering a relic.

Continuous transept. See *Transept.*

Corbel. A projecting stone or brick on the face of a wall which serves as a support (see *Corbel table frieze*).

Corbel table frieze. A series of small arches resting on corbels.

Cross church. See *Greek-cross plan.*

Cross-domed church (Kreuzkuppelkirche according to Wulff, *Handbuch*). A church plan whose core, enveloped on three sides by aisles and galleries, forms a cross; the core is

surmounted by a dome in the centre and four barrel-vaults resting on four strong corner piers; also, *église à croix* (in the older literature, sometimes referred to as ambulatory church).

Crossing. The space occupied by the intersection of the nave and transepts.

Cross-in-square (cross-inscribed). See *Quincunx.*

Cross transept. See *Transept.*

Crypt. In a church, a chamber or vaults beneath the main floor, not necessarily underground, usually containing graves or relics.

Cube capital. A capital resulting from the interpenetration of a cube placed over a hemispherical form.

Diaconicon. A room attached to or enclosed in the church; in Early Christian times, utilized for the reception of the congregation's offerings and serving as archive, vestry, and library; later used only for the latter functions (also, a sacristy).

Dome. A hemispherical vault supported by either a circular wall or, over a square space, by squinches or pendentives placed in the corners, the former transforming the square into an octagon, the latter into a circle (see: *squinch, pendentive*).

Dome on pendentives. See *Pendentive.*

Domed basilica. A church type on a square or short rectangular plan with a vaulted nave, aisles, and galleries; a dome surmounts the nave in its centre bay.

Domed octagon. A square plan, its corners bridged by squinches, which supports a dome on the resulting octagon (see: *Greek-cross domed octagon*).

Domical vault. See *Cloister-vault.*

Domus ecclesiae. A house serving the religious, administrative, and charitable needs of a congregation; a community centre (see *Oikos ekklesias*).

Drum. The circular or polygonal structure on which a dome is raised.

Dwarf transept. See *Transept.*

Entablature. The superstructure carried by columns, usually divided into three parts: architrave, frieze, and cornice (see *Architrave*).

Esonarthex. See *Narthex.*

Exedra. Any room opening full width into a larger, covered or uncovered space; a large niche.

Exonarthex. See *Narthex.*

Fastigium. Literally, the ridge of the roof or a gable; a structure, occurring in Constantinian basilicas, consisting of a colonnaded screen across the chord of the apse and centred either on a canopy or on a pedimented section.

Flos. The floral form adorning the middle of each face of the abacus of a Corinthian capital; also, *fleuron.*

Forecourt. See *Atrium.*

Frieze à billettes. A frieze composed of spool-shaped units set vertically.

Greek-cross domed octagon (opp. page, bottom). A mouthful designating the fusion of a centre bay in the shape of a domed octagon (see *Domed octagon*) with the barrel-vaulted arms of a Greek cross breaking through an ancillary belt of aisles and sometimes galleries, the whole enclosed in an outer square or rectangle; in the older literature, frequently referred to as a church with corner squinches (also, *église à trompes d'angle*[1]).

Greek-cross plan. A church plan forming a cross with arms of equal or nearly equal length; may be vaulted or unvaulted.

Groin-vault. The vault formed over a square bay by the interpenetration of two barrel-vaults of equal diameter and height, the lines of intersection (the groins) forming a diagonal cross; also known as a cross-vault.

Guilloche. An ornamental band composed of narrow strips flowing in interlaced curves with circular centres.

Haikal. Among Christian Arabs, the sanctuary part of a church.

Heliakon. A sun terrace.

Hollow tube construction. A vaulting construction consisting of cone-like hollow clay tubes, the narrow, closed end of one tube inserted into the wide, open end of another.

---

1. I am avoiding this term, which seems to me to allude only to a technical feature while disregarding the fusion of the Greek-cross plan with that of the domed octagon.

Hypogaeum. A subterranean tomb chamber (or group of tomb chambers) for private use.

Iconostasis. In a Byzantine church, the screen wall covered with icons which separates nave from chancel.

Impost block. A block placed between the capital of a column and the arches or vaults it supports.

Joggled. Notched.

Kyptikon. The Emperor's pew, if on gallery level.

Lavra. A cluster of cells or caves laid out for hermit monks, having in common a centre containing a church and sometimes a refectory.

Martyrium. A site which bears witness to the Christian faith, either by referring to an event in Christ's life or Passion, or by sheltering the grave of a martyr, a witness by virtue of having shed his blood; the structure erected over such a site.

Mensa. A table used for celebrating Mass; an altar table.

Mitatorium. The dressing-room of the Emperor, whether in a palace or church.

Naos. In modern Greek, a church; architecturally and liturgically, the core and sanctuary of a Byzantine centrally-planned church, i.e. the parts reserved for the performance of the liturgy.

Narthex. In Greek, a cane; architecturally, the transverse vestibule of a church either preceding nave and aisles as an inner narthex (esonarthex), or preceding the façade as an outer narthex (exonarthex); the exonarthex may also serve as the terminating transverse portico of a quadriporticus (see *Atrium*).

Nosokomion. Hospital or infirmary.

Nymphaeum. A fountain enclosure; as a rule, formed by a series of niches placed against or surmounting a wall.

Octaconch. A building composed of eight conchs (see *Conch*).

Oikos ekklesias. The Greek term for *domus ecclesia*.

Opaion. The circular opening at the apex of a dome.

Opus Alexandrinum. A pavement combining mosaic and opus sectile in guilloche design.

Opus listatum. Masonry composed of alternating (sometimes doubled) courses of brick and small blocks of stone.

Opus sectile. A covering for floor or wall consisting of marble slabs cut in a variety of shapes, generally geometric.

Pantokrator. Christ as ruler of the world.

Parekklesion. A chapel, flanking the church, the narthex, or both.

Pastophory. A room in an Early Christian or Byzantine church serving as a diaconicon or prothesis; as a rule, flanking the apse of the church.

Pelta. A shield-shaped design composed of a convex curve joined to two concave curves.

Pendentive. Architecturally, a triangular segment of a sphere, bordered by arches and resulting from the inter-penetration of a cubic space (bay or room, square in plan) and a hemisphere, the latter constructed from the circle circumscribed over the square of the plan. If the top of the

Greek-cross domed octagon

hemisphere is cut off horizontally, spherical sections are left between the bordering arches. These triangular sections – or pendentives – terminate in the circle inscribed in

the square of the plan. They thus form a base on which a dome can be placed, either directly or raised on a drum (a dome on pendentives). If, on the other hand, the hemisphere constructed over the circumscribed circle is continued from the pendentives to its apex, the result is a pendentive dome (also termed a sail-vault).

Pendentive dome. See *Pendentive.*

Pilaster. An engaged or semi-detached pier.

Presbyter. Literally, Elder; in the Early Christian church, a cleric exercising administrative and priestly functions; also, a parish priest.

Propylaeum. The entrance-gate building of a sacred precinct, whether church or Imperial palace.

Prothesis. The room attached to or enclosed in the church and serving for the preparation and storage of the species of the Eucharist before Mass; generally used also for the storage of the Eucharist after Mass.

Protomai capital. A capital with half-figures, usually animals, projecting from its four corners.

Pumpkin dome. A dome composed of curvilinear segments; also (Brit.) umbrella dome and melon dome.

Quadriporticus. See *Atrium.*

Quincunx.[1] A structure divided into nine bays, the centre bay a large square, the corner bays small squares, the remaining four bays rectangular; the centre bay, resting on four

---

1. The term is purloined from K. J. Conant, *A Brief Commentary on Early Medieval Church Architecture* (Baltimore, 1942), 15.

columns, is domed, the corner bays are either domed or groin-vaulted, the rectangular bays are, as a rule, barrel-vaulted; also referred to as cross-in-square, cross-inscribed, *croix inscrite.*

Recessed brick masonry. Masonry in which alternating brick courses are recessed from the wall plane and covered by mortar.

Refrigerium. In the Early Christian Church, a funeral banquet offered in commemoration of a martyr or an ordinary mortal.

Respond. The wall pilaster behind a column.

Rinceau. A scroll-like pattern of floral or plant design.

Salutatorium. A reception hall, in Roman terminology of the Emperor, in Christian of the bishop.

Sigma (pl. *sigmata*). In Roman and Byzantine terminology, a table of semicircular shape.

Skeuophylakion. 'Treasure house', sacristy; see also *Diaconicon.*

Solea. In an Early Christian or Byzantine church, a raised pathway projecting from the bema to the ambo.

Squinch (opposite page). A corbelling, usually a small arch or half-conical niche, which is placed across the corners of a square bay in order to form an octagon suitable for carrying an octagonal cloister-vault or a dome.

Stoa. A covered hall, its roof supported by one or more rows of columns parallel to the rear wall; in Latin, porticus.

Stylobate. A continuous base of stone, raised above floor level, from which rise the supports of the building, whether columns or piers.

Synthronon. In East Christian and Byzantine churches, the bench or benches reserved for the clergy; arranged either in a semicircle (sometimes amphitheatrically) in the apse or in straight rows on either side of the bema.

Squinch

Temenos. A sacred precinct.

Templon. In Middle Byzantine churches, a trabeated colonnade closing off the bema.

Tetraconch. A building composed of four conchs (see *Conch*).

Thermae. In the Roman Empire, a bathing establishment for public or private use.

Titulus. In the city of Rome, a *domus ecclesiae.*

Trabeation. A construction of horizontal beams, whether stone or wood.

Transept. The transverse unit of a basilican plan, as a rule inserted between nave and apse; it may be undivided (continuous transept) or divided into nave and aisles, continuing the division of the main body (cross transept); or it may consist of a centre bay continuing the nave together with wings, as high as the nave or lower, but always separated from the centre bay by colonnades (tripartite transept, or, with low wings, dwarf transept).

Tribelon. The triple arcade connecting the esonarthex with the nave, the term deriving from the three curtains (*tri-vela*) between the columns.

Triconch. A building composed of three conchs (see *Conch*).

Triconch transept. A transept with wings terminating in apses.

Tripartite transept. See *Transept.*

Twin cathedral. In Early Christian architecture, a cathedral of two halls or basilicas, their axes placed, as a rule, parallel to each other; the structures served different functions, as yet not fully understood.

Voussoir. A brick or wedge-shaped stone which forms one of the units of an arch.

SELECTED BIBLIOGRAPHY

The bibliography referring to specific periods or problems, or to individual buildings, is given in the Notes, chapter by chapter, the former usually in the first note, the latter as required. We thus dispense with bibliographies preceding the individual chapters.

I. POLITICAL, CULTURAL, AND ECCLESIASTICAL HISTORY

A. GENERAL STUDIES

Cambridge Ancient History, vol. 12, chapters 5, 6, 9, 10, 11, and 20. Cambridge, 1923 ff.

Cambridge Medieval History, vol. 1, chapters 1, 2, 4–6, 14, and 17; vol. 2, chapters 1, 2, and 9; all of vol. 4. New York and Cambridge, 1936 ff.

GIBBON, E. (ed. J. B. Bury). *The Decline and Fall of the Roman Empire*. 7 vols. London, 1900.

WISSOWA, G. *Pauly's Real-Encyklopädie der classischen Altertumswissenschaft, Neue Bearbeitung*. Stuttgart, 1894 ff.

B. EARLY CHRISTIAN

ALFÖLDI, A. *The Conversion of Constantine and Pagan Rome*. Oxford, 1948.

ALFÖLDI, A. *A Conflict of Ideas in the Late Roman Empire*. Oxford, 1952.

BAYNES, N. H. *Constantine the Great and the Christian Church (Proceedings of the British Academy, XV)*. London, 1929.

BROWN, P. *Augustine of Hippo*. Berkeley, 1967.

BROWN, P. *The Making of Late Antiquity*. Cambridge, Mass., and London, 1978.

BURKHARDT, J. *Die Zeit Konstantins des Grossen*. 2nd ed. Leipzig, 1880.

DIEHL, E. *Inscriptiones Latinae Christianae Veteres*. 3 vols. Berlin, 1961.

HARNACK, A. VON (ed. J. Moffatt). *The Expansion of Christianity*. New York and London, 1904 (*Die Mission und Ausbreitung des Christentums*, Leipzig, 1924).

MATTINGLY, H. *Christianity in the Roman Empire*. University of Otago, 1955.

MOMIGLIANO, A. (ed.). *The Conflict between Paganism and Christianity in the Fourth Century*. Oxford, 1963.

PIGANIOL, A. *L'empire chrétien 325–395*. Paris, 1947.

SETTON, K. M. *Christian Attitude towards the Emperor in the Fourth Century*. New York, 1941.

C. BYZANTIUM

BAYNES, N. H., and MOSS, H. ST L. B. *Byzantium*. Oxford, 1948 (Oxford paperback, 1961).

BRÉHIER, L. *Le monde byzantin*. 3 vols. Paris, 1947 ff.

BURY, J. B. *History of the Later Roman Empire*. 2 vols. London, 1923.

DIEHL, C. *Histoire de l'empire byzantin*. Paris, 1919.

GUERDAN, R. *Vie, grandeur et misères de Byzance*. Paris, 1954 (*Byzantium*, transl. D. L. B. Hartley, London, 1956; New York, Capricorn paperback, 1962).

JONES, A. H. M. *The Greek City from Alexander to Justinian*. Oxford, 1937.

MANGO, C. *Byzantium*. London, 1980.

OSTROGORSKY, G. *Geschichte des byzantinischen Staates*. Munich, 1940 (*History of the Byzantine State*, Oxford, 1956).

RUNCIMAN, S. *Byzantine Civilization*. London, 1933 (New York, Meridian paperback, 1962).

STEIN, E. *Geschichte des spätrömischen Reiches*. Vienna, 1928 (*Histoire du Bas-Empire*, ed. J. R. Palanque, 2 vols., Paris, 1949–59).

TREITINGER, O. *Die oströmische Kaiser- und Reichsidee*. Jena, 1938; 2nd ed., Darmstadt, 1956.

URE, P. N. *Justinian and his Age*. Harmondsworth, 1951.

VASILIEV, A. A. *Histoire de l'empire byzantin*. 2 vols. Paris, 1932 (trans. in *University of Wisconsin Studies in the Social Sciences and History*, nos. 13 and 14, 1928–9).

D. THE CHURCH

CASPAR, E. L. E. *Geschichte des Papsttums*. 2 vols. Tübingen, 1930–3.

FLICHE, A. and MARTIN, V. (ed.). *Histoire de l'église depuis les origines jusqu'à nos jours*, vols. 1–6. Paris, 1938 ff.

HEFELE, C. J. *History of the Councils of the Church*. London, 1871–96.

PIETRI, C. *Roma cristiana*. 2 vols. Rome, 1975.

RUNCIMAN, S. *The Eastern Schism*. Oxford, 1955.

E. PRIMARY SOURCES

Corpus scriptorum ecclesiasticorum latinorum. Vienna, 1866 ff.
Corpus scriptorum historiae byzantinae. Bonn, 1828–97.
EUSEBIUS (transl. J. E. L. Oulton). *The Ecclesiastical History (Loeb Classical Library)*. 2 vols.
EUSEBIUS. *Life of Constantine (Patrologia Graeca*, XX, 905 ff.).
EUSEBIUS (ed. I. A. Heikel). *Gesammelte Werke*, I. Berlin, 1898 (transl. H. Wace and P. Schaff, *A Select Library of Nicene and Post-Nicene Fathers, The Nicene Fathers*, I, New York, Oxford, and London, 1890).
Die griechischen christlichen Schriftsteller der ersten Jahrhunderte (Preussiche Akademie der Wissenschaften, Kirchenväter-Commission). Leipzig, 1897 ff.
MIGNE, J. P. *Patrologia Graeca*. Paris, 1857 ff.
MIGNE, J. P. *Patrologia Latina*. Paris, 1842 ff.

II. LITURGY

BATTIFOL, P. *Leçons sur la Messe*. Paris, 1919.
DIX, G. *The Shape of the Liturgy*. [London], 1947.
DUCHESNE, L. (trans. M. L. McClure). *Christian Worship*. London, 1949.
HANSSENS, J. *De Missa Rituum Orientalium (Institutiones Liturgicae de Ritibus Orientalibus*, II, III, appendix). Rome, 1930 ff.
JUNGMANN, J. A. *Missarum Sollemnia*. 2 vols. Vienna, 1948 (trans. F. A. Brunner, *The Mass of the Roman Rite*, New York, 1951 ff.).
The Orthodox Liturgy. London (Society for Promoting Christian Knowledge), 1939.

III. ART AND ARCHITECTURE

A. GENERAL STUDIES

CABROL, F., and LECLERCQ, H. *Dictionnaire d'archéologie chrétienne et de liturgie*. Paris, 1907–53.
CONANT, K. J. *A Brief Commentary on Early Medieval Church Architecture*. Baltimore, 1942.
DALTON, O. M. *East Christian Art*. Oxford, 1925.
DEICHMANN, F. W. *Versuch einer Darstellung der Grundrisstypen des Kirchenbaues . . . 1932*. Halle, Wittenberg, Würzburg, 1937.
DEICHMANN, F.W. *Einführung in die christliche Archäologie*. Darmstadt, 1983.
GLÜCK, H. *Die christliche Kunst des Ostens*. Berlin, 1923.
GRABAR, A. *Martyrium*. 2 vols. Paris, 1943–6.
GRABAR, A. *Archaeology*, II (1949), 95 ff.

KAUTZSCH, R. *Kapitellstudien (Studien zur spätantiken Kunstgeschichte)*. Berlin and Leipzig, 1936.
KHATCHATRIAN, A. *Les baptistères paleochrétiens*. Paris, 1962.
KITZINGER, E. *Byzantine Art in the Making*. London, 1977.
MACDONALD, W. *Early Christian and Byzantine Architecture*. New York, 1962.
ORLANDOS, A. *Hi Basiliki xylostegos tis mesogeiakis lekanis*. Athens, 1950–9.
Reallexikon für Antike und Christentum (ed. Th. Klauser). Stuttgart, 1950–62.
RICE, D. T. *The Beginnings of Christian Art*. Nashville and New York, 1957.
VOLBACH, W. F. (trans. C. Ligota). *Early Christian Art*. New York, 1962.
WARD PERKINS, J. B. *The Italian Element in Late Roman and Medieval Architecture – Annual Italian Lecture of the British Academy*, 1947 (*Proceedings of the British Academy*, XXXIII, 1947).
WULFF, O. *Altchristliche und Byzantinische Kunst (Handbuch der Kunstwissenschaft)*. Berlin, 1914–24.

B. EARLY CHRISTIAN

DAVIES, J. *The Origin and Development of Early Christian Church Architecture*. London, 1952.
DEICHMANN, F. *Frühchristliche Kirchen in Rom*. Basel, 1948.
DEICHMANN, F. W. *Ravenna*. 4 vols. Wiesbaden, 1958–76.
KIRSCH, J. P. *Die römischen Titelkirchen im Altertum (Studien zur Geschichte und Kultur des Altertums*, IX, 1, 2). Paderborn, 1918.
KRAUTHEIMER, R., and others. *Corpus Basilicarum Christianarum Romae*. Vatican City, 1939 ff.
MILLET, G. *L'école grecque dans l'architecture byzantine*. Paris, 1916.
VERZONE, P. *L'architettura religiosa dell'alto medio evo nell'Italia settentrionale*. Milan, 1942.
VIELLARD, R. *Recherches sur les origines de la Rome chrétienne*. Mâcon, 1941.

C. BYZANTIUM
AND THE EASTERN HINTERLANDS

BECKWITH, J. *The Art of Constantinople*. New York, 1961.
BECKWITH, J. *Early Christian and Byzantine Art (The Pelican History of Art)*. 2nd ed. Harmondsworth, 1979.
BRÉHIER, L. *L'art byzantin*. Paris, 1924.
BUTLER, H. C. (ed. E. Baldwin Smith). *Early Churches in Syria*. Princeton, 1929.

525

ĆURČIĆ, S. *Art and Architecture in the Balkans*. Boston, Mass., 1984.
DEICHMANN, F. *Studien zur Architektur Konstantinopels (Deutsches Beiträge zur Altertumswissenschaft)*. Baden-Baden, 1956.
DIEHL, C. *Manuel d'art byzantin*. 2 vols., 2nd ed. Paris, 1925.
DALTON, O. M. *Byzantine Art and Archaeology*. Oxford, 1911.
EBERSOLT, J. *Monuments d'architecture byzantine*. Paris, 1934.
EBERSOLT, J., and THIERS, A. *Les églises de Constantinople*. Paris, 1913.
HAMILTON, J. A. *Byzantine Architecture and Decoration*. London, 1933.
JANIN, R. *La géographie ecclésiastique de l'Empire Byzantin, première partie, Le siège de Constantinople et le patriarcat oecuménique, tome III, Les églises et les monastères*. Paris, 1953.
MANGO, C. *Byzantine Architecture*. New York, 1976.
MATHEWS, TH. F. *The Byzantine Churches of Istanbul. A Photographic Survey*. University Park and London, 1975.
MATHEWS, TH. F. *The Early Churches of Constantinople*. University Park and London, 1971.
MILLET, G. *L'art byzantin*, in A. Michel, *Histoire de l'art*, I, 127–301. Paris, 1905.
MILLET, G. *L'art chrétien d'Orient du milieu du XII au milieu du XV siècle*. Paris, 1908.
MÜLLER-WIENER, W. *Bildlexikon zur Topographie Istanbuls*. Tübingen, 1977.

Reallexikon zur Byzantinischen Kunst (ed. M. Restlé and K. Wessel). Stuttgart, 1966.
ROTT, H. *Kleinasiatische Denkmäler ... (Studien über christliche Denkmäler*, N.F. V, VI). Leipzig, 1908.
SCHNEIDER, A. M. *Byzanz – Vorarbeiten zur Topographie und Archäologie der Stadt (Istanbuler Forschungen*, VIII). Berlin, 1936.
VAN MILLINGEN, A., and others. *Byzantine Churches in Constantinople, Their History and Architecture*. London, 1912.
VOLBACH, W. F. *Art byzantin*. Paris, 1933.

D. PRIMARY SOURCES

CONSTANTINE PORPHYROGENETOS, *Book of Ceremonies (Patrologia Graeca*, CXII; *Bonn Corpus*, IX–X; A. Vogt, *Le Livre des Cérémonies*, Paris, 1935 ff. [Book I only]).
DUCHESNE, L. *Le Liber Pontificalis*. 3 vols. Paris, 1881–92, 1957.
MANGO, C. *The Art of the Byzantine Empire, 312–1453* (Sources and Documents in the History of Art Series, edited by H. W. Janson). Englewood Cliffs, New Jersey, 1972.
PROCOPIUS. *Loeb Classical Library*, 7 vols, ed. H. B. Dewing.
RICHTER, J. P. *Quellen der byzantinischen Kunstgeschichte (Quellenschriften für Kunstgeschichte und Kunsttechnik des Mittelalters und der Renaissance*, N.S. VIII). Vienna, 1897.
SCHLOSSER, J. *Quellenbuch zur Kunstgeschichte des abendländischen Mittelalters*. Vienna, 1896.

LIST OF ILLUSTRATIONS

177. Venice, Piazzetta, pier and capital, from Constantinople, H. Polyeuktos, 524–7 (Alinari)
178. Column with inlay, from Constantinople, H. Euphemia, sixth century. *Istanbul, Archaeological Museum* (German Archaeological Institute, Istanbul)
179. Column with inlay, from Constantinople, H. Polyeuktos, 524–7. *Istanbul, Archaeological Museum* (Elizabeth Harrison and Dumbarton Oaks)
180. Constantinople, H. Sergios and Bakchos, completed prior to 536. Plans (A) of ground floor, (B) of gallery (Van Millingen, *Churches*, 80)
181. Constantinople, H. Sergios and Bakchos, completed prior to 536. Exterior (Josephine Powell)
182. Constantinople, H. Sergios and Bakchos, completed prior to 536. Interior (Josephine Powell)
183. Constantinople, Yerebatan Cistern, fifth century. Vault (Josephine Powell)
184. Constantinople, H. Sergios and Bakchos, completed prior to 536. Capitals and entablature (Josephine Powell)
185. Constantinople, H. Sophia, 532–7. Composite capital (Hirmer Verlag, Munich)
186. Rome, Minerva Medica, *c.* 310, as in *c.* 1800. Exterior; etching by F. J. B. Kobell. *Munich, Graphische Sammlung* (Fototeca Unione, Rome)
187. Ravenna, S. Vitale, completed 546–8. Interior, facing apse (German Archaeological Institute, Rome)
188. Ravenna, S. Vitale, completed 546–8. Masonry (German Archaeological Institute, Rome)
189. Ravenna, S. Vitale, completed 546–8. Capitals in the chancel (Hirmer Verlag, Munich)
190. Ravenna, S. Vitale, completed 546–8. Vault of chancel (G. E. Kidder Smith)
191. Ravenna, S. Vitale, completed 546–8. Reconstruction of original marble revetment (Gerhard Kerff, Hamburg)
192. Ravenna, S. Vitale, completed 546–8. Exterior (L'Adriatica, Rimini)
193. Salonica, H. David, fifth century (last third). Isometric reconstruction (Lampl, based on Papahatzis, *Mnemeia*, figure on p. 22)
194. (A) Constantinople, Chalki gate, 532–6. Reconstruction (Lampl)
(B) Constantinople, Senate House, porch, after 532. Reconstruction (Lampl)
195. Constantinople, Holy Apostles, *c.* 536–50, as in *c.* 1100–50. *Paris, Bibliothèque Nationale* (gr. 1208, f. 3v)
196. Ephesus, St John, completed by 565. Plan (M. Büyükkolanci, *Ist. M.*, XXXII, 1982)
197. Ephesus, St John, completed by 565. South wall of west bay during rebuilding in 1963 (Osterr. Archäol. Institut, Vienna)
198. Ephesus, St John, completed by 565. Reconstructions of interior and exterior (H. Hörmann, *Forschungen in Ephesos*, IV, 3, figure 8)
199. Meriamlik (Meryemlik), 'domed' basilica, 471–94.

Plan (Lampl, adapted from E. Herzfeld and S. Guyer, *Meriamlik und Korykos*, figure 46)
200. Alahan Manastir (Alahan Klissi, Koja Kalessi), east church, late fifth(?) century. Plan (A. C. Headlam, *Ecclesiastical Sites in Isauria*, plate 1, 2)
201. Alahan Manastir (Alahan Klissi, Koja Kalessi), east church, late fifth(?) century. Interior of nave facing west (G. H. Forsyth, Kelsey Museum, University of Michigan)
202. Alahan Manastir (Alahan Klissi, Koja Kalessi), east church, late fifth(?) century. Exterior from the south-east (G. H. Forsyth, Kelsey Museum, University of Michigan)
203. Qasr Ibn Wardan, church, *c.* 564. South flank (F. W. Deichmann, Rome)
204. Qasr Ibn Wardan, palace, *c.* 564. Interior of apse (F. W. Deichmann, Rome)
205. Qasr Ibn Wardan, church, *c.* 564. North gallery, as in *c.* 1900 (Butler Archive, Princeton)
206. Qasr Ibn Wardan, church, *c.* 564. Ground-floor level (F. W. Deichmann, Rome)
207. Qasr Ibn Wardan, church, *c.* 564. Masonry (German Archaeological Institute, Rome)
208. Constantinople, H. Irene, begun 532. Exterior from the south-west (Fototeca Unione, Rome)
209. Constantinople, H. Irene, begun 532. Interior facing east (Josephine Powell)
210. Constantinople, H. Irene, begun 532. Exterior from the south-east (German Archaeological Institute, Istanbul)
211. Philippi, Basilica B, shortly before 540. Plan (P. Lemerle, *Philippes et la Macédoine orientale*, plate lvii)
212. Philippi, Basilica B, shortly before 540. Interior facing west (Fototeca Unione, Rome)
213. Philippi, Basilica B, shortly before 540. Base, capital, and impost block (C. L. Striker)
214. Gortyna, H. Titos, late sixth century. Isometric view (A. K. Orlandos, *Epetiris Byzantinōn Spoudōn*, III (1926), 307)
215. Sofia Cathedral, sixth–seventh centuries(?). Exterior (B. Stojadinov)
216. Sofia Cathedral, sixth–seventh centuries(?). Plan (Lampl, adapted from Mavrodinov (1959), figure 23)
217. Qasr Ibn Wardan, palace, *c.* 564. Exterior from the south (F. W. Deichmann, Rome)
218. Mount Sinai (Gebel Mûsa), monastery, founded *c.* 540. Air view (G. H. Forsyth, Kelsey Museum, University of Michigan)
219. Haïdra, fortress, sixth century. From the north (Thomas Schrunk)
220. R'safah, sixth century. Air view of town (Institut Français d'Archéologie de Beyrouth)
221. R'safah, tetraconch, before 553. Plan (J. Kollwitz, *Neue Deutsche Ausgrabungen*, 67)
222. R'safah, tetraconch, before 553. From the east (G. H. Forsyth, Kelsey Museum, University of Michigan)

536

404. Constantinople, Tekfur Sarayi, early fourteenth century. North-west façade (A. Frantz)
405. Constantinople, Tekfur Sarayi, early fourteenth century. Detail of north-west façade (A. Frantz)
406. Constantinople, Tekfur Sarayi, early fourteenth century. Detail of interior, lower part towards north (Olga Ford)

Author and publishers are grateful for careful work on the line drawings in the first place to Paul Lampl and subsequently to Sheila Gibson, Derek Martin, Ian Stewart, Paul White, and Vanessa Winchester.

INDEX

Words in *italic* are intended primarily as references to definitions. References to the Notes are given only where a reading of the text will not lead directly to a subject under discussion in the Note. Such references are given to the page on which the Note occurs, followed by the number of the chapter to which it belongs, and the number of the Note. Thus 472(5)[29] indicates page 472, Chapter 5, Note 29. Pointers to bibliography on a given site may be found by looking up the *text* reference in the *notes*; e.g. it will be seen from the index that Gračanica is

discussed on p. 436 of the text. If p. 436 is consulted in the form of the bold figures printed in the notes (pp. 455–515), the appropriate literature will be found.

Churches are indexed within towns in alphabetical order of the most important element of the dedication: e.g., at Constantinople, St John Studios will be found under Studios, St George under George. The dates following proper names refer in the case of rulers and church dignitaries to the span of their reign, otherwise to the life span.